Praise for

Inside the Microsoft Build Engine: Using MSBuild and Team Foundation Build, Second Edition

"Inside the Microsoft Build Engine: Using MSBuild and Team Foundation Build is a practical book covering all the essentials of MSBuild and the Team Foundation Server build system. But what makes the book extra valuable is its focus on real-life scenarios that often are hard to find a good, working solution for. In fact there is information in the book you're unlikely to find anywhere else. With the second edition of the book, the authors fill the gaps again, this time by covering the new TFS build workflow technology as well as MSBuild 4.0. It is an invaluable book that saves lots of time whenever you work with any aspect of automated builds in Visual Studio and TFS. This is a book I'll make sure to have with me all the time!"
-Mathias Olausson, ALM Consultant, QWise/Callista, Sweden

"As an ALM Consultant I come across many teams that are struggling with their build tools and processes. The second edition of Sayed and William's book is the perfect answer for these teams. Not only will it show you how to get your builds back on track, I challenge anyone not to be able to use the information in this book to improve their existing builds. It includes updated content focusing on the new Visual Studio 2010 release and is packed with practical examples you could start using straight away. You simply must include it in your technical library."
-Anthony Borton, Microsoft Visual Studio ALM MVP, Senior ALM trainer/consultant, Enhance ALM Pty Ltd, Australia

"The first edition of Inside the Microsoft Build Engine was a brilliant look at the internals of MSBuild, so it's fantastic to see Sayed and William updating it with all the new features in MSBuild 4.0 and also delving into the Team Foundation Server 2010 workflow based build process. It's also a real pleasure to see deployment with MSDeploy covered so that you can learn not only how to automate your builds, but also how to automate your deployments. A great book. Go out and get a copy now."
-Richard Banks, Visual Studio ALM MVP and Principal Consultant with Readify, Australia

"Did you know about the TaskFactory in MSBuild? If not, you're not alone - but you will know after reading this book. This book provides insights into the current technologies of the Microsoft Build Engine. Starting with background information about MSBuild, it covers also the necessary basics of Workflow Foundation which are applied during the description of advanced topics of Team Foundation Build. The level of detail is targeted to experienced build masters having a development background - even the overview is stuffed with new information, references, hints and best practices about MSBuild. Samples are provided as step-by-step guidance easy to follow inside Visual Studio. What I found astonishing is the practical focus of the samples such as web project deployment. I could have used at least half of them in my development projects! Simply put: A must read for all build experts that have to deal with MSBuild and the Team Foundation Server build engine who are not only interested in solutions but also background information!"
-Sven Hubert, AIT TeamSystemPro Team, Consultant, MVP Visual Studio ALM – www.tfsblog.de

i

"The reason that I only own one MSBuild/Team Build book is because there is no need for another. This book covers both topics from soup to nuts and is written in a way that allows new users to ramp up quickly. The real-world code examples used to illustrate the topics are useful in their own right. The Second Edition covers all of the changes in MSBuild 4.0 and all of the newness that is Team Build 2010. This is my 'go to' guide, and the only book on these topics that I recommend to my clients."
-Steve St Jean, Visual Studio ALM MVP, DevProcess (ALM) Consultant with Notion Solutions, an Imaginet Company

"Whether you consider yourself experienced or you are taking your first steps in the build and automation arena, this 2nd edition will prove a valuable read. Skilled MSBuild users will do well to remind themselves of the intricacies of MSBuild and learn of the new 4.0 features whilst novices are taken on a steady paced journey to quickly acquire the knowledge and confidence in developing successful solutions. This edition brings additional value to our ever changing profession in discussing MSDeploy and the new Windows Workflow 4.0 based Team Foundation Build. Regardless of your experience, I wholeheartedly recommend this book."
-Mike Fourie, Visual Studio ALM MVP and ALM Ranger, United Kingdom

"The first edition of this book had a perfect balance between a tutorial and a reference book. I say this as I used the book first to kick start my MS Build knowledge and then as reference whenever I needed information on some advanced topic. My main interest is Team Foundation Server and I learned MS Build more from necessity than an urge, hence I was very curious to see the 2nd edition. Sayed and William did not disappoint me - the four chapters on Team Build cover all points needed to customize builds. As a bonus there are three whole chapters on web deployment which is a recurrent request I hear during my consulting and presentations on TFS. If I had to summarize my opinion in a single sentence, I would just say `Buy the book, you won't regret it'."
-Tiago Pascoal, Visual Studio ALM MVP and Visual Studio ALM Ranger, Portugal

"Reliable and repeatable build processes are often the Achilles' heel of development teams. Often this is down to a lack of understanding of the underlying technologies and how they fit together. No matter which Continuous Integration (CI) tool you may be using, this book provides the fundamental information you need to establish solid build and deployment engineering practices and demystifies the various Microsoft technologies used along the way. This book is the essential reference for any team building software on the Microsoft.NET platform."
-Stuart Preston, Visual Studio ALM Ranger and Chief Technology Officer at RippleRock

"Successfully deploying application is one of the big challenges in today's modern software development. As applications become more complex to develop, they also become more complex to deploy. This well-written book provides us a deep-dive on how developers can improve their productivity and accomplish the business needs using Microsoft deployment technology: MSBuild, Web Deploy and Team Build. Microsoft provides us the right tools, and this book provides us the information we need to extract real value from these tools."
-Daniel Oliveira, MVP, Visual Studio ALM Ranger and ALM Consultant at TechResult

Inside the Microsoft® Build Engine: Using MSBuild and Team Foundation Build, Second Edition

Sayed Hashimi

William Bartholomew

PUBLISHED BY
Microsoft Press
A Division of Microsoft Corporation
One Microsoft Way
Redmond, Washington 98052-6399

Library of Congress Control Number: 2010940848
ISBN: 978-0-7356-4524-0

Printed and bound in the United States of America.

Microsoft Press books are available through booksellers and distributors worldwide. For further information about international editions, contact your local Microsoft Corporation office or contact Microsoft Press International directly at fax (425) 936-7329. Visit our Web site at www.microsoft.com/mspress. Send comments to mspinput@microsoft.com.

Acquisitions Editor: Devon Musgrave
Developmental Editor: Devon Musgrave
Project Editor: Iram Nawaz
Editorial Production: S4Carlisle Publishing Services
Technical Reviewer: Marc H. Young
Cover: Tom Draper Design

Body Part No. X17-29997

I would like to dedicate this book to my parents, Sayed A. Hashimi and Sohayla Hashimi, as well as my college advisor, Dr. Ben Lok. My parents have, over the course of the years, sacrificed a lot to give us the opportunity for us to be able to achieve our dreams. I can only hope that they are proud of the person that I have become. When I first met Ben, I wanted to get into a research program that he had going. Thankfully, he was willing to accept me. Ben helped show me how rewarding hard work can be, and he has enabled me to succeed in my career. When I look back on influences in my life, who are not relatives, he ranks at the top of my list. I am sure that I wouldn't be where I am had it not been for him.

—Sayed Ibrahim Hashimi

To my mother, Rosanna O'Sullivan, and my father, Roy Bartholomew, for their unfaltering support in all my endeavors.

—William Bartholomew

I would like to dedicate this book to my parents, Syama Mohana Rao Adharapurapu and Nalini Adharapurapu, my brother, Raghavendra Adharapurapu, my sister, Raga Sudha Vijjapurapu, and my wife, Deepti Ramakrishna.

—Pavan Adharapurapu

I dedicate this book to my wife, Samantha, and my daughters, Amelie and Madeline, as well as my parents, Leonea and Craig. Their love has no boundaries and their support has made me believe that I can accomplish anything.

—Jason Ward

Contents at a Glance

Part VII **Web Development Tool**

Table of Contents

What do you think of this book? We want to hear from you!

Microsoft is interested in hearing your feedback so we can continually improve our
books and learning resources for you. To participate in a brief online survey, please visit:

microsoft.com/learning/booksurvey

Part II   Customizing MSBuild

Part V **MSBuild in Visual C++ 2010**

Part VII **Web Development Tool**

Foreword

Often when people think about build, they think just about the act of compiling some source code – when I hit F5 in the IDE, it builds, right? Well yes, kind of. In a real production build system, there is so much more to it than that. There are many kinds of builds – F5, desktop, nightly, continuous, rolling, gated, buddy etc. The variety of build types is reflective of the important role build plays in the software development process and the varied ways it does so. Build is a key integration point in the process. It is where developers' work comes together; it is where developers hand off to test and where release hands off to operations. No wonder there are so many requirements on it.

As I mentioned, build is about a lot more than compiling the code. It can include making sure the right code is assembled, compiling, testing, version stamping, packaging, deployment and more. Of course, because software systems are all different and organizations are different, many of the activities need to be completely different. As a result, extensibility plays a major role. In TFS 2010, we increased the extensibility options by including a build workflow engine (based on the .NET Workflow Foundation) on top of the existing msbuild capabilities. Unfortunately, as flexibility increases, so does the amount you need to know to make sound decisions and fully automate your build workflow.

This book is a great resource to help you understand the variety of roles build plays in software development and how you can leverage msbuild and TFS. It will show you how to use "out of the box" solutions, provide guidance on when to customize, what the best customization approaches are and details on and examples of how to actually do it. I think it will be an invaluable resource to keep on your reference shelf.

Brian Harry

Technical Fellow

Team Foundation Server, Microsoft

Introduction

Build has historically been kind of like a black art, in the sense that there are just a few people who know and understand build, and are passionate about it. But in today's evolving environment that is changing. Now more and more people are becoming interested in build, and making it a part of their routine development activities. Today's applications are different from those that we were building five to ten years ago. Along with that the process by which we write software is different as well. Nowadays it is not uncommon for a project to have sophisticated build processes which include such things as code generation, code analysis, unit testing, automated deployment, etc. To deal with these changes developers are no longer shielded from the build process. Developers have to understand the build process so that they can leverage it to meet their needs.

Back in 2005 Microsoft released MSBuild, which is the build engine used to build most Visual Studio projects. That release was MSBuild 2.0. Since that release Microsoft has released two major versions of MSBuild—MSBuild 3.5 and MSBuild 4.0. In MSBuild 3.5 Microsoft released such goodness as multi-processor support, multi-targeting, items and properties being defined inside of targets and a few other things which brought MSBuild to where it needed to be. In MSBuild 4.0 there were a lot of really great features delivered. The feature which stands out the most is the support for building Visual C++ projects. Starting with Visual Studio 2010 your Visual C++ project files are in MSBuild format. Modifying MSBuild to be able to support building Visual C++ projects was a big effort on Microsoft's part, but they understood that the value they were delivering to customers would be worth it. Along with support for Visual C++ there were a number of significant feature add ons, such as support for BeforeTargets/AfterTargets, inline tasks, property functions, item functions and a new object model to name a few. During that same period Team Build has undergone a number of big changes.

Team Foundation Build (or Team Build as it is more commonly known) is now in its third version. Team Build 2005 and 2008 were entirely based on MSBuild using it for both build orchestration as well as the build process itself. While this had the advantage of just needing to learn one technology MSBuild wasn't suited for tasks such as distributing builds across multiple machines and performing complex branching logic. Team Build 2010 leverages the formidable combination of Workflow Foundation (for build orchestration) and MSBuild (for build processes) to provide a powerful, enterprise-capable, build automation tool. Team Build 2010 provides a custom Workflow Foundation service host that runs on the build servers that allows the build process to be distributed across multiple machines. The Workflow Foundation based process template can perform any complex branching and custom logic that is supported by Workflow Foundation, including the ability to call MSBuild based project files.

A common companion to build is deployment. In many cases the same script which builds your application is used to deploy it. This is why in this updated book we have a section, Part VII Web Deployment Tool, in which we dedicate three chapters to the topic. MSDeploy is a tool which was first released in 2009. It can be used to deploy websites, and other applications, to local and remote servers. In this section we will show you how to leverage MSDeploy and the Web Publishing Pipeline (WPP) in order to deploy your web applications. Two chapters are devoted to the theory of both MSDeploy and the WPP. There is also a cookbook chapter which shows real world examples of how to use these new technologies. Once you've automated your build and deployment process for the first time you will wonder why you didn't do that for all of your projects.

Who This Book Is For

This book is written for anyone who uses, or is interested in using, MSBuild or Team Build. If you are using Visual Studio to your applications then you are already using MSBuild. *Inside the Microsoft Build Engine* is for all developers and build masters using Microsoft technologies. If you are interested in learning more about how your applications are being built and how you can customize this process then you need this book. If you are using Team Build, or thinking of using it tomorrow, then this book is a must read. It will save you countless hours.

This book will help the needs of enterprise teams as well as individuals. You should be familiar with creating applications using Visual Studio. You are not required to be familiar with the build process, as this book will start from the basics and build on that. Because one of the most effective methods for learning is through examples, this book contains many examples.

Assumptions

To get the most from this book, you should meet the following profile:

- You should be an familiar with Visual Studio
- You should have experience with the technologies you are interested in building
- You should have a solid grasp of XML.

Organization of This Book

Inside the Microsoft Build Engine is divided into seven parts:

Part I, "Overview," describes all the fundamentals of creating and extending MSBuild project files. Chapter 1, "MSBuild Quick Start," is a brief chapter to get you started quickly with MSBuild. If you are already familiar with MSBuild then you can skip this chapter; its content will be covered in more detail within chapters 2 and 3. Chapter 2, "MSBuild Deep Dive, Part 1," discusses such things as static properties, static items, targets, tasks, and msbuild .exe usage. Chapter 3, "MSBuild Deep Dive, Part 2," extends on Chapter 2 with dynamic properties, dynamic items, how properties and items are evaluated, importing external files, extending the build process, property functions, and item functions.

Part II, "Customizing MSBuild," covers the two ways that MSBuild can be extended: custom tasks and custom loggers. Chapter 4, "Custom Tasks," covers all that you need to know to create your own custom MSBuild tasks. Chapter 5, "Custom Loggers," details how to create custom loggers and how to attach them to your build process.

Part III, "Advanced MSBuild Topics," discusses advanced MSBuild concepts. Chapter 6, "Batching and Incremental Builds," covers two very important topics, MSBuild batching and supporting incremental building. Batching is the process of categorizing items and processing them in batches. Incremental building enables MSBuild to detect when a target is up-to-date and can be skipped. Incremental building can drastically reduce build times for most developer builds. Chapter 7, "External Tools," provides some guidelines for integrating external tools into the build process. It also shows how NUnit and FXCop can be integrated in the build process in a reusable fashion.

Part IV, "MSBuild Cookbook," consists of two chapters that are devoted to real-world examples. Chapter 8, "Practical Applications, Part 1," contains several examples, including: setting the assembly version, customizing the build process in build labs, handling errors, and replacing values in configuration files. Chapter 9, "Practical Applications, Part 2," covers more examples, most of which are targeted toward developers who are building Web applications using .NET. It includes Web Deployment Projects, starting and stopping services, zipping output files, compressing Javascript file, and encrypting the web.config file.

Part V, "MSBuild in Visual C++ 2010" discusses how MSBuild powers various features of Visual C++ in light of Visual C++ 2010's switch to MSBuild for its build engine. Chapter 10, "MSBuild in Visual C++ 2010, Part 1" introduces the reader to the new .vcxproj file format for Visual C++ projects and illustrates the Visual C++ build process with a block diagram. Then it continues describing its features such as Build Parallelism, Property Sheets, etc. and how MSBuild enables these features. Of particular interest are the new File Tracker based Incremental Build and movement of Visual C++ Directories settings to a property sheet from the earlier Tools > Option page. Chapter 11, "MSBuild in Visual C++ 2010, Part 1" continues the theme of Chapter 10 by describing more Visual C++ features and the underlying MSBuild implementation. This includes Property Pages, Build Customizations, Platform and Platform Toolsets, project upgrade, etc. It also includes a discussion of all the default tasks, targets and property sheets that are shipped with Visual C++ 2010. Of particular interest is the section on multi-targeting which explains the exciting new feature in Visual C++ 2010 which allows building projects using older toolsets such as Visual C++ 2008 toolset. We describe both how to use this feature as well as how this feature is implemented using

MSBuild. Chapter 12, "Extending Visual C++ 2010" describes how you can extend the build system in various ways by leveraging the underlying MSBuild engine. Discussed in this chapter are authoring Build Events, Custom Build Steps, Custom Build Tool to customize Visual C++ build system in a simple way when the full power of MSBuild extensibility is not needed. This is followed by a discussion of adding a custom target and creating a Build Customization which allows you to use the full set of extensibility features offered by MSBuild. One of the important topics in this chapter deals with adding support for a new Platform or a Platform Toolset. The example of using the popular GCC toolset to build Visual C++ projects is used to drive home the point that extending platforms and platform toolsets is easy and natural in Visual C++ 2010.

Part VI, "Team Foundation Build," introduces Team Foundation Build (Team Build) in Chapter 13, "Team Build Quick Start". In this chapter we discuss the architectural components of Team Foundation Build and walkthrough the installation process and the basics of configuring it. In Chapter 14, "Team Build Deep Dive", we examine the process templates that ship with Team Build as well the Team Build API. Chapter 15, "Workflow Foundation Quick Start", introduces the basics of Workflow Foundation to enable customizing the build process. Chapter 16, "Process Template Customization", then leverages this knowledge and explains how to create customized build processes.

Part VII, "Web Deployment Tool" first introduces the Web Deployment Tool (MSDeploy) in Chapter 17 "Web Deployment Tool, Part 1". In that chapter we discuss what MSDeploy is, and how it can be used. We describe how MSDeploy can be used for "online deployment" in which you deploy your application to the target in real time and we discuss "offline deployments" in which you create a package which gets handed off to someone else for the actual deployment. In Chapter 18 "Web Deployment Tool, Part 2" we introduce the Web Publishing Pipeline (WPP). The WPP is the process which your web application follows to go from build output to being deployed on your remote server. It's all captured in a few MSBuild scripts, so it is very customizable and extensible. In that chapter we cover how you can customize and extend the WPP to suit your needs. Then in Chapter 19 "Web Deploy Practical Applications" we show many different examples of how you can use MSDeploy and WPP to deploy your packages. We cover such things as Publishing using MSBuild, parameterizing packages, deploying with Team Build, and a few others.

For Appendices A, B, and C please go to *http://oreilly.com/catalog/0790145301949/*.

System Requirements

The following list contains the minimum hardware and software requirements to run the code samples provided with the book.

- .NET 4.0 Framework

- Visual Studio 2010 Express Edition or greater

- 50 MB of available space on the installation drive

For Team Build chapters:

- Visual Studio 2010 Professional

- Some functionality (such as Code Analysis) requires Visual Studio 2010 Premium or Visual Studio 2010 Ultimate

- Access to a server running Team Foundation Server 2010

- Access to a build machine running Team Foundation Build 2010 (Chapter 13 walks you through installing this)

- A trial Virtual PC with Microsoft Visual Studio 2010 and Team Foundation Server 2010 RTM is available from *http://www.microsoft.com/downloads/en/details .aspx?FamilyID=509c3ba1-4efc-42b5-b6d8-0232b2cbb26e*

Code Samples

Follow these steps to install the code samples on your computer:

1. Navigate to *http://oreilly.com/catalog/0790145301949/*.

2. Click the Companion Content link.

3. You'll see instructions for downloading the files.

4. Copy the files to the following location on your computer.

Acknowledgements

The authors are happy to share the following acknowledgments.

Sayed Ibrahim Hashimi

Before I wrote my first book I thought that writing a book involved just a few people, but now having written my third book I realize how many different people it takes to successfully launch a book. Unfortunately with books most of the credit goes to the authors, but the others involved deserve much more credit than they are naturally given. As an author, the most we can do is thank them and mention their names here in the acknowledgements section. When I reflect on the writing of this book there are a lot of names, but there is one that stands out in particular, Dan Moseley. Dan is a part of the MSBuild team. He has gone way above and beyond what I could have ever imagined. I've never seen someone peer review a chapter as good, or as fast, as Dan has. Without Dan's invaluable insight the book would simply not be what it is today. In my whole career I've only encountered a few people who are as passionate about what they do as Dan. I hope that I can be as passionate about building products as he is.

Besides Dan I would like to first thank my co-authors and technical editor. William Bartholomew, who wrote the Team Build chapters, is a wonderful guy to work with. He is recognized as a Team Build expert, and I think his depth of knowledge shows in his work. Pavan Adharapurapu wrote the chapters covering Visual C++. When we first started talking about updating the book to cover MSBuild 4.0 to be honest I was a bit nervous. I was nervous because I had not written any un-managed code in more than 5 years, and because of that I knew that I could not write the content on Visual C++ and do it justice. Then we found Pavan. Pavan helped build the Visual C++ project system, and he pours his heart into everything that he does. Looking back I am confident that he was the best person to write those chapters and I am thankful that he was willing. Also I'd like to thank Jason Ward, who wrote a chapter on Workflow Foundation. Jason who has a great background in Workflow Foundation as well as Team Build was an excellent candidate to write that chapter. I started with the authors, but the technical editor, Marc Young deserves the same level of recognition. This having been my third book I was familiar with what a technical editor is responsible for doing. Their primary job is essentially to point out the fact that I don't know what I'm talking about, which Marc did very well. But Marc went beyond his responsibilities. Marc was the one who suggested that we organize all the sample code based on the chapters. At first I didn't really think it was a good idea, but he volunteered to reorganize the content and even redo a bunch of screen shots. I really don't think he knew what he was volunteering for! Now that it is over I wonder if he would volunteer again. I can honestly say that Marc was the best technical editor that I've ever worked with. His attention to detail is incredible, to the point that he was reverse engineering the code to validate some statements that I was making (and some were wrong). Before this book I knew what a technical editor was supposed to be, and now I know what a technical editor can be. Thanks to all of you guys!

As I mentioned at the beginning of this acknowledgement there are many others who came together to help complete this book besides those of us writing it. I'd like to thank Microsoft Press and everyone there who worked on it. I know there were some that were involved that I didn't even know of. I'd like to thank those that I do know of by name. Devon Musgrave, who also worked with us on the first edition, is a great guy to work with. This book really started with him. We were having dinner one night a while back and he said to me something along the lines of "what do you think of updating the book?" I knew that it would be a wonderful project and it was. Iram Nawaz who was the Project Editor of the book was just fantastic. She made sure that we stayed on schedule (sorry for the times I was late ☺) and was a great person to work with. The book wouldn't have made it on time if it was not for her. Along with these guys from Microsoft Press I would like to than the editors; Susan McClung and Nicole Schlutt for their perseverance to correct my bad writing.

There are several people who work on either the MSBuild/MSDeploy/Visual Studio product groups that I would like to thank as well. When the guys who built the technologies you are writing about help you, it brings the book to a whole new level. I would like to thank the following people for giving their valued assistance (in no particular order, and sorry if

I missed anyone); Jay Shrestha, Chris Mann, Andrew Arnott, Vishal Joshi, Bilal Aslam, Faith Allington, Ming Chen, Joe Davis and Owais Shaikh.

William Bartholomew

Firstly I'd like to thank my co-authors, Sayed, Pavan, and Jason, because without their contributions this book would not be as broad as it is. From Microsoft Press I'd like to thank Devon Musgrave, Ben Ryan, Iram Nawaz, Susan McClung, and the art team, for their efforts in converting our ideas into a publishable book. Thanks must go to Marc Young for his technical review efforts in ensuring that the procedures are easily followed, the samples work, and the book makes sense. Finally, I'd like to thank the Team Build Team, in particular Aaron Hallberg and Buck Hodges, for the tireless support.

Pavan Adharapurapu

A large number of people helped make this book happen. I would like to start off by thanking Dan Moseley, my manager at Microsoft who encouraged me to write the book and for providing thorough and detailed feedback for the chapters that I wrote. Brian Tyler, the architect of my team provided encouragement and great feedback. Many people from the Visual C and the project system teams here at Microsoft helped make the book a better one by providing feedback on their areas of expertise. In alphabetical order they are: Olga Arkhipova, Andrew Arnott, Ilya Biryukov, Felix Huang, Cliff Hudson, Renin John, Sara Joiner, Marian Luparu, Chris Mann, Bogdan Mihalcea, Kieran Mockford, Amit Mohindra, Li Shao. Any mistakes that remain are mine.

I would like to thank Devon Musgrave, Iram Nawaz, Susan McClung and Marc Young from Microsoft Press for their guidance and patience.

Finally, I would like to thank my wonderful wife Deepti who provided great support and understanding throughout the many weekends I spent locked up writing and revising the book. Deepti, I promise to make it up to you.

Jason Ward

First of all, I'd like to thank William Bartholomew for giving me the opportunity to contribute to this book. William displays an amazing amount of talent, passion and integrity in all his work. I'm honored to have his friendship as well as the opportunity to work with him on a daily basis.

I'd also like to thank Avi Pilosof and Rich Lowry for giving me the wonderful opportunity to work at Microsoft. From the moment I met them it was clear that moving my family half way around the world was the right thing to do. Their mentorship, passion, friendship and overarching goal of 'doing the right thing' has only further reinforced that working at Microsoft was everything I had hoped it would be. They are the embodiment of all things good at Microsoft.

Finally I'd like to thank the thousands of people working at Microsoft for producing the wonderful applications and experiences that millions of people around the world use and enjoy on a daily basis. It is truly an honor to work with you as we change the world.

Errata and Book Support

We've made every effort to ensure the accuracy of this book and its companion content. If you do find an error, please report it on our Microsoft Press site at oreilly.com:

1. Go to *http://microsoftpress.oreilly.com*.

2. In the Search box, enter the book's ISBN or title.

3. Select your book from the search results.

4. On your book's catalog page, under the cover image, you'll see a list of links. Click View/Submit Errata.

You'll find additional information and services for your book on its catalog page. If you need additional support, please e-mail Microsoft Press Book Support at *mspinput@microsoft.com*.

Please note that product support for Microsoft software is not offered through the addresses above.

We Want to Hear from You

At Microsoft Press, your satisfaction is our top priority, and your feedback our most valuable asset. Please tell us what you think of this book at:

http://www.microsoft.com/learning/booksurvey

The survey is short, and we read *every one* of your comments and ideas. Thanks in advance for your input!

Stay in Touch

Let's keep the conversation going! We're on Twitter: *http://twitter.com/MicrosoftPress*

Part I
Overview

Chapter 1
MSBuild Quick Start

When you are learning a new subject, it's exciting to just dive right in and get your hands dirty. The purpose of this chapter is to enable you to do just that. I'll describe all the key elements you need to know to get started using MSBuild. If you're already familiar with MSBuild, feel free to skip this chapter—all of the material presented here will be covered in later areas in the book as well, with the exception of the msbuild.exe usage details.

The topics covered in this chapter include the structure of an MSBuild file, properties, targets, items, and invoking MSBuild. Let's get started.

Project File Details

An MSBuild file—typically called an "MSBuild project file"—is just an XML file. These XML files are described by two XML Schema Definition (XSD) documents that are created by Microsoft: Microsoft.Build.Commontypes.xsd and Microsoft.Build.Core.xsd. These files are located in the %WINDIR%\Microsoft.NET\Framework*vNNNN*\MSBuild folder, where *vNNNN* is the version folder for the Microsoft .NET Framework 2.0, 3.5, or 4.0. If you have a 64-bit machine, then you will find those files in the Framework64 folder as well. (In this book, I'll assume you are using .NET Framework 4.0 unless otherwise specified. As a side note, a new version of MSBuild was not shipped with .NET Framework 3.0.) Microsoft .Build.Commontypes.xsd describes the elements commonly found in Microsoft Visual Studio-generated project files, and Microsoft.Build.Core.xsd describes all the fixed elements in an MSBuild project file. The simplest MSBuild file would contain the following:

```
<Project xmlns="http://schemas.microsoft.com/developer/msbuild/2003">
</Project>
```

This XML fragment will identify that this is an MSBuild file. All your content will be placed inside the Project element. Specifically, we will be declaring *properties*, *items*, *targets*, and a few other things directly under the Project element. When building software applications, you will always need to know two pieces of information: what is being built and what build parameters are being used. Typically, files are being built, and these would be contained in MSBuild items. Build parameters, like Configuration or OutputPath, are contained in MSBuild properties. We'll now discuss how to declare properties as well as targets, and following that we'll discuss items.

Properties and Targets

MSBuild properties are simply key-value pairs. The key for the property is the name that you will use to refer to the property. The value is its value. When you declare static properties, they are always contained in a *PropertyGroup* element, which occurs directly within the *Project* element. We will discuss dynamic properties (those declared and generated dynamically inside targets) in the next chapter. The following snippet is a simple example of declaring static properties:

```
<Project xmlns="http://schemas.microsoft.com/developer/msbuild/2003">
  <PropertyGroup>
    <AppServer>\\sayedApp</AppServer>
    <WebServer>\\sayedWeb</WebServer>
  </PropertyGroup>
</Project>
```

As previously stated, the *PropertyGroup* element, inside the *Project* element, will contain all of our properties. The name of a property is the XML tag name of the element, and the value of the property is the value inside the element. In this example, we have declared two properties, AppServer and WebServer, with the values \\sayedApp and \\sayedWeb, respectively. You can create as many *PropertyGroup* elements under the Project tag as you want. The previous fragment could have been defined like this:

```
<Project xmlns="http://schemas.microsoft.com/developer/msbuild/2003">
  <PropertyGroup>
    <AppServer>\\sayedApp</AppServer>
  </PropertyGroup>
  <PropertyGroup>
    <WebServer>\\sayedWeb</WebServer>
  </PropertyGroup>
</Project>
```

The MSBuild engine will process all elements sequentially within each *PropertyGroup* in the same manner. If you take a look at a project created by Visual Studio, you'll notice that many properties are declared. These properties have values that will be used throughout the build process for that project. Here is a region from a sample project that I created:

```
<Project DefaultTargets="Build"
    xmlns="http://schemas.microsoft.com/developer/msbuild/2003">
  <PropertyGroup>
    <Configuration Condition=" '$(Configuration)' == '' ">Debug</Configuration>
    <Platform Condition=" '$(Platform)' == '' ">AnyCPU</Platform>
    <ProductVersion>8.0.50727</ProductVersion>
    <SchemaVersion>2.0</SchemaVersion>
    <ProjectGuid>{A71540FD-9949-4AC4-9927-A66B84F97769}</ProjectGuid>
    <OutputType>WinExe</OutputType>
    <AppDesignerFolder>Properties</AppDesignerFolder>
    <RootNamespace>WindowsApplication1</RootNamespace>
    <AssemblyName>WindowsApplication1</AssemblyName>
  </PropertyGroup>
```

```
<PropertyGroup Condition=" '$(Configuration)|$(Platform)' == 'Debug|AnyCPU' ">
  <DebugSymbols>true</DebugSymbols>
  <DebugType>full</DebugType>
  <Optimize>false</Optimize>
  <OutputPath>bin\Debug\</OutputPath>
  <DefineConstants>DEBUG;TRACE</DefineConstants>
  <ErrorReport>prompt</ErrorReport>
  <WarningLevel>4</WarningLevel>
</PropertyGroup>
....
</Project>
```

You can see that values for the output type, the name of the assembly, and many others are defined in properties. Defining properties is great, but we also need to be able to utilize them, which is performed inside targets. We will move on to discuss Target declarations.

MSBuild fundamentally has two execution elements: tasks and targets. A task is the smallest unit of work in an MSBuild file, and a target is a sequential set of tasks. A task must always be contained within a target. Here's a sample that shows you the simplest MSBuild file that contains a target:

```
<Project xmlns="http://schemas.microsoft.com/developer/msbuild/2003">
  <Target Name="HelloWorld">
  </Target>
</Project>
```

In this sample, we have created a new target named HelloWorld, but it doesn't perform any work at this point because it is empty. When MSBuild is installed, you are given many tasks out of the box, such as Copy, Move, Exec, ResGen, and Csc. You can find a list of these tasks at the MSBuild Task Reference (*http://msdn2.microsoft.com/en-us/library/7z253716. aspx*). We will now use the Message task. This task is used to send a message to the logger(s) that are listening to the build process. In many cases this means a message is sent to the console executing the build. When you invoke a task in an MSBuild file, you can pass its input parameters by inserting XML attributes with values. These attributes will vary from task to task depending on what inputs the task is able to accept. From the documentation of the Message task (*http://msdn2.microsoft.com/en-us/library/6yy0yx8d.aspx*) you can see that it accepts a string parameter named Text. The following snippet shows you how to use the Message task to send the classic message "Hello world!"

```
<Project xmlns="http://schemas.microsoft.com/developer/msbuild/2003">
  <Target Name="HelloWorld">
    <Message Text="Hello world!" />
  </Target>
</Project>
```

Now we will verify that this works as expected. To do this, place the previous snippet into a file named HelloWorld.proj. Now open a Visual Studio command prompt, found in the Visual Studio Tools folder in the Start menu for Visual Studio. When you open this prompt, the path to msbuild.exe is already on the path. The command you will be invoking to start MSBuild is msbuild.exe. The basic usage for the command is as follows:

```
msbuild [INPUT_FILE] /t:[TARGETS_TO_EXECUTE]
```

So the command in our case would be

```
msbuild HelloWorld.proj /t:HelloWorld
```

This command says to execute the HelloWorld target, which is contained in the HelloWorld .proj file. The result of this invocation is shown in Figure 1-1.

```
C:\InsideMSBuild\Ch01>msbuild HelloWorld.proj /nologo
Build started 9/24/2010 5:55:31 PM.
Project "C:\InsideMSBuild\Ch01\HelloWorld.proj" on node 1 (default targets).
HelloWorld:
  Hello world!
Done Building Project "C:\InsideMSBuild\Ch01\HelloWorld.proj" (default targets).

Build succeeded.
    0 Warning(s)
    0 Error(s)
```

FIGURE 1-1 Result of HelloWorld target

> **Note** In this example, as well as all others in the book, we specify the /nologo switch. This simply avoids printing the MSBuild version information to the console and saves space in the book. Feel free to use it or not as you see fit.

We can see that the HelloWorld target is executed and that the message "Hello world!" is displayed on the console. The Message task also accepts another parameter, Importance. The possible values for this parameter are high, normal, or low. The Importance value may affect how the loggers interpret the purpose of the message. If you want the message logged no matter the verbosity, use the *high* importance level. We're discussing properties, so let's take a look at how we can specify the text using a property. I've extended the HelloWorld.proj file to include a few new items. The contents are shown here:

```
<Project xmlns="http://schemas.microsoft.com/developer/msbuild/2003">
  <Target Name="HelloWorld">
    <Message Text="Hello world!" />
  </Target>

  <PropertyGroup>
    <HelloMessage>Hello from property</HelloMessage>
  </PropertyGroup>
  <Target Name="HelloProperty">
    <Message Text="$(HelloMessage)" />
  </Target>
</Project>
```

I have added a new property, HelloMessage, with the value "Hello from property", as well as a new target, HelloProperty. The HelloProperty target passes the value of the property using the $(*PropertyName*) syntax. This is the syntax you use to evaluate a property. We can see this in action by executing the command `msbuild HelloWorld.proj /t:HelloProperty`. The result is shown in Figure 1-2.

```
C:\InsideMSBuild\Ch01>msbuild HelloWorld.proj /t:HelloProperty /nologo
Build started 9/24/2010 5:59:26 PM.
Project "C:\InsideMSBuild\Ch01\HelloWorld.proj" on node 1 (HelloProperty target(s)).
HelloProperty:
  Hello from property
Done Building Project "C:\InsideMSBuild\Ch01\HelloWorld.proj" (HelloProperty target(s)).

Build succeeded.
    0 Warning(s)
    0 Error(s)
```

FIGURE 1-2 Result of HelloProperty target

As you can see, the value of the property was successfully passed to the Message task. Now that we have discussed targets and basic property usage, let's move on to discuss how we can declare properties whose values are derived from other properties.

To see how to declare a property by using the value of an existing property, take a look at the project file, NestedProperties.proj:

```
<Project xmlns="http://schemas.microsoft.com/developer/msbuild/2003">
  <PropertyGroup>
    <Configuration Condition=" '$(Configuration)' == '' ">Debug</Configuration>
    <Platform Condition=" '$(Platform)' == '' ">AnyCPU</Platform>
    <DropLocation>
      \\sayedData\MSBuildExamples\Drops\$(Configuration)\$(Platform)\
    </DropLocation>
  </PropertyGroup>
  <Target Name="PrepareFilesForDrop">
    <Message Text="DropLocation : $(DropLocation)" />
  </Target>
</Project>
```

We can see here that three properties have been declared. On both the Configuration and Platform properties, a *Condition* attribute appears. We'll discuss this attribute later in this chapter. The remaining property, DropLocation, is defined using the values of the two previously declared items. The DropLocation property has three components: a constant value and two values that are derived from the Configuration and Platform properties. When the MSBuild engine sees the $(*PropertyName*) notation, it will replace that with the value of the specified property. So the evaluated value for DropLocation would be \\sayedData\MSBuildExamples\Drops\Debug\AnyCPU\. You can verify that by executing the PrepareFilesForDrop target with msbuild.exe. The reference for properties can be found at *http://msdn.microsoft.com/en-us/library/ms171458.aspx.*

When you use MSBuild, a handful of properties are available to you out of the box that cannot be modified. These are known as reserved properties. Table 1-1 contains all the reserved properties.

TABLE 1-1 Reserved Properties

Name	Description
MSBuildExtensionsPath	The full path where MSBuild extensions are located. By default, this is stored under %programfiles%\msbuild.
MSBuildExtensionsPath32	The full path where MSBuild 32-bit extensions are located. This typically is located under the Program Files folder. For 32-bit machines, this value will be the same as MSBuildExtensionsPath.
MSBuildExtensionsPath64*	The full path where MSBuild 64-bit extensions are located. This typically is under the Program Files folder. For 32-bit machines, this value will be empty.
MSBuildLastTaskResult*	This value holds the return value from the previous task. It will be *true* if the task completed successfully, and *false* otherwise.
MSBuildNodeCount	The number of nodes (processes) that are being used to build the projects. If the /m switch is not used, then this value will be 1.
MSBuildProgramFiles32*	This points to the 32-bit Program Files folder.
MSBuildProjectDefaultTargets	Contains the list of the default targets.
MSBuildProjectDirectory	The full path to the directory where the project file is located.
MSBuildProjectDirectoryNoRoot	The full path to the directory where the project file is located, excluding the root directory.
MSBuildProjectExtension	The extension of the project file, including the period.
MSBuildProjectFile	The name of the project file, including the extension.
MSBuildProjectFullPath	The full path to the project file.
MSBuildProjectName	The name of the project file, without the extension.
MSBuildStartupDirectory	The full path to the folder where the MSBuild process is invoked.
MSBuildThisFile*	The name of the file, including the extension but excluding the path, which contains the target that is currently executing.
MSBuildThisFileDirectory*	This is the full path to the directory that contains the file that is currently being executed.
MSBuildThisFileDirectoryNoRoot*	The same as MSBuildThisFileDirectory, except with the root removed.
MSBuildThisFileExtension*	The extension of the file that is currently executing.
MSBuildThisFileFullPath*	The full path to the file that is currently executing.
MSBuildThisFileName*	The name of the file, excluding the extension and path, of the currently executing file.
MSBuildToolsPath (MSBuildBinPath)	The full path to the location where the MSBuild binaries are located. For MSBuild 2.0, this property is named MSBuildBinPath; in MSBuild 3.5, it is deprecated.
MSBuildToolsVersion	The version of the tools being used to build the project. Possible values include 2.0, 3.5, and 4.0. The default value for this is 2.0.

* Denotes parameters new with MSBuild 4.0.

You would use these properties just as you would properties that you have declared in your own project file. To see an example of this, look at any Visual Studio–generated project file. When you create a new C# project, you will find the import statement `<Import Project="$(MSBuildToolsPath)\Microsoft.CSharp.targets" />` located near the bottom. This import statement uses the MSBuildToolsPath reserved property to resolve the full path to the Microsoft.CSharp.targets file and insert its content at this location. This is the file that drives the build process for C# projects. We will discuss its content throughout the remainder of this book. In Chapter 3, "MSBuild Deep Dive, Part 2," we discuss specifically how the Import statement is processed.

Items

Building applications usually means dealing with many files. Because of this, you use a specific construct when referencing files in MSBuild: items. Items are usually file-based references, but they can be used for other purposes as well. If you create a project using Visual Studio, you may notice that you see many *ItemGroup* elements as well as *PropertyGroup* elements. The *ItemGroup* element contains all the statically defined items. Static item definitions are those declared as a direct child of the *Project* element. Dynamic items, which we discuss in the next chapter, are those defined inside a target. When you define a property, you are declaring a key-value pair, which is a one-to-one relationship. When you declare items, one item can contain a list of many values. In terms of code, a property is analogous to a variable and an item to an array. Take a look at how an item is declared in the following snippet taken from the ItemsSimple.proj file:

```
<Project xmlns="http://schemas.microsoft.com/developer/msbuild/2003">
  <ItemGroup>
    <SolutionFile Include="..\InsideMSBuild.sln" />
  </ItemGroup>
  <Target Name="PrintSolutionInfo">
    <Message Text="SolutionFile: @(SolutionFile)" />
  </Target>
</Project>
```

In this file, there is an *ItemGroup* that has a subelement, *SolutionFile*. *ItemGroup* is the element type that all statically declared items must be placed within. The name of the subelement, *SolutionFile* in this case, is actually the item type of the item that is created. The *SolutionFile* element has an attribute, Include. This determines what values the item contains. Relating it back to an array, *SolutionFile* is the name of the variable that references the array, and the *Include* attribute is used to populate the array's values. The *Include* attribute can contain the following types of values (or any combination thereof): one distinct value, a list of values delimited with semicolons, or a value using wildcards. In this sample, the *Include* attribute contains one value. When you need to evaluate the contents of an item, you would use the @(*ItemType*) syntax. This is similar to the $(*PropertyName*) syntax for properties. To see this in action, take a look at the PrintSolutionInfo target. This target passes the value of the item into the Message task to be printed to the console. You can see the result of executing this target in Figure 1-3.

```
C:\InsideMSBuild\Ch01>msbuild ItemsSimple.proj /t:PrintSolutionInfo /nologo
Build started 9/24/2010 6:04:18 PM.
Project "C:\InsideMSBuild\Ch01\ItemsSimple.proj" on node 1 (PrintSolutionInfo target(s)).
PrintSolutionInfo:
  SolutionFile: ..\InsideMSBuild.sln
Done Building Project "C:\InsideMSBuild\Ch01\ItemsSimple.proj" (PrintSolutionInfo target(s)).

Build succeeded.
    0 Warning(s)
    0 Error(s)
```

FIGURE 1-3 PrintSolutionInfo result

In this case, the item *SolutionFile* contains a single value, so it doesn't seem very different from a property because the single value was simply passed to the Message task. Let's take a look at an item with more than one value. This is an extended version of the ItemsSimple .proj file shown earlier:

```
<Project xmlns="http://schemas.microsoft.com/developer/msbuild/2003">
  <ItemGroup>
    <SolutionFile Include="..\InsideMSBuild.sln" />
  </ItemGroup>
  <Target Name="PrintSolutionInfo">
    <Message Text="SolutionFile: @(SolutionFile)" />
  </Target>

  <ItemGroup>
    <Compile
     Include="Form1.cs;Form1.Designer.cs;Program.cs;Properties\AssemblyInfo.cs" />
  </ItemGroup>
  <Target Name="PrintCompileInfo">
    <Message Text="Compile: @(Compile)" />
  </Target>
</Project>
```

In the modified version, I have created a new item, Compile, which includes four values that are separated by semicolons. The PrintCompileInfo target passes these values to the Message task. When you invoke the PrintCompileInfo target on the MSBuild file just shown, the result will be Compile: Form1.cs;Form1.Designer.cs;Program.cs;Properties \AssemblyInfo.cs. It may look like the Message task simply took the value in the Include attribute and passed it to the Message task, but this is not the case. The Message task has a single input parameter, Text, as discussed earlier. This parameter is a string property. Because an item is a multivalued object, it cannot be passed directly into the Text property. It first has to be converted into a string. MSBuild does this for you by separating each value with a semicolon. In Chapter 2, I will discuss how you can customize this conversion process.

An item definition doesn't have to be defined entirely by a single element. It can span multiple elements. For example, the Compile item shown earlier could have been declared like this:

```
<ItemGroup>
  <Compile Include="Form1.cs" />
```

```
    <Compile Include="Form1.Designer.cs" />
    <Compile Include="Program.cs" />
    <Compile Include="Properties\AssemblyInfo.cs" />
  </ItemGroup>
```

In this version, each file is placed into the Compile item individually. These Compile elements could also have been contained in their own *ItemGroup* as well, as shown in the next snippet.

```
<ItemGroup>
  <Compile Include="Form1.cs" />
</ItemGroup>
<ItemGroup>
  <Compile Include="Form1.Designer.cs" />
</ItemGroup>
<ItemGroup>
  <Compile Include="Program.cs" />
</ItemGroup>
<ItemGroup>
  <Compile Include="Properties\AssemblyInfo.cs" />
</ItemGroup>
```

The end result of these declarations would all be the same. You should note that an item is an ordered list, so the order in which values are added to the item is preserved and may in some context affect behavior based on usage. When a property declaration appears after a previous one, the previous value is overwritten. Items act differently from this in that the value of the item is simply appended to instead of being overwritten. We've now discussed two of the three ways to create items. Let's look at using wildcards to create items.

Many times, items refer to existing files. If this is the case, you can use wildcards to automatically include files that meet the constraints of the wildcards. You can use three wildcard elements with MSBuild: ?, *, and **. The ? descriptor is used to denote that exactly one character can take its place. For example, the include declaration of b?t.cs could include values such as bat.cs, bot.cs, bet.cs, b1t.cs, and so on. The * descriptor can be replaced with zero or more characters (not including slashes), so the declaration b*t.cs could include values such as bat.cs, bot.cs, best.cs, bt.cs, etc. The ** descriptor tells MSBuild to search directories recursively for the pattern. In effect, "*" matches any characters except for "/" while "**" matches any characters, including "/". For example, Include="src***.cs" would include all files under the src folder (including subfolders) with the .cs extension.

Item Metadata

Another difference between properties and items is that items can have metadata associated with them. When you create an item, each of its elements is a full-fledged .NET object, which can have a set of values (metadata) associated with it. The metadata that is available on every item, which is called *well-known metadata,* is summarized in Table 1-2.

TABLE 1-2 Well-Known Metadata

Name	Description
Identity	The value that was specified in the Include attribute of the item after it was evaluated.
FullPath	Full path of the file.
RootDir	The root directory to which the file belongs, such as C:\.
Filename	The name of the file, not including the extension.
Extension	The extension of the file, including the period.
RelativeDir	Contains the path specified in the *Include* attribute, up to the final backslash (\).
Directory	Directory of the item, without the root directory.
RecursiveDir	This is the expanded directory path starting from the first ** of the include declaration. If no ** is present, then this value is empty. If multiple ** are present, then RecursiveDir will be the expanded value starting from the first **. This may sound peculiar, but it is what makes recursive copying possible.
ModifiedTime	The last time the file was modified.
CreatedTime	The time the file was created.
AccessedTime	The last time the file was accessed.

To access metadata values, you have to use this syntax:

```
@(ItemType->'%(MetadataName)')
```

ItemType is the name of the item, and MetadataName is the name of the metadata that you are accessing. This is the most basic syntax. To examine what types of values the well-known metadata returns, take a look at the file, WellKnownMetadata.proj, shown here:

```
<Project xmlns="http://schemas.microsoft.com/developer/msbuild/2003"
         ToolsVersion="4.0">
  <ItemGroup>
    <src Include="src\one.txt" />
  </ItemGroup>
  <Target Name="PrintWellKnownMetadata">

    <Message Text="===== Well known metadata ====="/>
    <!-- %40 = @ -->
    <!-- %25 = % -->
    <Message Text="%40(src->'%25(FullPath)'): @(src->'%(FullPath)')"/>
    <Message Text="%40(src->'%25(RootDir)'): @(src->'%(RootDir)')"/>
    <Message Text="%40(src->'%25(Filename)'): @(src->'%(Filename)')"/>
    <Message Text="%40(src->'%25(Extension)'): @(src->'%(Extension)')"/>
    <Message Text="%40(src->'%25(RelativeDir)'): @(src->'%(RelativeDir)')"/>
    <Message Text="%40(src->'%25(Directory)'): @(src->'%(Directory)')"/>
    <Message Text="%40(src->'%25(RecursiveDir)'): @(src->'%(RecursiveDir)')"/>
    <Message Text="%40(src->'%25(Identity)'): @(src->'%(Identity)')"/>
    <Message Text="%40(src->'%25(ModifiedTime)'): @(src->'%(ModifiedTime)')"/>
    <Message Text="%40(src->'%25(CreatedTime)'): @(src->'%(CreatedTime)')"/>
    <Message Text="%40(src->'%25(AccessedTime)'): @(src->'%(AccessedTime)')"/>

  </Target>
</Project>
```

> **Note** In order to use reserved characters, such as the % and @, you have to escape them. This is accomplished by the syntax %HV, where *HV* is the hex value of the character. This is demonstrated here with %25 and %40.

> **Note** In this example, we have specified the ToolsVersion value to be 4.0. This determines which version of the MSBuild tools will be used. Although not needed for this sample, we will be specifying this version number from this point forward. The default value is 2.0.

This MSBuild file prints the values for the well-known metadata for the src item. The result of executing the PrintWellKnownMetadata target is shown in Figure 1-4.

```
C:\InsideMSBuild\Ch01>msbuild WellKnownMetadata.proj /t:PrintWellKnownMetadata /nologo
Build started 9/24/2010 6:10:01 PM.
Project "C:\InsideMSBuild\Ch01\WellKnownMetadata.proj" on node 1 (PrintWellKnownMetadata target(s)
).
PrintWellKnownMetadata:
    ===== Well known metadata =====
  @(src->'%(FullPath)'): C:\InsideMSBuild\Ch01\src\one.txt
  @(src->'%(Rootdir)'): C:\
  @(src->'%(Filename)'): one
  @(src->'%(Extension)'): .txt
  @(src->'%(RelativeDir)'): src\
  @(src->'%(Directory)'): InsideMSBuild\Ch01\src\
  @(src->'%(RecursiveDir)'):
  @(src->'%(Identity)'): src\one.txt
  @(src->'%(ModifiedTime)'): 2010-09-08 22:15:12.4218750
  @(src->'%(CreatedTime)'): 2010-09-08 22:15:12.4218750
  @(src->'%(AccessedTime)'): 2010-09-08 22:15:12.4218750
Done Building Project "C:\InsideMSBuild\Ch01\WellKnownMetadata.proj" (PrintWellKnownMetadata targe
t(s)).

Build succeeded.
    0 Warning(s)
    0 Error(s)
```

FIGURE 1-4 PrintWellKnownMetadata result

The figure gives you a better understanding of the well-known metadata's usage. Keep in mind that this demonstrates the usage of metadata in the case where the item contains only a single value.

To see how things change when an item contains more than one value, let's examine MetadataExample01.proj:

```
<Project xmlns="http://schemas.microsoft.com/developer/msbuild/2003"
         ToolsVersion="4.0">
  <ItemGroup>
    <Compile Include="*.cs" />
  </ItemGroup>

  <Target Name="PrintCompileInfo">
    <Message Text="Compile fullpath: @(Compile->'%(FullPath)')" />
  </Target>
</Project>
```

In this project file we simply evaluate the FullPath metadata on the Compile item. From the examples with this text, the directory containing this example contains four files: Class1.cs, Class2.cs, Class3.c, and Class4.cs. These are the files that will be contained in the Compile item. Take a look at the result of the PrintCompileInfo target in Figure 1-5.

```
C:\InsideMSBuild\Ch01>msbuild MetadataExample01.proj /t:PrintCompileInfo /nologo
Build started 9/24/2010 6:18:39 PM.
Project "C:\InsideMSBuild\Ch01\MetadataExample01.proj" on node 1 (PrintCompileInfo target(s)).
PrintCompileInfo:
  Compile fullpath: C:\InsideMSBuild\Ch01\Class1.cs;C:\InsideMSBuild\Ch01\Class2.cs;C:\InsideMSBui
  ld\Ch01\Class3.cs;C:\InsideMSBuild\Ch01\Class4.cs
Done Building Project "C:\InsideMSBuild\Ch01\MetadataExample01.proj" (PrintCompileInfo target(s)).


Build succeeded.
    0 Warning(s)
    0 Error(s)
```

FIGURE 1-5 PrintCompileInfo result

You have to look carefully at this output to decipher the result. What is happening here is that a single string is created by combining the full path of each file, separated by a semicolon. The @(ItemType->'...%()...') syntax is an "Item Transformation." We will cover transformations in greater detail in Chapter 2. In the next section, we'll discuss conditions. Before we do that, take a minute to look at the project file for a simple Windows application that was generated by Visual Studio. You should recognize many things.

```xml
<Project DefaultTargets="Build"
xmlns="http://schemas.microsoft.com/developer/msbuild/2003" ToolsVersion="4.0">
  <PropertyGroup>
    <Configuration Condition=" '$(Configuration)' == '' ">Debug</Configuration>
    <Platform Condition=" '$(Platform)' == '' ">AnyCPU</Platform>
    <ProductVersion>8.0.50727</ProductVersion>
    <SchemaVersion>2.0</SchemaVersion>
    <ProjectGuid>{0F34CE5D-2AB0-49A9-8254-B21D1D2EFFA1}</ProjectGuid>
    <OutputType>WinExe</OutputType>
    <AppDesignerFolder>Properties</AppDesignerFolder>
    <RootNamespace>WindowsApplication1</RootNamespace>
    <AssemblyName>WindowsApplication1</AssemblyName>
  </PropertyGroup>
  <PropertyGroup Condition=" '$(Configuration)|$(Platform)' == 'Debug|AnyCPU' ">
    <DebugSymbols>true</DebugSymbols>
    <DebugType>full</DebugType>
    <Optimize>false</Optimize>
    <OutputPath>bin\Debug\</OutputPath>
    <DefineConstants>DEBUG;TRACE</DefineConstants>
    <ErrorReport>prompt</ErrorReport>
    <WarningLevel>4</WarningLevel>
  </PropertyGroup>
  <PropertyGroup Condition=" '$(Configuration)|$(Platform)' == 'Release|AnyCPU' ">
    <DebugType>pdbonly</DebugType>
    <Optimize>true</Optimize>
    <OutputPath>bin\Release\</OutputPath>
    <DefineConstants>TRACE</DefineConstants>
    <ErrorReport>prompt</ErrorReport>
    <WarningLevel>4</WarningLevel>
  </PropertyGroup>
  <ItemGroup>
    <Reference Include="System" />
    <Reference Include="System.Data" />
    <Reference Include="System.Deployment" />
    <Reference Include="System.Drawing" />
    <Reference Include="System.Windows.Forms" />
    <Reference Include="System.Xml" />
  </ItemGroup>
```

```xml
<ItemGroup>
  <Compile Include="Form1.cs">
    <SubType>Form</SubType>
  </Compile>
  <Compile Include="Form1.Designer.cs">
    <DependentUpon>Form1.cs</DependentUpon>
  </Compile>
  <Compile Include="Program.cs" />
  <Compile Include="Properties\AssemblyInfo.cs" />
  <EmbeddedResource Include="Properties\Resources.resx">
    <Generator>ResXFileCodeGenerator</Generator>
    <LastGenOutput>Resources.Designer.cs</LastGenOutput>
    <SubType>Designer</SubType>
  </EmbeddedResource>
  <Compile Include="Properties\Resources.Designer.cs">
    <AutoGen>True</AutoGen>
    <DependentUpon>Resources.resx</DependentUpon>
  </Compile>
  <None Include="Properties\Settings.settings">
    <Generator>SettingsSingleFileGenerator</Generator>
    <LastGenOutput>Settings.Designer.cs</LastGenOutput>
  </None>
  <Compile Include="Properties\Settings.Designer.cs">
    <AutoGen>True</AutoGen>
    <DependentUpon>Settings.settings</DependentUpon>
    <DesignTimeSharedInput>True</DesignTimeSharedInput>
  </Compile>
</ItemGroup>
<Import Project="$(MSBuildToolsPath)\Microsoft.CSharp.targets" />
<!-- To modify your build process, add your task
inside one of the targets below and uncomment it.
     Other similar extension points exist,
see Microsoft.Common.targets.
  <Target Name="BeforeBuild">
  </Target>
  <Target Name="AfterBuild">
  </Target>
  -->
</Project>
```

Simple Conditions

When you are building, you often have to make decisions based on conditions. MSBuild
allows almost every XML element to contain a conditional statement within it. The statement
would be declared in the *Condition* attribute. If this attribute evaluates to *false,* then the
element and all its child elements are ignored. In the sample Visual Studio project that was
shown at the end of the previous section, you will find the statement <Configuration
Condition=" '$(Configuration)' == '' ">Debug</Configuration>. In this declaration,
the condition is checking to see if the property is empty. If so, then it will be defined;
otherwise, the statement will be skipped. This is a method to provide a default overridable
value for a property. Table 1-3 describes a few common types of conditional operators.

TABLE 1-3 Simple Conditional Operators

Symbol	Description
==	Checks for equality; returns *true* if both have the same value.
!=	Checks for inequality; returns *true* if both do not have the same value.
Exists	Checks for the existence of a file. Returns *true* if the provided file exists.
!Exists	Checks for the nonexistence of a file. Returns *true* if the file provided is not found.

Because you can add a conditional attribute to any MSBuild element (excluding the Otherwise element), this means that we can decide to include entries in items as necessary. For example, when building ASP.NET applications, in some scenarios, you might want to include files that will assist debugging. Take a look at the MSBuild file, ConditionExample01.proj:

```
<Project xmlns="http://schemas.microsoft.com/developer/msbuild/2003"
        ToolsVersion="4.0">
  <PropertyGroup>
    <Configuration>Release</Configuration>
  </PropertyGroup>
  <ItemGroup>
    <Content Include="script.js"/>
    <Content Include="script.debug.js" Condition="$(Configuration)=='Debug'" />
  </ItemGroup>

  <Target Name="PrintContent">
    <Message Text="Configuration: $(Configuration)" />
    <Message Text="Content: @(Content)" />
  </Target>
</Project>
```

If we execute the command `msbuild ConditionExample01.proj /t:PrintContent`, the result would be what is shown in Figure 1-6.

```
C:\InsideMSBuild\Ch01>msbuild ConditionExample01.proj /t:PrintContent /nologo
Build started 9/24/2010 6:24:55 PM.
Project "C:\InsideMSBuild\Ch01\ConditionExample01.proj" on node 1 (PrintContent target(s)).
PrintContent:
  Configuration: Release
  Content: script.js
Done Building Project "C:\InsideMSBuild\Ch01\ConditionExample01.proj" (PrintContent target(s)).

Build succeeded.
    0 Warning(s)
    0 Error(s)
```

FIGURE 1-6 PrintContent target result

As you can see, because the Configuration value was not set to Debug, the script.debug.js file was not included in the Content item. Now we will examine the usage of the *Exists* function. To do this, take a look at the target _CheckForCompileOutputs, taken from the Microsoft .Common.targets file, a file included with MSBuild that contains most of the rules for building VB and C# projects:

```
<Target
    Name="_CheckForCompileOutputs">
```

```xml
    <!--Record the main compile outputs.-->
    <ItemGroup>
        <FileWrites
          Include="@(IntermediateAssembly)"
          Condition="Exists('@(IntermediateAssembly)')" />
    </ItemGroup>

    <!-- Record the .xml if one was produced. -->
    <PropertyGroup>
        <_DocumentationFileProduced
          Condition="!Exists('@(DocFileItem)')">false</_DocumentationFileProduced>
    </PropertyGroup>

    <ItemGroup>
        <FileWrites
          Include="@(DocFileItem)"
          Condition="'$(_DocumentationFileProduced)'=='true'" />
    </ItemGroup>

    <!-- Record the .pdb if one was produced. -->
    <PropertyGroup>
        <_DebugSymbolsProduced
           Condition="!Exists('@(_DebugSymbolsIntermediatePath)')">false
        </_DebugSymbolsProduced>
    </PropertyGroup>

    <ItemGroup>
        <FileWrites
          Include="@(_DebugSymbolsIntermediatePath)"
          Condition="'$(_DebugSymbolsProduced)'=='true'" />
    </ItemGroup>
</Target>
```

From the first FileWrites item definition, the condition is defined as Exists
(@(IntermediateAssembly)). This will determine whether the file referenced by the
IntermediateAssembly item exists on disk. If it doesn't, then the declaration task is
skipped. This was a brief overview of conditional statements, but it should be enough to
get you started. Let's move on to learn a bit more about targets.

Default/Initial Targets

When you create an MSBuild file, you will typically create it such that a target, or a set of
targets, will be executed most of the time. In this scenario, these targets can be specified
as default targets. These targets will be executed if a target is not specifically chosen to be
executed. Without the declaration of a default target, the first defined target in the logical
project file, after all imports have been resolved, is treated as the default target. A logical
project file is one with all Import statements processed. Using default target(s) is how Visual

Studio builds your managed project. If you take a look at Visual Studio–generated project files, you will notice that the Build target is specified as the default target:

```
<Project DefaultTargets="Build"
xmlns="http://schemas.microsoft.com/developer/msbuild/2003" ToolsVersion="4.0">
...
</Project>
```

As mentioned previously, you can have either one target or many targets be your default target(s). If the declaration contains more than one, the target names need to be separated by a semicolon. When you use a command such as msbuild ProjectFile.proj, because you have not specified a target to execute, the default target(s) will be executed. It's important to note that the list of DefaultTargets will be preserved, not modified, through an Import, provided that a project previously processed hasn't had a DefaultTargets list. This is one difference between DefaultTargets and InitialTargets. Values for InitialTargets are aggregated for all imports because each file may have its own initialization checks.

These targets listed in InitialTargets will always be executed even if the project file is imported by other project files. Similar to default targets, the initial targets list is declared as an attribute on the *Project* element with the name InitialTargets. If you take a look at the Microsoft.Common.targets file, you will notice that the target _CheckForInvalidConfigurationAndPlatform is declared as the initial target. This target will perform a couple sanity checks before allowing the build to continue. I would strongly encourage the use of default targets. InitialTargets should be used to verify initial conditions before the build starts and raises an error or warning if applicable. Next, we will discuss the command-line usage of the msbuild.exe command.

MSBuild.exe Command-Line Usage

In this section, we'll discuss the most important options when invoking msbuild.exe. When you invoke the msbuild.exe executable, you can pass many parameters to customize the process. We'll first take a look at the options that are available with MSBuild 2.0, and then we'll discuss what differences exist for MSBuild 3.5 and MSBuild 4.0. Table 1-4 summarizes the parameters you can pass to msbuild.exe. Many commands include a short version that can be used; these versions are listed in the table within parentheses.

TABLE 1-4 MSBuild.exe Command-Line Switches

Switch	Description
/help (/?)	Displays the usage information for msbuild.exe.
/nologo	Suppresses the copyright and startup banner.
/version (/ver)	Displays version information.
@file	Used to pick up response file(s) for parameters.

Switch	Description
/noautoresponse (/noautoresp)	Used to suppress automatically, including msbuild.rsp as a response file.
/target (/t)	Used to specify which target(s) should be built. If specifying more than one target, they should each be separated by a semicolon. Commas are valid separators, but semicolons are the ones most commonly used.
/property:<n>=<v> (/p)	Used to specify properties. If providing more than one property, they should each be separated by a semicolon. Property values should be specified in the format: *name=value*. These values would supersede any static property definitions. Commas are valid separators, but semicolons are the ones most commonly used.
/verbosity (/v)	Sets the verbosity of the build. The options are quiet (q), minimal (m), normal (n), detailed (d), and diagnostic (diag). This is passed to each logger, and the logger is able to make its own decision about how to interpret it.
/validate (/val)	Used to ensure that the project file is in the correct format before the build is started.
/logger (/l)	Attaches the specified logger to the build. This switch can be provided multiple times to attach any number of loggers. Also, you can pass parameters to the loggers with this switch.
/consoleloggerparameters (/clp)	Used to pass parameters to the console logger.
/noconsolelogger (/noconlog)	Used to suppress the usage of the console logger, which is otherwise always attached.
/filelogger (/fl)	Attaches a file logger to the build.
/fileloggerparameters (/flp)	Passes parameters to the file logger. If you want to attach multiple file loggers, you do so by specifying additional parameters in the switches /flp1, /flp2, /flp3, and so on.
/distributedFileLogger (/dl)	Used to attach a distributed logger. This is an advanced switch that you will most likely not use and that could have been excluded altogether.
/maxcpucount (/m)	Sets the maximum number of processes that should be used by msbuild.exe to build the project.
/ignoreprojectextensions (/ignore)	Instructs MSBuild to ignore the extensions passed.
/toolsversion (/tv)	Specifies the version of the .NET Framework tools that should be used to build the project.
/nodeReuse (/nr)	Used to specify whether nodes should be reused or not. Typically, there should be no need to specify this; the default value is optimal.

Switch	Description
/preprocess (/pp)*	This will output the complete logical file to either the console or to a specified file. To have the result written out to the file, use the syntax /pp:file.
	Usually, this file will build just as if you were building the original project (there are exceptions though, such as $(MSBuildThisFile)). The real purpose of this is to help diagnose a problem with the build by avoiding the need to jump between many different files. For example, if a particular property is getting overwritten somewhere, it is much easier to search for it in the single "preprocessed" file than it is to search for it in the many imported files.
/detailedSummary (/ds)*	It displays information about how the projects were scheduled to different CPUs. You can use this to help figure out how to make the build faster. For example, you can use this to determine which project was stalling other projects.

* Denotes parameters new with MSBuild 4.0.

From Table 1-4, the most commonly used parameters are target, property, and logger. You might also be interested in using the FileLogger switch. To give you an example, I will use an MSBuild file that we discussed earlier, the ConditionExample01.proj file. Take a look at the following command that will attach the file logger to the build process: msbuild ConditionExample01.proj /fl. Because we didn't specify the name of the log file to be written to, the default, msbuild.log, will be used. Using this same project file, let's see how to override the Configuration value. From that file, the Configuration value would be set to Release, but we can override it from the command line with the following statement: msbuild ConditionExample01.proj /p:Configuration=Debug /t:PrintContent. In this command, we are using the *p* (property) switch to provide a property value to the build engine, and we are specifying to execute the PrintContent target. The result is shown in Figure 1-7.

```
C:\InsideMSBuild\Ch01>msbuild ConditionExample01.proj /p:Configuration=Debug /t:PrintContent /nolog
o
Build started 9/24/2010 6:42:28 PM.
Project "C:\InsideMSBuild\Ch01\ConditionExample01.proj" on node 1 (PrintContent target(s)).
PrintContent:
    Configuration: Debug
    Content: script.js;script.debug.js
Done Building Project "C:\InsideMSBuild\Ch01\ConditionExample01.proj" (PrintContent target(s)).

Build succeeded.
    0 Warning(s)
    0 Error(s)
```

FIGURE 1-7 Specifying a property from the command line

The messages on the console show that the value for Configuration was indeed Debug, and as expected, the debug JavaScript file was included in the Content item. Now that you know the basic usage of the msbuild.exe command, we'll move on to the last topic: extending the build process.

Extending the Build Process

With versions of Visual Studio prior to 2005, the build was mostly a black box. The process by which Visual Studio built your applications was internal to the Visual Studio product itself. The only way you could customize the process was to use execute commands for pre- and post-build events. With this, you were able to embed a series of commands to be executed. You were not able to change how Visual Studio built your applications. With the advent of MSBuild, Visual Studio has externalized the build process and you now have complete control over it. Since MSBuild is delivered with the .NET Framework, Visual Studio is not required to build applications. Because of this, we can create build servers that do not need to have Visual Studio installed. We'll examine this by showing how to augment the build process. Throughout the rest of this book, we will describe how to extend the build process in more detail.

The pre- and post-build events mentioned earlier are still available, but you now have other options. The three main ways to add a pre- or post-build action are:

- Pre- and post-build events
- Override BeforeBuild/AfterBuild target
- Extend the BuildDependsOn list

The pre- and post-build events are the same as described previously. This is a good approach for backward compatibility and ease of use. Configuring this using Visual Studio doesn't require knowledge of MSBuild. Figure 1-8 shows the Build Events tab on the ProjectProperties page.

Here, you can see the two locations for the pre- and post-build events toward the center of the image. The dialog that is displayed is the post-build event command editor. This helps you construct the command. You define the command here, and MSBuild executes it for you at the appropriate time using the Exec task (*http://msdn2.microsoft.com/en-us/library/x8zx72cd.aspx*). Typically, these events are used to copy or move files around before or after the build.

Using the pre- and post-build event works fairly well if you want to execute a set of commands. If you need more control over what is occurring, you will want to manually modify the project file itself. When you create a new project using Visual Studio, the project file generated is an MSBuild file, which is an XML file. You can use any editor you choose, but if you use Visual Studio, you will have IntelliSense when you are editing it! With your solution loaded in Visual Studio, you can right-click the project, select Unload Project, right-click the project again, and select Edit. If you take a look at the project file, you will notice this statement toward the bottom of the file.

```
<!-- To modify your build process, add your task inside one
     of the targets below and uncomment it.
     Other similar extension points exist, see Microsoft.Common.targets.
  <Target Name="BeforeBuild">
  </Target>
  <Target Name="AfterBuild">
  </Target>
  -->
```

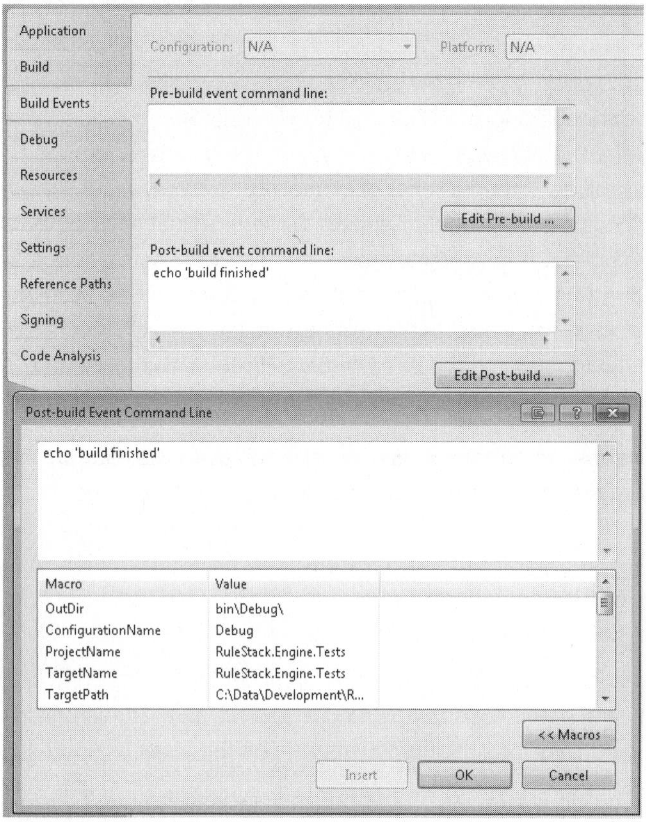

FIGURE 1-8 Build Events tab

From the previous snippet, we can see that there are predefined targets designed to handle these types of customizations. We can simply follow the directions from the project file, by defining the BeforeBuild or AfterBuild target. You will want to make sure that these definitions are **after** the *Import* element for the Microsoft.*.targets file, where * represents the language of the project you are editing. For example, you could insert the following AfterBuild target:

```
<Target Name="AfterBuild">
  <Message Text="Build has completed!" />
</Target>
```

When the build has finished, this target will be executed and the message 'Build has completed!' will be passed to the loggers. We will cover the third option, extending the BuildDependsOn list, in Chapter 3.

In this chapter, we have covered many features of MSBuild, including properties, items, targets, and tasks. Now you should have all that you need to get started customizing your build process. From this point on, the remainder of the book will work on filling in the details that were left out here so that you can become an MSBuild expert!

Chapter 2
MSBuild Deep Dive, Part 1

In the previous chapter, we gave a brief overview of all the key elements in MSBuild. In this chapter and the next, we'll examine most of those ideas in more detail. We'll discuss properties, items, targets, tasks, transformations, and much more. After you have completed this chapter, you will have a solid grasp of how to create and modify MSBuild files to suit your needs. After the next chapter, we'll explore ways to extend MSBuild as well as some advanced topics.

What is MSBuild? MSBuild is a general-purpose build system created by Microsoft and is used to build most Microsoft Visual Studio projects. MSBuild is shipped with the Microsoft .NET Framework. What this means is that you do *not* need to have Visual Studio installed in order to build your applications. This is very beneficial because you don't need to purchase licenses of Visual Studio for dedicated build machines, and it makes configuring build machines easier. Another benefit is that MSBuild will be installed on many machines. If .NET Framework 2.0 or later is available on a machine, so is a version of MSBuild. The following terms have been used to identify an MSBuild file: MSBuild file, MSBuild project file, MSBuild targets file, MSBuild script, etc. When you create an MSBuild file, you should follow these conventions for specifying the extension of the file:

- **.proj**   A project file
- **.targets**   A file that contains shared targets, which are imported into other files
- **.props**   Default settings for a build process
- **.tasks**   A file that contains UsingTask declarations

An MSBuild file is just an XML file. You can use any editor you choose to create and edit MSBuild files. The preferred editor is Visual Studio, because it provides IntelliSense on the MSBuild files as you are editing them. This IntelliSense will greatly decrease the amount of time required to write an MSBuild file. The IntelliSense is driven by a few XML Schema Definition (XSD) files. These XSD files, which are all in Visual Studio's XML directory, are Microsoft.Build.xsd, Microsoft.Build.Core.xsd, and Microsoft.Build.Commontypes.xsd. The Microsoft.Build.xsd file imports the other two files, and provides an extension point for task developers to include their own files. The Microsoft.Build.Core.xsd file describes all the fundamental elements that an MSBuild file can contain.

Microsoft.Build.Commonttypes.xsd defines all known elements; this is mainly used to describe the elements that Visual Studio–generated project files can contain. The XSD that is used is not 100 percent complete, but in most cases you will not notice that. Now that we have discussed what it takes to edit an MSBuild file, let's discuss properties in detail. If you are not familiar with invoking msbuild.exe from the command line, take a look back at Chapter 1, "MSBuild Quick Start"; this is not covered again here.

Properties

MSBuild has two main constructs for representing data: properties and items. A property is a key-value pair. Each property can have exactly one value. An item list differs from a property in that it can have many values. In programming terms, a property is similar to a scalar variable, and an item list is similar to an array variable, whose order is preserved. Properties are declared inside the *Project* element in a *PropertyGroup* element. We'll now take a look at how properties are declared. The following file, Properties01.proj, demonstrates declaration and usage of a property.

```
<Project xmlns=http://schemas.microsoft.com/developer/msbuild/2003
         ToolsVersion="4.0">

  <PropertyGroup>
    <Configuration>Debug</Configuration>
  </PropertyGroup>

  <Target Name="PrintConfig">
    <Message Text="Config: $(Configuration)" />
  </Target>

</Project>
```

As stated previously, we needed a *PropertyGroup* element, and the Configuration property was defined inside of that. By doing this we have created a new property named Configuration and given it the value *Debug*. When you create properties, you are not limited to defining only one property per *PropertyGroup* element. You can define any number of properties inside a single *PropertyGroup* element. In the target PrintConfig, the Message task is invoked in order to print the value of the Configuration property. If you are not familiar with what a target is, refer back to Chapter 1, "MSBuild Quick Start." You can execute that target with the command msbuild.exe Properties01.proj /t:PrintConfig. The results of this command are shown in Figure 2-1.

```
C:\InsideMSBuild\Ch02>msbuild Properties01.proj /t:PrintConfig /nologo
Build started 9/28/2010 9:52:48 PM.
Project "C:\InsideMSBuild\Ch02\Properties01.proj" on node 1 (PrintConfig target(s)).
PrintConfig:
  Config: Debug
Done Building Project "C:\InsideMSBuild\Ch02\Properties01.proj" (PrintConfig target(s)).

Build succeeded.
    0 Warning(s)
    0 Error(s)
```

FIGURE 2-1 PrintConfig target results

From the result in Figure 2-1, we can see that the correct value for the Configuration property was printed as expected. As properties are declared, their values are recorded in a top-to-bottom order. What this means is that if a property is defined, and then defined again, the last value will be the one that is applied. Take a look at a modified version of the previous example; this one is contained in the Properties02.proj file.

```
<Project xmlns=http://schemas.microsoft.com/developer/msbuild/2003
         ToolsVersion="4.0">

  <PropertyGroup>
    <Configuration>Debug</Configuration>
  </PropertyGroup>

  <PropertyGroup>
    <Configuration>Release</Configuration>
  </PropertyGroup>

  <Target Name="PrintConfig">
    <Message Text="Config: $(Configuration)" />
  </Target>

</Project>
```

In this example, we have declared the Configuration property once again, after the existing declaration, and specified that it have the value *Release*. Because the new value is declared *after* the previous one, we would expect the new value to hold. If you execute the PrintConfig target on this file, you will see that this is indeed the case. Properties in MSBuild can be declared any number of times. This is not an erroneous condition, and there is no way to detect this. Now we will look at another version of the previous file, a slightly modified one. Take a look at the contents of the following Properties03.proj file.

```
<Project xmlns=http://schemas.microsoft.com/developer/msbuild/2003
         ToolsVersion="4.0">

  <PropertyGroup>
    <Configuration>Debug</Configuration>
  </PropertyGroup>

  <PropertyGroup>
    <Configuration>Release</Configuration>
  </PropertyGroup>

  <Target Name="PrintConfig">
    <Message Text="Config: $(Configuration)"/>
  </Target>

  <PropertyGroup>
    <Configuration>CustomRelease</Configuration>
  </PropertyGroup>

</Project>
```

This example is a little different in the sense that there is a value for Configuration declared after the PrintConfig target. That value is *CustomRelease*. So if we execute the PrintConfig target, what should be the result, *Release* or *CustomRelease*? We can execute `msbuild.exe Properties03.proj /t:PrintConfig` to find out. The results of this command are shown in Figure 2-2.

```
C:\InsideMSBuild\Ch02>msbuild Properties03.proj /t:PrintConfig /nologo
Build started 9/28/2010 9:54:10 PM.
Project "C:\InsideMSBuild\Ch02\Properties03.proj" on node 1 (PrintConfig target(s)).
PrintConfig:
    Config: CustomRelease
Done Building Project "C:\InsideMSBuild\Ch02\Properties03.proj" (PrintConfig target(s)).

Build succeeded.
    0 Warning(s)
    0 Error(s)
```

FIGURE 2-2 PrintConfig result for Properties03.proj

As can be seen from the results in Figure 2-2, the value for Configuration that was printed was *CustomRelease*! How is this possible? It was defined after the PrintConfig target! This is because MSBuild processes the entire file for properties and items ***before*** any targets are executed. You can imagine all the properties being in a dictionary, and as the project file is processed, its values are placed in the dictionary. Property names are *not* case sensitive, so Configuration and CoNfiguratION would refer to the same property. After the entire file, including imported files, is processed, all the final values for statically declared properties and items have been resolved. Once all the properties and items have been resolved, targets are allowed to execute. We'll take a closer look at this process in the section entitled "Property and Item Evaluation," in Chapter 3, "MSBuild Deep Dive, Part 2."

> **Note** We will discuss importing files in Chapter 3.

Environment Variables

We have described the basic usage of properties. Now we'll discuss a few other related topics. When you are building your applications, sometimes you might need to extract values from environment variables. This is a lot simpler than you might imagine if you use MSBuild. You can access values, just as you would properties, for environment variables. For example, take a look at the following project file, Properties04.proj.

```
<Project xmlns=http://schemas.microsoft.com/developer/msbuild/2003
         ToolsVersion="4.0">

  <Target Name="PrintEnvVar">
    <Message Text="Temp: $(Temp)" />
    <Message Text="Windir: $(windir)" />
    <Message Text="VS100COMNTOOLS: $(VS100COMNTOOLS)" />
  </Target>

</Project>
```

In this example, we can see that no properties have been declared and no other files are imported. Inside the target, PrintEnvVar, we can see that we have made a few messages to print the values of some properties. These values are being pulled from the environment variables. When you use the $(*PropertyName*) syntax to retrieve a value, MSBuild will first look to see if there is a corresponding property. If there is, its value is returned. If there isn't, then it will look at the environment variables for a variable with the provided name. If such a variable exists, its value is returned. If you execute the command `msbuild.exe Properties04.proj /t:PrintEnvVar` you should see a result similar to that shown in Figure 2-3.

```
C:\InsideMSBuild\Ch02>msbuild Properties04.proj /t:PrintEnvVar /nologo
Build started 9/28/2010 9:57:37 PM.
Project "C:\InsideMSBuild\Ch02\Properties04.proj" on node 1 (PrintEnvVar target(s)).
PrintEnvVar:
    Temp: C:\Users\Ibrahim\AppData\Local\Temp
    Windir: C:\WINDOWS
    VS100COMNTOOLS: C:\Program Files\Microsoft Visual Studio 10.0\Common7\Tools\
Done Building Project "C:\InsideMSBuild\Ch02\Properties04.proj" (PrintEnvVar target(s)).

Build succeeded.
    0 Warning(s)
    0 Error(s)
```

FIGURE 2-3 Environment variable usage

As demonstrated in Figure 2-3, the values for the appropriate environment variables were printed as expected.

> **Note**   When MSBuild starts (that is, when msbuild.exe starts or when Visual Studio starts), all the environment variables and their values are captured *at that time*. So if a value for an environment variable changes after that, it will not be reflected in the build. Also, you should be aware that each project is isolated from environment variable changes and changes to the current directory that are made by other projects.

If you don't have Visual Studio 2010 installed on the machine running this file, then the value may be empty for the VS100COMNTOOLS property. As we just saw, you can get the value for an environment variable by using the property notation. Assigning a value to a property that has the same name as an environment variable has no effect on the environment variable itself. The $(*PropertyName*) notation can get a value from an environment variable, but it will never assign values to environment variables. Let's move on to discuss reserved properties.

Reserved Properties

There are a fixed number of reserved properties. These are properties that are globally available to every MSBuild script and that can never be overwritten. These properties are provided to users by the MSBuild engine itself, and many of them are very useful. These are summarized in Table 2-1.

TABLE 2-1 Reserved Properties

Name	Description
MSBuildProjectDirectory	The full path to the directory where the project file is located.
MSBuildProjectDirectoryNoRoot	The full path to the directory where the project file is located, excluding the root (for example, c:\).

Name	Description
MSBuildProjectFile	The name of the project file, including the extension.
MSBuildProjectExtension	The extension of the project file, including the period.
MSBuildProjectFullPath	The full path to the project file.
MSBuildProjectName	The name of the project file, without the extension.
MSBuildProjectDefaultTargets	Contains a list of the default targets.
MSBuildExtensionsPath	The full path to where MSBuild extensions are located. This is typically under the Program Files folder. Note that now this always points to the 32-bit location.
MSBuildExtensionsPath32	The full path to where MSBuild 32 bit extensions are located. This is typically under the Program Files folder. For 32-bit machines, this value will be the same as MSBuildExtensionsPath.
MSBuildExtensionsPath64 *	The full path to where MSBuild 64-bit extensions are located. This is typically under the Program Files folder. For 32-bit machines, this value will be empty.
MSBuildNodeCount	The maximum number of nodes (processes) that are being used to build the project. If the /m switch is not used, then this value will be 1. If you use the /m switch without specifying a number of nodes, then the default is the number of CPUs available.
MSBuildStartupDirectory	The full path to the folder where the MSBuild process was invoked.
MSBuildToolsPath (MSBuildBinPath)	The full path to the location where the MSBuild binaries are located. In MSBuild 2.0, this property is named MSBuildBinPath and is deprecated in MSBuild 3.5 and later. MSBuildBinPath and MSBuildToolsPath have the same value, but you should use only MSBuildToolsPath.
MSBuildToolsVersion	The version of the tools being used to build the project. Possible values include 2.0, 3.5, and 4.0. The default value is 2.0.
MSBuildLastTaskResult *	This contains *true* if the last executed task was a success (*task returned true*) and *false* if it ended in a failure. If a task fails, typically the build stops unless you specified ContinueOnError="true".
MSBuildProgramFiles32 *	This contains the path to the 32-bit Program Files folder. To get the value for the default Program Files folder, use $(ProgramFiles).
MSBuildThisFile *	Contains the file name, including the extension, of the file that contains the property usage. This differs from MSBuildProjectFile in that MSBuildProjectFile always refers to the file that was invoked, not any imported file name.
MSBuildThisFileDirectory *	The path of the folder of the file that uses the property. This is useful if you need to define any items whose location you know relative to the targets file.

Name	Description
MSBuildThisFileDirectoryNoRoot *	Same as MSBuildThisFileDirectory without the root (for example, InsideMSBuild\Ch02 instead of C:\InsideMSBuild\Ch02).
MSBuildThisFileExtension *	The extension of the file referenced by MSBuildThisFile.
MSBuildThisFileFullPath *	The full path to the file that contains the usage of the property.
MSBuildThisFileName *	The name of the file, excluding the extension, to the file that contains usage of the property.
MSBuildOverrideTasksPath *	MSBuild 4.0 introduces override tasks, which are tasks that force themselves to be used instead of any other defined task with the same name, and this property points to a file that contains the overrides. The override tasks feature is used internally to help MSBuild 4.0 work well with other versions of MSBuild.

* denotes parameters new with MSBuild 4.0.

> **Note** You are allowed to override the values for MSBuildExtensionsPath, as well as the 32- and 64-bit variants. This is useful in case you check shared tasks into source control and want to use those files.

You would use these properties in the same way as you would any other properties. In order to understand what types of values these properties are set to, I have created the following sample file, ReservedProperties01.proj, to print out all these values.

```
<Project xmlns=http://schemas.microsoft.com/developer/msbuild/2003
        ToolsVersion="4.0">
  <Target Name="PrintReservedProperties">
    <Message Text="MSBuildProjectDirectory: $(MSBuildProjectDirectory)" />
    <Message Text="MSBuildProjectDirectoryNoRoot: $(MSBuildProjectDirectoryNoRoot)" />
    <Message Text="MSBuildProjectFile: $(MSBuildProjectFile)" />
    <Message Text="MSBuildProjectExtension: $(MSBuildProjectExtension)" />
    <Message Text="MSBuildProjectFullPath: $(MSBuildProjectFullPath)" />
    <Message Text="MSBuildProjectName: $(MSBuildProjectName)" />
    <Message Text="MSBuildToolsPath: $(MSBuildToolsPath)" />
    <Message Text="MSBuildProjectDefaultTargets: $(MSBuildProjectDefaultTargets)" />
    <Message Text="MSBuildExtensionsPath: $(MSBuildExtensionsPath)" />
    <Message Text="MSBuildExtensionsPath32: $(MSBuildExtensionsPath32)" />
    <Message Text="MSBuildExtensionsPath64: $(MSBuildExtensionsPath64)" />
    <Message Text="MSBuildNodeCount: $(MSBuildNodeCount)" />
    <Message Text="MSBuildStartupDirectory: $(MSBuildStartupDirectory)" />
    <Message Text="MSBuildToolsPath: $(MSBuildToolsPath)" />
    <Message Text="MSBuildToolsVersion: $(MSBuildToolsVersion)" />
    <Message Text="MSBuildLastTaskResult: $(MSBuildLastTaskResult)" />
    <Message Text="MSBuildProgramFiles32: $(MSBuildProgramFiles32)" />
    <Message Text="MSBuildThisFile: $(MSBuildThisFile)" />
    <Message Text="MSBuildThisFileDirectory: $(MSBuildThisFileDirectory)" />
    <Message Text="MSBuildThisFileDirectoryNoRoot: $(MSBuildThisFileDirectoryNoRoot)" />
    <Message Text="MSBuildThisFileExtension: $(MSBuildThisFileExtension)" />
    <Message Text="MSBuildThisFileFullPath: $(MSBuildThisFileFullPath)" />
```

```
      <Message Text="MSBuildThisFileName: $(MSBuildThisFileName)" />
      <Message Text="MSBuildOverrideTasksPath: $(MSBuildOverrideTasksPath)" />
  </Target>
</Project>
```

If you execute this build file using the command msbuild.exe ReservedProperties01
.proj /t:PrintReservedProperties, you would see the results shown in Figure 2-4.

```
C:\InsideMSBuild\Ch02>msbuild ReservedProperties01.proj /t:PrintReservedProperties /nologo
Build started 9/28/2010 10:03:50 PM.
Project "C:\InsideMSBuild\Ch02\ReservedProperties01.proj" on node 1 (PrintReservedProperties targe
t(s)).
PrintReservedProperties:
  MSBuildProjectDirectory: C:\InsideMSBuild\Ch02
  MSBuildProjectDirectoryNoRoot: InsideMSBuild\Ch02
  MSBuildProjectFile: ReservedProperties01.proj
  MSBuildProjectExtension: .proj
  MSBuildProjectFullPath: C:\InsideMSBuild\Ch02\ReservedProperties01.proj
  MSBuildProjectName: ReservedProperties01
  MSBuildToolsPath: C:\WINDOWS\Microsoft.NET\Framework\v4.0.30319
  MSBuildProjectDefaultTargets:
  MSBuildExtensionsPath: C:\Program Files\MSBuild
  MSBuildExtensionsPath32: C:\Program Files\MSBuild
  MSBuildExtensionsPath64:
  MSBuildNodeCount: 1
  MSBuildStartupDirectory: C:\InsideMSBuild\Ch02
  MSBuildToolsPath: C:\WINDOWS\Microsoft.NET\Framework\v4.0.30319
  MSBuildToolsVersion: 4.0
  MSBuildLastTaskResult: true
  MSBuildProgramFiles32: C:\Program Files
  MSBuildThisFile: ReservedProperties01.proj
  MSBuildThisFileDirectory: C:\InsideMSBuild\Ch02\
  MSBuildThisFileDirectoryNoRoot: InsideMSBuild\Ch02\
  MSBuildThisFileExtension: .proj
  MSBuildThisFileFullPath: C:\InsideMSBuild\Ch02\ReservedProperties01.proj
  MSBuildThisFileName: ReservedProperties01
  MSBuildOverrideTasksPath:
Done Building Project "C:\InsideMSBuild\Ch02\ReservedProperties01.proj" (PrintReservedProperties t
arget(s)).

Build succeeded.
    0 Warning(s)
    0 Error(s)
```

FIGURE 2-4 Reserved properties

Most of these values are straightforward. You should note that the values relating to the
MSBuild file, with the exception of those starting with *MSBuildThis*, are always qualified
relative to the MSBuild file that is invoking the entire process. This becomes clear when you
use the *Import* element to import additional MSBuild files. For the *MSBuildThis* properties,
those values always refer to the file that contains the element. We will take a look at
importing external files in the next chapter.

Command-Line Properties

You can also provide properties through the command line. As stated in Chapter 1, we can
use the /property switch (short version /p) to achieve this. We will see how this works now.
When you use the /p switch, you must specify the values in the format /p:*<n>*=*<v>*, where
<n> is the name of the property and *<v>* is its value. You can provide multiple values by
separating the pairs by a semicolon or a comma. We will demonstrate a simple case with the
following project file, Properties05.proj.

```
<Project xmlns=http://schemas.microsoft.com/developer/msbuild/2003
        ToolsVersion="4.0">
```

```
<Target Name="PrintInfo">
  <Message Text="AssemblyName: $(AssemblyName)" />
  <Message Text ="OutputPath: $(OutputPath)" />
</Target>

</Project>
```

Because there are no values for AssemblyName or OutputPath, it would be pointless to execute this MSBuild file. If we pass them in through the command line, you can see their values. If you specify values for AssemblyName and OutputPath with the command `msbuild.exe Properties05.proj /t:PrintInfo /p:AssemblyName=Sedo.Namhu .Common;OutputPath="deploy\Release\\"`, then the result would be what is shown in Figure 2-5.

```
C:\InsideMSBuild\Fundamentals>msbuild.exe Properties05.proj /t:PrintInfo /p:AssemblyName=Sedo.Namhu
.Common;OutputPath="deploy\Release\"  /nologo
Build started 5/13/2010 11:57:34 PM.
Project "C:\InsideMSBuild\Fundamentals\Properties05.proj" on node 1 (PrintInfo target(s)).
PrintInfo:
  AssemblyName: Sedo.Namhu.Common
  OutputPath: "deploy\Release\"
Done Building Project "C:\InsideMSBuild\Fundamentals\Properties05.proj" (PrintInfo target(s)).

Build succeeded.
    0 Warning(s)
    0 Error(s)
```

FIGURE 2-5 PrintInfo result for Properties05.proj

From Figure 2-5, we can see that the values for the properties that were provided at the command line were successfully passed through. Note in this example that we passed the OutputPath contained in quotes and the end is marked with \\ because \" is an escaped quote mark ("). In this case, the quotes are optional, but if you are passing values containing spaces, then they are required. When you provide a value for a property through the command line, it takes precedence over all other static property declarations. To demonstrate this, take a look at a different version of this file, Properties06.proj, with the values defined.

```
<Project xmlns=http://schemas.microsoft.com/developer/msbuild/2003
         ToolsVersion="4.0">

  <PropertyGroup>
    <AssemblyName>assemblyName</AssemblyName>
  </PropertyGroup>

  <Target Name="PrintInfo">
    <Message Text="AssemblyName: $(AssemblyName)" />
    <Message Text ="OutputPath: $(OutputPath)" />
  </Target>

  <PropertyGroup>
    <OutputPath>outputPath</OutputPath>
  </PropertyGroup>

</Project>
```

In this file, we have specified a value for both AssemblyName and OutputPath. To show that the location of the property with respect to targets doesn't affect the result, I have placed one value at the beginning of the file and the other at the end. If you execute the command `msbuild.exe Properties06.proj /t:PrintInfo /p:AssemblyName=Sedo.Namhu .Common;OutputPath="deploy\Release\\"`, the result would be the same as that shown in Figure 2-5. Command-line properties are special properties and have some special behavior that you should be aware of:

- Command-line properties cannot have their values changed (except through dynamic properties, which is covered in the next section).

- The values get passed to all projects through the MSBuild task.

- Their values take precedence over all other property type values, including environment variables and toolset properties. The MSBuild toolset defines what version of the MSBuild tools will be used. For example, you can use v2.0, v3.5, or v4.0.

Thus far, we have covered pretty much everything you need to know about static properties. Now we'll move on to discuss dynamic properties.

Dynamic Properties

When you create properties in your build scripts, static properties will be good enough most of the time. But there are many times when you need to either create new properties or to modify the values of existing properties during the build within targets. These types of properties can be called dynamic properties. Let's take a look at how we can create and use these properties.

In MSBuild 2.0, there was only one way to create dynamic properties, and that was using the CreateProperty task. In MSBuild 3.5 and 4.0, there is a much cleaner approach that you should use, which we cover right after our discussion on the CreateProperty task. Before we discuss how we can use CreateProperty, we have to discuss how to get a value from a task out to the MSBuild file calling it. When a task exposes a value to MSBuild, this is known as an Output property. MSBuild files can extract output values from tasks using the *Output* element. The *Output* element must be placed inside the tags of the task to extract the value. A task can see only those items and properties passed into it explicitly. This is by design and makes it easier to maintain and reuse tasks. To demonstrate this, take a look at the following project file.

```
<Project xmlns=http://schemas.microsoft.com/developer/msbuild/2003
        ToolsVersion="4.0">

  <Target Name="PrintProperty">
    <Message Text="AssemblyName: $(AssemblyName)" />

    <CreateProperty Value="Sedodream.Build.Tasks">
```

```
      <Output TaskParameter="Value" PropertyName="AssemblyName" />
    </CreateProperty>

    <Message Text="AssemblyName: $(AssemblyName)" />
  </Target>

</Project>
```

In this file, the PrintProperty target first prints the value for AssemblyName, which hasn't been defined so it should be empty. Then the CreateProperty task is used to define the AssemblyName property. Let's take a close look at this so we can fully understand the invocations. The statement `<CreateProperty Value="Sedodream.Build.Tasks">` invokes CreateProperty and initializes the property named Value to Sedodream.Build.Tasks. The inner statement, <Output TaskParameter="Value" PropertyName="AssemblyName" />, populates the MSBuild property AssemblyName with the value for the .NET property Value. The *Output* element must declare a TaskParameter, which is the name of the task's .NET property to output, and can either contain a value of *PropertyName* or *ItemName*, depending on whether it is supposed to output a property or item, respectively. In this case, we are emitting a property so we use the value *PropertyName*. Looking back at the example shown previously, we would expect that after the CreateProperty task executes, the property AssemblyName will be set to *Sedodream.Build.Tasks*. The result of the PrintProperty target is shown in Figure 2-6.

```
C:\InsideMSBuild\Ch02>msbuild Properties07.proj /t:PrintProperty /nologo
Build started 9/28/2010 10:24:24 PM.
Project "C:\InsideMSBuild\Ch02\Properties07.proj" on node 1 (PrintProperty target(s)).
PrintProperty:
  AssemblyName:
  AssemblyName: Sedodream.Build.Tasks
Done Building Project "C:\InsideMSBuild\Ch02\Properties07.proj" (PrintProperty target(s)).

Build succeeded.
    0 Warning(s)
    0 Error(s)
```

FIGURE 2-6 PrintProperty results

From the results shown in Figure 2-6, we can see that the value for AssemblyName was set, as expected, by the CreateProperty task. In this example, we are creating a property that did not exist previously, but the CreateProperty task also can modify the value for existing properties. If you use the task to output a value to a property that already exists, then it will be overwritten. This is true unless a property is reserved. Command-line parameters cannot be overwritten by statically declared properties, only by properties within targets.

If you are using MSBuild 3.5 or 4.0, you can use the CreateProperty task, but there is a cleaner method. You can place *PropertyGroup* declarations directly inside of targets. With this new approach, you can create static and dynamic properties in the same manner. The cleaner version of the previous example is shown as follows. This is contained in the Properties08.proj file.

```
<Project xmlns=http://schemas.microsoft.com/developer/msbuild/2003
        ToolsVersion="4.0">
```

```
<Target Name="PrintProperty">
  <Message Text="AssemblyName: $(AssemblyName)" />

  <PropertyGroup>
    <AssemblyName>Sedodream.Build.Tasks</AssemblyName>
  </PropertyGroup>

  <Message Text="AssemblyName: $(AssemblyName)" />
</Target>
```

```
</Project>
```

The results of the preceding project file are identical to the example shown in Properties07 .proj, but the syntax is much clearer. This is the preferred approach to creating dynamic properties. This syntax is not supported by MSBuild 2.0, so be sure not to use it in such files. Now that we have thoroughly covered properties, we'll move on to discuss items in detail.

Items

When software is being built, files and directories are used heavily. Because of the usage and importance of files and directories, MSBuild has a specific construct to support these. This construct is items. In the previous section, we covered properties. As stated previously, in programming terms, properties can be considered a regular scalar variable. This is because a property has a unique name and a single value. An item can be thought of as an array. This is because an item has a single name but can have multiple values. Properties use *PropertyGroup* to declare properties; similarly, items use an *ItemGroup* element. Take a look at the following very simple example from Items01.proj.

```
<Project xmlns=http://schemas.microsoft.com/developer/msbuild/2003
         ToolsVersion="4.0">

  <ItemGroup>
    <SourceFiles Include="src\one.txt" />
  </ItemGroup>

  <Target Name="Print">
    <Message Text="SourceFiles: @(SourceFiles)" />
  </Target>

</Project>
```

As stated previously, statically declared items will be inside an *ItemGroup* element. The value for the *Include* attribute determines what values get assigned to the item. Of the few types of values that can be assigned to the *Include* attribute, we'll start with the simplest. The simplest value for *Include* is a text value. In the previous sample, one item, SourceFiles, is declared. The SourceFiles item is set to include one file, which is located at src\one.txt. To get the value of an item, you use the @(*ItemType*) syntax. In the Print target this is used on the SourceFiles item. The result of the `Print` target is shown in Figure 2-7.

```
C:\InsideMSBuild\Ch02>msbuild Items01.proj /t:Print /nologo
Build started 9/28/2010 10:26:35 PM.
Project "C:\InsideMSBuild\Ch02\Items01.proj" on node 1 (Print target(s)).
Print:
    SourceFiles: src\one.txt
Done Building Project "C:\InsideMSBuild\Ch02\Items01.proj" (Print target(s)).

Build succeeded.
    0 Warning(s)
    0 Error(s)
```

FIGURE 2-7 Print target result for Items01.proj

From the result shown in Figure 2-7, you can see that the file was assigned to the SourceFiles item as expected. From this example, an item seems to behave exactly as a property; this is because we assigned only a single value to the item. The behavior changes when there are more values assigned to the item. The following example is a modified version of the previous example. This modified version is contained in the Items02.proj file.

```
<Project xmlns=http://schemas.microsoft.com/developer/msbuild/2003
        ToolsVersion="4.0">

  <ItemGroup>
    <SourceFiles Include="src\one.txt" />
    <SourceFiles Include="src\two.txt" />
  </ItemGroup>

  <Target Name="Print">
    <Message Text="SourceFiles: @(SourceFiles)" />
  </Target>

</Project>
```

In this version, the SourceFiles item type is declared twice. When more than one item declaration is encountered, the values are appended to each other instead of overwritten like properties. Alternatively, you could have declared the SourceFiles item on a single line by placing both values inside the *Include* attribute, separated by a semicolon. So the previous sample would be equivalent to the following one. With respect to item declarations, ordering is significant and preserved.

```
<Project xmlns="http://schemas.microsoft.com/developer/msbuild/2003"
        ToolsVersion="4.0">

  <ItemGroup>
    <SourceFiles Include="src\one.txt;src\two.txt" />
  </ItemGroup>

  <Target Name="Print">
    <Message Text="SourceFiles: @(SourceFiles)" />
  </Target>

</Project>
```

If you execute the Print target on this file, the result will be what is shown in Figure 2-8.

```
C:\InsideMSBuild\Ch02>msbuild Items02.proj /t:Print /nologo
Build started 9/28/2010 10:28:25 PM.
Project "C:\InsideMSBuild\Ch02\Items02.proj" on node 1 (Print target(s)).
Print:
    SourceFiles: src\one.txt;src\two.txt
Done Building Project "C:\InsideMSBuild\Ch02\Items02.proj" (Print target(s)).

Build succeeded.
    0 Warning(s)
    0 Error(s)
```

FIGURE 2-8 Print target results for Items02.proj

In this version, we have supplied two values into the SourceFiles item. If you look at the documentation for the Message task, you will notice that the Text property is a string. Fundamentally, there are two types of values in MSBuild: single-valued values and multi-valued values. These are known as *scalar values* and *vector values,* respectively. Properties are scalar values, and items are vector values. What happens when we have a vector value that we need to pass to a task that is accepting only scalar values? MSBuild will first flatten the item before sending it to the task. The value that is passed to the Text property on the Message can be only a single-valued parameter, not a multi-valued one. The @*(ItemType)* operator flattens the SourceFiles item for us, before it is sent into the task. When using @*(ItemType)*, if there is only one value inside the item, that value is used. If there is more than one value contained by the item, then all values are combined, separated by a semicolon by default. Flattening an item is the most basic example of an item transformation. We'll discuss this topic, and using custom separators, in more detail in the section entitled "Item Transformations," later in this chapter. For now, let's move on to see how items are more commonly used.

 Note MSBuild doesn't recognize file types by extension as some other build tools do. Also, be aware that item lists do not have to point to files; they can be any type of list-based value. We will see examples of this throughout this book.

Copy Task

A very common scenario for builds is copying a set of files from one place to another. How can we achieve this with MSBuild? There are several ways to do this, which we will demonstrate in this chapter. Before we discuss how to copy the files, we'll first take a close look at the Include statement of an item. I have created some sample files shown in the following tree, which we will use for the remainder of the chapter.

```
C:\InsideMSBuild\Ch02
|
|  . . .
|
+---src
```

```
¦   one.txt
¦   two.txt
¦   three.txt
¦   four
¦
+---sub
        sub_one.txt
        sub_two.txt
        sub_three.txt
        sub_four.txt
```

Previously, I said that three types of values can be contained in the Include declaration of an item:

1. A single value

2. Multiple values separated by a ";"

3. Declared using wildcards

We have shown how 1 and 2 work, so now we'll discuss 3—using wildcards to declare items. These wildcards always resolve values to items on disk. There are three wildcard declarations: *, **, and ?. You may already be familiar with these from usage in other tools, but we will quickly review them once again here. The * descriptor is used to declare that either zero or more characters can be used in its place. The ** descriptor is used to search directories recursively, and the ? is a placeholder for only one character. Effectively, the "*" descriptor matches any characters except for "/" while "**" descriptor matches any characters, including "/". For example, if *file.*proj* used this declaration, the following values would meet the criteria: *file.csproj, file.vbproj, file.vdproj, file.vcproj, file.proj, file.mproj, file.1proj*, etc. In contrast, *file.?proj* will allow only one character to replace the ? character. Therefore, from the previous list of matching names, only *file.mproj* and *file.1proj* meet those criteria. We will examine the ** descriptor shortly in an example. Take a look at the snippet from the following Copy01 .proj file.

```
<Project xmlns="http://schemas.microsoft.com/developer/msbuild/2003"
        ToolsVersion="4.0">

  <ItemGroup>
    <SourceFiles Include="src\*" />
  </ItemGroup>

  <Target Name="PrintFiles">
    <Message Text="SourceFiles: @(SourceFiles)" />
  </Target>

</Project>
```

In this example, we have used the * syntax to populate the SourceFiles item. Using this syntax, we would expect all the files in the src\ folder to be placed into the item. In order to verify this, you can execute the PrintFiles target. If you were to do this, the result would be

the statement 'SourceFiles: src\four.txt;src\one.txt;src\three.txt;src\two
.txt'—so we were able to successfully populate the item. Back to the ** wildcard: take a look
at the following portion of the Copy02.proj file.

```
<Project xmlns="http://schemas.microsoft.com/developer/msbuild/2003"
        ToolsVersion="4.0">

  <ItemGroup>
    <SourceFiles Include="src\**\*.txt" />
  </ItemGroup>

  <Target Name="PrintFiles">
    <Message Text="SourceFiles: @(SourceFiles)" />
  </Target>
</Project>
```

In this version of the SourceFiles declaration, we used the ** descriptor to denote that the
src\ folder should be searched recursively for files matching the pattern *.txt. We could
have stayed with the * pattern here as well, but I changed it for demonstration. We would
expect all the files in the src\ and src\sub\ folder to be placed into the SourceFiles item. If you
execute the PrintFiles target on this file, you would get the result shown in Figure 2-9.

```
C:\InsideMSBuild\Ch02>msbuild Copy02.proj /t:PrintFiles /nologo
Build started 9/28/2010 10:30:19 PM.
Project "C:\InsideMSBuild\Ch02\Copy02.proj" on node 1 (PrintFiles target(s)).
PrintFiles:
  SourceFiles: src\four.txt;src\one.txt;src\sub\sub_four.txt;src\sub\sub_one.txt;src\sub\sub_three
  .txt;src\sub\sub_two.txt;src\three.txt;src\two.txt
Done Building Project "C:\InsideMSBuild\Ch02\Copy02.proj" (PrintFiles target(s)).

Build succeeded.
    0 Warning(s)
    0 Error(s)
```

FIGURE 2-9 PrintFiles result for Copy02.proj

As expected, the SourceFiles item does contain all the files in both of those folders. Now that
we have discussed items declared using wildcards, we'll revert to the topic of copying files.

In order to copy files from one location to another, we can use the built-in Copy task. This
task has a few different input parameters, which are summarized in Table 2-2.

TABLE 2-2 Copy Task Parameters

Name	Description
SourceFiles	Contains the files that should be copied.
DestinationFolder	The path to the folder where the files should be copied. If this parameter is specified, then the DestinationFiles parameter cannot be used.
DestinationFiles	Contains the locations where the files should be copied to. If this is used, there must be a one-to-one correspondence between this list and the SourceFiles list. Also, if this is used, the DestinationFolder parameter cannot be used.
CopiedFiles	Output parameter that contains the files that were successfully copied.

Name	Description
SkipUnchangedFiles	If true, then only changed files, based on their timestamp and size, will be copied. Otherwise, all files will be copied.
OverwriteReadOnlyFiles	If true, then read-only files will be overwritten. Otherwise, read-only files will not be overwritten.
Retries *	The number of times that the copy should be retried if previous attempts fail. The default value is 0. This can be used to make builds more robust if multiple projects tend to copy a file to the same place.
RetryDelayMilliseconds *	The delay, in milliseconds, between any retries.
UseHardlinksIfPossible *	If true, then hard links are created instead of actually copying the files. This is useful for speeding up the file copying process as well as saving disk space. One downside to hard links is the increased likelihood for file locks.

* denotes new parameters with MSBuild 4.0

When you use the Copy task, you will always use the SourceFiles property to define what files should be copied. As for the location where the files will be copied to, you have a choice of using *either* DestinationFolder *or* DestinationFiles. The only time you should use DestinationFolder instead of DestinationFiles is when you are copying files into the same destination directory. Take a look at the following complete version of the Copy01.proj; the **bold** delineates the added parts.

```
<Project xmlns="http://schemas.microsoft.com/developer/msbuild/2003"
        ToolsVersion="4.0">

  <ItemGroup>
    <SourceFiles Include="src\*" />
  </ItemGroup>

  <PropertyGroup>
    <Dest>dest\</Dest>
  </PropertyGroup>

  <Target Name="PrintFiles">
    <Message Text="SourceFiles: @(SourceFiles)" />
  </Target>
  <Target Name="CopyFiles">
    <Copy SourceFiles="@(SourceFiles)"
        DestinationFolder="$(Dest)" />
  </Target>
</Project>
```

This file now contains a CopyFiles target, which invokes the Copy task in order to copy the files in the src folder to the dest folder. Notice that the Dest property ends with a slash; when creating properties that point to directories, it is a best practice to declare them ending in a trailing slash. A forward or backward slash will work equally well. In this example, the DestinationFolder property is used to specify the folder into which the files should be copied. If you execute the CopyFiles target, the result will be what is shown in Figure 2-10.

```
C:\InsideMSBuild\Ch02>msbuild Copy01.proj /t:CopyFiles /nologo
Build started 9/28/2010 10:31:57 PM.
Project "C:\InsideMSBuild\Ch02\Copy01.proj" on node 1 (CopyFiles target(s)).
CopyFiles:
  Creating directory "dest".
  Copying file from "src\four.txt" to "dest\four.txt".
  Copying file from "src\one.txt" to "dest\one.txt".
  Copying file from "src\three.txt" to "dest\three.txt".
  Copying file from "src\two.txt" to "dest\two.txt".
Done Building Project "C:\InsideMSBuild\Ch02\Copy01.proj" (CopyFiles target(s)).


Build succeeded.
    0 Warning(s)
    0 Error(s)
```

FIGURE 2-10 CopyFiles result for Copy01.proj

From the result shown in Figure 2-10, we can see that the files were copied successfully. We can now take a look at how we can copy files from more than one folder to another location. In order to achieve this, we will use DestinationFiles instead of the DestinationFolder property. We could use DestinationFolder along with batching, an advanced technique discussed in Chapter 6, "Batching and Incremental Builds." For now, we will use the DestinationFiles approach. The completed version of the Copy02.proj file is shown here:

```xml
<Project xmlns="http://schemas.microsoft.com/developer/msbuild/2003"
         ToolsVersion="4.0">

  <ItemGroup>
    <SourceFiles Include="src\**\*.txt" />
  </ItemGroup>

  <PropertyGroup>
    <Dest>$(MSBuildProjectDirectory)\dest\</Dest>
  </PropertyGroup>

  <Target Name="PrintFiles">
    <Message Text="SourceFiles: @(SourceFiles)" />
  </Target>
  <Target Name="CopyFiles">
    <Copy SourceFiles="@(SourceFiles)"
          DestinationFiles=
          "@(SourceFiles->'$(Dest)%(RecursiveDir)%(Filename)%(Extension)')" />
  </Target>
</Project>
```

In this sample, the portions in **bold** are the regions that have been added. This MSBuild file declares the SourceFiles item to include all the files in the src\ folder as well as all folders underneath it. In the CopyFiles target, the DestinationFiles parameter is used to specify the location where the files are to be copied to. The value for the DestinationFiles is called an item transformation on the SourceFiles item. We'll take a closer look at these later in this chapter. Item transformations also depend on item metadata, which we will discuss in the next section. Until we cover those subjects, we cannot fully examine this example, so we will revisit it later in this chapter. With that being said, we can at least execute the CopyFiles target to see if it does work as expected. The result of this invocation is captured in Figure 2-11.

```
C:\InsideMSBuild\Ch02>msbuild Copy02.proj /t:CopyFiles /nologo
Build started 9/28/2010 10:35:11 PM.
Project "C:\InsideMSBuild\Ch02\Copy02.proj" on node 1 (CopyFiles target(s)).
CopyFiles:
    Creating directory "C:\InsideMSBuild\Ch02\dest".
    Copying file from "src\four.txt" to "C:\InsideMSBuild\Ch02\dest\four.txt".
    Copying file from "src\one.txt" to "C:\InsideMSBuild\Ch02\dest\one.txt".
    Creating directory "C:\InsideMSBuild\Ch02\dest\sub".
    Copying file from "src\sub\sub_four.txt" to "C:\InsideMSBuild\Ch02\dest\sub\sub_four.txt".
    Copying file from "src\sub\sub_one.txt" to "C:\InsideMSBuild\Ch02\dest\sub\sub_one.txt".
    Copying file from "src\sub\sub_three.txt" to "C:\InsideMSBuild\Ch02\dest\sub\sub_three.txt".
    Copying file from "src\sub\sub_two.txt" to "C:\InsideMSBuild\Ch02\dest\sub\sub_two.txt".
    Copying file from "src\three.txt" to "C:\InsideMSBuild\Ch02\dest\three.txt".
    Copying file from "src\two.txt" to "C:\InsideMSBuild\Ch02\dest\two.txt".
Done Building Project "C:\InsideMSBuild\Ch02\Copy02.proj" (CopyFiles target(s)).

Build succeeded.
    0 Warning(s)
    0 Error(s)
```

FIGURE 2-11 Result of the CopyFiles task for Copy02.proj

From the result shown in Figure 2-11, we can see that the files from src\ and src\sub\ were successfully copied into the dest folder. Now we'll move on to discuss item metadata, which is another distinction between items and properties.

Well-Known Item Metadata

When you create items, each value in an item also has a set of metadata associated with it. This is another difference between items and properties. A property is a key-value pair, but each element in an item is much richer than a property. Each of these can have zero or more metadata values associated with them. These metadata are also key-value pairs. For files and directories, you are given a set of metadata automatically. These are well-known metadata. They are read-only and are summarized in Table 2-3.

TABLE 2-3 Well-Known Metadata

Name	Description
FullPath	Full path of the file.
RootDir	The root directory to which the file belongs, such as c:\.
Filename	The name of the file, not including the extension.
Extension	The extension of the file, including the period.
RelativeDir	Contains the path specified in the *Include* attribute, up to the final backslash (\).
Directory	Directory of the item, without the root directory.
RecursiveDir	This is the expanded directory path starting from the first ** of the include declaration. If no ** is present, then this value is empty. If multiple ** are present, then *RecursiveDir* will be the expanded value starting from the first **. This may sound peculiar, but it is what makes recursive copying possible.
Identity	The value that was specified in the *Include* attribute of the item.
ModifiedTime	The last time the file was modified.
CreatedTime	The time the file was created.
AccessedTime	The last time the file was accessed.

> **Note** For well-known metadata, the *Include* value of the item needs to be a path for the values to be populated.

We will now see how we can use these, and later in the chapter we'll discuss custom metadata. In order to demonstrate using well-known metadata, take a look at the following simple project. This is taken from the file WellKnownMetadata.proj.

```
<Project xmlns="http://schemas.microsoft.com/developer/msbuild/2003"
         ToolsVersion="4.0">
  <ItemGroup>
    <src Include="src\one.txt" />
  </ItemGroup>
  <Target Name="PrintWellKnownMetadata">

    <Message Text="===== Well known metadata =====" />
    <!-- %40 = @ -->
    <!-- %25 = % -->
    <Message Text="%40(src->'%25(FullPath)'): @(src->'%(FullPath)')" />
    <Message Text="%40(src->'%25(Rootdir)'): @(src->'%(Rootdir)')" />
    <Message Text="%40(src->'%25(Filename)'): @(src->'%(Filename)')" />
    <Message Text="%40(src->'%25(Extension)'): @(src->'%(Extension)')" />
    <Message Text="%40(src->'%25(RelativeDir)'): @(src->'%(RelativeDir)')" />
    <Message Text="%40(src->'%25(Directory)'): @(src->'%(Directory)')" />
    <Message Text="%40(src->'%25(RecursiveDir)'): @(src->'%(RecursiveDir)')" />
    <Message Text="%40(src->'%25(Identity)'): @(src->'%(Identity)')" />
    <Message Text="%40(src->'%25(ModifiedTime)'): @(src->'%(ModifiedTime)')" />
    <Message Text="%40(src->'%25(CreatedTime)'): @(src->'%(CreatedTime)')" />
    <Message Text="%40(src->'%25(AccessedTime)'): @(src->'%(AccessedTime)')" />

  </Target>
</Project>
```

> **Note** In order to use reserved characters such as % and @, you have to escape. This is accomplished by the syntax *%HV*, where *HV* is the hex value of the character. This is demonstrated in this code sample with %25 and %40.

From the preceding project, one item is created: the src item. This item purposefully contains only a single file, one.txt. In order to extract a single metadata value from an item, you can use the @(*ItemType*->'%(*MetadataName*)') syntax, where *ItemType* is the name of the item and *MetadataName* is the name of the metadata to extract. We can see that in the PrintWellKnownMetadata target, all the well-known values from Table 2-3 are printed. The @(*ItemType*->'%(*MetadataName*)') syntax is a simplified version of an item transformation, which we will discuss in the next section. If you execute the PrintWellKnownMetadata target on this file, the result will be what is shown in Figure 2-12.

```
C:\InsideMSBuild\Ch02>msbuild WellKnownMetadata.proj /t:PrintWellKnownMetadata /nologo
Build started 9/28/2010 10:37:07 PM.
Project "C:\InsideMSBuild\Ch02\WellKnownMetadata.proj" on node 1 <PrintWellKnownMetadata target(s)
>.
PrintWellKnownMetadata:
  ===== Well known metadata =====
  @(src->'%(FullPath)'): C:\InsideMSBuild\Ch02\src\one.txt
  @(src->'%(Rootdir)'): C:\
  @(src->'%(Filename)'): one
  @(src->'%(Extension)'): .txt
  @(src->'%(RelativeDir)'): src\
  @(src->'%(Directory)'): InsideMSBuild\Ch02\src\
  @(src->'%(RecursiveDir)'):
  @(src->'%(Identity)'): src\one.txt
  @(src->'%(ModifiedTime)'): 2010-09-08 21:45:13.6875000
  @(src->'%(CreatedTime)'): 2010-09-08 21:45:13.6875000
  @(src->'%(AccessedTime)'): 2010-09-08 21:45:13.6875000
Done Building Project "C:\InsideMSBuild\Ch02\WellKnownMetadata.proj" <PrintWellKnownMetadata targe
t(s)>.

Build succeeded.
    0 Warning(s)
    0 Error(s)
```

FIGURE 2-12 Well-known metadata

The result in Figure 2-12 demonstrates most of the well-known metadata that are available to be used for files and directories. One metadata value that needs further explanation is *RecursiveDir*. In order to see this value being populated, you need to create an item with the ** wildcard declaration. To see this, we can examine a slightly modified version of the previous file, the following WellKnownMetadata02.proj file.

```xml
<Project xmlns="http://schemas.microsoft.com/developer/msbuild/2003"
         ToolsVersion="4.0">
  <ItemGroup>
    <src Include="src\**\sub_one.txt" />
  </ItemGroup>
  <Target Name="PrintWellKnownMetadata">

    <Message Text="===== Well known metadata =====" />
    <!-- %40 = @ -->
    <!-- %25 = % -->
    <Message Text="%40(src->'%25(FullPath)'): @(src->'%(FullPath)')" />
    <Message Text="%40(src->'%25(Rootdir)'): @(src->'%(Rootdir)')" />
    <Message Text="%40(src->'%25(Filename)'): @(src->'%(Filename)')" />
    <Message Text="%40(src->'%25(Extension)'): @(src->'%(Extension)')" />
    <Message Text="%40(src->'%25(RelativeDir)'): @(src->'%(RelativeDir)')" />
    <Message Text="%40(src->'%25(Directory)'): @(src->'%(Directory)')" />
    <Message Text="%40(src->'%25(RecursiveDir)'): @(src->'%(RecursiveDir)')" />
    <Message Text="%40(src->'%25(Identity)'): @(src->'%(Identity)')" />
    <Message Text="%40(src->'%25(ModifiedTime)'): @(src->'%(ModifiedTime)')" />
    <Message Text="%40(src->'%25(CreatedTime)'): @(src->'%(CreatedTime)')" />
    <Message Text="%40(src->'%25(AccessedTime)'): @(src->'%(AccessedTime)')" />

  </Target>
</Project>
```

The section that has changed from the previous version has been put in bold. I have modified this to use the ** qualifier, but at the same time to allow only a single file to be in the item. If you were to execute this MSBuild file, you would see results very similar to the previous one, but the main difference in the output is the line @(src->'%(RecursiveDir)'): sub\. As Table 2-3 states, *RecursiveDir* will take the value that matches the ** declaration. In this case, the value used was *sub*, which is exactly what we would expect. The summary in Table 2-3 is not entirely correct for *RecursiveDir,* but it is more concise than the correct definition. To understand the behavior of *RecursiveDir,* take a look at the following code block, and its explanation, which is contained in WellKnownMetadata03.proj.

```xml
<Project xmlns="http://schemas.microsoft.com/developer/msbuild/2003"
         ToolsVersion="4.0">
  <ItemGroup>
    <src Include="src\**\sub\sub_one.txt" />
  </ItemGroup>
  <Target Name="PrintWellKnownMetadata">

    <Message Text="===== Well known metadata =====" />
    <!-- %40 = @ -->
    <!-- %25 = % -->
    <Message Text="%40(src->'%25(FullPath)'): @(src->'%(FullPath)')" />
    <Message Text="%40(src->'%25(Rootdir)'): @(src->'%(Rootdir)')" />
    <Message Text="%40(src->'%25(Filename)'): @(src->'%(Filename)')" />
    <Message Text="%40(src->'%25(Extension)'): @(src->'%(Extension)')" />
    <Message Text="%40(src->'%25(RelativeDir)'): @(src->'%(RelativeDir)')" />
    <Message Text="%40(src->'%25(Directory)'): @(src->'%(Directory)')" />
    <Message Text="%40(src->'%25(RecursiveDir)'): @(src->'%(RecursiveDir)')" />
    <Message Text="%40(src->'%25(Identity)'): @(src->'%(Identity)')" />
    <Message Text="%40(src->'%25(ModifiedTime)'): @(src->'%(ModifiedTime)')" />
    <Message Text="%40(src->'%25(CreatedTime)'): @(src->'%(CreatedTime)')" />
    <Message Text="%40(src->'%25(AccessedTime)'): @(src->'%(AccessedTime)')" />

  </Target>
</Project>
```

The line that has been changed is bold, and the part to make note of is that part of the path is specified after the ** declaration on the src item. If you print the *RecursiveDir* value for this new item, you will get the same result of '@(src->'%(RecursiveDir)'): sub\', so the result was the same even though we specified the subdirectory name after the **. This is because the RecursiveDir metadata doesn't examine what the item specification declared after the initial **. It looks at the item specification, finds the first occurrence of **, and returns the remaining section of the path from that specification. If you have multiple **s in a single item specification, it wouldn't affect the result of the RecursiveDir; it would still behave as I described by finding the first occurrence of the ** and return the path that follows. Now that we have discussed well-known metadata in depth, we will move on to discuss custom metadata followed by item transformations.

Custom Metadata

When you declare items that point to files or directories, you get a set of metadata for free—this is the well-known metadata that we discussed in the previous section. What if you have the need to associate some additional data with an item? You can do this; they are called custom metadata and they behave exactly the same as well-known metadata, with the exception that well-known metadata are read-only. When you declare an item, you will associate the metadata with its declaration. In this section, we will describe how to create and use custom metadata in your build scripts.

Metadata behaves similarly to properties in the sense that they are key-value pairs. So each piece of metadata, custom or not, has a name, which is the key, and a value, which is untyped as for property values but "cast" as needed to pass into tasks. For statically created items, you will declare the metadata as a child of the item element itself. The metadata key is the element name, and the value of the metadata is the value of the XML element. For example, take a look at the following project file, Metadata01.proj.

```xml
<Project xmlns="http://schemas.microsoft.com/developer/msbuild/2003"
         ToolsVersion="4.0">

  <ItemGroup>
    <Server Include="Server1">
      <Type>2008</Type>
      <Name>SVR01</Name>
      <AdminContact>Sayed Ibrahim Hashimi</AdminContact>
    </Server>
    <Server Include="Server2">
      <Type>2003</Type>
      <Name>SVR02</Name>
      <AdminContact>Sayed Y. Hashimi</AdminContact>
    </Server>
    <Server Include="Server3">
      <Type>2008</Type>
      <Name>SVR03</Name>
      <AdminContact>Nicole Woodsmall</AdminContact>
    </Server>
    <Server Include="Server4">
      <Type>2003</Type>
      <Name>SVR04</Name>
      <AdminContact>Keith Tingle</AdminContact>
    </Server>
  </ItemGroup>

  <Target Name="PrintInfo" Outputs="%(Server.Identity)">
    <Message Text="Server: @(Server)" />
    <Message Text="Admin: @(Server->'%(AdminContact)')" />
  </Target>

</Project>
```

In this project file, we have declared an item, Server, which will have three metadata values associated with it. If you take a look at each item's declaration, you will see that each has three XML child elements: *Type, Name,* and *AdminContact.* Each of these is custom metadata, and after the item is created, you can access those values using the same syntax as you would with well-known metadata. You can have any number of metadata elements declared. Also, you should note that if your item's declaration uses wildcards, then each item value created from the *Include* will have the attached metadata. You are not limited to text in declaring these values; you can use any MSBuild statements as a metadata value declaration. In the previous project file, there is one target, PrintInfo, which, as it is named, prints the information for the Server item. This target uses another technique called batching, which in this case will cause the target to be executed once per each value in Server. We will thoroughly examine batching in Chapter 6. If you execute this target, the result will be what is shown in Figure 2-13.

```
C:\InsideMSBuild\Ch02>msbuild Metadata01.proj /t:PrintInfo /nologo
Build started 9/28/2010 10:41:54 PM.
Project "C:\InsideMSBuild\Ch02\Metadata01.proj" on node 1 (PrintInfo target(s)).
PrintInfo:
  Server: Server1
  Admin: Sayed Ibrahim Hashimi
PrintInfo:
  Server: Server2
  Admin: Sayed Y. Hashimi
PrintInfo:
  Server: Server3
  Admin: Nicole Woodsmall
PrintInfo:
  Server: Server4
  Admin: Keith Tingle
Done Building Project "C:\InsideMSBuild\Ch02\Metadata01.proj" (PrintInfo target(s)).


Build succeeded.
    0 Warning(s)
    0 Error(s)
```

FIGURE 2-13 PrintInfo target results on Metadata01.proj

The PrintInfo target extracts custom metadata values in the same way as well-known metadata values are extracted. Figure 2-13 demonstrates that this does work exactly as expected. Well-known metadata are always read-only, whereas custom metadata are not. Therefore, if you provide a value for already-existing metadata, that value will be overwritten. For instance, consider the following taken from Metadata02.proj.

```xml
<Project xmlns="http://schemas.microsoft.com/developer/msbuild/2003"
         ToolsVersion="4.0">
  <ItemGroup>
    <Server Include="Server1">
      <Type>2008</Type>
      <Name>SVR01</Name>
      <AdminContact>Adam Barr</AdminContact>
      <AdminContact>Kim Abercrombie</AdminContact>
    </Server>
  </ItemGroup>

  <Target Name="PrintInfo" Outputs="%(Server.Identity)">
    <Message Text="Server: @(Server)" />
    <Message Text="Admin: @(Server->'%(AdminContact)')" />
  </Target>
</Project>
```

Notice that the Server item defines *AdminContact* twice, with the second value equal to "Kim Abercrombie". If you execute the PrintInfo target, the result for @(Server->'%(AdminContact)') would be "Kim Abercrombie" instead of "Adam Barr".

Item Transformations

When you are using MSBuild, there are many times that you would like to take an existing item, modify it a bit, and then pass it to a task. For example, if you are copying a set of files from one place to another, you would like to take an item that points to an existing set of files, change its location to point to the destination, and then give it to the Copy task for the DestinationFiles property. MSBuild has a mechanism for this behavior built in: this process is called item transformations, and we will discuss it in detail in this section. A transformation can be expressed as $A \Rightarrow A'$, where A is the original item and A' is the transformed item. Transformations always create new item lists and never modify the original item list. The most important thing to remember is that A and A' will always have the same number of elements. This is because the transformation is processed on each element to generate the new item. A transformation can be visualized as that shown in Figure 2-14.

Item Transformation

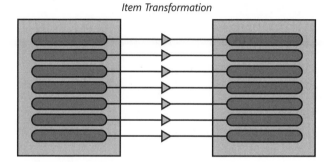

FIGURE 2-14 Item transformation visualization

As stated previously, the visualization in Figure 2-14 reemphasizes that an item transformation is a one-to-one translation.

Now that we have defined what an item transformation is, we will take a look at the transformation syntax and explain how it can be effectively used. Here is the syntax:

```
@(ItemType->'TransformExpression[TransformExpression...]'[,Separator])
```

where *ItemType* is the name of the item being transformed, *TransformExpression* is a transform expression, and *Separator* is an optional parameter that will be used as the separator between values.

> **Note** Elements contained in *[]* are optional.

The default value for the separator is ";". You can use the syntax `@(ItemType,[Separator])` where you do not declare any expressions but only override the separator. The three acceptable types of transform expression are summarized in Table 2-4.

TABLE 2-4 Transform Expressions

Type	Description	Example
Text	Any plain text	c:\test
Property	Property value extraction expression	$(Configuration)
Item Metadata	Item metadata extraction expression	%(FullPath)

As stated, there are only three possible types of transform expressions, and we will demonstrate all of them in this section. You should note that there is no restriction on what type/order transform expressions are declared in the transformation. To start our discussion on transformations, we will examine the following file, Transformation01.proj.

```
<Project xmlns="http://schemas.microsoft.com/developer/msbuild/2003"
        ToolsVersion="4.0"
        DefaultTargets="All">
  <ItemGroup>
    <SourceFiles Include="src\**\*" ></SourceFiles>
  </ItemGroup>

  <PropertyGroup>
    <DestFolder>copy\</DestFolder>
  </PropertyGroup>

  <!-- %40 = @ -->
  <!-- %25 = % -->
  <Target Name="PrintSourceFiles">
    <Message Text="%40(SourceFiles):"
             Importance="high" />
    <Message Text="@(SourceFiles)" />
  </Target>
  <Target Name="Demo01">
    <Message Text="%40(SourceFiles->'%25(Filename)'):"
             Importance="high" />
    <Message Text="@(SourceFiles->'%(Filename)')" />
  </Target>
  <Target Name="Demo02">
    <Message Text="%40(SourceFiles->'%25(Filename)%25(Extension)'):"
             Importance="high"/>
    <Message Text="@(SourceFiles->'%(Filename)%(Extension)')" />
  </Target>
  <Target Name="Demo03">
    <Message Text="%40(SourceFiles->'%25(Filename)%25(Extension).bak'):"
             Importance="high" />
    <Message Text="@(SourceFiles->'%(Filename)%(Extension).bak')" />
  </Target>

  <ItemGroup>
    <Transform01
      Include="@(SourceFiles->'$(DestFolder)%(RecursiveDir)%(Filename)%(Extension)')" />
  </ItemGroup>
```

```
<Target Name="Demo04">
  <Message Text="%40(Transform01):"
           Importance="high" />
  <Message Text="@(Transform01)" />
  <Message Text="===== Copying files ====="
           Importance="high" />
  <Copy SourceFiles="@(SourceFiles)" DestinationFiles="@(Transform01)" />
</Target>

<Target Name="All"
        DependsOnTargets="PrintSourceFiles;Demo01;Demo02;Demo03;Demo04" />

</Project>
```

At the top of the project file, there is one item as well as one property declared. The item, SourceFiles, points to some files that will be used throughout the example. The property, DestFolder, contains a path to where some files should be copied. There is another item defined toward the bottom of the file, which we will discuss later. This file contains five relevant targets, one of which, PrintSourceFiles, prints out the list of files in the SourceFiles item for reference when executing the other targets. Each of these targets essentially contains one transformation that you should understand. The All target is declared simply to execute the other targets for demonstration here. In the following list, we will describe these targets and the transformations' purpose.

Demo01

The transformation on the SourceFiles target is defined as @(SourceFiles->'%(Filename)'). This will transform the SourceFiles item list into a list containing the *Filename* metadata value. If you recall from Table 2-2, this is the file name, with no path information and no extension.

Demo02

The transformation in this target, @(SourceFiles->'%(Filename)%(Extension)'), extends the previous transformation to add the extension, using the *Extension* well-known metadata.

Demo03

The transformation in this target, @(SourceFiles->'%(Filename)%(Extension).bak'), demonstrates how we can use a combination of metadata values along with free text. This transformation adds .bak to the end of the name of the file.

Demo04

This target is a little different in the sense that it doesn't actually contain the transformation itself. This target uses the Transform01 item, which is a transformed version of the SourceFiles item. The transformation to create this item is defined as

@(SourceFiles->'$(DestFolder)%(RecursiveDir)%(Filename)%(Extension)'). In this transformation, we create a new item that uses the DestFolder path to create a list of file paths where the SourceFiles files should be copied to. Because the SourceFiles item can contain items in subfolders, it uses the *RecursiveDir* metadata value to re-create the appropriate directory structure in the DestFolder.

This file starts with a very simple example and then builds on it. These four transformations describe the three types of transform expressions that are available. Now let's take a look at the result of executing all these targets, which is shown in Figure 2-15.

In the result shown in Figure 2-15, you can take a look at each transformation and make sure that it performs the transformation that you would expect. Also, for the Demo04 target, we can see that the files were successfully copied into the appropriate location.

```
C:\InsideMSBuild\Ch02>msbuild Transformation01.proj /t:All /nologo
Build started 9/28/2010 10:43:56 PM.
Project "C:\InsideMSBuild\Ch02\Transformation01.proj" on node 1 (All target(s)).
PrintSourceFiles:
  @(SourceFiles):
  src\four.txt;src\one.txt;src\sub\sub_four.txt;src\sub\sub_one.txt;src\sub\sub_three.txt;src\sub\
  sub_two.txt;src\three.txt;src\two.txt
Demo01:
  @(SourceFiles->'%(Filename)'):
  four;one;sub_four;sub_one;sub_three;sub_two;three;two
Demo02:
  @(SourceFiles->'%(Filename)%(Extension)'):
  four.txt;one.txt;sub_four.txt;sub_one.txt;sub_three.txt;sub_two.txt;three.txt;two.txt
Demo03:
  @(SourceFiles->'%(Filename)%(Extension).bak'):
  four.txt.bak;one.txt.bak;sub_four.txt.bak;sub_one.txt.bak;sub_three.txt.bak;sub_two.txt.bak;thre
  e.txt.bak;two.txt.bak
Demo04:
  @(Transform01):
  copy\four.txt;copy\one.txt;copy\sub\sub_four.txt;copy\sub\sub_one.txt;copy\sub\sub_three.txt;cop
  y\sub\sub_two.txt;copy\three.txt;copy\two.txt
  ===== Copying files =====
  Creating directory "copy".
  Copying file from "src\four.txt" to "copy\four.txt".
  Copying file from "src\one.txt" to "copy\one.txt".
  Creating directory "copy\sub".
  Copying file from "src\sub\sub_four.txt" to "copy\sub\sub_four.txt".
  Copying file from "src\sub\sub_one.txt" to "copy\sub\sub_one.txt".
  Copying file from "src\sub\sub_three.txt" to "copy\sub\sub_three.txt".
  Copying file from "src\sub\sub_two.txt" to "copy\sub\sub_two.txt".
  Copying file from "src\three.txt" to "copy\three.txt".
  Copying file from "src\two.txt" to "copy\two.txt".
Done Building Project "C:\InsideMSBuild\Ch02\Transformation01.proj" (All target(s)).

Build succeeded.
    0 Warning(s)
    0 Error(s)
```

FIGURE 2-15 Transformation01.proj result

We will now revisit a previous example, the one contained in the following Copy02.proj file.

```
<Project xmlns="http://schemas.microsoft.com/developer/msbuild/2003"
         ToolsVersion="4.0">

  <ItemGroup>
    <SourceFiles Include="src\**\*.txt" />
  </ItemGroup>

  <PropertyGroup>
    <Dest>$(MSBuildProjectDirectory)\dest\</Dest>
  </PropertyGroup>

  <Target Name="PrintFiles">
    <Message Text="SourceFiles: @(SourceFiles)" />
```

```
    </Target>
    <Target Name="CopyFiles">
      <Copy SourceFiles="@(SourceFiles)"
            DestinationFiles=
            "@(SourceFiles->'$(Dest)%(RecursiveDir)%(Filename)%(Extension)')" />
    </Target>
</Project>
```

We'll now fully describe the Copy statement in this build file. Let's dissect the *DestinationFiles* value. This value, @(SourceFiles->'$(Dest)%(RecursiveDir)%(Filename)%(Extension)'), is a transform. The components of the value are:

- $(Dest)

- %(RecursiveDir)

- %(Filename)

- %(Extension)

where *$(Dest)* is an evaluation of the Dest property, and the others are evaluations for metadata values on the SourceFiles item. From this transformation, there is only one static value, which is the value for *$(Dest)*. Aside from that, all the values will be taken from the metadata for each item element. These metadata values were previously discussed in this chapter. The output of the CopyFiles target is shown in Figure 2-16.

```
C:\InsideMSBuild\Ch02>msbuild Copy02.proj /t:CopyFiles /nologo
Build started 9/28/2010 10:47:20 PM.
Project "C:\InsideMSBuild\Ch02\Copy02.proj" on node 1 (CopyFiles target(s)).
CopyFiles:
    Creating directory "C:\InsideMSBuild\Ch02\dest".
    Copying file from "src\four.txt" to "C:\InsideMSBuild\Ch02\dest\four.txt".
    Copying file from "src\one.txt" to "C:\InsideMSBuild\Ch02\dest\one.txt".
    Creating directory "C:\InsideMSBuild\Ch02\dest\sub".
    Copying file from "src\sub\sub_four.txt" to "C:\InsideMSBuild\Ch02\dest\sub\sub_four.txt".
    Copying file from "src\sub\sub_one.txt" to "C:\InsideMSBuild\Ch02\dest\sub\sub_one.txt".
    Copying file from "src\sub\sub_three.txt" to "C:\InsideMSBuild\Ch02\dest\sub\sub_three.txt".
    Copying file from "src\sub\sub_two.txt" to "C:\InsideMSBuild\Ch02\dest\sub\sub_two.txt".
    Copying file from "src\three.txt" to "C:\InsideMSBuild\Ch02\dest\three.txt".
    Copying file from "src\two.txt" to "C:\InsideMSBuild\Ch02\dest\two.txt".
Done Building Project "C:\InsideMSBuild\Ch02\Copy02.proj" (CopyFiles target(s)).

Build succeeded.
    0 Warning(s)
    0 Error(s)
```

FIGURE 2-16 CopyFiles target result on Copy02.proj

From the output, we can see that eight files were successfully copied to the destination as expected. Now we will examine the first copy message in more detail to describe the transformation. In this example, the original item was specified as *src\four.txt* and it was transformed into the file on the right side. In the transformed specification, the *$(Dest)* value was assigned c:\InsideMSBuild\Ch02\dest\; the *%(RecursiveDir)* did not return a value, so it was an empty string; the *%(Filename)* evaluated to the value "four"; and *%(Extension)* became .txt. If you take a look at the output for the files in the subdirectory, you can see that the *%(RecursiveDir)* metadata returned the path correctly. Now we have covered what you need to know about item transformations, which are used extensively throughout MSBuild files.

In this chapter, we have introduced a lot of material, including properties, items, metadata, and transformations. Now we will move on to the next chapter, in which we will continue this discussion and add the topics of dynamic properties and dynamic items. In the next chapter, you will learn how properties and items are evaluated, and how to import other MSBuild files and extend the build process.

Chapter 3
MSBuild Deep Dive, Part 2

In the previous chapter, we discussed a variety of topics, including static properties, static items, and transformations. In this chapter, we will extend that discussion and conclude with a foundation that is required to successfully use MSBuild. We will start by discussing dynamic properties and items. We will also see how properties and items are evaluated as well as how you can extend your own build process. Following this chapter, we will discuss custom tasks, custom loggers, and other advanced topics.

Dynamic Properties and Items

Many times when building software, static items and properties, those defined outside of targets, will do the job fine. For example, most of the time you know what files you are building and the possible values for Configuration. From that you can determine what files need to be built. Despite this, there are many instances where you will need to create properties and items as your build is occurring. For example, if you want to build your product and then copy the binaries from the output path to another location you will need to be able to discover those created files. Properties and items that are created as your build process is executing are called dynamic properties and dynamic items. In this section, we will examine how to use these dynamic values.

 Note In MSBuild 2.0, you were limited to creating dynamic properties and items with the tasks CreateProperty and CreateItem, respectively. They are now obsolete.

Dynamic Properties and Items: MSBuild 3.5

MSBuild 3.5 introduced the ability to use the *PropertyGroup* and *ItemGroup* elements inside targets. With this enhancement, we can declare dynamic properties and items just as we would normally declare them. You can see how dynamic properties are created in the following example taken from Dynamic01.proj.

```
<Project xmlns="http://schemas.microsoft.com/developer/msbuild/2003"
         ToolsVersion="4.0"
         DefaultTargets="All">

  <PropertyGroup>
    <Configuration>Debug</Configuration>
  </PropertyGroup>
```

```
<Target Name="PrintConfig">
  <Message Text="Config: $(Configuration)" />
</Target>

<Target Name="PrintConfig2">
  <PropertyGroup>
    <Configuration>Release</Configuration>
  </PropertyGroup>

  <Message Text="Config: $(Configuration)" />
</Target>

<Target Name="All" DependsOnTargets="PrintConfig;PrintConfig2" />
</Project>
```

If you execute the All target, which simply executes the other targets, the result is that shown in Figure 3-1.

```
C:\InsideMSBuild\Ch03>msbuild Dynamic01.proj /t:All /nologo
Build started 9/9/2010 10:12:41 PM.
Project "C:\InsideMSBuild\Ch03\Dynamic01.proj" on node 1 (All target(s)).
PrintConfig:
  Config: Debug
PrintConfig2:
  Config: Release
Done Building Project "C:\InsideMSBuild\Ch03\Dynamic01.proj" (All target(s)).

Build succeeded.
    0 Warning(s)
    0 Error(s)
```

FIGURE 3-1 Dynamic property result

As you can see from the result shown in Figure 3-1, the value for the Configuration property was overridden dynamically inside the PrintConfig2 target. The usage of PropertyGroup is not limited to modifying values for existing properties; you can create new properties as well.

To demonstrate that new properties can be created, the previous example has been modified. Take a look at the new file, Dynamic02.proj, which is shown next.

```
<Project xmlns="http://schemas.microsoft.com/developer/msbuild/2003"
         ToolsVersion="4.0"
         DefaultTargets="All">

  <PropertyGroup>
    <Configuration>Debug</Configuration>
  </PropertyGroup>

  <Target Name="PrintConfig">
    <Message Text="Config: $(Configuration)" />
  </Target>

  <Target Name="PrintConfig2">
    <PropertyGroup>
      <Configuration>Release</Configuration>
      <OutputPath>$(Configuration)\dest\</OutputPath>
    </PropertyGroup>

    <Message Text="Config: $(Configuration)" />
```

```
    <Message Text="OutputPath: $(OutputPath)" />
  </Target>

  <Target Name="All" DependsOnTargets="PrintConfig;PrintConfig2" />
</Project>
```

In this example, the changed areas have been highlighted. Inside the PrintConfig2 target a new property, OutputPath, is created using the *PropertyGroup* element. This new property will contain the value of the Configuration property followed by *dest*. After that, the newly created property and the value of the Configuration property are printed out. Figure 3-2 shows the result of running this script.

```
C:\InsideMSBuild\Ch03>msbuild Dynamic02.proj /t:All /nologo
Build started 9/9/2010 10:19:40 PM.
Project "C:\InsideMSBuild\Ch03\Dynamic02.proj" on node 1 (All target(s)).
PrintConfig:
  Config: Debug
PrintConfig2:
  Config: Release
  OutputPath: Release\dest\
Done Building Project "C:\InsideMSBuild\Ch03\Dynamic02.proj" (All target(s)).

Build succeeded.
    0 Warning(s)
    0 Error(s)
```

FIGURE 3-2 Results for Dynamic02.proj

From the results shown in Figure 3-2, you can see that the OutputPath property was indeed created and initialized successfully. Now that we have discussed dynamic properties, we can take a look at how dynamic items are created.

The problem with static items is that the value for static items is *always* evaluated *before* any target executes. Thus, if you need an item to contain any generated files, you must create the item dynamically. To create dynamic items, you can use the *ItemGroup* element inside a target. Inside a target, the *ItemGroup* element even has some new features. You are able to remove values from an item and you can modify the metadata value for an item. Doing so was not possible using MSBuild 2.0. Consider the following sample, which is contained in the Metadata01.proj file.

```
<Project xmlns="http://schemas.microsoft.com/developer/msbuild/2003"
        ToolsVersion="4.0">
  <ItemGroup>
    <Server Include="Server1">
      <Type>2008</Type>
      <Name>SVR01</Name>
      <AdminContact>Sayed Ibrahim Hashimi</AdminContact>
    </Server>
    <Server Include="Server2">
      <Type>2003</Type>
      <Name>SVR02</Name>
      <AdminContact>Sayed Y. Hashimi</AdminContact>
    </Server>
    <Server Include="Server3">
      <Type>2008</Type>
      <Name>SVR03</Name>
```

```
          <AdminContact>Nicole Woodsmall</AdminContact>
        </Server>
        <Server Include="Server4">
          <Type>2003</Type>
          <Name>SVR04</Name>
          <AdminContact>Keith Tingle</AdminContact>
        </Server>
      </ItemGroup>

      <Target Name="PrintInfo">
        <Message Text="%(Server.Identity) : %(Server.AdminContact)" />

        <!-- just for new line -->
        <Message Text=" " />
        <Message Text="Overriding AdminContact" Importance="high" />
        <!-- Override the AdminContact if it is set to Keith Tingle -->
        <ItemGroup>
          <Server Condition="'%(Server.AdminContact)' == 'Keith Tingle'">
            <AdminContact>Sayed Ibrahim Hashimi</AdminContact>
          </Server>
        </ItemGroup>
        <Message Text="%(Server.Identity) : %(Server.AdminContact)" />

        <Message Text=" "/>
        <Message Text="Removing item" Importance="high" />
        <!-- Remove an item   -->
        <ItemGroup>
          <Server Remove="Server2" />
        </ItemGroup>
        <Message Text="%(Server.Identity) : %(Server.AdminContact)" />

        <!--<Message Text="Server: @(Server)" />
        <Message Text="Admin: @(Server->'%(AdminContact)')" />-->
      </Target>
    </Project>
```

In this MSBuild file, we have created an item type, Server, which contains a list of values relating to servers. Each item value contains some custom metadata that describes it, including AdminContact. Inside the PrintInfo target, the ItemGroup declaration of the Server item is redefining the AdminContact metadata value, but only for items whose AdminContact is set to the value 'Kim Abercrombie'. If the condition was not placed on the Server item type, then it would affect all the Server item values. Following that, you can see how an item value is removed. Now we can see if all this works by executing the PrintInfo target of this MSBuild file. The results are shown in Figure 3-3.

As you can see from the output, first the value for the AdminContact metadata was modified for one of the values and then an item value was removed from the Server item type. Now that we have seen how dynamic items are created, we will move on to a more realistic example.

Consider this typical scenario: After you build a project, you would like to copy all the files in the output directory to another location. I will show you how this can be achieved

```
C:\InsideMSBuild\Ch03>msbuild Metadata01.proj /t:PrintInfo /nologo
Build started 9/9/2010 10:39:17 PM.
Project "C:\InsideMSBuild\Ch03\Metadata01.proj" on node 1 (PrintInfo target(s))

PrintInfo:
  Server1 : Sayed Ibrahim Hashimi
  Server2 : Sayed Y. Hashimi
  Server3 : Nicole Woodsmall
  Server4 : Keith Tingle

  Overriding AdminContact
  Server1 : Sayed Ibrahim Hashimi
  Server2 : Sayed Y. Hashimi
  Server3 : Nicole Woodsmall
  Server4 : Sayed Ibrahim Hashimi

  Removing item
  Server1 : Sayed Ibrahim Hashimi
  Server3 : Nicole Woodsmall
  Server4 : Sayed Ibrahim Hashimi
Done Building Project "C:\InsideMSBuild\Ch03\Metadata01.proj" (PrintInfo target
(s)).

Build succeeded.
    0 Warning(s)
    0 Error(s)
```

FIGURE 3-3 Metadata01.proj result

using dynamic items. In the sample files, I have created a simple Windows application, WindowsApplication2. In the .csproj file for the project, I have added this functionality. The following sample shows an abbreviated version of the WindowsApplication2.csproj file, which contains all the added portions.

```xml
<Project ToolsVersion="4.0"
  DefaultTargets="Build"
  xmlns="http://schemas.microsoft.com/developer/msbuild/2003">
        ...

  <Import Project="$(MSBuildToolsPath)\Microsoft.CSharp.targets" />

  <!-- Extend build to copy the files in output dir -->
  <PropertyGroup>
    <BuildDependsOn>
      $(BuildDependsOn);
      CopyOutputFiles
    </BuildDependsOn>
    <OutputCopyFolder>$(MSBuildProjectDirectory)\CustomOutput\</OutputCopyFolder>
  </PropertyGroup>
  <Target Name="CopyOutputFiles">
    <!-- Dynamically create the item because these files
         are created during build -->
    <ItemGroup>
      <OutputFiles Include="$(OutputPath)**\*" />
    </ItemGroup>
    <MakeDir Directories="$(OutputCopyFolder)" />
    <Copy SourceFiles="@(OutputFiles)"
          DestinationFiles=
  "@(OutputFiles->'$(OutputCopyFolder)%(RecursiveDir)%(FileName)%(Extension)')" />
  </Target>
</Project>
```

In this snippet, I first re-declare the BuildDependsOn property; this is the property that contains the list of targets that will be executed when the build target runs. I extend this value by using a reference to itself using the $(BuildDependsOn) declaration. So I take the current list of targets and add the CopyOutputFiles target to the end of the list. We will talk more about this later in this chapter; the important part to understand now is that this target will be executed *after* the project has been built. Take a look at the usage of the ItemGroup inside the CopyOutputFiles target. The *Include* value on this picks up all the files in the OutputPath as well as subfolders. These files are placed into a new item named OutputFiles. Following this, the additional output directory is created if it doesn't exist, and then the files are copied to this new location. The Copy task is passed a value of @(OutputFiles->'$ (OutputCopyFolder)%(RecursiveDir)%(FileName)%(Extension)') for the DestinationFiles parameter. If you recall from the previous chapter, this is an Item Transformation. In this transformation, we place all the files under the OutputCopyFolder directory in the same relative location to where they are in the OutputPath folder. We achieve this by using the RecursiveDir well-known metadata. We can see if this works by building the project. I will execute the Rebuild target to ensure that all artifacts from previous builds are removed. The result of this is shown in Figure 3-4.

```
C:\InsideMSBuild\Ch03\WindowsApplication2>msbuild WindowsApplication2.csproj /t:Rebuild /nologo
Build started 9/11/2010 10:18:02 PM.
Project "C:\InsideMSBuild\Ch03\WindowsApplication2\WindowsApplication2.csproj" on node 1 (Rebuild
target(s)).
CoreClean:
    Deleting file "C:\InsideMSBuild\Ch03\WindowsApplication2\bin\Debug\WindowsApplication2.exe".
    Deleting file "C:\InsideMSBuild\Ch03\WindowsApplication2\bin\Debug\WindowsApplication2.pdb".
    Deleting file "C:\InsideMSBuild\Ch03\WindowsApplication2\obj\Debug\WindowsApplication2.Propertie
    s.Resources.resources".
    Deleting file "C:\InsideMSBuild\Ch03\WindowsApplication2\obj\Debug\GenerateResource-ResGen.read.
    1.tlog".
    Deleting file "C:\InsideMSBuild\Ch03\WindowsApplication2\obj\Debug\GenerateResource-ResGen.write
    .1.tlog".
    Deleting file "C:\InsideMSBuild\Ch03\WindowsApplication2\obj\Debug\WindowsApplication2.exe".
    Deleting file "C:\InsideMSBuild\Ch03\WindowsApplication2\obj\Debug\WindowsApplication2.pdb".
CustomAfterClean:
    Deleting file "C:\InsideMSBuild\Ch03\WindowsApplication2\CustomOutput\WindowsApplication2.exe".
    Deleting file "C:\InsideMSBuild\Ch03\WindowsApplication2\CustomOutput\WindowsApplication2.pdb".
    Removing directory "C:\InsideMSBuild\Ch03\WindowsApplication2\CustomOutput\".
CoreResGen:
    C:\Program Files\Microsoft SDKs\Windows\v6.0A\bin\ResGen.exe /useSourcePath /r:c:\WINDOWS\Micros
    oft.NET\Framework\v2.0.50727\mscorlib.dll /r:"c:\Program Files\Reference Assemblies\Microsoft\Fr
    ame                                                                          .Framework\v3.5
    \Sy     Removed to save space                                                '27\System.Data
    .d.                                                                          .WINDOWS\Micros
    oft.NET\Framework\v2.0.50727\System.dll /r:c:\WINDOWS\Microsoft.NET\Framework\v2.0.50727\System.
    Drawing.dll /r:c:\WINDOWS\Microsoft.NET\Framework\v2.0.50727\System.Windows.Forms.dll /r:c:\WIND
CoreCompile:
    C:\WINDOWS\Microsoft.NET\Framework\v4.0.30319\Csc.exe /noconfig /nowarn:1701,1702 /nostdlib+ /er
    rorreport:prompt /warn:4 /define:DEBUG;TRACE /reference:c:\WINDOWS\Microsoft.NET\Framework\v2.0.
    50'                                                                          .mework\v3.5\Sy
    ste     Removed to save space                                               ork\v3.5\System
    .Da                                                                          )727\System.Dat
    a.dll /reference:c:\WINDOWS\Microsoft.NET\Framework\v2.0.50727\System.Deployment.dll /reference:
    c:\WINDOWS\Microsoft.NET\Framework\v2.0.50727\System.dll /reference:c:\WINDOWS\Microsoft.NET\Pra
CopyFilesToOutputDirectory:
    Copying file from "obj\Debug\WindowsApplication2.exe" to "bin\Debug\WindowsApplication2.exe".
    WindowsApplication2 -> C:\InsideMSBuild\Ch03\WindowsApplication2\bin\Debug\WindowsApplication2.e
    xe
    Copying file from "obj\Debug\WindowsApplication2.pdb" to "bin\Debug\WindowsApplication2.pdb".
AfterBuild:
    Build has completed!
CopyOutputFiles:
    Creating directory "C:\InsideMSBuild\Ch03\WindowsApplication2\CustomOutput\".
    Copying file from "bin\Debug\WindowsApplication2.exe" to "C:\InsideMSBuild\Ch03\WindowsApplicati
    on2\CustomOutput\WindowsApplication2.exe".
    Copying file from "bin\Debug\WindowsApplication2.pdb" to "C:\InsideMSBuild\Ch03\WindowsApplicati
    on2\CustomOutput\WindowsApplication2.pdb".
Done Building Project "C:\InsideMSBuild\Ch03\WindowsApplication2\WindowsApplication2.csproj" (Rebu
ild target(s)).

Build succeeded.
    0 Warning(s)
    0 Error(s)
```

FIGURE 3-4 Build of WindowsApplication2.csproj

In the log shown in Figure 3-4, you can see that the CopyOutputFiles target was called after the build target executed and you can see that the files were copied into the folder specified. One other thing to note about this project file is that I extend the clean process to remove these files. The relevant elements added to the project file are shown in the following snippet.

```
<!-- Extend clean process to delete created files -->
<PropertyGroup>
  <CleanDependsOn>
    $(CleanDependsOn);
    CustomAfterClean
  </CleanDependsOn>
</PropertyGroup>
<Target Name="CustomAfterClean">
  <ItemGroup>
    <CopiedFilesToDelete Include="$(OutputCopyFolder)**\*" />
  </ItemGroup>
  <Delete Files="@(CopiedFilesToDelete)" />
  <RemoveDir Directories="$(OutputCopyFolder)" />
</Target>
```

If you extend the build process to create additional files, you should *always* extend the clean process to remove these files. MSBuild will clean up all the files it generates, but you are responsible for cleaning yours. If you are implementing incremental building, you should pay particular attention to this advice. This is because projects that are not properly cleaned may result in incorrect builds when building incrementally. We will talk more about incremental building in Chapter 6, "Batching and Incremental Builds." In this example, I have manually created files as a separate step, but sometimes there is a better way.

For C# or Visual Basic .NET (VB.NET) projects, there is a simple way to have your files automatically deleted for you. If you are creating files early in the build process, you can add files that should be deleted on clean by appending them to the FileWrites item. This is an item that the C# and VB.NET MSBuild files use to determine which files need to be deleted the next time the project is cleaned. The contents of this item are written into a file named $(MSBuildProjectFile).FileListAbsolute.txt in the intermediate output path folder. You can use this method only if you are appending the value to the FileWrites list before the Clean/IncrementalClean target is executed and the file resides under the output path folder. This is a great way to make sure that generated code files are deleted at the appropriate time. This is discussed in more detail in Chapter 8, "Practical Applications, Part 1."

Removing Items

Previously, it was mentioned that you can remove values from items using the *ItemGroup* element. In MSBuild 2.0, once a value was placed inside an item, there was no way to remove it, so items were append-only. The remove function was added in MSBuild 3.5. This is facilitated by a new attribute, Remove, on the *ItemGroup* element. This is supported for dynamic items only. I will demonstrate this with dynamic items. The usage of this is shown in the following Dynamic03.proj file.

```
<Project xmlns="http://schemas.microsoft.com/developer/msbuild/2003"
        ToolsVersion="4.0">
  <PropertyGroup>
    <SourceRoot>src\</SourceRoot>
  </PropertyGroup>
  <ItemGroup>
    <SrcFiles Include="$(SourceRoot)**\*" />
  </ItemGroup>

  <Target Name="Build">
    <Message Text="SrcFiles: @(SrcFiles)" />
    <Message Text="Removing from item" Importance="high" />
    <ItemGroup>
      <SrcFiles Remove="$(SourceRoot)sub\*" />
    </ItemGroup>
    <Message Text="SrcFiles: @(SrcFiles)" />
  </Target>

</Project>
```

In this sample, SrcFiles is initially created to include all files in and under the *src* folder. Then in the Build target, all the files in the *src\sub* folder are removed from the SrcFiles item. You can see that this works as described by examining the results shown in Figure 3-5.

```
C:\InsideMSBuild\Ch03>msbuild Dynamic03.proj /t:Build /nologo
Build started 9/11/2010 10:37:59 PM.
Project "C:\InsideMSBuild\Ch03\Dynamic03.proj" on node 1 (Build target(s)).
Build:
  SrcFiles: src\four.txt;src\one.txt;src\sub\sub_four.txt;src\sub\sub_one.txt;src\sub\sub_three.tx
t;src\sub\sub_two.txt;src\three.txt;src\two.txt
  Removing from item
  SrcFiles: src\four.txt;src\one.txt;src\three.txt;src\two.txt
Done Building Project "C:\InsideMSBuild\Ch03\Dynamic03.proj" (Build target(s)).

Build succeeded.
    0 Warning(s)
    0 Error(s)
```

FIGURE 3-5 Demonstration of removing values from items

The results here are pretty straightforward; several files were removed from SrcFiles after the *ItemGroup* element was processed by the MSBuild engine. We will now move on to cover the order that properties and items are evaluated in MSBuild.

Property and Item Evaluation

When the MSBuild engine begins to process a build file, it is evaluated in a top-down fashion in a multi-pass manner. These passes are described in order in the following list:

0. Load all environment and global properties, and toolset properties. In Microsoft Visual Studio 2010, for example, C++ defines several properties in the MSBuild 4.0 toolset.

1. Evaluate properties and process imports as encountered

2. Evaluate item definitions

3. Evaluate items

4. Evaluate using tasks

5. Start build and reading targets

The first step is numbered 0 (no, it's not a typo) because it doesn't pertain to processing the file but is important in its evaluation. The first pass (numbered 1) is to populate all static properties and to process all import statements. As an import statement is encountered, the contents of the import file are duplicated inline into the current project file. When an import is encountered, the current directory is temporarily set to the directory where the imported file resides, for use when processing imports found within the imported file. This occurs only during the processing of the import statement. This is performed to ensure that import elements are processed correctly. For relative paths in items, the directory of the invoked MSBuild file is always used. This current directory is not maintained while any targets in the imported files are executed. We will discuss the directory issue later in this chapter, but first we will take a look at properties and items.

In this section, we will focus on the process in which properties and items are populated. Then in the next section, we will take a look at importing external files. As stated previously, MSBuild will process your file in multiple passes. The first pass is to process all imports and properties. These items are evaluated as they are encountered. Following this, items are evaluated. You should note that if you create a property that references an item, the value of the property is evaluated when it is used. What this means is that at the time you reference the property, the item reference is evaluated and expanded. Therefore, if the item changes, so can the property. To start our discussion of property and item evaluation, we will work our way through a very simple case. Take a look at the following Eval01.proj file.

```
<Project xmlns="http://schemas.microsoft.com/developer/msbuild/2003"
         ToolsVersion="4.0"
         DefaultTargets="PrintInfo">

  <PropertyGroup>
    <PropOne>one</PropOne>
    <PropTwo>$(PropThree)</PropTwo>
    <PropThree>three</PropThree>
    <PropFour>$(PropThree)</PropFour>
  </PropertyGroup>

  <Target Name="PrintInfo">
    <Message Text="PropOne: $(PropOne)" />
    <Message Text="PropTwo: $(PropTwo)" />
    <Message Text="PropThree: $(PropThree)" />
    <Message Text="PropFour: $(PropFour)" />
  </Target>
</Project>
```

Since all these properties do not depend on items, we would expect all of them to be evaluated at the same time from top to bottom. Two properties in this file, which are in bold in the code, depend on the value of PropThree. One of the properties, PropTwo, occurs before PropThree, and the other, PropFour, occurs after PropThree. In the only target, PrintInfo, we simply print the values for each of these four properties. This printout is shown in Figure 3-6.

```
C:\InsideMSBuild\Ch03>msbuild Eval01.proj /t:PrintInfo /nologo
Build started 9/11/2010 10:43:01 PM.
Project "C:\InsideMSBuild\Ch03\Eval01.proj" on node 1 (PrintInfo target(s)).
PrintInfo:
  PropOne: one
  PropTwo:
  PropThree: three
  PropFour: three
Done Building Project "C:\InsideMSBuild\Ch03\Eval01.proj" (PrintInfo target(s)).

Build succeeded.
    0 Warning(s)
    0 Error(s)
```

FIGURE 3-6 PrintInfo target on Eval01.proj

In the result shown here, take note of two things. The first is that PropTwo doesn't have a value; this is because PropThree did not have a value when it was populated. The other significant observation here is that PropFour was successfully populated with the value from PropThree. This is because the declaration of PropFour occurs after the definition for PropThree. Now let's take a look at the same example, using items instead of properties. The following contents are taken from the Eval02.proj file.

```
<Project xmlns="http://schemas.microsoft.com/developer/msbuild/2003"
         DefaultTargets="PrintInfo" ToolsVersion="4.0">

  <ItemGroup>
    <ItemOne Include="One" />
    <ItemTwo Include="@(ItemThree)" />
    <ItemThree Include="Three" />
    <ItemFour Include="@(ItemThree)" />
  </ItemGroup>

  <Target Name="PrintInfo">
    <Message Text="ItemOne: @(ItemOne)" />
    <Message Text="ItemTwo: @(ItemTwo)" />
    <Message Text="ItemThree: @(ItemThree)" />
    <Message Text="ItemFour: @(ItemFour)" />
  </Target>
</Project>
```

This example simply replaced all the properties in the previous file with items. Since they are all items, they will be evaluated in a similar manner as the properties were in the previous example. The output, as you might expect, is the same as the previous one as well, so it is not listed a second time. Instead, we will look at properties and items together.

For a slightly more interesting example, we will take a look at what happens when we introduce properties and items together. You will find the contents of a new example in the following Eval03.proj file. As you look at this, try to guess what the output of the PrintInfo target will be for this file.

```xml
<Project xmlns="http://schemas.microsoft.com/developer/msbuild/2003"
        ToolsVersion="4.0"
        DefaultTargets="PrintInfo">

  <PropertyGroup>
    <OutputPathCopy>$(OutputPath)</OutputPathCopy>
  </PropertyGroup>

  <ItemGroup>
    <OutputPathItem Include="$(OutputPath)" />
  </ItemGroup>

  <PropertyGroup>
    <Configuration>Debug</Configuration>
    <OutputPath>bin\$(Configuration)\</OutputPath>
  </PropertyGroup>

  <Target Name="PrintInfo">
    <Message Text="Configuration: $(Configuration)" />
    <Message Text="OutputPath: $(OutputPath)"/>
    <Message Text="OutputPathCopy: $(OutputPathCopy)" />
    <Message Text="OutputPathItem: @(OutputPathItem)" />
  </Target>

</Project>
```

The two important elements in this project file are the first property and item declared, OutputPathCopy and OutputPathItem, respectively. Both of these are declared before the property on which both depend. That property is the OutputPath property. In the PrintInfo target, all the properties and the single item are printed out. You will find the results of that target in Figure 3-7.

```
C:\InsideMSBuild\Ch03>msbuild Eval03.proj /t:PrintInfo /nologo
Build started 9/11/2010 10:46:31 PM.
Project "C:\InsideMSBuild\Ch03\Eval03.proj" on node 1 (PrintInfo target(s)).
PrintInfo:
  Configuration: Debug
  OutputPath: bin\Debug\
  OutputPathCopy:
  OutputPathItem: bin\Debug\
Done Building Project "C:\InsideMSBuild\Ch03\Eval03.proj" (PrintInfo target(s)).

Build succeeded.
    0 Warning(s)
    0 Error(s)
```

FIGURE 3-7 PrintInfo result on Eval03.proj

As mentioned previously, the interesting pieces of this are the OutputPathCopy property and the OutputPathItem item. If you take a look at the preceding figure, you can see that the value was placed into OutputPathItem but not into OutputPathCopy. This is because the item's final value was evaluated after the OutputPath property was declared. This is because the OutputPath property doesn't depend on an item. This section should have given you a good idea of how properties and items are evaluated by MSBuild. We'll now discuss how you can import other files.

Importing Files

MSBuild natively supports importing project files or targets. In fact, this is how Visual Studio builds your projects. In this section, we will see how this works and how you can take advantage of it in your build process. To reuse the contents of other files, you must use the *Import* element. This element must be placed directly inside the *Project* element, at the same level as a Target element. You specify the file that is to be imported by using the *Project* attribute. The only other attribute that can be placed on the *Import* element is the *Condition* attribute, as with most other MSBuild elements. These are the only two attributes that can be specified for the Import element. If you take a look at any C# project created by Visual Studio, you will find the following declaration:

```
<Import Project="$(MSBuildToolsPath)\Microsoft.CSharp.targets" />
```

> **Note** With MSBuild 4.0, you can now wrap up one or more Import elements inside an ImportGroup element. This is the only occasion that the import doesn't have to be an immediate child of the Project element.

This imports the Microsoft.CSharp.targets file; the reserved property MSBuildToolsPath is used to resolve the full path to this file. This file is created by Microsoft to fully describe the build process for C# projects. Other managed projects have their own build scripts that are imported into their own project files. The Microsoft.CSharp.targets file, like Microsoft .VisualBasic.targets (used for VB.NET projects), describes all the steps to build the project while the actual project file describes what is being built. These files then import the shared file Microsoft.Common.targets, which contains the common steps to build managed projects. This explains why there is not a single target in project files generated by Visual Studio. All the targets required to build managed projects are imported from another file. We will now move on to discuss how to import external files.

When MSBuild processes an import statement, the current working directory is set to the directory of the imported project file. This is necessary to correctly resolve the location of paths declared in import elements or inside the *UsingTask* element. In addition, the imported file is then expanded inline at the location where the *Import* element occurs. This can be visualized by the image shown in Figure 3-8.

> **Note** With MSBuild 4.0, you can use the new `/preprocess` (`/pp`) switch to examine the contents of the project that MSBuild uses. This will contain all imports. In order to write the contents to a file, you can use the notation `/pp:filename.txt`, where *filename.txt* is the file to write to.

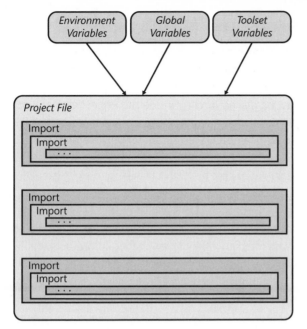

FIGURE 3-8 Project file import visualization

When the MSBuild engine processes a build file, it builds a representation of it in memory. When files are imported, the in-memory representation is made to include the contents of the imported file. We will now take a look at how Visual Studio behaves in building your managed projects by reviewing the contents of the following two MSBuild files: Import01 .proj and Import01.targets.

```
<!-- Import01.proj -->
<Project xmlns="http://schemas.microsoft.com/developer/msbuild/2003"
         ToolsVersion="4.0"
         DefaultTargets="All">

  <PropertyGroup>
    <SourceRoot>$(MSBuildProjectDirectory)\src\</SourceRoot>
    <Configuration>Debug</Configuration>
  </PropertyGroup>
  <ItemGroup>
    <SourceFiles Include="$(SourceRoot)\*" />
  </ItemGroup>

  <Import Project="$(MSBuildProjectDirectory)\Import01.targets" />

  <Target Name="PrintOutputPath">
    <Message Text="OutputPath: $(OutputPath)" />
    <Message Text="MSBuildProjectFile: $(MSBuildProjectFile)" />
  </Target>
  <Target Name="All"
          DependsOnTargets="PrintInfo;PrintOutputPath" />
</Project>
```

```
<!-- Import01.targets -->
<Project xmlns="http://schemas.microsoft.com/developer/msbuild/2003"
         ToolsVersion="4.0">

  <Target Name="PrintInfo">
    <Message Text="SourceRoot: $(SourceRoot)" />
    <Message Text="Configuration: $(Configuration)" />
    <Message Text="SourceFiles: @(SourceFiles)" />
  </Target>

  <PropertyGroup>
    <OutputPath>bin\$(Configuration)\</OutputPath>
  </PropertyGroup>

</Project>
```

In this example, the Import01.proj imports the Import01.targets file; the import statement has been highlighted here. This is a simplified view of how managed projects are built. With managed projects, the project file that is generated by Visual Studio defines all the properties and items to be built, and an imported file defines how to build those values. So in this example, Imports01.proj (project file) represents the project file created by Visual Studio, and the Import01.targets (targets file) represents the build file that is imported by those generated projects, based on the language that this file changes. Back to the example, the project file defines a few properties as well as an item. Along with these, the target PrintOutputPath is defined, which prints out the value for the OutputPath, which is defined in the targets file. The targets file defines the aforementioned property and defines a target, PrintInfo, which prints out the values for those items defined in the project file. I will execute both targets, PrintInfo and PrintOutputPath, by executing the All target. The results of this are shown in Figure 3-9.

```
C:\InsideMSBuild\Ch03>msbuild Import01.proj /t:All /nologo
Build started 9/11/2010 10:49:26 PM.
Project "C:\InsideMSBuild\Ch03\Import01.proj" on node 1 (All target(s)).
PrintInfo:
  SourceRoot: C:\InsideMSBuild\Ch03\src\
  Configuration: Debug
  SourceFiles: C:\InsideMSBuild\Ch03\src\\four.txt;C:\InsideMSBuild\Ch03\src\\one.txt;C:\InsideMSB
  uild\Ch03\src\\three.txt;C:\InsideMSBuild\Ch03\src\\two.txt
PrintOutputPath:
  OutputPath: bin\Debug\
  MSBuildProjectFile: Import01.proj
Done Building Project "C:\InsideMSBuild\Ch03\Import01.proj" (All target(s)).

Build succeeded.
    0 Warning(s)
    0 Error(s)
```

FIGURE 3-9 Import01.proj results

Here are some things to note:

1. All items and properties defined in Import01.proj *before* the *Import* element are available to Import01.targets.

2. All items and properties defined in Import01.targets are available to Import01.proj *after* the *Import* element.

3. All properties and targets are defined from top to bottom, and the last definition that occurs is the value that persists.

4. Targets are executed after all items, properties, and imports are evaluated.

Because of the first item in the previous list, the target PrintInfo was able to print out the values for the properties and items in Import01.proj successfully. Because of the second item in the previous list, the target PrintOutputPath was able to get the value for the OutputPath that was defined in Import01.targets. The third point was not demonstrated here, but it is important to understand it. Any file can define any property except reserved properties, and any target it desires. Because a property or a target can have only one in-memory representation, the last definition encountered is the value that will be used to build the project. The last point listed, that targets begin execution after all static items and properties are processed, is very important as well. By the time any target is executed, the MSBuild engine has already completed creating its in-memory representation of the build script. This means that when a target executes, it has no connection back to the file that contains it. It could have been defined in any file that was imported.

We will now examine another set of files that will help us further understand how build files behave when importing other files. This example will be demonstrated by two new files, Import02.proj and Import02.targets. In this example, the Import02.targets file is stored in a subfolder named Import. The following sample shows the complete definition of both these files.

```
<!-- Import02.proj -->
<Project xmlns="http://schemas.microsoft.com/developer/msbuild/2003"
         ToolsVersion="4.0"
         DefaultTargets="All">

  <Target Name="PrintPath">
    <Message Text="MSBuildProjectFullPath: $(MSBuildProjectFullPath)" />
  </Target>

  <Import Project="Import\Import02.targets" />

  <Target Name="All"
          DependsOnTargets="PrintPath;PrintPathImport;PrintCompile" />
</Project>

<!-- Import02.targets -->
<Project xmlns="http://schemas.microsoft.com/developer/msbuild/2003"
         ToolsVersion="4.0">

  <ItemGroup>
    <Compile Include="Class1.cs" />
  </ItemGroup>

  <Target Name="PrintPathImport">
    <Message Text="MSBuildProjectFullPath: $(MSBuildProjectFullPath)" />
  </Target>
```

```
<Target Name="PrintCompile">
  <Message Text="Compile: @(Compile)" />
  <Message Text="Compile.Fullpath: @(Compile->'%(Fullpath)','%0a%0d')" />
</Target>

</Project>
```

Both of these files contain a target that prints the value of the MSBuildProjectFullPath reserved property. This is to demonstrate the fact that all the properties and items, including built-in properties, have defined values before those targets execute. Also, in the imported file, an item named Compile is defined, which includes a single file named Class1.cs. This file resides in the same folder as the Import02.targets. Can you guess what the results of the PrintCompile target would be? If you execute all these targets, the results would be as shown in Figure 3-10.

```
C:\InsideMSBuild\Ch03>msbuild Import02.proj /t:All /nologo
Build started 9/11/2010 11:04:19 AM.
Project "C:\InsideMSBuild\Ch03\Import02.proj" on node 1 (All target(s)).
PrintPath:
  MSBuildProjectFullPath: C:\InsideMSBuild\Ch03\Import02.proj
PrintPathImport:
  MSBuildProjectFullPath: C:\InsideMSBuild\Ch03\Import02.proj
PrintCompile:
  Compile: Class1.cs
  Compile.Fullpath: C:\InsideMSBuild\Ch03\Class1.cs
Done Building Project "C:\InsideMSBuild\Ch03\Import02.proj" (All target(s)).

Build succeeded.
    0 Warning(s)
    0 Error(s)
```

FIGURE 3-10 Import02.proj result

If you take a look at the results shown in Figure 3-10, you can see that the value for the MSBuildProjectFullPath property evaluates to the same value regardless of the file that contains the target that prints it. This exemplifies the fact that the file that contains a target has no effect on the values for properties and items. If you need to get the name/path of the current file, then you can use the reserved properties MSBuildThisFile and related reserved properties. For the full list, see the section entitled "Reserved Properties," in Chapter 2, "MSBuild Deep Dive, Part 1."

The imported file also contains another target, PrintCompile, which prints out the value for the Compile item defined in that file. The file that is included in the Compile item is the Class1.cs file. This file resides in the Import folder. If you look at the Import02.targets file, it is obvious that the Compile item is attempting to include that Class1.cs file. The printed value for that path to that file does not place it in the Import folder. Instead, it references the folder of the outermost file, the Import02.proj file. If an imported file declares items to files, it will always be defined relative to the file that the MSBuild process starts with. If you need to declare items in files that will be imported, they should be defined using properties that are defined in the importing file, or you can explicitly define them using MSBuildThisFile and related properties. We have covered how to import external files in some detail. Throughout the remainder of this text, we will be using this technique. We'll now move on to discuss how you can extend the build process for managed projects.

Extending the Build Process

MSBuild aims to expose the build process and to allow users to completely customize the process. MSBuild does indeed achieve both of these goals, and it does a good job of it! We will now take a close look at that build process and see how it can be extended.

When you create a managed project using Visual Studio, toward the bottom of the project file, you will find an import statement such as the following one, which was taken from a C# project.

```
<Import Project="$(MSBuildToolsPath)\Microsoft.CSharp.targets" />
```

This statement imports another known file that defines *how* C# projects are built. This project file is shipped along with MSBuild, which is delivered as a part of the Microsoft .NET Framework. The contents of the project files created by Visual Studio define only properties and items; there are no targets included in that file. All the targets for building managed projects are contained in those shared files provided with MSBuild. If you need to extend the build process, you can do so by modifying the project file itself. The four most common ways to extend the build process for managed projects are (listed in order of ease of use):

1. PreBuildEvent and PostBuildEvent

2. Override BeforeBuild, AfterBuild, and similar targets

3. Target Hooks (i.e. BeforeTargets and AfterTarget)

4. Target injection

In versions of Visual Studio prior to 2005, the only way to extend the build process was to define a command, such as a batch file or external program, which would be executed before or after the build was completed. These are the pre-build event and post-build event respectively. These "events" are implemented using plain MSBuild properties and targets; there is no event construct in MSBuild files. These build events are still supported in current versions of Visual Studio, for backward compatibility and because the Visual Studio user interface already supports this concept. You can enter these commands in Visual Studio on each project's Properties page, on the build tab, as shown in Figure 3-11.

From the user interface shown in Figure 3-11, you can insert a set of commands that will be executed before or after the build executes. This is captured in MSBuild simply as a property; the two properties that are used to capture these values are PreBuildEvent and PostBuildEvent. These properties will be defined in the project file itself. This method is the simplest one to extend the build process, but also the least powerful. I would suggest avoiding this technique. A better approach would be one of the other techniques. We will now discuss the second option.

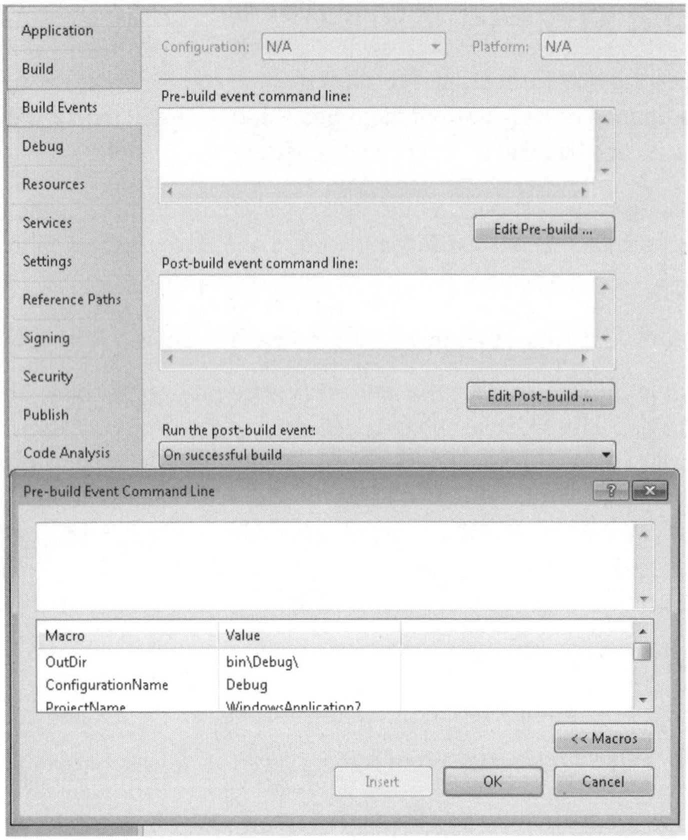

FIGURE 3-11 Build events in Visual Studio

After the PreBuildEvent and PostBuildEvent properties, the next option is to override existing targets that were created as extension points. Previously, I showed that the C# projects import a project file named Microsoft.CSharp.targets; other managed languages define their own shared file. All these files will then import another file, Microsoft.Common.targets. This file, which contains all the common elements in building managed projects, defines many targets that were created simply to be overridden. For example, if you take a look at a project file created by Visual Studio, you will see a comment like the following.

```
<!-- To modify your build process, add your task inside one of
     the targets below and uncomment it.
     Other similar extension points exist,
     see Microsoft.Common.targets.
<Target Name="BeforeBuild">
</Target>
<Target Name="AfterBuild">
</Target>
-->
```

These and other targets are defined as empty targets in the Microsoft.Common.targets file. The following list shows 14 such targets:

- BeforeBuild

- AfterBuild

- BeforeRebuild

- AfterRebuild

- BeforeResolveReferences

- AfterResolveReferences

- BeforeResGen

- AfterResGen

- BeforeCompile

- AfterCompile

- BeforeClean

- AfterClean

- BeforePublish

- AfterPublish

All these targets are simply extension points and will be executed at the appropriate time. If you define a target with the same name *after* the import element, then your target will override the default empty target. For example, consider the following project file.

```
<Project DefaultTargets="Build"
xmlns="http://schemas.microsoft.com/developer/msbuild/2003" ToolsVersion="4.0">
   ...

  <Import Project="$(MSBuildToolsPath)\Microsoft.CSharp.targets" />
<!-- To modify your build process, add your task inside one of
     the targets below and uncomment it.
     Other similar extension points exist,
     see Microsoft.Common.targets.
<Target Name="BeforeBuild">
</Target>
<Target Name="AfterBuild">
</Target>
-->
  <Target Name="AfterBuild">
    <Message Text="Build has completed!" Importance="high" />
  </Target>

  ...

</Project>
```

In the preceding snippet, the AfterBuild target was defined to invoke the Message task with the statement "Build has completed!" If you build this, you will see the message printed to the console after the project has been built. If you do not see the message when you are building in Visual Studio, you may need to increase the verbosity used by Visual Studio. This is defined in the Options dialog under the Project and Solutions, Build and Run node.

The option just described is a great way to extend the build process, and I highly recommend using it. The only problem with this technique is that only one AfterBuild, or any of those targets listed previously, can be defined at once. Because of this, if two or more imports are processed that define the same target, then the previous definition will be overridden. So if you are creating reusable build scripts, this technique is not suitable. Instead, you can use target hooks or target injection. Now we will discuss the target hooks.

MSBuild 4.0 added a new concept called target hooks. With this came two new attributes on the *Target* element: *BeforeTargets* and *AfterTargets*. Many times when you are creating a target, you don't care about the exact time that it executes, but you just want it to execute before or after one or more targets. *BeforeTargets* and *AfterTargets* easily facilitate this. When you author a target and you know one or more targets it should execute after, you can specify them in a semicolon-separated list in the *AfterTargets* attribute. And the idea applies for targets that should be executed before the target; just put them inside the *BeforeTargets* value. For example, consider the simple project file, BeforeAfter01.proj, shown next.

```
<Project xmlns="http://schemas.microsoft.com/developer/msbuild/2003"
         ToolsVersion="4.0"
         DefaultTargets="Build">

  <Target Name="Build">
    <Message Text="Build target"/>
  </Target>

  <Target Name="GenerateCode" BeforeTargets="Build">
    <Message Text="GenerateCode target"/>
  </Target>

  <Target Name="CustomCopyOutput" AfterTargets="Build">
    <Message Text="CustomCopyOutput target"/>
  </Target>

</Project>
```

In this file, there are three targets defined, in no particular order, and each just prints a message stating that the target has executed. The default target is the Build target. The GenerateCode target uses the *BeforeTargets* attribute to ensure that it is executed before the Build target, and the CustomCopyOutput target uses *AfterTargets*, specifying Build so that it executes after the Build target. Figure 3-12 shows the result of executing `msbuild.exe BeforeAfter01.proj /t:Build`.

```
C:\InsideMSBuild\Ch03>msbuild BeforeAfter01.proj /t:Build /nologo
Build started 9/11/2010 10:52:10 PM.
Project "C:\InsideMSBuild\Ch03\BeforeAfter01.proj" on node 1 (Build target(s)).
GenerateCode:
  GenerateCode target
Build:
  Build target
CustomCopyOutput:
  CustomCopyOutput target
Done Building Project "C:\InsideMSBuild\Ch03\BeforeAfter01.proj" (Build target(s)).

Build succeeded.
    0 Warning(s)
    0 Error(s)
```

FIGURE 3-12 BeforeAfter01.proj

As you can see, we were able to extend the behavior of the Build target without modifying it. This approach works even if you are extending targets that are defined outside the current file. For example, you can use this approach when you edit your C# or VB.NET project files even though most targets are defined inside the Microsoft.Common.targets file.

Let's define how *BeforeTargets* and *AfterTargets* behave a bit more precisely. In this discussion, the target listed in *BeforeTargets* and *AfterTargets* is X. *BeforeTargets* means that when target X is about to run the first time, even if its condition evaluates to *false,* then run *BeforeTargets* before it if it hasn't run already. *AfterTargets* is very similar to this, and it can be defined as follows: After target X runs for the first time, or if it was invoked and its condition was false, then run *AfterTargets* if it hasn't run already.

If you specified more than one target inside the *BeforeTargets* or *AfterTargets* attribute, then you are not guaranteed that they will be executed in that order. For example, take a look at the BeforeAfter02.proj file shown next.

```xml
<Project xmlns="http://schemas.microsoft.com/developer/msbuild/2003"
         ToolsVersion="4.0">

  <Target Name="CustomBuild" BeforeTargets="Prebuild1;Prebuild2">
    <Message Text="CustomBuild target"/>
  </Target>

  <Target Name="Prebuild1">
    <Message Text="Prebuild1 target"/>
  </Target>

  <Target Name="Prebuild2">
    <Message Text="Prebuild2 target"/>
  </Target>

</Project>
```

The Prebuild1 and Prebuild2 targets are free to execute in any order. The fact that they are defined as `Prebuild1,Prebuild2` has no effect on the order of execution. To clarify, Prebuild2 may execute before Prebuild1; the *BeforeTargets* declaration has no effect on that. If you want a dependency there, then you must handle that accordingly.

This is a great approach, but it does have some drawbacks. Since these concepts were introduced with MSBuild 4.0, you cannot use this method with any previous version, and the target you define has to know to inject itself into the build process. Many times, you are dealing with the other case: That is, you have a target that has already been defined and you want to inject that target into your existing build process. Target injection solves both of these concerns, and we will discuss that now.

Target injection is the most flexible option when extending the build process. It is also the least intuitive and most difficult method. With that being said, it is pretty easy once you see how it works. If you take a look at the Microsoft.Common.targets, the file that is at the core of building managed projects, you will see targets defined like the one that follows.

```
<Target
    Name="Build"
    Condition=" '$(_InvalidConfigurationWarning)' != 'true' "
    DependsOnTargets="$(BuildDependsOn)"
    Outputs="$(TargetPath)" />
```

If you take a look at this target, you will quickly notice that it doesn't actually do anything—it's an empty target. You might wonder, what is the purpose of creating a target that doesn't do anything? What this empty target does do, however, is specify a set of targets that must be executed before it is. These targets are placed in the *DependsOnTargets* attribute as $(BuildDependsOn). Immediately above the declaration for the Build target is the following property declaration.

```
<PropertyGroup>
    <BuildDependsOn>
        BeforeBuild;
        CoreBuild;
        AfterBuild
    </BuildDependsOn>
</PropertyGroup>
```

This specifies the value for the BuildDependsOn property, which is a list of targets that must be executed before the Build target is allowed to execute. It is no coincidence that these target names are placed into a property instead of declared inline in the *Target* element. The reason that they were placed inside a property was as an extension point. Because they are placed in a property, you can override the value, thereby extending the build process. We will now take a look at how we can inject a target inside the build process, using the Build target as an example. When you utilize these properties, odds are that you don't want to simply override the value for BuildDependsOn but add to it. From the samples, I have created a Windows Forms project named WindowsApplication1.csproj. Inside that project file, you will find the following statement:

```
<Project DefaultTargets="Build"
         xmlns="http://schemas.microsoft.com/developer/msbuild/2003"
         ToolsVersion="4.0">
...
```

```xml
<Import Project="$(MSBuildToolsPath)\Microsoft.CSharp.targets" />

<PropertyGroup>
  <BuildDependsOn>
    $(BuildDependsOn);
    CustomAfterBuild
  </BuildDependsOn>
</PropertyGroup>

<Target Name="CustomAfterBuild">
  <Message Text="Inside CustomAfterBuild target"
          Importance="high" />
</Target>
...
</Project>
```

In the preceding snippet, you see that the Microsoft.CSharp.targets file is imported, which then imports Microsoft.Common.targets. The Microsoft.Common.targets file defines the BuildDependsOn property, so it is available after that import statement. *After* the *Import* element, you can see that the BuildDependsOn property was re-declared. It is very important that this declaration comes after the *Import* element. If you declared a value for BuildDependsOn before the *Import* element, then it would simply be overwritten in the imported file. As stated previously in this chapter, that last definition for a property is the one that is used.

Looking back at the declaration for BuildDependsOn just shown, you can see that the new value for the property is declared using the value for the property itself. If you append to a dependency property by referencing the current value, you do not have to worry if the current value is empty. In this case, the resulting dependency property will have extra semicolons, which is not a problem. What this notation does is allow you to take an existing property and append, or prepend, to it. In this case, we have appended the target CustomAfterBuild to the BuildDependsOn property. When MSBuild begins to process the Build target, it will first execute all targets on the TargetDependsOn list, and therefore execute the list of targets that we specified. We can see if this works by simply building the WindowsApplication1.csproj file. The definition for the CustomAfterBuild target follows. The results of the command `msbuild.exe WindowsApplication1.csproj` are shown in Figure 3-13.

```
C:\InsideMSBuild\Ch03\WindowsApplication1>msbuild WindowsApplication1.csproj /nologo
Build started 10/6/2010 11:03:19 PM.
Project "C:\InsideMSBuild\Ch03\WindowsApplication1\WindowsApplication1.csproj" on node 1 (default
targets).
CoreResGen:
  All outputs are up-to-date.
CoreCompile:
Skipping target "CoreCompile" because all output files are up-to-date with respect to the input fi
les.
_CopyAppConfigFile:
Skipping target "_CopyAppConfigFile" because all output files are up-to-date with respect to the i
nput files.
CopyFilesToOutputDirectory:
  WindowsApplication1 -> C:\InsideMSBuild\Ch03\WindowsApplication1\bin\Debug\WindowsApplication1.e
  xe
CustomAfterBuild:
  Inside CustomAfterBuild target
Done Building Project "C:\InsideMSBuild\Ch03\WindowsApplication1\WindowsApplication1.csproj" (defa
ult targets).

Build succeeded.
    0 Warning(s)
    0 Error(s)
```

FIGURE 3-13 Target injection on Build

From the results, you can see that we were able to successfully inject our target into this process. After looking through the Microsoft.Common.targets file, I was able to find several dependency properties available for your use. Those are listed in Table 3-1.

TABLE 3-1 Predefined Target Dependency Properties

BuildDependsOn	CreateSatelliteAssembliesDependsOn
CoreBuildDependsOn	PrepareForRunDependsOn
RebuildDependsOn	UnmanagedRegistrationDependsOn
RunDependsOn	CleanDependsOn
PrepareForBuildDependsOn	CoreCleanDependsOn
GetFrameworkPathsDependsOn	PostBuildEventDependsOn
PreBuildEventDependsOn	PublishDependsOn
UnmanagedUnregistrationDependsOn	PublishOnlyDependsOn
ResolveReferencesDependsOn	PublishBuildDependsOn
GetRedistListsDependsOn	BuiltProjectOutputGroupDependsOn
ResolveAssemblyReferencesDependsOn	DebugSymbolsProjectOutputGroupDependsOn
PrepareResourcesDependsOn	DocumentationProjectOutputGroupDependsOn
PrepareResourceNamesDependsOn	SatelliteDllsProjectOutputGroupDependsOn
ResGenDependsOn	SourceFilesProjectOutputGroupDependsOn
CoreResGenDependsOn	ContentFilesProjectOutputGroupDependsOn
CompileLicxFilesDependsOn	SGenFilesOutputGroupDependsOn
CompileDependsOn	DesignTimeResolveAssemblyReferencesDependsOn
GetTargetPathDependsOn	AssignTargetPathsDependsOn
CreateCustomManifestResourceNamesDependsOn	ComputeIntermediateSatelliteAssembliesDependsOn
GenerateManifestsDependsOn	GetCopyToOutputDirectoryItemsDependsOn

 Note These properties do not apply to C++ projects because they do not import the Microsoft.Common.targets file. For C++ projects, you will have to use target hooks.

As you can see, there are many places where you can place customizations to the build process in an unobtrusive, safe, and supported manner. The names of these properties are for the most part self-explanatory. I will not expand on these here, but if you need more information, you should go directly to the source: the Microsoft.Common.targets file. You should also know that the Microsoft.CSharp.targets file and other files for managed languages do define a few other dependency properties that can be used. They will not be listed here. Throughout this text, we will be using this procedure, so you will become familiar with it.

There is an important difference between how target hooks (*BeforeTargets* and *AfterTargets*) work, compared to target injection (*DependsOnTargets*), and that relate to the behavior exhibited when the condition on the target evaluates to *false*. When using target hooks, if the condition on the target that is being hooked onto is false, the targets declaring

BeforeTargets and *AfterTargets* will still be executed (if they haven't already, of course). This is not the case when you use *DependsOnTargets*. If the target that is being extended has a condition that evaluates to *false*, the *DependsOnTargets* property is ignored.

> **Note** A target will be executed only once during a build. For example, if the Compile target has already executed, then if the build encounters a CallTarget task for Compile after that, it will be skipped. This is by design.

Now that we have discussed how to extend the build process, let's discuss a couple of new features with MSBuild 4.0: property functions and item functions.

Property Functions and Item Functions

With previous versions of MSBuild, if you needed to perform simple, common operations on properties and items, you always needed to invoke a custom task. In MSBuild 4.0, however, there is support for many common tasks. For instance, if you want to compute the length of a string or extract a substring for a property, you shouldn't need to use a task. Well, now you don't have to because you can use property functions to do things like this. Also, with MSBuild 4.0, item functions have been introduced. You can use item functions to alleviate some of the need for batching, which many MSBuild users have found to be difficult to understand. We will cover both of these features in this section, starting with property functions.

Property Functions

As we just mentioned, property functions can be used to perform a set of simple operations that previously would have required a custom task. There are three types of property functions, which are outlined in Table 3-2. Each of these types has its own unique syntax, which we will cover in this section.

TABLE 3-2 Types of Property Functions

Type	Description
String property functions	Since all properties are represented as strings, you can call any instance method from the *String* class on your properties.
Static property functions	During a build, there is a set of common classes on which you can call static methods, or properties. For example, you can call any static method or property on *System.String*, *System.Int16*, and so on. For a full list of these classes, along with a few specific other items, see *http://msdn.microsoft.com/en-us/library/dd633440.aspx*.
MSBuild property functions	This is a set of functions that have been created specifically for use during builds. They perform a variety of operations such as basic arithmetic, logical operations, etc.

String Property Functions

Because you can access either the instance properties of the property or instance methods with string property functions, two syntaxes will be used. To access an instance property, then you will use the following syntax:

$({*PropertyName*}.{*InstanceProperty*})

where *{PropertyName}* is the MSBuild property name and *{InstanceProperty}* is the name of the string instance property that you want to access. For example, if you wanted to find the length of the Configuration property, you would use $(Configuration.Length).

In order to access an instance method of the *String* class, you would use the following syntax:

$({*PropertyName*}.{*MethodName*}([parameter*s*]))

where *{PropertyName}* is the name of the property, and *{MethodName}* is the name of the string method that you want to call. If you need to pass in any parameters, you would do so using the optional *[parameters]*. For example, either $(Configuration.ToLower()) or $(Configuration.Substring(0,2)) would be valid.

One of the really useful features of property functions is that you can chain the commands together. For example, if you wanted to perform a substring on the OutputPath property and then see if the results ends with a '\', you would use the statement $(OutputPath .Substring(0,10).EndsWith('\')). Here, you can see that we first invoke the *Substring* method on the OutputPath property and then the *EndsWith* method. In order to give you a better idea of this in action, take a look at the contents of the following code snippet, from the PropertyFunctions01.proj file.

```
<Project xmlns="http://schemas.microsoft.com/developer/msbuild/2003"
        ToolsVersion="4.0"
        DefaultTargets="Demo">

  <PropertyGroup>
    <Configuration Condition=" '$(Configuration)' == '' ">Debug</Configuration>
    <OutputPath>bin\Debug\</OutputPath>
  </PropertyGroup>


  <Target Name="Demo">
    <Message Text="Configuration: $(Configuration)" Importance="high"/>
    <Message Text="OutputPath: $(OutputPath)" Importance="high"/>
    <Message Text="==============================================================="
                  Importance="high" />
    <Message Text="OutputPath length: $(OutputPath.Length)"/>
    <Message Text="OutputPath ends with '\': $(OutputPath.EndsWith('\'))"/>
    <Message Text="OutputPath no trailing slash: $(OutputPath.TrimEnd('\'))"/>
    <Message Text="OutputPath no trailing slash ends with Configuration:
                  $(OutputPath.TrimEnd('\').EndsWith('$(Configuration)'))"/>
    <Message Text="OutputPath root:
```

```
            $(OutputPath.TrimEnd('\').Replace($(Configuration),''))"/>
    <Message Text="OutputPath root no trailing slash:
        $(OutputPath.TrimEnd('\').Replace($(Configuration),'').TrimEnd('\'))"/>
  </Target>

</Project>
```

In this project file, we have created one target, Demo, which uses property functions in a variety of ways. Take a look at the result shown in Figure 3-14.

```
C:\InsideMSBuild\Ch03>msbuild PropertyFunctions01.proj /t:Demo /nologo
Build started 10/25/2010 9:46:31 PM.
Project "C:\InsideMSBuild\Ch03\PropertyFunctions01.proj" on node 1 (Demo target(s)).
Demo:
  Configuration: Debug
  OutputPath: bin\Debug\
  ===================================================================
  OutputPath length: 10
  OutputPath ends with '\': True
  OutputPath no trailing slash: bin\Debug
  OutputPath no trailing slash ends with Configuration: True
  OutputPath root: bin\
  OutputPath root no trailing slash: bin
Done Building Project "C:\InsideMSBuild\Ch03\PropertyFunctions01.proj" (Demo target(s)).

Build succeeded.
    0 Warning(s)
    0 Error(s)
```

FIGURE 3-14 Result of Demo Target in PropertyFunctions01.proj

From Figure 3-14 and its corresponding sample, you can see how powerful property functions become when you chain them together.

Static Property Functions

Along with the string property functions, you can access static members of many system classes. Some of those classes include *System.DateTime, System.Math, System.String, and System .StringComparer,* among many others. For a full list of these classes, you can visit *http://msdn .microsoft.com/en-us/library/dd633440.aspx.* Along with these functions, there are also a number of specific static methods and properties in other classes which you can access. For example, you can call many methods on the System.IO.File and System.IO.Directory classes.

Just like string functions, you can access either methods or properties. The syntax when accessing a static property would be as follows:

$({*ClassName*}::{*PropertyName*})

where *{ClassName}* is the full class name (such as *System.DateTime*) and *{PropertyName}* is the name of the static property that you want to access.

To access a method, you would use similar syntax:

$({ClassName}::{MethodName}([parameters]))

where *{ClassName}* is the class name and *{MethodName}* is the name of the method. If you have any parameters to pass in, you would place those inside the parenthesis. Take a look at the following code, from the PropertyFunctions02.proj file.

```
<Project xmlns="http://schemas.microsoft.com/developer/msbuild/2003"
         ToolsVersion="4.0"
         DefaultTargets="Demo">

  <Target Name="Demo">
    <Message Text="DateTime.Now: $([System.DateTime]::Now)"/>
    <Message Text="Days in month: $([System.DateTime]::DaysInMonth(2011,2))"/>
    <Message Text="New Guid: $([System.Guid]::NewGuid())"/>
    <Message Text="IsMatch:
     $([System.Text.RegularExpressions.Regex]::IsMatch('someInputHere','.*In.*'))"/>
    <Message Text="Framework path: $([Microsoft.Build.Utilities.ToolLocationHelper]::
        GetPathToDotNetFramework(
            Microsoft.Build.Utilities.TargetDotNetFrameworkVersion.Version40))"/>
    <Message Text="MSBuild.exe path:
              $([Microsoft.Build.Utilities.ToolLocationHelper]::GetPathToSystemFile(
                'msbuild.exe'))"/>
  </Target>
</Project>
```

In this example, you can see a few different ways to use static property functions. Figure 3-15 shows the result if you execute the Demo target.

```
C:\InsideMSBuild\Ch03>msbuild PropertyFunctions02.proj /t:Demo /nologo
Build started 10/31/2010 11:19:39 PM.
Project "C:\InsideMSBuild\Ch03\PropertyFunctions02.proj" on node 1 (Demo target(s)).
Demo:
  DateTime.Now: 10/31/2010 11:19:39 PM
  Days in month: 28
  New Guid: 51788b4b-6a35-431a-8afa-71a9509d0934
  IsMatch: True
  Framework path: C:\Windows\Microsoft.NET\Framework\v4.0.30319
  mspaint.exe path: C:\Windows\system32\mspaint.exe
Done Building Project "C:\InsideMSBuild\Ch03\PropertyFunctions02.proj" (Demo target(s)).

Build succeeded.
    0 Warning(s)
    0 Error(s)
```

FIGURE 3-15 Result of the Demo target in the PropertyFunctions02.proj file.

MSBuild Property Functions

The last kind of property functions are MSBuild property functions; these are a set of special methods that can be called using the following syntax:

```
$([MSBuild]::{MethodName}([parameters]))
```

where *{MethodName}* is the name of the method and *[parameters]* are the parameters that you are sending in.

Table 3-3 lists the MSBuild property functions.

TABLE 3-3 MSBuild Property Functions

Function Signature	Description
double Add(double a, double b)	Adds two doubles
long Add(long a, long b)	Adds two longs
double Subtract(double a, double b)	Subtracts two doubles

Function Signature	Description
long Subtract(long a, long b)	Subtracts two longs
double Multiply(double a, double b)	Multiplies two doubles
long Multiply(long a, long b)	Multiplies two longs
double Divide(double a, double b)	Divides two doubles
long Divide(long a, long b)	Divides two longs
double Modulo(double a, double b)	Returns the result of a % b
long Modulo(long a, long b)	Returns the result of a % b
string Escape(string unescaped)	Escapes the string using the MSBuild escaping rules
string Unescape(string escaped)	Unescapes the string using the MSBuild escaping rules
int BitwiseOr(int first, int second)	Returns the result of first | second
int BitwiseAnd(int first, int second)	Returns the result of first & second
int BitwiseXor(int first, int second)	Returns the result of first ^ second
int BitwiseNot(int first)	Returns the result of ~first

Along with these methods, there are a handful of other methods that you can call. For more information on these, take a look at *http://msdn.microsoft.com/en-us/library/dd633440.aspx*. To see how to use MSBuild property functions, see the following code snippet, which was taken from the PropertyFunctions03.proj file.

```xml
<Project xmlns="http://schemas.microsoft.com/developer/msbuild/2003"
         ToolsVersion="4.0"
         DefaultTargets="Demo">

  <Target Name="Demo">
    <Message Text="Add: $([MSBuild]::Add(5,9))"/>
    <Message Text="Subtract01: $([MSBuild]::Subtract(90,768))"/>
    <Message Text="Mult01: $([MSBuild]::Multiply(4,9))"/>
    <Message Text="Div01: $([MSBuild]::Divide(100,5.2))"/>
  </Target>
</Project>
```

After executing the Demo target, the result is shown in Figure 3-16.

```
C:\InsideMSBuild\Ch03>msbuild PropertyFunctions03.proj /t:Demo /nologo
Build started 10/19/2010 10:29:13 PM.
Project "C:\InsideMSBuild\Ch03\PropertyFunctions03.proj" on node 1 (Demo target(s)).
Demo:
  Add: 14
  Subtract01: -678
  Mult01: 36
  Div01: 19.2307692307692
Done Building Project "C:\InsideMSBuild\Ch03\PropertyFunctions03.proj" (Demo target(s)).

Build succeeded.
    0 Warning(s)
    0 Error(s)
```

FIGURE 3-16 Result of the Demo target in PropertyFunctions03.proj

Now that we have discussed property functions, let's take a look at item functions.

Item Functions

Item functions are exactly what they sound like: functions on an item list that you can call directly from your MSBuild script. For example, you can filter an item list for its distinct value, or filter an item list based on a metadata value, and a few other operations. Table 3-4 summarizes the item functions that you can call.

TABLE 3-4 Item Functions

Function	Description
DirectoryName	Returns a list of the directory names of each value in the item list
Metadata	Returns the values for the metadata name specified
DistinctWithCase	Returns the distinct (case-sensitive) values from the item list
Distinct	Returns the distinct (case-insensitive) values from the item list
ClearMetadata	Returns an item list whose values do not contain any metadata
WithMetadataValue	Returns the values from the item list that have a value defined for the given metadata value
AnyHaveMetadataValue	Returns *true* if any value in the item list has a value for the given metadata name, otherwise false

The syntax when using item functions is as follows:

```
@({ItemListName}->{ItemFunctionName}([parameters]))
```

where *{ItemListName}* is the name of the item list, and *{ItemFunctionName}* is the name of the item function to invoke. If you need any parameters, then you can pass them inside the parentheses. When you are using item functions, you should keep in mind that you are executing a function over a set of values. Therefore, in many cases, the result will be a list of results. Take a look at the following code snippet, from the ItemFunctions01.proj file.

```
<Project xmlns="http://schemas.microsoft.com/developer/msbuild/2003"
        ToolsVersion="4.0"
        DefaultTargets="Demo">

  <ItemGroup>
    <None Include="one.txt;two.txt;three.txt;One.txt"/>

    <Reference Include="System;">
      <Private>True</Private>
    </Reference>
    <Reference Include="System.Data">
      <Private>False</Private>
    </Reference>
    <Reference Include="System.Deployment">
      <Private>True</Private>
    </Reference>
  </ItemGroup>

  <Target Name="Demo">
```

```
        <Message Text="None: @(None)" Importance="high"/>
        <Message Text="Reference: @(Reference)" Importance="high"/>
        <Message Text="===================================================="/>
        <Message Text="Distinct: @(None->Distinct())"/>
        <Message Text="DistinctWithCase: @(None->DistinctWithCase())"/>
        <Message Text="Metadata: @(Reference->Metadata('Private'))"/>
    </Target>
</Project>
```

Figure 3-17 shows the results of executing the Demo target from ItemFunctions01.proj. From this sample, you can see how to execute item functions.

```
C:\InsideMSBuild\Ch03>msbuild ItemFunctions01.proj /t:Demo /nologo
Build started 10/19/2010 11:05:27 PM.
Project "C:\InsideMSBuild\Ch03\ItemFunctions01.proj" on node 1 (Demo target(s)).
Demo:
  None: one.txt;two.txt;three.txt;One.txt
  Reference: System;System.Data;System.Deployment
  ====================================================
  Distinct: one.txt;two.txt;three.txt
  DistinctWithCase: one.txt;two.txt;three.txt;One.txt
  Metadata: True;False;True
Done Building Project "C:\InsideMSBuild\Ch03\ItemFunctions01.proj" (Demo target(s)).

Build succeeded.
    0 Warning(s)
    0 Error(s)
```

FIGURE 3-17 Result of the Demo target in Itemfunctions01.proj

In this and the previous chapter, a lot of material was covered, and I don't expect you to master it by simply reading these chapters. Mastery can be achieved only by using these ideas in your own MSBuild scripts. The remainder of the book will use these chapters as a basis on which to craft your knowledge of MSBuild. In these two chapters, we have covered 90 percent of what you need to know to make MSBuild do what you need 90 percent of the time. The rest of the material in the book will make up for the gaps that were left out here and define how you customize your build process.

Part II
Customizing MSBuild

Chapter 4
Custom Tasks

MSBuild is shipped with many built-in tasks, and there are many tasks that are available by third parties. Even with these, there may be times where you need to write your own task. In this chapter, we will take a look at how custom tasks are created and used. In the next chapter, we will cover custom loggers. Before you create a new task, you should make sure that you cannot reuse an already existing task to fulfill your needs. Here is a list of a few open-source task repositories where you can find MSBuild tasks:

- MSBuild Extension Pack (*http://msbuildextensionpack.codeplex.com/*)
- Microsoft SDC Tasks (*http://sdctasks.codeplex.com/*)
- MSBuild Community Tasks (*http://msbuildtasks.tigris.org*)

 Note The MSBuild Extension Pack is the preferred task repository. First, check there for a task that you might need.

Custom tasks allow you to write Microsoft .NET Framework code that can be used in your build process. Custom tasks have all the same abilities that built-in tasks have. We will also discuss inline tasks, which enable you to create tasks without compiling an assembly and then use them like any other task. There are many advantages to using inline tasks: You don't have to compile them, they are easy to maintain, and easy to share, just to name a few. Until this chapter, we have created only MSBuild project files; in this chapter, we will focus primarily on how your tasks can be written to be used effectively with MSBuild.

Custom Task Requirements

Essentially the only requirement of a custom task is to implement the Microsoft.Build.Framework.ITask interface. This interface contains two properties and one method. The class diagram for that interface is shown in Figure 4-1.

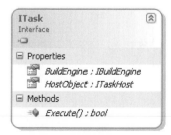

FIGURE 4-1 ITask interface

The two properties, BuildEngine and HostObject, will be set by the MSBuild engine itself. These will be set when the task is constructed by the MSBuild engine. The contract for the *Execute* method is that if it returns *true*, then the task was a success; otherwise, it is treated as a failure. Except in disastrous cases, such as running out of memory, the task should not throw an exception. If a problem occurs, it should log an error and then return *false*.

Creating Your First Task

As many other texts do, we will create a Hello World example. This simple example, which follows, was taken from the HelloWorld.cs file.

```
public class HelloWorld : ITask
{
    public IBuildEngine BuildEngine
    { get; set; }
    public ITaskHost HostObject
    { get; set; }

    public bool Execute()
    {
        // set up support for logging
        TaskLoggingHelper loggingHelper = new TaskLoggingHelper(this);
        loggingHelper.LogMessageFromText(
            "Hello MSBuild", MessageImportance.High);

        return true;
    }
}
```

In this first example, we have created a HelloWorld task that outputs the message *Hello MSBuild* to the loggers attached to MSBuild. This is achieved by using an instance of the *TaskLoggingHelper* class. In this case, we have directly implemented the ITask interface. The only piece that we are really interested in is the implementation of the *Execute* method. Despite this being pretty simple, I will show you an even simpler way to create this task, but we will first take a look at how we can integrate this task into an MSBuild project file, HelloWorld01.proj, which follows.

```
<Project xmlns="http://schemas.microsoft.com/developer/msbuild/2003"
         ToolsVersion="4.0"
         DefaultTargets="Demo">

  <UsingTask AssemblyFile="$(MSBuildProjectDirectory)\..\Examples.Tasks.dll"
             TaskName="HelloWorld" />

  <Target Name="Demo">
    <HelloWorld />
  </Target>
</Project>
```

When you create a new task, you have to declare that you are going to use it. This is achieved by the *UsingTask* element. The *UsingTask* element has only a few possible attributes, which are summarized in Table 4-1.

> **Note** If you have more than one task with the same *TaskName* value declared, the first one encountered is the one that will be used.

TABLE 4-1 *UsingTask* **Attributes**

Name	Description
TaskName	The class name of the task that is to be used. If there is a naming conflict, this value should be specified using the full namespace. If there is a conflict, then unexpected results might occur.
	This is a required property.
AssemblyFile	Specifies the location of the assembly that contains the task to be loaded. This must be a full path. This will result in the assembly being loaded by the *System.Reflection.Assembly.LoadFrom* method.
	Either this attribute or *AssemblyName* must be used, but not both. Of the two, *AssemblyFile* is the most used attribute.
AssemblyName	Name of the assembly that contains the task to be loaded. Using this property will result in the assembly being loaded by the *System.Reflection.Assembly.Load* method. You would use this if your task's assembly is in the global assembly cache (GAC). If you are deploying a task assembly publicly, you generally should put it in the GAC.
	Either this attribute or *AssemblyFile* must be used, but not both. Of the two options, *AssemblyFile* is used most commonly.
TaskFactory*	This specifies the class in the assembly that is responsible for creating new instances of the task. This is primarily used for inline tasks, which we will cover in the section entitled "Inline Tasks," later in this chapter.

* Denotes an attribute that was introduced with MSBuild 4.0.

In this example, UsingTask references the Example.Tasks.dll in the parent directory. This is because the project file is placed in a folder in the output directory. This will be explained in more detail later in this chapter. After you have declared that you are going to reference the task, with a *UsingTask* element, you are free to invoke the task inside any targets. The preceding sample file shows a single target, Demo. This target executes the task with the statement <HelloWorld />. Since this task doesn't have any inputs or outputs, we do not need to specify any attributes or children in the XML. This is all that is required to invoke this task. The result of executing the Demo target from this build file is shown in Figure 4-2.

```
C:\InsideMSBuild\Ch04\bin\Debug\Samples>msbuild HelloWorld01.proj /t:Demo /nologo
Build started 9/12/2010 10:40:18 AM.
Project "C:\InsideMSBuild\Ch04\bin\Debug\Samples\HelloWorld01.proj" on node 1 (Demo target(s)).
Demo:
  Hello MSBuild
Done Building Project "C:\InsideMSBuild\Ch04\bin\Debug\Samples\HelloWorld01.proj" (Demo target(s))
.

Build succeeded.
    0 Warning(s)
    0 Error(s)
```

FIGURE 4-2 HelloWorld01.proj execution

As you can see from Figure 4-2, the Hello World message was successfully printed on the console.

Even though this example was pretty simple, it can be even simpler by using the classes *Microsoft.Build.Utilities.Task, Microsoft.Build.Utilities.ToolTask,* and *Microsoft.Build.Utilities .AppDomainIsolatedTask.* Typically, when you create a new task, you should extend one of these classes instead of implementing the ITask interface yourself, unless you must extend another class. Table 4-2 shows a brief description that can help you decide which of these classes to extend.

TABLE 4-2 Common Task Abstract Classes

Class Name	When to Extend
Task	Most MSBuild tasks will extend this class. This class should be extended whenever your task does not wrap an executable.
ToolTask	Extend this class when you are creating a task that will wrap a call to an **.exe** file. It includes all the functionally of the *Task* class, because it derives from it, but adds support for running external programs.
AppDomainIsolatedTask	When you need your task to be loaded in its own app domain, then you should use this as your base class. A typical reason to derive from this class is if you need to use a task that is contained in an assembly that was created during the executing build process. Deriving from this class will mean that the task will be loaded in a new app domain, which will be unloaded after you're done. It is uncommon to derive from this class. If MSBuild is loaded in Microsoft Visual Studio, then tasks can be locked. The lock will remain until Visual Studio is closed. If the build was run on the command line, then it will be locked between builds unless you set **/nodereuse** to *false.*

When you extend one of these classes, all you have to do is implement the *Execute* method. The abstract class will create the required properties in the ITask interface. In the case of the Hello World example, we would pick the Task class to extend. We can create a new task, HelloWorld02. This new, simpler implementation is shown as follows.

```
public class HelloWorld02 : Task
{
    public override bool Execute()
    {
        Log.LogMessageFromText("Hello MSBuild from Task!", MessageImportance.High);
        return true;
    }
}
```

In this new implementation, the only requirement is to implement the *Execute* method. By using one of these abstract classes, we can focus on what the task is supposed to accomplish. Also, you may have noticed that logging the Hello World statement is different from the previous implementation. This is because those helper classes also define a property, Log, which is of the type Microsoft.Build.Utilities. TaskLoggingHelper, which makes logging much easier. Now that we have briefly described how to create simple MSBuild tasks, we will discuss how values can be passed into and out of MSBuild tasks. Later in this chapter, we'll discuss how to extend the *ToolTask* class.

Task Input/Output

When you create custom MSBuild tasks, they will most likely need to accept some input and/or provide some output values. Inside your task, these are implemented with normal .NET properties that may be decorated with attributes. Don't confuse these with MSBuild properties. We will first examine a very simple example and then move on to discuss more realistic tasks. Building on the HelloWorld02 task, I've created a new task, HelloWorld03, which accepts two input parameters. Those input parameters are FirstName and LastName. The definition of the HelloWorld03 task is shown as follows.

```
public class HelloWorld03 : Task
{
    [Required]
    public string FirstName
    { get; set; }

    public string LastName
    { get; set; }

    public override bool Execute()
    {
        Log.LogMessage(string.Format("Hello {0} {1}", FirstName, LastName));

        return true;
    }
}
```

As you can see, both of the properties here were defined as any other .NET property would be. You may have noticed that the FirstName property has a *Required* (Microsoft.Build .Framework.Required) attribute attached to it. As the name states, this is a property that is required to be set before the task is allowed to be executed. This is checked by MSBuild itself. If a user attempts to invoke a task without providing values for all required parameters, then the task will fail.

Any property that has a writeable property is available as an MSBuild input parameter. There are some limitations on the type, but we will discuss that later in this chapter. Now we can see how we can provide values to these custom input parameters from an MSBuild project file; see the following example, which is taken from HelloWorld03.proj.

```
<Project xmlns="http://schemas.microsoft.com/developer/msbuild/2003"
         ToolsVersion="4.0"
         DefaultTargets="Demo">

  <UsingTask AssemblyFile="$(MSBuildProjectDirectory)\..\Examples.Tasks.dll"
             TaskName="HelloWorld03" />

  <Target Name="Demo">
    <HelloWorld03 FirstName="Mike" LastName="Murphy" />
  </Target>
</Project>
```

When you provide values as input into an MSBuild task, you will always provide those values using XML attributes, where the attribute name is the name of the .NET property and the attribute value is the value that the .NET property should be set to. From this example, we can see that the *FirstName* and *LastName* attributes correspond to the names of the .NET properties that we created in the task previously. If you execute the Demo target in this MSBuild file, you would see the result shown in Figure 4-3.

```
C:\InsideMSBuild\Ch04\bin\Debug\Samples>msbuild HelloWorld03.proj /t:Demo /nologo
Build started 9/13/2010 9:53:26 PM.
Project "C:\InsideMSBuild\Ch04\bin\Debug\Samples\HelloWorld03.proj" on node 1 (Demo target(s)).
Demo:
  Hello Mike Murphy
Done Building Project "C:\InsideMSBuild\Ch04\bin\Debug\Samples\HelloWorld03.proj" (Demo target(s))
.

Build succeeded.
    0 Warning(s)
    0 Error(s)
```

FIGURE 4-3 HelloWorld03 example

As we expected, the values were successfully passed into that task and were then passed to the console logger. Now we can see how to pass a value from a task back to the calling MSBuild project file. Once again I've modified the previous task and created a new one, HelloWorld04, which exposes an output property named Message. The class is shown as follows:

```
public class HelloWorld04 : Task
{
    [Required]
    public string FirstName
    { get; set; }

    public string LastName
    { get; set; }

    [Output]
    public string Message
    { get; set; }

    public override bool Execute()
    {
        Message = string.Format("Fullname: {0} {1}", FirstName, LastName);
        Log.LogMessage(string.Format("Hello {0} {1}", FirstName, LastName));

        return true;
    }
}
```

Just like inputs, outputs are simply .NET properties. Output properties must be decorated with the *Microsoft.Build.Framework.Output* attribute. When you extract a value from a task you will always use an *Output* element as a child of the task node itself. An example of this is demonstrated in the following sample, HelloWorld04.proj.

```
<Project xmlns=http://schemas.microsoft.com/developer/msbuild/2003
        ToolsVersion="4.0"
        DefaultTargets="Demo">
```

```
<UsingTask AssemblyFile="$(MSBuildProjectDirectory)\..\Examples.Tasks.dll"
           TaskName="HelloWorld4" />

<Target Name="Demo">

  <HelloWorld4 FirstName="Mike" LastName="Murphy">
    <Output PropertyName="PropFromTask" TaskParameter="Message" />
  </HelloWorld4>

  <Message Text ="From task: $(PropFromTask)" />

</Target>
</Project>
```

If the task you are using has multiple outputs, then you can declare multiple *Output* elements. The *Output* element has three attributes, in addition to the *Condition* attribute, which are briefly outlined in Table 4-3.

TABLE 4-3 Output Element Attributes

Attribute	Description
TaskParameter	This is the name of the .NET property that you are accessing the value of. This is a required attribute.
PropertyName	The name of the MSBuild property in which the value should be placed. Either this or *ItemName* must be used, but not both.
ItemName	The name of the MSBuild item list in which the values should be placed. Either this or *PropertyName* must be used, but not both.

In the HelloWorld04 example, we are outputting the value of the Message property on the task into an MSBuild property named PropFromTask. This is why we use the *PropertyName* attribute instead of *ItemName*. This syntax takes getting used to, but is easy to use after that. Now let's take a look at a more realistic task.

All the custom tasks that we have discussed thus far were variations of the HelloWorld task. We will now take a look at a few tasks that are actually useful in your own build scripts. We will start with the GetDate task. This is a task that returns the current date in a specified format. This task is shown in the following code block.

```
public class GetDate : Task
{
    public string Format
    { get; set; }

    [Output]
    public string Date
    { get; private set; }

    public override bool Execute()
    {
        DateTime now = DateTime.Now;
```

```
        Date = now.ToString(Format, null);
        return true;
    }
}
```

This task defines an optional input parameter, Format. (This is an optional parameter because it is not decorated with the *Required* attribute.) A single output property is declared, named Date, which is a string representation of the time in which the task was invoked. We can see this used in the following GetDate01.proj file.

```xml
<Project xmlns=http://schemas.microsoft.com/developer/msbuild/2003
        ToolsVersion="4.0"
        DefaultTargets="Demo">

  <UsingTask AssemblyFile="$(MSBuildProjectDirectory)\..\Examples.Tasks.dll"
    TaskName="GetDate" />

  <Target Name="Demo">
    <GetDate>
      <Output PropertyName="DateUnformatted" TaskParameter="Date" />
    </GetDate>

    <GetDate Format="yyyyMMdd.hh.ss">
      <Output PropertyName="DateValue" TaskParameter="Date" />
    </GetDate>

    <PropertyGroup>
      <FolderName>$(MSBuildProjectName)_$(DateValue)</FolderName>
    </PropertyGroup>

    <Message Text="DateUnformatted value: $(DateUnformatted)" />
    <Message Text="DateValue value: $(DateValue)" />
    <Message Text="FolderName value: $(FolderName)" />
  </Target>

</Project>
```

In this example, we are invoking the GetDate task twice, once without specifying a format and the other with a format passed in. The values are stored in MSBuild properties named *DateUnformatted* and *DateValue,* and then these values are passed to the Message task. The result of this build file is shown in Figure 4-4.

```
C:\InsideMSBuild\Ch04\bin\Debug\Samples>msbuild GetDate01.proj /t:Demo /nologo
Build started 9/13/2010 10:22:39 PM.
Project "C:\InsideMSBuild\Ch04\bin\Debug\Samples\GetDate01.proj" on node 1 (Demo target(s)).
Demo:
  DateUnformatted value: 9/13/2010 10:22:39 PM
  DateValue value: 20100913.10.39
  FolderName value: GetDate01_20100913.10.39
Done Building Project "C:\InsideMSBuild\Ch04\bin\Debug\Samples\GetDate01.proj" (Demo target(s)).

Build succeeded.
    0 Warning(s)
    0 Error(s)
```

FIGURE 4-4 GetDate01 example

In this demonstration, we have shown how we can pass values into and out of the task.

To recap, when you pass a value into a task, it is always passed in as an attribute on the task's element. Output values will be exposed to the build script by using an *Output* element as a child of the *Task* element. We will now move on to discuss what types are supported.

Supported Task Input and Output Types

Task inputs and outputs are the only means by which a project file can communicate with a task. A task will not have access to any properties or items that are not passed into it. This is by design, so that it is easy to see what information is passed into and out of the task by reading the project file. When you create values that can be passed into and out of tasks, there are a variety of types that are supported. Since XML is the representation that all MSBuild scripts are stored in, all values must be able to be converted to and from a string. As mentioned in Chapter 2, "MSBuild Deep Dive, Part 1," there are fundamentally two types of values that are supported by MSBuild: scalar values and vector values. For vector values, an *array* of acceptable scalar types is allowed. Table 4-4 summarizes what types are supported to be passed through MSBuild tasks.

TABLE 4-4 Types Supported for MSBuild Inputs and Outputs

Type	Description
String	String values are simply passed back and forth directly, no conversion necessary.
ITaskItem	This interface (Microsoft.Build.Framework.ITaskItem) is a part of MSBuild itself. It is typically used when referencing files and for item value members. If an MSBuild task needs to deal with items as input or output, then they should be exposed by ITaskItem properties. It will allow you to pass items with metadata on them to the task; it also allows the task to set or modify metadata on the item and then return those items back into the build process.
Value	MSBuild will allow you to pass value types back and forth from task to script. The conversion support is limited to subclasses of ITaskItem and those types that the *System.Convert.ChangeType* method is able to convert from and to strings. Those types are: bool, byte, char, DateTime, Decimal, Double, int, long, sbyte, short, Single, uint, ulong, and ushort.
	Arrays of these types are acceptable as well.
	When using the bool type, acceptable values include *true, false, on, off, yes,* and *no,* and when used with the ! operator, such as *!true.*

In the tasks that we have created thus far, we have shown only task inputs and outputs using string values. From the value types listed in Table 4-4, you can see that there are many other types of values that we can pass into and out of tasks. When you create task properties of any supported type, you don't have to worry about the conversion between string and the actual type. The MSBuild engine will take care of this automatically. The most interesting type listed in Table 4-4 is the ITaskItem type. This is shipped with MSBuild, in the *Microsoft .Build.Framework* assembly, and is heavily used in tasks. In the next task, we will demonstrate using objects of this type.

The next sample we will discuss is the TempFile task. This task creates a temp file and returns its locations to the calling build script. The location value is passed as the property TempFilePath, which is declared as an ITaskItem. The class definition is shown as follows.

```
public class TempFile : Task
{
    [Output]
    public ITaskItem TempFilePath
    { get; private set; }

    public override bool Execute()
    {
        string path = System.IO.Path.GetTempFileName();

        TempFilePath = new TaskItem(path);
        return true;
    }
}
```

Inside the *Execute* method, we get the full path to a new temporary file, and create a new TaskItem object that refers to it and assign it to the TempFilePath property. The *TaskItem* class is the class that you should use when you have to create new objects that implement ITaskItem. The constructor being called is TaskItem(string itemSpec). The itemSpec (item specification) parameter is the representation of the value passed in the *Include* attribute in an MSBuild file. After the value for TempFilePath is set, the task returns *true* to indicate that the task completed without errors. You can see this task being used in the corresponding sample file, TempFile01.proj, as follows:

```
<Project xmlns=http://schemas.microsoft.com/developer/msbuild/2003
        ToolsVersion="4.0"
        DefaultTargets="Demo">

  <UsingTask AssemblyFile="$(MSBuildProjectDirectory)\..\Examples.Tasks.dll"
          TaskName="TempFile" />

  <Target Name="Demo">
    <TempFile>
      <Output ItemName="TestFile" TaskParameter="TempFilePath" />
    </TempFile>

    <Message Text="TestFile: @(TestFile)" />
    <Message Text="TestFile.Filename: @(TestFile->'%(Filename)')" />
    <Message Text="TestFile.Extension: @(TestFile->'%(Extension)')" />

  </Target>

</Project>
```

As with every custom task, we first declare that we are going to be using the task with a UsingTask statement. This makes the TempFile task available for use. In the example, the value from the task is placed into an item named TestFile, and then a few messages are sent to the logger. The output of the Demo target is shown in Figure 4-5.

As can be seen from this sample, the task successfully created a temp file and returned its path back to the calling MSBuild file. Since we place the value from the task into an item, we could retrieve values for metadata of that item as well. In the TempFile task, the TempFilePath was declared as an ITaskItem, which is the preferred method. If a consuming MSBuild script places a value into an item, it is automatically converted into a representation using ITaskItem. So in this example the difference is trivial, but you should generally use ITaskItem when you expect to expose properties to be items in consuming scripts.

```
C:\InsideMSBuild\Ch04\bin\Debug\Samples>msbuild TempFile01.proj /t:Demo /nologo
Build started 9/13/2010 10:59:40 PM.
Project "C:\InsideMSBuild\Ch04\bin\Debug\Samples\TempFile01.proj" on node 1 (Demo target(s)).
Demo:
    TestFile: C:\Documents and Settings\Marc\Local Settings\Temp\tmp48.tmp
    TestFile.Filename: tmp48
    TestFile.Extension: .tmp
Done Building Project "C:\InsideMSBuild\Ch04\bin\Debug\Samples\TempFile01.proj" (Demo target(s)).

Build succeeded.
    0 Warning(s)
    0 Error(s)
```

FIGURE 4-5 TempFile task demonstration

Using objects that are ITaskItems is preferred because you are able to pass a richer object to and from a task. Objects of this type can have metadata associated with it, which the task can interact with. We will discuss this concept in more detail in the next section.

Using Arrays with Task Inputs and Outputs

We have now discussed various topics about passing values into and out of tasks; one of the only issues that we have not discussed is passing vector values into and out of tasks. We will discuss that now, by examining a real MSBuild task. This task was taken from my open-source task repository, Sedodream Tasks, which is available at Codeplex at *http://sedodream .codeplex.com/.* The task that we will demonstrate is a custom Move task. If you are using MSBuild 4.0, there is a built-in Move task that you can use, but for previous versions, there wasn't one. This task was designed to work similar to the Copy task in the sense that it has a similar set of inputs, outputs, and behavior. The properties that are declared by the task are shown in the following code snippet.

```
[Required]
public ITaskItem[] SourceFiles
{ get; set; }

public ITaskItem[] DestinationFiles
{ get; set; }

public ITaskItem DestinationFolder
{ get; set; }

[Output]
public ITaskItem[] MovedFiles
{ get; private set; }
```

```
[Output]
public long[] FileLengths
{ get; private set; }
```

From these properties, there are three that are declared as arrays of ITaskItem objects and the remaining as a scalar ITaskItem. These could have been created using string[], but this would limit the information that we could gather from the values. Specifically, a string object cannot have any metadata associated with it, whereas ITaskItem objects can. You will find an example of the usage of this task in the following file, MoveExample01.proj.

```xml
<Project xmlns="http://schemas.microsoft.com/developer/msbuild/2003"
         ToolsVersion="4.0"
         DefaultTargets="Demo">

  <UsingTask AssemblyFile="$(MSBuildProjectDirectory)\..\Examples.Tasks.dll"
             TaskName="Move" />

  <PropertyGroup>
    <SampleFilesPath>$(MSBuildProjectDirectory)\sampleFiles\</SampleFilesPath>
    <DestPath>$(MSBuildProjectDirectory)\dest\</DestPath>
  </PropertyGroup>

  <ItemGroup>
    <SampleFiles Include="$(SampleFilesPath)**\*.txt"
                 Exclude="$(SourceFolder)**\.svn\**\*" />
  </ItemGroup>

  <Target Name="Demo">
    <Move SourceFiles="@(SampleFiles)"
          DestinationFiles=
          "@(SampleFiles->'$(DestPath)%(RecursiveDir)%(Filename)%(Extension)')">
    </Move>
  </Target>

</Project>
```

In this example, we create a new item, SampleFiles, and pass that into the SourceFiles property for the Move task. The value for DestinationFiles is a transformation of the SourceFiles item. When you use tasks that have inputs that should have a one-to-one correspondence, it is common for one of them to be a transformation of the other. This is what is shown here. Previously, we mentioned that the ITaskItem type of objects can have metadata; we will now discuss that in more detail. In the code for a custom task, you can get and set the values for an item's metadata by using the *GetMetadata* and *SetMetadata* methods, respectively. We will see this at work in the sample task I created, MetadataExample.

In order to demonstrate clearly how you can use metadata on items passed into and out of custom tasks, I have created a sample task, MetadataExample, that demonstrates this. This task is very simple and is shown in its entirety as follows.

```
public class MetadataExample : Task
{
    [Required]
    public ITaskItem[] ServerList
    { get; set; }

    [Output]
    public ITaskItem[] Result
    { get; set; }

    public override bool Execute()
    {
        if (ServerList.Length > 0)
        {
            Result = new TaskItem[ServerList.Length];

            for(int i=0; i<Result.Length; i++)
            {
                ITaskItem item = ServerList[i];
                ITaskItem newItem = new TaskItem(item.ItemSpec);
                string fullpath = item.GetMetadata("Fullpath");

                newItem.SetMetadata("ServerName", item.GetMetadata("Name"));
                newItem.SetMetadata("DropLoc", item.GetMetadata("DropLocation"));

                newItem.SetMetadata("IpAddress", string.Format("127.0.0.{0}", i+10));
                Result[i] = newItem;
            }
        }
        return true;
    }
}
```

In this task, we have two properties, both of which are declared as ITaskItem[]. ServerList is a required input parameter and Result is the output parameter. In the *Execute* method, we get some values from the metadata and use it to populate values into the Result item. We can see this in action in the following MetadataExample01.proj file.

```
<Project xmlns="http://schemas.microsoft.com/developer/msbuild/2003"
         ToolsVersion="4.0"
         DefaultTargets="Demo">

  <UsingTask AssemblyFile="$(MSBuildProjectDirectory)\..\Examples.Tasks.dll"
             TaskName="MetadataExample" />

  <PropertyGroup>
    <ConfigFileRoot>$(MSBuildProjectDirectory)\sampleConfigFiles\</ConfigFileRoot>
  </PropertyGroup>
  <ItemGroup>
    <Server Include="$(ConfigFileRoot)server1.app.config">
      <Name>server1</Name>
      <DropLocation>D:\Drops\</DropLocation>
    </Server>
    <Server Include="$(ConfigFileRoot)server2.app.config">
```

```
            <Name>server2</Name>
            <DropLocation>E:\Builds\Drops\</DropLocation>
        </Server>
        <Server Include="$(ConfigFileRoot)server3.app.config">
            <Name>server3</Name>
            <DropLocation>D:\Data\DropDir\</DropLocation>
        </Server>
        <Server Include="$(ConfigFileRoot)server4.app.config">
            <Name>server4</Name>
            <DropLocation>D:\Projects\DropLocation\</DropLocation>
        </Server>
    </ItemGroup>


    <Target Name="Demo">

        <MetadataExample ServerList="@(Server)">
            <Output ItemName="ServerIpList" TaskParameter="Result" />
        </MetadataExample>

        <Message Text="ServerIpList: @(ServerIpList)" />

        <Message
            Text="Server: %(ServerIpList.ServerName)
    %(ServerIpList.DropLoc)
    %(ServerIpList.IpAddress)" />
    </Target>

</Project>
```

In this project file, we have created an item named Server and attached a value for Name and DropLocation metadata for each item. Inside the Demo target of this project file, we invoke the MetadataExample task and pass in the Server item. Then we place the output of the task into an item named ServerIpList with the *Output* element. Finally, we print a message to display the custom metadata values that the task set. If you execute this project file, you would see the results shown in Figure 4-6.

```
C:\InsideMSBuild\Ch04\bin\Debug\Samples>msbuild MetadataExample01.proj /t:Demo /nologo
Build started 9/14/2010 10:03:44 PM.
Project "C:\InsideMSBuild\Ch04\bin\Debug\Samples\MetadataExample01.proj" on node 1 (Demo target(s)
).
Demo:
  ServerIpList: C:\InsideMSBuild\Ch04\bin\Debug\Samples\sampleConfigFiles\server1.app.config;C:\In
  sideMSBuild\Ch04\bin\Debug\Samples\sampleConfigFiles\server2.app.config;C:\InsideMSBuild\Ch04\bi
  n\Debug\Samples\sampleConfigFiles\server3.app.config;C:\InsideMSBuild\Ch04\bin\Debug\Samples\sam
  pleConfigFiles\server4.app.config
  Server: server1
    D:\Drops\
    127.0.0.10
  Server: server2
    E:\Builds\Drops\
    127.0.0.11
  Server: server3
    D:\Data\DropDir\
    127.0.0.12
  Server: server4
    D:\Projects\DropLocation\
    127.0.0.13
Done Building Project "C:\InsideMSBuild\Ch04\bin\Debug\Samples\MetadataExample01.proj" (Demo targe
t(s)).


Build succeeded.
    0 Warning(s)
    0 Error(s)
```

FIGURE 4-6 Using metadata

If you look at the results shown here, you can see that we were able to successfully pass metadata into and out of a task. Note that once an item value has been passed to a task, any modifications to it are not reflected back into the MSBuild file. So if you use the *SetMetadata* method on an item that was passed into the task by an input, it will *not* be reflected back in the calling MSBuild file. Now that we have discussed all that you need to know to pass values in and out of tasks, we will discuss inline tasks and then move on to extending the *ToolTask* class, which we briefly touched on earlier.

Inline Tasks

As you can see, writing a task is pretty easy, but sometimes it is inconvenient to write the task, store the source of that task, compile it into an assembly, and then deploy that assembly into your build process. It would be a lot simpler if you could just write the task inside an MSBuild file and let MSBuild take care of the rest. With MSBuild 4.0, you can do just that. This new feature is known as *inline tasks,* and we will cover those now, and then move on to look at an easy way to create tasks that wrap command-line tools.

First, I will show you what a very simple inline task looks like and how to use it. After that, we will go over the details. Similar to the previous sections, the first inline task that we create will be a *Hello World* task. Take a look at the following snippet, which is contained in the Hello-IT-01.proj file.

```
<Project xmlns="http://schemas.microsoft.com/developer/msbuild/2003"
        ToolsVersion="4.0"
        DefaultTargets="Demo">

  <UsingTask
    TaskName="HelloWorldIt01"
    TaskFactory="CodeTaskFactory"
    AssemblyFile="$(MSBuildToolsPath)\Microsoft.Build.Tasks.v4.0.dll" >
    <Task>
      <Code Type="Fragment" Language="cs">
        <![CDATA[
        Log.LogMessage("Hello MSBuild");
        ]]>
      </Code>
    </Task>
  </UsingTask>

  <Target Name="Demo">
    <HelloWorldIt01 />
  </Target>
</Project>
```

Here, I have used a *UsingTask* element, which you are already familiar with, but added some new things to it. We've already discussed all its attributes in Table 4-1, but we didn't tell you about the *Code* element that you can declare under it. This is where you would place your code. This task is written in C#, which is why we have a *cs* value for the *Language* attribute. We will go over this soon, along with the *TaskFactory* attribute of the *UsingTask* element. The value for the *TaskName* attribute in the *UsingTask* element is set to HelloWorldIt01, which is the name of the class that gets generated for you. If you were writing this as a typical compiled task, then it would be the name of the class, just like HelloWorld was the name of the first take we created in this chapter. In order to call this task, you would do the same thing if it was a compiled task. The results of the msbuild Hello-IT-01.proj /t:Demo command are shown in Figure 4-7.

```
C:\InsideMSBuild\Ch04\Samples>msbuild Hello-IT-01.proj /t:Demo /nologo
Build started 9/14/2010 10:56:50 PM.
Project "C:\InsideMSBuild\Ch04\Samples\Hello-IT-01.proj" on node 1 (Demo target(s)).
Demo:
  Hello MSBuild
Done Building Project "C:\InsideMSBuild\Ch04\Samples\Hello-IT-01.proj" (Demo target(s)).

Build succeeded.
    0 Warning(s)
    0 Error(s)
```

FIGURE 4-7 HelloWorld inline task

As you can see from this figure, the result of the HelloWorldIt01 task is the same as the compiled task HelloWorld01 that we created earlier.

Now that you have seen how to create and use an inline task, we will take a close look at the different ways of creating inline tasks. First, let's discuss creating inline tasks in different languages. So far, we have only covered C#, but you can create inline tasks in different languages. You can create them in any language you want, but the ones supported by default are C# and VB.NET. In order to create inline tasks in any other language, you will have to create a new task factory or find it online. If you are using C# for the *Language* attribute, the following case-insensitive values are valid: *c#, cs,* and *csharp.* For VB.NET, the following case-insensitive values are allowed: *vb, vbs, visualbasic,* and *vbscript.*

> **Note** The allowed values for the *Language* attribute are derived from the *System.CodeDom .Compiler.CompilerInfo* class.

As an example, here is the VB.NET version of the previous inline task, in a bit more verbose fashion so that it is obvious that it is not C#.

```
<Project xmlns="http://schemas.microsoft.com/developer/msbuild/2003"
         ToolsVersion="4.0"
         DefaultTargets="Demo">

  <UsingTask
    TaskName="HelloWorldIt02"
    TaskFactory="CodeTaskFactory"
    AssemblyFile="$(MSBuildToolsPath)\Microsoft.Build.Tasks.v4.0.dll" >
    <Task>
      <Code Type="Fragment" Language="vb">
        <![CDATA[
```

```
          Dim message As String
          message = String.Format("{0} {1}{2}", "Hello", "World",", from VB.NET")
          Log.LogMessage(message)
        ]]>
      </Code>
    </Task>
  </UsingTask>

  <Target Name="Demo">
    <HelloWorldIt02 />
  </Target>
</Project>
```

If you execute the Demo target, the result is just "Hello World, from VB.NET". We will
not show any more samples in VB.NET for the remainder of the book, but converting C#
examples should be pretty straightforward. We will now move on to discuss how parameters,
both input and output, are handled for inline tasks.

Just like compiled tasks, inline tasks can have both input and output parameters. In fact, your
parameters can be as rich as they are with normal compiled tasks. If you want your tasks
to contain parameters, then you will have to use the *ParameterGroup* element to define
them. Take a look at the new inline task that is created in the next snippet from the file
PrintMessage01.proj.

```
<Project xmlns="http://schemas.microsoft.com/developer/msbuild/2003"
         ToolsVersion="4.0"
         DefaultTargets="Demo">

  <UsingTask
    TaskName="PrintMessage"
    TaskFactory="CodeTaskFactory"
    AssemblyFile="$(MSBuildToolsPath)\Microsoft.Build.Tasks.v4.0.dll" >
    <ParameterGroup>
      <Message Required="true"/>
    </ParameterGroup>
    <Task>
      <Code Type="Fragment" Language="c#">
        <![CDATA[
          Log.LogMessageFromText(Message,MessageImportance.High);
        ]]>
      </Code>
    </Task>
  </UsingTask>

  <Target Name="Demo">
    <PrintMessage Message="Print this message" />
  </Target>

  <Target Name="DemoNoMessage">
    <PrintMessage />
  </Target>
</Project>
```

In this snippet, a new task, PrintMessage, was defined inline, which just logs the string provided in the Message property. It does this by using the Log helper object from the *Microsoft.Build.Utilities.Task* class, which is the base class for all inline tasks. We will discuss this more soon. In this project file, I have created the PrintMessage task, and it uses the *ParameterGroup* element to define the lone Message parameter, which is marked as required by setting the *Required* attribute to *true*. The default value for this is *false*. Figure 4-8 shows the result of executing the command msbuild PrintMessage01.proj /t:Demo /nologo.

```
C:\InsideMSBuild\Ch04\Samples>msbuild PrintMessage01.proj /t:Demo /nologo
Build started 9/15/2010 9:32:21 PM.
Project "C:\InsideMSBuild\Ch04\Samples\PrintMessage01.proj" on node 1 (Demo target(s)).
Demo:
  Print this message
Done Building Project "C:\InsideMSBuild\Ch04\Samples\PrintMessage01.proj" (Demo target(s)).


Build succeeded.
    0 Warning(s)
    0 Error(s)
```

FIGURE 4-8 PrintMessage Demo target result

The Demo target calls the PrintMessage task and passes it the value *"Print this message"* for the *Message* attribute. In that project file, the other target, DemoNoMessage, just calls the PrintMessage task as we were invoking the HelloWorld tasks previously, without passing in any parameters. In this case, the build should fail in the same way that it would for a compiled task because the required parameter is not specified. If you execute that target, you will see the failure message shown in Figure 4-9.

```
C:\InsideMSBuild\Ch04\Samples>msbuild PrintMessage01.proj /t:DemoNoMessage /nologo
Build started 9/15/2010 9:40:05 PM.
Project "C:\InsideMSBuild\Ch04\Samples\PrintMessage01.proj" on node 1 (DemoNoMessage target(s)).
C:\InsideMSBuild\Ch04\Samples\PrintMessage01.proj(26,5): error MSB4044: The "PrintMessage" task wa
s not given a value for the required parameter "Message".
Done Building Project "C:\InsideMSBuild\Ch04\Samples\PrintMessage01.proj" (DemoNoMessage target(s)
) -- FAILED.

Build FAILED.

"C:\InsideMSBuild\Ch04\Samples\PrintMessage01.proj" (DemoNoMessage target) (1) ->
(DemoNoMessage target) ->
  C:\InsideMSBuild\Ch04\Samples\PrintMessage01.proj(26,5): error MSB4044: The "PrintMessage" task
was not given a value for the required parameter "Message".

    0 Warning(s)
    1 Error(s)
```

FIGURE 4-9 PrintMessage DemoNoMessage target result

From the result shown in this figure, you can see that you get the exact same error message that you would have if you were using a normal task. We have discussed input parameters; let's now take a look at how we can create a task that also creates an output parameter.

The sample file, CreateGuid01.proj, contains the contents shown in the following code section.

```
<Project xmlns="http://schemas.microsoft.com/developer/msbuild/2003"
         ToolsVersion="4.0"
         DefaultTargets="Demo">

  <UsingTask
    TaskName="CreateGuid01"
```

```
    TaskFactory="CodeTaskFactory"
    AssemblyFile="$(MSBuildToolsPath)\Microsoft.Build.Tasks.v4.0.dll" >
    <ParameterGroup>
      <Id Output="true"/>
    </ParameterGroup>
    <Task>
      <Code Type="Fragment" Language="cs">
        <![CDATA[
          Id = Guid.NewGuid().ToString();
        ]]>
      </Code>
    </Task>
  </UsingTask>

  <Target Name="Demo">
    <CreateGuid01>
      <Output PropertyName="MyId" TaskParameter="Id"/>
    </CreateGuid01>
    <Message Text="MyId: $(MyId)"/>
  </Target>
</Project>
```

In this file, we have created a new inline task, CreateGuid01, and that task has declared an output parameter, Id. The fact that the Id parameter has the value *Output="true"* makes it an output parameter. Then, inside the Demo target, we invoke that task and extract the value for Id and place it into the MyId property, just as we would have done if we were using a normal task. Figure 4-10 shows the results of executing that target.

```
C:\InsideMSBuild\Ch04\Samples>msbuild CreateGuid01.proj /t:Demo /nologo
Build started 9/15/2010 9:45:58 PM.
Project "C:\InsideMSBuild\Ch04\Samples\CreateGuid01.proj" on node 1 (Demo target(s)).
Demo:
  MyId: ed7edbf3-269f-4a22-87e6-92b67a1c94e3
Done Building Project "C:\InsideMSBuild\Ch04\Samples\CreateGuid01.proj" (Demo target(s)).

Build succeeded.
    0 Warning(s)
    0 Error(s)
```

FIGURE 4-10 CreateGuid01 demo

You can see that we were able to use the result of the output parameter inside the project file, as we expected. Thus far, we have not discussed what type of properties (.NET properties, that is) we are creating. If you do not specify a type for a property (input or output), then it will default to being a string. But you can specify the type by using the *ParameterType* attribute on the parameter declaration. In this attribute, you should specify the full name of the type that you want to use, and it can be any valid type. We discussed the supported types in the section entitled "Supported Task Input and Output Types," earlier in this chapter.

Take a look at the new inline task, Add01, that we created from the Add01.proj file. This task just takes two numbers, adds them, and places the result into an output parameter.

```
<Project xmlns="http://schemas.microsoft.com/developer/msbuild/2003"
        ToolsVersion="4.0"
        DefaultTargets="Demo">
```

```xml
    <UsingTask
      TaskName="Add01"
      TaskFactory="CodeTaskFactory"
      AssemblyFile="$(MSBuildToolsPath)\Microsoft.Build.Tasks.v4.0.dll" >
      <ParameterGroup>
        <Value1 ParameterType="System.Double" Required="true"/>
        <Value2 ParameterType="System.Double" Required="true"/>
        <Sum ParameterType="System.Double" Output="true"/>
      </ParameterGroup>
      <Task>
        <Code Type="Fragment" Language="cs">
          <![CDATA[
            Sum = Value1 + Value2;
          ]]>
        </Code>
      </Task>
    </UsingTask>

    <Target Name="Demo">
      <PropertyGroup>
        <x>1.2</x>
        <y>3.4</y>
      </PropertyGroup>
      <Add01 Value1="$(x)" Value2="$(y)">
        <Output PropertyName="Result" TaskParameter="Sum"/>
      </Add01>
      <Message Text="$(x) + $(y) = $(Result)"/>
    </Target>
</Project>
```

This task declares three properties—Value1, Value2, and Sum—all of which are declared as being of type System.Double (double). Then, inside the Demo target, we showed the task at work. It was able to add the two values provided and placed the result into the output parameter. We will not show the result here, but if you want to see it in action, you can execute the command msbuild Add01.proj /t:Demo.

Thus far, all the inline tasks that we have created used only scalar values (those with only one value), but we will now take a look at a task that uses a vector value. Previously, you saw the CreateGuid01 task that created one globally unique identifier (GUID), but what if you need more than one? Then you create a new inline task for just that purpose. The CreateGuid02 task handles this. It is capable of creating many IDs and placing them into an output parameter, which is defined as an array of strings. The task and a sample target are shown in the next snippet from the CreateGuid02.proj file.

```xml
<Project xmlns="http://schemas.microsoft.com/developer/msbuild/2003"
         ToolsVersion="4.0"
         DefaultTargets="Demo">

  <UsingTask
    TaskName="CreateGuid02"
    TaskFactory="CodeTaskFactory"
    AssemblyFile="$(MSBuildToolsPath)\Microsoft.Build.Tasks.v4.0.dll" >
```

```
  <ParameterGroup>
    <NumToCreate ParameterType="System.Int32" Required="true" />
    <Guids ParameterType="System.String[]" Output="true" />
  </ParameterGroup>
  <Task>
    <Code Type="Fragment" Language="cs">
      <![CDATA[
          List<string> guids = new List<string>();
          for (int i = 0; i < NumToCreate; i++)
          {
              guids.Add(Guid.NewGuid().ToString());
          }
          Guids = guids.ToArray();
      ]]>
    </Code>
  </Task>
</UsingTask>

<Target Name="Demo">
  <CreateGuid02 NumToCreate="1">
    <Output ItemName="Id01" TaskParameter="Guids" />
  </CreateGuid02>
  <Message Text="Id01: @(Id01)" />

  <CreateGuid02 NumToCreate="4">
    <Output ItemName="Id02" TaskParameter="Guids" />
  </CreateGuid02>
  <Message Text=" "/>
  <Message Text="Id02: @(Id02)" />
</Target>
</Project>
```

The CreateGuid02 task has two parameters defined: one input and one output. The input parameter, NumToCreate, is a required parameter, and it is used to determine how many new IDs to create. The other parameter, Guids, is the resulting list of IDs, and it's marked with the *Output="true"* value. Take a look at the *ParameterType="System.String[]"* attribute declaration, which is saying that the Guids property (a .NET property) will be defined as an array of strings. Then, inside the body of the task, a *List<string>* object is used to contain the values, and at the end of the task, the Guids property is assigned the value of *guids.ToArray()*, as shown in Figure 4-11.

```
C:\InsideMSBuild\Ch04\Samples>msbuild CreateGuid02.proj /t:Demo /nologo
Build started 9/15/2010 10:08:39 PM.
Project "C:\InsideMSBuild\Ch04\Samples\CreateGuid02.proj" on node 1 (Demo target(s)).
Demo:
  Id01: 7f91532e-b4f3-4f45-8cc2-f481b4f8ec01

  Id02: b3f3eef8-8aad-432d-9e48-fac5f08cc110;4a3576ac-8cea-47ee-9fd1-61209eff7cc2;0d76a0ea-3383-4e
  20-839e-aea89y5ya65eb;eab8fade-866d-4e8c-b75b-f23c405cad3a
Done Building Project "C:\InsideMSBuild\Ch04\Samples\CreateGuid02.proj" (Demo target(s)).

Build succeeded.
    0 Warning(s)
    0 Error(s)
```

FIGURE 4-11 CreateGuid02 inline task result

In the Demo target, we invoke the CreateGuid02 task twice. The first time, we use it to create just one value and placed that into the Id01 item. You could have placed this into a property if you wanted, but we placed it into an item here for consistency. The second invocation specified that four values should be created. You can verify that this was the case by looking at the result in Figure 4-11. By now, you should be pretty comfortable with task parameters. Let's look at some other aspects of inline tasks.

There are a couple other issues that we have not yet discussed, which are very important because the tasks that we have created have been very basic. To give a better idea, let's discuss what is happening internally. At runtime, MSBuild uses the CodeDOM to generate a class from your inline task, which it then compiles and loads just like any other task.

> **Note** For more info on CodeDOM, you can visit the reference at *http://msdn.microsoft.com/ en-us/library/y2k85ax6.aspx*.

Let's take a look at what that class looks like. In the next snippet, you will find the class that was automatically created for us to implement the CreateGuid02 task. It has been formatted a bit to preserve space for printing.

```
namespace InlineCode {
    using System;
    using System.Collections;
    using System.Collections.Generic;
    using System.Text;
    using System.Linq;
    using System.IO;
    using Microsoft.Build.Framework;
    using Microsoft.Build.Utilities;

    public class CreateGuid02 : Microsoft.Build.Utilities.Task {
        private bool _Success = true;
        public virtual bool Success {
            get { return _Success; }
            set { _Success = value; }
        }

        private int _NumToCreate;
        public virtual int NumToCreate
            {
            get { return _NumToCreate; }
            set { _NumToCreate = value; }
        }

        private string[] _Guids;
        public virtual string[] Guids
            {
            get { return _Guids; }
            set { _Guids = value; }
        }

        public override bool Execute()
            {
            List<string> guids = new List<string>();
```

```
            for (int i = 0; i < NumToCreate; i++)
            {
                guids.Add(Guid.NewGuid().ToString());
            }
            Guids = guids.ToArray();

            return _Success;
        }
    }
}
```

From this, you can see how your tasks are created. The parameters are declared as you would have declared them, and then the body of the task is placed inside the *Execute* method. One thing to take note of here is that you don't see the *[Required]* and *[Output]* attributes; these are handled separately, but they do behave as expected. The other thing that you should notice are the namespaces that have been declared as being used via using statements at the top of the class. You will always have these namespaces at your disposal. If you need more, you can insert more with the *Using* element under the task element. For example, if you wanted to use the *Regex* class from the *System.Text.RegularExpressions* namespace without qualifying its name, then you can add the using System.Text.RegularExpressions; statement to the generated class. The Replace01 inline task from Replace01.proj, shown next, shows how you would accomplish this.

```xml
<Project xmlns="http://schemas.microsoft.com/developer/msbuild/2003"
         ToolsVersion="4.0"
         DefaultTargets="Demo">

  <UsingTask
    TaskName="Replace01"
    TaskFactory="CodeTaskFactory"
    AssemblyFile="$(MSBuildToolsPath)\Microsoft.Build.Tasks.v4.0.dll" >
    <ParameterGroup>
      <Input Required="true"/>
      <Pattern Required="true"/>
      <Replacement Required="true"/>
      <Result Output="true"/>
    </ParameterGroup>
    <Task>
      <Using Namespace="System.Text.RegularExpressions" />
      <Code Type="Fragment" Language="cs">
        <![CDATA[
          Result = Regex.Replace(Input, Pattern, Replacement);
        ]]>
      </Code>
    </Task>
  </UsingTask>

  <Target Name="Demo">
    <Replace01 Input="This is a ssn 123-45-7894 value"
               Pattern="\d{3}\-\d{2}\-\d{4}"
               Replacement="***-**-****">
      <Output PropertyName="MaskedSsnString" TaskParameter="Result"/>
```

```
      </Replace01>
      <Message Text="MaskedSsnString: $(MaskedSsnString)"/>
    </Target>
</Project>
```

In this example, I use the Replace01 task to mask a Social Security value that is contained in a string. Now that we have covered using statements, you might be wondering how you can add references to other assemblies. You do this with the *Reference* element under Task.

It is very similar to *Using,* but instead of a *Namespace* attribute, it has an *Include* attribute. To clarify this, we will take a look at a sample. In the Example.Tasks project file, I have created a simple static class, *ExampleValues,* shown here.

```
namespace Examples.Tasks
{
    public static class ExampleValues
    {
        public const string Name = "Example-values";
    }
}
```

In this class, I just create a const property, Name, that I access from the inline task that I create. This task, Ref01, is defined in the IT-Ref01.proj file in the Samples directory of the Example.Tasks project. The contents of that file are shown here.

```
<Project xmlns="http://schemas.microsoft.com/developer/msbuild/2003"
        ToolsVersion="4.0"
        DefaultTargets="Demo">

  <UsingTask
    TaskName="Ref01"
    TaskFactory="CodeTaskFactory"
    AssemblyFile="$(MSBuildToolsPath)\Microsoft.Build.Tasks.v4.0.dll" >
    <ParameterGroup>
      <Value Output="true"/>
    </ParameterGroup>
    <Task>
      <Reference Include="$(MSBuildProjectDirectory)\..\Examples.Tasks.dll" />
      <Using Namespace="Examples.Tasks"/>
      <Code Type="Fragment" Language="cs">
        <![CDATA[
          Value = ExampleValues.Name;
        ]]>
      </Code>
    </Task>
  </UsingTask>

  <Target Name="Demo">
    <Ref01>
      <Output PropertyName="Result" TaskParameter="Value"/>
    </Ref01>
    <Message Text="Result: $(Result)"/>
  </Target>
</Project>
```

In this sample, the Ref01 task is defined, and it uses the *Reference* element to let MSBuild know where the assembly is that should be referenced when building the Ref01 task. Along with that, I also insert a using statement for the namespace *Examples.Tasks*. That way, I do not have to qualify the *ExampleValues* class when I use it. Then, inside the Demo target, I simply use the task as I normally would have. You can see the result of executing that target in Figure 4-12.

```
C:\InsideMSBuild\Ch04\bin\Debug\Samples>msbuild IT-Ref01.proj /t:Demo /nologo
Build started 9/15/2010 10:56:10 PM.
Project "C:\InsideMSBuild\Ch04\bin\Debug\Samples\IT-Ref01.proj" on node 1 (Demo target(s)).
Demo:
  Result: Example-values
Done Building Project "C:\InsideMSBuild\Ch04\bin\Debug\Samples\IT-Ref01.proj" (Demo target(s)).

Build succeeded.
    0 Warning(s)
    0 Error(s)
```

FIGURE 4-12 Ref01 InlineTasks result

From this figure, you can see that we were able to successfully reference another assembly when the inline task was built. We've covered default inline tasks pretty well. We will now move on to cover what a TaskFactory is.

TaskFactory

In the previous examples for inline tasks that we have shown, you might have been wondering about the attribute *TaskFactory="CodeTaskFactory"*, which we assigned to each *UsingTask* element. The task factory, which this attribute refers to, is the object that is responsible for creating instances of those tasks dynamically. As was mentioned previously, you can create inline tasks with managed languages by default, and these use the CodeDOM to compile those at run time. You are not limited to using inline tasks in this way. You can create your own task factory to allow you to author your own inline tasks in whatever language you choose. For example, if you download the MSBuild Extension Pack (available from *http://msbuildextensionpack.codeplex.com/*), then you can author inline tasks using IronRuby or IronPython. To author tasks with those languages, you need to use a task factory called DlrTaskFactory, which is contained in the extension pack.

If you want to be able to author inline tasks in a language that is not supported, you can do that by creating your own task factory, which is straightforward. In this section, we will discuss a very basic task factory that can be used to execute batch files. This task factory is not very useful because the Exec task already exists, but it will introduce you to the concepts of creating your own task factory. To create a new task factory, all that you need to do is implement the Microsoft.Build.Framework.ITaskFactory interface. This interface has two properties and a handful of methods that you will need to implement. That interface is shown in Figure 4-13.

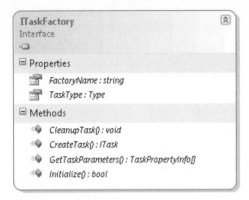

FIGURE 4-13 ITaskFactory interface

We will now go over all these properties and methods. In Table 4-5, you will see the descriptions of the two properties of the ITaskFactory interface.

TABLE 4-5 ITaskFactory Properties

Property	Description
FactoryName	This is the name of the factory, such as DlrTaskFactory, CodeTaskFactory, or BatchFileTaskFactory. This is the name that you will need to use inside the MSBuild files to specify which task factory should be used. Most implementations will return just the name of the task factory class.
TaskType	This returns the type for the task that this factory will create.

These properties are pretty straightforward, so we will not go over them in detail. We will now discuss the four methods that are defined in that interface. Let's start with the *Initialize* method:

```
bool Initialize(string taskName, IDictionary<string, TaskPropertyInfo> parameterGroup,
string taskBody, IBuildEngine taskFactoryLoggingHost);
```

When your task factory is created by the MSBuild engine, it will be constructed using the default constructor, so make sure that you have one defined, and then the *Initialize* method will be called to prepare it. TaskName is the name of the task which is being created; this is the value of the *TaskName* attribute from the *UsingTask* element. Depending on the implementation, you may be able to ignore this. The container for all the parameters that are being passed into the task is called parameterGroup. If your *UsingTask* element declares a parameter, then the parameters will all be contained in the parameterGroup property. Typically, you will want to take those values and store them because you will return those same values in the *GetTaskParameters* method. Since the MSBuild script will pass in the parameters into the *Initialize* method, many times you will just return those parameters as is, but you are given a chance to modify them if your task factory requires it. The only remaining method is the *CleanupTask* method, which is called when the task is no longer needed and can be disposed of. Now that we have discussed all the methods that you will need to implement, let's take a look at an example and then we will go a bit deeper. In the following code block, you'll find the contents of the BatchFileTaskFactory.cs file.

```
public class BatchFileTaskFactory : ITaskFactory
{
    protected string TaskXmlBody
    { get; set; }

    protected IDictionary<string, TaskPropertyInfo> ParameterGroup
    { get; private set; }

    public virtual void CleanupTask(ITask task)
    {
        Contract.Requires(task != null);
        // If  the task is disposable then dispose it
        IDisposable disposableTask = task as IDisposable;
        if (disposableTask != null)
        {
            disposableTask.Dispose();
        }
    }

    public virtual ITask CreateTask(IBuildEngine taskFactoryLoggingHost)
    { return new BatchFileTask(this.TaskXmlBody); }

    public string FactoryName
    {
        get { return this.GetType().Name; }
    }

    public virtual TaskPropertyInfo[] GetTaskParameters()
    { return this.ParameterGroup.Values.ToArray(); }

    public virtual bool Initialize(
        string taskName,
        IDictionary<string, TaskPropertyInfo> parameterGroup,
        string taskBody,
        IBuildEngine taskFactoryLoggingHost)
    {
        Contract.Requires(!string.IsNullOrEmpty(taskName));
        Contract.Requires(parameterGroup != null);
        Contract.Requires(taskBody != null);
        Contract.Requires(taskFactoryLoggingHost != null);

        this.TaskXmlBody = taskBody;
        this.ParameterGroup = parameterGroup;

        return true;
    }

    public Type TaskType
    {
        get { return typeof(BatchFileTask); }
    }
}
```

By looking at this sample task factory and the descriptions for the properties and methods that we just discussed, what is happening is pretty straightforward. There is no magic happening here. When an inline task element is being encountered for the first time, MSBuild will call the task factory to create an instance of that inline task and then call the *Initialize* method. *Initialize* will essentially be "passed" everything contained in the *UsingTask* element. After that, MSBuild will call the *CreateTask* method to create a specific instance of the task for that usage of the task. After the instance is created, all the parameters passed into the task element in the target will be assigned as they would a normal task. Then the task is executed, and finally, if any *Output* elements are present, they will be processed.

If you take a look at the *CreateTask* method, you will see that we are creating a new instance of BatchFileTask and passing it the task body contents. This class is simply an implementation of the ITask interface that we create. You can create and return any object that implements the ITask interface, including those tasks that already exist. Even though you could return tasks that already exist, the odds are that you will create a new task specifically to execute the behavior contained in the task body. For instance, if you created a Perl task factory, you could create a task that could execute the Perl scripts contained in the body of the task. In this case, we will just execute the batch file. The definition of BatchFileTask is shown in its entirety in the next code section.

```
public class BatchFileTask : Task
{
    public BatchFileTask(string xmlBody)
    {
        this.InitalizeFromXml(xmlBody);
    }

    private string Filepath
    { get; set; }

    public string Message
    { get; set; }

    public int ExitCode
    { get; set; }

    private void InitalizeFromXml(string xmlBody)
    {
        if (!string.IsNullOrWhiteSpace(xmlBody))
        {
            // parse the doc, should look like this <Script Filepath="..."/>
            XDocument doc = XDocument.Parse(xmlBody);
            XNamespace xnamespace =
                @"http://schemas.microsoft.com/developer/msbuild/2003";
            var node = (from n in doc.Elements(xnamespace + "Script")
                        select n).SingleOrDefault();
            if (node != null)
            {
                this.Filepath = node.Attribute("Filepath").Value;
            }
        }
    }
}
```

```
public override bool Execute()
{
    if (!string.IsNullOrWhiteSpace(Filepath))
    {
        // make sure the file exists
        if (!File.Exists(this.Filepath))
        {
            Log.LogError("Batch file not found at [{0}]", this.Filepath);
        }
        else
        {
            Log.LogMessage(
                MessageImportance.High,
                "Executing batch file from [{0}]",
                this.Filepath);
            string cmdFilepath = ToolLocationHelper.GetPathToSystemFile("cmd.exe");
            Process process = new Process();
            process.StartInfo = new ProcessStartInfo(this.Filepath);
            process.StartInfo.UseShellExecute = true;
            process.StartInfo.CreateNoWindow = true;
            process.Start();
            process.WaitForExit();
            int exitCode = process.ExitCode;
            if (exitCode != 0)
            {
                Log.LogError(
                    "Non-zero exit code [{0}] from batch file [{1}]",
                    exitCode,
                    this.Filepath);
            }
            // you could set this via a parameter
            // process.StartInfo.WorkingDirectory
        }
    }

    return !this.Log.HasLoggedErrors;
}
}
```

The only thing that makes this task different from a normal task is the way that it's created. In this case, there is no default constructor, so it can't be used outside a task factory. The XML fragment that is contained inside the body of the task from an inline task declaration must be passed to it.

Note If you want to create a dynamic task, you might be interested in learning about the Microsoft.Build.Framework.IGeneratedTask interface. By implementing this interface, you do not have to specify that your task can be passed in any parameters. When you use this interface, properties can be retrieved or set on the task using the *GetPropertyValue* and *SetPropertyValue* methods instead of declaring the parameters at the time the task is defined.

IGeneratedTask is a bad choice of name because the tasks are not really generated; regular tasks are implemented internally with a task factory. A better name, perhaps, would have been IDynamicTask.

We've covered inline tasks and task factories pretty well up to this point. There is more to know about task factories, but we will not cover all the details here. If you need more information, a good place to look is the MSDN reference for MSBuild. We will now switch back to standard tasks and discuss the *ToolTask* class.

Extending ToolTask

There are many instances in which you need to invoke an .exe file in your build process. There is a task, the Exec task, which allows you to execute any command. This works great and is used throughout the MSBuild community. If you find yourself executing the same .exe file on several occasions, then it may be worth writing a custom task to execute the command. Custom tasks that wrap up executables have many advantages to simply using the Exec task. Some of those benefits are outlined in the following list:

- Ease of use   Since custom tasks have specific properties for inputs and outputs, they are very easy to use.

- Better input validation   You can write .NET code to validate the parameters that the script is requesting be sent to the executable.

- Easier path resolution   Sometimes you may not know where the .exe file resides. You may have to search the registry or examine a set of folders. This is typically performed more easily in code than in an MSBuild script.

- Pre- and post-processing   Because you are creating a custom task, you can perform actions before and/or after the execution of the executable.

- Parsing stdout and stderr   The *ToolTask* class can detect errors and warnings from messages that are sent into the stdout and stderr streams.

- Enables task execution skipping   By overriding the *SkipTaskExecution* method, you can programmatically determine if the task should be skipped.

When you have decided to write a custom task to wrap an executable file, you should consider extending the *ToolTask* class. This class, which is in the *Microsoft.Build.Utilities* assembly, was designed specifically for this. The class diagram for the *ToolTask* abstract class is shown in Figure 4-14, which was generated with the MSBuild 3.5 assemblies.

As shown in the previous diagram, the *ToolTask* class extends the task class. This class implements the *Execute* method from the task class, but it does define one abstract method and one abstract property that need to be implemented. Those are the *GenerateFullPathToTool* method and the ToolName property. There are many other methods and properties that are relevant in this class, and we will discuss some of those now. We will discuss only the methods and properties with which you are likely to interact.

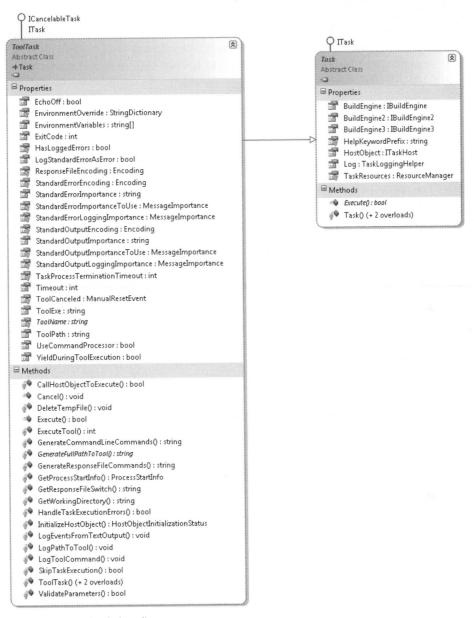

FIGURE 4-14 *ToolTask* class diagram

ToolTask Methods

- *Cancel*   This method is called to cancel the task execution. Once this method is called by MSBuild, if the task does not complete, it will be forcefully terminated.

- *DeleteTempFile*   This is simply a helper method that can be used to delete files. The advantage of using this method is that it doesn't fail the build if the file can't be deleted; it only warns and continues.

- *ExecuteTool*   This is the method called that will execute the tool based on the values from the input parameters.

- *GenerateFullPathToTool*   You will have to implement this method. The return value, as the name suggests, is the full path to the tool that you are executing.

- *GenerateCommandLineCommands*   This is used to generate any parameters that are passed to the command. The return value will be appended to the full tool path for the command that will be executed. This value, along with the response file, if provided, is passed to the System.Diagnostics.ProcessStartInfo(string, string) constructor as the command-line arguments.

- *GenerateResponseFileCommands*   If your tool accepts a response file for initialization, then you can return a string that contains the values that should be contained in a response file sent to the tool. These commands will be written to a temporary file and then passed to the tool. When you use this method, you may also need to override the *GetResponseFileSwitch* method. A typical reason for preferring a response file is that you can pass many parameters. If you pass parameters on the command line, you are typically limited to 8 Kb, imposed by cmd.exe.

- *GetProcessStartInfo*   This method is used to initialize the information that will be used to create the process when the tool is executed.

- *GetResponseFileSwitch*   If the tool that you are invoking accepts a response file, then you need to override this method if you want to supply a response file to it. If the tool simply accepts the file path as the response file, then you do not need to override this method; that is the default behavior. If the tool requires a switch to process the response file, then override this method to create the switch to be passed to the tool.

- *GetWorkingDirectory*   If you need to specify the working directory of the tool, then override this method to override the working directory to use. If *null* is returned from this method, then the current directory will be used as the working directory. This is the default behavior.

- *HandleTaskExecutionErrors*   This method will be called after the command completes with a nonzero exit code. The return value of this method is used as the return value of the task itself. If you have a scenario where you would like to conditionally ignore certain exit codes, then you can override this method and examine the exit code and decide to return *true* or *false*. There exist tools that return nonzero exit codes even when the tool succeeds. If you return *true,* then the build will proceed as if there were no error.

- *SkipTaskExecution*   The return value of this method will determine if the command should actually be executed. If this method returns *false,* then the task will be executed; otherwise it will not. If the task execution is skipped due to the return value of this method, it will not be treated as an error but as an intended response. The default implementation of this method simply returns *false.* You can use this opportunity to do custom dependency checking, and skip the task if everything is up to date.

- *ValidateParameters*   This is an empty method that can be used to validate any input parameters that have been passed to the task. If this method returns *false,* then the task will automatically fail. By default, this method simply returns *true.* If your task accepts inputs, then you can place your input validation in this method and it will be called by the default implementation of the *Execute* method. If the *Execute* method is overridden, then this validation method should be called near the beginning of the process.

ToolTask Properties

- EchoOff   If this property is set to *true,* then command-line echoing will be turned off.

- EnvironmentVariables   This property is an array of key/value pairs, where the key is the name of the environment variable and the value is the value of the environment variable. These values are passed to the spawned process. If a value exists in both the regular environment block and in this set of values, then the value defined in this array will be used.

- ExitCode   Contains the exit code of the tool. This is an MSBuild Output property, so its value will be available to build files using the task.

- LogStandardErrorAsError   If the value for this property is *true,* then any message received in the standard error stream will be logged as an error.

- ResponseFileEncoding   Contains the encoding that should be used to write out the response file. The default value for this is System.Text.Encoding.UTF8.

- StandardErrorEncoding   Contains the encoding value that should used for error output. The default value for this is the default encoding of the system running the task.

- StandardErrorImportance   Contains the MessageImportance level that tool errors will be logged at. The default value for this is *MessageImportance.High.*

- StandardErrorImportanceToUse   Gets the effective importance that standard error messages will be logged at.

- StandardErrorLoggingImportance   Contains the MessageImportance level for messages sent to the standard error stream. The default value for this is *MessageImportance.Normal.*

- StandardOutputEncoding   Contains the encoding of the standard output stream. The default value for this is the default value of the machine running the task.

- StandardOutputImportance   Contains the encoding of the standard output stream. The default value for this is *MessageImportance.Normal*.

- StandardOutputImportanceToUse   Gets the effective importance that the standard output messages will be logged at.

- StandardOutputLoggingImportance   Contains the MessageImportance level that messages sent to the standard output will be logged at. The default value for this is *MessageImportance.Low*.

- TaskProcessTerminationTimeout   This property is the timeout period, in milliseconds, that the task will be given after the *Cancel* method is called and before the process is forcefully terminated.

- ToolCanceled   This property is used to signal when a tool is canceled.

- Timeout   Contains the amount of the time that the task will be allowed to run. If the task exceeds the initial value, set prior to execution, then it will be stopped, and the task will fail. This value is given in milliseconds.

- ToolExe   This property serves as an alternative to the ToolName property. The problem with the ToolName property is that it is read-only, so there is no option to change the name of the .exe file; this property introduces that option. If this is specified, it will take precedence over ToolName.

- ToolName   Contains the name of the executable file to run. This should not include the path, just the name of the actual executable file. If ToolExe is specified, then that value is used in place of this.

- ToolPath   Contains the full path to the folder where the tool is located. If this property returns a value, then the result from the *GenerateFullPathToTool* method is ignored.

- UseCommandProcessor   When this property is set to *true,* the tool task will be executed using the command processor; otherwise, the tool task will be placed in a batch file and executed.

- YieldDuringToolExecution   If this property is set to *true,* then while the tool is executing, it will yield so that other projects can continue to build. If you have long-running tasks, then you should set this value to *true* so that you can have build times.

The MSBuild team has created this helper class to ensure that wrapping an existing .exe file is very simple. This is because there are many preexisting tools that can be very useful during the build process. If you are writing a task that will invoke an executable, you should extend this base class so you can focus on what is important and not on the plumbing of calling it.

In order to demonstrate how we can effectively use this class, I will create a new task that wraps up an .exe file that is delivered with Visual Studio, which is the MakeZipExe.exe executable. Before we take a look at the task that will be created for this executable, let's take a look at the usage for this tool, as shown in Figure 4-15.

```
C:\InsideMSBuild>makezipexe
Microsoft (R) Zip File to Exe converter version 1.0
Copyright (C) Microsoft Corporation 2005. All rights reserved.

Usage:
        -zipfile:filename
                Path to the zip file to turn into an exe.
        -output:filename
                Path to the .exe file to generate. If this is not specified,
                then an .exe file with the same name as the input file (but
                with the .exe extension) will be used.
        -overwrite
                Overwrite the output the file if it exists.
        -?
                This help screen.
```

FIGURE 4-15 MakeZipExe.exe usage

This tool has only a few parameters that can be provided but is certainly a useful tool, so it should pose as a good demonstration task. From the usage of the tool, we can see that we should create three properties that will be sent to the tool: Zipfile, OutputFile, and Overwrite. The only required property will be Zipfile, because this is the only required parameter by the tool itself. Now we can take a look at the following task definition.

```csharp
public class MakeZipExe : ToolTask
{
    private const string ExeName = "makezipexe.exe";

    public MakeZipExe()
    {
        Overwrite = false;
    }

    [Required]
    public ITaskItem Zipfile { get; set; }
    public ITaskItem OutputFile { get; set; }
    public bool Overwrite { get; set; }

    protected override bool ValidateParameters()
    {
        base.Log.LogMessageFromText("Validating arguments", MessageImportance.Low);

        if (!File.Exists(Zipfile.GetMetadata("FullPath")))
        {
            string message = string.Format("Missing ZipFile: {0}", Zipfile);
            base.Log.LogError(message, null);
            return false;
        }
        if (File.Exists(OutputFile.GetMetadata("FullPath")) && !Overwrite)
        {
            string message = string.Format("Output file {0}, Overwrite false.",
                OutputFile);
            base.Log.LogError(message, null);
            return false;
        }

        return base.ValidateParameters();
    }
}
```

```csharp
protected override string GenerateFullPathToTool()
{
    string path = ToolPath;
    // If ToolPath was not provided by the MSBuild script try to find it.
    if (string.IsNullOrEmpty(path))
    {
        using (RegistryKey key = Registry.LocalMachine.OpenSubKey(
            @"SOFTWARE\Microsoft\VisualStudio\10.0\Setup\VS"))
        {
            if (key != null)
            {
                string keyValue =
                    key.GetValue("EnvironmentDirectory", null).ToString();
                path = keyValue;
            }
        }
    }
    if (string.IsNullOrEmpty(path))
    {
        using (RegistryKey key = Registry.LocalMachine.OpenSubKey(
            @"SOFTWARE\Microsoft\VisualStudio\9.0\Setup\VS"))
        {
            if (key != null)
            {
                string keyValue =
                    key.GetValue("EnvironmentDirectory", null).ToString();
                path = keyValue;
            }
        }
    }
    if (string.IsNullOrEmpty(path))
    {

        using (RegistryKey key = Registry.LocalMachine.OpenSubKey
            (@"SOFTWARE\Microsoft\VisualStudio\8.0\Setup\VS"))
        {
            if (key != null)
            {
                string keyValue =
                    key.GetValue("EnvironmentDirectory", null).ToString();
                path = keyValue;
            }
        }

    }
    if (string.IsNullOrEmpty(path))
    {
        Log.LogError("VisualStudio install directory not found",
            null);

        return string.Empty;
    }
    string fullpath = Path.Combine(path, ToolName);
    return fullpath;
}
```

```
protected override string GenerateCommandLineCommands()
{
    StringBuilder sb = new StringBuilder();
    if (Zipfile != null)
    {
        sb.Append(
            string.Format("-zipfile:{0} ",
            Zipfile.GetMetadata("FullPath")));
    }
    if (OutputFile != null)
    {
        sb.Append(
            string.Format("-output:{0} ",
            OutputFile.GetMetadata("FullPath")));
    }
    if (Overwrite)
        sb.Append("-overwrite:true ");

    return sb.ToString();
}
protected override string ToolName
{
    get { return ExeName; }
}
}
```

One of the things to take note of here is the usage of ITaskItem. Earlier in this chapter, we mentioned that you should try to employ objects of this type for properties that refer to files and directories. This task overrides the abstract ToolName property to return the name of the file to be executed. Along with this property, three methods—*ValidateParameters, GenerateFullPathToTool,* and *GenerateCommandLineCommands*—are overridden. In most implementations extending *ToolTask,* these methods will be found. *ValidateParameters* is used to validate the input provided from the calling script and to throw meaningful errors for invalid input. *GenerateFullPathToTool* is an abstract method and must be implemented by the concrete class. *GenerateCommandLineCommands* is the method that will be called to determine what values will be passed into the command as parameters. If you have a tool that doesn't accept any parameters, then you do not need to implement this method. If you noticed, we did not have to define the *Execute* or *ExecuteTool* methods; this is because *ToolTask* implements these methods by calling the other methods declared in this class. Now we can see how this task can be used.

Using this task is no different from using a task that extends Task or directly implements ITask. You have to declare that you are interested in using the task with the *UsingTask* statement and then invoke it in a target. I have created the following example file, MakeZipExe01.proj.

```
<Project xmlns="http://schemas.microsoft.com/developer/msbuild/2003"
         ToolsVersion="4.0"
         DefaultTargets="Demo">
```

```
<UsingTask AssemblyFile="$(MSBuildProjectDirectory)\..\Examples.Tasks.dll"
           TaskName="MakeZipExe"/>

<Target Name="Demo">
  <MakeZipExe ZipFile="Sample.zip"
              OutputFile="Sample.exe"
              Overwrite="true"
              ToolPath="$(DevEnvDir)">

  </MakeZipExe>
</Target>
</Project>
```

In this simple execution of the task, we invoke the MakeZipExe task inside the Demo target. We specify the zipfile that should be the source for the self-extracting zipfile and where the output needs to be written to. If you execute the Demo target, you will see that the Sample .exe file is successfully created. In the results captured in Figure 4-16, I increased the verbosity of the console logger to "detailed" in order to display the relevant messages.

```
C:\InsideMSBuild\Ch04\bin\Debug\Samples>msbuild MakeZipExe01.proj /t:Demo /clp:v=detailed /nologo
Build started 10/4/2010 10:12:12 PM.
Project "C:\InsideMSBuild\Ch04\bin\Debug\Samples\MakeZipExe01.proj" on node 1 (Demo target(s)).
Building with tools version "4.0".
Target "Demo" in project "C:\InsideMSBuild\Ch04\bin\Debug\Samples\MakeZipExe01.proj" (entry point)
:
Using "MakeZipExe" task from assembly "C:\InsideMSBuild\Ch04\bin\Debug\Samples\..\Examples.Tasks.d
ll".
Task "MakeZipExe"
  Validating arguments
  command-line = -zipfile:C:\InsideMSBuild\Ch04\bin\Debug\Samples\Sample.zip -output:C:\InsideMSBu
  ild\Ch04\bin\Debug\Samples\Sample.exe -overwrite:true
  C:\Program Files\Microsoft Visual Studio 10.0\Common7\IDE\makezipexe.exe -zipfile:C:\InsideMSBui
  ld\Ch04\bin\Debug\Samples\Sample.zip -output:C:\InsideMSBuild\Ch04\bin\Debug\Samples\Sample.exe
  -overwrite:true
  Microsoft (R) Zip File to Exe converter version 1.0
  Copyright (C) Microsoft Corporation 2005. All rights reserved.

  exe file generation successful.
Done executing task "MakeZipExe".
Done building target "Demo" in project "MakeZipExe01.proj".
Done Building Project "C:\InsideMSBuild\Ch04\bin\Debug\Samples\MakeZipExe01.proj" (Demo target(s))
.

Build succeeded.
    0 Warning(s)
    0 Error(s)
```

FIGURE 4-16 MakeZipExe task demonstration

From the image in Figure 4-16, we can see that the MakeZipExe tool was successfully discovered and invoked with the expected parameters. Also, the result file, Sample.exe, was correctly created. Now that we have introduced how you can quickly and effectively create custom MSBuild tasks that wrap command-line tools, we'll move on to discuss the little-known topic of debugging MSBuild tasks.

Debugging Tasks

When you write custom MSBuild tasks, you are writing managed code, and hooking into an existing process, the MSBuild engine. Even though MSBuild tasks are very easy to write, you will inevitably run into times when they do not behave as you expect. This will be the case especially when you are writing complex tasks. When this time arrives, you will need to debug your tasks, which we discuss in this section.

When you need to debug your custom MSBuild tasks, you will find that there are primarily three ways to debug these tasks. Ultimately, the goal when debugging tasks is to have all the tools available when one is debugging .NET applications. We should be able to use Visual Studio to debug custom tasks. The following are three ways that you can debug tasks:

1. Examine the content of the log.

2. Use Debugger.Launch() to prompt for debugger attachment.

3. Start MSBuild as an external program, and debug normally.

The first technique, examining the log, is obviously the simplest, but it will also provide the least amount of information. Also, it is not an interactive process; you simply examine the log file that was generated. You can increase the number of messages that your task logs to discover more about its behavior, and you can increase the verbosity of the loggers. If you set the verbosity to be "diagnostic," then all properties and items are dumped by the logger.

We will now discuss the second option, the *Debugger.Launch()* method. When you are trying to debug an MSBuild task, one technique that I have seen employed is to add the statement `System.Diagnostics.Debugger.Launch()`. Typically, you will place this statement inside the *Execute* method. When this statement is encountered, you will be prompted about attaching a debugger to the process. After this, you can start executing the build script that you would like to debug that invokes the task you are trying to debug. You should be prompted with a dialog similar to the one shown in Figure 4-17.

FIGURE 4-17 Debugger selection dialog

From this dialog, you can choose Visual Studio as the debugger. Following this, you can set breakpoints, step into methods, and all the other benefits that you are accustomed to except for Edit and Continue. This is a great technique to employ, but it has at least the following drawbacks:

- You have to change the task (adding a Debugger.Launch() statement).
- There is no support for Edit and Continue.

The way to get around these issues is to employ the last method, which is starting MSBuild as an external program. Once you create a task and a build script that exercises the task, you can use Visual Studio to start the MSBuild.exe executable on the specified build script and to use the debugger to debug it. This is similar to but not exactly the same as the previous approach. In the Debug pane of the Project properties, you will see an option called Start External Program; this is the option that we will use. I will show you how to achieve this by debugging a task contained in the samples, the MetadataExample task that we discussed earlier.

Normally when I am writing tasks, I create a set of sample MSBuild scripts that can be used to exercise and demonstrate the task usage of the task. If it is possible, I place these samples in the project that contains the task itself. The reason for this is that it allows me to be able to maintain the task and the samples in one place. Another reason is that it makes it a little simpler to debug the tasks. For sample scripts I set the files to be copied to the output directory. Another reason that you will want to do so is so that you can execute the MSBuild scripts in their output folders and know that you are using the latest version of the task. In the samples, this folder is named *Samples*. This is why you have seen *UsingTask* statements such as:

```
<UsingTask AssemblyFile="$(MSBuildProjectDirectory)\..\Examples.Tasks.dll"
           TaskName="AspnetRegsql"/>
```

In this example, we know that we will be executing this script from the output directory and it is contained in a directory named *Samples*. So the *Example.Tasks.dll* assembly is located in the directory above the current project; this is why I use the '. .' in the *AssemblyFile* attribute. Another advantage of taking this approach is that if your sample scripts need dummy files to go along with them, you can place them all inside that folder and set the Copy To Output Directory option appropriately. You can set the attribute directly inside Visual Studio in the Properties grid. You can see this in Figure 4-18.

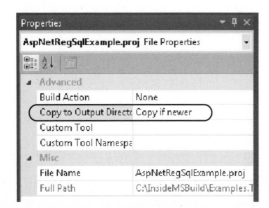

FIGURE 4-18 Copy To Output Directory

In this figure, I have set the value of Copy To Output Directory to be Copy If Newer, but you could also set it to Copy Always; either should work. Now we can debug the MetadataExample task. I will use the following MetadataExample01.proj file to demonstrate this.

```xml
<Project xmlns="http://schemas.microsoft.com/developer/msbuild/2003"
         ToolsVersion="4.0"
         DefaultTargets="Demo">

  <UsingTask AssemblyFile="..\Examples.Tasks.dll"
             TaskName="MetadataExample"/>

  <PropertyGroup>
    <ConfigFileRoot>$(MSBuildProjectDirectory)\sampleConfigFiles\</ConfigFileRoot>
  </PropertyGroup>
  <ItemGroup>
    <Server Include="$(ConfigFileRoot)server1.app.config">
      <Name>server1</Name>
      <DropLocation>D:\Drops\</DropLocation>
    </Server>
    <Server Include="$(ConfigFileRoot)server2.app.config">
      <Name>server2</Name>
      <DropLocation>E:\Builds\Drops\</DropLocation>
    </Server>
    <Server Include="$(ConfigFileRoot)server3.app.config">
      <Name>server3</Name>
      <DropLocation>D:\Data\DropDir\</DropLocation>
    </Server>
    <Server Include="$(ConfigFileRoot)server4.app.config">
      <Name>server4</Name>
      <DropLocation>D:\Projects\DropLocation\</DropLocation>
    </Server>
  </ItemGroup>

  <Target Name="Demo">
    <MetadataExample ServerList="@(Server)">
      <Output ItemName="ServerIpList" TaskParameter="Result" />
    </MetadataExample>

    <Message Text="ServerIpList: @(ServerIpList)"/>

    <Message
      Text="Server: %(ServerIpList.ServerName)
  %(ServerIpList.DropLoc)
  %(ServerIpList.IpAddress)"/>
  </Target>
</Project>
```

For the project that contains this task (in this case, Examples.Tasks), go to the Properties page for the project by selecting Properties from the Project menu. On the Debug tab, we have to specify that we want to invoke MSBuild, which will load our assembly when it detects the UsingTask statement referencing it. The following list describes three settings that you should be aware of:

- **Start external program**   You should select this value and provide the full path to the msbuild.exe file. Make sure to pick the correct version of MSBuild that you are intending to use. These files are located in the directory %Windows%\Microsoft.

NET\Framework\v3.5\ and %Windows%\Microsoft.NET\Framework\v4.0.30319\ for MSBuild 3.5 and MSBuild 4.0, respectively.

- **Command line arguments**   Here, you should place the path to the MSBuild sample file that invokes the task that you are trying to debug. Also, you can provide any properties or other switches to the msbuild.exe executable. I typically also attach a FileLogger item in case I might need to examine it to determine what was happening before or after the task was invoked. For instance, you may need to examine the log to determine what other targets were executed.

- **Working directory**   You should set this to the full path where the sample script lies, which should be under the output directory of the tasks' project itself.

You should note that these values are not stored in the project file but in the user file, so if you are working in a team, it should not affect any of the others working with you. You can see the value that I set this to for the MetadataExample task in Figure 4-19.

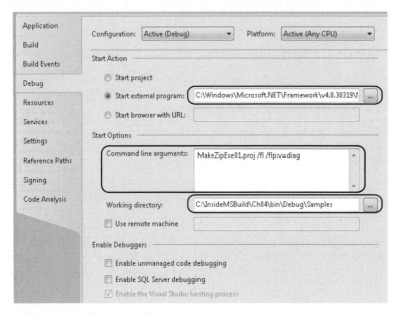

FIGURE 4-19 Project properties

Here, I've highlighted the areas listed previously. In this example, I am using MSBuild 4.0 on the MetadataExample01.proj file. After you have set these values correctly, all you have to do is set breakpoints where you want to stop and then hit F5! From there, you can step through the task and use all the tools that Visual Studio makes available to you.

Now we have covered everything you need to know to efficiently and effectively write custom MSBuild tasks. In this chapter, we have discussed getting started writing tasks, handling task input and output, what task base classes are available, debugging tasks, and more. Writing custom MSBuild tasks is one way to extend MSBuild itself; the other way is to write custom loggers. In the next chapter, we will cover custom loggers in detail. Following that chapter, we will start the MSBuild cookbook section.

Chapter 5
Custom Loggers

We have identified that there are two ways to extend MSBuild: by custom tasks and custom loggers. In the previous chapter, we covered custom tasks; in this chapter, we will discuss custom loggers. We'll start by discussing what loggers are available by default and how they can be used. After that, we'll take a look at what it takes to write and use a new custom logger. Now let's get started.

Overview

One of the most important aspects of a build tool is its logging support. You can create the best build tool ever, but if the logging mechanism doesn't meet the needs of consumers, then it will never be used. MSBuild has a great deal of flexibility with respect to loggers. There are two loggers that are shipped with MSBuild: the console logger and the file logger. We will cover these two loggers in the next two sections. A logger is an object that can accept and respond to build events. For example, throughout this book we have been sending messages to the loggers using the Message task.

The Message task has two properties: Text and Importance. The Text property contains the message that is to be logged, and the Importance a value indicating the priority of the message. When this task is executed, the MSBuild engine will raise an event on each attached logger sending both pieces of information. Individual loggers are allowed to interpret how messages with high importance versus those with low importance are to be handled. This importance level, along with the verbosity setting for the logger, typically determines how the message is logged. Each logger can have its own verbosity setting, which plays a role in what messages are logged and how. In the case of the console logger, messages with high importance are highlighted, whereas those with low importance are suppressed when the verbosity setting is set to normal, the default value.

We can now take a look at how different messages are passed through to the console logger using the Message task. The next block contains the content of the Logging01.proj project file.

```
<Project xmlns="http://schemas.microsoft.com/developer/msbuild/2003"
         ToolsVersion="4.0"
         DefaultTargets="Demo">

  <Target Name="Demo">
    <Message Text="high importance message" Importance="high" />
    <Message Text="normal importance message" Importance="normal" />
    <Message Text="low importance message" Importance="low" />
  </Target>

</Project>
```

In this project file, the single target, Demo, contains three calls to the Message task. Each task has a different setting for the Importance attribute. If you execute the command `msbuild Logging01.proj /t:Demo`, the result will be what is shown in Figure 5-1.

```
C:\InsideMSBuild\Ch05\bin\Debug\Samples>msbuild Logging01.proj /t:Demo /nologo
Build started 9/17/2010 9:23:57 PM.
Project "C:\InsideMSBuild\Ch05\bin\Debug\Samples\Logging01.proj" on node 1 (Demo target(s)).
Demo:
  high importance message
  normal importance message
Done Building Project "C:\InsideMSBuild\Ch05\bin\Debug\Samples\Logging01.proj" (Demo target(s)).

Build succeeded.
    0 Warning(s)
    0 Error(s)
```

FIGURE 5-1 Message importance demonstration 1

In Figure 5-1, you will see that only the messages with high importance and normal importance are shown. The message with a low-importance level is suppressed. This is a decision made by the console logger, based on the importance of the message as well as the verbosity setting of the logger. Also, notice that the message with high importance is printed in a more noticeable color. In the next section, we will cover the console logger in detail. For now let's just say that the extra command line switch `/clp:v=d` increases the verbosity setting of the console logger. If you execute the command `msbuild Logging01.proj /t:Demo /clp:v=d`, then the result would be what is shown in Figure 5-2.

```
C:\InsideMSBuild\Ch05\bin\Debug\Samples>msbuild Logging01.proj /t:Demo /clp:v=d /nologo
Build started 9/17/2010 9:29:11 PM.
Project "C:\InsideMSBuild\Ch05\bin\Debug\Samples\Logging01.proj" on node 1 (Demo target(s)).
Building with tools version "4.0".
Target "Demo" in project "C:\InsideMSBuild\Ch05\bin\Debug\Samples\Logging01.proj" (entry point):
Using "Message" task from assembly "Microsoft.Build.Tasks.v4.0, Version=4.0.0.0, Culture=neutral,
PublicKeyToken=b03f5f7f11d50a3a".
Task "Message"
  high importance message
Done executing task "Message".
Task "Message"
  normal importance message
Done executing task "Message".
Task "Message"
  low importance message
Done executing task "Message".
Done building target "Demo" in project "Logging01.proj".
Done Building Project "C:\InsideMSBuild\Ch05\bin\Debug\Samples\Logging01.proj" (Demo target(s)).

Build succeeded.
    0 Warning(s)
    0 Error(s)
```

FIGURE 5-2 Message importance demonstration 2

From the results shown in Figure 5-2, you can see that there is much more information logged to the console compared to Figure 5-1. Not only is the low importance message logged but much more information as well. We will now discuss the two loggers that are shipped with MSBuild.

Console Logger

When you invoke msbuild.exe, the console logger will be attached by default; you can disable this by using the /noconsolelogger (/noconlog) switch. You can set the verbosity of the console logger using the /verbosity (/v) switch when using msbuild.exe. The defined values for the verbosity are shown in Table 5-1.

TABLE 5-1 **Logger Verbosity**

Long Name	Short Name
Quiet	q
Minimal	m
Normal	n
Detailed	d
Diagnostic	diag

When you are specifying the verbosity for either of these loggers, you can use the long name or the short name. A common practice is to set the verbosity of the console logger to Minimal and attach file loggers with higher verbosities. That way the console shows the progress and errors/warnings, and a log file is available for diagnosis. The console logger accepts only a few parameters and they are outlined in Table 5-2. The parameters are passed by the /consoleloggerparameters (/clp) switch.

TABLE 5-2 **Console Logger Parameters**

Name	Description
PerformanceSummary	When passed as a parameter, the console logger will output messages that show the amount of time spent building tasks, targets, and projects. If you are trying to profile long running builds, this may be very useful.
NoSummary	When passed, this suppresses the errors and warnings summary that is typically displayed at the end of the log.
NoItemAndPropertyList	Indicates to not display the values for properties and items that are typically shown at the start of the build log when using the diagnostic verbosity setting.
Verbosity	Overrides the verbosity for the console logger.
Summary	Shows errors and warnings summary at the end of the log.
ErrorsOnly	Shows only errors.
WarningsOnly	Shows only warnings.
ShowCommandLine	Shows TaskCommandLineEvent messages. This is raised when the *TaskLoggingHelper.LogCommandLine* method is invoked.
ShowTimestamp	Displays a timestamp to every message.
ShowEventId	Displays the event ID for started, finished, and message events.
ForceNoAlign	Does not align the text to the size of the console buffer.
DiableMPLogging	Disables the multiprocessor logging style of output when running in non-multiprocessor mode.
EnableMPLogging	Enables the multiprocessor logging style even when running in non-multiprocessor mode. This logging style is on by default.
DisableConsoleColor*	When you provide this switch, all text written to the console will use the default color.

* denotes parameters new with MSBuild 4.0.

When you are using the console logger, you will typically not need to pass any of these parameters with the exception of the verbosity parameter. In the previous section, the command `msbuild Logging01.proj /t:Demo /clp:v=d` was demonstrated to increase the verbosity of the console logger. Now we know that the `/clp:v=d` switch sets the verbosity of the console logger to detailed. You can pass additional parameters by separating them with a semicolon. For example, you can extend the previous command to include event IDs and a performance summary by using `msbuild Logging01.proj /t:Demo /nologo /clp:v=d; ShowEventId;Summary;PerformanceSummary`. Now let's take a look at the file logger.

File Logger

The other logger that is shipped with MSBuild is the file logger, which logs messages to a file. With MSBuild 4.0, a set of command-line switches are provided to attach a file logger. In order to attach a file logger, you can use the /fl switch and the /flp switch to specify its parameters, similar to the /clp switch. For example, you can use the command `msbuild Logging01.proj /fl` to attach a file logger without specifying any parameters. You can also use /fl[*n*] and /flp[*n*], where *n* ranges from 1 to 9 in order to attach additional file loggers. When you use these switches, /flp1 corresponds to /fl1 and /flp4 to /fl4. If you specify parameters using /flp[*n*], then the /fl[*n*] is implied, so it is optional; so if you pass /flp4, then you do not have to pass /fl4 as well. In case you were wondering what the difference is between using a file logger and piping the content of the console to a file, it's mainly that you can attach multiple file loggers.

The command `msbuild Logging01.proj /fl /fl1 /fl2 /fl3` will attach four file loggers. These will produce four different logs: msbuild.log, msbuild1.log, msbuild2.log, and msbuild3.log. When you don't specify a file name, then the default is msbuild*[n]*.log, where *[n]* corresponds to /fl[*n*]. Since we didn't specify any parameters, they would all log the same content. We will cover the available parameters after we discuss the MSBuild 2.0 syntax.

If you are using .NET 2.0, you have to use the /logger (/l) switch to attach the file logger. The syntax for that is switch is `/l:<LoggerClassName>, <LoggerAssembly>[;LoggerParameters]`.

The values in that syntax are described as:

- **LoggerClassName**   The name of the logger class. A partial or full namespace is acceptable but not required.

- **LoggerAssembly**   The assembly that contains the logger. This can be either the path to the assembly or the assembly name.

- **LoggerParameters**   The string that should be passed to the logger as the value for the Parameters property. This is passed to the logger *exactly* as declared. These must be interpreted by the logger itself.

In order to attach the file logger in MSBuild 2.0, you will use the syntax `/l:FileLogger,Microsoft.Build.Engine[,LoggerParameters]`. The *LoggerParameters* value is an optional string that will be passed to the file logger. Here is an example of building the Logging01.proj with a file logger attached to the build process: `msbuild Logging01.proj /l:FileLogger,Microsoft.Build.Engine`.

When you are using MSBuild 2.0, the default verbosity of the file logger is Normal; in MSBuild 3.5 and later, it is Detailed. In order to change the verbosity level, you can pass it as a value in the parameters. We will discuss this after we take a look at the available parameters. Now that we have described how to attach the file logger to a build process, take a look at all the parameters that can be sent to the file logger, as described in Table 5-3.

TABLE 5-3 FileLogger Parameters

Parameter Name	Description
Append	If a log file already exists, it will be appended to instead of overwritten. You do not need to specify a value for this parameter; its existence will set it. In fact, if you specify a value, even *false*, it will be ignored!
Encoding	Used to specify the encoding that will be used to write the log file. This is interpreted by the *System.Text.Encoding.GetEncoding(string)* method. The default value is the default encoding for the system.
Logfile	Specifies the path to where the log file will be written. The default value is *msbuild.log*.
Verbosity	Used to specify the value for the verbosity of the logger. This uses the same values as mentioned previously. The default value is *Normal* for MSBuild 2.0 and *Detailed* for MSBuild 3.5.

> **Note** Along with these values, all parameters for ConsoleLogger can be provided as well, but there are some differences in default values. For example, text coloring is off as well as word wrapping.

You can specify the parameters using the /flp switch. You can set the verbosity to diagnostic by the command `msbuild Overview01.proj /fl /flp:v=diag`. The same for 2.0 syntax is `msbuild Overview01.proj /l:FileLogger,Microsoft.Build.Engine;v=diag`.

Building on the previous example, the command to attach a file logger that logs in diagnostic mode to a file named overview.log would be `msbuild Overview01.proj /fl /flp:Verbosity=diag;logfile=overview.log` in MSBuild 3.5 syntax. In MSBuild 2.0 syntax, that would be `msbuild Overview01.proj /l:FileLogger,Microsoft.Build .Engine; V=diag;logfile=overview.log`. You should note that when you are using MSBuild, you are free to attach any number of loggers as you desire; you can even attach more than one instance of the same logger. For example, a common scenario is to attach a file logger reading only errors and warnings, minimal verbosity, and another at a higher verbosity. This is a good idea because the log on minimal verbosity can be used to quickly determine where build errors occur, and the other(s) can be used to determine how to resolve them. The syntax to use for that would be `msbuild Overview01.proj /flp:v=m;logfile=overview.minimal.log /flp1:v=d;logfile=overview.detailed.log`. Now that we have discussed the preexisting loggers, let's move on to discuss creating custom loggers.

ILogger Interface

Before we can discuss how to create new loggers, we must first take a look at what loggers are. A logger is any object that implements the *ILogger* (Microsoft.Build.Framework.ILogger) interface. This is a simple interface; it contains only two properties and two methods. The class diagram for this interface is shown in Figure 5-3.

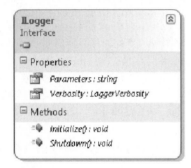

FIGURE 5-3 *ILogger* interface

The Verbosity property determines the level of detail that should be included in the log. If the verbosity is set by using the `/verbosity (/v)` switch on msbuild.exe, then this value is passed to each attached logger, but it can be overridden by parameters passed to individual loggers as well. The values for this are (in the order of least detail to most): Minimal, Quiet, Normal, Detailed, and Diagnostic. It is up to the writer of the logger to interpret what these values mean and how they change what events are being logged. MSBuild doesn't use verbosity at all itself. It just passes it on to loggers. (Some loggers also accept verbosity just for them, like the console and file loggers.) The loggers can ignore it completely. Also, you should know that the build (that is, the MSBuild files) cannot tell what the verbosity is and modify what is logged based on that.

The Parameters property is a string property that contains all the parameters that are sent to the logger. It is also the responsibility of the logger to parse the string for individual values. Typically, the string that is passed is parsed by loggers as key-value pairs separated by a semicolon. Loggers do not currently have the strongly typed properties interface that tasks do. Instead, they are passed the properties string directly and have to parse it themselves. We will now discuss creating custom loggers.

Creating Custom Loggers

There are three ways to create a new custom logger:

1. Implement the *ILogger* interface

2. Extend the abstract *Microsoft.Build.Utilities.Logger* class

3. Extend an existing logger

In Figure 5-3, we showed the *ILogger* interface, which all loggers must implement. The abstract *Logger* class has been provided to serve as a base class for new loggers. This class implements all the requirements of the *ILogger* interface except overriding the *Initialize* method, which is left to subclasses. The third option is most likely the simplest; all you have to do is extend an existing logger and override a specific behavior. We will see how to utilize all three methods in this chapter.

We will first take a look at implementing the *ILogger* interface. We previously discussed the Parameters and Verbosity properties, so we will now look at the *Initialize* method. The signature for this method is `void Initialize(Microsoft.Build.Framework. IEventSource eventSource)`. This method is called by the MSBuild engine before the build process begins. The passed-in object, *EventSource,* can be used to register build events that the logger is interested in. The event source is a class that contains a number of events, one per logging message type. By registering an event handler for these events, we get access to the event when it is raised by the MSBuild engine. Those events are summarized in Table 5-4.

TABLE 5-4 *IEventSource* **Build Events**

Name	Description
MessageRaised	Raised when a build registers a message.
WarningRaised	Raised when a warning occurs.
ErrorRaised	Raised when a build error occurs.
BuildStarted	Raised when the build starts.
BuildFinished	Raised when the build is completed.
ProjectStarted	Raised when a project is starting to build.
ProjectFinished	Raised when a project is finished building.
TargetStarted	Raised when a target is started.
TargetFinished	Raised when a target is finished building.
TaskStarted	Raised when a task is starting to execute.
TaskFinished	Raised when a task is finished executing.
AnyEventRaised	Raised when any build event occurs. In other words, all events raise their specific handler, and then raise an *AnyEvent*. If you have a simple logger, you can just subscribe to *AnyEventRaised* only.

Name	Description
CustomEventRaised	Raised when a custom build event occurs. This is used when an event doesn't fall into any other category; for instance, the *ExternalProjectStarted* event. This is used in the following way: 1. The user derives from *CustomBuildEventArgs* to define a new event args 2. Their tasks can fire it as desired. 3. MSBuild will route it. This exists so that you can pass arbitrary information to your logger. For this to work, you must follow the following rules: ■ The class must be serializable. ■ Implementation should be loadable by any node; that is, be careful if you put it in the same assembly as a task because one node could use *AssemblyFile* during the build, so the event args are found, but the other node uses *AssemblyName* and the type may not be found.
StatusEventRaised	Raised when a status event occurs. Status events include build started, build finished, target started, target finished, and so on.

Custom loggers can attach handlers to any number of these events. Each of these event handlers passes a specific subclass of *BuildEventArgs*. For example, a *TargetStarted* event will be passed a *BuildTargetStarted* event argument. The class diagram for this class is shown in Figure 5-4.

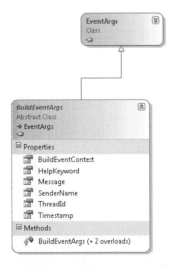

FIGURE 5-4 *BuildEventArgs* class diagram

All the event arguments that are passed to each individual event handler will contain at least this information; some will contain even more data. For example the *BuildWarningEventArgs* object contains additional information that helps identify where in the build script the warning was raised.

The samples contain the complete source to the IndentFileLogger. This is a very simple logger that logs messages with indentation depending on when the message was received. This is implemented using an int that keeps track of the current indentation. When a started event (for example, *ProjectStarted* or *TargetStarted*) is encountered, the indent level is increased. Conversely, when a finished event is encountered, then the indent level is decreased. The reason for discussing this logger is not the implementation, but how the results are logged to demonstrate the order in which these events are raised. When building the sample solution with this logger attached, the first section of the log is shown as follows. Note that some lines were truncated to fit this page.

```
BuildStarted:Build started.
    ProjectStarted:Project "InsideMSBuild.sln" (default targets):
        BuildMessage:Building with tools version "2.0".
        TargetStarted:Target "ValidateSolutionConfiguration" ...
            BuildMessage:Task "Error" skipped, due to false condition; ...
            BuildMessage:Task "Warning" skipped, due to false condition; ...
            BuildMessage:Using "Message" task from assembly ...
            TaskStarted:Task "Message"
                BuildMessage:Building solution configuration ...
                TaskFinished:Done executing task "Message".
            TargetFinished:Done building target ...
        TargetStarted:Target "ValidateToolsVersions" ...
            BuildMessage:Task "Error" skipped, due to false condition; ...
            TargetFinished:Done building target "ValidateToolsVersions" ...
        TargetStarted:Target "ValidateProjects" ...
            BuildMessage:Task "Message" skipped, due to false condition; ...
                    .
                    .
                    .
            TargetFinished:Done building target "ValidateProjects" ...
        TargetStarted:Target "Build" ...
            BuildMessage:Using "MSBuild" task from assembly ...
            TaskStarted:Task "MSBuild"
            BuildMessage:Global Properties:
            BuildMessage:  BuildingSolutionFile=true
```

IndentFileLogger starts each log message with the event type that raised it. From the preceding output, you can see the order in which these events are raised. *BuildStarted* will be followed by *ProjectStarted*, then *TargetStarted* and any task-related events inside of that. Messages, errors, warnings, and status events can be raised at any point during the build process. We will move on to discuss creating custom loggers by taking a look at a very simple logger, HelloLogger.

HelloLogger will not accept any parameters, and it will ignore the Verbosity setting. We will leave that for other examples later in this chapter. The *Initialize* method for this logger is shown as follows.

```
public void Initialize(IEventSource eventSource)
{
    // always writes to a log with this name
```

```
    string logFile = "hello.log";
    if (File.Exists(logFile))
    { File.Delete(logFile); }

    // initialize the writer
    writer = new StreamWriter(logFile);
    writer.AutoFlush = true;
    //this writer must be closed in the Shutdown() method

    // register to the events you are interested in here
    eventSource.AnyEventRaised += AnyEventRaised;
    eventSource.BuildStarted += BuildStarted;
    eventSource.BuildFinished += BuildFinished;
    eventSource.CustomEventRaised += CustomEvent;
    eventSource.ErrorRaised += ErrorRaised;
    eventSource.MessageRaised += MessageRaised;
    eventSource.ProjectStarted += ProjectStarted;
    eventSource.ProjectStarted += ProjectFinished;
    eventSource.StatusEventRaised += StatusEvent;
    eventSource.TargetStarted += TargetStarted;
    eventSource.TargetFinished += TargetFinished;
    eventSource.TaskStarted += TaskStarted;
    eventSource.TaskFinished += TaskFinished;
    eventSource.WarningRaised += WarningRaised;
}
```

In this method, we first initialize the writer to the file that will contain the contents of the log. Following that, we attach an event handler to all the available build events. Even though each event is assigned a distinct handler in this logger, each delegate performs the same operation: `writer.WriteLine(GetLogMessage(e));`. In the next code snippet, you can see the definition for the *ILogger* parameters, the *Shutdown* method, and a couple of helper methods. From the event handlers, only the *BuildStarted* event handler is shown; the other event handlers are implemented similarly. The full source is available with the code samples for this text.

```
void BuildStarted(object sender, BuildStartedEventArgs e)
{ writer.WriteLine(GetLogMessage("BuildStarted",e)); }

/// <summary>
/// This is set by the MSBuild engine
/// </summary>
public string Parameters
{ get; set; }

/// <summary>
/// Called by MSBuild engine to give you a chance to
/// perform any cleanup
/// </summary>
public void Shutdown()
{
    // close the writer
    if (writer != null)
    {
        writer.Flush();
```

```
        writer.Close();
        writer = null;
    }
}

public LoggerVerbosity Verbosity
{ get; set; }

protected string GetLogMessage(string eventName, BuildEventArgs e)
{
    if (string.IsNullOrEmpty(eventName)){ throw new ArgumentNullException("eventName"); }

    string eMessage = string.Format("{0}\t{1}\t{2}",
        eventName,
        FormatString(e.Message),
        FormatString(e.HelpKeyword)
        );
    return eMessage;
}

protected string FormatString(string str)
{
    string result = string.Empty;
    if (!string.IsNullOrEmpty(str))
    {
        result = str.Replace("\t", "    ")
            .Replace("\r\n", "\r\n\t\t\t\t");
    }
    return result;
}
```

From the previous snippet, we can see that the Verbosity and Parameters properties are implemented even though they are not used. Inside the *Shutdown* method is where the writer to the log file is closed out. The only other elements in this class are a couple of helper methods to get the log message from a build event argument, as well as a method to format the message for the logger. From the folder InsideMSBuild\Ch05\bin\Debug\Samples\, the command to build the Unittest.Proj1.csproj with HelloLogger attached would be

```
msbuild.exe ..\..\..\unittest\Unittest.Proj1\Unittest.Proj1.csproj
/l:HelloLogger,..\Examples.Loggers.dll.
```

If you execute this command, you will see a file, hello.log, written to the working directory. This is the log created by this logger. A portion of this log is shown next with some of the lines truncated.

```
BuildStarted     Build started.
StatusEvent      Build started.
AnyEventRaised   Build started.
MessageRaised    Overriding target "GetFrameworkPaths" in project ...
AnyEventRaised   Overriding target "GetFrameworkPaths" in project ...
MessageRaised    Overriding target "SatelliteDllsProjectOutputGroup" ...
AnyEventRaised   Overriding target "SatelliteDllsProjectOutputGroup" ...
ProjectStarted   Project "Unittest.Proj1.csproj" (default targets):
```

```
ProjectFinished  Project "Unittest.Proj1.csproj" (default targets):
StatusEvent      Project "Unittest.Proj1.csproj" (default targets):
AnyEventRaised   Project "Unittest.Proj1.csproj" (default targets):
MessageRaised    Building with tools version "4.0".
AnyEventRaised   Building with tools version "4.0".
TargetStarted    Target "_CheckForInvalidConfigurationAndPlatform" in file ...
StatusEvent      Target "_CheckForInvalidConfigurationAndPlatform" in file ...
AnyEventRaised   Target "_CheckForInvalidConfigurationAndPlatform" in file ...
MessageRaised    Task "Error" skipped, due to false condition; ...
AnyEventRaised   Task "Error" skipped, due to false condition; ...
MessageRaised    Task "Warning" skipped, due to false condition; ...
AnyEventRaised   Task "Warning" skipped, due to false condition; ...
MessageRaised    Using "Message" task from assembly ...
AnyEventRaised   Using "Message" task from assembly ...
TaskStarted      Task "Message"
StatusEvent      Task "Message"
AnyEventRaised   Task "Message"
MessageRaised    Configuration=Debug
AnyEventRaised   Configuration=Debug
TaskFinished     Done executing task "Message".
```

From the log file, we can see that HelloLogger successfully logged the build process as expected. Now that we've shown an example of creating a completely new MSBuild logger, we'll move on to discuss employing one of the other methods of creating custom loggers mentioned previously.

Extending the *Logger* Abstract Class

The definition for an MSBuild logger is that it implements the *ILogger* interface. You don't need to implement this interface directly; you can extend the *Logger* abstract class instead. When you extend this class, you need to provide the definition only for the *Initialize* method. The class diagram for the *Logger* class is shown in Figure 5-5.

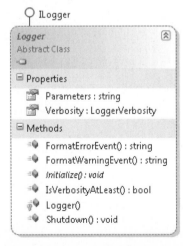

FIGURE 5-5 *Logger* class diagram

From Figure 5-5, you can see that there are three helper methods that can be used to help the logging process. Those methods are summarized in Table 5-5.

TABLE 5-5 Logger Methods

Name	Description
FormatErrorEvent	This can be used to format a BuildErrorEventArgs object into a readable string.
FormatWarningEvent	This can be used to format a BuildWarningEventArgs object into a readable string.
IsVerbosityAtLeast	Can be used to determine if the current verbosity setting of the logger is greater than the value passed in.

We will now create a simple logger that extends the Logger class and that makes use of both Verbosity and Parameters. This logger builds on the previous example and is called HelloLogger2.

The HelloLogger2 logger will parse the parameters as well as use the verbosity setting to determine what messages should be placed in the log file. In this logger, the Initialize method has changed a little bit; the most significant change is that the method InitializeParameters is called. The next snippet contains this method and a few supporting methods. In the snippet, I have bolded a few key elements that we will discuss.

```
public override void Initialize(IEventSource eventSource)
{
    // parse the values passed in as parameters
    InitializeParameters();

    if (string.IsNullOrEmpty(LogFile))
    {
        //apply default log name here
        LogFile = "hello2.log";
    }

    if (File.Exists(LogFile))
    { File.Delete(LogFile); }

    // initialize the writer
    writer = new StreamWriter(LogFile);

    // register to the events you are interested in here
        eventSource.BuildStarted += BuildStarted;
        eventSource.BuildFinished += BuildFinished;
        eventSource.CustomEventRaised += CustomEvent;
        eventSource.ErrorRaised += ErrorRaised;
        eventSource.MessageRaised += MessageRaised;
        eventSource.ProjectStarted += ProjectStarted;
        eventSource.ProjectStarted += ProjectFinished;
        eventSource.TargetStarted += TargetStarted;
        eventSource.TargetFinished += TargetFinished;
```

```csharp
        eventSource.TaskStarted += TaskStarted;
        eventSource.TaskFinished += TaskFinished;
        eventSource.WarningRaised += WarningRaised;
}
/// <summary>
/// Read values form <c>Parameters</c> string and populate
/// other properties.
/// </summary>
protected virtual void InitializeParameters()
{
    try
    {
        if (!string.IsNullOrEmpty(Parameters))
        {
            // Parameters string should be in the format:
            //   Prop1=value1;Prop2=value2;Prop3=value;...
            foreach (string paramString in
                this.Parameters.Split(new char[] {';'}))
            {
                // now we have Prop1=value1
                string[] keyValue =
                    paramString.Split(new char[] {'='});
                if (keyValue == null || keyValue.Length < 2)
                {
                    continue;
                }
                // keyValue[0] = Prop1
                // keyValue[1] = value1
                this.ProcessParam(keyValue[0].ToLower(), keyValue[1]);
            }
        }
    }
    catch (Exception e)
    {
        throw new LoggerException(
            string.Format(
                "Unable to initialize parameters; message={0}",
                e.Message),
                e);
    }
}


/// <summary>
/// Method that will process the parameter value.
/// If either <code>name</code> or
/// <code>value</code> is empty then this parameter
/// will not be processed.
/// </summary>
/// <param name="name">name of the paramater</param>
/// <param name="value">value of the parameter</param>
protected virtual void ProcessParam(string name, string value)
{
    try
    {
        if (!string.IsNullOrEmpty(name) &&
```

```
        !string.IsNullOrEmpty(value))
    {
        switch (name.Trim().ToUpper())
        {
            case ("LOGFILE"):
            case ("L"):
                this.LogFile = value;
                break;

            case ("VERBOSITY"):
            case ("V"):
                ProcessVerbosity(value);
                break;
        }
    }
}
catch (Exception e)
{
    string message = string.Format(
        "Unable to process parameters;[name={0}, value={1}] message={2}",
        name, value, e.Message);
    throw new LoggerException(message, e);
}
}


/// <summary>
/// This will set the verbosity level from the parameter
/// </summary>
/// <param name="level"></param>
protected virtual void ProcessVerbosity(string level)
{
    if (!string.IsNullOrEmpty(level))
    {
        switch (level.Trim().ToUpper())
        {
            case ("QUIET"):
            case ("Q"):
                this.Verbosity = LoggerVerbosity.Quiet;
                break;

            case ("MINIMAL"):
            case ("M"):
                this.Verbosity = LoggerVerbosity.Minimal;
                break;

            case ("NORMAL"):
            case ("N"):
                this.Verbosity = LoggerVerbosity.Normal;
                break;

            case ("DETAILED"):
            case ("D"):
                this.Verbosity = LoggerVerbosity.Detailed;
                break;
```

```
            case ("DIAGNOSTIC"):
            case ("DIAG"):
                this.Verbosity = LoggerVerbosity.Diagnostic;
                break;
        }
    }
}
```

The first highlighted line is found inside the *InitializeParameters* method, which calls the *ProcessParam* method for each parameter passed in. Once the Parameters string has been parsed, we have to interpret what it contains. The *InitializeParameters* method splits the string into an array of strings containing key-value pairs. As mentioned previously, the format of the Parameters string is entirely up to the logger. By convention, I have chosen to separate elements by a semicolon and to specify name-values in the format *<name>=<value>*. Unless you have a specific requirement that would not allow this, you should do the same.

The next highlight is on the usage of the LoggerException. This is a special type of exception that the MSBuild engine specifically handles. MSBuild loggers should throw this type of exception instead of any other exceptions. When this exception is thrown, it gives the MSBuild engine a chance to gracefully shut down the process. Once this exception is caught, the *Shutdown* method on all attached loggers will be called before the msbuild.exe process exits. If any other type of exception is thrown, MSBuild considers this a bug in the logger and logs the call stack to the console to help you to fix the bug.

The final item highlighted is the *ProcessVerbosity* method. This method is called inside the *ProcessParam* method to initialize the value for the verbosity. If a logger supports its own verbosity setting, one other than the current verbosity for the entire build, then it must do so through the parameters string. If you remember from the previous discussion, the default verbosity setting is determined from the /verbosity (/v) switch for msbuild.exe. This logger is able to have a different verbosity if a *Verbosity (V)* value is passed through the parameters string. If you create your own logger, you should be able to reuse the definition of this method to take care of this parameter for you.

We have now discussed how the parameters are parsed, so we can take a look at how the verbosity influences what log messages are sent to the log file. I based the types of messages that were being logged on messages that the console logger logs. There are two types of messages that you always want to log: Errors and Warnings. The next code snippet contains the handlers for these two events, as well as the BuildStarted and BuildFinished handlers.

```
void ErrorRaised(object sender, BuildErrorEventArgs e)
{
    // always write out errors
    writer.WriteLine(GetLogMessage("ErrorRaised", e));
}
void WarningRaised(object sender, BuildWarningEventArgs e)
{
    // always log warnings
```

```
        writer.WriteLine(GetLogMessage("WarningRaised", e));
}
void BuildStarted(object sender, BuildStartedEventArgs e)
{
    if (IsVerbosityAtLeast(LoggerVerbosity.Normal))
    {
        writer.WriteLine(GetLogMessage("BuildStarted", e));
    }
}
void BuildFinished(object sender, BuildFinishedEventArgs e)
{
    if (IsVerbosityAtLeast(LoggerVerbosity.Normal))
    {
        writer.WriteLine(GetLogMessage("BuildFinished", e));
    }
}
```

In the previous snippet, you can see that the errors and warnings are always written to the log, as previously mentioned. The BuildStarted and BuildFinished events are not always written to the log. These messages should be passed only if the verbosity is set to Normal or higher. This is accomplished by the bold "if" statements. If the events are paired, for instance *BuildStarted* and *BuildFinished,* you should make sure that the required verbosity for both messages is the same. In the previous snippet, both handlers check to see that the verbosity is set to Normal or higher. Of all the event handlers in this logger, the only handler that is a bit different is the *MessageRaised* event. The definition for that handler is shown in the next snippet.

```
void MessageRaised(object sender, BuildMessageEventArgs e)
{
    bool logMessage = false;

    switch (e.Importance)
    {
        case MessageImportance.High:
            logMessage = IsVerbosityAtLeast(LoggerVerbosity.Minimal);
            break;
        case MessageImportance.Normal:
            logMessage = IsVerbosityAtLeast(LoggerVerbosity.Normal);
            break;
        case MessageImportance.Low:
            logMessage = IsVerbosityAtLeast(LoggerVerbosity.Detailed);
            break;
        default:
            throw new LoggerException(
                string.Format(
                "Unrecognized value for MessageImportance: [{0}]",
                e.Importance));
    }

    if (logMessage)
    {
        writer.WriteLine(GetLogMessage("MessageRaised", e));
    }
}
```

The reason why this event handler is different from the others is that the *BuildMessageEventArgs* has an importance associated with it. Because of this, we have to examine the verbosity as well as the importance set for the message. This event is raised by the Message task, through an instance of the *Microsoft.Build.Utilities.TaskLoggingHelper* class. The value for the importance on the event argument comes from the Importance parameter passed to the Message task. Using this logger is similar to using the previous logger. In the next image, you can see how we attach HelloLogger2 with a log file named unittest.diag.log and a Verbosity setting of Diagnostic.

```
C:\InsideMSBuild\Ch05\bin\Debug\Samples>msbuild ..\..\..\unittest\Unittest.Proj1\Unittest.Proj1.csp
roj /t:Rebuild /l:HelloLogger2,..\Examples.Loggers.dll;logfile=unittest.diag.log;v=diag /nologo
Build started 9/19/2010 9:23:20 PM.
Project "C:\InsideMSBuild\Ch05\unittest\Unittest.Proj1\Unittest.Proj1.csproj" on node 1 (Rebuild t
arget(s)).
CoreClean:
  Deleting file "C:\InsideMSBuild\Ch05\unittest\Unittest.Proj1\bin\Debug\Unittest.Proj1.dll".
  Deleting file "C:\InsideMSBuild\Ch05\unittest\Unittest.Proj1\bin\Debug\Unittest.Proj1.pdb".
  Deleting file "C:\InsideMSBuild\Ch05\unittest\Unittest.Proj1\bin\Debug\nunit.framework.dll".
  Deleting file "C:\InsideMSBuild\Ch05\unittest\Unittest.Proj1\bin\Debug\nunit.framework.xml".
  Deleting file "C:\InsideMSBuild\Ch05\unittest\Unittest.Proj1\obj\Debug\ResolveAssemblyReference.
  cache".
  Deleting file "C:\InsideMSBuild\Ch05\unittest\Unittest.Proj1\obj\Debug\Unittest.Proj1.dll".
  Deleting file "C:\InsideMSBuild\Ch05\unittest\Unittest.Proj1\obj\Debug\Unittest.Proj1.pdb".
CoreCompile:
  C:\WINDOWS\Microsoft.NET\Framework\v4.0.30319\Csc.exe /noconfig /nowarn:1701,1702 /nostdlib+ /er
  rorreport:prompt /warn:4 /define:DEBUG;TRACE /reference:c:\WINDOWS\Microsoft.NET\Framework\v2.0.
  50727\mscorlib.dll /reference:"C:\InsideMSBuild\Contrib\NUnit 2.5.7\bin\net-2.0\framework\nunit.
  framework.dll" /reference:"c:\Program Files\Reference Assemblies\Microsoft\Framework\v3.5\System
  .Core.dll" /reference:"c:\Program Files\Reference Assemblies\Microsoft\Framework\v3.5\System.Dat
  a.DataSetExtensions.dll" /reference:c:\WINDOWS\Microsoft.NET\Framework\v2.0.50727\System.Data.dl
  l /reference:c:\WINDOWS\Microsoft.NET\Framework\v2.0.50727\System.dll /reference:c:\WINDOWS\Micr
  osoft.NET\Framework\v2.0.50727\System.Xml.dll /reference:"c:\Program Files\Reference Assemblies\
  Microsoft\Framework\v3.5\System.Xml.Linq.dll" /debug+ /debug:full /filealign:512 /optimize- /out
  :obj\Debug\Unittest.Proj1.dll /target:library Properties\AssemblyInfo.cs TestOperators.cs
_CopyFilesMarkedCopyLocal:
  Copying file from "C:\InsideMSBuild\Contrib\NUnit 2.5.7\bin\net-2.0\framework\nunit.framework.dl
  l" to "bin\Debug\nunit.framework.dll".
  Copying file from "C:\InsideMSBuild\Contrib\NUnit 2.5.7\bin\net-2.0\framework\nunit.framework.xm
  l" to "bin\Debug\nunit.framework.xml".
CopyFilesToOutputDirectory:
  Copying file from "obj\Debug\Unittest.Proj1.dll" to "bin\Debug\Unittest.Proj1.dll".
  Unittest.Proj1 -> C:\InsideMSBuild\Ch05\unittest\Unittest.Proj1\bin\Debug\Unittest.Proj1.dll
  Copying file from "obj\Debug\Unittest.Proj1.pdb" to "bin\Debug\Unittest.Proj1.pdb".
Done Building Project "C:\InsideMSBuild\Ch05\unittest\Unittest.Proj1\Unittest.Proj1.csproj" (Rebui
ld target(s)).

Build succeeded.
    0 Warning(s)
    0 Error(s)
```

FIGURE 5-6 HelloLogger2 usage

We can see that the logger was successfully attached to the build process and the expected log file was indeed created. Now that we have covered many details of creating custom loggers, we'll see how we can extend ConsoleLogger to create new loggers.

Extending Existing Loggers

In the previous section, we saw how we could create new loggers by implementing the *ILogger* interface and extending the *Logger* abstract class. The only other method to create a new logger is to extend an existing logger. We'll now see how to accomplish this by extending the console logger. The console logger can be used as a basis for various loggers, not just those that log to the console. You may be surprised to find out that the *FileLogger* class extends the *ConsoleLogger* class! In some cases, you could consider encapsulation (composition) instead of derivation. If you have too many levels of derived classes, it can be problematic to maintain. Some reasons that you should consider extending this class are outlined here.

- **Ease of Creation**   From the three methods listed previously for creating new loggers, extending an existing logger is the easiest method.

- **Automatic Indentation**   The console logger already has a sophisticated means for indenting the log messages to logically group log messages, as well as implementing rules to know when to show certain events. It's quite a lot of work to make a logger produce output that looks good. When you extend the console logger, you can get this functionality for free.

- **Consistent Verbosity Interpretation**   Because you are extending the console logger, you can let it determine what log messages need to be logged based on the verbosity setting instead of doing it manually.

Because of the advantages of extending the console logger, you should give it strong consideration before you implement the same logic. The console logger has five properties, which are summarized in Table 5-6.

TABLE 5-6 ConsoleLogger Properties

Name	Type	Description
Parameters	string	The property that contains the parameter string that was passed to the logger.
ShowSummary	bool	If true, then a summary of errors and warnings will be written by the logger.
SkipProjectStartedText	bool	If true, then the log message stating that a project that is beginning to build is not written by the logger.
Verbosity	Microsoft.Build. Framework, LoggerVerbosity	Determines the amount of detail that should be contained in the log. Possible values: *Quiet, Minimal, Normal, Detailed,* and *Diagnostic.*
WriteHandler	delegate	The delegate that will be called to physically write log statements. In custom implementations that are not logging to the console, you will need to override this property.

The values for the properties listed in this table will affect what statements will be logged and how they will be logged. For example, if your logger should never show the summary text, then you should set the value for ShowSummary to *false* and not allow it to be overridden. The most interesting property is the WriteHandler property. This is the delegate that will be called to place the messages into the log. The declaration for this delegate is `public delegate void WriteHandler(string message)`. If the console logger determines that a message should be logged based on event and verbosity, then this delegate is invoked to perform the write into the log. If you are creating a new logger to write to a destination other than the console, you will have to override this value. This is performed in the CustomFileLogger, which we'll now take a look at.

The CustomFileLogger is a new custom logger that, as its name suggests, writes its log to a file. It extends ConsoleLogger and overrides *WriteHandler* to achieve this. Earlier we stated the indentation is taken care of by the base class. When you override the *WriteHandler* method, the indentation has already been placed in the output. All *WriteHandler* can do is write the text of the log message. You cannot access the current indent level. The properties of this logger, as well as the *Initialize* and *Shutdown* methods, are shown in the next snippet.

```csharp
protected string LogFile { get; set; }
protected bool Append { get; set; }
protected StreamWriter FileWriter {get;set;}

public override void Initialize(Microsoft.Build.Framework.IEventSource eventSource, int
nodeCount)
{
    // default value
    Append = false;

    ParseCustomParameters();
    base.Initialize(eventSource, nodeCount);

    if (string.IsNullOrEmpty(LogFile))
    {
        // default value
        LogFile = "custom.build.log";
    }

    FileWriter = new StreamWriter(LogFile, Append);
    FileWriter.AutoFlush = true;

    base.WriteHandler = new WriteHandler(HandleWrite);
}

public override void Shutdown()
{
    base.Shutdown();
    if (FileWriter != null)
    {
        FileWriter.Close();
        FileWriter = null;
    }
}
```

In the *Initialize* method, you can see that it calls *ParseCustomParameters*, which will extract the values that have been passed through the logger's parameters. We will see this method shortly. In addition to this, the important items in that method are: base.Initialize is called, the file writer is initialized, and *WriteHandler* is overridden to point to the *HandleWrite* method. In the *Shutdown* method, the file writer is closed out to ensure that the stream is closed gracefully. Now we can take a look at how the parameters are parsed out; the related methods are shown here.

```
public virtual void ParseCustomParameters()
{
    if (!string.IsNullOrEmpty(Parameters))
    {
        string[] paramPairs = Parameters.Split(';');
        for (int i = 0; i < paramPairs.Length; i++)
        {
            if (paramPairs[i].Length > 0)
            {
                string[] paramPair = paramPairs[i].Split('=');
                if (!string.IsNullOrEmpty(paramPair[0]))
                {
                    if (paramPair.Length > 1)
                    {
                        ApplyParam(paramPair[0], paramPair[1]);
                    }
                    else
                    {
                        ApplyParam(paramPair[0], null);
                    }
                }
            }
        }
    }
}

public virtual void ApplyParam(string paramName, string paramValue)
{
    if (!string.IsNullOrEmpty(paramName))
    {
        string paramNameUpper = paramName.ToUpperInvariant();
        switch (paramNameUpper)
        {
            case "LOGFILE":
            case "L":
                LogFile = paramValue;
                break;

            case "APPEND":
                if (string.Compare(paramValue, "true", true) == 0)
                {
                    Append = true;
                }
                else
                {
                    Append = false;
                }
                break;
        }
    }
}
```

Inside the *ParseCustomParameters* method, I have bolded two lines of code. The first bold line, **string[] paramPairs = Parameters.Split(';')**, splits up the string based on ";" characters. This creates an array of strings that contain key-value pairs in the format *<name>=<value>*. The other bold line is **string[] paramPair = paramPairs[i].Split('=')**. This separates the key-value string into a key and value; then these values are interpreted by the *ApplyParam* method. I point these statements out to reinforce the fact that the logger itself is completely responsible for parsing and interpreting what the values in the string mean. Even the value for the verbosity is not automatically processed by the Logger class, but it is by the ConsoleLogger class.

Now that we have seen how CustomFileLogger was created, we can see how to use it. In order to attach this logger, as with any custom logger, we will use the /l (/logger) switch on msbuild.exe. We can see an example of attaching this logger in Figure 5-7, which shows the beginning of a build with this logger. The command for this from the \InsideMSBuild\Ch05\bin\Debug\Samples\ folder is

```
msbuild ..\..\..\..\Ch04\Examples.Tasks.csproj /t:Rebuild /l:CustomFileLogger,..\Examples.
Loggers.dll,
```

```
C:\InsideMSBuild\Ch05\bin\Debug\Samples>msbuild ..\..\..\..\Ch04\Examples.Tasks.csproj /t:Rebuild /
l:CustomFileLogger,..\Examples.Loggers.dll /nologo
Build started 9/19/2010 10:17:22 PM.
Project "C:\InsideMSBuild\Ch04\Examples.Tasks.csproj" on node 1 (Rebuild target(s)).
CoreClean:
  Deleting file "C:\InsideMSBuild\Ch04\bin\Debug\Samples\sampleFiles\four.txt".
  Deleting file "C:\InsideMSBuild\Ch04\bin\Debug\Samples\sampleFiles\one.txt".
  Deleting file "C:\InsideMSBuild\Ch04\bin\Debug\Samples\sampleFiles\sub\sub_four.txt".
  Deleting file "C:\InsideMSBuild\Ch04\bin\Debug\Samples\sampleFiles\sub\sub_one.txt".
  Deleting file "C:\InsideMSBuild\Ch04\bin\Debug\Samples\sampleFiles\sub\sub_three.txt".
  Deleting file "C:\InsideMSBuild\Ch04\bin\Debug\Samples\sampleFiles\sub\sub_two.txt".
  Deleting file "C:\InsideMSBuild\Ch04\bin\Debug\Samples\sampleFiles\three.txt".
  Deleting file "C:\InsideMSBuild\Ch04\bin\Debug\Samples\sampleFiles\two.txt".
  Deleting file "C:\InsideMSBuild\Ch04\bin\Debug\Samples\AspNetRegSqlExample.proj".
  Deleting file "C:\InsideMSBuild\Ch04\bin\Debug\Samples\Batch-File01.cmd".
  Deleting file "C:\InsideMSBuild\Ch04\bin\Debug\Samples\BatchTf01.proj".
  Deleting file "C:\InsideMSBuild\Ch04\bin\Debug\Samples\GetDate01.proj".
  Deleting file "C:\InsideMSBuild\Ch04\bin\Debug\Samples\HelloWorld02.proj".
  Deleting file "C:\InsideMSBuild\Ch04\bin\Debug\Samples\HelloWorld01.proj".
  Deleting file "C:\InsideMSBuild\Ch04\bin\Debug\Samples\HelloWorld04.proj".
  Deleting file "C:\InsideMSBuild\Ch04\bin\Debug\Samples\IT-Ref01.proj".
  Deleting file "C:\InsideMSBuild\Ch04\bin\Debug\Samples\IT-Ruby01.proj".
  Deleting file "C:\InsideMSBuild\Ch04\bin\Debug\Samples\MakeZinExe01.proj".
```

FIGURE 5-7 CustomFileLogger usage example

In Figure 5-7, we can see that the build for the Example.Tasks project is invoked with the new custom logger attached to the process. Since the build successfully started, we know that MSBuild was able to create a new instance of the logger and attach it to the process. If you repeat this command, you will see that a new log file, custom.build.log, has been created. We didn't specify a value for LogFile, so the default value is used, which is custom.build .log. As shown with the file logger, it is useful to attach multiple loggers to the build process. In order to do so, you simply use multiple /l switches. You can see this in action in Figure 5-8. The command here is

```
msbuild ..\..\..\..\Ch04\Examples.Tasks.csproj /t:Rebuild /l:CustomFileLogger,..\Examples.
Loggers.dll;v=m;logfile=custom.minimal.log /l:CustomFileLogger,..\Examples.Loggers.
dll;v=diag;logfile=custom.diag.log
```

```
C:\InsideMSBuild\Ch05\bin\Debug\Samples>msbuild ..\..\..\..\Ch04\Examples.Tasks.csproj /t:Rebuild /
l:CustomFileLogger,..\Examples.Loggers.dll;v=m;logfile=custom.minimal.log /l:CustomFileLogger,..\Ex
amples.Loggers.dll;v=diag;logfile=custom.diag.log /nologo
Build started 9/19/2010 10:27:15 PM.
Project "C:\InsideMSBuild\Ch04\Examples.Tasks.csproj" on node 1 (Rebuild target(s)).
CoreClean:
  Deleting file "C:\InsideMSBuild\Ch04\bin\Debug\Samples\sampleFiles\four.txt".
  Deleting file "C:\InsideMSBuild\Ch04\bin\Debug\Samples\sampleFiles\one.txt".
  Deleting file "C:\InsideMSBuild\Ch04\bin\Debug\Samples\sampleFiles\sub\sub_four.txt".
  Deleting file "C:\InsideMSBuild\Ch04\bin\Debug\Samples\sampleFiles\sub\sub_one.txt".
  Deleting file "C:\InsideMSBuild\Ch04\bin\Debug\Samples\sampleFiles\sub\sub_three.txt".
  Deleting file "C:\InsideMSBuild\Ch04\bin\Debug\Samples\sampleFiles\sub\sub_two.txt".
  Deleting file "C:\InsideMSBuild\Ch04\bin\Debug\Samples\sampleFiles\three.txt".
  Deleting file "C:\InsideMSBuild\Ch04\bin\Debug\Samples\sampleFiles\two.txt".
  Deleting file "C:\InsideMSBuild\Ch04\bin\Debug\Samples\AspNetRegSqlExample.proj".
  Deleting file "C:\InsideMSBuild\Ch04\bin\Debug\Samples\Batch-File01.cmd"
```

FIGURE 5-8 Attaching multiple CustomFileLoggers

The MSBuild command demonstrated in Figure 5-8 shows how we can attach two instances of the CustomFileLogger to the build process. One is set to a Minimal verbosity setting and the other to Diagnostic mode. The file custom.minimal.log will be used to quickly identify errors and warnings, and the custom.diag.log file can be used to diagnose the build process. With this content, we have now covered extending existing loggers, which was the third option for creating new custom loggers. Extending the console logger in this fashion is a good idea, but it does have some limitations. The most difficult limitation to deal with for some loggers is the fact that you are simply logging lines of text; you don't really have an idea of the state of the process. This is because the console logger is handling this and then simply calling into *WriteHandler* to handle writing text to the log file. One example where you would need to know which event caused messages to be logged would be if you were using XmlLogger. In order to create the correct XML element, you need to know what build event occurred. We will see how to do this now.

FileLoggerBase and **XmlLogger**

In order to demonstrate a realistic logger that doesn't extend ConsoleLogger, I will show you XmlLogger. The full source for this logger is available at my open-source MSBuild project, *http://codeplex.com/sedodream*, as well as in the samples provided with this text. By default, MSBuild will create a text-based log, but if you are going to feed this log to other applications for processing or presentation, it might be easier if you had an XML-based log. Since one doesn't ship with MSBuild, you can write your own. In this section, we will do just that.

Before we get into the implementation of the XmlLogger, take a look at the output from the logger shown next. The command, executed from the \InsideMSBuild\Ch05\bin\Debug\ Samples directory, is:

```
msbuild Properties04.proj /l:XmlLogger,..\Examples.Loggers.dll
```

The resulting XML file (with formatting changes to fit this layout) is shown in the next snippet.

```
<MSBuild>
  <Build Started="8/15/2010 1:39:09 PM"
         Verbosity="Normal"
         Finished="8/15/2010 1:39:09 PM"
         Succeeded="True">
```

```
    <Message>Build started.</Message>
    <Project Name="C:\InsideMSBuild\Ch05\bin\Debug\Samples\Properties04.proj"
             Message="Project &quot;Properties04.proj&quot; (default targets):"
             Started="8/15/2010 1:39:09 PM"
             Finished="8/15/2010 1:39:09 PM">
      <Target Started="8/15/2010 1:39:09 PM"
              Name="PrintEnvVar"
              Message="Target &quot;PrintEnvVar&quot; in project &quot;
                        C:\InsideMSBuild\Ch05\bin\Debug\Samples\Properties04.proj
                        &quot; (entry point):"
              Finished="8/15/2010 1:39:09 PM" Succeeded="True">
        <Task Started="8/15/2010 1:39:09 PM" Name="Message"
              Finished="8/15/2010 1:39:09 PM">
          <Message Importance="Normal">
                  Temp: C:\Users\Ibrahim\AppData\Local\Temp</Message>
        </Task>
        <Task Started="8/15/2010 1:39:09 PM" Name="Message"
              Finished="8/15/2010 1:39:09 PM">
          <Message Importance="Normal">Windir: C:\Windows</Message>
        </Task>
        <Task Started="8/15/2010 1:39:09 PM" Name="Message"
              Finished="8/15/2010 1:39:09 PM">
          <Message Importance="Normal">
            VS100COMNTOOLS: C:\Program Files (x86)\Microsoft Visual Studio
                    10.0\Common7\Tools\</Message>
        </Task>
      </Target>
    </Project>
    <Message>Build succeeded.</Message>
  </Build>
</MSBuild>
```

We will start our discussion by taking a look at the XmlLogger's base class *FileLoggerBase*. This is an abstract class that I have written to assist in the creation of file-based loggers. In Figure 5-9, you will find a class diagram for the XmlLogger.

From the class diagram, we can see that the *FileLoggerBase* class extends from the *Microsoft .Build.Utilities.Logger* class. The *FileLoggerBase* class adds some common functionality that will make creating loggers easier; most notably, it will read the values for the parameters shown in Table 5-7.

TABLE 5-7 *FileLoggerBase* **Known Properties**

Parameter	Description
LogFile	The name of the file to which the log should be written.
Verbosity	The verbosity setting for the logger. These can be specified by full name or short name.
Append	Value that determines if the file should be appended to, if it exists, or overwritten. If *false*, then the file will be overwritten if it exists.
ShowSummary	Value that determines if a summary should be displayed in the log. It is up to each concrete logger to determine how this affects the behavior of the application.

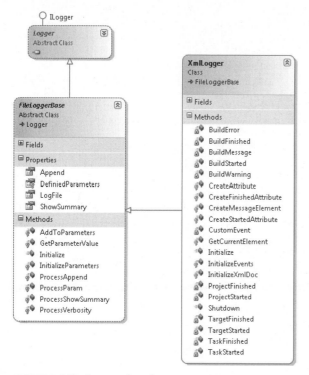

FIGURE 5-9 XmlLogger class diagram

When parameters are passed to the logger on the command line, they are made available in the Parameters property in the *ILogger* interface. This property is a string and needs to be parsed by each logger. *FileLoggerBase* will parse parameters that are passed in the format paramName=value;paramName2=value2;…. This is performed when the *Initialize* method is called. Now that we have discussed what *FileLoggerBase* basically takes care of, let's take a look at the XmlLogger implementation.

The XmlLogger uses a set of stacks to keep track of what needs to be written out to the XML document at the end of the build. The following example shows the definition of the *Initialize* method in the XmlLogger.

```
public override void Initialize(IEventSource eventSource)
{
        errorList = new List<string>();
        warningList = new List<string>();

        buildElements = new Stack<XmlElement>();
        projectElements = new Stack<XmlElement>();
        targetElements = new Stack<XmlElement>();
        taskElements = new Stack<XmlElement>();
        buildTypeList = new Stack<BuildType>();
```

```
        // apply default values
        LogFile = "build.log.xml";
        Append = false;
        ShowSummary = false;

        // have base init the parameters
        base.Initialize(eventSource);

        this.InitializeEvents(eventSource);

        this.InitializeXmlDoc();
}
```

In this method, we let the *FileLoggerBase* class take care of parsing the logger parameters, after which the class fields are initialized. In the *InitializeEvents* method, the build event handlers are registered with *IEventSource*. The following example shows the definition of the *InitializeEvents* method.

```
protected void InitializeEvents(IEventSource eventSource)
{
    try
    {
            eventSource.BuildStarted += this.BuildStarted;
            eventSource.BuildFinished += this.BuildFinished;
            eventSource.ProjectStarted += this.ProjectStarted;
            eventSource.ProjectFinished += this.ProjectFinished;
            eventSource.TargetStarted += this.TargetStarted;
            eventSource.TargetFinished += this.TargetFinished;
            eventSource.TaskStarted += this.TaskStarted;
            eventSource.TaskFinished += this.TaskFinished;
            eventSource.ErrorRaised += this.BuildError;
            eventSource.WarningRaised += this.BuildWarning;
            eventSource.MessageRaised += this.BuildMessage;
    }
    catch (Exception e)
    {
        string message = string.Format(
            "Unable to initialize events; message={0}",
            e.Message);
        throw new LoggerException(message, e);
    }
}
```

In the preceding snippet, you will notice in the catch block that it converts the Exception to one of type LoggerException. This is important because if your logger raises another exception, then it will be difficult to identify the logger as the reason for the build failure. Of the 14 events defined in the *Microsoft.Build.Framework.IEventSource* interface, XmlLogger registers to receive notification of 11 events. Figure 5-10 shows a class diagram for the *IEventSource* interface, which lists all the available build events. Table 5-4 includes specific information regarding these events.

IEventSource
Interface

□ Events

- ⚡ *AnyEventRaised*
- ⚡ *BuildFinished*
- ⚡ *BuildStarted*
- ⚡ *CustomEventRaised*
- ⚡ *ErrorRaised*
- ⚡ *MessageRaised*
- ⚡ *ProjectFinished*
- ⚡ *ProjectStarted*
- ⚡ *StatusEventRaised*
- ⚡ *TargetFinished*
- ⚡ *TargetStarted*
- ⚡ *TaskFinished*
- ⚡ *TaskStarted*
- ⚡ *WarningRaised*

FIGURE 5-10 *IEventSource* interface

After the events are registered with the event source, the logger will move on to initialize the XML document itself in the *InitializeXmlDoc* method. Since we have discussed how this logger is initialized, we can move on to take a look at a few of the handlers themselves. In the following example, you will see the definition for the *BuildStarted* and *ProjectStarted* events. In production code, exceptions would be properly handled.

```
void BuildStarted(object sender, BuildStartedEventArgs e)
{
    buildTypeList.Push(BuildType.Build);

    XmlElement buildElement = xmlDoc.CreateElement("Build");

    rootElement.AppendChild(buildElement);
    buildElement.Attributes.Append(
        CreateStartedAttribute(e.Timestamp));
    buildElement.Attributes.Append(
        CreateAttribute("Verbosity", this.Verbosity.ToString()));

    if (this.Parameters != null &&
        base.IsVerbosityAtLeast(LoggerVerbosity.Detailed))
    {
        // log all the parameters that were passed to the logger
        XmlElement paramElement =
            xmlDoc.CreateElement("LoggerParameters");
        buildElement.AppendChild(paramElement);
        foreach (string current in DefiniedParameters)
        {
            XmlElement currentElement =
                xmlDoc.CreateElement("Parameter");
            currentElement.InnerText =
```

```
                        current + "=" + GetParameterValue(current);
                paramElement.AppendChild(currentElement);
            }
        }

        buildElement.AppendChild(CreateMessageElement(e.Message));

        buildElements.Push(buildElement);
    }

    void ProjectStarted(object sender, ProjectStartedEventArgs e)
    {
        buildTypeList.Push(BuildType.Project);

        XmlElement projectElement = xmlDoc.CreateElement("Project");
        projectElements.Push(projectElement);

        buildElements.Peek().AppendChild(projectElement);

        projectElement.Attributes.Append(
            CreateAttribute("Name", e.ProjectFile));

        projectElement.Attributes.Append(
            CreateAttribute("Message", e.Message));
        projectElement.Attributes.Append(
            CreateStartedAttribute(e.Timestamp));

        if (base.IsVerbosityAtLeast(LoggerVerbosity.Detailed))
        {
            projectElement.Attributes.Append(
                CreateAttribute("SenderName", e.SenderName));
        }

        if (base.IsVerbosityAtLeast(LoggerVerbosity.Diagnostic))
        {
            XmlElement propertiesElement =
                xmlDoc.CreateElement("Properties");
            projectElement.AppendChild(propertiesElement);

            foreach (DictionaryEntry current in e.Properties)
            {
                if (current.Equals(null) ||
                    current.Key == null ||
                    string.IsNullOrEmpty(current.Key.ToString()) ||
                    current.Value == null ||
                    string.IsNullOrEmpty(current.Value.ToString()))
                {
                    continue;
                }
                XmlElement newElement =
                    xmlDoc.CreateElement(current.Key.ToString());
                newElement.InnerText = current.Value.ToString();
                propertiesElement.AppendChild(newElement);
            }
        }
    }
```

As was stated previously, each logger must interpret what the logger verbosity means. In the two preceding methods, you can see that in a few locations, the verbosity is checked before actions are performed. An example of attaching XmlLogger to a build is shown in Figure 5-11.

```
C:\InsideMSBuild\Ch05\bin\Debug\Samples>msbuild ..\..\..\..\Ch04\Examples.Tasks.csproj /t:Rebuild /
l:XmlLogger,..\Examples.Loggers.dll;v=d;logfile=build.detailed.xml /nologo
Build started 9/20/2010 9:56:19 PM.
Project "C:\InsideMSBuild\Ch04\Examples.Tasks.csproj" on node 1 (Rebuild target(s)).
CoreClean:
  Deleting file "C:\InsideMSBuild\Ch04\bin\Debug\Samples\sampleFiles\four.txt".
  Deleting file "C:\InsideMSBuild\Ch04\bin\Debug\Samples\sampleFiles\one.txt".
  Deleting file "C:\InsideMSBuild\Ch04\bin\Debug\Samples\sampleFiles\sub\sub_four.txt".
  Deleting file "C:\InsideMSBuild\Ch04\bin\Debug\Samples\sampleFiles\sub\sub_one.txt".
  Deleting file "C:\InsideMSBuild\Ch04\bin\Debug\Samples\sampleFiles\sub\sub_three.txt".
  Deleting file "C:\InsideMSBuild\Ch04\bin\Debug\Samples\sampleFiles\sub\sub_two.txt".
  Deleting file "C:\InsideMSBuild\Ch04\bin\Debug\Samples\sampleFiles\three.txt".
  Deleting file "C:\InsideMSBuild\Ch04\bin\Debug\Samples\sampleFiles\two.txt".
  Deleting file "C:\InsideMSBuild\Ch04\bin\Debug\Samples\AspNetRegSqlExample.proj".
  Deleting file "C:\InsideMSBuild\Ch04\bin\Debug\Samples\Batch-File01.cmd".
  Deleting file "C:\InsideMSBuild\Ch04\bin\Debug\Samples\BatchTf01.proj".
  Deleting file "C:\InsideMSBuild\Ch04\bin\Debug\Samples\GetDate01.proj".
  Deleting file "C:\InsideMSBuild\Ch04\bin\Debug\Samples\HelloWorld02.proj".
  Deleting file "C:\InsideMSBuild\Ch04\bin\Debug\Samples\HelloWorld01.proj".
  Deleting file "C:\InsideMSBuild\Ch04\bin\Debug\Samples\HelloWorld04.proj".
  Deleting file "C:\InsideMSBuild\Ch04\bin\Debug\Samples\IT-Ref01.proj".
  Deleting file "C:\InsideMSBuild\Ch04\bin\Debug\Samples\IT-Ruby01.proj".
```

FIGURE 5-11 XmlLogger

In the build command shown in the Figure 5-11, XmlLogger was attached to the build process. The parameters for that instance specified that the verbosity be set to Detailed and that the log file be placed at build.detailed.xml. This was indeed the behavior and can be confirmed by executing this same statement. Now that we have examined XmlLogger, we can move on to briefly discuss debugging custom loggers.

Debugging Loggers

Custom loggers are very easy to write, and for the most part, they are easy to implement as well. Still, if you are creating new loggers, you may need to debug the behavior. Debugging custom loggers is very similar to debugging custom tasks. Just like debugging custom tasks, there are three methods that can be used to debug loggers:

1. Examine the contents of the log.

2. Use Debugger.Launch().

3. Start MSBuild as an external program.

The simplest and least informative approach is the first one, which entails simply examining the contents of the log to determine the behavior of the logger. If you decide to use this technique, you may want to set the verbosity of the logger to either Detailed or Diagnostic, if possible. This method can be used only for very simple issues and for those that allow the logger to be properly initialized. If there is an initialization error when creating a logger, the build process is aborted and no log is written. Unlike the other approaches, this is non-interactive and there is no debugger. For the other two techniques, the Microsoft Visual Studio debugger will be used.

In the second option, the Debugger.Launch() technique, is that when the statement is executed, a dialog will be shown to attach a debugger once you attach Visual Studio to the build process. This dialog is shown in Figure 5-12.

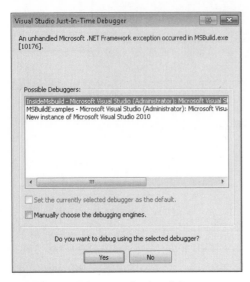

FIGURE 5-12 Debugger selection dialog

After you have completed this, Visual Studio will be attached to the process and it will stop at any breakpoints you set. Normal debugging will continue from here. The pros and cons of this approach were covered in the previous chapter, so they will not be repeated here.

The last approach, starting MSBuild as an external program, is the same as covered in the previous chapter, but we will quickly review this here as well. For the project that contains the logger, you can change the Debug Start Action. All the settings can be set on the Properties page for the Project under the Debug tab. On this tab, there are three values that you will need to fill in: Start External Program, Command Line Arguments, and Working Directory. The value for Start External Program should contain the full path to the executable that you want to run; in this case the full path to msbuild.exe. The Command Line Arguments value should contain the project file to build, the statement to attach the logger, and any other properties that you want to pass. The working directory should be set to any known directory, but ideally to a directory under the output folder for the project. This may simplify the project file used for debugging. For a more detailed description of these, you can refer back to Chapter 4, "Custom Tasks." A sample set of properties to debug CustomFileLogger is shown in Figure 5-13.

The values that were discussed previously are highlighted in Figure 5-13. Now we have discussed the three main ways that you can debug custom MSBuild loggers.

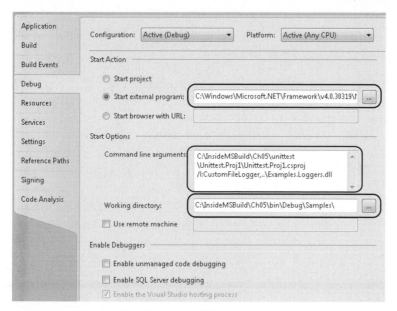

FIGURE 5-13 Debug settings for CustomFileLogger

As you've seen in this chapter, creating MSBuild loggers is very easy and very powerful. We have covered a lot of material in this chapter, including creating loggers, passing values to loggers, extending existing loggers, and debugging loggers. If you need to create new MSBuild loggers, you should now have a great arsenal with which to do so. The best way to learn how to create good loggers is by creating loggers. I strongly suggest simply diving in and getting started. You should note that there is another kind of logger that you can create, distributed loggers, which was intended for multiprocessor builds. In addition, there are two other advanced interfaces, *INodeLogger* and *IForwardingLogger,* which you can implement, but these are for very specific cases and will not be covered here. These types of loggers are more complex and suitable for only a limited set of applications, so we will not cover them in this book. In the next chapter, we will cover two very important but very elusive subjects: batching and incremental building. Knowing about these topics will turn good build scripts into great ones.

Part III
Advanced MSBuild Topics

Chapter 6
Batching and Incremental Builds

Batching and incremental building are two very important yet potentially confusing topics. In this chapter, we will describe these two topics in great detail. Batching, at a high level, allows you to repeatedly perform an action over a set of inputs. Incremental building is a process that enables MSBuild to determine when target outputs are already up to date and can be skipped. These two topics are advanced and closely related to each other. After you read this chapter, you will be able to take your build scripts to the next level.

Batching Overview

During a build process, you typically deal with many files, and very often you need to handle files that are categorized. For instance, you have files that are sent to the compiler, files that are resources, files that are references, and so on. Because of how common this is, MSBuild has a construct that is designed for it. Since MSBuild is a declarative language, as opposed to an imperative one, there must be a way to describe the operation you desire and let MSBuild take care of the looping for you. This concept is referred to as *batching*. Batching is an advanced topic that can be confusing, but it is also very powerful. Batching is a mechanism for placing items into groups, also referred to as batches, based on matching metadata. Batching always occurs on metadata; items with the same value for batched metadata will reside in the same batch. You can think of these batches as buckets; each bucket represents a set of files with the same values for the batched metadata. There are two kinds of batching: task batching and target batching. Task batching is where you execute a given task once per batch, and target batching is where a target is executed once per batch. Task batching is far more useful than target batching. Note that batches are not required to contain more than one item; many times, they include only one.

Here is an example, taken from the file Batching01.proj.

```
<Project xmlns="http://schemas.microsoft.com/developer/msbuild/2003"
        ToolsVersion=-"4.0">
  <PropertyGroup>
    <SourceFolder>src\</SourceFolder>
  </PropertyGroup>

  <ItemGroup>
    <SourceFiles Include="$(SourceFolder)*.txt" />
  </ItemGroup>
```

```
    <Target Name="TaskBatching">
      <!-- Transforms items into single string -->
      <Message Text="--------------------------------------------" />
      <Message Text="Not batched @(SourceFiles->'%(FullPath)')" />
      <!-- Invokes message task per each batch -->
      <Message Text="--------------------------------------------" />
      <Message Text="Batched %(SourceFiles.FullPath)" />
    </Target>
</Project>
```

In this project, we declare the SourceFiles item to include all files ending in .txt located in the src folder. Figure 6-1 depicts the file/folder structure in which the project file is located.

```
─src
  │    01.txt
  │    02.txt
  │    03.txt
  │    04.txt
  │
  └──sub
          sub_01.txt
          sub_02.txt
          sub_03.txt
          sub_04.txt
```

FIGURE 6-1 Directory structure

From this image, we can expect that the SourceFiles item will contain the four files in the src folder. Inside the TaskBatching target, you can see that we simply invoke the message task a few times. We can examine the output closely and describe where the batching is occurring. The result is shown in Figure 6-2.

```
C:\InsideMSBuild\Ch06>msbuild Batching01.proj /t:TaskBatching /nologo
Build started 9/22/2010 9:37:18 PM.
Project "C:\InsideMSBuild\Ch06\Batching01.proj" on node 1 (TaskBatching target(s)).
TaskBatching:
  --------------------------------------------
  Not batched C:\InsideMSBuild\Ch06\src\01.txt;C:\InsideMSBuild\Ch06\src\02.txt;C:\InsideMSBuild\C
  h06\src\03.txt;C:\InsideMSBuild\Ch06\src\04.txt
  --------------------------------------------
  Batched C:\InsideMSBuild\Ch06\src\01.txt
  Batched C:\InsideMSBuild\Ch06\src\02.txt
  Batched C:\InsideMSBuild\Ch06\src\03.txt
  Batched C:\InsideMSBuild\Ch06\src\04.txt
Done Building Project "C:\InsideMSBuild\Ch06\Batching01.proj" (TaskBatching target(s)).

Build succeeded.
    0 Warning(s)
    0 Error(s)
```

FIGURE 6-2 TaskBatching target result

From the previous output, the most important thing to notice is that the statement <Message Text="Not batched @(SourceFiles->'%(FullPath)')" /> resulted in a single invocation of the Message task. This is obvious because the prefix Not batched is presented only once. On the other hand, the other statement, <Message Text="Batched %(SourceFiles .FullPath)" />, resulted in the Message task being executed four times, once for each file. Strictly speaking, it is once per batch, where the batch is defined by the metadata FullPath for SourceFiles. Because the *FullPath* value will be unique for each file (in this case), it creates batches that contain only one item. To describe this in a diagram, you can think of a target (without batching), as shown in Figure 6-3.

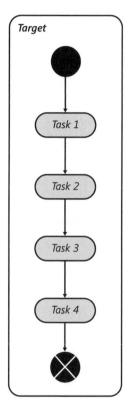

FIGURE 6-3 Visualization diagram of target (without batching)

In unbatched targets, each task is executed one after another until all the tasks have been executed. In contrast to this, when a batched task is encountered, the batches are created, and then each batch is passed to the task and executed. Note that the execution of these batches is not performed in parallel; each batch is processed *one after the other*. However, conceptually they are run in parallel, in the sense that no batch can see changes to items or properties made by another batch that ran before it. After each batch has been processed, execution continues. This is shown in Figure 6-4.

As shown in Figure 6-4, the MSBuild engine will automatically create the batches and pass the items into the task that is being batched. In the previous example, we created batches with only one item. Now, let's take a little closer look at how batches work. We will first examine task batching and then move on to target batching.

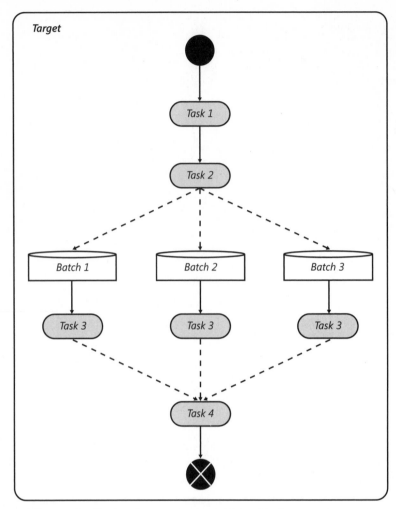

FIGURE 6-4 Visualization diagram of target (with batching)

Task Batching

As stated previously, task batching is the process of invoking the same individual task multiple times, each time with a subset of the original input items, where the input is defined by the batches created for the task. See the following example, which is contained in the Batching02.proj file.

```
<Project xmlns="http://schemas.microsoft.com/developer/msbuild/2003"
        ToolsVersion="4.0">
  <PropertyGroup>
    <SourceFolder>src\</SourceFolder>
  </PropertyGroup>
```

```xml
<ItemGroup>
  <SourceFiles Include="$(SourceFolder)01.txt">
    <CopyToOutputDirectory>Always</CopyToOutputDirectory>
  </SourceFiles>
  <SourceFiles Include="$(SourceFolder)02.txt">
    <CopyToOutputDirectory>PreserveNewest</CopyToOutputDirectory>
  </SourceFiles>
  <SourceFiles Include="$(SourceFolder)03.txt">
    <CopyToOutputDirectory>Always</CopyToOutputDirectory>
  </SourceFiles>
  <SourceFiles Include="$(SourceFolder)04.txt">
    <CopyToOutputDirectory>PreserveNewest</CopyToOutputDirectory>
  </SourceFiles>
</ItemGroup>

<Target Name="TaskBatching">
  <!-- Transforms items into single string -->
  <Message Text="--------------------------------------------" />
  <Message Text="Not batched @(SourceFiles->'%(CopyToOutputDirectory)')" />
  <!-- Invokes message task once per each batch -->
  <Message Text="--------------------------------------------" />
  <Message Text="Batched %(SourceFiles.CopyToOutputDirectory)" />
</Target>

<Target Name="TargetBatching" Outputs="%(SourceFiles.CopyToOutputDirectory)">
  <Message Text="CopyToOutputDirectory: %(SourceFiles.CopyToOutputDirectory)" />
  <Message Text="@(SourceFiles)" />
</Target>

</Project>
```

In this example, we first declare one item, SourceFiles, with four elements. Each element has the metadata CopyToOutputDirectory specified. Two elements have CopyToOutputDirectory set to Always, and the other two have it set to PreserveNewest. We'll examine the result of the TaskBatching target. This target, which is a copy of the previous example, invokes the Message task for the SourceFiles item once without batching, and then once with batching using the CopyToOutputDirectory item metadata. In Figure 6-5, you will find the result of executing this target.

```
C:\InsideMSBuild\Ch06>msbuild Batching02.proj /t:TaskBatching /nologo
Build started 9/22/2010 9:50:13 PM.
Project "C:\InsideMSBuild\Ch06\Batching02.proj" on node 1 (TaskBatching target(s)).
TaskBatching:
  --------------------------------------------
  Not batched Always;PreserveNewest;Always;PreserveNewest
  --------------------------------------------
  Batched Always
  Batched PreserveNewest
Done Building Project "C:\InsideMSBuild\Ch06\Batching02.proj" (TaskBatching target(s)).

Build succeeded.
    0 Warning(s)
    0 Error(s)
```

FIGURE 6-5 TaskBatching target result

The output is interesting. In the first invocation, we can see that the values for the CopyToOutputDirectory metadata were simply appended to each other and passed to the Message task, as expected. In the last invocation, we can see that the expression

%(SourceFiles.CopyToOutputDirectory) was evaluated into two distinct values, Always and PreserveNewest, and the Message task was invoked only once for each of those values.

Now that we have described batching and looked at some trivial examples, we will take a look at some more realistic applications of batching. The following example, TaskBatching01.proj, will take a set of files and then copy those files to a set of directories.

```xml
<Project xmlns="http://schemas.microsoft.com/developer/msbuild/2003">
  <PropertyGroup>
    <SourceFolder>src\</SourceFolder>
    <DestFolder>dest\</DestFolder>
  </PropertyGroup>

  <ItemGroup>
    <SourceFiles Include="$(SourceFolder)*.txt" />
    <Dest Include="$(DestFolder)One" />
    <Dest Include="$(DestFolder)Two" />
    <Dest Include="$(DestFolder)Three" />
    <Dest Include="$(DestFolder)Four" />
    <Dest Include="$(DestFolder)Five" />
  </ItemGroup>

  <Target Name="CopyAll">
    <!-- Task batching to copy files -->
    <Copy SourceFiles ="@(SourceFiles)"
          DestinationFolder="%(Dest.FullPath)" SkipUnchangedFiles="false" />
    <!-- Task batching to print message -->
    <Message Text="Fullpath: %(Dest.FullPath)" />
  </Target>

</Project>
```

In this example, we have defined two properties, SourceFolder and DestFolder. The SourceFolder contains the path to the folder that contains all the files that we would like to copy. The directory structure is the same as that shown in Figure 6-1. The DestFolder property contains the top-level path to the folder where the files will be copied into—actually, into folders under the DestFolder. From that file, take a look at the following item declaration.

```xml
<ItemGroup>
  <SourceFiles Include="$(SourceFolder)*.txt" />
  <Dest Include="$(DestFolder)One" />
  <Dest Include="$(DestFolder)Two" />
  <Dest Include="$(DestFolder)Three" />
  <Dest Include="$(DestFolder)Four" />
  <Dest Include="$(DestFolder)Five" />
</ItemGroup>
```

This creates the SourceFiles item, which contains all the files that are to be copied. Then it declares the Dest item, which contains a list of folders, under DestFolder. This is an example of using an item that doesn't point to a list of files. In this case, it points to a list of directories.

You can use an item for any list-based value, not only files and directories. Now let's zero in on the statement:

```
<Copy SourceFiles ="@(SourceFiles)"
    DestinationFolder="%(Dest.FullPath)" SkipUnchangedFiles="false" />
```

> **Note** SkipUnchangedFiles is set to *false* only for demonstrative purposes, to ensure that every file is copied each time.

In this task declaration, the expression %(Dest.FullPath) will cause the Copy task to be invoked once per batch, where the batches are created by an expansion of the FullPath metadata of the Dest item. Since the FullPath is unique, it will be executed once per element in Dest, so this expression is equivalent to the following set of statements.

```
<Copy SourceFiles="@(SourceFiles)"
    DestinationFiles="$(DestFolder)One" SkipUnchangedFiles="false" />
<Copy SourceFiles="@(SourceFiles)"
    DestinationFiles="$(DestFolder)Two" SkipUnchangedFiles="false" />
<Copy SourceFiles="@(SourceFiles)"
    DestinationFiles="$(DestFolder)Three" SkipUnchangedFiles="false" />
<Copy SourceFiles="@(SourceFiles)"
    DestinationFiles="$(DestFolder)Four" SkipUnchangedFiles="false" />
<Copy SourceFiles="@(SourceFiles)"
    DestinationFiles="$(DestFolder)Five" SkipUnchangedFiles="false" />
```

So we would expect all the files in SourceFiles to be copied into each of the four folders in DestFolder. The output of executing the CopyAll target is shown in Figure 6-6.

```
C:\InsideMSBuild\Ch06>msbuild TaskBatching01.proj /t:CopyAll /nologo
Build started 9/22/2010 10:05:53 PM.
Project "C:\InsideMSBuild\Ch06\TaskBatching01.proj" on node 1 (CopyAll target(s)).
CopyAll:
    Creating directory "C:\InsideMSBuild\Ch06\dest\One".
    Copying file from "src\01.txt" to "C:\InsideMSBuild\Ch06\dest\One\01.txt".
    Copying file from "src\02.txt" to "C:\InsideMSBuild\Ch06\dest\One\02.txt".
    Copying file from "src\03.txt" to "C:\InsideMSBuild\Ch06\dest\One\03.txt".
    Copying file from "src\04.txt" to "C:\InsideMSBuild\Ch06\dest\One\04.txt".
    Creating directory "C:\InsideMSBuild\Ch06\dest\Two".
    Copying file from "src\01.txt" to "C:\InsideMSBuild\Ch06\dest\Two\01.txt".
    Copying file from "src\02.txt" to "C:\InsideMSBuild\Ch06\dest\Two\02.txt".
    Copying file from "src\03.txt" to "C:\InsideMSBuild\Ch06\dest\Two\03.txt".
    Copying file from "src\04.txt" to "C:\InsideMSBuild\Ch06\dest\Two\04.txt".
    Creating directory "C:\InsideMSBuild\Ch06\dest\Three".
    Copying file from "src\01.txt" to "C:\InsideMSBuild\Ch06\dest\Three\01.txt".
    Copying file from "src\02.txt" to "C:\InsideMSBuild\Ch06\dest\Three\02.txt".
    Copying file from "src\03.txt" to "C:\InsideMSBuild\Ch06\dest\Three\03.txt".
    Copying file from "src\04.txt" to "C:\InsideMSBuild\Ch06\dest\Three\04.txt".
    Creating directory "C:\InsideMSBuild\Ch06\dest\Four".
    Copying file from "src\01.txt" to "C:\InsideMSBuild\Ch06\dest\Four\01.txt".
    Copying file from "src\02.txt" to "C:\InsideMSBuild\Ch06\dest\Four\02.txt".
    Copying file from "src\03.txt" to "C:\InsideMSBuild\Ch06\dest\Four\03.txt".
    Copying file from "src\04.txt" to "C:\InsideMSBuild\Ch06\dest\Four\04.txt".
    Creating directory "C:\InsideMSBuild\Ch06\dest\Five".
    Copying file from "src\01.txt" to "C:\InsideMSBuild\Ch06\dest\Five\01.txt".
    Copying file from "src\02.txt" to "C:\InsideMSBuild\Ch06\dest\Five\02.txt".
    Copying file from "src\03.txt" to "C:\InsideMSBuild\Ch06\dest\Five\03.txt".
    Copying file from "src\04.txt" to "C:\InsideMSBuild\Ch06\dest\Five\04.txt".
    Fullpath: C:\InsideMSBuild\Ch06\dest\One
    Fullpath: C:\InsideMSBuild\Ch06\dest\Two
    Fullpath: C:\InsideMSBuild\Ch06\dest\Three
    Fullpath: C:\InsideMSBuild\Ch06\dest\Four
    Fullpath: C:\InsideMSBuild\Ch06\dest\Five
Done Building Project "C:\InsideMSBuild\Ch06\TaskBatching01.proj" (CopyAll target(s)).

Build succeeded.
    0 Warning(s)
    0 Error(s)
```

FIGURE 6-6 CopyAll target result

From Figure 6-6, we can see that each file in the SourceFiles item was indeed copied to the individual directories defined in DestFolder. If you set the verbosity of the logger to Detailed, you will see that the Copy task was executed five times. Now that we have discussed task batching, we will move on to discuss target batching.

Target Batching

Target batching is similar to task batching in that an operation is invoked once per batch. *Task batching* is the process of invoking an individual task once per batch; target batching is executing a target once per batch. Target batching is driven entirely by the *Outputs* attribute of the target. Based on the batches created, the target is executed once per batch. Target batching is not used very much in practice, but task batching is. Take a look at the following file, TargetBatching01.proj, for a simple example.

```
<Project xmlns="http://schemas.microsoft.com/developer/msbuild/2003"
         ToolsVersion="4.0">
  <PropertyGroup>
    <SourceFolder>src\</SourceFolder>
  </PropertyGroup>

  <ItemGroup>
    <SourceFiles Include="$(SourceFolder)*.txt" />
  </ItemGroup>

  <Target Name="PrintMessage"
          Outputs="%(SourceFiles.Fullpath)">
    <Message Text="PrintMessage started" />
    <Message Text="@(SourceFiles)" />
  </Target>
</Project>
```

In the target PrintMessage, the value *%(SourceFiles.FullPath)* in the *Output* attribute means that the batches will be created using the FullPath metadata of the SourceFiles item. Then these batches will be used to represent the SourceFiles item. During each of the resulting target executions, as the batches are referred to using the SourceFiles item, it no longer contains all items, but instead a subset of the original item list being used with each batch. Take a look at the result of executing the PrintMessage target, as shown in Figure 6-7.

From the result shown in Figure 6-7, we can see that PrintMessage target was indeed invoked once per batch—that is, four times—for SourceFiles. Also, note that when target batching occurs, only the items in each batch are available when the item itself is referenced. For example, in the PrintMessage target, @(SourceFiles) is actually passed to the Message task, but only the files in the batch are printed.

Now that we have a better idea of target batching, we will examine an example that is a little easier to relate to. The following TargetBatching02.proj file demonstrates how to build a solution file for each of the defined configurations.

```
C:\InsideMSBuild\Ch06>msbuild TargetBatching01.proj /t:PrintMessage /nologo
Build started 9/22/2010 10:25:51 PM.
Project "C:\InsideMSBuild\Ch06\TargetBatching01.proj" on node 1 (PrintMessage target(s)).
PrintMessage:
  PrintMessage started
  src\01.txt
PrintMessage:
  PrintMessage started
  src\02.txt
PrintMessage:
  PrintMessage started
  src\03.txt
PrintMessage:
  PrintMessage started
  src\04.txt
Done Building Project "C:\InsideMSBuild\Ch06\TargetBatching01.proj" (PrintMessage target(s)).

Build succeeded.
    0 Warning(s)
    0 Error(s)
```

FIGURE 6-7 PrintMessage target result

```
<Project xmlns="http://schemas.microsoft.com/developer/msbuild/2003"
         ToolsVersion="4.0">
  <PropertyGroup>
    <SourceRoot>$(MSBuildProjectDirectory)\TestProjects\</SourceRoot>
  </PropertyGroup>

  <ItemGroup>
    <BuildFile Include="$(SourceRoot)TestProj1.sln" />
    <Config Include="Debug configuration">
      <Configuration>Debug</Configuration>
    </Config>
    <Config Include="Release configuration">
      <Configuration>Release</Configuration>
    </Config>
  </ItemGroup>

  <Target Name="BuildAll"
          Outputs="%(Config.Configuration)">

    <Message Text="Start building for configuration: %(Config.Configuration)" />
    <MSBuild Projects="@(BuildFile)"
             Properties="Configuration=%(Config.Configuration)"
             Targets="Rebuild" />
  </Target>
</Project>
```

The solution file is referenced in the BuildFile item. The other item, Config, defines the values for the configuration that should be used. These values are defined in the Configuration metadata. The BuildAll target is the one that builds the solution for each defined configuration. The batching is achieved by the attribute *Outputs="%(Config.Configuration)"*. The *Outputs* attribute is also related to incremental building, which is discussed later in this chapter. Target batching is a different use of this attribute. So the BuildAll target will be executed once per unique value of the Configuration metadata for the Config item, which is Debug and Release. If you execute the command msbuild TargetBatching02.proj /t:BuildAll, you will notice that the target BuildAll is indeed invoked once for Debug and once for Release. This configuration value is passed through to the build file using the Properties parameter on the MSBuild task. We have now provided an overview of task and target batching; the next section will describe the behavior of build scripts when combining task and target batching.

Combining Task and Target Batching

In this section, we will demonstrate ways to use task and target batching together. In this discussion, we will examine the following sample project file, Batching03.proj.

```xml
<Project xmlns="http://schemas.microsoft.com/developer/msbuild/2003"
         ToolsVersion="4.0">
  <ItemGroup>
    <Server Include="Server1">
      <Type>2008</Type>
      <Name>SVR01</Name>
      <AdminContact>Sayed Ibrahim Hashimi</AdminContact>
    </Server>
    <Server Include="Server2">
      <Type>2003</Type>
      <Name>SVR02</Name>
      <AdminContact>Sayed Y. Hashimi</AdminContact>
    </Server>
    <Server Include="Server3">
      <Type>2008</Type>
      <Name>SVR03</Name>
      <AdminContact>Nicole Woodsmall</AdminContact>
    </Server>
    <Server Include="Server4">
      <Type>2003</Type>
      <Name>SVR04</Name>
      <AdminContact>Keith Tingle</AdminContact>
    </Server>
  </ItemGroup>

  <Target Name="TaskBatching">
    <Message Text="%40(Server->'%25(Name)'): @(Server->'%(Name)')" />
    <Message Text="=========================================" />
    <!--
      Task Batching here using the Name metadata.
      Notice that Message task is invoked once per unique batch
      The same applies for %(Server.Type) below.
    -->
    <Message Text="%25(Server.Name): %(Server.Name)" />
    <Message Text="=========================================" />
    <Message Text="%25(Server.Type): %(Server.Type)" />
    <Message Text="=========================================" />
  </Target>

  <!--
    NOTE: Others targets defined here.
  -->
</Project>
```

This listing does not contain the full source for the project file; a few targets have not been shown yet. Instead, they will be covered separately later in this section. In this target, we have declared an item, Server, which contains references to four servers, each with three values for custom metadata. The custom metadata defined are Type, Name, and AdminContact. Following that there are four targets, which we will examine in detail now. The TaskBatching target demonstrates task batching once again. The first message statement, `<Message Text="%40(Server->'%25(Name)'): @(Server->'%(Name)')" />`, is a statement that does not start batching because that syntax results in the Server item being transformed into a single string and then passed to the Message task. This was inserted to print out the values to the logger. Following that, we first batch using the Name metadata with `<Message Text="%25(Server.Name): %(Server.Name)" />` and then similarly with the Type metadata. You can see the results of the TaskBatching target with the command `msbuild Batching03.proj /t:TaskBatching` in Figure 6-8.

```
C:\InsideMSBuild\Ch06>msbuild Batching03.proj /t:TaskBatching /nologo
Build started 9/23/2010 8:59:24 PM.
Project "C:\InsideMSBuild\Ch06\Batching03.proj" on node 1 (TaskBatching target(s)).
TaskBatching:
  @(Server->'%(Name)'): SUR01;SUR02;SUR03;SUR04
  =============================================
  %(Server.Name): SUR01
  %(Server.Name): SUR02
  %(Server.Name): SUR03
  %(Server.Name): SUR04
  =============================================
  %(Server.Type): 2008
  %(Server.Type): 2003
  =============================================
Done Building Project "C:\InsideMSBuild\Ch06\Batching03.proj" (TaskBatching target(s)).

Build succeeded.
    0 Warning(s)
    0 Error(s)
```

FIGURE 6-8 Result of TaskBatching target

From the result shown in Figure 6-8, we can see that, as expected, there were four batches created for the Server.Name property and two distinct groups created from the Server.Type value. To reiterate: When the batching is performed, MSBuild will identify the unique values in the batching expression and create the required groups. Now, we will move on to the targets that involve target batching.

In the next snippet, the TargetBatching01 target is declared, which is also defined inside the Batching03.proj file. Other sections of this file were shown previously.

```
<Target Name="TargetBatching01" Outputs="%(Server.Name)">
  <Message Text="===== TargetBatching01 ============" />
  <Message Text="%25(Server.Name): %(Server.Name)" />
  <Message Text="%25(Server.Type): %(Server.Type)" />
  <Message Text="Server: @(Server)" />
  <Message Text="================================" />
</Target>
```

The TargetBatching01 target creates batches with the Server.Name property. This is due to the attribute *Outputs="%(Server.Name)"* being present. When we execute this target, we would expect that it is executed once for each unique value for Server.Name. Since each name value is defined as being unique, we should see this target executed four times. The result is shown in Figure 6-9.

```
C:\InsideMSBuild\Ch06>msbuild Batching03.proj /t:TargetBatching01 /nologo
Build started 9/23/2010 9:01:37 PM.
Project "C:\InsideMSBuild\Ch06\Batching03.proj" on node 1 (TargetBatching01 target(s)).
TargetBatching01:
    ===== TargetBatching01 =============
  %(Server.Name): SVR01
  %(Server.Type): 2008
  Server: Server1
    ===============================
TargetBatching01:
    ===== TargetBatching01 =============
  %(Server.Name): SVR02
  %(Server.Type): 2003
  Server: Server2
    ===============================
TargetBatching01:
    ----- TargetBatching01 --------------
  %(Server.Name): SVR03
  %(Server.Type): 2008
  Server: Server3
    ===============================
TargetBatching01:
    ===== TargetBatching01 =============
  %(Server.Name): SVR04
  %(Server.Type): 2003
  Server: Server4
    ===============================
Done Building Project "C:\InsideMSBuild\Ch06\Batching03.proj" (TargetBatching01 target(s)).

Build succeeded.
    0 Warning(s)
    0 Error(s)
```

FIGURE 6-9 TargetBatching01 result

We can see that the target was indeed executed four times, once for each Server item, because the Server.Name value is unique. The TargetBatching02 target is a carbon copy of the TargetBatching01 target, with the exception of the *Output* attribute. The TargetBatching02 target node contains the attribute *Outputs="%(Server.Type)"*, which means that we will execute that target once for each unique set of value for the Type metadata on the Server item. The result of this target invocation is shown in Figure 6-10.

```
C:\InsideMSBuild\Ch06>msbuild Batching03.proj /t:TargetBatching02 /nologo
Build started 9/23/2010 9:13:56 PM.
Project "C:\InsideMSBuild\Ch06\Batching03.proj" on node 1 (TargetBatching02 target(s)).
TargetBatching02:
    ===== TargetBatching02 =============
  %(Server.Name): SVR01
  %(Server.Name): SVR03
  %(Server.Type): 2008
  Server: Server1;Server3
    ===============================
TargetBatching02:
    ----- TargetBatching02 --------------
  %(Server.Name): SVR02
  %(Server.Name): SVR04
  %(Server.Type): 2003
  Server: Server2;Server4
    ===============================
Done Building Project "C:\InsideMSBuild\Ch06\Batching03.proj" (TargetBatching02 target(s)).

Build succeeded.
    0 Warning(s)
    0 Error(s)
```

FIGURE 6-10 TargetBatching02 target

In the TargetBatching01 target, each target was executing with a context of a single value for the Server item. This is because the batching produced batches with only one item. In this sample, we are batching over the Type metadata, which has two unique values, among four different item values. If you look at the previous result, you can see that the statement `<Message Text="%25(Server.Name): %(Server.Name)" />` produces two values to be printed. This is because there are two items in both of the batches. This is an example of target batching on Server.Type and task batching on Server.Name. In the next section, we will discuss multi-value batches in more detail.

Multi-batching

When you get started with batching, it takes time to understand its behavior, and even more effort to utilize it effectively. Batching over multiple values requires a deep understanding of how batching works. In this section, we will take a closer look at batching, mostly through a series of examples.

We will first examine what the behavior is when we perform task batching with two different items. When a batched statement is encountered, MSBuild will create unique batches based on the *item itself* and the value for the metadata. What this means is that when you are using qualified batching statements, no batch will contain references to more than one item. A qualified batching statement is one that declares the item type as well as the metadata name. It is possible to batch without specifying the item type inside the %(EXPRESSION); we cover this in the section entitled "Batching Using Shared Metadata," later in this chapter. In the next snippet, you will find the contents of the Batching04.proj file. The complete source is not shown here; a few targets are shown later in this section.

```xml
<Project xmlns="http://schemas.microsoft.com/developer/msbuild/2003"
         ToolsVersion="4.0">
  <ItemGroup>
    <!-- Test1 items -->
    <Test1 Include="One">
      <a>A1</a>
      <b>B</b>
      <c>C</c>
    </Test1>
    <Test1 Include="Two">
      <a>A</a>
      <b>B1</b>
      <c>C</c>
    </Test1>
    <Test1 Include="Three">
      <a>A1</a>
      <b>B1</b>
      <c>C1</c>
    </Test1>
    <!-- Test2 items -->
    <Test2 Include="Four">
      <a>A</a>
      <b>B1</b>
      <c>C1</c>
    </Test2>
    <Test2 Include="Five">
      <a>A1</a>
      <b>B</b>
      <c>C2</c>
    </Test2>
    <Test2 Include="Six">
      <a>A</a>
      <b>B</b>
      <c>C2</c>
```

```
    </Test2>
  </ItemGroup>

  <Target Name="Task01">
    <Message Text="%25(Test1.a): %(Test1.a)" />
    <Message Text="------------------------------------" />
    <Message Text="%25(Test2.a): %(Test2.a)" />
    <Message Text="------------------------------------" />
    <Message Text=
      "%25(Test1.a): %(Test1.a) || %25(Test2.a): %(Test2.a)" />
  </Target>

  <!--
    NOTE: Others targets defined here.
  -->
</Project>
```

In this project file, there are two items declared, Test1 and Test2, both of which have metadata values for a, b, and c. In the Task01 target, the values for the a metadata are batched first separately, then together. The result from executing this target, shown in Figure 6-11, might be different from what you expect.

```
C:\InsideMSBuild\Ch06>msbuild Batching04.proj /t:Task01 /nologo
Build started 9/23/2010 9:24:14 PM.
Project "C:\InsideMSBuild\Ch06\Batching04.proj" on node 1 (Task01 target(s)).
Task01:
  %(Test1.a): A1
  %(Test1.a): A
  ------------------------------------
  %(Test2.a): A
  %(Test2.a): A1
  ------------------------------------
  %(Test1.a): A1 || %(Test2.a):
  %(Test1.a): A || %(Test2.a):
  %(Test1.a):    || %(Test2.a): A
  %(Test1.a):    || %(Test2.a): A1
Done Building Project "C:\InsideMSBuild\Ch06\Batching04.proj" (Task01 target(s)).

Build succeeded.
    0 Warning(s)
    0 Error(s)
```

FIGURE 6-11 Batching04.proj Task01 result

As you can see from the result in Figure 6-11, both items have the values *A* and *A1* for the a metadata. When they are batched together with the statement <Message Text="%25(Test1.a): %(Test1.a) || %25(Test2.a): %(Test2.a)"/>, the result is that the Message task is invoked four times, twice for the values on Test1 and twice for the values on Test2. When there are values for Test1, the values for Test2 are empty, and vice versa. This is why the message task outputs values for only Test1 or Test2, but never for both at once. We can get a better perspective of target batching by examining the result from the Target01 target. Target01 is shown in the next snippet, and it is defined in the Batching04 .proj as well.

```
<Target Name="Target01"
        Outputs="%(Test1.a)%(Test2.a)">
  <Message Text="%25(Test1.a): %(Test1.a) "/>
  <Message Text="%25(Test1.Identity) %(Test1.Identity)" />
  <Message Text="------------------------------------" />
```

```
    <Message Text="%25(Test2.a): %(Test2.a)" />
    <Message Text="%25(Test2.Identity) %(Test2.Identity)" />
</Target>
```

The result of executing this target is shown in Figure 6-12. In this example, I also print the value for the Identity metadata, which shows which items are included in the batch.

From the result shown in Figure 6-12, you can see that the Target01 target was executed four times, just like the Message task of the previous example. Just as in the previous invocation, when a value existed for Test1, there was none for Test2. We can now take a look at batching to build multiple configurations.

```
C:\InsideMSBuild\Ch06>msbuild Batching04.proj /t:Target01 /nologo
Build started 9/23/2010 9:37:05 PM.
Project "C:\InsideMSBuild\Ch06\Batching04.proj" on node 1 (Target01 target(s)).
Target01:
  %(Test1.a): A1
  %(Test1.Identity) One
  %(Test1.Identity) Three
  ----------------------------------------
  %(Test2.a):
  %(Test2.Identity)
Target01:
  %(Test1.a): A
  %(Test1.Identity) Two
  ----------------------------------------
  %(Test2.a):
  %(Test2.Identity)
Target01:
  %(Test1.a):
  %(Test1.Identity)
  ----------------------------------------
  %(Test2.a): A
  %(Test2.Identity) Four
  %(Test2.Identity) Six
Target01:
  %(Test1.a):
  %(Test1.Identity)
  ----------------------------------------
  %(Test2.a): A1
  %(Test2.Identity) Five
Done Building Project "C:\InsideMSBuild\Ch06\Batching04.proj" (Target01 target(s)).


Build succeeded.
    0 Warning(s)
    0 Error(s)
```

FIGURE 6-12 Batching04.proj Target01 result

Using Batching to Build Multiple Configurations

Many situations exist when you might need to build a set of projects for a set of defined configuration values. We'll examine how to do this now. The basic idea here is that you'll use the MSBuild task in order to build each project while passing in the Configuration property value. All the values for the configuration should be placed in an item so that they can be expanded using batching. The contents of the Batching05.proj file are shown in the next snippet.

```
<Project xmlns="http://schemas.microsoft.com/developer/msbuild/2003"
         ToolsVersion="4.0">
  <PropertyGroup>
    <SourceRoot>TestProjects\</SourceRoot>
    <OutputRoot>..\BUILD\BuildTemp\</OutputRoot>
  </PropertyGroup>
```

```xml
<ItemGroup>
  <AllConfigurations Include="Debug configuration">
    <Configuration>Debug</Configuration>
  </AllConfigurations>
  <AllConfigurations Include="Release configuration">
    <Configuration>Release</Configuration>
  </AllConfigurations>

  <OutputPath Include="$(OutputRoot)One\">
    <Path>$(OutputRoot)One\</Path>
  </OutputPath>
  <OutputPath Include="$(OutputRoot)Two\">
    <Path>$(OutputRoot)Two\</Path>
  </OutputPath>
</ItemGroup>

<ItemGroup>
  <Projects Include="$(SourceRoot)TestProj1\TestProj1.csproj" />
  <Projects Include="$(SourceRoot)TestProj2\TestProj2.csproj" />
  <Projects Include="$(SourceRoot)TestProj3\TestProj3.csproj" />
</ItemGroup>

<!-- Show an example of the Configuration batching deal -->
<Target Name="Task01">
  <!-- Build each project for each defined configuration -->
  <MSBuild Projects="@(Projects)"
           Properties="Configuration=%(AllConfigurations.Configuration)"
           Targets="Build"
           ToolsVersion="4.0"
           />
</Target>

<!--
 NOTE: Others targets defined here.
 -->

</Project>
```

In this file, there are two noteworthy items: Projects and AllConfigurations, described as follows:

- **Projects**   Contains a list of projects that should be built

- **AllConfigurations**   Contains the values for all the configurations that should be used during the build process

The Task01 target shown in the previous snippet demonstrates task batching. This target builds all the projects for the defined configuration values. This is achieved by calling the MSBuild task and passing in all the projects to be built, along with the value for the configuration. If you take a look at MSBuild task invocation, it uses the notation

@(Projects), which will send a list of projects to a single MSBuild task. The beginning of the build process for the Task01 target is shown in Figure 6-13.

From the result shown in Figure 6-13, you can see that the TestProj1 started building and then the TestProj2 started to build after that. If the full log were shown here, you would see that the TestProj3 project then started building. Figure 6-13 shows that the configuration used for the build was Debug. The remainder of the build not shown in Figure 6-13 is building using *Release* as the Configuration value. This works because the only value used for batching was *%(AllConfigurations.Configuration)*.

```
C:\InsideMSBuild\Ch06>msbuild Batching05.proj /t:Task01 /nologo
Build started 9/23/2010 10:04:23 PM.
Project "C:\InsideMSBuild\Ch06\Batching05.proj" on node 1 (Task01 target(s)).
Project "C:\InsideMSBuild\Ch06\Batching05.proj" (1) is building "C:\InsideMSBuild\Ch06\TestProject
s\TestProj1\TestProj1.csproj" (2) on node 1 (Build target(s)).
CoreResGen:
  C:\Program Files\Microsoft SDKs\Windows\v7.0A\bin\ResGen.exe /useSourcePath /r:c:\WINDOWS\Micros
  oft.NET\Framework\v2.0.50727\mscorlib.dll /r:c:\WINDOWS\Microsoft.NET\Framework\v2.0.50727\Syste
  m.Data.dll /r:c:\WINDOWS\Microsoft.NET\Framework\v2.0.50727\System.Deployment.dll /r:c:\WINDOWS\
  Microsoft.NET\Framework\v2.0.50727\System.dll /r:c:\WINDOWS\Microsoft.NET\Framework\v2.0.50727\S
  ystem.Drawing.dll /r:c:\WINDOWS\Microsoft.NET\Framework\v2.0.50727\System.Windows.Forms.dll /r:c
  :\WINDOWS\Microsoft.NET\Framework\v2.0.50727\System.Xml.dll /compile Properties\Resources.resx,o
  bj\Debug\TestProj1.Properties.Resources.resources
CoreCompile:
  C:\WINDOWS\Microsoft.NET\Framework\v4.0.30319\Csc.exe /noconfig /nowarn:1701,1702 /nostdlib+ /er
  rorreport:prompt /warn:4 /define:DEBUG;TRACE /reference:c:\WINDOWS\Microsoft.NET\Framework\v2.0.
  50727\mscorlib.dll /reference:c:\WINDOWS\Microsoft.NET\Framework\v2.0.50727\System.Data.dll /ref
  erence:c:\WINDOWS\Microsoft.NET\Framework\v2.0.50727\System.Deployment.dll /reference:c:\WINDOWS
  \Microsoft.NET\Framework\v2.0.50727\System.dll /reference:c:\WINDOWS\Microsoft.NET\Framework\v2.
  0.50727\System.Drawing.dll /reference:c:\WINDOWS\Microsoft.NET\Framework\v2.0.50727\System.Windo
  ws.Forms.dll /reference:c:\WINDOWS\Microsoft.NET\Framework\v2.0.50727\System.Xml.dll /debug+ /de
  bug:full /optimize- /out:obj\Debug\TestProj1.exe /resource:obj\Debug\TestProj1.Properties.Resour
  ces.resources /target:winexe Form1.cs Form1.Designer.cs Program.cs Properties\AssemblyInfo.cs Pr
  operties\Resources.Designer.cs Properties\Settings.Designer.cs
CopyFilesToOutputDirectory:
  Copying file from "obj\Debug\TestProj1.exe" to "bin\Debug\TestProj1.exe".
  TestProj1 -> C:\InsideMSBuild\Ch06\TestProjects\TestProj1\bin\Debug\TestProj1.exe
  Copying file from "obj\Debug\TestProj1.pdb" to "bin\Debug\TestProj1.pdb".
Done Building Project "C:\InsideMSBuild\Ch06\TestProjects\TestProj1\TestProj1.csproj" (Build targe
t(s)).

Project "C:\InsideMSBuild\Ch06\Batching05.proj" (1) is building "C:\InsideMSBuild\Ch06\TestProject
s\TestProj2\TestProj2.csproj" (3) on node 1 (Build target(s)).
CoreResGen:
  C:\Program Files\Microsoft SDKs\Windows\v7.0A\bin\ResGen.exe /useSourcePath /r:c:\WINDOWS\Micros
  oft.NET\Framework\v2.0.50727\mscorlib.dll /r:c:\WINDOWS\Microsoft.NET\Framework\v2.0.50727\Syste
  m.Data.dll /r:c:\WINDOWS\Microsoft.NET\Framework\v2.0.50727\System.Deployment.dll /r:c:\WINDOWS\
  Microsoft.NET\Framework\v2.0.50727\System.dll /r:c:\WINDOWS\Microsoft.NET\Framework\v2.0.50727\S
  ustem.Drawing.dll /r:c:\WINDOWS\Microsoft.NET\Framework\v2.0.50727\System.Windows.Forms.dll /r:c
```

FIGURE 6-13 Batching05.proj Task01 result

For a more complicated variation of the previous example, we will use an example where you need to build a set of projects for all the defined configurations, and you need to set the output path for each configuration to a different location. We can achieve this by a careful application of target batching. The next snippet, taken from Batching05.proj, contains the Target02 target, which demonstrates this.

```
<Target Name="Target01"
        Outputs="%(AllConfigurations.Configuration)">
  <!-- Build each project for each defined configuration -->
  <MSBuild Projects="@(Projects)"
           Properties="Configuration=%(AllConfigurations.Configuration)"
           Targets="Rebuild"
           ToolsVersion="4.0"
           />
```

```
</Target>
<Target Name="Target02" Outputs="%(Projects.Identity)">
  <PropertyGroup>
    <_CurrentProjectFilename>%(Projects.Filename)</_CurrentProjectFilename>
    <_CurrentProjectFullpath>%(Projects.Fullpath)</_CurrentProjectFullpath>
    <_CurrentOutputPath>$(OutputRoot)$(_CurrentProjectFilename)\</_CurrentOutputPath>
  </PropertyGroup>

  <MSBuild Projects="$(_CurrentProjectFullpath)"
    Properties="Configuration=%(AllConfigurations.Configuration);
    OutputPath=$(_CurrentOutputPath)%(AllConfigurations.Configuration)\"
    Targets="Rebuild"
    ToolsVersion="4.0"
    />
</Target>
```

The previous snippet contains two targets, which both build for all configurations. The Target02 target also specifies the output path. We will focus on Target02. In this target, I have chosen to batch with the Projects item instead of the AllConfigurations item. This is because I will need to use some other metadata values from the Projects, such as the file name. To accommodate for the change, I then batch the MSBuild task over all values for AllConfigurations. In that target, you will notice properties defined in the following way.

```
<PropertyGroup>
  <_CurrentProjectFilename>%(Projects.Filename)</_CurrentProjectFilename>
</PropertyGroup>
```

This takes the current value for the Filename for Projects item and places it into the property named _CurrentProjectFilename. Since we are batching the target on Projects.Identity, we know that the evaluation of that statement will be processed over only a single item value. This is needed because the statement %(Projects.Identity) cannot be used directly in the MSBuild task invocation. If this had been done, the task invocation would have been batched using two items, Projects and AllConfigurations. As stated previously, each batch will contain only one value. Because we need the value of Projects and AllConfigurations, we create properties to refer to needed Projects values and use those instead. In the MSBuild task used in that target, we are passing the Configuration property as well as the OutputPath property. So we will build for all configurations, and we override the output path while doing so. If we build that target, the result would be similar to that shown in Figure 6-14.

From the result shown in Figure 6-14, you can see that TestProj1 started building first for Debug, and then for Release. Following that, the TestProj2 project began building. We'll now move on to discuss another form of batching that was briefly mentioned before: batching using multiple expressions.

```
C:\InsideMSBuild\Ch06>msbuild Batching05.proj /t:Target02 /nologo
Build started 9/23/2010 10:18:34 PM.
Project "C:\InsideMSBuild\Ch06\Batching05.proj" on node 1 (Target02 target(s)).
Project "C:\InsideMSBuild\Ch06\Batching05.proj" (1) is building "C:\InsideMSBuild\Ch06\TestProject
s\TestProj1\TestProj1.csproj" (2) on node 1 (Build target(s)).
CoreResGen:
  C:\Program Files\Microsoft SDKs\Windows\v7.0A\bin\ResGen.exe /useSourcePath /r:c:\WINDOWS\Micros
  oft.NET\Framework\v2.0.50727\mscorlib.dll /r:c:\WINDOWS\Microsoft.NET\Framework\v2.0.50727\Syste
  m.Data.dll /r:c:\WINDOWS\Microsoft.NET\Framework\v2.0.50727\System.Deployment.dll /r:c:\WINDOWS\
  Microsoft.NET\Framework\v2.0.50727\System.dll /r:c:\WINDOWS\Microsoft.NET\Framework\v2.0.50727\S
  ystem.Drawing.dll /r:c:\WINDOWS\Microsoft.NET\Framework\v2.0.50727\System.Windows.Forms.dll /r:c
  :\WINDOWS\Microsoft.NET\Framework\v2.0.50727\System.Xml.dll /compile Properties\Resources.resx,o
  bj\Debug\TestProj1.Properties.Resources.resources
CoreCompile:
  C:\WINDOWS\Microsoft.NET\Framework\v4.0.30319\Csc.exe /noconfig /nowarn:1701,1702 /nostdlib+ /er
  rorreport:prompt /warn:4 /define:DEBUG;TRACE /reference:c:\WINDOWS\Microsoft.NET\Framework\v2.0.
  50727\mscorlib.dll /reference:c:\WINDOWS\Microsoft.NET\Framework\v2.0.50727\System.Data.dll /ref
  erence:c:\WINDOWS\Microsoft.NET\Framework\v2.0.50727\System.Deployment.dll /reference:c:\WINDOWS
  \Microsoft.NET\Framework\v2.0.50727\System.dll /reference:c:\WINDOWS\Microsoft.NET\Framework\v2.
  0.50727\System.Drawing.dll /reference:c:\WINDOWS\Microsoft.NET\Framework\v2.0.50727\System.Windo
  ws.Forms.dll /reference:c:\WINDOWS\Microsoft.NET\Framework\v2.0.50727\System.Xml.dll /debug+ /de
  bug:full /optimize- /out:obj\Debug\TestProj1.exe /resource:obj\Debug\TestProj1.Properties.Resour
  ces.resources /target:winexe Form1.cs Form1.Designer.cs Program.cs Properties\AssemblyInfo.cs Pr
  operties\Resources.Designer.cs Properties\Settings.Designer.cs
CopyFilesToOutputDirectory:
  Copying file from "obj\Debug\TestProj1.exe" to "..\BUILD\BuildTemp\TestProj1\Debug\TestProj1.exe
  ".
  TestProj1 -> C:\InsideMSBuild\Ch06\TestProjects\BUILD\BuildTemp\TestProj1\Debug\TestProj1.exe
  Copying file from "obj\Debug\TestProj1.pdb" to "..\BUILD\BuildTemp\TestProj1\Debug\TestProj1.pdb
  "
Done Building Project "C:\InsideMSBuild\Ch06\TestProjects\TestProj1\TestProj1.csproj" (Build targe
t(s)).

Project "C:\InsideMSBuild\Ch06\Batching05.proj" (1) is building "C:\InsideMSBuild\Ch06\TestProject
s\TestProj1\TestProj1.csproj" (2:2) on node 1 (Build target(s)).
CoreResGen:
  C:\Program Files\Microsoft SDKs\Windows\v7.0A\bin\ResGen.exe /useSourcePath /r:c:\WINDOWS\Micros
  oft.NET\Framework\v2.0.50727\mscorlib.dll /r:c:\WINDOWS\Microsoft.NET\Framework\v2.0.50727\Syste
  m.Data.dll /r:c:\WINDOWS\Microsoft.NET\Framework\v2.0.50727\System.Deployment.dll /r:c:\WINDOWS\
  Microsoft.NET\Framework\v2.0.50727\System.dll /r:c:\WINDOWS\Microsoft.NET\Framework\v2.0.50727\S
  ystem.Drawing.dll /r:c:\WINDOWS\Microsoft.NET\Framework\v2.0.50727\System.Windows.Forms.dll /r:c
  :\WINDOWS\Microsoft.NET\Framework\v2.0.50727\System.Xml.dll /compile Properties\Resources.resx,o
  bj\Release\TestProj1.Properties.Resources.resources
CoreCompile:
  C:\WINDOWS\Microsoft.NET\Framework\v4.0.30319\Csc.exe /noconfig /nowarn:1701,1702 /nostdlib+ /er
  rorreport:prompt /warn:4 /define:TRACE /reference:c:\WINDOWS\Microsoft.NET\Framework\v2.0.50727\
  mscorlib.dll /reference:c:\WINDOWS\Microsoft.NET\Framework\v2.0.50727\System.Data.dll /reference
  :c:\WINDOWS\Microsoft.NET\Framework\v2.0.50727\System.Deployment.dll /reference:c:\WINDOWS\Micro
  soft.NET\Framework\v2.0.50727\System.dll /reference:c:\WINDOWS\Microsoft.NET\Framework\v2.0.5072
  7\System.Drawing.dll /reference:c:\WINDOWS\Microsoft.NET\Framework\v2.0.50727\System.Windows.For
  ms.dll /reference:c:\WINDOWS\Microsoft.NET\Framework\v2.0.50727\System.Xml.dll /debug:pdbonly /o
  ptimize+ /out:obj\Release\TestProj1.exe /resource:obj\Release\TestProj1.Properties.Resources.res
  ources /target:winexe Form1.cs Form1.Designer.cs Program.cs Properties\AssemblyInfo.cs Propertie
  s\Resources.Designer.cs Properties\Settings.Designer.cs
CopyFilesToOutputDirectory:
  Copying file from "obj\Release\TestProj1.exe" to "..\BUILD\BuildTemp\TestProj1\Release\TestProj1
  .exe".
  TestProj1 -> C:\InsideMSBuild\Ch06\TestProjects\BUILD\BuildTemp\TestProj1\Release\TestProj1.exe
  Copying file from "obj\Release\TestProj1.pdb" to "..\BUILD\BuildTemp\TestProj1\Release\TestProj1
  .pdb".
Done Building Project "C:\InsideMSBuild\Ch06\TestProjects\TestProj1\TestProj1.csproj" (Build targe
t(s)).

Project "C:\InsideMSBuild\Ch06\Batching05.proj" (1) is building "C:\InsideMSBuild\Ch06\TestProject
s\TestProj2\TestProj2.csproj" (3) on node 1 (Build target(s)).
```

FIGURE 6-14 Batching05.proj Target02 result

Batching Using Multiple Expressions

Thus far, we have covered different ways of batching, but none of them have shown the behavior if there are multiple batching expressions for the same item. When you have multiple batching statements for the same item, such as `<Message Text="Type: %(Server.Type) Env: %(Server.Env)"/>`, then the MSBuild engine will create unique batches based on all metadata being batched. Here, you will find the Batching09.proj file; some targets were removed because we will be discussing them later in this section.

```
<Project xmlns="http://schemas.microsoft.com/developer/msbuild/2003"
        ToolsVersion="4.0">
  <ItemGroup>
    <Server Include="Server1">
      <Type>2008</Type>
```

```
          <Name>SVR01</Name>
          <AdminContact>Sayed Ibrahim Hashimi</AdminContact>
          <Env>PROD</Env>
      </Server>
      <Server Include="Server2">
        <Type>2003</Type>
        <Name>SVR02</Name>
        <AdminContact>Sayed Y. Hashimi</AdminContact>
        <Env>UAT</Env>
      </Server>
      <Server Include="Server3">
        <Type>2008</Type>
        <Name>SVR03</Name>
        <AdminContact>Nicole Woodsmall</AdminContact>
        <Env>PROD</Env>
      </Server>
      <Server Include="Server4">
        <Type>2003</Type>
        <Name>SVR04</Name>
        <AdminContact>Keith Tingle</AdminContact>
        <Env>DEV</Env>
      </Server>
    </ItemGroup>

    <Target Name="PrintTypeEnv">
      <!-- Batches over Type and Env -->
      <Message Text="Type: %(Server.Type) Env: %(Server.Env)"/>
    </Target>

    <!--
    NOTE: Others targets defined here.
    -->
</Project>
```

The PrintTypeEnv target uses batching for the Type and Env metadata from the Server item list. In this case, the batches will be formed by unique combinations of Type and Env metadata. If you execute the command msbuild Batching09.proj /t:PrintTypeEnv, the result would be what is shown in Figure 6-15.

```
C:\InsideMSBuild\Ch06>msbuild Batching09.proj /t:PrintTypeEnv /nologo
Build started 9/23/2010 10:25:53 PM.
Project "C:\InsideMSBuild\Ch06\Batching09.proj" on node 1 (PrintTypeEnv target(s)).
PrintTypeEnv:
  Type: 2008 Env: PROD
  Type: 2003 Env: UAT
  Type: 2003 Env: DEV
Done Building Project "C:\InsideMSBuild\Ch06\Batching09.proj" (PrintTypeEnv target(s)).

Build succeeded.
    0 Warning(s)
    0 Error(s)
```

FIGURE 6-15 PrintTypeEnv target results

In this case, there are three unique combinations of the Type and Env metadata, and there are two item values with Type=2008 and Env=PROD. Because of this, the Message task was invoked three times. This behavior is a little different from the examples in the section entitled "Multi-batching," earlier in this chapter. In that section, there were multiple batches created because different metadata was used from different item lists. In this case, we are using multiple metadata values from the same item list.

Here, you will find the other targets from the Batching09.proj file, which were omitted from the previously shown snippet.

```
<Target Name="PrintTypeName">
  <!-- Batches over Type and Name -->
  <Message Text="Type: %(Server.Type) Name: %(Server.Name)"/>
</Target>
<Target Name="PrintTypeNameEnv">
  <!-- Batches over Type, Name and Env -->
  <Message Text="Type: %(Server.Type) Name: %(Server.Name) Env: %(Server.Env)"/>
</Target>
```

These two targets also demonstrate batching with multiple values from the same item. Take a look at the results of the command `msbuild Batching09.proj /t:PrintTypeName;PrintTypeNameEnv`, shown in Figure 6-16.

```
C:\InsideMSBuild\Ch06>msbuild Batching09.proj /t:PrintTypeName;PrintTypeNameEnv /nologo
Build started 9/23/2010 10:33:50 PM.
Project "C:\InsideMSBuild\Ch06\Batching09.proj" on node 1 (PrintTypeName;PrintTypeNameEnv target(s
)).
PrintTypeName:
  Type: 2008 Name: SUR01
  Type: 2003 Name: SUR02
  Type: 2008 Name: SUR03
  Type: 2003 Name: SUR04
PrintTypeNameEnv:
  Type: 2008 Name: SUR01 Env: PROD
  Type: 2003 Name: SUR02 Env: UAT
  Type: 2008 Name: SUR03 Env: PROD
  Type: 2003 Name: SUR04 Env: DEV
Done Building Project "C:\InsideMSBuild\Ch06\Batching09.proj" (PrintTypeName;PrintTypeNameEnv targ
et(s)).

Build succeeded.
  0 Warning(s)
  0 Error(s)
```

FIGURE 6-16 PrintTypeName and PrintTypeNameEnv target results

In the first target, PrintTypeName, the batching is using the Type and Name metadata values. Since the Name metadata is unique, we would expect that the Message task be executed once for each value in the Server item list. From the results shown in Figure 6-16, you can see that this is indeed the case. This also holds true for the PrintTypeNameEnv target, which extends the first target by also batching on the Env metadata value. There is no limit on the number of metadata values that can be used for a task. Now we will take a look at why MSBuild allows batching expressions to be expressed without an item list name.

Batching Using Shared Metadata

The concept of shared metadata is not well known; it is a set of metadata that is common across more than one item type. For example, in VB.NET and C# project files, many different items can have a value for the DependentUpon metadata. There are scenarios in which you would like to batch using different item types that have identical metadata—that is, batching using shared metadata.

In all the examples we have discussed thus far, we have always qualified the item type in the batching expression. For example, we recently used the expression %(Projects.Identity). In this expression, the item type was Projects and we were batching on the Identity metadata. Consider this example: As you create projects in Microsoft Visual Studio, several item types allow a value for the *CopyToOutputDirectory* value. Some item types that support this include EmbeddedResource, Compile, Content, and so on. Instead of handling each set of files individually, it would be ideal if we could act on them all at once. You can do this by declaring a metadata expression without the item type. You will see this in the following Batching06.proj file.

```xml
<Project xmlns="http://schemas.microsoft.com/developer/msbuild/2003"
        ToolsVersion="4.0"
        DefaultTargets="PrintInfo">
  <ItemGroup>
    <None Include="None01.txt">
      <CopyToOutputDirectory>PreserveNewest</CopyToOutputDirectory>
    </None>
    <None Include="None02.txt">
      <CopyToOutputDirectory>Always</CopyToOutputDirectory>
    </None>
    <None Include="None03.txt;None4.txt">
      <CopyToOutputDirectory>PreserveNewest</CopyToOutputDirectory>
    </None>
    <Compile Include="src01.cs;src02.cs;src03.cs">
      <CopyToOutputDirectory>PreserveNewest</CopyToOutputDirectory>
    </Compile>
    <Compile Include="src04.cs;src05.cs">
      <CopyToOutputDirectory>Always</CopyToOutputDirectory>
    </Compile>
  </ItemGroup>

  <Target Name="PrintInfo">
    <Message Text="%(CopyToOutputDirectory): @(None) @(Compile)" />
    <Message Text="====" />
    <Message Text="PreserveNewest: @(Compile) @(None)"
             Condition="'%(CopyToOutputDirectory)'=='PreserveNewest'" />
    <Message Text="Always: @(Compile) @(None)"
             Condition="'%(CopyToOutputDirectory)'=='Always'" />
  </Target>
</Project>
```

Inside the PrintInfo target, the Message task is invoked with the expression %(CopyToOutputDirectory). The CopyToOutputDirectory metadata is being referenced without an item type specified. When this is the case, at least one item type must be passed to the task so that the MSBuild engine knows what item type(s) to use for batching. In this case, the Message task is referencing the None and Compile items, so it will create unique batches for CopyToOutputDirectory consisting of items from both the None and Compile item types. This works because both item types have the shared metadata CopyToOutputDirectory. You can see the result of executing this target in Figure 6-17.

```
C:\InsideMSBuild\Ch06>msbuild Batching06.proj /t:PrintInfo /nologo
Build started 9/24/2010 7:43:22 PM.
Project "C:\InsideMSBuild\Ch06\Batching06.proj" on node 1 (PrintInfo target(s)).
PrintInfo:
  PreserveNewest: None01.txt;None03.txt;None4.txt src01.cs;src02.cs;src03.cs
  Always: None02.txt src04.cs;src05.cs
  ====
  PreserveNewest: src01.cs;src02.cs;src03.cs None01.txt;None03.txt;None4.txt
  Always: src04.cs;src05.cs None02.txt
Done Building Project "C:\InsideMSBuild\Ch06\Batching06.proj" (PrintInfo target(s)).

Build succeeded.
    0 Warning(s)
    0 Error(s)
```

FIGURE 6-17 Common metadata batching, example 1

From the result shown in Figure 6-17, we can see that the statement `<Message Text="%(CopyToOutputDirectory): @(None) @(Compile)"/>` was executed once for the value *PreserveNewest* and once for *Always*. Also during the batching, values from both None and Compile item types were placed in the same batch. Because of this, we can create steps in our build process that don't discriminate based on an item type, only on one of its metadata values. If you do use this, you must ensure that every value in each referenced item type has declared the used metadata value. For example, if the result in Figure 6-17 had an additional ItemGroup declaration before the PrintInfo target, such as

```
<ItemGroup>
  <Compile Include="src06.cs" />
</ItemGroup>
```

then the target would fail, showing the error message in Figure 6-18.

```
C:\InsideMSBuild\Ch06>msbuild Batching06.proj /t:PrintInfo /nologo
Build started 9/24/2010 7:48:41 PM.
Project "C:\InsideMSBuild\Ch06\Batching06.proj" on node 1 (PrintInfo target(s)).
C:\InsideMSBuild\Ch06\Batching06.proj(27,5): error MSB4096: The item "src06.cs" in item list "Comp
ile" does not define a value for metadata "CopyToOutputDirectory".  In order to use this metadata,
 either qualify it by specifying %(Compile.CopyToOutputDirectory), or ensure that all items in thi
s list define a value for this metadata.
Done Building Project "C:\InsideMSBuild\Ch06\Batching06.proj" (PrintInfo target(s)) -- FAILED.

Build FAILED.

"C:\InsideMSBuild\Ch06\Batching06.proj" (PrintInfo target) (1) ->
(PrintInfo target) ->
  C:\InsideMSBuild\Ch06\Batching06.proj(27,5): error MSB4096: The item "src06.cs" in item list "Co
mpile" does not define a value for metadata "CopyToOutputDirectory".  In order to use this metadat
a, either qualify it by specifying %(Compile.CopyToOutputDirectory), or ensure that all items in t
his list define a value for this metadata.

    0 Warning(s)
    1 Error(s)
```

FIGURE 6-18 Common metadata batching error

This is one difference in behavior from the batching methods that we already discussed. In all previous cases, if an item value did not have the specified metadata value defined, it would be treated as empty. In this case, it causes the build to fail. If you need to use this type of batching but you are not sure if all the item values have defined the metadata, then you may have to provide a default value. You can use the new *ItemDefinitionGroup* element to provide this for you. The following Batching07.proj file demonstrates this behavior.

```
<Project xmlns="http://schemas.microsoft.com/developer/msbuild/2003"
        ToolsVersion="4.0"
        DefaultTargets="PrintInfo">
  <ItemGroup>
```

```xml
    <None Include="None01.txt">
      <CopyToOutputDirectory>PreserveNewest</CopyToOutputDirectory>
    </None>
    <None Include="None02.txt">
      <CopyToOutputDirectory>Always</CopyToOutputDirectory>
    </None>
    <None Include="None03.txt;None4.txt">
      <CopyToOutputDirectory>PreserveNewest</CopyToOutputDirectory>
    </None>
    <Compile Include="src01.cs;src02.cs;src03.cs">
      <CopyToOutputDirectory>PreserveNewest</CopyToOutputDirectory>
    </Compile>
    <Compile Include="src04.cs;src05.cs">
      <CopyToOutputDirectory>Always</CopyToOutputDirectory>
    </Compile>
  </ItemGroup>

  <ItemGroup>
    <Compile Include="src06.cs" />
  </ItemGroup>

  <ItemDefinitionGroup>
    <Compile>
      <CopyToOutputDirectory>Never</CopyToOutputDirectory>
    </Compile>
  </ItemDefinitionGroup>

  <Target Name="PrintInfo">
    <ItemGroup>
      <Compile Include="src07.cs" />
      <Compile Include="src08.cs">
        <CopyToOutputDirectory>Always</CopyToOutputDirectory>
      </Compile>
    </ItemGroup>

    <Message Text="%(CopyToOutputDirectory): @(None) @(Compile)" />
    <Message Text="====" />
    <Message Text="PreserveNewest: @(Compile) @(None)"
             Condition="'%(CopyToOutputDirectory)'=='PreserveNewest'" />
    <Message Text="Always: @(Compile) @(None)"
             Condition="'%(CopyToOutputDirectory)'=='Always'" />
    <Message Text="Never: @(Compile) @(None)"
             Condition="'%(CopyToOutputDirectory)'=='Never'" />
  </Target>
</Project>
```

This file declares a few values for the Compile item type that have not defined the CopyToOutputDirectory metadata value. A default value is provided via the ItemDefinitionGroup declaration. I've highlighted the changed regions. The result of executing the PrintInfo target in this file is shown in Figure 6-19.

From this result, we can see that the default value was successfully applied and we were able to use batching with unique values of the common metadata value.

```
C:\InsideMSBuild\Ch06>msbuild Batching07.proj /t:PrintInfo /nologo
Build started 9/24/2010 8:50:07 PM.
Project "C:\InsideMSBuild\Ch06\Batching07.proj" on node 1 (PrintInfo target(s)).
PrintInfo:
  PreserveNewest: None01.txt;None03.txt;None4.txt src01.cs;src02.cs;src03.cs
  Always: None02.txt src04.cs;src05.cs;src08.cs
  Never:  src06.cs;src07.cs
  ====
  PreserveNewest: src01.cs;src02.cs;src03.cs None1.txt;None03.txt;None4.txt
  Always: src04.cs;src05.cs;src08.cs None02.txt
  Never: src06.cs;src07.cs
Done Building Project "C:\InsideMSBuild\Ch06\Batching07.proj" (PrintInfo target(s)).

Build succeeded.
    0 Warning(s)
    0 Error(s)
```

FIGURE 6-19 Common metadata batching, example 2

Another method of achieving the same result would be to use the ability to dynamically update an item's metadata value using ItemGroup inside a target. The following Batching08.proj file removes the *ItemDefinitionGroup* element and replaces its functionality with this other technique.

```xml
<Project xmlns="http://schemas.microsoft.com/developer/msbuild/2003"
         ToolsVersion="4.0"
         DefaultTargets="PrintInfo">
  <ItemGroup>
    <None Include="None01.txt">
      <CopyToOutputDirectory>PreserveNewest</CopyToOutputDirectory>
    </None>
    <None Include="None02.txt">
      <CopyToOutputDirectory>Always</CopyToOutputDirectory>
    </None>
    <None Include="None03.txt;None4.txt">
      <CopyToOutputDirectory>PreserveNewest</CopyToOutputDirectory>
    </None>
    <Compile Include="src01.cs;src02.cs;src03.cs">
      <CopyToOutputDirectory>PreserveNewest</CopyToOutputDirectory>
    </Compile>
    <Compile Include="src04.cs;src05.cs">
      <CopyToOutputDirectory>Always</CopyToOutputDirectory>
    </Compile>
  </ItemGroup>

  <ItemGroup>
    <Compile Include="src06.cs" />
  </ItemGroup>

  <Target Name="PrintInfo">
    <ItemGroup>
      <Compile Include="src07.cs" />
      <Compile Include="src08.cs">
        <CopyToOutputDirectory>Always</CopyToOutputDirectory>
      </Compile>
    </ItemGroup>

    <ItemGroup>
      <Compile Condition="'%(Compile.CopyToOutputDirectory)'==''">
        <CopyToOutputDirectory>Never</CopyToOutputDirectory>
      </Compile>
    </ItemGroup>
```

```
    <Message Text="%(CopyToOutputDirectory): @(None) @(Compile)" />
    <Message Text="====" />
    <Message Text="PreserveNewest: @(Compile) @(None)"
            Condition="'%(CopyToOutputDirectory)'=='PreserveNewest'" />
    <Message Text="Always: @(Compile) @(None)"
            Condition="'%(CopyToOutputDirectory)'=='Always'" />
    <Message Text="Never: @(Compile) @(None)"
            Condition="'%(CopyToOutputDirectory)'=='Never'" />
  </Target>
</Project>
```

In this demonstration, I have highlighted in bold the text that has changed. You can see that the *ItemGroup* element is used inside the PrintInfo target. In this case, we are providing a value for the CopyToOutputDirectory metadata if its value is empty. This is implemented with task batching and as a condition. The difference between this approach and the ItemDefinitionGroup approach is this: ItemDefinitionGroup will provide a true default value, in the sense that it applies even for item values defined later in the build process, whereas the replacement approach modifies only currently defined item values. We will now move on to discuss incremental building, another great feature of MSBuild, which is little known.

Incremental Building

As products grow into giants, so do their build times. For a large code base, a build time of a few hours is not uncommon. Knowing this, there must be a way to ensure that only components that have changed, or depend on changed components, be built. This is accomplished through incremental building. Incremental building allows the MSBuild engine to determine which targets can be skipped, or even partially skipped. This then enables faster build times in most cases. In this section, we will discuss how you can take advantage of this in your own build scripts.

We have seen in target batching that the Output parameter of the *Target* element contains the batching statement. On the *Target* element, there is also an *Input* attribute; when both of these values are present, incremental building is enabled. In this case, the MSBuild engine will examine the timestamps of the input files and compare them to the timestamps of the files provided in the outputs value. If the outputs were created after the inputs, then the target is skipped. We can now take a look at this in action.

The Incremental01.proj file demonstrates incremental building. It copies a set of files from one location to another. If the files are up to date, then the target that performs the copy is skipped. This file is shown next.

```
<Project xmlns="http://schemas.microsoft.com/developer/msbuild/2003"
        ToolsVersion="4.0">
  <PropertyGroup>
    <SourceFolder>$(MSBuildProjectDirectory)\src\</SourceFolder>
```

```
      <DestFolder>$(MSBuildProjectDirectory)\dest\</DestFolder>
  </PropertyGroup>

  <ItemGroup>
    <SourceFiles Include="$(SourceFolder)*.txt" />
  </ItemGroup>

  <Target Name="CopyFilesToDest"
    Inputs="@(SourceFiles)"
    Outputs="@(SourceFiles->'$(DestFolder)%(RecursiveDir)%(Filename)%(Extension)')">
    <Copy SourceFiles="@(SourceFiles)"
      DestinationFiles=
        "@(SourceFiles->'$(DestFolder)%(RecursiveDir)%(Filename)%(Extension)')" />
  </Target>

  <Target Name="CleanDestFolder">
    <ItemGroup>
      <_FilesToDelete Include="$(DestFolder)**\*"/>
    </ItemGroup>
    <Delete Files="@(_FilesToDelete)" />
  </Target>
</Project>
```

In this build script, we have declared two targets, CopyFilesToDest and CleanDestFolder. The important target here is CopyFilesToDest. The inputs for that target are specified as @(SourceFiles), and outputs as @(SourceFiles->'$(DestFolder)%(RecursiveDir)%(Filename)%(Extension)'), which is a transformation of the SourceFiles item. If the files in the output location are newer than the source files, then we would expect this target to be skipped. The CleanDestFolder target can be used to delete the output files. Take a look at the result of the command msbuild Incremental01.proj /t:CleanDestFolder;CopyFilesTo Dest, shown in Figure 6-20.

```
C:\InsideMSBuild\Ch06>msbuild Incremental01.proj /t:CleanDestFolder;CopyFilesToDest /nologo
Build started 9/24/2010 9:21:49 PM.
Project "C:\InsideMSBuild\Ch06\Incremental01.proj" on node 1 (CleanDestFolder;CopyFilesToDest targ
et(s)).
CleanDestFolder:
  Deleting file "C:\InsideMSBuild\Ch06\dest\01.txt".
  Deleting file "C:\InsideMSBuild\Ch06\dest\02.txt".
  Deleting file "C:\InsideMSBuild\Ch06\dest\03.txt".
  Deleting file "C:\InsideMSBuild\Ch06\dest\04.txt".
CopyFilesToDest:
  Copying file from "C:\InsideMSBuild\Ch06\src\01.txt" to "C:\InsideMSBuild\Ch06\dest\01.txt".
  Copying file from "C:\InsideMSBuild\Ch06\src\02.txt" to "C:\InsideMSBuild\Ch06\dest\02.txt".
  Copying file from "C:\InsideMSBuild\Ch06\src\03.txt" to "C:\InsideMSBuild\Ch06\dest\03.txt".
  Copying file from "C:\InsideMSBuild\Ch06\src\04.txt" to "C:\InsideMSBuild\Ch06\dest\04.txt".
Done Building Project "C:\InsideMSBuild\Ch06\Incremental01.proj" (CleanDestFolder;CopyFilesToDest
target(s)).

Build succeeded.
    0 Warning(s)
    0 Error(s)
```

FIGURE 6-20 CopyFilesToDest result 1

In this example, I purposefully deleted all the output files by calling the CleanDestFolder target before the CopyFilesToDest target. I do this to ensure that the target is called, which can be seen in the result in Figure 6-20. From that output, we can see that the files were successfully copied from the source location to the destination. Now what would happen if we ran that target again, without first calling the CleanDestFolder target? The result is shown in Figure 6-21.

```
C:\InsideMSBuild\Ch06>msbuild Incremental01.proj /t:CopyFilesToDest /nologo
Build started 9/24/2010 9:24:17 PM.
Project "C:\InsideMSBuild\Ch06\Incremental01.proj" on node 1 (CopyFilesToDest target(s)).
CopyFilesToDest:
Skipping target "CopyFilesToDest" because all output files are up-to-date with respect to the inpu
t files.
Done Building Project "C:\InsideMSBuild\Ch06\Incremental01.proj" (CopyFilesToDest target(s)).


Build succeeded.
    0 Warning(s)
    0 Error(s)
```

FIGURE 6-21 CopyFilesToDest result 2

As the result shows, the target was successfully skipped because all the outputs were up to
date with respect to the inputs. This basic implementation serves as the basis for incremental
building and is the key to efficient build scripts. The targets shipped by Microsoft to build
managed projects use incremental building extensively. If you make modifications to the
build, your targets should also support this when possible. If you extend the build process for
a managed project to use custom targets that create files, you should also make sure those
files are deleted when the project is cleaned. We will take a look at this specific example in
Chapter 8, "Practical Applications, Part 1." It's very important that your incremental build
works properly—that is, that it does not touch any files. This is not only because it makes
your life easier as a developer, but also because it's highly antisocial in the context of a larger
build: Subsequent (correctly authored) build steps will be triggered to run because you
touched those files. Sometimes inputs and outputs alone will not enable you to properly
implement incremental builds. For example, if a task operates on files that have transitive
dependencies, such as C++ header files, then you may not be able to (or may not want to) list
all of them in inputs and outputs. In this scenario, you must bypass the inputs and outputs list
and let the task do the timestamp checking for itself before it is run. The GenerateResource
task behaves in this manner because .resx files can refer to other files.

Partially Building Targets

When incremental building is utilized, you may run into times when a target is up to date
for some files, but not all. You shouldn't have to completely rebuild the target simply to
take care of a few files, and indeed, you do not—MSBuild will take care of this for you
automatically. This is called partially building targets.

The best way to describe how partial building works is to demonstrate it. We'll start by
examining the build script shown in the next snippet.

```
<Project xmlns="http://schemas.microsoft.com/developer/msbuild/2003"
         ToolsVersion="4.0" DefaultTargets="CopyFilesToDest">
  <PropertyGroup>
    <SourceFolder>src\</SourceFolder>
    <DestFolder>dest\</DestFolder>
  </PropertyGroup>
```

```
  <ItemGroup>
    <SourceFiles Include="$(SourceFolder)*.txt" />
  </ItemGroup>

  <Target Name="CopyFilesToDest"
    Inputs="@(SourceFiles)"
    Outputs="@(SourceFiles->'$(DestFolder)%(RecursiveDir)%(Filename)%(Extension)')">
    <Copy SourceFiles="@(SourceFiles)"
      DestinationFiles=
        "@(SourceFiles->'$(DestFolder)%(RecursiveDir)%(Filename)%(Extension)')" />
  </Target>

  <Target Name="CleanDestFolder">
    <ItemGroup>
      <_FilesToDelete Include="$(DestFolder)**\*"/>
    </ItemGroup>
    <Delete Files="@(_FilesToDelete)" />
  </Target>

  <Target Name="DeleteSomeRandomFiles">
    <ItemGroup>
      <_PartialFilesToDelete Include="$(DestFolder)01.txt;$(DestFolder)03.txt"/>
    </ItemGroup>
    <Delete Files="@(_PartialFilesToDelete)" />
  </Target>
</Project>
```

This script, Incremental02.proj, is a modification of the previous example from Incremental01 .proj. The change is the addition of a new target, DeleteSomeRandomFiles. This target will clean out some of the files in the dest folder, but not all of them. Assuming that the CopyFilesToDest target has been run previously without being cleaned, the result of the command msbuild Incremental02.proj /t: DeleteSomeRandomFiles;CopyFilesToDest is shown in Figure 6-22.

```
C:\InsideMSBuild\Ch06>msbuild Incremental02.proj /t:DeleteSomeRandomFiles;CopyFilesToDest /nologo
Build started 9/24/2010 9:42:45 PM.
Project "C:\InsideMSBuild\Ch06\Incremental02.proj" on node 1 (DeleteSomeRandomFiles;CopyFilesToDes
t target(s)).
DeleteSomeRandomFiles:
  Deleting file "dest\01.txt".
  Deleting file "dest\03.txt".
CopyFilesToDest:
Building target "CopyFilesToDest" partially, because some output files are out of date with respec
t to their input files.
  Copying file from "src\01.txt" to "dest\01.txt".
  Copying file from "src\03.txt" to "dest\03.txt".
Done Building Project "C:\InsideMSBuild\Ch06\Incremental02.proj" (DeleteSomeRandomFiles;CopyFilesT
oDest target(s)).

Build succeeded.
    0 Warning(s)
    0 Error(s)
```

FIGURE 6-22 Partially building targets

If you take a look at the result shown in Figure 6-22, you will see the message Building target "CopyFilesToDest" partially, because some output files are out of date with respect to their input files. Since the DeleteSomeRandomFiles target deleted only a couple of the generated files, the ones that were not deleted were still up to date. Therefore, those files do not need to be rebuilt. MSBuild automatically recognized this and executed CopyFilesToDest only for the outdated inputs. Following that statement, you can see that two files were copied to the destination location. Since some of the files were up to date, the batch that was sent to the CopyFilesToDest target contained only the out-of-date files. When the inputs and outputs contain the same number of values, MSBuild will match input to output in a 1:1 fashion. For example, it will assume that the first value in the input corresponds to the first value of the output, and the second input value to the second output value, and so on. Using this process, MSBuild is able to determine specifically what set of inputs are out of date with respect to outputs, and process only those item values. Typically, you will not have to be concerned with partial building because MSBuild will take care of it, but you should be aware of it.

In this chapter, we have covered an advanced technique—batching. Batching will allow you to create build scripts that take full advantage of the MSBuild engine. When you create build scripts, you should remember that batching is available and use it when it can serve a purpose. Along with batching, we have discussed incremental building, which allows for drastically reduced build times for most builds. For any complex build scripts, incremental building must be implemented. Now that we have covered batching and incremental building, in the next chapter we will take a look at how external tools can be used in the build process. We will discuss some guidelines for using external tools, as well as show how to correctly integrate a few tools.

Chapter 7
External Tools

When you are using MSBuild, sometimes there is no specific task that provides the functionality that you need. At those times, you will have to use one of the many existing tools that can and should be used to assist in builds and deployments. Some of the most commonly used tools include FxCop, StyleCop, NUnit, and so on. In this chapter, I will describe how external tools can be effectively consumed by MSBuild. We'll examine a few commonly used tools and discuss how to integrate them into your build process. We'll first describe how these can simply be invoked in build scripts and then describe a way to create reusable targets files for tools. Also, we will discuss some guidelines for reusable build scripts.

Exec Task

The simplest method to invoke an existing tool is by using the Exec task. This task is shipped with MSBuild, and it can be used to execute any program or command. This is the task that is used to execute the PreBuild and PostBuild events as well. There are several properties in this task, which are summarized in Table 7-1.

TABLE 7-1 Exec Task Properties

Name	Description
Command	The command that is to be executed. This is the only *required* parameter.
WorkingDirectory	Specifies the working directory.
Timeout	Specifies the timeout, in milliseconds. After the amount of time specified has passed, the command will be terminated. There is no timeout by default, so a command will be allowed to execute indefinitely.
ExitCode	Output property containing the exit code returned by the execute command.
IgnoreExitCode	If true, then the Exec task will not fail the build based on the exit code. Otherwise, the build is failed for any nonzero exit code.
	Currently, there is a bug related to this such that, if this value is set to *true* and an error message has been logged, the build should fail, but it doesn't.
Outputs	An input/output parameter that contains the output items from the task. This is not set by the Exec task itself but made available to be set by the consumer. This parameter is needed only for output inferral. When a target is skipped, MSBuild tries to create all the properties and items that the target would have created if it had run. For custom tasks, this is possible only if the output is also an input. So this should be set to whatever the outputs for the executed command would be if the task were run, so that MSBuild can properly determine dependencies. This is output inferral. By exposing the outputs as an input as well, output inferral is supported. Generally, you will not have to worry about this.

Name	Description
StdErrEncoding	An input/output parameter that specifies the encoding that is used for the standard error stream. The default value is almost always sufficient; it is the current OEM encoding or else ANSI. These possible values are code page names for the desired encoding, for example UTF-8 and UTF-32.
StdOutEncoding	An input/output parameter that specifies the encoding that is used for the standard output stream. These possible values are code page names for the desired encoding, for example UTF-8 and UTF-32.
IgnoreStandardErrorWarningFormat	If true, the output is not examined for *standard* errors and warnings.
CustomErrorRegularExpression	If provided, this will be the regular expression pattern used to determine if an error occurred. MSBuild will attempt to examine the output of the executing tool for errors and warnings. For standard compliant tools, this is automatic. For tools that do not log using the standard conventions (e.g., GCC compiler), then you can provide an expression to detect the errors. Also, you may need to provide an expression for the CustomWarningRegularExpression parameter. Typically, you should use this in conjunction with the IgnoreStandardErrorWarningFormat parameter.
CustomWarningRegularExpression	If provided, this will be the regular expression pattern used to determine that a warning occurred. See the note in the CustomErrorRegularExpression description about how MSBuild processes the executables output. Typically, you should use this in conjunction with the IgnoreStandardErrorWarningFormat parameter.

The most commonly used Exec properties are Command, IgnoreExitCode, and WorkingDirectory. In the next code fragment, you will see a very simple usage of this task. This is from the Exec01.proj file.

```
<Project xmlns="http://schemas.microsoft.com/developer/msbuild/2003"
        ToolsVersion="4.0">
  <Target Name="Demo">
    <Exec Command="echo Hello MSBuild" />
  </Target>
</Project>
```

In this demonstration, we are simply invoking the echo command to pass a message to the console. When you use the Exec task, the contents of the command are placed in a .cmd file and passed to cmd.exe for execution. We can verify that this was successfully executed by examining the result shown in Figure 7-1.

```
C:\InsideMSBuild\Ch07>msbuild Exec01.proj /t:Demo /nologo
Build started 9/11/2010 4:02:53 PM.
Project "C:\InsideMSBuild\Ch07\Exec01.proj" on node 1 (Demo target(s)).
Demo:
  echo Hello MSBuild
  Hello MSBuild
Done Building Project "C:\InsideMSBuild\Ch07\Exec01.proj" (Demo target(s)).

Build succeeded.
    0 Warning(s)
    0 Error(s)
```

FIGURE 7-1 Exec result

From this result, we can see that the Exec task executed the provided command and the
message was sent to the console. You should use the Exec task to invoke an executable when
a task doesn't exist to invoke it for you. For example, you should use the Exec task to invoke
svcutil.exe, from the Windows SDK, but not csc.exe because the Csc task wraps the csc.exe
executable. A few of the reasons why custom tasks are easier to use is that they can expose
a specific set of properties that the tool can use, the output may be cleaner, and the task may
be able to discover where the .exe is located. Many existing build processes are captured in
non-MSBuild scripts, and the Exec task can be used to invoke those scripts. By doing this, you
can slowly migrate your build process to MSBuild instead of employing an "all or nothing"
approach.

> **Note** In case you are interested in how the Exec task works, here are some details. The Exec
> task takes the content of the Command parameter, places it into a temporary file, and then runs
> cmd.exe on that file. What this means is that you can use things like multiple lines, environment
> variables, and so on. Another implication of this is that because this is running in a child process
> (cmd.exe), any changes to environment variables will last only until the task is done.

One common usage of the Exec task, especially when using MSBuild 2.0, is to invoke the
attrib command. This command can be used to change a file's attributes. When applications
are under development, many files are marked as read-only due to the source control
provider. This is great for development, but sometimes it causes problems for a build process
that might copy and replace files with other ones. If you are using MSBuild 3.5, or later,
the Copy task now has a property called OverwriteReadOnlyFiles, which can be used to
bypass the copy read-only file problem. With MSBuild 2.0, you would have to change the
file's attribute to be writeable. An example of this would be replacing resource files at build
time, or replacing JavaScript files for Web projects. The following Exec02.proj file contains
an example demonstrating using the attrib command.

```
<Project xmlns="http://schemas.microsoft.com/developer/msbuild/2003"
         ToolsVersion="4.0">
  <ItemGroup>
    <SrcFiles Include="src\*" />
  </ItemGroup>
  <Target Name="Demo">
    <Message Text="SrcFiles: @(SrcFiles)" />
    <Message Text="%0a%0dMaking files Readonly" Importance="high" />
    <!-- Make SrcFiles Readonly -->
```

```
      <Exec Command="attrib %(SrcFiles.Identity) +R" />

      <!-- Display the attributes -->
      <Exec Command="attrib %(SrcFiles.Identity)" />

      <Message Text="%0a%0dMaking files writeable" Importance="high" />
      <!-- Make SrcFiles Writeable -->
      <Exec Command="attrib %(SrcFiles.Identity) -R" />

      <!-- Display the attributes -->
      <Exec Command="attrib %(SrcFiles.Identity)" />
    </Target>
</Project>
```

This file declares a single item, SrcFiles, and a single target, Demo. Inside the Demo target, the attrib command is used to apply the read-only flag, display file attributes, remove read-only attributes, and finally display the attributes one last time. The result of invoking this build script is captured in Figure 7-2.

```
C:\InsideMSBuild\Ch07>msbuild Exec02.proj /t:Demo /nologo
Build started 9/11/2010 4:09:54 PM.
Project "C:\InsideMSBuild\Ch07\Exec02.proj" on node 1 (Demo target(s)).
Demo:
  SrcFiles: src\four.txt;src\one.txt;src\three.txt;src\two.txt

Making files Readonly
   attrib src\four.txt +R
   attrib src\one.txt +R
   attrib src\three.txt +R
   attrib src\two.txt +R
   attrib src\four.txt
   A      R       C:\InsideMSBuild\Ch07\src\four.txt
   attrib src\one.txt
   A      R       C:\InsideMSBuild\Ch07\src\one.txt
   attrib src\three.txt
   A      R       C:\InsideMSBuild\Ch07\src\three.txt
   attrib src\two.txt
   A      R       C:\InsideMSBuild\Ch07\src\two.txt

Making files writeable
   attrib src\four.txt -R
   attrib src\one.txt -R
   attrib src\three.txt -R
   attrib src\two.txt -R
   attrib src\four.txt
   A              C:\InsideMSBuild\Ch07\src\four.txt
   attrib src\one.txt
   A              C:\InsideMSBuild\Ch07\src\one.txt
   attrib src\three.txt
   A              C:\InsideMSBuild\Ch07\src\three.txt
   attrib src\two.txt
   A              C:\InsideMSBuild\Ch07\src\two.txt
Done Building Project "C:\InsideMSBuild\Ch07\Exec02.proj" (Demo target(s)).

Build succeeded.
    0 Warning(s)
    0 Error(s)
```

FIGURE 7-2 Exec02.proj result

As you can see, the attrib command was successfully invoked to set and clear the read-only flag. Now that the read-only attribute has been cleared, we are free to copy any file on top of this one. Another common usage of the Exec task is to interact with source control providers. With more common source control providers, you may be able to find custom tasks, but tasks for all providers are not available. You may have to use the Exec task to perform the operation for you. We will now conclude our discussion of the Exec task and move on to cover the MSBuild task.

MSBuild Task

When you are building products, there will be many instances where you simply want to build an existing MSBuild file. This could be an MSBuild file that you authored or one that was created by a third-party tool for you. Of course, you could use the Exec task to perform this, but a better option is to use the MSBuild task. This is another task that is delivered along with MSBuild itself. As the name suggests, it will invoke MSBuild on the specified file(s). Some of the advantages of using this task instead of the Exec task include increased performance, better integration, and ease of use. One of the main advantages of using the MSBuild task is that you can make sure that the same project is not built multiple times concurrently. For example, if you have projects A and B, which both reference project C, if both A and B run the Exec task on C, then there would be two copies of C building at once unless you used the MSBuild task. This would cause file access issues and build breaks, which is why you shouldn't start msbuild.exe inside a build. The properties for this task are outlined in Table 7-2.

TABLE 7-2 MSBuild Task Properties

Name	Description
BuildInParallel	If true, then the projects will be built in parallel if possible. The default value for this is *false*. The Microsoft.Common.targets file passes a default value of *true* for this property when using the MSBuild task. To make your projects build in parallel, you need to use the /m command-line switch to ensure that more than one processor can be used.
Projects	Project file(s) to be built. If you specify more than one, either pass it in as an item list or as a semicolon-delimited list.
Properties	Optional semicolon-delimited list of properties in the format `<n>=<v>`, where *<n>* is the name of the property and *<v>* is the value. These are global properties and treated the same as properties passed to the msbuild.exe command using the `/property` (`/p`) switch. You can also add properties using the Properties or AdditionalProperties project item metadata.
RemoveProperties	A semicolon-delimited list of properties to remove. This is a new property of MSBuild 4.0.
RebaseOutputs	If this is true, then any relative paths from the built projects' Target outputs will be adjusted to that of the calling project. The default value for this is *false*.
RunEachTargetSeparately	If true, then each target will be executed independent of the other targets in the Target property. If not building in parallel, then each project will be built once for each target. If building in parallel, then all projects will be built together for each target. If an error occurs during a target and this is set to *false*, subsequent targets are allowed to execute instead of the entire task execution terminated. The default value for this is *false*. It is more efficient to leave this value as *false;* otherwise, the engine will be called to build each target in turn, rather than giving it a list.

Name	Description
SkipNonexistentProjects	If this is set to *true,* then if a project doesn't exist, it is skipped instead of raising an error. The default value for this is *false.*
StopOnFirstFailure	The default value for this is *false.* If set to *false* and you are building projects A and B, if A fails, then project B will begin building. If you are building targets t1 and t2, if t1 fails, then t2 will start.
	If this is set to *true* and an error occurs, the task invocation will be stopped. This works only if you are building single proc (as under the covers, it is implemented in the task; that is, the task has to give each project to the engine one at a time if it is going to have a chance to stop before the end).
TargetAndPropertyListSeparators	Can be used to change the default semicolon separator for properties and targets.
TargetOutputs	Output parameter that contains the outputs from the specified targets that were built.
Targets	Specifies the target(s) to be built. If providing more than one value, then it should be a semicolon-delimited list just as when using the `/target` `(/t)` switch with msbuild.exe.
ToolsVersion	Determines which version of tools will be used to build the project. Valid values are 2.0, 3.5, and 4.0. The default value is 2.0. This determines the version of the tasks and targets that are used to build your project. Note that Microsoft.Common. targets also has a property named TargetFrameworkVersion that can be used to target other framework versions. These are not the same. TargetFrameworkVersion is a regular property used by the common Microsoft targets files. If your ToolsVersion is 2.0, then the TargetFrameworkVersion must be 2.0 as well.
UnloadProjectsOnCompletion	Obsolete. Do not use.
UseResultsCache	Obsolete. Do not use.

From the properties listed in Table 7-2, the most commonly used are Projects, Targets, Properties, and TargetOutputs. We will demonstrate the usage of all these properties in this section. The following snippet shows the contents of two project files: MSBuildTask01.proj and MSBuildTask01_external.proj.

MSBuildTask01.proj

```
<Project xmlns="http://schemas.microsoft.com/developer/msbuild/2003"
         ToolsVersion="4.0"
         DefaultTargets="Demo">

  <Target Name="Demo">
    <Message Text="Inside Demo target" />
    <MSBuild Projects="MSBuildTask01_external.proj"
             Targets="PrintMessage" />
  </Target>

</Project>
```

MSBuildTask01_external.proj

```
<Project xmlns="http://schemas.microsoft.com/developer/msbuild/2003"
         ToolsVersion="4.0">

  <Target Name="PrintMessage">
    <Message Text="Hello MSBuild" />
  </Target>
</Project>
```

The MSBuildTask01.proj file contains a single target, Demo. This is the one that we will be invoking from the MSBuild command line. This target uses the MSBuild task to call the PrintMessage target contained in the MSBuildTask01_external.proj file. If you executed the command msbuild MSBuildTask01.proj /t:Demo, the result would be what is shown in Figure 7-3.

```
C:\InsideMSBuild\Ch07>msbuild MSBuildTask01.proj /t:Demo /nologo
Build started 9/11/2010 4:20:07 PM.
Project "C:\InsideMSBuild\Ch07\MSBuildTask01.proj" on node 1 (Demo target(s)).
Demo:
    Inside Demo target
Project "C:\InsideMSBuild\Ch07\MSBuildTask01.proj" (1) is building "C:\InsideMSBuild\Ch07\MSBuildT
ask01_external.proj" (2) on node 1 (PrintMessage target(s)).
PrintMessage:
    Hello MSBuild
Done Building Project "C:\InsideMSBuild\Ch07\MSBuildTask01_external.proj" (PrintMessage target(s))
.

Done Building Project "C:\InsideMSBuild\Ch07\MSBuildTask01.proj" (Demo target(s)).

Build succeeded.
    0 Warning(s)
    0 Error(s)
```

FIGURE 7-3 MSBuildTask01.proj result

From these results, you can see that the PrintMessage target was called using the MSBuild task from the Demo target. Now that we have seen how to use the MSBuild task, we'll take a look at how we can send properties into a project.

When you invoke the MSBuild task, the properties and items of the calling MSBuild file are *not* passed through to the projects by the MSBuild task. This is by design. You can pass property values using the Properties parameter of the MSBuild task. You cannot pass items through, but you can use Properties to initialize items inside the project being built. These properties are global properties. They are treated in the same manner as properties that are passed into msbuild.exe using the /p switch; that is, they cannot be overwritten by static values declared in the project file that will be processed by the MSBuild task. Building a project with a different set of properties causes it to build again; it has a different identity. Building a project with the same set of properties causes the build to be skipped. In the following code section, you will find the contents of the MSBuildTask02.proj file, which is a modified version of the previous example.

```
<Project xmlns="http://schemas.microsoft.com/developer/msbuild/2003"
         ToolsVersion="4.0"
         DefaultTargets="Demo">
```

```
  <Target Name="Demo">
    <Message Text="Inside Demo target" />
    <MSBuild Projects="$(MSBuildProjectFullPath)"
             Targets="PrintMessage"
             Properties="SourceName=PrintMessage Target"
             />
  </Target>

  <Target Name="PrintMessage">
    <Message Text="Hello MSBuild from: $(SourceName)" />
  </Target>
</Project>
```

The difference between this example and the previous one is that in this example, a value
for SourceName is passed by the Properties parameter, which is indicated in bold in this
code snippet. As stated in Table 7-2, properties should be passed in the format <n>=<v>.
In this case, the name of the property that we are passing is SourceName and the value is
"PrintMessage target". If we were to pass more than one value, we would have to delimit the
name-value pairs with a semicolon. You can see the result of building the Demo target of this
file in Figure 7-4.

```
C:\InsideMSBuild\Ch07>msbuild MSBuildTask02.proj /t:Demo /nologo
Build started 9/11/2010 4:26:06 PM.
Project "C:\InsideMSBuild\Ch07\MSBuildTask02.proj" on node 1 (Demo target(s)).
Demo:
    Inside Demo target
Project "C:\InsideMSBuild\Ch07\MSBuildTask02.proj" (1) is building "C:\InsideMSBuild\Ch07\MSBuildT
ask02.proj" (1:2) on node 1 (PrintMessage target(s)).
PrintMessage:
    Hello MSBuild from: PrintMessage Target
Done Building Project "C:\InsideMSBuild\Ch07\MSBuildTask02.proj" (PrintMessage target(s)).

Done Building Project "C:\InsideMSBuild\Ch07\MSBuildTask02.proj" (Demo target(s)).


Build succeeded.
    0 Warning(s)
    0 Error(s)
```

FIGURE 7-4 MSBuildTask02.proj result

You can see from this result that the SourceName property was successfully passed from the
calling file into the project being built. As you might have noticed, in this case the project
file is performing a build on itself, using the MSBuild task. But the behavior would have been
the same even if it had been building a different file. We can now move on to take a look at
a more realistic example.

A very common scenario is creating an MSBuild file that will be used as the "master" build
file. What this means is that you will have one MSBuild file that is responsible for building
a set of project files, as well as any other steps before, after, or between project builds. You
can achieve this by using the MSBuild task. The next example, taken from MSBuildTask03
.proj, uses the MSBuild task to build two sample unit test projects. The full source for this file
is shown in the following example.

```
<Project xmlns="http://schemas.microsoft.com/developer/msbuild/2003"
         ToolsVersion="4.0"
         DefaultTargets="BuildAll">
  <PropertyGroup>
```

```
        <UnitTestSrcRoot>unittest\</UnitTestSrcRoot>
    </PropertyGroup>
    <ItemGroup>
        <UnitTestProjects
            Include="$(UnitTestSrcRoot)Unittest.Proj1\Unittest.Proj1.csproj" />
        <UnitTestProjects
            Include="$(UnitTestSrcRoot)Unittest.Proj2\Unittest.Proj2.csproj" />
    </ItemGroup>

    <PropertyGroup>
        <!-- BuildAll convention used here but these could be named anything. -->
        <BuildAllDependsOn>
            BeforeBuildAll;
            CoreBuildAll;
            AfterBuildAll
        </BuildAllDependsOn>
    </PropertyGroup>
    <Target Name="BuildAll" DependsOnTargets="$(BuildAllDependsOn)" />

    <Target Name="CoreBuildAll">
        <MSBuild Projects="@(UnitTestProjects)"
                Targets="Rebuild"
                Properties="Configuration=Release">
            <Output ItemName="unitTestBuildOutputs" TaskParameter="TargetOutputs" />
        </MSBuild>

        <Message Text="unitTestBuildOutputs:%0a%0d@(unitTestBuildOutputs,'%0a%0d')" />
    </Target>

    <Target Name="BeforeBuildAll">
        <Message Text="Before BuildAll" Importance="high" />
    </Target>

    <Target Name="AfterBuildAll">
        <Message Text="After BuildAll" Importance="high" />
    </Target>
</Project>
```

In this project, I have defined an item, UnitTestProjects, which contains the two projects that are to be built. These projects are built inside the CoreBuildAll target using the MSBuild task. If you take a look at that task invocation, you will see that we are building the Release configurations of the specified projects. Also, you can see that we're placing the output value from the TargetOutputs parameter into the unitTestBuildOutputs item. The TargetOutputs value will expose any values defined as Outputs on *explicitly* called targets. In this case, we are explicitly calling only the Rebuild target. If you take a look at the definition for that target, from the Microsoft.Common.targets file, you will see what is contained in the next snippet.

```
<Target
    Name="Rebuild"
    Condition=" '$(_InvalidConfigurationWarning)' != 'true' "
    DependsOnTargets="$(RebuildDependsOn)"
    Outputs="$(TargetPath)" />
```

This target has defined the Outputs value to be *$(TargetPath),* which is a property pointing to the location of the output file. This will be the value that is transferred into the unitTestBuildOutputs item. You will see that I have defined a target to be executed before and after the project is built, using BeforeBuildAll and AfterBuildAll. You can see this in action by executing the command `msbuild MSBuildTask03.proj /t:BuildAll`. The last bit of the result of this is shown in Figure 7-5.

```
t.rroj1.dll /target:library rroperties\HssemplyInro.cs lestuperators.cs
_CopyFilesMarkedCopyLocal:
  Copying file from "C:\InsideMSBuild\Contrib\nunit2.2\nunit.framework.dll" to "bin\Release\nunit.
  framework.dll".
  Copying file from "C:\InsideMSBuild\Contrib\nunit2.2\nunit.framework.xml" to "bin\Release\nunit.
  framework.xml".
CopyFilesToOutputDirectory:
  Copying file from "obj\Release\Unittest.Proj1.dll" to "bin\Release\Unittest.Proj1.dll".
  Unittest.Proj1 -> C:\InsideMSBuild\Ch07\unittest\Unittest.Proj1\bin\Release\Unittest.Proj1.dll
  Copying file from "obj\Release\Unittest.Proj1.pdb" to "bin\Release\Unittest.Proj1.pdb".
Done Building Project "C:\InsideMSBuild\Ch07\unittest\Unittest.Proj1\Unittest.Proj1.csproj" (Rebui
ld target(s)).

Project "C:\InsideMSBuild\Ch07\MSBuildTask03.proj" (1) is building "C:\InsideMSBuild\Ch07\unittest
\Unittest.Proj2\Unittest.Proj2.csproj" (3) on node 1 (Rebuild target(s)).
CoreClean:
  Creating directory "obj\Release\".
CoreCompile:
  C:\Windows\Microsoft.NET\Framework\v4.0.30319\Csc.exe /noconfig /nowarn:1701,1702 /nostdlib+ /er
  rorreport:prompt /warn:4 /define:TRACE /reference:C:\Windows\Microsoft.NET\Framework\v2.0.50727\
  mscorlib.dll /reference:C:\InsideMSBuild\Contrib\nunit2.2\nunit.framework.dll /reference:"C:\Pro
  gram Files (x86)\Reference Assemblies\Microsoft\Framework\v3.5\System.Core.dll" /reference:"C:\P
  rogram Files (x86)\Reference Assemblies\Microsoft\Framework\v3.5\System.Data.DataSetExtensions.d
  ll" /reference:C:\Windows\Microsoft.NET\Framework\v2.0.50727\System.Data.dll /reference:C:\Windo
  ws\Microsoft.NET\Framework\v2.0.50727\System.dll /reference:C:\Windows\Microsoft.NET\Framework\v
  2.0.50727\System.Xml.dll /reference:"C:\Program Files (x86)\Reference Assemblies\Microsoft\Frame
  work\v3.5\System.Xml.Linq.dll" /debug:pdbonly /filealign:512 /optimize+ /out:obj\Release\Unittes
  t.Proj2.dll /target:library TestStirng.cs Properties\AssemblyInfo.cs
_CopyFilesMarkedCopyLocal:
  Copying file from "C:\InsideMSBuild\Contrib\nunit2.2\nunit.framework.dll" to "bin\Release\nunit.
  framework.dll".
  Copying file from "C:\InsideMSBuild\Contrib\nunit2.2\nunit.framework.xml" to "bin\Release\nunit.
  framework.xml".
CopyFilesToOutputDirectory:
  Copying file from "obj\Release\Unittest.Proj2.dll" to "bin\Release\Unittest.Proj2.dll".
  Unittest.Proj2 -> C:\InsideMSBuild\Ch07\unittest\Unittest.Proj2\bin\Release\Unittest.Proj2.dll
  Copying file from "obj\Release\Unittest.Proj2.pdb" to "bin\Release\Unittest.Proj2.pdb".
Done Building Project "C:\InsideMSBuild\Ch07\unittest\Unittest.Proj2\Unittest.Proj2.csproj" (Rebui
ld target(s)).

CoreBuildAll:
  unitTestBuildOutputs:
C:\InsideMSBuild\Ch07\unittest\Unittest.Proj1\bin\Release\Unittest.Proj1.dll
C:\InsideMSBuild\Ch07\unittest\Unittest.Proj2\bin\Release\Unittest.Proj2.dll
AfterBuildAll:
  After BuildAll
Done Building Project "C:\InsideMSBuild\Ch07\MSBuildTask03.proj" (BuildAll target(s)).

Build succeeded.
    0 Warning(s)
    0 Error(s)
```

FIGURE 7-5 MSBuildTask03.proj result

From the result captured in Figure 7-5, you can see that both unit tests were successfully built using the MSBuild task. Furthermore, you can see that the result assemblies were placed into the unitTestBuildOutputs item as expected. Now we have demonstrated how we can utilize the MSBuild task in order to build child projects. You should note that if you want to take advantage of the multiprocessor support that MSBuild has, you must invoke msbuild.exe using the /maxcpucount (/m) switch, and when using the MSBuild task, you should set the BuildInParallel value to *true*. The MSBuild task also supports a set of known metadata that can be used during the build process: Properties, AdditionalProperties, and ToolsVersion.

Thus far, we have discussed the Exec task and the MSBuild task. Now, we'll move on to discuss error message formats. If you have many projects that will utilize the same tools, then you should create reusable scripts to make integration of the tools simpler.

MSBuild and Visual Studio Known Error Message Formats

When a tool is executed that outputs some text, MSBuild will examine the text for errors and warnings. Many tools use a known format to report these messages. By default, MSBuild will examine the text and report errors and/or warnings based on the output. This behavior can be changed or disabled by using these parameters on the Exec task: IgnoreStandardErrorWarningFormat, CustomErrorRegularExpression, and CustomWarningRegularExpression.

> **Note** If you do decide to use your own regular expression to detect error and warnings, then you should know that MSBuild will look at the result *one line at a time*. Even if your custom regex would match something across multiple lines, it will not behave that way because of how MSBuild processes that text.

Take a look at the following four messages, which are all properly formatted and will be recognized by MSBuild and Microsoft Visual Studio.

```
Main.cs(17,20): warning CS0168: The variable 'foo' is declared but never used

C:\dir1\foo.resx(2) : error BC30188: Declaration expected.

cl : Command line warning D4024 : unrecognized source file type 'foo.cs', object . . .

error CS0006: Metadata file 'System.dll' could not be found.
```

These messages conform to the special five-part format shown in Figure 7-6. The order of these parts is important and should not change.

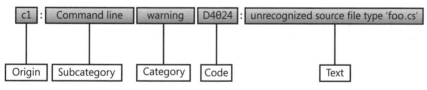

FIGURE 7-6 Known message format

Now we will describe each of the components of this format:

- **Origin (Required)** Origin can be blank. If present, the origin is usually a tool name, such as "cl" in one of the examples. But it could also be a file name, such as "Main.cs," shown in another example. If it is a file name, then it must be an absolute or a relative file name, followed by an optional parenthesized line/column information in one of the following forms:

    ```
    (line) or (line-line) or (line-col) or (line,col-col) or (line,col,line,col)
    ```

Lines and columns start at 1 in a file; that is, the beginning of a file is 1, and the leftmost column is 1. If the Origin is a tool name, then it must not change based on locale; that is, it needs to be locale-neutral.

- **Subcategory (Optional)**   Subcategory is used to classify the category itself further; it should not be localized.

- **Category (Required)**   Category must be either "error" or "warning". Case does not matter. As with origin, category must not be localized.

- **Code (Required)**   Code identifies an application-specific error code/warning code. Code must not be localized and it must not contain spaces.

- **Text**   User-friendly text that explains the error, and it must be localized if you cater to multiple locales.

When MSBuild calls command-line tools (for instance, csc.exe or vbc.exe), it looks at the output emitted by the tool to the standard out and standard error streams. Any lines that match the error format that I just described will be treated specially; that is, lines that are recognized as errors or warnings will be turned into build errors and warnings, respectively.

To see the real benefit of this, you have to be building from within Visual Studio. Because MSBuild treats these messages specially, they get logged as first-class warnings and errors in the Visual Studio task list. If the Origin specifies line/column information, then double-clicking the message will take you to the source of the error in the offending file.

Creating Reusable Build Elements

When you are integrating tools into your build process that serve as key elements in a build, then you should consider creating reusable elements that can be consumed by various products. Creating reusable build elements is different, and more difficult, than the content that we have covered thus far. When you are creating these scripts, there are a few rules that you should follow. We will point out how the scripts that we create in this chapter adhere to the guidelines outlined in the following list:

1. Needs to be self-contained

2. Process needs to be transparent and extensible to the consumer

3. Overridable behavior

4. A contract should be defined and validated

The first rule, "Needs to be self-contained," means that all the necessary steps to perform the desired actions are captured in the defined script. This does not mean that the script cannot make assumptions (these are covered by rule #4), but it does mean that the tool's build script cannot modify values of the calling build script. For example, if you have a build script for public use that defines how to invoke FxCop, then the FxCop script file should not change the value for the BuildDependsOn property, even though this is tempting. Instead, the importing build script should place the FxCop target(s) into that property.

The second consideration, "Process needs to be transparent and extensible to the consumer," means that the entire process needs to be able to be modified to suit the needs of the caller. For example, similar to the Microsoft.Common.targets, target dependency lists should be exposed as properties so that consumers can extend them to inject their own targets. For example, the Microsoft.Common.targets contains properties such as BuildDependsOn, CompileDependsOn, ResolveReferencesDependsOn, PrepareResourceNamesDependsOn, and many others. By exposing such properties, callers can easily change the process of the script itself. With MSBuild 4.0, you get this by default with BeforeTargets and AfterTargets. However, DependsOn properties are still good to use because there is a slight difference. With DependsOn properties, you can redefine all dependencies, but with BeforeTargets and AfterTargets, you cannot. There are a few disadvantages to using DependsOn properties, though, which are outlined as follows:

1. The target must explicitly define its DependsOnTargets value in a property.

2. If the property is carelessly overwritten, unexpected results will occur.

3. You can only prepend or append; you cannot inject a step in the middle.

Because of these limitations, this solution is not ideal, either, but it is better than any other option currently available.

The third rule, "Overridable behavior," is for the most part built into MSBuild. This is because every target that is imported into a file can be overridden by simply re-declaring that target at some point after the Import statement that initially defines it. Because of this, you should be wary of creating MSBuild scripts that have targets with an excessive number of task invocations. Just as when you write code, when your targets grow too large, then they should be re-factored. If your targets are more fine-grained, then others can easily override a target to customize the behavior. If a target performs many different actions, it is difficult for others to override because they don't want to have to rewrite the entire target just to change a small section.

> **Note** You can use the command-line switch `/preprocess` (`/pp`) to write out the entire MSBuild file to a file. This would include all the imported targets, properties, and items. Sometimes this is very helpful to do because it shows what targets are being used.

Now we can move on to the final guideline, "A contract should be defined and validated." Of all the rules, this is the one that is most interesting. Most frameworks, such as the Microsoft .NET Framework and Microsoft Windows Communication Foundation (WCF), have a clear mechanism for defining a contract between a consumer and a provider. Unfortunately, MSBuild doesn't have such a mechanism. Despite this limitation, we need a way to declare an agreement between these two parties, and that agreement should be validated. In reusable .targets files, the data are always provided by the caller and the essential behavior is always described by the callee. Because the callee needs to know what data to act upon, the correct properties and items need to be made available to it. Also, the validation logic can be placed inside a target, which is called before the essential actions are performed. If you are validating static items, then you can place these validation targets inside the InitialTargets declaration. We will see this implemented in all the target files in this chapter. When you are creating target files, there is a convention that you should be aware of and make sure to follow: You should prefix with an underscore all properties, items, and target names that should be considered internal implementation details. By doing so, you are letting the caller know that its behavior is subject to change or might even be removed in newer versions. A future version of MSBuild might support some type of scoping mechanism that can be used to work around this issue. This convention is followed by all target files provided by Microsoft. Now that we have outlined some guidelines, we can take a look at what it takes to integrate some specific tools into our build process.

NUnit

If you are not familiar with NUnit, it is an open-source unit testing framework. It is very similar to the unit testing tools that are available in the team versions of Visual Studio, which have specific tasks and targets. You can learn more about NUnit at its homepage, *nunit.org*. NUnit is not the only alternative to Visual Studio tests; another tool is xUnit.net, and there are many others. If you are using NUnit to test your applications, then you should automate running NUnit as a part of your build process. You can achieve this in a few different ways. One of the best options is to use the NUnit task that is available from the MSBuild Extension Pack. We will first take a look at this task and then describe how to effectively utilize it. Table 7-3 describes the properties that are available on the NUnit task.

TABLE 7-3 NUnit Task Properties

Name	Description
Assemblies	Contains the assemblies that the NUnit task will examine. You can also pass in the full path to a Visual Studio project, if it ends in one of these extensions: .csproj, .vbproj, .vjsproj, or .vcproj. Another option here is to pass an NUnit project file. This is the only *required* input.
IncludeCategory	Specifies the NUnit test case category or categories that should be executed. If you decorate your test cases with an *NUnit.Framework.Category* attribute, then this feature may be useful. If you are providing multiple values, then they should be separated by a *comma*. This corresponds to the /include command-line parameter of nunit-console.exe.

Name	Description
ExcludeCategory	Specifies the NUnit test case category or categories that should be excluded from test execution. If you are passing more than one value for this, they should be *comma*-separated. This corresponds to the `/exclude` command-line parameter.
OutputXmlFile	This is where the test results XML file will be stored. This is not a required input, but you should always set this. If this is not set, then the file will be placed in a file named TestResult.xml in the working directory. This corresponds to the /xml parameter.
ErrorOutputFile	If provided, this file will be populated with any messages that are sent to the standard error stream. This corresponds to the /err parameter.
NoShadow	By default, NUnit will execute all of your test cases on shadow copies of your assemblies. These are typically contained in the "%temp%\nunit20\ShadowCopyCache\" folder. This behavior can be disabled by providing a value of `true` for this property. This corresponds to the /noshadow command-line parameter.
Configuration	Using this, you can specify the value for configuration that the test cases should be run against. This corresponds to the `/config` command-line parameter.
NoThread	If a value of *true* is provided for this property, then the test cases will be executed in the same thread. The default value for this is *false.* This corresponds to the /thread parameter.

Note Other properties exist for this task as well. For the full list, see the documentation for the MSBuild Extension Pack.

To demonstrate using this task, I have created a simple class containing some test cases, as shown in the following class definition.

```
namespace Unittest.Proj1
{
    using NUnit.Framework;

    [TestFixture]
    public class TestOperators
    {
        [Test]
        public void TestAddition()
        {
            int result = 1 + 1;
            Assert.AreEqual(2, result);

            result = 100 + 1;
            Assert.AreEqual(101, result);
```

```
        result = 1005 + (-1);
        Assert.AreEqual(1004, result);
    }
    [Test]
    public void TestSubtraction()
    {
        int result = 1 - 1;
        Assert.AreEqual(0, result);

        result = 100 - 1;
        Assert.AreEqual(99, result);

        result = 1005 - (-1);
        Assert.AreEqual(1006, result);
    }
  }
}
```

This class is located in the Unittest.Proj1 project. Now we need to create an MSBuild file that can be used to execute the unit tests in that project for us using the NUnit task, shown in the following nunitExample.proj file.

```
<Project xmlns="http://schemas.microsoft.com/developer/msbuild/2003"
         ToolsVersion="4.0"
         DefaultTargets="UnitTest">

  <PropertyGroup>
    <ExtensionTasksPath>
      $(MSBuildThisFileDirectory)\..\Contrib\ExtensionPack\4.0\
    </ExtensionTasksPath>
  </PropertyGroup>
  <Import Project="$(ExtensionTasksPath)MSBuild.ExtensionPack.tasks"/>

  <ItemGroup>
    <UnitTestProjects
      Include="$(MSBuildProjectDirectory)\unittest\Unittest.Proj1\Unittest.Proj1.csproj">
    </UnitTestProjects>
  </ItemGroup>

  <PropertyGroup>
    <NUnitResultFile>$(MSBuildProjectDirectory)\nunit-result.xml</NUnitResultFile>
  </PropertyGroup>

  <Target Name="UnitTest">
    <!-- Build all the projects in UnitTestProjects -->
    <MSBuild Projects="@(UnitTestProjects)" />
    <!-- Execute the test cases, if any fail so will the build -->
    <NUnit Assemblies="@(UnitTestProjects)"
           ToolPath="..\Contrib\NUnit 2.5.7\bin\net-2.0" />

  </Target>
</Project>
```

In this MSBuild file, I have declared the UnitTestProjects item and included the Unittest.Proj1 .csproj file.

> **Note** In the previous example, the MSBuild Extension Pack was referenced from a relative folder, but if you have installed the extension pack on your machine, then you could have used the MSBuildExtensionsPath property. This property points to the suggested location for third-party targets and tasks. They should be located in a directory under that path which typically points to the folder C:\Program Files\MSBuild. Also, there is a related property, MSBuildExtensionsPath32, which is for tasks and targets that have 32- and 64-bit versions.

In the UnitTest target, the default target for this file, I first build the project, and then I invoke the NUnit task against it. In this example, I have chosen, for simplicity, to pass the project file as the NUnit input file. Also, notice that I provide the path to nunit-console.exe via the ToolPath property, which is available on any task extending the *Microsoft.Build.Utilities .ToolTask* class. The listing shown in Figure 7-7 captures the last portion of the results you get when you execute the command `msbuild nunitExample.proj /t:UnitTest /clp:v=d`. In this case, we are setting the verbosity of the console logger to detailed (/clp:v=d) in order to output the NUnit messages.

```
d" depends on it):
Done building target "CoreBuild" in project "Unittest.Proj1.csproj".
Target "AfterBuild" in file "C:\Windows\Microsoft.NET\Framework\v4.0.30319\Microsoft.Common.target
s" from project "C:\InsideMSBuild\Ch07\unittest\Unittest.Proj1\Unittest.Proj1.csproj" (target "Bui
ld" depends on it):
Done building target "AfterBuild" in project "Unittest.Proj1.csproj".
Target "Build" in file "C:\Windows\Microsoft.NET\Framework\v4.0.30319\Microsoft.Common.targets" fr
om project "C:\InsideMSBuild\Ch07\unittest\Unittest.Proj1\Unittest.Proj1.csproj" (entry point):
Done building target "Build" in project "Unittest.Proj1.csproj".
Done Building Project "C:\InsideMSBuild\Ch07\unittest\Unittest.Proj1\Unittest.Proj1.csproj" (defau
lt targets).

Done executing task "MSBuild".
Using "NUnit" task from assembly "C:\InsideMSBuild\Ch07\..\..\Contrib\ExtensionPack\4.0\MSBuild.Exte
nsionPack.dll".
Task "NUnit"
  Command:
  C:\InsideMSBuild\Contrib\NUnit 2.5.7\bin\net-2.0\nunit-console.exe /nologo C:\InsideMSBuild\Ch07
  \unittest\Unittest.Proj1\Unittest.Proj1.csproj
  The "NUnit" task is using "nunit-console.exe" from "C:\InsideMSBuild\Contrib\NUnit 2.5.7\bin\net
  -2.0\nunit-console.exe".
  ProcessModel: Default    DomainUsage: Default
  Execution Runtime: Default

  Tests run: 2, Errors: 0, Failures: 0, Inconclusive: 0, Time: 0.0670039 seconds
    Not run: 0, Invalid: 0, Ignored: 0, Skipped: 0

  Dir
Done executing task "NUnit".
Done building target "UnitTest" in project "nunitExample.proj".
Done Building Project "C:\InsideMSBuild\Ch07\nunitExample.proj" (UnitTest target(s)).

Build succeeded.
    0 Warning(s)
    0 Error(s)
```

FIGURE 7-7 NUnitExample.proj passing result

From the output shown, we can see that the Unittest.Proj1.csproj file was built, and then the test cases executed via the NUnit task. If any test cases failed, then the build itself would have failed. To demonstrate this behavior, uncomment the following failing test case in the *TestOperators* class.

```
[Test]
public void TestDivide()
{
    int numerator = 100;
    int divisor = 20;
    int result = numerator / divisor;
    Assert.AreEqual(6, result);
}
```

To see how a failing test would affect the build, execute the nunitExample.proj more times. The result is shown in Figure 7-8.

As stated, since there was at least one failing test case, the entire build failed. The failures are also summarized at the end of the build. Now that we've described how we can use the NUnit task, we can take a look at how we can create a reusable targets file to simplify the process of invoking it.

```
C:\InsideMSBuild\Ch07>msbuild nunitExample.proj /t:UnitTest /nologo
Build started 9/11/2010 5:30:17 PM.
Project "C:\InsideMSBuild\Ch07\nunitExample.proj" on node 1 (UnitTest target(s)).
Project "C:\InsideMSBuild\Ch07\nunitExample.proj" (1) is building "C:\InsideMSBuild\Ch07\unittest\
Unittest.Proj1\Unittest.Proj1.csproj" (2) on node 1 (default targets).
CoreCompile:
  C:\Windows\Microsoft.NET\Framework\v4.0.30319\Csc.exe /noconfig /nowarn:1701,1702 /nostdlib+ /er
  rorreport:prompt /warn:4 /define:DEBUG;TRACE /reference:C:\Windows\Microsoft.NET\Framework\v2.0.
  50727\mscorlib.dll /reference:C:\InsideMSBuild\Contrib\nunit2.2\nunit.framework.dll /reference:"
  C:\Program Files (x86)\Reference Assemblies\Microsoft\Framework\v3.5\System.Core.dll" /reference
  :"C:\Program Files (x86)\Reference Assemblies\Microsoft\Framework\v3.5\System.Data.DataSetExtens
  ions.dll" /reference:C:\Windows\Microsoft.NET\Framework\v2.0.50727\System.Data.dll /reference:C:
  \Windows\Microsoft.NET\Framework\v2.0.50727\System.dll /reference:C:\Windows\Microsoft.NET\Frame
  work\v2.0.50722\System.Xml.dll /reference:"C:\Program Files (x86)\Reference Assemblies\Microsoft
  \Framework\v3.5\System.Xml.Linq.dll" /debug+ /debug:full /filealign:512 /optimize- /out:obj\Debu
  g\Unittest.Proj1.dll /target:library Properties\AssemblyInfo.cs TestOperators.cs
CopyFilesToOutputDirectory:
  Copying file from "obj\Debug\Unittest.Proj1.dll" to "bin\Debug\Unittest.Proj1.dll".
  Unittest.Proj1 -> C:\InsideMSBuild\Ch07\unittest\Unittest.Proj1\bin\Debug\Unittest.Proj1.dll
  Copying file from "obj\Debug\Unittest.Proj1.pdb" to "bin\Debug\Unittest.Proj1.pdb".
Done Building Project "C:\InsideMSBuild\Ch07\unittest\Unittest.Proj1\Unittest.Proj1.csproj" (defau
lt targets).

UnitTest:
  ..\Contrib\NUnit 2.5.7\bin\net-2.0\nunit-console.exe /nologo C:\InsideMSBuild\Ch07\unittest\Unit
  test.Proj1\Unittest.Proj1.csproj
  ProcessModel: Default      DomainUsage: Default
  Execution Runtime: Default
  ..F.
  Tests run: 3, Errors: 0, Failures: 1, Inconclusive: 0, Time: 0.0790045 seconds
    Not run: 0, Invalid: 0, Ignored: 0, Skipped: 0

  Errors and Failures:
  1) Test Failure : Unittest.Proj1.TestOperators.TestDivide

      expected:<6>
      but was:<5>
  at Unittest.Proj1.TestOperators.TestDivide() in c:\InsideMSBuild\Ch07\unittest\Unittest.Proj1\Te
  stOperators.cs:line 38

C:\InsideMSBuild\Ch07\nunitExample.proj(26,5): error MSB6006: "nunit-console.exe" exited with code
 1.
Done Building Project "C:\InsideMSBuild\Ch07\nunitExample.proj" (UnitTest target(s)) -- FAILED.

Build FAILED.
```

FIGURE 7-8 NUnitExample.proj failing result

I have created a reusable targets file, nunit.targets, which can be used across products. I will show portions of the file in this chapter, but you can see it in its entirety in the sample sources. The following snippet contains some key elements of this file.

```
<Target Name="ValidateNUnitSettings">
  <!-- Validate assumptions that are contracted  -->

  <Error Condition="'$(NUnitOutputDir)'==''"
    Text="NUnitOutputDir property not defined" />

  <Error Condition="'@(NUnitAssemblies)'==''"
    Text="NUnitAssemblies not defined" />
  <Error Condition="'%(NUnitAssemblies.ProjectName)'==''"
    Text="Atleast 1 item in NuitAssemblies doesn't have metadata 'ProjectName' defined." />
  <Error Condition="!Exists('%(NUnitAssemblies.FullPath)')"
    Text="Couldn't locate assembly at: %(NUnitAssemblies.FullPath)" />
```

```xml
  <Error Condition="
!Exists('$(GenericBuildRoot)Contrib\NUnit 2.5.7\bin\net-2.0\nunit-console.exe')"
Text="Couldn't locate nunit-console.exe at:
$(GenericBuildRoot)Contrib\NUnit 2.5.7\bin\net-2.0\nunit-console.exe"/>
</Target>

<PropertyGroup>
  <!-- Declare target dependencies here -->
  <UnitTestDependsOn>
    $(UnitTestDependsOn);
    BeforeUnitTest;
    ValidateNUnitSettings;
    UnitTestCore;
    DetectNUnitFailures;
    ReportNUnitFailures;
    AfterUnitTest;
  </UnitTestDependsOn>
  <UnitTestCleanDependsOn>
    $(UnitTestCleanDependsOn);
    BeforeUnitTestClean;
    CoreUnitTestClean;
    AfterUnitTestClean;
  </UnitTestCleanDependsOn>
</PropertyGroup>

<Target Name="UnitTest"
    Inputs="%(NUnitAssemblies.Identity)"
    Outputs="@(NUnitAssemblies->'$(NUnitOutputDir)%(ProjectName).UNITTEST.xml')"
    DependsOnTargets="$(UnitTestDependsOn)" />

<Target Name="UnitTestCore" Outputs="%(NUnitAssemblies.Identity)">
  <Message Text="Start UnitTest for @(NUnitAssemblies->'%(Fullpath)')" />

  <MakeDir  Condition="!Exists('$(NUnitOutputDir)')"
            Directories="$(NUnitOutputDir)" />

  <Message
    Condition="'$(GenBuildDebugMode)'=='true'"
    Text="Calling NUnit on:%0a%0d@(NunitAssemblies,'%0a%0d')" />

  <PropertyGroup>
    <NUnitContinueOnError
      Condition="'$(NUnitContinueOnError)'==''">true</NUnitContinueOnError>
  </PropertyGroup>
  <!--
  Don't rely on NUnit stopping build on failed unit test, we have more work afterwards
  -->

  <ItemGroup>
    <_NUnitReportFiles
      Include="@(NUnitAssemblies->'$(NUnitOutputDir)%(ProjectName).unittest.xml')" />
  </ItemGroup>
</Target>
```

```
<Target Name="CleanUnitTest"
        DependsOnTargets="$(UnitTestCleanDependsOn)" />
<Target Name="CoreUnitTestClean">
  <MakeDir Directories="$(NUnitOutputDir)"
           Condition="!Exists('$(NUnitOutputDir)')" />
  <ItemGroup>
    <_OldNUnitResultFiles Include="$(NUnitOutputDir)**\*.unittest.xml" />
    <_OldNUnitResultFiles Include="$(NUnitOutputDir)**\*.FAILED.xml" />
  </ItemGroup>

  <Delete Files="@(_OldNUnitResultFiles)" />
</Target>
```

You can see the contract defined, in MSBuild terms, inside the ValidateNUnitSettings target. This target will be executed before the UnitTest target gets executed; this is because it is contained in the value of the UnitTestDependsOn property. Inside this target, there are five error statements, each with conditional statements. These conditions define the contract that this file defines. If any of these erroneous conditions is detected, then the execution will fail. The following list describes the details of the contract that are asserted in that target.

1. A property named NUnitOutputDir is defined and not empty.

2. An item called NUnitAssemblies is defined.

3. Each item value in NUnitAssemblies contains a value for ProjectName metadata.

4. Each file in NUnitAssemblies exists on disk.

5. The nunit-console.exe file exists in the expected folder.

By using this contract, we have defined how a calling project file will feed data into this file. In return, this file will provide the core behavior required to execute the NUnit test cases contained in the provided assemblies. You should note that when declaring a condition such as Condition= "'$(NUnitContinueOnError)'==''", you should always wrap each term in quotes. If you do not, you may run into situations where the condition may not evaluate as expected. Now we can see how the other requirements for reusable targets files are achieved in this sample.

All the requirements for using the nunit.targets file are contained in the validation target shown previously. One of the requirements is that a list of assemblies be provided for which NUnit will be executed with. If you were authoring this file, you might be tempted to inject the UnitTest target directly into the BuildDependsOn property. This would make the assumption that the file was being consumed by a typical managed project file and would be a violation of the first rule outlined. The calling MSBuild file is entirely responsible for injecting the UnitTest target into its build, not the other way around. Also, your targets files, which are made publically available, should not override or even assume the existence of targets provided in Microsoft.Common.targets such as BeforeBuild, BeforeCompile, and so on.

How does this targets file meet the requirements for transparency and extensibility? That is achieved through the use of dependency properties, namely UnitTestDependsOn and UnitTestCleanDependsOn. These properties are used to define the set of steps to be executed in order for their corresponding targets to be executed. For example, the UnitTest target declares its dependency list as DependsOnTargets=$(UnitTestDependsOn). By using these, we externalize the steps required to execute the UnitTest and CleanUnitTest targets. Now that we've discussed how this targets file meets the requirements laid out previously, we can now examine how to use it.

Now that we've created a reusable targets file for invoking NUnit, we'll see how this can be utilized by calling MSBuild scripts. The following file, UnittestBuild.proj, demonstrates the usage of this file.

```xml
<Project xmlns="http://schemas.microsoft.com/developer/msbuild/2003"
        ToolsVersion="4.0"
        DefaultTargets="Build">
  <PropertyGroup>
    <SourceRoot>$(MSBuildProjectDirectory)\</SourceRoot>
    <UnitTestRoot>$(SourceRoot)unittest\</UnitTestRoot>
    <OutDirName>bin\</OutDirName>
    <Configuration>Debug</Configuration>
    <NUnitOutputDir>$(SourceRoot)BuildTemp\</NUnitOutputDir>
    <GenericBuildRoot>$(SourceRoot)\..\</GenericBuildRoot>
  </PropertyGroup>

  <ItemGroup>
    <UnitTestProjects
      Include="$(UnitTestRoot)Unittest.Proj1\Unittest.Proj1.csproj">
      <ProjectName>Unittest.Proj1</ProjectName>
    </UnitTestProjects>
    <UnitTestProjects
      Include="$(UnitTestRoot)Unittest.Proj2\Unittest.Proj2.csproj">
      <ProjectName>Unittest.Proj2</ProjectName>
    </UnitTestProjects>
  </ItemGroup>

  <PropertyGroup>
    <BuildDependsOn>
      $(BuildDependsOn);
      Clean;
      CoreBuild;
      UnitTest
    </BuildDependsOn>
  </PropertyGroup>
  <Target Name="Build" DependsOnTargets="$(BuildDependsOn)" />
  <Target Name="Clean">
    <MSBuild Projects="@(UnitTestProjects)" Targets="Clean" />
  </Target>
  <Target Name="CoreBuild">
```

```
  <!--
    Build the NUnit assemblies & put the
    assemblies in the NUnitAssemblies Item -->
  <MSBuild Projects="@(UnitTestProjects)">
    <Output ItemName="NUnitAssemblies"
            TaskParameter="TargetOutputs" />
  </MSBuild>
</Target>

<PropertyGroup>
  <RebuildDependsOn>
    $(RebuildDependsOn);
    Clean;
    Build
  </RebuildDependsOn>
</PropertyGroup>
<Target Name="Rebuild"
        DependsOnTargets="$(RebuildDependsOn)" />
<Import
  Project="nunit.targets" />

<PropertyGroup>
  <UnitTestDependsOn>
    CustomBeforeUnitTest;
    $(UnitTestDependsOn);
  </UnitTestDependsOn>
</PropertyGroup>

<Target Name="CustomBeforeUnitTest">
  <Message Text="NUnitAssemblies:%0a%0d@(NUnitAssemblies,'%0a%0d')"
           Importance="high" />
</Target>
</Project>
```

In this example, we have created a sample build file that builds a couple of projects and then sends the resulting assemblies to the NUnit task. I've made bold the text where I declare the UnitTestProjects item, which contains the projects that we are testing. Following that, you can see that the UnitTest target is placed into the BuildDependsOn list after the projects are to be built. Inside the CoreBuild target, the NUnitAssemblies item is created using the TargetOutputs of the MSBuild task, which is used to build the projects. Also, you can see that we inject the CustomBeforeUnitTest target into the list of targets required to execute before the UnitTest target. You should note that this must be defined after the Import statement for the nunit.targets file. If you build this project file, the result will be what is shown in Figure 7-9; only a portion of the result is shown here to conserve space.

The test cases in both projects were executed successfully. Since all the test cases passed, the build was allowed to continue. Also, you can see that CustomBeforeUnitTest was successfully injected into the build process at the appropriate time. Now we have demonstrated how we can integrate NUnit into the build process in a reusable means, we'll move on to discuss FxCop.

```
CustomBeforeUnitTest:
  NUnitAssemblies:
C:\InsideMSBuild\Ch07\unittest\Unittest.Proj1\bin\Debug\Unittest.Proj1.dll
C:\InsideMSBuild\Ch07\unittest\Unittest.Proj2\bin\Debug\Unittest.Proj2.dll
UnitTestCore:
  Start UnitTest for C:\InsideMSBuild\Ch07\unittest\Unittest.Proj1\bin\Debug\Unittest.Proj1.dll
  C:\InsideMSBuild\Ch07\..\..\Contrib\NUnit 2.5.7\bin\net-2.0\nunit-console.exe /nologo C:\InsideMSB
  uild\Ch07\unittest\Unittest.Proj1\bin\Debug\Unittest.Proj1.dll /xml=C:\InsideMSBuild\Ch07\BuildT
  emp\Unittest.Proj1.unittest.xml
  ProcessModel: Default    DomainUsage: Single
  Execution Runtime: Default
  . .
  Tests run: 2, Errors: 0, Failures: 0, Inconclusive: 0, Time: 0.0620035 seconds
    Not run: 0, Invalid: 0, Ignored: 0, Skipped: 0

UnitTestCore:
  Start UnitTest for C:\InsideMSBuild\Ch07\unittest\Unittest.Proj2\bin\Debug\Unittest.Proj2.dll
  C:\InsideMSBuild\Ch07\..\..\Contrib\NUnit 2.5.7\bin\net-2.0\nunit-console.exe /nologo C:\InsideMSB
  uild\Ch07\unittest\Unittest.Proj2\bin\Debug\Unittest.Proj2.dll /xml=C:\InsideMSBuild\Ch07\BuildT
  emp\Unittest.Proj2.unittest.xml
  ProcessModel: Default    DomainUsage: Single
  Execution Runtime: Default
  . .
  Tests run: 1, Errors: 0, Failures: 0, Inconclusive: 0, Time: 0.0540031 seconds
    Not run: 0, Invalid: 0, Ignored: 0, Skipped: 0

DetectNUnitFailures:
  Reading Xml Document "C:\InsideMSBuild\Ch07\BuildTemp\Unittest.Proj1.unittest.xml".
  XmlRead Result: ""
  _NUnitFailures:
DetectNUnitFailures:
  Reading Xml Document "C:\InsideMSBuild\Ch07\BuildTemp\Unittest.Proj2.unittest.xml".
  XmlRead Result: ""
  _NUnitFailures:
UnitTest:
Skipping target "UnitTest" because all output files are up-to-date with respect to the input files
UnitTest:
Skipping target "UnitTest" because all output files are up-to-date with respect to the input files

Done Building Project "C:\InsideMSBuild\Ch07\UnittestBuild.proj" (default targets).

Build succeeded.
    0 Warning(s)
    0 Error(s)
```

FIGURE 7-9 UnittestBuild.proj result

FxCop

FxCop is a code analysis tool created by Microsoft, which can help identify potential problem areas and can help enforce best practices. We will discuss how we can integrate FxCop into the build process here. There also is an FxCop task, provided by the MSBuild Extension Pack, which is similar to the NUnit task. We will use this task to execute the FxCop tool against the binaries of our projects. In the following example, we will execute FxCop against the Examples.Tasks and Example.Loggers project. Another related tool, which we will not demonstrate here, is StyleCop. StyleCop is a source code analysis tool; it examines the actual source files to ensure that styling guidelines are followed and to spot potential rule violations.

Similar to integrating NUnit, a targets file, fxcop.targets, has been created to take care of the heavy lifting for us. This file also has a validation target, ValidateFxCopSettings, which is shown in the following snippet.

```
<Target Name="ValidateFxCopSettings" DependsOnTargets="SetupFxCopProperties">
  <Error Condition="'@(FxCopAssemblies)'==''"
        Text="%40(FxCopAssemblies) not defined"/>
  <Error Condition="!Exists('%(FxCopAssemblies.Fullpath)')"
        Text="Path not found (FxCopAssemblies): [%(FxCopAssemblies.Fullpath)]"/>
```

```
  <Error Condition="'$(FxCopContribRoot)'==''"
         Text="%24(FxCopContribRoot) is not defined"/>
  <Error Condition="!Exists($(FxCopContribRoot))"
         Text="Path not found(FxCopContribRoot): [$(FxCopContribRoot)]"/>

  <Error Condition="'$(FxCopOutputRoot)'==''"
         Text="%24(FxCopOutputRoot) is not defined"/>
  <Error Condition="!Exists($(FxCopOutputRoot))"
         Text="Path not found(FxCopOutputRoot): [$(FxCopOutputRoot)]"/>
</Target>
```

Based on this target, we can see what this file requires for successful integration. The file that consumes the fxcop.targets file, FxCop_Examples.proj, is very similar to the one for the NUnit example; it is shown next.

```
<Project xmlns="http://schemas.microsoft.com/developer/msbuild/2003"
         DefaultTargets="Build">
  <PropertyGroup>
    <SourceRoot>$(MSBuildProjectDirectory)\</SourceRoot>
    <ContribRoot>..\Contrib\</ContribRoot>
    <FxCopOutputRoot>$(SourceRoot)BuildTemp\FxCopTemp\</FxCopOutputRoot>
    <Configuration>debug</Configuration>
  </PropertyGroup>

  <PropertyGroup>
    <_TaskOutputRoot>$(SourceRoot)Examples.Tasks\</_TaskOutputRoot>
    <_LoggerOutputRoot>$(SourceRoot)Examples.Loggers\</_LoggerOutputRoot>
  </PropertyGroup>

  <ItemGroup>
    <FxCopProjects
      Include="$(_TaskOutputRoot)Examples.Tasks.csproj">
      <Outputs>$(_TaskOutputRoot)bin\$(Configuration)\Examples.Tasks.dll</Outputs>
    </FxCopProjects>
    <FxCopProjects
      Include="$(_LoggerOutputRoot)Examples.Loggers.csproj">
      <Outputs>$(_LoggerOutputRoot)bin\$(Configuration)\Examples.Loggers.dll</Outputs>
    </FxCopProjects>

    <FxCopAssemblies Include="@(FxCopProjects->'%(Outputs)')" />
  </ItemGroup>

  <PropertyGroup>
    <BuildDependsOn>
      $(BuildDependsOn);
      CoreBuild;
      RunFxcop;
    </BuildDependsOn>
    <RebuildDependsOn>
      Clean;
      $(BuildDependsOn)
    </RebuildDependsOn>
  </PropertyGroup>
  <Target Name="Rebuild" DependsOnTargets="$(RebuildDependsOn)"/>
  <Target Name="Build" DependsOnTargets="$(BuildDependsOn)" />
```

```xml
  <Target Name="Clean">
    <MSBuild Projects="@(FxCopProjects)" Targets="Clean" />
  </Target>
  <Target Name="CoreBuild"
          Inputs="@(FxCopProjects)"
          Outputs="@(FxCopAssemblies)">
    <MSBuild Projects="@(FxCopProjects)" />
  </Target>

  <PropertyGroup>
    <CleanDependsOn>
      $(CleanDependsOn);
      CleanFxCop;
    </CleanDependsOn>
  </PropertyGroup>
  <Target Name="Clean" DependsOnTargets="$(CleanDependsOn)">
    <MSBuild Projects="@(FxCopProjects)" Targets="Clean" />
  </Target>
  <!-- Extension Pack required for fxcop.targets file -->
  <PropertyGroup>
    <ExtensionTasksPath>$(MSBuildThisFileDirectory)\..\Contrib\ExtensionPack\4.0\
    </ExtensionTasksPath>
  </PropertyGroup>
  <Import Project="$(ExtensionTasksPath)MSBuild.ExtensionPack.tasks"/>
  <Import
    Project="fxcop.targets"/>

  <PropertyGroup>
    <RunFxCopDependsOn>
      $(RunFxCopDependsOn);
      CoreBuild;
      CustomAfterFxCop
    </RunFxCopDependsOn>
  </PropertyGroup>

    <Target Name="CustomAfterFxCop">
    <Message Text="FxCop executed."
             Importance="high" />
  </Target>
</Project>
```

From the sample build script, you can see how easy it is to consume this targets file. In the previous snippet, I have highlighted a few key areas, some of which we will discuss here. Inside the CoreBuild target, the MSBuild task is used to build the projects. It is important to note that the CoreBuild target declares values for both Inputs and Outputs. Because of this, the target will support incremental building and will be executed only if it is out of date. This is critical in large builds. Sometimes you may have to make changes to your build to support this, but it is well worth it and is a best practice. The RunFxCop target is injected into the build process by placing it into the list of targets to execute during a build by extending the BuildDependsOn property. Along with this, the CustomAfterFxCop target is injected into the list of targets that will be executed after the RunFxCop target executes. We can see the results of building this script with the command msbuild.exe FxCop_Example.proj /t:Build in Figure 7-10.

```
g* /debug:full /filealign:512 /optimize- /out:obj\Debug\Examples.Loggers.dll /target:library Cus
tomFileLogger.cs FileLoggerBase.cs HelloLogger.cs HelloLogger2.cs IndentFileLogger.cs Properties
\AssemblyInfo.cs SimpleFileLogger.cs XmlLogger.cs "C:\Users\Ibrahim\AppData\Local\Temp\.NETFrame
work.Version=v4.0.AssemblyAttributes.cs"
_CopyOutOfDateSourceItemsToOutputDirectory:
    Copying file from "C:\InsideMSBuild\Ch07\Examples.Loggers\Samples\log4net.msbuild.xml" to "bin\D
ebug\Samples\log4net.msbuild.xml".
CopyFilesToOutputDirectory:
    Copying file from "obj\Debug\Examples.Loggers.dll" to "bin\Debug\Examples.Loggers.dll".
    Examples.Loggers -> C:\InsideMSBuild\Ch07\Examples.Loggers\bin\Debug\Examples.Loggers.dll
    Copying file from "obj\Debug\Examples.Loggers.pdb" to "bin\Debug\Examples.Loggers.pdb".
Done Building Project "C:\InsideMSBuild\Ch07\Examples.Loggers\Examples.Loggers.csproj" (default ta
rgets).

CoreFxcop:
    FxCop begin analysis on: C:\InsideMSBuild\Ch07\Examples.Tasks\bin\debug\Examples.Tasks.dll;C:\In
sideMSBuild\Ch07\Examples.Loggers\bin\debug\Examples.Loggers.dll
    ..\Contrib\Microsoft FxCop 1.36\fxcopcmd.exe /d:"..\Contrib\MSBuildCommunityTasks" /f:"C:\Inside
MSBuild\Ch07\Examples.Tasks\bin\debug\Examples.Tasks.dll" /f:"C:\InsideMSBuild\Ch07\Examples.Log
gers\bin\debug\Examples.Loggers.dll" /o:"C:\InsideMSBuild\Ch07\BuildTemp\FxCopTemp\fxcopResult.x
ml" /oXsl:"..\Contrib\Microsoft FxCop 1.36\Xml\FxCopReport.xsl" /r:"..\Contrib\Microsoft FxCop 1
.36\Rules\UsageRules.dll" /r:"..\Contrib\Microsoft FxCop 1.36\Rules\SecurityRules.dll" /r:"..\Co
ntrib\Microsoft FxCop 1.36\Rules\PortabilityRules.dll" /r:"..\Contrib\Microsoft FxCop 1.36\Rules
\PerformanceRules.dll" /r:"..\Contrib\Microsoft FxCop 1.36\Rules\MobilityRules.dll" /r:"..\Contr
ib\Microsoft FxCop 1.36\Rules\InteroperabilityRules.dll" /r:"..\Contrib\Microsoft FxCop 1.36\Rul
es\GlobalizationRules.dll" /r:"..\Contrib\Microsoft FxCop 1.36\Rules\DesignRules.dll" /s
DetectFxCopError:
    FxCop HTML Report File: C:\InsideMSBuild\Ch07\BuildTemp\FxCopTemp\fxcopResult.xml.html
    Reading Xml Document "C:\InsideMSBuild\Ch07\BuildTemp\FxCopTemp\fxcopResult.xml".
    XmlRead Result: "14"
    Reading Xml Document "C:\InsideMSBuild\Ch07\BuildTemp\FxCopTemp\fxcopResult.xml".
    XmlRead Result: "56"
    Reading Xml Document "C:\InsideMSBuild\Ch07\BuildTemp\FxCopTemp\fxcopResult.xml".
    XmlRead Result: "0"
    FxCopCriticalErrors: 14
    FxCopErrors: 56
    FxCopCriticalWarnings: 0
C:\InsideMSBuild\Ch07\fxcop.targets(121,5): error : FxCopCriticalErrors detected, count: 14 [C:\In
sideMSBuild\Ch07\FxCop_Examples.proj]
Done Building Project "C:\InsideMSBuild\Ch07\FxCop_Examples.proj" (Build target(s)) -- FAILED.


Build FAILED.

"C:\InsideMSBuild\Ch07\FxCop_Examples.proj" (Build target) (1) ->
(DetectFxCopError target) ->
    C:\InsideMSBuild\Ch07\fxcop.targets(121,5): error : FxCopCriticalErrors detected, count: 14 [C:\
InsideMSBuild\Ch07\FxCop_Examples.proj]

    0 Warning(s)
    1 Error(s)
```

FIGURE 7-10 RunFxCop result

There were a few FxCop errors detected during the build process; because of this, the build itself was stopped, as expected. We never have an opportunity to see if the CustomAfterFxCop target executes; therefore, it is not displayed in Figure 7-10. From the results shown, you can also see that the full path to the FxCop HTML report is passed for developers to use in order to help fix all the FxCop-related errors.

Now that we have seen how to use the fxcop.targets file, we can take a closer look at the file itself. The full source is delivered along with the other examples for this book. For this book, we will discuss some of the contents of that file here. In the next snippet, you will find the list of targets that make up the dependencies for the RunFxCop target.

```
<PropertyGroup>
  <RunFxCopDependsOn>
    SetupFxCopProperties;
    CopySourceFiles;
    ValidateFxCopSettings;
    BeforeFxCop;
    CoreFxCop;
    DetectFxCopError;
    AfterFxcop
  </RunFxCopDependsOn>
</PropertyGroup>
```

The two most important targets from the previous list are ValidateFxCopSettings and CoreFxCop, which are shown in bold in the code. The validate target declares the contract for consumers and ensures that it is adhered to, and the CoreFxCop target executes FxCop on the input specified. We have already seen the definition for the ValidateFxCopSettings target; in the following snippet, we will see the CoreFxCop target.

```xml
<Target Name="CoreFxcop"
        Inputs="@(FxCopAssemblies)"
        Outputs="$(FxCopReportFile)">
  <Message Text="FxCop begin analysis on: @(FxCopAssemblies)"
           Importance="high"/>
  <Message Text="FxCopReportFile: $(FxCopReportFile)"
           Importance="low"/>

  <MSBuild.ExtensionPack.CodeQuality.FxCop
    TaskAction="Analyse"
    Files="@(FxCopAssemblies)"

    ShowSummary="true"
    FxCopPath="$(MSBuildThisFileDirectory)\..\Contrib\Microsoft FxCop 1.36\FxCopCmd.exe"
    OutputFile="$(FxCopReportFile)" />


  <ItemGroup>
    <_FxCopReportFileItem Include="$(FxCopReportFile)"/>
  </ItemGroup>
  <PropertyGroup>
    <_FxCopHtmlReportFile>@(_FxCopReportFileItem->'%(Fullpath).html')</_FxCopHtmlReportFile>
  </PropertyGroup>

  <!-- Create human friendly version -->
  <XslTransformation
    XmlInputPaths="$(FxCopReportFile)"
    XslInputPath="$(FxCopTransformFile)"
    OutputPaths="$(_FxCopHtmlReportFile)" />

</Target>
```

This target invokes the FxCop task with the provided values. This invocation results in an XML file being written that contains the results of the analysis. This file is used later in the build process to detect FxCop failures. After the FxCop target completes executing, that same XML file is fed into the XslTransformation task, which is provided with MSBuild, to create a human-readable version of the FxCop report. Similar to the CoreBuild target shown earlier, the CoreFxCop target defines values for Inputs and Outputs; this will allow the target to be skipped if all FxCopAssemblies are older than the FxCopReportFile file. The remaining aspects of this file are specific implementation details and will not be discussed here.

In this chapter, we have discussed a few different ways that you can invoke tools external to your build process. We have also discussed how you can create reusable build elements for build processes that will be repeated from project to project. This chapter concludes our coverage of MSBuild in this fashion. The next two chapters will take a cookbook-style approach to delivering material.

Part IV
MSBuild Cookbook

Chapter 8
Practical Applications, Part 1

In the previous chapters, we have presented the material that you will need to extend and customize your build process. Stating how to do something and giving an example of doing it are two entirely different things. In order to provide the most benefit, this chapter and the next one are dedicated to providing practical examples that can be used in your build process. In this chapter, we will discuss examples such as setting an assembly version, handling errors, extending the clean process, and a few more.

Setting the Assembly Version

A common scenario when building projects is the need to set the version information for an assembly. You can easily accomplish this with the MSBuild Extension Pack (*http://msbuildextensionpack.codeplex.com/*). When you download and install the extension pack, it installs all the files into the $(MSBuildExtensionsPath)\ExtensionPack folder. Those files include MSBuild.ExtensionPack.VersionNumber.targets, which you will need to import into your project to help you set the version information. If you are using version control, then I suggest that you place the files under version control so that all of your developers do not have to install the extension pack. In my sample, you will see how to set the version information as if the files were under version control.

After you've downloaded and installed the extension pack, you can copy the files under the ExtensionPack to a folder with a known location relative to the project for which you want to set the version. In my example, I created a sample WPF application, WpfApplication1, and placed the files inside a Contrib folder at the same level as the projects folder. Then I edited the project file, WpfApplication1.csproj, to include the following snippet after the Import for Microsoft.CSharp.targets.

```
<PropertyGroup>
  <ExtensionTasksPath>..\Contrib\ExtensionPack\4.0\</ExtensionTasksPath>
</PropertyGroup>

<Import Project="$(ExtensionTasksPath)MSBuild.ExtensionPack.VersionNumber.targets"
        Condition=" '$(BuildingInsideVisualStudio)'!='true' " />

<PropertyGroup Condition=" '$(BuildingInsideVisualStudio)'!='true' ">
  <AssemblyMajorVersion>2</AssemblyMajorVersion>
  <AssemblyMinorVersion>5</AssemblyMinorVersion>
  <AssemblyFileMajorVersion>2</AssemblyFileMajorVersion>
  <AssemblyFileMinorVersion>5</AssemblyFileMinorVersion>
  <AssemblyInfoSpec>Properties\AssemblyInfo.cs</AssemblyInfoSpec>
</PropertyGroup>
```

First, I declare the ExtensionTasksPath property, which is required if you want to use the MSBuild Extension Pack from a location other than the MSBuildExtensionsPath. After that, I import the MSBuild.ExtensionPack.VersionNumber.targets file. This is the targets file that knows how to edit the AssemblyInfo.cs file to inject the correct version information. All we have to do is to declare some properties and it will take care of the rest for us. You can read that file for a full list of properties that it supports, but I have shown a few of them in the previous snippet. The properties that I set include the following: AssemblyMajorVersion, AssemblyMinorVersion, AssemblyFileMajorVersion, AssemblyFileMinorVersion, and AssemblyInfoSpec. The first two properties correspond to the first two numbers of AssemblyVersion, and the next two relate to the first two values for AssemblyFileVersion. The last property identifies where the AssemblyInfo.cs file can be found.

Also, you may notice that I have placed a condition on the import for the version number targets file as well as the property group containing those properties, `Condition="'$(BuildingInsideVisualStudio)'!='true' "`. By including this property, we will not run this task while the developers are building inside Microsoft Visual Studio. So when we run our builds from a command line, through Team Build, or any other Continuous Integration (CI) tool, the versioning task will be executed. Now all we have to do is build the project, and the version information will be taken care of for us. When I built the WpfApplication1 project and attached a FileLogger, the following statement was contained in the log.

```
Target "UpdateAssemblyInfoFiles" in file "C:\InsideMSBuild\Ch08\SetAssemblyVersion\Contrib\
ExtensionPack\4.0\
MSBuild.ExtensionPack.VersionNumber.targets" from project "C:\InsideMSBuild\Ch08\
SetAssemblyVersion\WpfApplication1
\WpfApplication1.csproj" (target "CoreCompile" depends on it):
Building target "UpdateAssemblyInfoFiles" completely.
Output file "obj\x86\Debug\WpfApplication1.exe" does not exist.
Using "AssemblyInfo" task from assembly "C:\InsideMSBuild\Ch08\SetAssemblyVersion\Contrib\
ExtensionPack\
4.0\MSBuild.ExtensionPack.dll".
Task "AssemblyInfo"
  Updating assembly info for Properties\AssemblyInfo.cs
        Updating major version to 2
        Updating minor version to 5
        Update method is DateString
        Updating build number to 0912
        Update method is AutoIncrement
        Updating revision number to 01
        Final assembly version is 2.5.0912.01
        Updating major version to 2
        Updating minor version to 5
        Update method is DateString
        Updating build number to 0912
        Update method is AutoIncrement
        Updating revision number to 01
        Final assembly version is 2.5.0912.01
Done executing task "AssemblyInfo".
```

From the log statement, you can see that the version properties were set twice, once for the assembly version and again for the file version. If you examined the assembly, you would see that these properties were indeed set as reported. In this example, I did not override any other properties that could be set by the task, but there are many others. Take a look at the documentation provided along with the download for more information regarding its usage.

We will revisit this in another example that shows how to set the version properties for more than one project file to the same value. The drawback of using this task is that it modifies a source file, which is a bad practice. One reason is because the source file must be checked out in order to build. A better solution would be to remove the assembly attributes from the AssemblyInfo.cs file and instead have a task that would be executed before the Compile target. This task would then create a new file, in the intermediate folder, that contains the attributes for the assembly and is appended to the Compile item list. Then the file should be appended to the FileWrites list so it can be removed on a clean. For more specific information regarding cleaning, see the example in the section entitled "Extending the Clean," later in this chapter.

Building Multiple Projects

When you are working in a team environment, you will typically want a little more control when building your applications than just building the solution. For example, many applications are now using generated code, running code analysis tools, executing test cases, and so on. When you need to create a build process, there are typically two approaches that you can take:

- Write a build file that builds the solution
- Create a build file that builds the projects individually

The main difference between the two is that when you build a solution file, you don't have control over what happens as the solution builds each individual project. You can supplement the solution's build process by adding steps before and after the solution is built. If you don't need this fine-grained control over the actual building, then I would suggest that you take this approach. The obvious advantage of using the Solution file is that this is the file used by Visual Studio. So when you use msbuild.exe on a solution file, you should get the exact same build that you would within Visual Studio. The major drawback is that solution files are very limited; for example, you cannot change the build process, and solution files can't be nested. In this section, we will demonstrate both techniques.

We have discussed the MSBuild task (the one that builds MSBuild projects) in the previous chapter. We will need to utilize this task in order to build the solution and projects. There have been some enhancements to the MSBuild task in version 3.5. The MSBuild task is able to process properties contained in an item's metadata instead of just accepting values as the

Properties input parameter. The following list presents three ways to pass properties into the MSBuild task.

1. As values in the Properties parameter of the MSBuild task

2. Item metadata named Properties

3. Item metadata named AdditionalProperties

The second option will always take precedence over the first, if both are supplied, so use only one or the other. The third option, however, can be used in conjunction with either the first or the second. Effectively, if a Properties metadata value is found on a project file passed to the MSBuild task, then any properties contained in the Properties input parameter on the MSBuild task itself will be *ignored*. The third option is always appended to either value from the first two options. Take a look at the contents of the following MSBuildTaskProperties.proj file.

```
<Project xmlns="http://schemas.microsoft.com/developer/msbuild/2003"
         ToolsVersion="4.0"
         DefaultTargets="Build">

  <PropertyGroup>
    <ExternalProjectFile>External.proj</ExternalProjectFile>
  </PropertyGroup>

  <ItemGroup>
    <!-- No values for Properties or AdditionalProperties -->
    <Projects Include="$(ExternalProjectFile)" />

    <!-- Only values for Properties -->
    <Projects Include="$(ExternalProjectFile)">
      <Properties>
        Name=One;
        Source=PropertiesMD;
      </Properties>
    </Projects>

    <!-- Only values for AdditionalProperties -->
    <Projects Include="$(ExternalProjectFile)">
      <AdditionalProperties>
        Name=Two;
        Source=AdditionalPropertiesMD;
      </AdditionalProperties>
    </Projects>

    <!-- Values for both Properties and AdditionalProperties -->
    <Projects Include="$(ExternalProjectFile)">
      <Properties>
        Name=Three;
        Source=PropertiesMD;
      </Properties>
      <AdditionalProperties>
        Name=Three;
```

```
          Source=AdditionalPropertiesMD;
        </AdditionalProperties>
      </Projects>
  </ItemGroup>

  <Target Name="Build">
    <!-- Execute the PrintInfo target for all projects in Projects -->
    <MSBuild Properties="Name=propertiesMSBuildTask"
             Projects="@(Projects)"
             Targets="PrintInfo"
             />
  </Target>

</Project>
```

This project will call the PrintInfo target of the External.proj file. This file is shown in the next snippet.

```
<Project xmlns="http://schemas.microsoft.com/developer/msbuild/2003"
         ToolsVersion="4.0"
         DefaultTargets="Build">

  <PropertyGroup>
    <!-- Defaults here -->
    <Name>none</Name>
    <Source>none</Source>
  </PropertyGroup>

  <Target Name="PrintInfo">
    <!-- Prints the values of the Name & Source properties -->
    <Message Text="Name: $(Name)"/>
    <Message Text="Source: $(Source)"/>
  </Target>
</Project>
```

Toward the top of the External.proj project file, two properties are declared, Name and Source. We will be overriding these values, but default values were provided in the case that they were not overridden. The MSBuildTaskProperties.proj project file declares an item type, Projects, which contains a list of projects to be built. All the item values point to the External .proj file using the property ExternalProjectFile. If you look at how the Projects items are declared, you will see that the four item declarations demonstrate four different ways that values can be passed using the Properties and AdditionalProperties metadata. One item contains no values for either, the second only values for Properties, the third only values for AdditionalProperties, and the last has values for both. Inside the Build target, we use the MSBuild task to execute the PrintInfo target, which prints the value for the Name and Source properties.

The output shown in Figure 8-1 demonstrates the difference between these three methods of providing properties. From the results, you can see that values from both the Properties and AdditionalProperties metadata values were used while building the projects.

```
C:\InsideMSBuild\Ch08>msbuild MSBuildTaskProperties.proj /t:Build /nologo
Build started 9/12/2010 2:11:45 PM.
Project "C:\InsideMSBuild\Ch08\MSBuildTaskProperties.proj" on node 1 (Build target(s)).
Project "C:\InsideMSBuild\Ch08\MSBuildTaskProperties.proj" (1) is building "C:\InsideMSBuild\Ch08\
External.proj" (2) on node 1 (PrintInfo target(s)).
PrintInfo:
  Name: propertiesMSBuildTask
  Source: none
Done Building Project "C:\InsideMSBuild\Ch08\External.proj" (PrintInfo target(s)).

Project "C:\InsideMSBuild\Ch08\MSBuildTaskProperties.proj" (1) is building "C:\InsideMSBuild\Ch08\
External.proj" (2:2) on node 1 (PrintInfo target(s)).
PrintInfo:
  Name: One
  Source: PropertiesMD;
Done Building Project "C:\InsideMSBuild\Ch08\External.proj" (PrintInfo target(s)).

Project "C:\InsideMSBuild\Ch08\MSBuildTaskProperties.proj" (1) is building "C:\InsideMSBuild\Ch08\
External.proj" (2:3) on node 1 (PrintInfo target(s)).
PrintInfo:
  Name: Two
  Source: AdditionalPropertiesMD;
Done Building Project "C:\InsideMSBuild\Ch08\External.proj" (PrintInfo target(s)).

Project "C:\InsideMSBuild\Ch08\MSBuildTaskProperties.proj" (1) is building "C:\InsideMSBuild\Ch08\
External.proj" (2:4) on node 1 (PrintInfo target(s)).
PrintInfo:
  Name: Three
  Source: AdditionalPropertiesMD;
Done Building Project "C:\InsideMSBuild\Ch08\External.proj" (PrintInfo target(s)).

Done Building Project "C:\InsideMSBuild\Ch08\MSBuildTaskProperties.proj" (Build target(s)).


Build succeeded.
    0 Warning(s)
    0 Error(s)
```

FIGURE 8-1 Build target results

I would suggest using the Properties metadata very carefully because when it is used, the values for the Properties parameter on the MSBuild task are completely ignored. If you mistakenly use this and you continue to pass properties directly into the MSBuild task, it may be difficult to track down the cause of errors. Using AdditionalProperties is very safe. When these values are present, they take precedence, but values passed directly into the MSBuild task are allowed as well. After we discuss how we can build the projects using the solution file, we will exercise these new behaviors when we build the projects individually. The advantage of using the Properties metadata, or AdditionalProperties, is that you can pass different sets of properties to different projects, whereas using the *Properties* attribute always passes the same global properties to all projects specified in the MSBuild task.

We will start by looking at building a solution file from an MSBuild project using the MSBuild task. One idea when creating a master build file is that you want to perform steps before and after the build. In the next code block, you will find the contents of the ExampleBuild_Sln.proj file.

```xml
<Project xmlns="http://schemas.microsoft.com/developer/msbuild/2003"
        ToolsVersion="4.0"
        DefaultTargets="FullBuild">

  <ItemGroup>
    <!-- define all the configurations that we should build -->
    <AllConfigurations Include="Debug" />
    <AllConfigurations Include="Release" />
  </ItemGroup>

  <ItemGroup>
    <SolutionToBuild Include="SampleSolution\SampleSolution.sln" />
  </ItemGroup>
```

```xml
<PropertyGroup>
  <FullBuildDependsOn>
    $(FullBuildDependsOn);
    BeforeBuild;
    CoreBuild;
    AfterBuild
  </FullBuildDependsOn>
  <FullRebuildDependsOn>
    $(FullRebuildDependsOn);
    Clean;
    FullBuild
  </FullRebuildDependsOn>
</PropertyGroup>

<Target Name="FullBuild"
        DependsOnTargets="$(FullBuildDependsOn)" />
<Target Name="BeforeBuild">
  <!-- TODO: Get latest source from version control -->
  <!-- TODO: Generate code -->
</Target>
<Target Name="AfterBuild">
  <!-- TODO: Unit tests -->
  <!-- TODO: Code Analysis -->
</Target>

<Target Name="CoreBuild">
  <MSBuild
    Projects="@(SolutionToBuild)"
    BuildInParallel="true"
    Properties="Configuration=%(AllConfigurations.Identity)" />
</Target>

<Target Name="FullRebuild"
        DependsOnTargets="$(FullRebuildDependsOn)" />
<Target Name="Clean">
  <!-- Clean for each configuration -->
  <MSBuild
    Projects="@(SolutionToBuild)"
    BuildInParallel="true"
    Properties="Configuration=%(AllConfigurations.Identity)"
    Targets="Clean"
    />
</Target>

</Project>
```

This is the project that is used to build the solution file. In this file, the main target, FullBuild, similar to the Microsoft.Common.targets Build target, performs no actions itself. It simply sets up a set of dependent targets to be executed. This list of targets is contained in the FullBuildDependsOn property. I have chosen to do this to make it easier to perform steps before or after the build process. The actual build takes place in the CoreBuild target. In this target, the MSBuild task is invoked on the SolutionToBuild item type. Also, you should note that we are specifying the Properties="Configuration=%(AllConfigurations.Identity)" so that the correct configuration value is passed to the project. By doing so, the MSBuild task will be invoked using task batching for all the values defined in the AllConfigurations item type. In this case, we will build the solution in Debug and Release mode. If you execute the command `msbuild.exe ExampleBuild_Sln.proj`, you will see that the solution was indeed built for Debug and Release configuration values.

When you build the solution file, you don't have much control over the build process. For example, if you need to set the assembly version by providing values for the AssemblyFileMajorVersion, AssemblyMajorVersion, and other related properties, this cannot be easily achieved because you cannot pass properties to individual projects to be used during the build. In contrast, when building each project, this is easily achieved by using the MSBuild task. In the next example, I will build the projects themselves while setting the assembly file version for all projects. The next snippet shows the relevant changes to the previous example. The full source can be found in the ExampleBuild_Projects.proj file.

```xml
<ItemGroup>
  <!--
  Properties and AdditionalProperties metadata are automatically
  passed when using the MSBuild task.
  If Properties metadata exists it takes precedence over and REPLACES
  any value for Properties provided to the MSBuild task itself.
  -->
  <ProjectsToBuild Include="SampleSolution\ClassLibrary1\ClassLibrary1.csproj">
    <AdditionalProperties>
      AssemblyFileMajorVersion=2;AssemblyMajorVersion=2;
      AssemblyFileMinorVersion=6;AssemblyMinorVersion=6
    </AdditionalProperties>
  </ProjectsToBuild>
  <ProjectsToBuild Include="SampleSolution\ClassLibrary2\ClassLibrary2.csproj">
    <AdditionalProperties>
      AssemblyFileMajorVersion=2;AssemblyMajorVersion=2;
      AssemblyFileMinorVersion=6;AssemblyMinorVersion=6
    </AdditionalProperties>
  </ProjectsToBuild>
  <ProjectsToBuild Include="SampleSolution\WpfApplication1\WpfApplication1.csproj">
    <AdditionalProperties>
      AssemblyFileMajorVersion=3;AssemblyMajorVersion=3;
      AssemblyFileMinorVersion=91;AssemblyMinorVersion=91
    </AdditionalProperties>
  </ProjectsToBuild>
  <ProjectsToBuild Include="SampleSolution\WindowsFormsApplication1\
WindowsFormsApplication1.csproj">
    <AdditionalProperties>
      AssemblyFileMajorVersion=3;AssemblyMajorVersion=3;
      AssemblyFileMinorVersion=91;AssemblyMinorVersion=91
    </AdditionalProperties>
  </ProjectsToBuild>
  <ProjectsToBuild Include="SampleSolution\unittest\Unittest.Proj1\Unittest.Proj1.csproj">
  </ProjectsToBuild>
  <ProjectsToBuild Include="SampleSolution\unittest\Unittest.Proj2\Unittest.Proj2.csproj">
  </ProjectsToBuild>
</ItemGroup>
<Target Name="CoreBuild">
```

```
  <MSBuild
    Projects="@(ProjectsToBuild)"
    BuildInParallel="true"
    Properties="Configuration=%(AllConfigurations.Identity)"
    />
</Target>

<Target Name="Clean">
  <!-- Clean for each configuration -->
  <MSBuild
    Projects="@(ProjectsToBuild)"
    BuildInParallel="true"
    Properties="Configuration=%(AllConfigurations.Identity)"
    Targets="Clean" />
</Target>
```

In this example, instead of using the SolutionToBuild item, a new item, ProjectsToBuild, is declared. (Note that these names are arbitrary—you could have named them whatever you wanted.) This item contains the list of projects that should be built. If you take a look at the declaration, you will notice that an AdditionalProperties metadata value is defined for some of the item values. As previously mentioned, if an item that you are passing to the MSBuild task contains metadata values for either Properties or AdditionalProperties, then these will be used as properties while building the project. This is a feature that has been available since MSBuild 3.5. To achieve the same with MSBuild 2.0, you would have to build each project individually and pass the properties in the *Properties* attribute. When using MSBuild 3.5 or later, one major drawback (besides usability) of this approach is that you would not be able to take advantage of building in parallel. In order for the MSBuild to build projects in parallel, all the projects must be passed into a single instance of the MSBuild task. MSBuild is not able to parallelize multiple declarations of the MSBuild task. Also, to take advantage of parallel build, you would need to specify that the property BuildInParallel be set to *true*, as well as invoking msbuild.exe with the /m switch.

The properties defined here for a few of the ProjectsToBuild item values determine what the major and minor version values should be. If you recall from the sample shown in the section entitled "Setting the Assembly Version," earlier in this chapter, these are properties that will be used by the AssemblyInfo task to set the assembly and file version of the created assembly. The command `msbuild ExampleBuild_Projects.proj /t:FullBuild` can be used to build all of the projects. The assemblies with version information also would be correctly stamped with the expected version numbers. I will not display the log here because of its size.

Attaching Multiple File Loggers

We have discussed creating and using loggers in detail in Chapter 5, "Custom Loggers." We mentioned that you could attach several instances of the file logger to the build process by using the notation /fl *[n]*, where *[n]* is an optional value in the range 1–9. If you use the switch /flp *[n]* without a corresponding /fl *[n]*, then the corresponding /fl *[n]* is implied and can be omitted. In that chapter, we didn't expand on why you would want to do this, but we will here. When a developer is kicking off a build process, a good set of loggers to have attached is outlined in Table 8-1.

TABLE 8-1 Loggers to Attach to a Typical Build

Type	Setting
ConsoleLogger	Verbosity = minimal and display summary
FileLogger	Verbosity = detailed
FileLogger	errorsonly
FileLogger	warningsonly

We purposefully turn down the verbosity of the console logger to show only the most important log messages. This is because it is typically difficult to gain any insight on a decent-sized build from the console logger, as well as for performance reasons. It is much faster to write to a file and then to the console. Builds that write a lot of information to the console take longer than those that do not. This reduced amount of information is fine because we attach a file logger to capture the remaining information into a file, so if needed, the results are always available there. Two other instances of the file logger are suggested, one to capture errors and the other for warnings. This allows the developers to be able to pinpoint specific information about errors and warnings, in order to clear them out. To summarize, there are really two reasons to have logs: to see progress and to diagnose problems. In order to see the progress, the build should log to the console as well as have a low verbosity. In order to diagnose problems, the logs need to be written to a file and have detailed information. Take a look at the command shown next, which builds the WpfApplication1 project, under the SetAssemblyVersion folder, with the loggers described in Table 8-1.

```
msbuild.exe /clp:verbosity=minimal /clp:summary
 /flp:verbosity=detailed;logfile=build.detailed.log
 /flp1:errorsonly;logfile=build.errors.log
 /flp2:warningsonly;logfile=build.warnings.log
 /m /p:BuildInParallel=true
 WpfApplication1.csproj /t:rebuild
```

In the command shown previously, we passed the appropriate parameters to the msbuild.exe to attach the desired loggers. Along with this, we specified the /m switch as well as defined the BuildInParallel value as *true*. Because of this, the projects will be built in parallel instead of serially.

Creating a Logger Macro

Because you generally want to attach the same set of loggers to a build process, we need a way to make it easier to attach all the loggers. One way that you might have guessed is to create a batch file; another is to create a DOS macro to perform the same action. A DOS macro is one of the lesser-known features of the command prompt. You can create and manage macros using the DOSKEY command.

We can create a parameterized macro that can automatically attach these loggers for us. In this case, we would need to create a macro with the following command.

```
doskey build=msbuild.exe /clp:verbosity=minimal /clp:summary
/flp:verbosity=detailed;logfile=build.detailed.log
/flp1:errorsonly;logfile=build.errors.log
/flp2:warningsonly;logfile=build.warnings.log
/m /p:BuildInParallel=true
$*
```

The previous command will create a new macro named *build* that executes msbuild.exe, which is assumed to be on the path, while attaching the loggers declared. You should take note of the usage of the *$** symbol. When you invoke a macro, the *$** symbol will be replaced with any text following the macro name on the command line. In our previous example, the command would have been simplified to `build WpfApplication1.csproj /t:Rebuild`. In this case, the *$** would have been replaced with the value 'WpfApplication1.csproj `/t:Rebuild`.' Once you create this macro, it is very easy to attach the same set of loggers to each build that you perform. One drawback to using a macro, however, is that the macro declaration lasts only for the duration of the command prompt. When the command prompt closes, the macros created in it will no longer be available. You are able to save the macros to a file using a command such as `doskey /macros > FileName`, where *FileName* is the name of the file to store the macros in. When you start a new command prompt, you can load the macros using the command `doskey /macrofile = FileName`. You could place this file under source control and have developers load it when the command prompt is opened.

Custom Before/After Build Steps in the Build Lab

There are scenarios when you would like to execute a set of steps before or after a build executes, but only on certain machines. On build machines, for example, you may want to encrypt config files, or obfuscate your code every time a Visual Studio project is built. The Microsoft.Common.targets file exposes this functionality. Inside that file, there are two import statements, one at the very top and the other at the very end:

```
<Import Project="$(CustomBeforeMicrosoftCommonTargets)"
        Condition="Exists('$(CustomBeforeMicrosoftCommonTargets)')"/>

<Import Project="$(CustomAfterMicrosoftCommonTargets)"
        Condition="Exists('$(CustomAfterMicrosoftCommonTargets)')"/>
```

These statements will import a file, if it exists, at the locations contained in the CustomBeforeMicrosoftCommonTargets and CustomAfterMicrosoftCommonTargets properties. The default values for these locations are %ProgramFiles32%\MSBuild\v*NNNN*\ Custom.Before.Microsoft.Common.targets and %ProgramFiles32%\MSBuild\v*NNNN*\Custom

.After.Microsoft.Common.targets, where *NNNN* is the version of MSBuild being used, which depends on your tools version. If you place an MSBuild file at either of those locations, it will be picked up at the appropriate time. If you do create such files, keep in mind that they will be processed by *every* build of a managed Visual Studio project that is executed on that machine. Also, it is worth noting that because you can have only one of each of these files, it is not typically useful to share various customizations.

> **Note**   With MSBuild 4.0, you can also place import files in %Program Files%\msbuild\4.0\
> Microsoft.Common.targets\ImportBefore\ and %Program Files%\msbuild\4.0\Microsoft
> .Common.targets\ImportAfter\, and the files will be automatically imported at the top
> of the Microsoft.Common.targets file for those in ImportBefore, and at the bottom
> of that file for ImportAfter. Unlike CustomBeforeMicrosoftCommonTargets and
> CustomAfterMicrosoftCommonTargets, you cannot change the path, but you can include more
> than one file. You will have to decide which method to use depending on your needs.

You can also override the CustomBeforeMicrosoftCommonTargets and CustomAfterMicrosoftCommonTargets properties to point to other locations. When you override these values, you should always provide the full path to the files. If you want the override to be machine-wide, then you could create these as environment variables. For a demonstration, I have created the following file, CustomAfter.proj.

```xml
<Project xmlns="http://schemas.microsoft.com/developer/msbuild/2003"
        ToolsVersion="4.0">
  <!--
  Insert custom steps into the build process
  -->
  <PropertyGroup>
    <BuildDependsOn>
      CustomBefore;
      $(BuildDependsOn);
      CustomAfter;
    </BuildDependsOn>
  </PropertyGroup>

  <Target Name="CustomBefore">
    <Message Text="Inside CustomBefore" Importance="high" />
  </Target>
  <Target Name="CustomAfter">
    <Message Text="Inside CustomAfter" Importance="high" />
  </Target>
</Project>
```

In this file, I extend the build process by injecting the CustomBefore and targets into the build dependency list. From the C:\InsideMSBuild\Ch08\SetAssemblyVersion\ WpfApplication1 directory, the following command was executed:

```
msbuild WpfApplication1.csproj /p:CustomAfterMicrosoftCommonTargets=C:\
InsideMSBuild\Ch08\CustomAfter.proj.
```

The end of the build is shown in Figure 8-2.

```
rk.dll" /reference:"C:\Program Files (x86)\Reference Assemblies\Microsoft\Framework\.NETFramewor
k\v4.0\Profile\Client\System.Core.dll" /reference:"C:\Program Files (x86)\Reference Assemblies\M
icrosoft\Framework\.NETFramework\v4.0\Profile\Client\System.Data.DataSetExtensions.dll" /referen
ce:"C:\Program Files (x86)\Reference Assemblies\Microsoft\Framework\.NETFramework\v4.0\Profile\C
lient\System.Data.dll" /reference:"C:\Program Files (x86)\Reference Assemblies\Microsoft\Framewo
rk\.NETFramework\v4.0\Profile\Client\System.dll" /reference:"C:\Program Files (x86)\Reference As
semblies\Microsoft\Framework\.NETFramework\v4.0\Profile\Client\System.Xaml.dll" /reference:"C:\P
rogram Files (x86)\Reference Assemblies\Microsoft\Framework\.NETFramework\v4.0\Profile\Client\Sy
stem.Xml.dll" /reference:"C:\Program Files (x86)\Reference Assemblies\Microsoft\Framework\.NETFr
amework\v4.0\Profile\Client\System.Xml.Linq.dll" /reference:"C:\Program Files (x86)\Reference As
semblies\Microsoft\Framework\.NETFramework\v4.0\Profile\Client\WindowsBase.dll" /debug+ /debug:f
ull /filealign:512 /optimize- /out:obj\x86\Debug\WpfApplication1.exe /resource:obj\x86\Debug\Wpf
Application1.g.resources /resource:obj\x86\Debug\WpfApplication1.Properties.Resources.resources
/target:winexe App.xaml.cs MainWindow.xaml.cs Properties\AssemblyInfo.cs Properties\Resources.De
signer.cs Properties\Settings.Designer.cs C:\InsideMSBuild\Ch08\SetAssemblyVersion\WpfApplicatio
n1\obj\x86\Debug\MainWindow.g.cs C:\InsideMSBuild\Ch08\SetAssemblyVersion\WpfApplication1\obj\x8
6\Debug\App.g.cs "C:\Users\Ibrahim\AppData\Local\Temp\.NETFramework,Version=v4.0,Profile=Client.
AssemblyAttributes.cs"
CopyFilesToOutputDirectory:
  Copying file from "obj\x86\Debug\WpfApplication1.exe" to "bin\Debug\WpfApplication1.exe".
  WpfApplication1 -> C:\InsideMSBuild\Ch08\SetAssemblyVersion\WpfApplication1\bin\Debug\WpfApplica
  tion1.exe
  Copying file from "obj\x86\Debug\WpfApplication1.pdb" to "bin\Debug\WpfApplication1.pdb".
CustomAfter:
  Inside CustomAfter
Done Building Project "C:\InsideMSBuild\Ch08\SetAssemblyVersion\WpfApplication1\WpfApplication1.cs
proj" (default targets).

Build succeeded.
    0 Warning(s)
    0 Error(s)
```

FIGURE 8-2 External build customization demonstration

From Figure 8-2, you can see that the targets were successfully injected into the build process and executed at the appropriate time. I chose to override the CustomAfterMicrosoftCommonTargets property from the command line for this example (because I don't want this to execute with every Visual Studio project build), but you could have placed this file in the previously mentioned location to have it automatically executed. If you do use this procedure, keep in mind that if you need to inject steps into the build process using the technique shown here, you must do this in the After targets file, not the Before targets file. If you override a property such as BuildDependsOn in a file that is imported in the Before targets file, then it will be overridden by the value contained in Microsoft.Common.targets itself.

Handling Errors

As you create project files, you may need to perform some custom steps in case an error occurs. MSBuild has a specific element that can be used for this exact task: the *OnError* element. If you use the *OnError* element, it must be the last element found inside the *Target* element that contains it. If this is not the case, then the build will be stopped before any target is executed. Some good examples of when you may want to use this are when you want to free resources that may have been taken by a previous target, send an email alert that the build has failed, create a work item to track the failed build, or undo checkout. The VB.NET/C# build process uses this to run build events that are supposed to be executed on compilation error. Team Build 2008 uses the *OnError* element in two places: in the CallCompile and CoreTest targets. If an error occurs, then either the SetBuildBreakProperties or SetTestBreakProperties target is called. Following this, the OnBuildBreak target is executed to create a failure work item that will be assigned to a team member. The *OnError* element has a parameter called ExecuteTargets, which contains one or more targets that should be executed if the target fails. If you specify more than one target, then the value should be a semicolon-delimited list. Targets will be executed in the sequence that they are declared in the ExecuteTargets list. In the file HandleErrors01.proj, we demonstrate using this element. The contents of this file are shown in the following snippet.

```
<Project xmlns="http://schemas.microsoft.com/developer/msbuild/2003"
        ToolsVersion="4.0"
        DefaultTargets="Build">
  <Target Name="Build">
    <!--
    This target simulates a target which fails.
    -->
    <Error Text="An error occurred" />

    <OnError ExecuteTargets="HandleErrors" />
  </Target>

  <Target Name="HandleErrors">

    <Message Text="An error has occurred and the build will fail"
            Importance="high" />

    <!-- TODO: Email error details -->

    <!-- TODO: Create a Work Item for fixing the build -->
  </Target>
</Project>
```

This sample uses the *OnError* element in order to execute the HandleErrors target if an error occurs during the Build target. The Build target uses the Error task to purposefully raise an error during the target. Figure 8-3 contains the results of executing the Build target.

```
C:\InsideMSBuild\Ch08>msbuild HandleErrors01.proj /t:Build /nologo
Build started 9/12/2010 3:06:58 PM.
Project "C:\InsideMSBuild\Ch08\HandleErrors01.proj" on node 1 (Build target(s)).
C:\InsideMSBuild\Ch08\HandleErrors01.proj(8,5): error : An error occurred
HandleErrors:
  An error has occurred and the build will fail
Done Building Project "C:\InsideMSBuild\Ch08\HandleErrors01.proj" (Build target(s)) -- FAILED.

Build FAILED.

"C:\InsideMSBuild\Ch08\HandleErrors01.proj" (Build target) (1) ->
(Build target) ->
  C:\InsideMSBuild\Ch08\HandleErrors01.proj(8,5): error : An error occurred

    0 Warning(s)
    1 Error(s)
```

FIGURE 8-3 *OnError* demonstration

Figure 8-3 shows that the build failed, as expected, when the Error task was called, and the HandleErrors target was called after this error occurred. In this case, I simply sent some text to the log using the Message task, but your error handlers can be much more sophisticated. If there are many instances of the *OnError* element, then they are handled in sequence, one after the other. If an error occurs inside a target that is handling an error, then another error is logged and the build is stopped, unless that target has an *OnError* element. In that case, the specified target or targets will be called. If any other targets were pending to be executed by the *OnError* element, they are abandoned, and the build is simply stopped.

Replacing Values in Config Files

There will be many times that you will need to update an application's configuration file at build time. For example, you may need to update a connection string or the logging level. In order to update the configuration, we can use a set of XML-related tasks that is available from the MSBuild Extension Pack. You can find these at *http://msbuildextensionpack.codeplex.com/*. In this example, I am going to update the config file for the sample WpfApplication1 project, under the UpdateConfig folder. The contents of the app.config file for that project are shown next.

```xml
<?xml version="1.0" encoding="utf-8" ?>
<configuration>
  <appSettings>
    <add key="helpUrl" value="http://www.sedodream.com" />
  </appSettings>
</configuration>
```

In this configuration file, I would like to do two things: update the configuration appSettings value and add a new setting that will contain an email address that can be used for help. We will have to create a new target, UpdateConfig, to perform these modifications for us. We will also need to inject this target into the build process by placing the following declaration after the Import statement for Microsoft.CSharp.targets.

```xml
<PropertyGroup>
  <ExtensionTasksPath>..\..\..\Contrib\ExtensionPack\4.0\</ExtensionTasksPath>
</PropertyGroup>

<Import Project="$(ExtensionTasksPath)MSBuild.ExtensionPack.tasks"/>

<PropertyGroup>
  <BuildDependsOn  Condition="'$(BuildingInsideVisualStudio)'!='true'">
    $(BuildDependsOn);
    UpdateConfig
  </BuildDependsOn>
</PropertyGroup>
```

In this example, you can see that I import the MSBuild Extension Pack so that I can use the XmlFile task that it contains to update the config file. After that, the Build target is extended by appending the UpdateConfig target to its dependency list. Once again, the condition `'$(BuildingInsideVisualStudio)'!='true'` is used to make sure that the UpdateConfig target is not run while building inside Visual Studio. When we build the project from the command line, the UpdateConfig target will be called after the project is built. We introduced this technique in Chapter 3, "MSBuild Deep Dive, Part 2." This target is shown in the following snippet.

```xml
<Target Name="UpdateConfig" DependsOnTargets="CoreBuild">
  <!-- Create an item that points to the dest config file -->
  <ItemGroup>
    <_DestConfigFile
      Include="@(AppConfigWithTargetPath->'$(OutDir)%(TargetPath)')"/>
  </ItemGroup>
  <PropertyGroup>
    <_UpdateXPath>/configuration/appSettings/add[@key='helpUrl']</_UpdateXPath>
    <_HelpEmailXPath>/configuration/appSettings/add[@key='helpEmail']</_HelpEmailXPath>
    <_HelpEmail>sayed.hashimi@gmail.com</_HelpEmail>
  </PropertyGroup>
  <Message Text="Updating config file %(_DestConfigFile.FullPath)"
           Importance="low"/>

  <!-- Update existing element -->
  <MSBuild.ExtensionPack.Xml.XmlFile
    TaskAction="UpdateAttribute"
    File="%(_DestConfigFile.FullPath)"
    XPath="$(_UpdateXPath)"
    Key="value"
    Value="http://sedotech.com/help"/>

  <!-- Insert a new 'add' element that has a 'key' attribute. -->
  <MSBuild.ExtensionPack.Xml.XmlFile
    TaskAction="AddElement"
    File="%(_DestConfigFile.FullPath)"
    XPath="/configuration/appSettings"
    Element="add"
    Key="key"
    Value="helpEmail" />

  <!-- Add a 'value' attribute to the new 'add' element. -->
  <MSBuild.ExtensionPack.Xml.XmlFile
    TaskAction="AddAttribute"
    File="%(_DestConfigFile.FullPath)"
    XPath="$(_HelpEmailXPath)"
    Key="value"
    Value="$(_HelpEmail)"/>
</Target>
```

In this target, I used the AppConfigWithTargetPath item to resolve the full path to the location where the configuration file was being placed after a build has been executed. Specifically, the item's TargetPath metadata value is being used to pinpoint this location. This item is declared in the Microsoft.Common.targets file. The location where the config file is finally placed is captured in the _DestConfigFile item. This item, and a few properties that are declared in this target, all start with an underscore. This is a convention that is used to denote that the element being declared is internal and should not be referenced by others. This convention is followed by all the targets files shipped by Microsoft.

The first notable action in the target is the usage of the XmlFile task. This task can be used to perform modifications to an XML file, including *AddAttribute, AddElement, RemoveAttribute, RemoveElement, UpdateAttribute,* and *UpdateElement.* The action will be decided with the value for TaskAction. You can use this task to update existing XML elements by setting the value for an element or setting the value for an attribute. In this case, we want to modify the helpUrl element `<add key="helpUrl" value="http://internal.sedotech.com/help"/>` and place the correct URL into the value attribute. The XPath to locate this element, which is contained in the _UpdateXPath property, is `/configuration/appSettings/add [@key='helpUrl']`. This is passed to the XmlFile task into the XPath input parameter. For more information about this task, see the MSBuild Extension Pack site.

Following this update, we need to insert a new element that contains an email address that can be used for support. This setting should be placed in the helpEmail app setting. In order to achieve this with the extension pack tasks, we first need to create a new XML element, using the XmlFile task with the TaskAction set to *AddElement,* to contain the value, and then update its value using the *AddAttribute TaskAction* value. After these steps are performed, the process has been completed. The following config file results show the Debug configuration.

```xml
<?xml version="1.0" encoding="utf-8"?>
<configuration>
  <appSettings>
    <add key="helpUrl" value="http://www.sedodream.com" />
    <add key="helpEmail" value="sayed.hashimi@gmail.com" />
  </appSettings>
</configuration>
```

From the resulting configuration file shown, we can see that we were able to successfully make the needed modifications at build time. You can use a similar technique to assist in automating your own modifications. Another technique for creating or modifying configuration files is to perform an XSL transformation to generate them. You can use the XslTransform task, which is shipped with MSBuild 4.0. This was briefly demonstrated in Chapter 7, "External Tools," when discussing FxCop.

Extending the Clean

Whenever you extend the build process to generate files, you must make sure that those files get cleaned up when the clean process is executed. Two primary ways of performing this are:

- Appending to the FileWrites item list
- Injecting custom targets into the clean process

The Microsoft.Common.targets file maintains a list of files that needs to be removed when the Clean target is executed; this list is the FileWrites list. It is written to disk in the base intermediate output path (i.e., obj\Debug) as the *ProjectFileName*.FileListAbsolute .txt file, where *ProjectFileName* is the name of the project file, including the extension. You can add values to the FileWrites item list if you need files deleted that were generated by

custom steps in your build process. You should never manually edit the *ProjectFileName*
.FileListAbsolute.txt file. Take a look at the segment from the ExtendClean\WpfExtendClean
.csproj file shown next.

```
<PropertyGroup>
  <BuildDependsOn>
    CustomBeforeBuild;
    $(BuildDependsOn);
  </BuildDependsOn>
</PropertyGroup>

<Target Name="CustomBeforeBuild">
  <ItemGroup>
    <_UserConfigFile Include="user.config" />
  </ItemGroup>
  <!-- Since this is before build, OutputPath directory may not yet exist -->
  <MakeDir Directories="$(OutputPath)"/>
  <!-- Copy user.config to OutputPath, if the user.config file exists -->
  <Copy Condition="Exists('@(_UserConfigFile)')"
        SourceFiles="@(_UserConfigFile)"
        DestinationFiles="@(_UserConfigFile->'$(OutputPath)user.config')">
    <Output ItemName="_CopiedUserFiles" TaskParameter="CopiedFiles"/>
  </Copy>
  <ItemGroup>
    <FileWrites Include="@(_CopiedUserFiles)"/>
  </ItemGroup>
</Target>
```

Here, we are extending the build process by injecting the CustomBeforeBuild target to be
executed before the Build target. The CustomBeforeBuild target is very straightforward: It
copies the user.config file, if it exists, to *OutputPath*. Following this, the file is appended to
the FileWrites item. Because of this, when a clean is executed, we would expect that this
file would be automatically deleted for us. The results of executing the command `msbuild`
`WpfExtendClean.csproj /t:Build;Clean` are shown in Figure 8-4.

```
CoreClean:
    Deleting file  "C:\InsideMSBuild\Ch08\ExtendClean\WpfExtendClean\bin\Debug\user.config".
    Deleting file  "C:\InsideMSBuild\Ch08\ExtendClean\WpfExtendClean\bin\Debug\WpfExtendClean.exe".
    Deleting file  "C:\InsideMSBuild\Ch08\ExtendClean\WpfExtendClean\bin\Debug\WpfExtendClean.pdb".
    Deleting file  "C:\InsideMSBuild\Ch08\ExtendClean\WpfExtendClean\obj\x86\Debug\ResolveAssemblyRef
    erence.cache".
    Deleting file  "C:\InsideMSBuild\Ch08\ExtendClean\WpfExtendClean\obj\x86\Debug\MainWindow.baml".
    Deleting file  "C:\InsideMSBuild\Ch08\ExtendClean\WpfExtendClean\obj\x86\Debug\MainWindow.g.cs".
    Deleting file  "C:\InsideMSBuild\Ch08\ExtendClean\WpfExtendClean\obj\x86\Debug\App.g.cs".
    Deleting file  "C:\InsideMSBuild\Ch08\ExtendClean\WpfExtendClean\obj\x86\Debug\WpfExtendClean_Mar
    kupCompile.cache".
    Deleting file  "C:\InsideMSBuild\Ch08\ExtendClean\WpfExtendClean\obj\x86\Debug\WpfExtendClean.g.r
    esources".
    Deleting file  "C:\InsideMSBuild\Ch08\ExtendClean\WpfExtendClean\obj\x86\Debug\WpfExtendClean.Pro
    perties.Resources.resources".
    Deleting file  "C:\InsideMSBuild\Ch08\ExtendClean\WpfExtendClean\obj\x86\Debug\GenerateResource.r
    ead.1.tlog".
    Deleting file  "C:\InsideMSBuild\Ch08\ExtendClean\WpfExtendClean\obj\x86\Debug\GenerateResource.w
    rite.1.tlog".
    Deleting file  "C:\InsideMSBuild\Ch08\ExtendClean\WpfExtendClean\obj\x86\Debug\WpfExtendClean.exe
    ".
    Deleting file  "C:\InsideMSBuild\Ch08\ExtendClean\WpfExtendClean\obj\x86\Debug\WpfExtendClean.pdb
    ".
Done Building Project "C:\InsideMSBuild\Ch08\ExtendClean\WpfExtendClean\WpfExtendClean.csproj" (Bu
ild;Clean target(s)).

Build succeeded.
    0 Warning(s)
    0 Error(s)
```

FIGURE 8-4 Clean target results

From the results shown in Figure 8-4, you can see that the user.config file was deleted when we executed the Clean target. This is exactly what we needed. One thing that you should note when using this technique: If your build step adds to the FileWrites item list, it must do so every time it would have written the file, even if it didn't because the file was up to date. For example, the output assembly goes into the FileWrites item list even if the project is up to date, in which case the compiler would not have been run. Because the *ProjectFileName* .FileListAbsolute.txt file is written for every build, you need to include the up-to-date files so that the next time the Clean target runs, it will delete the files.

Since this works so well, you may be wondering why we would discuss any other method. The reason is that this technique has some limitations:

- Files to be deleted must be under the output path.
- You must append to the FileWrites item early in the build process.

The first limitation is straightforward: If the file is not under the output path, it will not be deleted. This is for safety reasons; that way you cannot delete files by mistake. The second limitation states that you must append to the FileWrites item early in the build process. More specifically, you must append your values to the FileWrites item before the Clean or IncrementalClean target executes. When either of these targets gets executed, the clean file, the file that persists the FileWrites item, is written to disk. Despite these limitations, there are many cases in which you will be able to effectively use this technique. If you are not able to use this technique, however, then you can extend the clean process itself manually. Another advantage to cleaning manually is that you don't have to predict the files that were written. You can just blow away a whole directory, or use a wildcard expression.

There are some cases when you will be creating or copying files either later in the build process or to locations that are outside the output path that will need to be cleaned up as well. For instance, you may need to copy some of the outputs to different locations. In these cases, you will have to inject targets into the clean process to manage this manually.

Extending the clean process manually is similar to how the build process is extended. You have the following options: override an existing blank target such as BeforeClean, inject a target into the clean process, or use BeforeTargets or AfterTargets against the Clean target. If you choose the first option, you can override either the BeforeClean or the AfterClean target. This is similar to how the BeforeBuild or AfterBuild target can be overridden, as discussed in Chapter 3.

In Visual Studio Project files, you will find an import statement similar to the following, which is for C# project files.

```
<Import Project="$(MSBuildToolsPath)\Microsoft.CSharp.targets" />
```

Any customizations to the build or clean process should be declared after this statement to ensure that they are not overwritten. The following snippet shows how we can override the BeforeClean and AfterClean targets.

```
<Target Name="BeforeClean">
  <Message Text="This target is called before the clean begins"/>
  <!-- Place clean customizations here -->
</Target>
<Target Name="AfterClean">
  <Message Text="This target is called after the clean completes"/>
  <!-- Place clean customizations here -->
</Target>
```

When you override either of these two targets, they will be called at the appropriate time. If you are creating customizations to a specific project file, this is a great way to go. If you are creating reusable MSBuild scripts, then you must choose one of the other two options instead of taking this approach. This is because if the same target gets declared more than once, then the last target declared will be the definition that is used. All other target declarations will be ignored.

In order to inject a target into the clean process, the CleanDependsOn property is extended. This is demonstrated by the following snippet, taken from the ExtendClean\ ClassLibraryExtendClean.csproj file.

```
<PropertyGroup>
  <BuildDependsOn>
    $(BuildDependsOn);
    CustomAfterBuild
  </BuildDependsOn>

  <CleanDependsOn>
    $(CleanDependsOn);
    CustomClean
  </CleanDependsOn>

  <_OutputCopyLocation>$(OutputPath)..\..\CustomOutput\</_OutputCopyLocation>
</PropertyGroup>

<Target Name="CustomAfterBuild">
  <ItemGroup>
    <_FilesToCopy Include="$(OutputPath)**\*"/>
  </ItemGroup>
  <Message Text="_FilesToCopy: @(_FilesToCopy)" Importance="high"/>

  <Message Text="DestFiles:
        @(_FilesToCopy->'$(_OutputCopyLocation)%(RecursiveDir)%(Filename)%(Extension)')"/>

  <Copy SourceFiles="@(_FilesToCopy)"
        DestinationFiles=
        "@(_FilesToCopy->'$(_OutputCopyLocation)%(RecursiveDir)%(Filename)%(Extension)')"/>
</Target>

<Target Name="CustomClean">
  <Message Text="Inside CustomClean" Importance="high"/>
  <ItemGroup>
    <_CustomFilesToDelete Include="$(_OutputCopyLocation)**\*"/>
  </ItemGroup>
```

```
    <Delete Files="@(_CustomFilesToDelete)"/>
</Target>
```

In this snippet, we are re-declaring the CleanDependsOn property and appending the CustomClean target to its value. Also, BuildDependsOn is similarly extended to copy some files to another location. By extending the CleanDependsOn property when the Clean target is executed, the CustomClean target will be called at the end of the process. Inside the CustomClean target, I create an item, _CustomFilesToDelete, which will contain all the files that need to be deleted. These files are then deleted using the Delete task. Figure 8-5 contains the results of executing the Build target followed by the Clean target.

```
Version=v4.0.AssemblyAttributes.cs"
CopyFilesToOutputDirectory:
  Copying file from "obj\Debug\ClassLibraryExtendClean.dll" to "bin\Debug\ClassLibraryExtendClean.
  dll".
  ClassLibraryExtendClean -> C:\InsideMSBuild\Ch08\ExtendClean\ClassLibraryExtendClean\bin\Debug\C
  lassLibraryExtendClean.dll
  Copying file from "obj\Debug\ClassLibraryExtendClean.pdb" to "bin\Debug\ClassLibraryExtendClean.
  pdb".
CustomAfterBuild:
  _FilesToCopy: bin\Debug\ClassLibraryExtendClean.dll;bin\Debug\ClassLibraryExtendClean.pdb
  DestFiles: ClassLibraryExtendClean.dll;ClassLibraryExtendClean.pdb
  Copying file from "bin\Debug\ClassLibraryExtendClean.dll" to "bin\Debug\..\..\CustomOutput\Class
  LibraryExtendClean.dll".
  Copying file from "bin\Debug\ClassLibraryExtendClean.pdb" to "bin\Debug\..\..\CustomOutput\Class
  LibraryExtendClean.pdb".
CoreClean:
  Deleting file "C:\InsideMSBuild\Ch08\ExtendClean\ClassLibraryExtendClean\bin\Debug\ClassLibraryE
  xtendClean.dll".
  Deleting file "C:\InsideMSBuild\Ch08\ExtendClean\ClassLibraryExtendClean\bin\Debug\ClassLibraryE
  xtendClean.pdb".
  Deleting file "C:\InsideMSBuild\Ch08\ExtendClean\ClassLibraryExtendClean\obj\Debug\ClassLibraryE
  xtendClean.dll".
  Deleting file "C:\InsideMSBuild\Ch08\ExtendClean\ClassLibraryExtendClean\obj\Debug\ClassLibraryE
  xtendClean.pdb".
CustomClean:
  Inside CustomClean
  Deleting file "bin\Debug\..\..\CustomOutput\ClassLibraryExtendClean.dll".
  Deleting file "bin\Debug\..\..\CustomOutput\ClassLibraryExtendClean.pdb".
Done Building Project "C:\InsideMSBuild\Ch08\ExtendClean\ClassLibraryExtendClean\ClassLibraryExten
dClean.csproj" (Build;Clean target(s)).

Build succeeded.
    0 Warning(s)
    0 Error(s)
```

FIGURE 8-5 Extending the clean process

Figure 8-5 shows that the CustomClean target was called when expected and deleted the files that were copied in the CustomAfterBuild target. It is easy to forget about cleaning up files that your custom process creates or copies, but this is very important. If you do not clean up these files correctly, then you may encounter unexpected results during your build process. For instance, targets may continue to be skipped because of incremental building, even after the clean target has been executed.

In this chapter, we discussed a few very common build customizations, such as setting the version for an assembly and extending the clean process. We will continue these types of examples in the next chapter as well. Following that chapter, we will start examining materials related to Microsoft Visual C++.

Chapter 9
Practical Applications, Part 2

In the previous chapter, we started presenting some possible applications of MSBuild that you can use in your own build process. In this chapter, we'll examine some examples geared towards Web applications. Some of the examples in this chapter include starting and stopping services, encrypting the web.config file, and compressing JavaScript files.

Starting and Stopping Services

There are several instances where either your build or deployment process relies on services to be running. In these cases, you should ensure that the services are installed and started before they are needed. It's very easy to start and stop services from MSBuild.

You can use the Exec command to execute the command `net start` or `net stop` to start and stop services. A better alternative for this is to use the WindowsService task from the MSBuild Extension Pack. The MSBuild Extension Pack can be found at *http://msbuildextensionpack.codeplex.com/*. Using this task, you can perform many actions relating to services in a unified manner. This task supports these actions: start, stop, install, uninstall, disable, set manual start, set automatic start, check if a service exists, and update service identity. For complete information regarding this task, see the documentation provided with the tasks. When you install the MSBuild Extension Pack, the documentation file is placed in the same directory as the task assembly, which is typically %Program Files%\MSBuild\ExtensionPack. The following project file, Services01.proj, demonstrates this task.

```
<Project xmlns="http://schemas.microsoft.com/developer/msbuild/2003"
  ToolsVersion="4.0"
  DefaultTargets="StartService">

  <!-- Extension Pack required for fxcop.targets file -->
  <PropertyGroup>
    <ExtensionTasksPath>$(MSBuildThisFileDirectory)\..\Contrib\ExtensionPack\4.0\</ExtensionTasksPath>
  </PropertyGroup>
  <Import Project="$(ExtensionTasksPath)MSBuild.ExtensionPack.tasks"/>

  <Target Name="StartService">
    <!--
      The convention when using the MSBuild Extension Pack is to
      fully qualify the task name to avoid any possible collision with
      other tasks.
    -->
    <MSBuild.ExtensionPack.Computer.WindowsService
      TaskAction="Start"
      ServiceName="aspnet_state" />
```

```
        <!-- Similar to the command -->
        <!-- <Exec Command="net start aspnet_state" IgnoreExitCode="true" /> -->
    </Target>
    <Target Name="StopService">
        <MSBuild.ExtensionPack.Computer.WindowsService
            TaskAction="Stop"
            ServiceName="aspnet_state"/>

        <!-- Similar to the command -->
        <!-- <Exec Command="net stop aspnet_state" IgnoreExitCode="true" /> -->
    </Target>
</Project>
```

This task accepts a TaskAction parameter that describes what action the task is to perform. In order to start a service, TaskAction should be set to Start, and the name of the service, which is required, is provided in the ServiceName parameter. Similarly, to stop a service, Stop should be the TaskAction parameter.

If you execute the command `msbuild Services01.proj /t:StartService;StopService`, the result will be what is shown in Figure 9-1. You will need to execute this in a command line that has administrator privileges.

```
C:\InsideMSBuild\Ch09>msbuild Services01.proj /t:StartService;StopService /nologo
Build started 9/19/2010 5:56:59 PM.
Project "C:\InsideMSBuild\Ch09\Services01.proj" on node 1 (StartService;StopService target(s)).
StartService:
    Starting: aspnet_state on 'IBRAHIM-P55' - Stopped...
    Started: aspnet_state
StopService:
    Stopping: aspnet_state on 'IBRAHIM-P55' - Running...
    Please wait, Service state: aspnet_state on 'IBRAHIM-P55' - StopPending...
    Stopped: aspnet_state on 'IBRAHIM-P55'
Done Building Project "C:\InsideMSBuild\Ch09\Services01.proj" (StartService;StopService target(s))
.

Build succeeded.
    0 Warning(s)
    0 Error(s)
```

FIGURE 9-1 Starting and stopping services

In Figure 9-1, the WindowsService task is used to start and then stop the aspnet_state service. You might use this when you deploy a Web application that depends on the ASP.NET state service. When you deploy an application that has dependencies such as services, you must make sure that the dependencies, along with the application, are in a usable state when the deployment completes.

Web Deployment Project Overview

When you create Web sites and Web applications (both referred to as *Web applications* from this point) using Microsoft Visual Studio, it is a good idea to also use Web Deployment Projects (WDP) to assist in preparing the application for deployment. WDP is not installed by default with Visual Studio, but it is an add-in that you can download for free. You can download it by going to *http://www.microsoft.com/downloads* and searching for "Web Deployment Projects". The page name should be listed as "Visual Studio 2010 Web Deployment Projects." This add-in is supported by Microsoft, and you are encouraged to use it.

The following is a list of features that are provided with WDP:

- Automatic pre-compilation with the build process.

- WDP files are MSBuild files, so they are extensible.

- Various options exist regarding assembly generation, including:

  - Single assembly for all outputs

  - One assembly per folder

  - All pages and control outputs to a single assembly

  - Separate assembly for each page and control output

- Ability to sign assemblies.

- Ability to set assembly version.

When you are building and debugging your Web applications using Visual Studio, you place your markup in one file and the code behind the markup in a separate file. You could take the contents of the directory as is and allow Microsoft Internet Information Services (IIS) to compile the pages in place. The obvious problem to the approach is that you expose the code for your Web application on the Web server that is running it. A much better option is to pre-compile the application into one or many assemblies and deploy those along with the page files. A WDP can be used for this as well as the other tasks listed previously.

After you have installed the WDP add-in, you can create a new WDP in Visual Studio by right-clicking the desired Web application and selecting Add Web Deployment Project. This will show a dialog that prompts you for the name and location of the Web deployment project. Once you add the project, you will see it in Solution Explorer, similar to the one shown in Figure 9-2.

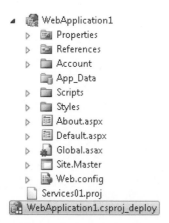

FIGURE 9-2 Web Deployment Projects in Solution Explorer

The WDP shows up in Visual Studio as any other project would. When you create WDP projects, the name typically ends in "_deploy" and the extension on the file is .wdproj. Unlike most other project types, there will never be any project items, such as files or folders, placed under this node in Visual Studio. This is just an MSBuild project file with some Visual Studio GUI support. When you build or rebuild the solution, the WDP will also be built. As a best practice, you should disable building WDP projects for Debug configurations because WDP builds may be lengthy. You can do this from the Configuration Manager in Visual Studio. You can always right-click the WDP to explicitly build it even if the current configuration is set to Debug. If you double-click the WDP, you will be presented with a dialog that consists of four pages: Compilation, Output Assemblies, Signing, and Deployment. From each of these pages, you can assign properties to customize that portion of the deployment process. For instance, take a look at the Output Assemblies page shown in Figure 9-3.

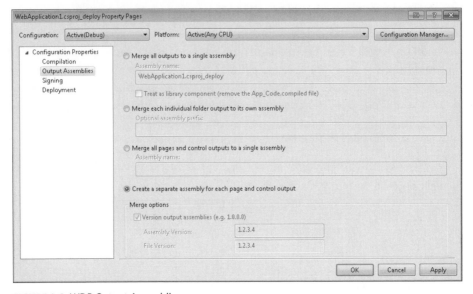

FIGURE 9-3 WDP Output Assemblies page

From the dialog in Figure 9-3, the option specified is to create one assembly named WebApplication1.csproj_deploy, and the assembly will be stamped with the value 1.2.3.4 for both assembly and file version. All the customizations on these pages are stored in the MSBuild project file for the WDP. Note that all the options specified for all four pages are specific to the Configuration and Platform selected in the drop-down lists toward the top of the dialog. You can even define new configurations, or platforms, to meet your needs. For instance, you may want to sign your assemblies that are going into production environments but not elsewhere. In this case, you could create a new configuration, Production, that has this setting enabled and configured.

We have discussed what WDPs are and the fact that they are MSBuild files. We will now take a closer look at a WDP file. In order to view the content of a WDP, you can right-click the WDP node and select Open Project File. The following sample WDP file is taken from WebApplication1.csproj_deploy.wdproj.

```xml
<Project xmlns="http://schemas.microsoft.com/developer/msbuild/2003"
         ToolsVersion="4.0"
         DefaultTargets="Build">
  <PropertyGroup>
    <Configuration Condition=" '$(Configuration)' == '' ">Debug</Configuration>
    <Platform Condition=" '$(Platform)' == '' ">AnyCPU</Platform>
    <ProductVersion>10.0.30319</ProductVersion>
    <SchemaVersion>2.0</SchemaVersion>
    <ProjectGuid>{C4AC8379-E059-4C19-894D-AA6A849D3CA2}</ProjectGuid>
    <SourceWebPhysicalPath>..\WebApplication1</SourceWebPhysicalPath>
    <SourceWebProject>
      {3161B34E-AE96-4095-B397-3259E5A9EC9E}|Ch09\WebApplication1\WebApplication1.csproj
    </SourceWebProject>
    <SourceWebVirtualPath>/WebApplication1.csproj</SourceWebVirtualPath>
    <TargetFrameworkVersion>v4.0</TargetFrameworkVersion>
  </PropertyGroup>
  <PropertyGroup Condition=" '$(Configuration)|$(Platform)' == 'Debug|AnyCPU' ">
    <DebugSymbols>true</DebugSymbols>
    <OutputPath>.\Debug</OutputPath>
    <EnableUpdateable>true</EnableUpdateable>
    <UseMerge>true</UseMerge>
    <SingleAssemblyName>WebApplication1.csproj_deploy</SingleAssemblyName>
  </PropertyGroup>
  <PropertyGroup Condition=" '$(Configuration)|$(Platform)' == 'Release|AnyCPU' ">
    <DebugSymbols>false</DebugSymbols>
    <OutputPath>.\Release</OutputPath>
    <EnableUpdateable>true</EnableUpdateable>
    <UseMerge>true</UseMerge>
    <SingleAssemblyName>WebApplication1.csproj_deploy</SingleAssemblyName>
  </PropertyGroup>
  <ItemGroup>
    <ProjectReference Include="..\WebApplication1\WebApplication1.csproj">
      <Project>{3161B34E-AE96-4095-B397-3259E5A9EC9E}</Project>
      <Name>WebApplication1</Name>
    </ProjectReference>
  </ItemGroup>
  <ItemGroup Condition="'$(Configuration)|$(Platform)' == 'Debug|AnyCPU'">
    <AssemblyAttributes Include="AssemblyFileVersion">
      <Value>1.2.3.4</Value>
    </AssemblyAttributes>
    <AssemblyAttributes Include="AssemblyVersion">
      <Value>1.2.3.4</Value>
    </AssemblyAttributes>
  </ItemGroup>
  <Import
    Project=
    "$(MSBuildExtensionsPath)\Microsoft\WebDeployment\v10.0\Microsoft.WebDeployment.targets"
    />

  <PropertyGroup>
    <OutputPath>Out_01\$(Configuration)\</OutputPath>
  </PropertyGroup>
</Project>
```

From the WDP shown here, you can see that all the values entered through the Visual Studio user interface are indeed captured in MSBuild format. Because of this, you can easily customize and/or extend the process. In fact, in this example, the output path has been customized using the OutputPath property to be Out_01\$(Configuration)\. This file is similar to a C# or VB.NET project in the sense that another file, Microsoft.WebDeployment.targets, which defines the build process, is imported. If you want to get a deeper understanding of the WDPs, you should take a look at that file.

I've already mentioned that when you build a solution that contains a WDP, the WDP will also be built automatically, if it is enabled for that configuration. You can also use msbuild .exe to manually build the WDP as you would any other MSBuild project file. When you build the WDP, you will notice that all the files that are contained in or under the source root for your Web application will be included in the deployment. The source root is captured in the SourceWebPhysicalPath property. This is because WDPs can support either Web sites or Web applications. If you would like to exclude files from being included in the deployment, you can use the ExcludeFromBuild item. For instance, in the WebApplication1_02.csproj_deploy .wdproj file, which extends the previous example, the following customizations have been inserted.

```
<ItemGroup>
  <!-- Use the ExcludeFromBuild item to exclude files from being deployed -->
  <ExcludeFromBuild
    Include="$(SourceWebPhysicalPath)\WebApplication1.csproj" />
  <ExcludeFromBuild
    Include="$(SourceWebPhysicalPath)\WebApplication1.csproj.user" />
  <ExcludeFromBuild
    Include="$(SourceWebPhysicalPath)\CustomOut\**\*" />
  <ExcludeFromBuild
    Include="$(SourceWebPhysicalPath)\**\.svn\**\*" />
</ItemGroup>

<PropertyGroup>
  <!-- Customize output location using the OutputPath property -->
  <OutputPath>Out_02\$(Configuration)\</OutputPath>
</PropertyGroup>
```

In these customizations, the following files will be excluded: the Web applications project file, the Web applications user file, the contents of the CustomOut folder, which is a copy of the bin folder, and any files related to version control. Because the WDP will pick up all files under the SourceWebPhysicalPath directory, this will include any artifacts that are placed there by your source control provider. In the case of Subversion, you should exclude those files contained within a .svn folder using the declaration shown previously. Typically, a snapshot of the Web directory is made and the build is then processed from that directory. This takes place in the following _CopyBeforeBuild target.

```
<Target Name="_CopyBeforeBuild"
        Condition=" '$(EnableCopyBeforeBuild)' == 'true' or '@(ExcludeFromBuild)' != ''  "
        DependsOnTargets="$(_CopyBeforeBuildDependsOn)">
```

```xml
  <ItemGroup>
    <_WDPAllExtraFilesUnderTempFolder
      Condition="'$(CopyBeforeBuildTargetPath)' != ''"
      Include="$(CopyBeforeBuildTargetPath)\**" />
    <_WDPAllExtraFilesUnderTempFolder
      Remove="@(_WebFiles->'$(CopyBeforeBuildTargetPath)\%(DestinationRelativePath)')" />
  </ItemGroup>
  <!--Remove all extra files in the temp folder that's not in the @
(FilesForPackagingFromProject-->
  <Delete Files="@(_WDPAllExtraFilesUnderTempFolder)"  />

  <!--This method support incremental copy instead of wipe out everytime-->
  <!--We already expand the path as relative path to the project, there is no need for
sourceDirectory-->
  <CopyPipelineFiles
    PipelineItems="@(_WebFiles)"
    SourceDirectory="$(MSBuildProjectDirectory)"
    TargetDirectory="$(CopyBeforeBuildTargetPath)"
    SkipMetadataExcludeTrueItems="True"
    UpdateItemSpec="False"
    DeleteItemsMarkAsExcludeTrue ="True">
    <Output
      TaskParameter="UpdatedPipelineItems"
      ItemName="_WebFilesCopied"/>
  </CopyPipelineFiles>

  <CreateProperty Value="$(CopyBeforeBuildTargetPath)">
    <Output TaskParameter="Value"
            PropertyName="_AspNetCompilerSourceWebPath" />
  </CreateProperty>

  <CallTarget Targets="$(OnAfter_CopyBeforeBuild)"
              RunEachTargetSeparately="false" />
</Target>
```

From this target, we can see that the CopyPipelineFiles task is called to copy the files. The _WebFiles item contains the files which will be copied. This item is populated in a dependent target, _CollectFilesForCopyBeforeBuild, taking into account files that should be excluded. Also note that at the end of the target, the _AspNetCompilerSourceWebPath property is declared to point to the new directory that was just created. Initially, it points to the full path of the SourceWebPhysicalPath. This path is passed to the AspNetCompiler task, which is a custom task that calls aspnet_compiler.exe. There are also some scenarios in which you may want to remove files from the output Web after the build. In this case, you can define an item type to contain these files, and then you can override the AfterBuild target to delete these files. For example, take a look at the following snippet.

```xml
<ItemGroup>
  <RemoveAfterBuild Include="$(OutputPath)\obj\" />
  <RemoveAfterBuild Include="$(OutputPath)\My Project\" />
</ItemGroup>
```

```
<Target Name="AfterBuild">
  <RemoveDir Directories="@(RemoveAfterBuild)" />
</Target>
```

The difference between this approach and the ExcludeFromBuild approach is that these files will be removed after the build process instead of being excluded from it. So if you needed files to be available during your build process but those files are not required by the application to run, then you should use the RemoveAfterBuild approach.

Zipping Output Files, Then Uploading to an FTP Site

In this sample, the files in the output folder are first compressed into a zip file and then uploaded to an FTP site. This sample uses these tasks from third parties: DNZip and Ftp. Both of these tasks are shipped with the MSBuild Extension Pack. The parameters for those tasks are outlined in Tables 9-1 and 9-2.

TABLE 9-1 DNZip Task Parameters

Name	Description
TaskAction	Valid values include *AddFiles*, *Create*, and *Extract*.
CompressFiles	A parameter that contains files to zip. Either this or CompressPath should be used, but not both. If both are specified, then CompressPath will be ignored.
CompressPath	The path that contains the files to be compressed. Either this or CompressFiles should be used, but not both. If both are specified, CompressPath will be ignored.
CompressionLevel	Sets the compression level to be used. There are three typical values; *Default*, *BestSpeed*, and *BestCompression*. Unsurprisingly, the default is *Default*. A number of uncommonly used values include *Level0*, *Level1*, *Level2*, *Level3*, *Level4*, *Level5*, *Level6*, *Level7*, *Level8*, and *Level9*. The *None* value means no compression at all, *Level1* is the least amount of compression, and *Level9* is the most.
ExtractPath	The path where the zip file is extracted.
Password	Sets the password used to create the zip file.
RemoveRoot	The root to remove from the zip path. This path should be a part of the files that are being compressed, not the target path. *Note that this is case-sensitive.*
ZipFileName	A required parameter that is the name of the zip file to be created.

TABLE 9-2 Ftp Task Parameters

Name	Description
TaskAction	Valid values include *UploadFiles*, *DownloadFiles*, *DeleteFiles*, *DeleteDirectory*, and *CreateDirectory*.
FileNames	The list of files that need to be transferred.
Host	The host to connect to. This should not include the *ftp://* prefix.
Port	The port used to connect to the FTP server.

Name	Description
RemoteDirectoryName	The remote path that will be opened on the FTP server.
UserName	The user name used to connect to the FTP server.
Password	The password to be used when connecting to the FTP site.

In the following snippet, you will find the contents of the ZipOutputFiles target taken from the WebApplication1_ftp01.csproj_deploy.wdproj file.

```
<Target Name="ZipOutputFiles" DependsOnTargets="Build">
  <ItemGroup>
    <_FilesToZip
        Include="$(OutputPath)**\*"
        Exclude="$(OutputPath)obj\**\*;$(OutputPath)bin\Samples\**\*"/>
    <!-- Create an item so we can get full path -->
    <_ZipOutputPathItem Include="$(OutputPath)" />
  </ItemGroup>
  <!--
Zip task requires that we have the full path
to the working directory, so create an item
from OutputPath to get that value.
-->
  <PropertyGroup>
    <_ZipOutputPathFull>%(_ZipOutputPathItem.Fullpath)</_ZipOutputPathFull>
    <!-- Get Date/Time to create unique .zip file name -->
    <_DateTime>$([System.DateTime]::Now.ToString('ddMMyyyy_hh_ss'))</_DateTime>
</PropertyGroup>

  <ItemGroup>
    <_ZipFile Include="$(OutputPath)..\$(_DateTime)_outputs.zip" />
  </ItemGroup>

  <MSBuild.ExtensionPack.Compression.DNZip
    TaskAction="Create"
    CompressFiles="@(_FilesToZip->'%(FullPath)')"
    ZipFileName="@(_ZipFile)"
    RemoveRoot="$(_ZipOutputPathFull)" />
</Target>
```

Notice that this target has declared that it depends on the Build target, so the Build target will be executed before this target is allowed to begin. The item _FilesToZip is created to contain all the files that should be placed in the zip file. In order to create a unique zip file name, the current date and time will be a part of the zip file name. To get this value, a property function is used. Then the Zip task is used to create the zip file. Note that the RemoveRoot is set to the *full path* of the OutputPath folder. This is necessary to create the zip file with the correct hierarchy. The resulting zip file is written to disk in the location contained in the _ZipFile item. Now that the file has been zipped, all that is left is to transfer the file using FTP. The related elements are shown next.

```
<PropertyGroup>
  <FtpFilesDependsOn>
    Build;
    ValidateFtpFilesSettings;
    ZipOutputFiles;
  </FtpFilesDependsOn>
</PropertyGroup>
<Target Name="FtpFiles" DependsOnTargets="$(FtpFilesDependsOn)">
  <!-- Ensure _ZipFile is not empty -->
  <Error Condition="'@(_ZipFile)'==''"
         Text="_ZipFile is required" />

  <MSBuild.ExtensionPack.Communication.Ftp
      TaskAction="UploadFiles"
      Host="$(FtpRoot)"
      FileNames="%(_ZipFile.FullPath)"
      UserName="$(FtpUsername)"
      UserPassword="$(FtpPassword)"
      RemoteDirectoryName="$(FtpDirectory)" />
</Target>

<Target Name="ValidateFtpFilesSettings">
  <Error Condition="'$(FtpRoot)'==''"
         Text="FtpRoot property is required" />
  <Error Condition="'$(FtpUsername)'==''"
         Text="FtpUsername property is required" />
  <Error Condition="'$(FtpPassword)'==''"
         Text="FtpPassword property is required" />
</Target>
```

The target being executed is the FtpFiles target, which depends on the targets contained in the FtpFilesDependsOn property. The main targets contained in that list are Build, ValidateFtpFilesSettings, and ZipOutputFiles. The ValidateFtpFilesSettings target ensures that the properties FtpRoot, FtpUsername, and FtpPassword are not empty. In this example, they are passed in to MSBuild from the command line using the /p switch. In the FtpFiles target, the FtpUpload task is used to perform the actual upload. You could execute this target using the command `msbuild WebApplication1_ftp01.csproj_deploy.wdproj /t:FtpFiles /fl /p:FtpRoot=FTP_HOST;FtpUsernameFTP_USERNAME;ftpPassword=FTP_ PASSWORD,FtpDirectory=FTP_DIRECTORY`. The *UPPER_CASE* values are values provided by you.

Compressing JavaScript Files

If your Web applications are deploying JavaScript files, then you should process those files through a JavaScript compressor before they are placed on the IIS server. A freely available one, JSMin, can be found at *http://www.crockford.com/javascript/jsmin.html*. JSMin offers significant compression results without modifying the actual source that is executed. Instead, it performs noninvasive operations such as remove comments and remove unnecessary white space. The JSCompress task available as a part of the MSBuildCommunityTasks compresses JavaScript files by relying on Jazmin, which is a C# port of JSMin.

The WebApplication1 project from the samples includes a Scripts folder that contains some JavaScript source files. These files were taken from the open-source Dojo project, which is available at *http://dojotoolkit.org*. To demonstrate compressing JavaScript, take a look at the WDP named WebApplication1_javascript.csproj_deploy.wdproj, which will automatically compress JavaScript files if Configuration is set to Release. The additions that were made to the file are shown next.

```
<PropertyGroup>
  <!-- aspnet_regiis.exe requires a path without the trailing slash -->
  <_OutputPathNoTrailingSlash>Out_JS01\$(Configuration)</_OutputPathNoTrailingSlash>
  <!-- Customize output location using the OutputPath property -->
  <OutputPath>$(_OutputPathNoTrailingSlash)\</OutputPath>
  <_WebProject>$(SourceWebPhysicalPath)\WebApplication1.csproj</_WebProject>
</PropertyGroup>
<!--
JSCompress task is contained in MSBuildCommunityTasks
This is a required to use the community tasks from a custom location.
-->
<PropertyGroup>  <MSBuildCommunityTasksPath>$(MSBuildThisFileDirectory)\..\Contrib\
MSBuildCommunityTasks\</MSBuildCommunityTasksPath>
</PropertyGroup>
<Import Project="$(MSBuildThisFileDirectory)\..\Contrib\MSBuildCommunityTasks\MSBuild.
Community.Tasks.targets" />
<PropertyGroup>
  <BuildDependsOn Condition=" '$(Configuration)'=='Release' ">
    BuildWebProject;
    $(BuildDependsOn);
    CompressJavascript
  </BuildDependsOn>
</PropertyGroup>
<Target Name="CompressJavascript">
  <ItemGroup>
    <_JSFilesToCompress Include="$(OutputPath)Scripts\**\*.js" />
  </ItemGroup>
  <JSCompress Files="@(_JSFilesToCompress)" />
</Target>
<Target Name="BuildWebProject">
  <MSBuild
    Projects="$(_WebProject)"
    Properties="Configuration=$(Configuration);Platform=$(Platform)" />
</Target>
```

In this sample, the target will be executed only if the Configuration property is set to Release. The CompressJavaScript target uses the JSCompress task to compress the JavaScript files contained in the Scripts folder. The available parameters for that task are summarized in Table 9-4.

TABLE 9-4 JSCompress Task Parameters

Name	Description
Files	Input parameter that will contain the list of files to be compressed
CompressedFiles	Output container containing the list of files that were compressed
Encoding	The encoding of the files

In this example, we pass the JavaScript files into the Files parameter using the
_JSFilesToCompress item. If you execute the command `msbuild`
`WebApplication1_javascript01.csproj_deploy.wdproj /p:Configuration=Release`,
then at the end of the build, you will notice what is shown in Figure 9-4.

Because of the usage of the JSCompress task, the size of the JavaScript files was reduced
from 74.4 Kb to 30.5 Kb. Since websites are using more and more JavaScript, compressing the
source files is becoming more important. It is recommended that you allow developers to
edit human-friendly files while at the same time automating your deployments to compress
the JavaScript files, as shown here.

```
Copying obj\Release\TempBuildDir\bin\WebApplication1_03.csproj_deploy.dll to C:\InsideMSBuild\Ch
09\Out_JS01\Release\bin\WebApplication1_03.csproj_deploy.dll.
Copying obj\Release\TempBuildDir\Scripts\Chart2D.js to C:\InsideMSBuild\Ch09\Out_JS01\Release\Sc
ripts\Chart2D.js.
Copying obj\Release\TempBuildDir\Scripts\DataGrid.js to C:\InsideMSBuild\Ch09\Out_JS01\Release\S
cripts\DataGrid.js.
Copying obj\Release\TempBuildDir\Scripts\dijit-all.js to C:\InsideMSBuild\Ch09\Out_JS01\Release\
Scripts\dijit-all.js.
Copying obj\Release\TempBuildDir\Scripts\dojo.js.uncompressed.js to C:\InsideMSBuild\Ch09\Out_JS
01\Release\Scripts\dojo.js.uncompressed.js.
Skip copying obj\Release\TempBuildDir\Styles\Site.css to C:\InsideMSBuild\Ch09\Out_JS01\Release\
Styles\Site.css, File C:\InsideMSBuild\Ch09\Out_JS01\Release\Styles\Site.css is up to date
ToggleDebugCompilation:
  Updating Web.config <compilation> element debug attribute to 'False'.
  Successfully updated Web.config <compilation> element debug attribute to 'False'.
CompressJavascript:
  Compressing JavaScript in "Out_JS01\Release\Scripts\Chart2D.js".
  Compressing JavaScript in "Out_JS01\Release\Scripts\DataGrid.js".
  Compressing JavaScript in "Out_JS01\Release\Scripts\dijit-all.js".
  Compressing JavaScript in "Out_JS01\Release\Scripts\dojo.js.uncompressed.js".
Done Building Project "C:\InsideMSBuild\Ch09\WebApplication1_03.csproj_deploy.wdproj" (default tar
gets).


Build succeeded.
    0 Warning(s)
    0 Error(s)
```

FIGURE 9-4 CompressJavaScript example

Encrypting web.config

A built-in tool is available that you can use to encrypt sections of your web.config file.
This tool is aspnet_regiis.exe and it ships with the Microsoft .NET Framework. It was
introduced in version 2.0. This tool can be used for many different purposes; in this section,
we will limit the discussion to using it to encrypt the web.config file.

When a section of the web.config file (or machine.config for that matter) is encrypted using
the aspnet_regiis.exe tool, it is done such that the section will be decrypted on the fly during
the lifetime of the Web application. The encryption is transparent to the application code.
When you use aspnet_regiis.exe to encrypt the configuration file, you will use the -pef switch
to indicate what section needs to be encrypted. In this example, we will also use a WDP,
an extension of those previously discussed. The WDP file for this example can be found in
the WebApplication1_encWebConfig.csproj_deploy.wdproj file. The customizations that were
made to the file are shown in the following snippet.

```
<PropertyGroup>
  <!-- aspnet_regiis.exe requires a path without the trailing slash -->
```

```xml
    <_OutputPathNoTrailingSlash>Out_Enc01\$(Configuration)</_OutputPathNoTrailingSlash>
    <!-- Customize output location using the OutputPath property -->
    <OutputPath>$(_OutputPathNoTrailingSlash)\</OutputPath>
    <_WebProject>$(SourceWebPhysicalPath)\WebApplication1.csproj</_WebProject>
</PropertyGroup>

<PropertyGroup>
  <BuildDependsOn>
    BuildWebProject;
    $(BuildDependsOn);
    EncryptWebConfig
  </BuildDependsOn>
</PropertyGroup>
<Target Name="EncryptWebConfig">
  <!-- Get the .NET 4.0 path -->
  <GetFrameworkPath>
    <Output PropertyName="_Net40Path" TaskParameter="FrameworkVersion40Path" />
  </GetFrameworkPath>

  <PropertyGroup>
    <_AspNetRegIisExe>&quot;$(_Net40Path)\aspnet_regiis.exe&quot;</_AspNetRegIisExe>
    <_pef>-pef &quot;connectionStrings&quot;</_pef>
    <_out>&quot;$(_OutputPathNoTrailingSlash)&quot;</_out>
  </PropertyGroup>
  <Exec Command="$(_AspNetRegIisExe) $(_pef) $(_out)"/>
</Target>
<Target Name="BuildWebProject">
  <MSBuild
    Projects="$(_WebProject)"
    Properties="Configuration=$(Configuration);Platform=$(Platform)" />
</Target>
```

As you can see, the build process was extended by injecting the EncryptWebConfig target to the end of the BuildDependsOn target. Inside that target, the GetFrameworkPath task is used to determine where the .NET Framework 4.0 is installed. The properties for that task, which are all outputs, are summarized in Table 9-5.

TABLE 9-5 GetFrameworkPath Parameters

Name	Description
FrameworkVersion11Path	Returns the path for the .NET 1.1 assemblies
FrameworkVersion20Path	Returns the path for the .NET 2.0 assemblies
FrameworkVersion30Path	Returns the path for the .NET 3.0 assemblies
FrameworkVersion35Path	Returns the path for the .NET 3.5 assemblies
FrameworkVersion40Path	Returns the path for the .NET 4.0 assemblies
Path	Returns the path for the .NET assemblies being used for the build process

This example uses the GetFrameworkPath task to determine where .NET 4.0 is installed because the aspnet_regiss.exe is located in that directory. After that, the following command is executed.

```
"%Framework4.0%\aspnet_regiis.exe" -pef "connectionStrings"
"Out_Enc01\Debug".
```

After that, the original connectionStrings node from the web.config is transformed into

```
<connectionStrings configProtectionProvider="RsaProtectedConfigurationProvider">
  <EncryptedData Type="http://www.w3.org/2001/04/xmlenc#Element"
    xmlns="http://www.w3.org/2001/04/xmlenc#">
    <EncryptionMethod Algorithm="http://www.w3.org/2001/04/xmlenc#tripledes-cbc" />
    <KeyInfo xmlns="http://www.w3.org/2000/09/xmldsig#">
      <EncryptedKey xmlns="http://www.w3.org/2001/04/xmlenc#">
        <EncryptionMethod Algorithm="http://www.w3.org/2001/04/xmlenc#rsa-1_5" />
        <KeyInfo xmlns="http://www.w3.org/2000/09/xmldsig#">
          <KeyName>Rsa Key</KeyName>
        </KeyInfo>
        <CipherData>
          <CipherValue>jHA75XUfC9PK7dyN4nSZZV1jNsTYfOS2BUudEmo8Fl3+vAYxRDkowZJ/g4wU
            hJanj2HCalnhwHKfBZvaHmlQej9nYnsssYg3v0r89LvAkHoXz4fUclg6ywjWYkyvadqyBog
            S1GRsdwLhtGRgdkeF6I76w40o9wCOkxolFYYara4=</CipherValue>
        </CipherData>
      </EncryptedKey>
    </KeyInfo>
    <CipherData>
      <CipherValue>YyzhkAEVtYsWIykmXZJqzXeDvVJNGKX/Xk6hcWA+dcITBM/4qYKsBoxx2nn69iEa
      /5hvSoOX1UQFe6fF5YuiziHYOI+n7TNKUJbAt4SIHOwGZYIy72Mbkjw7lmEEPXRO1YymocZtnlPbi
      aagNscvuLOoSvfR1zFrb4JNHuUwgIQFjeq3lEMGNzThuqoPjl+Csgmgrbc6EVx9C5jubfUSLiW8UZ
      /raVTu2cHVk+Hslj0twkIUkP6CkcPRiGA3wvfjI1+KMfUaBB5IRIX1jjQV2cObgQbgcyZTzA3jyR3
      fSOXpKZzHJ3IYvnOFXTpY/TfB7fHPEg8x0yHZ43cMlf2hCcd1O4RteWT9jSX3rNbvZCS8Y2/81qJH
      AYbZUft1KRgQwLSB/KDep6g=</CipherValue>
    </CipherData>
  </EncryptedData>
</connectionStrings>
```

> **Note** If you want to invoke the aspnet_regiis tool to perform encryption, then the build must be executed with administrator rights; that is, you must use an elevated command prompt. Otherwise, you will receive an error.

Now the connection strings have been encrypted. You can encrypt several other sections of the web.config as well. You should encrypt only the sections that contain sensitive information because encrypted sections do carry a performance penalty when being used by the application. If you are encrypting the web.config on a build server, then you have to make sure that the machine key is the same for the build server as the IIS server, or else the section(s) will not be successfully unencrypted.

Building Dependent Projects

If you are using a Web Application Project (WAP) as opposed to a website, then there is one major flaw in the process followed by the Microsoft.WebDeployment.targets file. The WAP is never built; it is assumed to have already been built. In the case of this example, if the WebApplication1 project was not built and you executed the command msbuild WebApplication1.csproj_deploy.wdproj, the result would be what is shown in Figure 9-5.

```
C:\InsideMSBuild\Ch09>msbuild WebApplication1.csproj_deploy.wdproj /nologo
Build started 9/21/2010 10:44:14 PM.
Project "C:\InsideMSBuild\Ch09\WebApplication1.csproj_deploy.wdproj" on node 1 (default targets).
ResolveAssemblyReferences:
    Primary reference "WebApplication1".
        Could not find dependent files. Expected file "C:\InsideMSBuild\Ch09\WebApplication1\bin\Web
Application1.dll" does not exist.
        Could not find dependent files. The system cannot find the path specified. (Exception from H
RESULT: 0x80070003)
        Resolved file path is "C:\InsideMSBuild\Ch09\WebApplication1\bin\WebApplication1.dll".
        Reference found at search location "".
AspNetCompiler:
    C:\Windows\Microsoft.NET\Framework\v4.0.30319\aspnet_compiler.exe -v /WebApplication1.csproj -p
    C:\InsideMSBuild\Ch09\WebApplication1 -u -f -d obj\Debug\TempBuildDir
/WebApplication1.csproj/global.asax(1): error ASPPARSE: Could not load type 'WebApplication1.Globa
l'. [C:\InsideMSBuild\Ch09\WebApplication1.csproj_deploy.wdproj]
Done Building Project "C:\InsideMSBuild\Ch09\WebApplication1.csproj_deploy.wdproj" (default target
s) -- FAILED.

Build FAILED.

"C:\InsideMSBuild\Ch09\WebApplication1.csproj_deploy.wdproj" (default target) (1) ->
(AspNetCompiler target) ->
  /WebApplication1.csproj/global.asax(1): error ASPPARSE: Could not load type 'WebApplication1.Glo
bal'. [C:\InsideMSBuild\Ch09\WebApplication1.csproj_deploy.wdproj]

    0 Warning(s)
    1 Error(s)
```

FIGURE 9-5 WDP failure

Since the WAP is not being built, the AspNetCompiler task fails because it was unable to load a type that was contained inside the WAP. In order to work around this problem, we will have to build the WAP. Additionally, we must build the WAP *before* the _CopyBeforeBuild target is executed; otherwise, a copy of the Web files will be created that doesn't contain the built assemblies. Take a look at the following definition of the BuildDependsOn property from Microsoft.WebDeployment.targets.

```
<PropertyGroup>
    <BuildDependsOn>
        _PrepareForBuild;
        ResolveProjectReferences;
        _ResolveReferences;
        ResolveReferences;
        _CheckExcludeWAPObjFolderFromBuild;
        _CopyBeforeBuild;
        BeforeBuild;
        AspNetCompiler;
        BeforeMerge;
        AspNetMerge;
        AfterMerge;
        CopyToOutputDir;
        ReplaceWebConfigSections;
        CreateVirtualDirectory;
        AfterBuild
    </BuildDependsOn>
</PropertyGroup>
```

The important thing to notice here is that the BeforeBuild target is positioned *after* the _CopyBeforeBuild target in the dependency list. We cannot use the BeforeBuild target to build the WAP because it needs to be built prior to the copying step. Instead, we have to extend the BuildDependsOn property and inject that step at the very beginning. The WebApplication1_03.csproj_deploy.wdproj demonstrates this, and the snippet is shown on the following page.

```
<PropertyGroup>
   <!-- Customize output location using the OutputPath property -->
   <OutputPath>Out_JS01\$(Configuration)\</OutputPath>
   <_WebProject>$(SourceWebPhysicalPath)\WebApplication1.csproj</_WebProject>
</PropertyGroup>

<PropertyGroup>
   <BuildDependsOn>
     BuildWebProject;
     $(BuildDependsOn)
   </BuildDependsOn>
</PropertyGroup>

<Target Name="BuildWebProject">
   <MSBuild
     Projects="$(_WebProject)"
     Properties="Configuration=$(Configuration);Platform=$(Platform)" />
</Target>
```

In this file, the BuildDependsOn property has been prepended to contain the BuildWebProject target, which builds the WAP. Now that these customizations have been created, the WAP is not assumed to have been built, and each time the WDP project is built, the WAP will be built, ensuring that it is up to date with respect to the source files. When you are building the solution file, you do not have to worry about this because Visual Studio will build the projects in the correct order.

Deployment Using Web Deployment Projects

There are many approaches to deploying your applications to various environments. In this sample, I'll demonstrate how you can extend the WDP to assist your deployment process. The approach that I demonstrate is fairly simplistic and has some limitations, which we will discuss. Later in the book, we will discuss the Web Deployment Tool, aka MSDeploy. This tool can be used for more robust deployments, but it may not be necessary for simple, copy-based deployments. The following target is taken from the WebApplication1_deploy01 .csproj_deploy.wdproj file.

```
<Target Name="DeployToServer" DependsOnTargets="BuildWebProject;Build">
   <PropertyGroup>
     <_ServerName>Ibrahim-P55</_ServerName>
     <_VDirName>Sample01</_VDirName>
     <_ServerDeployPath>\\$(_ServerName)\D$\Stage\$(_VDirName)\</_ServerDeployPath>
     <_ServerLocalPath>D:\Stage\$(_VDirName)\</_ServerLocalPath>
     <_ReplaceExisting>true</_ReplaceExisting>
   </PropertyGroup>
```

```
<!-- Create dir if it doesn't exist -->
<MakeDir Directories="$(_ServerDeployPath)" />

<!-- Copy files -->
<ItemGroup>
  <_FilesToDeploy
    Include="$(OutputPath)**\*"
    Exclude="$(OutputPath)obj\**\*;$(OutputPath)bin\Samples\**\*" />
</ItemGroup>

<Message Text="Copying files to remote server [$(_ServerName)]" />
<Copy SourceFiles="@(_FilesToDeploy)"
     DestinationFiles=
     "@(_FilesToDeploy->'$(_ServerDeployPath)%(RecursiveDir)%(Filename)%(Extension)')" />

<CreateVirtualDirectory
  Alias = "$(_VDirName)"
  ServerName ="$(_ServerName)"
  Path = "$(_ServerLocalPath)"
  ReplaceExisting = "$(_ReplaceExisting)" />

</Target>
<PropertyGroup>
  <_WebProject>$(SourceWebPhysicalPath)\WebApplication1.csproj</_WebProject>
</PropertyGroup>
<Target Name="BuildWebProject">
  <MSBuild
    Projects="$(_WebProject)"
    Properties="Configuration=$(Configuration);Platform=$(Platform)" />
</Target>
```

The first thing to notice about the DeployToServer target is that it depends on the Build target. In this target, a few properties are first declared that will be used throughout the target. The _ServerName property contains the name of the server to which the application is to be deployed. After the properties are declared, the destination folder is created (if it doesn't already exist) by using the MakeDir task. Then a set of files is copied to the server. Finally, the CreateVirtualDirectory task is used to create a virtual directory on the remote machine. The parameters of this task are summarized in Table 9-6.

TABLE 9-6 CreateVirtualDirectory Task Parameters

Name	Description
Alias	Required parameter that contains the name of the virtual directory to create.
Path	Required parameter that contains the location where the virtual directory will point. This should be a path used on the remote machine, not a path relative to the build machine. For instance, D:\Stage\Sample01, rather than \\sayed-762\D$\Stage\Sample01.

Name	Description
MetabaseProperties	Any additional metabase properties that should be set can be passed here. The name of the property should be placed in the Include attribute and the value of the property is a metadata named *Value*. For example, the following item type, VirtualDirectoryMetabaseProperties, could be passed to MetabaseProperties to set EnabledirBrowsing and AccessWrite to true on the virtual directory:

```
<ItemGroup>
 <VirtualDirectoryMetabaseProperties
    Include="EnableDirBrowsing">
   <value>true</value>
 </VirtualDirectoryMetabaseProperties>
 <VirtualDirectoryMetabaseProperties
    Include="AccessWrite">
   <value>true</value>
 </VirtualDirectoryMetabaseProperties>
</ItemGroup>
```

Name	Description
ReplaceExisting	If set to *true,* then this will allow any existing virtual directory to be replaced. The default value for this is *false.*
ServerName	Name of the server on which the virtual directory is being created. This defaults to *localhost.*
SiteId	The ID for the website on which the virtual directory will be installed. The default value for this is 1. Typically, you have to worry about this only if your IIS server is hosting multiple websites.

In the example shown previously, the CreateVirtualDirectory task is used to create a virtual directory named Sample01 on the server sayed_762. The contents of this virtual directory are placed at D:\stage\Sample01 on the IIS server. When the command `msbuild WebApplication1_deploy01.csproj_deploy.wdproj /t:DeployToServer` was executed, the files were copied to the remote server and the virtual directory was created.

This sample shows how you can deploy a Web application to a remote server. Every deployment process is different, and each has its own pros and cons. This should get you started with your own deployment process. This approach has the following limitations:

- The process running the build must have Administrator rights to the IIS server.

- IIS must have read/write access to the folder where the files are being placed.

- Copying files one by one can be very slow.

- If you encrypt the web.config file on the build machine, you must make sure that the machine key is the same on the build server as the IIS server.

Because of these limitations, this exact approach may not suit your needs, but this should not prevent you from creating your own deployment process using the WDPs.

In this chapter, we have introduced the WDPs. Some limitations and workarounds of the WDPs were discussed. Following that, we covered a few examples that you may be able to use in your current build and deployment process for Web applications. This chapter concludes the MSBuild material. Starting in the next chapter, we'll begin our discussion of Team Foundation Build.

Part V
MSBuild in Visual C++ 2010

Chapter 10
MSBuild in Visual C++ 2010, Part 1

With Microsoft Visual Studio 2010, Visual C++ has joined the long list of project types that use MSBuild as their build engine. This should be exciting news to all those who maintain large and complex Visual C++ build setups—in fact, to anyone who builds Visual C++ projects using more than just the Build, Rebuild, and Clean menu items from the IDE. This is because MSBuild brings with it extensive customizability, extensibility, transparency, and logging capabilities. Further, MSBuild is highly scalable and has superior performance even with large solutions. What's more, a large and growing user base means that you can expect MSBuild to gain significant capabilities and fine-tuning going forward. And any changes to MSBuild will be made free to Visual C++ as well, automatically.

MSBuild replaces VCBuild, which has been the build system for Visual C++ since Visual Studio 2002. VCBuild is specific to only Visual C++ projects. VCBuild was the right tool for its time because it simplified the old makefile-based build system. But VCBuild allowed only a limited amount of customizability. Also, VCBuild was a black box in that it provided limited insight to the developer into the build process. With the move to MSBuild, VCBuild has been retired permanently.

In Part V written by Pavan Adharapurapu, Chapters 10 and 11 discuss various Visual C++ build features—old and new—powered by MSBuild. Chapter 12 discusses advanced topics on extending the Visual C++ build system in various ways. Think of this chapter and the next as a tour of the new Visual C++ build system and Chapter 12 as a cookbook for Visual C++ build extensibility. These three chapters are written for build lab engineers who spend their time creating and managing Visual C++ build setups. However, they are also useful to anyone who is curious about how Visual C++ projects get built.

It is assumed that you have basic knowledge of MSBuild. That said, pointers to the relevant MSBuild topics are provided where necessary.

The New .vcxproj Project File

Visual C++ projects are now in MSBuild format. To distinguish them from older formats, the Visual C++ projects have been given the new .vcxproj extension (as comparison, the older VCBuild-based project files used the .vcproj[1] extension). Let us open a .vcxproj file to see what it contains. First, create a simple Visual C++ Win32 Console Application using the New Project Wizard in the Integrated Development Environment (IDE) by clicking File, New, and

---

[1] See the section entitled "Migrating from Visual C++ 2008 and Earlier to Visual C++ 2010," in Chapter 11 for details on how to convert a .vcproj file to .vcxproj.

then Project. Then, open the .vcxproj in an editor like Notepad or in Visual Studio Editor itself by unloading the project in Solution Explorer and choosing Edit *YourProjectName*.vcxproj from the context menu. The code snippet here shows the first few lines of a newly created Visual C++ console project called MyVcProject.vcxproj.

```xml
<?xml version="1.0" encoding="utf-8"?>
<Project DefaultTargets="Build" ToolsVersion="4.0"
         xmlns="http://schemas.microsoft.com/developer/msbuild/2003">
  <ItemGroup Label="ProjectConfigurations">
    <ProjectConfiguration Include="Debug|Win32">
      <Configuration>Debug</Configuration>
      <Platform>Win32</Platform>
    </ProjectConfiguration>
    <ProjectConfiguration Include="Release|Win32">
      <Configuration>Release</Configuration>
      <Platform>Win32</Platform>
    </ProjectConfiguration>
  </ItemGroup>
  <PropertyGroup Label="Globals">
    <ProjectGuid>{1AAC3B55-6C1B-4D5D-9EC1-215FC580EFF8}</ProjectGuid>
    <Keyword>Win32Proj</Keyword>
    <RootNamespace>MyVCProject</RootNamespace>
  </PropertyGroup>
  <Import Project="$(VCTargetsPath)\Microsoft.Cpp.Default.props" />
  <PropertyGroup Condition="'$(Configuration)|$(Platform)'=='Debug|Win32'"
                 Label="Configuration">
    <ConfigurationType>Application</ConfigurationType>
    <UseDebugLibraries>true</UseDebugLibraries>
    <CharacterSet>Unicode</CharacterSet>
  </PropertyGroup>
...
```

You can clearly see various MSBuild elements, such as Properties, ItemGroups, and Imports, in the file. Over and above the MSBuild format, the .vcxproj file follows a particular structure in the ordering of the top-level elements. This ordering is motivated by the sequential evaluation behavior of MSBuild and the need to allow user-defined elements to override system defaults. If you are interested in the details of the .vcxproj format, see the blog post by the author titled "A Guide to .vcxproj and .props File Structure," on the Visual Studio team blog (*http://blogs.msdn.com/b/visualstudio*).

Building the project through the IDE is done exactly as before: Simply right-click the project node in Solution Explorer, and then choose the Build option or use the Build menu on the IDE toolbar. Under the covers, the IDE invokes MSBuild to build the project.

Building on the command line is done using the following command; this is similar to building any other MSBuild project.

```
msbuild.exe MyVcProject.vcxproj
```

Since we did not specify any target, MSBuild executes the default target which, as defined by the *DefaultTargets* element in the previous code block above, is the Build target. You can also pass many switches to msbuild.exe to control its execution. See the section entitled "MSBuild .exe Command-Line Usage," in Chapter 1, "MSBuild Quick Start," for the list of all the available switches.

As expected, the IDE build and the command-line build are exactly the same. One obvious implication is that you don't need Visual Studio 2010 installed on the build lab machines. You can build all your Visual C++ 2010 projects with just the Microsoft .NET Framework 4.0 and the Windows SDK v7.1 installed (the former gives you the MSBuild framework, whereas the latter gets you the Visual C++ targets, tasks, and tools).

Anatomy of the Visual C++ Build Process

Figure 10-1 is a block diagram showing the Visual C++ and MSBuild components inside and outside the Visual Studio IDE and how they function together. It also orders the control and data flow in a typical edit-build IDE session.

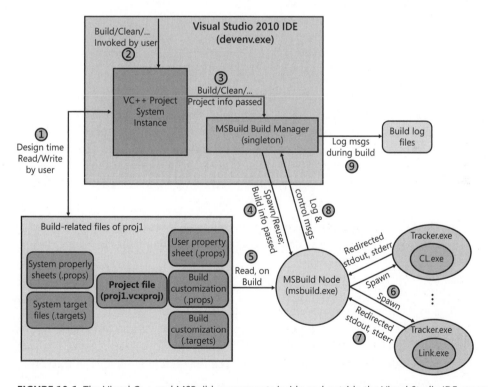

FIGURE 10-1 The Visual C++ and MSBuild components inside and outside the Visual Studio IDE process

Now we will describe what is going on, in the numerical order defined in the figure:

1. The user edits the build-related files during design time, chiefly using the Property Pages user interface. The Property Pages user interface is described in the section entitled "Property Pages," in Chapter 11. We call the project file (.vcxproj), the property sheets (.props), and the targets files (.targets) as build-related files since they exist primarily to support the build process. We will cover property sheets in the section entitled "Property Sheets," later in this chapter; but for now, consider these as MSBuild files used to share settings (a term we will use to collectively refer to properties, item definition metadata and sometime to also include item metadata) among multiple projects, such as how header files (.h) files are used to share class declarations among multiple class files (.cpp). Apart from the build-related files, the user also edits—directly or indirectly—other files such as source code files and the purely design-time files like filters file (.vcxproj.filters), Intellisense database files, Rule files, and so on. These files are not shown in the figure. Note that while the source files are read by the tools such as the compiler, the purely design-time files are never touched during build.

2. The user invokes a build operation such as Build, Clean, or Rebuild via the IDE. This command goes to the Visual C++ project system. The Visual C++ project system is an in-memory object model of the project artifacts (such as items, properties, and property sheets). It also acts as an intermediary between the user interface and the underlying MSBuild-based build system. The project system instance exists only when at least one Visual C++ project is loaded in the solution.

3. The Visual C++ project system relays the build operation requested by the user to the MSBuild Build Manager. The MSBuild Build Manager is a singleton that manages builds for various project systems such as Visual C++, C#, and Microsoft Visual Basic in the IDE. The Build Manager doesn't do the build itself but acts as a coordinating station for other MSBuild components, which perform the actual work of building. When a single project is built, the Build Manager dynamically spawns a single MSBuild Node (or reuses[2] an existing one) during build time.

4. The MSBuild Node is a process that appears in the Task Manager as msbuild.exe. This component performs the actual build by scheduling and executing the targets and tasks defined in the project.

5. To perform the build operation, the MSBuild Node reads the build-related files of the project.

6. Some of the tasks executed in the build may invoke external tools such as the compiler (cl.exe), linker (link.exe), etc. More accurately, these tasks actually wrap the tool processes inside Tracker.exe, which is an MSBuild-infrastructure component used to support accurate incremental build. See the section entitled "File Tracker–Based Incremental Build," later in this chapter, for more details.

---

[2] See the section entitled "Build Parallelism," later in this chapter, for more details on MSBuild Node reuse.

7. The MSBuild Node captures the output and error messages from the tool processes by redirecting the *stdout* and *stderr* streams of the Tracker.exe process.

8. The MSBuild Node reports the messages from step 7, control messages, and build metrics to the Build Manager.

9. The Build Manager writes the log messages to the build log files.

As is apparent from this description, the Visual C++ build is done out-of-proc[3]. This is required for providing different build environments for different projects and for realizing parallel builds.

For a command-line build, you simply invoke MSBuild.exe supplying the project file and specifying MSBuild switches. MSBuild.exe then reads the build-related files and spawns off (or reuses) the Nodes as in the IDE case. No project system components are created in the command-line build case. The build process uses only the build files to perform the build. Thus, whether you perform an IDE build or a command-line build, the results are identical.

Diagnostic Output

Diagnostic output is probably the most common way of diagnosing problems in a build that has already happened. MSBuild provides an adjustable and easily accessible way of capturing the build output. Adjustability here refers to the configurability of the amount of output that is emitted; this is referred to as *verbosity* by MSBuild. See the section entitled "MSBuild.exe Command-Line Usage," in Chapter 1, for details. As the referenced section mentions, MSBuild supports five verbosity levels: quiet, minimal, normal, detailed, and diagnostic, listed in increasing order of the amount of output generated.

In the IDE, you can change the verbosity level of the output logged to both the Output window as well as the log file via Tools, Options, Projects and Solutions, and Build and Run (see Figure 10-2). Although the first property (MSBuild Project Build Output Verbosity) is applicable to all project types, the second one (MSBuild Project Build Log File Verbosity) is valid only for Visual C++ projects (because the other project types do not create build log files).

The build log file's location is specified by the Build Log File property in the Property Pages user interface located under Configuration Properties/General/Build Log File (see Figure 10-3).

For the command-line case, you can use verbosity and logfile parameters with the /fileLoggerParameters switch (short form /flp) to specify the verbosity and log file path for the file logger. For example, `msbuild.exe /flp:logfile=MyLog.log;verbosity=diagnostic MyVcProject.vcxproj` builds the MyVcProject project and generates the MyLog.log build log file containing information at the diagnostic verbosity level.

---

[3] Design time builds, such as Design Time Assembly Resolution (DTAR) and Intellisense compiler builds, are done in process but are still coordinated by the Build Manager.

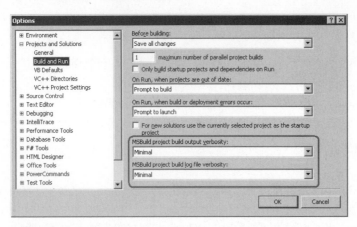

FIGURE 10-2 Configuring the build output and build log verbosity in the IDE

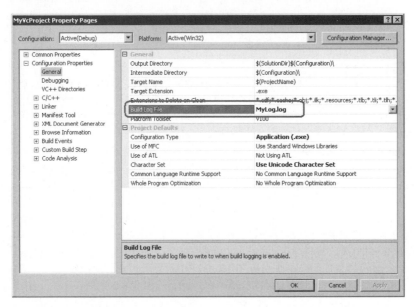

FIGURE 10-3 The Build Log File property

Build Parallelism

Generally speaking, there are two types of build parallelisms that can be exploited in Visual C++—the project level and the file level[4].

---

4 There is a kind of parallelism that is achieved at the task level by using the *YieldDuringToolExecution* keyword. It helps the build go faster by "overdriving" MSBuild Nodes when they've started long-running tools like CL. However, it is an implementation artifact and should not be construed as being at the same level as the other two types of parallelism described here.

1. Project-level parallelism allows multiple projects to be built in parallel, while adhering to project dependency restrictions.

2. File-level parallelism allows groups of source files to be compiled in parallel in a project.

MSBuild supports and controls project-level parallelism. Enabling file-level parallelism, on the other hand, is up to the individual task authors. The CL task (the Visual C++ task that compiles C++ source files) is the only Visual C++ task that supports file-level parallelism. If enabled, it invokes the compiler tool with the /MP switch, which instructs the compiler to compile source files with multiple instances of itself (the number of instances can be configured). Thus, in the case of the compiler, file-level parallelism is achieved by using an enabling feature in the compiler tool. Most often, file-level parallelism in a tool task (a term we will use in this chapter to refer to Visual C++ tasks that invoke an external command-line tool, in a separate process, to perform their job) depends on concurrency features in the underlying tool.

In Visual C++, the user can enable project- and file-level parallelism (for the compiler) as well as configure the degree of parallelism for each of them. This is described in the following section.

Configuring Project- and File-Level Build Parallelism

In the IDE, project-level build parallelism can be configured by setting the Maximum Number Of Parallel Project Builds setting under Tools/Options/Project and Solutions/Build and Run (the same as in Visual Studio 2008), as shown in Figure 10-4. This text field accepts an integer between 1 and 32 (inclusive) and denotes the number of projects that MSBuild will attempt to build in parallel. This number can be more than the number of physical processor cores. Visual Studio defaults this value to the available number of cores on your machine. Note that this setting is stored per-user and per-computer and not in the project file, so it applies to all solutions that the user can access on the computer. Sometimes you may want to have different settings for different solutions, but unfortunately, the user interface does not allow you to do that.

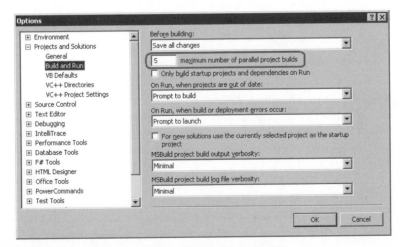

FIGURE 10-4 Configuring parallel project builds in the IDE

As explained in the section entitled "Anatomy of the Visual C++ Build Process," earlier in this chapter, MSBuild Nodes do the actual execution of targets during a build. Each MSBuild Node is a separate process (msbuild.exe). MSBuild dynamically creates a number of MSBuild Nodes up to the value of the user interface (UI) setting described previously. These nodes would build different projects in parallel. Note that MSBuild Nodes can be reused for building different projects. The MSBuild Node process generally lingers for 15 minutes after finishing a build assigned to it. If some other build is started before it exits, then the Build Manager can enlist the node for this new build job rather than create a new node. The Build Manager uses a handshaking protocol with the MSBuild Node to query its availability and to sign it on.

On the command line, project-level build parallelism is enabled by using the /m switch (full form /maxcpucount). Since the IDE setting is not stored in the project file, you need to pass the /m switch for a command-line build; otherwise, a parallel project build is not performed. In other words, only one CPU is used for the build. So, when building a solution, keep in mind to always use the /m switch to reap the benefits of project-level build parallelism. Hopefully, this switch will be enabled by default in future versions of MSBuild. The /m switch takes a number that denotes the maximum number of projects that MSBuild should attempt to build in parallel. If no number is specified with the /m switch, MSBuild defaults to the total number of cores on the machine. Note that this is different from not specifying the /m switch at all, in which case MSBuild uses just one core. The following command invokes MSBuild to build a solution with up to four projects simultaneously built at any given time. If at least one project dependency exists among the five projects, then the degree of concurrency will be less than four.

```
msbuild /m:4 Foo.sln
```

When trying to build projects in parallel, MSBuild will ensure that project dependencies are respected. Therefore, if a Visual C++ project called A has a project dependency to another Visual C++ project called B, then A will not be built until B has finished building. Project dependencies are explicitly specified using items of the *ProjectReference* type, as shown in the code snippet from A.vcxproj.

```
<ItemGroup>
    <ProjectReference Include="B.vcxproj" />
</ItemGroup>
```

Implicit reference to another project by referencing its output assembly will not be recognized as a dependency by MSBuild. In other words, if project A references project B only via a dependency on B.dll, then MSBuild will not infer that A cannot be built before B. Wherever possible, it is recommended that you use project references to capture project dependency relationships.

The previous discussion was about project-level parallelism. Now, let us talk about file-level parallelism. For Visual C++ and Visual C++/CLI projects, only the CL task supports file-level parallelism. As mentioned previously, the CL task depends on the /MP switch of the compiler tool (cl.exe) to enable file-level parallelism. File-level parallelism was supported in

Visual C++ 2008 as well, using the same /MP feature in the compiler. Note that the /MP option applies to compilations but not to linking or link-time code generation. The /MP option is incompatible with some compiler options and language features such as the /Gm (incremental compilation) option, files that use #import, and so on. See the MSDN documentation for more details about this at *http://msdn.microsoft.com/en-us/library/bb385193.aspx*.

Unlike the project-level parallelism case, the settings in the IDE for enabling and configuring the degree of file-level parallelism are distinct. The Multi-processor Compilation property, located under Configuration Properties/C/C++/General, controls whether file-level parallel compilation is on or off (see Figure 10-5). When switching it on, make sure you choose All Configurations and All Platforms, so that it is enabled for all project configurations (unless you want to enable it only for a specific project configuration).

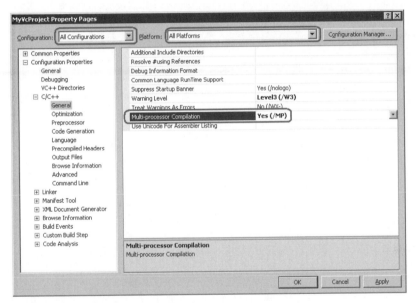

FIGURE 10-5 Enabling file-level parallel compilation in the IDE

Setting the value of this property in the Project Properties user interface writes the MultiProcessorCompilation item definition metadata for the ClCompile item definition in the project file. Item definition metadata are described in the section entitled "Batching Using Shared Metadata," in Chapter 6, "Batching and Incremental Builds**."** Item definition groups and item definition metadata are used frequently in Visual C++ to provide default values for item properties. Continuing with the UI setting, if you enabled this setting for all project configurations, then the metadata is written individually for each project configuration, as shown in the following snippet. Since this metadata is written to the project file, we can infer that this setting is project-specific.

```
<ItemDefinitionGroup Condition="'$(Configuration)|$(Platform)'=='Debug|Win32'">
   <ClCompile>
```

```
    <MultiProcessorCompilation>true</MultiProcessorCompilation>
  </ClCompile>
</ItemDefinitionGroup>
<ItemDefinitionGroup Condition="'$(Configuration)|$(Platform)'=='Release|Win32'">
  <ClCompile>
    <MultiProcessorCompilation>true</MultiProcessorCompilation>
  </ClCompile>
</ItemDefinitionGroup>
```

Once multi-processor compilation is enabled, we can set exactly how many simultaneous compilations should happen. This can be set using the Maximum Concurrent C++ Compilations property under Tools/Options/Projects and Solutions/ Visual C++ Project Settings (see Figure 10-6). Note that setting this property has no effect without enabling the Multi-processor Compilation property described previously. This property takes any nonnegative value. A value of 0 is equivalent to setting it to the number of cores on the machine.

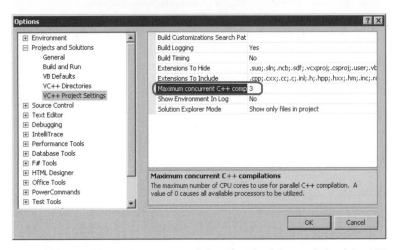

FIGURE 10-6 Enabling concurrent compilations for Visual C++ and Visual C++/CLI projects

This setting is again a per-user and per-computer property and is not stored in the project file. However, you can manually define the ProcessorNumber item definition metadata under the ClCompile item definition in the project file to achieve the same effect, as shown in the following code snippet. If you don't have MultiProcessorCompilation defined, then this property has no effect.

```
<ItemDefinitionGroup Condition="'$(Configuration)|$(Platform)'=='Debug|Win32'">
    <ClCompile>
        <MultiProcessorCompilation>true</MultiProcessorCompilation>
        <ProcessorNumber>3</ProcessorNumber>
    </ClCompile>
</ItemDefinitionGroup>
```

For a command-line build, you don't have to do anything special to switch on file-level parallel compilation if the two ClCompile item definition metadata

MultiProcessorCompilation and ProcessorNumber are defined in any of the project files. These values will be used during the build. If, however, these metadata are not defined, or if they are defined in the project files but you want to override them, then we need to supply them on the command line. However, MSBuild allows you to define only properties on the command line (using the /p switch), not item definition metadata. Fortunately, these two item definition metadata are bound to two properties, respectively. This binding ensures that setting these two item definition metadata is equivalent to setting these two properties, respectively (and to the same value). This binding is set in the Visual C++ system target files and property sheets. These equivalent properties are MultiprocessorCompilation (yes, the same name) for the MultiprocessorCompilation metadata and CL_MPCount for the ProcessorNumber metadata. Thus, you can use the following command line to switch on file-level parallelism and instruct the CL compiler to perform up to three parallel compiles.

```
msbuild /p:MultiProcessorCompilation=true;CL_MPCount=3 MyVcProject.vcxproj
```

Optimally configuring project- and file-level parallelism requires analysis of the bottlenecks in the solution build. The /detailedsummary switch to msbuild.exe produces information that helps in just this analysis. See the blog post entitled "MSBuild 4 Detailed Build Summary," on the MSBuild team blog (*http://blogs.msdn.com/b/msbuild/*) for more information on this. Other strategies for optimally configuring build parallelism can be found in the blog post entitled "Tuning C++ Build Parallelism in VS2010," on the same blog site.

A lot was described in this section. We summarize all this information in Tables 10-1 and 10-2. We use the notation *ClCompile\MultiProcessorCompilation* to refer to the MultiProcessorCompilation metadata of the ClCompile item definition.

TABLE 10-1 Summary of Enabling and Configuring Project- and File-Level Build Parallelism in the IDE

Type of Parallelism	Configure	User Interface Path	Scope	Default	Persisted in Project File?	Property/ Item Definition Metadata
			IDE			
Project-level	Enable	Tools/Options/ Projects and Solutions/Build and Run/Maximum Number Of Parallel Project Builds. Set the value of this property as > 1 to enable, 1 to disable	Per-user, per-machine	Enabled	No	None available
	# of nodes, when enabled	Same property as above	Same as above	# of cores	No	None available

Type of Parallelism	Configure	IDE					
		User Interface Path	Scope	Default	Persisted in Project File?	Property/ Item Definition Metadata	
File-level	Enable	Project Properties/ Configuration Properties/C/ C++/General, Multi-processor Compilation	Per-project [configuration]	Disabled	Yes	ClCompile\ MultiProcessorCompilation	
	# of concurrent compiles, when enabled	Tools/ Options/ Projects and Solutions/ Visual C++ Project Settings, Maximum Concurrent C++ Compilations Setting to 0 is equivalent to setting to available # of cores	Per-user per-machine	0 (≡ # of cores)	No	ClCompile\ ProcessorNumber	

TABLE 10-2 **Summary of Enabling and Configuring Project- and File-Level Build Parallelism on the Command Line**

Type of Parallelism	Configure	Command Line	
		Switch	Default
Project-level	Enable	/m	Disabled
	# of nodes, when enabled	/m:2 creates up to 2 MSBuild Nodes, e.g.	# of cores
File-level	Enable	/p: MultiProcessorCompilation=true	Value of ClCompile\ MultiProcessorCompilation from project files
	# of concurrent compiles, when enabled	/p: CL_MPCount=2 performs up to 2 parallel compilations per project.	Value of ClCompile\ ProcessorNumber from project files

File Tracker–Based Incremental Build

Incremental Build

Incremental build of a project means reusing the results of the preceding build while processing only the changes made to the project since the preceding build. An important corollary to this is that if nothing changed since the last build, then no processing occurs (other than some checks). This saves time over a complete build since we don't have to process items that haven't changed. MSBuild supports an accurate incremental build.

Recast in MSBuild terms, incremental build reduces to running only those tasks whose inputs have changed since the last build. Such a scheme can be implemented only when (1) we know the complete set of input files a task consumes; and (2) we know whether an input file has been modified since the last build. The second problem is easy to solve by comparing the current timestamp values of the input files with the values for the preceding build. The first problem, on the other hand, is more difficult. To understand why, consider the CL task that compiles .cpp files in a project to .obj binaries. The CL task needs to run whenever any of the .cpp files is changed directly or if any of the .h files included (or even the .h files that these in turn include, and so on) is touched. The .h files referred by the .cpp files may not be part of the project, but they are still consumed by the CL task, so there is no one place where the list of all such files is statically stored. So how does MSBuild solve the problem of finding the complete set of input files to a task? The answer is File Tracker.

File Tracker

File Tracker, a new feature in MSBuild 4.0, is a "file up-to-date check" infrastructure that powers MSBuild's incremental build feature. File Tracker, as the name implies, tracks read and write accesses to files made by a process. Most of the Visual C++ tools, such as cl.exe and link.exe, are run in their own separate processes by the corresponding tasks. The tool tasks don't create the tool process directly. They create the File Tracker executable—the Tracker.exe process—and hand over the responsibility of executing the tool to it. File Tracker wraps these tool processes and keeps track of all the files read by and written to by the process (and any other process it spawns) in a lightweight manner. File Tracker achieves this by detouring several Win32 file access application programming interface (API) calls such as CreateFile and CopyFile, recording the access, and then passing on the call to the operating system normally. This eavesdropping means that MSBuild doesn't have to depend on the user supplying the list of inputs and outputs that a task consumes (as was the case in MSBuild 3.5). File Tracker then writes the list of these file paths in tracking log files (with the extension .tlog) in the project's intermediate directory. Tlog files are in a human-readable format although in the normal course of events, the only reason that you should ever need to look at the log files themselves is to satisfy your curiosity.

When a task is scheduled to run during an incremental build, MSBuild compares the timestamp-on-disk for the input files to the timestamp-on-disk for the output files. A set of input and output files is judged to be up to date if the oldest output is newer than the newest input. If the set of files is not up to date, the task is run; otherwise, it is not. Notice that we only used timestamps on disk for checking the up-to-date status. Because of this, no timing information is ever written to the tlog files.

One way to get a task to participate in an incremental build is to make it File Tracker–enabled. Architecturally, this means that the class that implements the task behavior needs to use the File Tracker API to submit its tool for tracking. Note that the File Tracker API has been published by Microsoft for use by anyone. See the class *Microsoft.Build.Utilities.FileTracker* in the Microsoft.Build.Utilities.v4.0.dll assembly. Instead of interacting with the File Tracker API, you can simply derive from the *Microsoft.Build.CPPTasks.TrackedVCToolTask* class (available in the Microsoft.Build.CPPTasks.Common.dll assembly). By abstracting out most of the File Tracker interaction, this class makes it easier to create your own File Tracker–enabled task that invokes an external tool. Be aware of the fact that although this class is public, the details of inheriting from this class are not straightforward. Most likely, it will become easier in later editions of MSBuild. In Visual C++ 2010, all tool tasks, like CL and Link (the Visual C++ task that links object libraries), are File Tracker–enabled. Hence, they are capable of participating in an incremental build. Other tasks are not. In fact, if all tasks were File Tracker–enabled by default, then we could never write simple logging tasks such as one that would log some message during a build. Such tasks have no inputs and hence will always be up to date and never run a second time.

When building using MSBuild.exe from the command line, an up-to-date check is done on the level of the individual tools—CL will look only at its tracking logs, RC will look only at its tracking logs, and so on. If CL skips building, that has no impact on whether or not RC skips (except in the case of tools that depend on each other's outputs—for example, if CL does not skip, Link will also be forced to rebuild because the obj files will now be out of date).

In the IDE, there is also a "fast up-to-date check," which does a project-level check of the up-to-date status of the solution, and only spawns a project build if the up-to-date check fails. This up-to-date check also (among other checks) uses the File Tracker API to do a very simple all reads vs. all writes comparison; if the project is determined to be at all out of date, it triggers a build and the decision of whether to skip falls back to the more fine-grained dependency checking provided by the individual tasks.

We also need to mention that it is up to the individual tool tasks to determine how they use the File Tracker API to implement an incremental build. It is possible to do a very fine-grained incremental build, as is demonstrated by CL. The cl.exe tool (invoked by the CL task) produces one .obj file for each .cpp file and its imports. The linker combines the .obj files into the final dll/exe binary. Now, if a build is invoked on a project and only one .cpp file was changed, the CL task passes *only* this changed .cpp file to the cl.exe compiler to produce the corresponding .obj file. Thus, CL task runs optimized even in the case when some of its inputs have changed. The Link task on the other hand always processes all its inputs.

Trust Visual C++ Incremental Build

Visual C++ supported incremental builds even in earlier editions. It used the dependency checker infrastructure that stored relationships between the source files—for example, the cpp files, class definitions, and header files—in a database file (.idb) on the first compile and used it to make decisions on future incremental builds. However, it has never been very reliable. This was further aggravated by the fact that VCBuild did not have good logging capabilities and it was very hard to tell what caused a rebuild when the user didn't expect it to happen. And if the user did figure it out somehow, it was not clear at all how to fix it as the user had very little influence on how VCbuild worked. However, because of the way that File Tracker captures input and output file information by automatically working behind the scenes, incremental builds in Visual C++ 2010 are extremely reliable. Incremental builds in Visual C++ 2010 are also way faster than the incremental builds in Visual C++ 2008, in part because MSBuild checks timestamps in parallel.

We cannot overemphasize the fact that in Visual C++ 2010, incremental builds can be *trusted*. That means that you can use them for real builds, not just ad-hoc builds, which can improve your productivity considerably in some cases. If you're doing clean builds (a "rebuild"), question why. There's rarely a good reason to do so.

Troubleshooting

Say that an incremental build (in the IDE or command line) is taking longer than expected. From the build log file, you see that a tool task that you did not expect to run has actually run. This means that one of the build input files for the tool had changed since the last build. How do you go about knowing the exact files that changed? The answer is by looking in the same build log file. When the verbosity level is cranked up to "detailed" or "diagnostic," detailed information about the task (and target) execution will be written to the log files. You will find that not only can you get to know about the files that were found to be modified since the last build, you can also know about the .tlog files that were read by the tool task to determine the up-to-date status.

Property Sheets

Property sheets are a powerful way of sharing settings among multiple projects, which relieves you from defining those settings in each individual project. This is analogous to how header files are used to share type declarations among multiple class files. A Visual C++ property sheet is an MSBuild file that has a .props extension by convention (the extension used to be .vsprops for non-MSBuild property sheets in earlier versions of Visual Studio). A property sheet can contain any valid MSBuild elements, although it generally only contains settings (in the form of properties and item definition metadata) and references to other property sheets. A property sheet can be included in a project file or another property sheet; the inclusion is done via MSBuild's Import statement.

A project file (or property sheet) that imports a property sheet is said to "inherit" the imported settings. The term *inherit* alludes to class inheritance, where the subclass inherits the behavior of the superclass. In the case of property sheets, you inherit project settings.

In the IDE, the property sheets hierarchy is displayed by the Property Manager tool window (accessed by browsing to View/Property Manager or View/Other Windows/Property Manager if your IDE is not set up with Visual C++ development settings). This tool window also allows you to add, remove, or reorder user-added property sheets. Figure 10-7 shows the Property Manager containing a hierarchy of property sheets. Property sheets can be added for individual project configurations. In Figure 10-7, we see that the user has added two property sheets—ps1 and ps2—to the debug configuration. Further, he or she has added the same property sheet (named "Common") to both ps1 and ps2. The tool window buttons and context menu on each node expose functionality for adding a new or existing property sheet.

FIGURE 10-7 The Property Manager window showing a property sheet hierarchy

Some of the property sheets in Figure 10-7 have a different icon than the rest. The icons are used to distinguish between the System and User property sheets (as explained in Chapter 11). Application, Unicode Support, and Core Windows Libraries are system property sheets added by default to every Visual C++ project. Microsoft.Cpp.Win32.user is not a system property sheet. However, it is also added by default to every Visual C++ project.

Double-clicking a property sheet in the Property Manager brings up a Property Pages user interface that allows you to view and edit values of settings defined in the property sheet. More details are found in the section entitled "Property Pages," in Chapter 11.

If we look inside the project file, we will see imports for the property sheets, as shown in the following code snippet. The system property sheets from the Property Manager are not found in this snippet since they are imported at the top of the project file via some other property sheet (see the next section, "System Property Sheets and User Property Sheets," for more on this).

```
<ImportGroup Label="PropertySheets"
            Condition="'$(Configuration)|$(Platform)'=='Debug|Win32'">
   <Import Project="$(UserRootDir)\Microsoft.Cpp.$(Platform).user.props"
          Condition="exists('$(UserRootDir)\Microsoft.Cpp.$(Platform).user.props')"
          Label="LocalAppDataPlatform" />
   <Import Project="ps1.props" />
   <Import Project="ps2.props" />
  </ImportGroup>
  <ImportGroup Label="PropertySheets"
            Condition="'$(Configuration)|$(Platform)'=='Release|Win32'">
   <Import Project="$(UserRootDir)\Microsoft.Cpp.$(Platform).user.props"
          Condition="exists('$(UserRootDir)\Microsoft.Cpp.$(Platform).user.props')"
          Label="LocalAppDataPlatform" />
  </ImportGroup>
```

Note that the path used in the Import statement is relative to the *importing* element and not necessarily to the project directory. Notice that the display ordering in the Property Manager is the *reverse* of the textual ordering in the project file. This is for backward compatibility.

The property sheets ps1 and ps2 import common.props unconditionally. The snippet here shows how common.props is imported in ps1.props.

```
<ImportGroup Label="PropertySheets">
    <Import Project="common.props" />
</ImportGroup>
```

This is generally the pattern followed in Visual C++. Only the top-level property sheets are conditionally imported into the project file using a project configuration–based condition. The property sheets, on the other hand, do not use project configuration–based conditions while importing their own property sheets. This ensures that the property sheets can be used across multiple projects with varying project configurations.

A project could import multiple property sheets and many of these property sheets could define a particular property. Of course, the final value of this property would be determined by MSBuild's evaluation algorithm. However, many times you would need to know exactly which property sheets define a particular property and where they occur in the import hierarchy. The hard way to do this is to manually traverse the import chain while searching for the property definitions. An easier way is to use the /preprocess switch with msbuild.exe. This switch causes msbuild.exe to print out a unified file that contains the contents of all imports (and not just property sheet imports) inline and with their boundaries marked. Keep in mind to use this feature when you find yourself navigating a large import hierarchy.

System Property Sheets and User Property Sheets

Consider a newly created Visual C++ console project. Various settings have to be defined before this project can be built. For example, we need to set the output directory where the final binaries will reside, the name of the output file(s), and so on. Further, we may also want to set the values for tool switches (for example, the compiler warning level, optimization preference, the linker output name, and so on). Furthermore, these common settings need to be defined for every single project. This is a textbook scenario that calls for the use of property sheets, and that is exactly what Visual C++ does. Visual C++ defines multiple property sheets containing settings for common properties and tool options. When you create a new project, these property sheets are imported into the new project by default. Such property sheets are called *System Property Sheets*. These show up in the Property Manager with an icon that looks like a computer with a sheet in front of it (see Figure 10-7).

The System Property Sheets are pulled into a Visual C++ project via the following two imports, which you can find at the beginning of your project file (note that these are not successive lines in the project file; they are separated by other lines).

```
<Import Project="$(VCTargetsPath)\Microsoft.Cpp.Default.props" />
<Import Project="$(VCTargetsPath)\Microsoft.Cpp.props" />
```

The section entitled "Default Visual C++ Property Sheets," in Chapter 11 explains many of the System Property Sheets and also tells how they are imported by default into every Visual C++ project.

Unlike System Property Sheets, which are shipped by Microsoft and are imported by default into every wizard-generated project, User Property Sheets are generally those that have been added by the user to a single project or a limited set of projects. The User Property Sheets contain settings that the user would explicitly like the project to inherit. As Figure 10-7 shows, the Property Manager imports User Property Sheets *after* the System Property Sheets (again, the display order is the reverse of the textual order). This ensures that user-specified values for settings override default system values, which is generally what is intended.

Note that it is not possible to edit property values using the Property Pages user interface for System Property Sheets; you can do so only for User Property Sheets. Keep in mind, however, that the values displayed in System Property Sheets can change based on other setting changes, such as a change in the active platform, etc.

In Figure 10-7, we see the User Property Sheet Microsoft.CppWin32.user.props. This is the only User Property Sheet added by default to every newly created Visual C++ project. The next section covers the function of this property sheet.

Visual C++ Directories

Visual C++ Directories is the settings pane where you can set the IDE equivalents of command-line environment variables of *PATH, INCLUDE, LIBPATH,* and other variables. These denote the directories where one can find executables, include files, libraries, and other elements referenced by the source code. The typical usage is to point them to SDK elements that are installed on the box—thus, they define the computer-specific roots that are then used by the rest of the system to keep the project files independent of things like C:\Program Files.

These are very important variables that can dramatically affect the results of a build. In Visual C++ 2008, these settings would be set via Tools/Options, as shown in Figure 10-8. The values set via this pane were stored in the VCComponents.dat file located at %LOCALAPPDATA%\ Microsoft\VisualStudio\9.0. Since it is in the LocalAppData directory, it meant that the settings were per-user and per-machine. The VCComponents.dat file was in INI format, not the Extensible Markup Language (XML) of a .vcproj file; and the importing of this file was done by some custom code inside vcbuild.exe and the IDE.

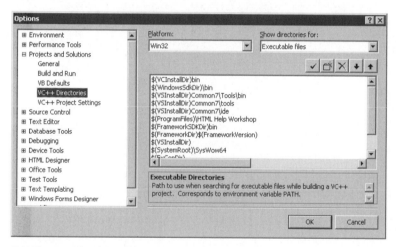

FIGURE 10-8 Visual C++ Directories in Visual C++ 2008

In Visual C++ 2010, the same pane would display a message saying that the pane is now deprecated. So, what happened to the Visual C++ Directories settings?

In Visual Studio 2010, the Visual C++ Directories have been moved to—you guessed it—a property sheet. If you open up the Property Manager view to see the property sheets associated with any Visual C++ 2010 project (see Figure 10-7, earlier in this chapter), you'll see that one of the property sheets is named Microsoft.Cpp.Win32.User. In the project file itself, you can clearly see this property sheet imported for all project configurations (see the code snippet following Figure 10-7).

You can set values for the variables by bringing the Property Pages user interface (as shown in Figure 10-9) on this property sheet in the Property Manager (to access this, right-click the property sheet and choose Properties). Click on the Visual C++ Directories node in the left pane of the Property Pages window. This will reveal the current values for the Visual C++ Directories properties. You will notice that the default values are the same as in Visual Studio 2008. You can edit these properties in the same way as any other project property (including using the macro editor as shown—something that is not possible in Visual C++ 2008).

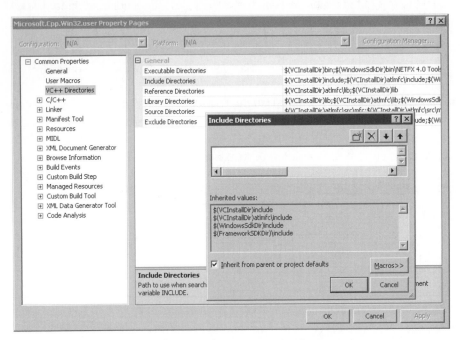

FIGURE 10-9 The Visual C++ Directory settings are now set using property pages.

The Microsoft.Cpp.Win32.User property sheet is located in the same LocalAppData directory (%LocalAppData%\Microsoft\MSBuild\v4.0) as the VCComponents.dat file. All new projects import this by default. When you convert older projects using the Visual Studio 2010 Conversion Wizard, this property sheet is once again added by default. Thus, when you define settings in this property sheet (by using the Property Pages user interface spawned from *any* Visual C++ 2010 project's Property Manager), they get written to this common property sheet. This means that you are in effect changing these settings for all Visual C++ 2010 projects on your machine. Thus, you are effectively editing the Visual C++ Directories in the same global way that you could before using Tools/Options. However, the new part of this is that if you don't want these global settings for one or more of your projects, you can delete this property sheet import (via the Property Manager) and simply add a new property sheet in which you can then define the custom Visual C++ Directory settings. Since this new property sheet is imported only into one particular project, the new settings will not affect the other projects, which will continue to use the values in the Microsoft.Cpp.Win32.User property sheet. Alternatively, you can keep the Microsoft.Cpp.Win32.User property sheet, but add your custom property sheet while making sure that it is imported later in the evaluation model (this should happen by default when you add it through the Property Manager). This will ensure that your custom settings will override the ones defined in the Microsoft.Cpp. Win32.User property sheet.

There are multiple reasons that Microsoft changed the mechanism of defining and storing Visual C++ Directories:

- **Ability to define different Visual C++ Directories settings per project**   In Visual Studio 2008, all projects had to share the same Visual C++ Directories settings. There was no way to prevent it. With the new property sheet approach, you can not only have global settings but can also selectively override it in individual projects.

- **Enlistment-friendly**   Moving Visual C++ Directories to a property sheet makes it easy to check in your entire project system—not just the source files, but the build system as well. This makes it possible to go to a new machine with only the source control system installed and to check out the project system and build. Such a scenario would have been difficult if your build system depended on per-machine settings, as was the case with VCComponents.dat.

- **Consistency in storing settings**   This is a minor but satisfying reason. VCComponents.dat was an INI-based file that was different from the .vcproj file format, whereas the Microsoft.Cpp.Win32.User property sheet is an MSBuild file. Not just that, it is consistent with the way other settings are stored in the project system (namely inside property sheets).

Finally, a note about the Import/Export Settings feature of the IDE. With the move from Tools/Options to property sheets, Visual C++ Directories are no longer considered part of the Visual C++ Settings in Visual Studio 2010 that can be imported or exported via Tools/ Import and Export Settings. These settings are meant for IDE-specific configuration settings, and Visual C++ Directories are now integrated directly into the build process via the property sheet mechanism. When you import settings from Visual Studio 2008 (where Visual C++ Directories is part of the settings), these settings are migrated into the Microsoft.Cpp.Win32. User property sheet.

Chapter 11
MSBuild in Visual C++ 2010, Part 2

In this chapter, we continue the discussion of Visual C++ features powered by MSBuild that we started in the last chapter.

Property Pages

Property pages are the primary way that you change the properties of the project (such as the project name) or set switches for the various build tools such as CL.exe (warning level, optimization, and so on). Property pages have been a standard feature of the Visual C++ project system for a long time, but in Visual C++ 2010, the underlying architecture has been completely redone to allow for extensibility. It is now possible to add a property page for your own tool and have it be treated like a first-class citizen by the project system. (By "first-class citizen," I mean the project system will treat your custom tool like it would any of the shipped tools like the compiler, linker, and so on.) Also, with the move to MSBuild, the semantic meaning of the property values and the way they are computed has changed. This section will describe these changes.

Reading and Writing Property Values

Figure 11-1 shows a snapshot of the property pages focused on properties for the Linker tool.

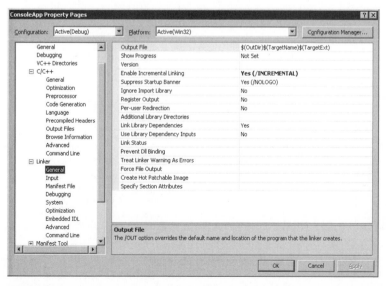

FIGURE 11-1 Property pages for the project node showing the Linker options under the General category

This window was obtained by right-clicking the project node in Solution Explorer and choosing Properties from the context menu. In addition to viewing properties for a project, you can view the properties for a property sheet in the Property Manager tool window or for a file in Solution Explorer. In fact, you can select multiple nodes and request the property pages. In such a case, the value shown for a property is the common part (which possibly could be empty) of the values of this property for the entities selected. For this multi-selection property page, you can even edit the value, which results in each of the entities in the multi-selection getting this property value.

In the preceding paragraph, we talked about property values without actually defining what this term refers to. What value is shown for a particular property, say the Enable Incremental Linking property shown in Figure 11-1, for a project, as opposed to a property sheet? Would it be the same or different? Where is the value sourced from? Let us explain. First, let us call the file-on-disk underlying the node from which the Property Pages window was spawned as the *context*. Therefore, for the project node, the context would be the .vcxproj file, whereas for a particular property sheet, it would be the underlying .props file. Also, to keep the discussion concrete, consider a project that imports three property sheets, as shown on the left side of Figure 11-2. The figure shows all definitions of a property named q, whose definitions are spread across multiple files. On the right side is the "logical project," which is obtained by substituting the contents of the property sheet at the point where it is imported in the project file. It is this logical project that MSBuild uses when it evaluates a project. By the way, the /preprocess option to msbuild.exe that was mentioned in the section entitled "Property Sheets," in Chapter 10, "MSBuild in Visual C++ 2010, Part 1," outputs this very same logical project. It also marks the boundaries of the inline content so that it is easy to see the contributions of each import.

There are three ways of storing settings in an MSBuild file: properties, item definition metadata, and item metadata. We will refer to all three simply as *properties* unless we say otherwise.

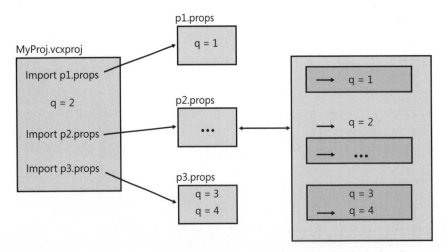

FIGURE 11-2 A project-property sheets hierarchy and the corresponding logical project

You can think of project evaluation as a process wherein MSBuild travels line by line in the logical project and when it comes across a property definition, it overwrites any previous definitions of that property in a big table that it maintains. Of course, this is a simplification of the evaluation process, but you get the idea. This *linear evaluation* model is in contrast with the *late evaluation* model followed by VCBuild. Since this is an important change likely to cause confusion to users transitioning from VCBuild to MSBuild, let us take an example to illustrate it. Consider the following property declarations. They are in MSBuild syntax, but assume that you have equivalent definitions in VCBuild syntax also.

```
<PropertyGroup>
    <A>1</A>
    <B>$(A)</B>
    <A>2</A>
</PropertyGroup>
```

When MSBuild is finished evaluating the project containing this snippet, the value of the property B ends up as 1; all expressions are expanded and values substituted as and when they are encountered. Under VCBuild evaluation, however, B would end up with a value of 2. This is because VCBuild does not expand non-literal expressions until the very end of the evaluation, by which time it would have overwritten the value of A to 2.

With the background set, let us tell you how the value that you see in the property pages is computed. The value shown for a property in the property page is the value obtained by evaluating the logical project up to the last definition of the property in the context file. It is the value that MSBuild would see when it reaches that point during the project evaluation. Since the project is not evaluated to the end, we call this *partial evaluation*. Thus, property pages show a value that is obtained by a *context-specific, partial evaluation* of the project.

In the above description, we conveniently left out the case when a property may not be defined in the context at all. In such a case, where will the partial evaluation stop? The answer is that Visual C++ will evaluate up to the *standard location* for the property; that is, the location in the context where the property would normally be defined. The standard location is defined by the Rule file for that property, which is explained later in this section. For now, assume that for every property, there is a location in the context where it will normally be written by the Integrated Development Environment (IDE) when it is set for the first time. The value shown in the property pages is bold if there is at least one definition of the property in the context; otherwise, it is not bold. Most of the properties for the project and property sheets are unbolded because those values are coming from the system property sheets included at the beginning of the project.

Table 11-1 shows the value shown for the property q for every context in the setup shown in Figure 11-2. Bold font is used to indicate that the property value would appear bolded in the property pages. The value of q for all contexts except p2.props is bold since it is defined in all contexts except p2.

TABLE 11-1   Values of the Property q as Computed by the Property Pages for Different Contexts

Context	Value of q	Reason
MyProj.vcxproj	2	The property q is defined in context.
p1.props	1	The property q is defined in context.
p2.props	2	The property q is not defined in context. Context-specific partial evaluation up to the standard location would result in the value 2, since this is the value stated in the definition immediately preceding the standard location.
p3.props	4	The property q is defined in context.

One final thing to mention is that the values shown in the property pages are the unevaluated values and not the evaluated values. So if the definition of q mentioned in the project file listed *$(foo)* as its value, then the property pages for the project context would show *$(foo)* (even if *foo* was declared to be, say 10, somewhere earlier). This is because property pages allow editing a property value and you cannot edit evaluated values. Hence, it makes more sense to display the unevaluated values. It would probably be helpful if the evaluated value was also shown, but in a read-only mode. However, that would make the property pages more complex.

The preceding paragraphs explained how reads are handled. As far as writing is concerned, it is simpler. When you edit a property value in the property pages, the last definition of the property in the context is overwritten with the new value. If there is no definition at all of the property, then we create a new definition with the entered value at the standard location.

While defining a property value, we can use the help of the Property Editor (by selecting Edit… from the drop-down list in the value column; this is not available for enumeration properties). See Figure 11-3. In the property editor, there is a Macros button, which expands the editor to show a list of macros. These *macros* are essentially properties defined in the logical project before the point of definition of the current property (or its standard location, if it is not yet defined). The values shown for the macros are the values obtained by partial evaluation to this point. Macros are useful because you can use the appropriate macro to define your property. For example, I can define my property q as *$(foo)* after checking that the value of the macro *foo* is appropriate.

Coming back to the value displayed in the property pages, why do we obtain this value from partial evaluation? Why not show the value from full evaluation (let's call them final values)? After all, the build uses the final values when it passes these to the various tasks and targets. The reasoning is as follows:

We edit property values because we would like to change the contribution of the context to the whole project. For this, we need to know what the current contribution of the context is.

If we were to show the final values in the property pages, it would not be of much use. You would see the same value regardless of the context. Further, modifying a value on the property page for a particular context and hitting apply may not change anything on the property page if the property is overridden in some other property sheet down the line. In such a case, the value shown in the property page would be the same even after you modify it.

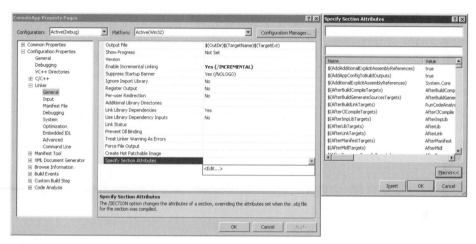

FIGURE 11-3 Property value editor along with Macros

Note that you can get the final values of properties by building the project from the command line (not the IDE) with the /verbosity switch set to *diagnostic* and then looking in the generated build log file. It will have all the properties and their final *evaluated* values (although it will not include the property values defined inside targets). If none of your targets files define properties, then you can also see the final value, albeit unevaluated, in the Property Pages user interface when the context is the project file.

Before we end this section, we would like to mention the property page architecture. The property pages in Visual C++ 2010 are data-driven and extensible. Each node under the Configuration Properties node in the left pane in Figure 11-1 is called a *Rule* and is driven by an Extensible Application Markup Language (XAML) file called the *Rule file*. The Rule file defines the categories and properties in the Rule. The Rule file also defines the location in the project file (or property sheet) where the value of the properties should be written (called the "standard location" in the previous discussion). You can see the Rule files for C/C++, Linker, and so on, at %ProgramFiles%\MSBuild\Microsoft.Cpp\v4.0\1033[1]. Details on the format of a Rule file can found in a blog post by the author titled "Platform extensibility - Part 2" on the VS Project Team Blog (*http://blogs.msdn.com/b/vsproject*). In the next chapter, we will show how to author a Rule file for a custom tool.

---

[1] Replace 1033 with the appropriate locale ID for non-English-language editions of Microsoft Visual Studio.

Build Customizations

We all know about the compiler tool, which is one of the most important tools run during the build of a Visual C++ project. Let us see how the compiler tool is surfaced to the user in the IDE:

- We can use the project's Property Pages user interface to set compiler options (that apply to all C++ source files in the project).

- When you add a new .cpp file to a project, the IDE immediately understands it to be of type ClCompile and knows that this item is consumed by the compiler. The Item Type property under Configuration Properties/General shows the value *C/C++ Compiler*.

- You can bring up the property pages on a .cpp file and it will show you all Compiler properties that can be set on it. The property pages show only the compiler properties because the IDE knows that this file is consumed only by the compiler tool.

Setting aside for a while what we have discussed previously, consider how we could integrate a custom tool into the build process. Perhaps you plan to add files with a custom extension, such as .foo, and you need to process them using your custom tool during build. Is that possible, and if so, what would you need to do?

It is easy to make your tool run at build time. Just write a task that will invoke your tool passing along the files which end in the extension .foo. Compile your task to an assembly. Then write a targets file that refers to your task. Use the *BeforeTargets* or *AfterTargets* attribute for your target to hook it up to the build-time target execution sequence. If you set BeforeTargets="Build", for example, your target will be run before the Build target. But what about setting properties for this tool? What if different projects, or even different .foo files, need different tool settings? Clearly, we don't want to manually type them in the project file. It would be nice to have property pages for the custom tool so that users can set tool properties just as they do for the compiler tool. In fact, it would be great if the custom tool was treated exactly like the compiler tool, both at design time and build time. Is this possible?

It is, with the Build Customization feature. It was called Custom Build Rule in earlier editions; it has been renamed to reflect its changed file format and the underlying architecture. Build customization provides the following benefits:

- Full design time integration; that is, property pages and item recognition
- Build time integration
- Ability to declaratively express your target using XAML syntax

The project system treats Build Customizations as first-class citizens. That is, it treats them just as it would the compiler tool or the linker tool. So how do you go about creating a Build Customization?

A Build Customization is described by the following three files. It might be useful to look at one of the two Build Customizations that are shipped with Visual C++ 2010 while reading what follows next. These are the License Compiler (LC) and Microsoft Macro Assembler (MASM) Build Customizations, which deal with .licx and .masm files, respectively. You can find the files for these in the $(VCTargetsPath)\BuildCustomizations directory (where the default for $(VCTargetsPath) is %programfiles%\MSBuild\Microsoft.Cpp\v4.0).

- An XAML file ending in the .xml extension that describes the property page schema for your tool. This is the Rule file explained in the section entitled "Property Pages," earlier in this chapter. This describes what properties your tool has and under what categories they are organized. This file also defines the file extensions that your tool would like to claim as its own. This file is optional if you don't want design-time integration. This Rule file causes a new node to be created in the Property Pages user interface similar to the C/C++ nodes or the Link node. This new node will expose the properties of your custom tool.

- A .props file that contains the default values for the properties listed in the above .xml file. This file is optional if you don't need to set default values.

- A .targets file that defines your target. This target, like any MSBuild target, contains one or more tasks. Presumably, one of the tasks is the main one, which processes all files with the custom extension. Most often, this task invokes an external command-line tool.

  The target also includes a reference to the above .xml file. This means that if this targets file is imported into a project, the property page xml file is automatically pulled in.

  This targets file is the only mandatory file required for the definition of a Build Customization. Indeed, if there is no target to be run, then it can't be called a customization of the build.

If your target's main job is to invoke an external tool, whose properties are described in the .xml Rule file, then MSBuild has a feature that makes it easy for you to define such a task without writing any code whatsoever. MSBuild provides the *XamlTaskFactory* which dynamically generates a task class whose switches, inputs, and outputs are inferred from a Rule file. This task is automatically wired to execute your tool, whose command line you specify in the .props file. Finally, this task is compiled on the fly, so it looks to MSBuild like any regular task. So you have a task without writing any code! This is helpful since you don't have to check into your source control repository a precompiled .dll with your custom task. The shipped LC and MASM Build Customizations use this approach. Note that if you don't have a Rule file, then you can't use *XamlTaskFactory*. Your targets file needs to refer to a compiled task or an inline task (see the section entitled "Inline Tasks," in Chapter 4, "Custom Tasks") or a task that uses some other task factory, such as the C#/VB task factory.

In the next chapter, we will actually walk you through the creation of these three files, but for now, we will limit ourselves to explaining how these enable the functionality that they do.

Once you have authored these three files, you need to add your Build Customization to the project so that it can take effect. The way to do this is use the Build Customization user interface available via the Build Customizations… context menu on the project node in Solution Explorer (see Figure 11-4). Use the Find Existing… button to browse to the directory location where your Build Customization is located and select it. Notice that the Build Customization window shows the two Build Customizations that are shipped with Microsoft Visual Studio 2010.

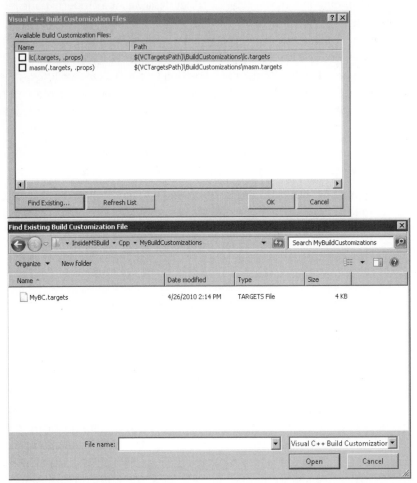

FIGURE 11-4 Using the Build Customization user interface to add the MyBC Build Customization

When you add a Build Customization using this user interface, the targets file and the property sheet are imported into the project file under the ExtensionTargets and ExtensionSettings ImportGroups, respectively. The xml file is pulled in via the targets file, so it is not added directly to the project. This is shown in Figure 11-5.

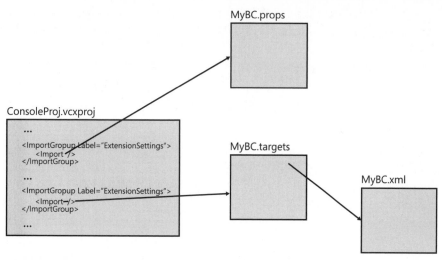

FIGURE 11-5 Result of adding a Build Customization using the IDE

Platforms and Platform Toolsets

Visual C++ 2010 allows you to target multiple platforms and platform toolsets. We will first define the terms *platform* and *toolset* before explaining how Visual C++ supports them:

- **Platform**:   *Hardware configuration* that requires special design-time, build, debug, and deploy consideration. Win32 (x86), x64, Xbox, and ARM are examples of platforms. The tasks, targets, and tools required to build for a particular platform could be completely different from those required to build for a different platform.

- **Toolset**:   *Software configuration* that requires special design-time and build consideration. More concretely, a toolset represents a complete set of build tools such as compiler, linker, and so on, along with the software libraries used to build your application. A toolset is normally labeled by its version, so the set of C++ tools and libraries that are shipped with Visual C++ 2010 (henceforth called "v100") is a different toolset compared to the set of C++ tools and libraries that were shipped with Visual C++2008 (henceforth referred to as "v90"). There could be multiple toolsets for a given platform. Under the Win32 platform, v100 and v90 could be two toolsets. The tasks and targets to execute for a particular platform toolset may be different from those of a different platform toolset.

You can view the active platform and the platform toolset for a project from the property pages (see Figure 11-6). However, you can only change the active Platform Toolset from this user interface. Changing the Platform selection in this user interface simply changes the values of the displayed properties to correspond to the new platform. It does not actually change the active platform for the project. To actually change the active platform for the project, you need to use the Configuration Manager. To do this, click the Configuration

Manager… button on the upper-right corner of the Property Pages user interface and then use the Platform drop-down list for the project.

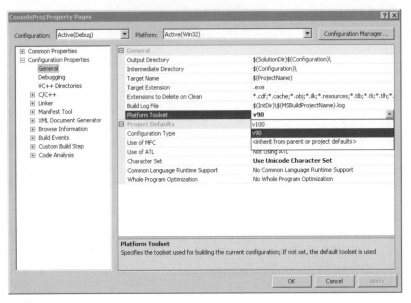

FIGURE 11-6 Viewing the platform and platform toolset in the property pages

Configuration Manager is also the place to add another of the installed platforms on the machine to a project. To do so, choose the <New…> option from the Platform drop-down list. This opens a small window (shown in Figure 11-7) containing a New Platform drop-down list. This drop-down list shows you the list of all installed platforms on your machine, from which you can choose one that has not already been added to your project.

The active platform for a project is saved in the .sln file, whereas the platform toolset is stored as the PlatformToolset property in the individual project file.

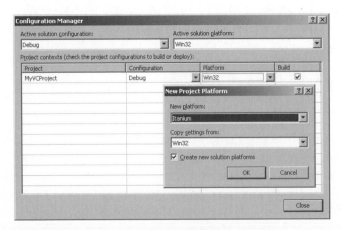

FIGURE 11-7 Adding a new installed platform to a project

Now we discuss what is involved in supporting multiple platforms/platform toolsets. To support multiple platforms and platform toolsets, Visual C++ needs to do the following:

- **Build time**   Invoke the right targets for the right platform/platform toolset.

- **Design time**   The properties and their values shown in the property pages must be platform/platform toolset–specific.

Visual C++ uses a simple architecture to support this. In fact, the same architecture can be used to add support for new platforms and platform toolsets. Visual C++ considers every folder in the $(VCTargetsPath)\Platforms directory to represent a platform (see Figure 11-8). In fact, these are the entries shown in the drop-down list in Figure 11-7. Inside each platform directory, there is a PlatformToolsets directory. Visual C++ considers all directories under this folder to represent the platform toolsets available for that particular platform. Once again, these are the entries that are shown in the Platform Toolset drop-down list in the property pages (see Figure 11-6).

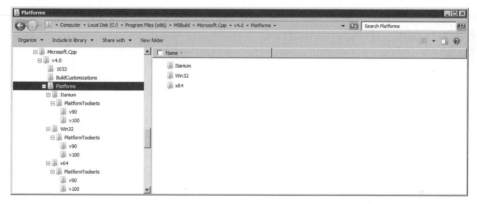

FIGURE 11-8 The installed platforms and platform toolsets are located in the $(VCTargetsPath)\Platforms directory root.

The platform and platform toolset folder can contain any number of .targets, .props, and .xml files. When present, they represent the targets, property defaults, and Rules that are applicable to the particular platform/platform toolset. At any given time, Visual C++ is using the files from the directories corresponding to the active platform and platform toolset. When you change either of them, Visual C++ automatically switches to the directory corresponding to the new platform/platform toolset. This importing will change the property page structure (via the Rule files), default property page values (via the .props files), and the build (via the .targets files) to correspond to the new selection. A change in the platform/ platform toolset also causes a re-evaluation, which in turn causes the property values to be updated in the Property Pages user interface.

The same mechanism can be used to add support for a completely new platform or platform toolset. All you need to do is author the appropriate .targets/.props/.xml files and place them in newly created directories under the Platforms (or PlatformToolsets, as appropriate) folder. In the section entitled "Adding a New Platform/Platform Toolset," in Chapter 12, "Extending Visual C++," we will show you how to author these files.

Native and Managed Multi-targeting

Multi-targeting is the ability to use the current version of Visual Studio to build your application using multiple installed platform toolsets or frameworks (see the previous section for the definition of a toolset). For native C++ applications, it means the ability to build using the Visual C++ 2010 toolset (v100), the Visual C++2008 toolset (v90), or even others. We will call this feature *Native multi-targeting*. For Visual C++ CLR applications, the term *multi-targeting* refers to the ability to use tools from any version of the Microsoft .NET Framework, v1.0 through v4.0. We shall call this *Managed multi-targeting*. Visual C++ had the ability to do managed multi-targeting in earlier editions of Visual Studio as well. However, Visual C++ 2010 is the first edition to support native multi-targeting.

Native Multi-targeting

Large ISV vendors often build their products using multiple versions of toolsets because not all of their customers use the latest toolset version. Until now, this required the ISVs to maintain multiple versions of their project files and use corresponding editions of Visual Studio to build their application so as to produce binaries that targeted different toolsets. However, with Visual C++ 2010, you can use the same IDE to build using the v100 toolset as well as the v90 toolset. Note that you need to have Visual Studio 2008 installed on the same machine to target the v90 toolset[2]. Visual Studio 2010 supports only v90 and v100 toolsets by default, although it is possible to author support for any platform toolset as explained in the section entitled "Platforms and Platform Toolsets," earlier in this chapter.

Native multi-targeting can be enabled both from the IDE and the command line. In the IDE, native multi-targeting is obtained by changing the Platform Toolset property, as described in the previous section. To build using the v90 toolset, simply set the "Platform Toolset" property under Configuration Properties/General to v90 as shown in Figure 11-6. To make all configurations use the same toolset, select All Configurations and All Platforms from the drop-down lists at the top of the property page window. To target multiple projects, multi-select them in Solution Explorer while bringing up the property pages and set the same property.

When you save the project, the PlatformToolset property gets written to the project file holding the version of the toolset that was selected.

```
<PropertyGroup Condition="'$(Configuration)|$(Platform)'=='Debug|Win32'"
               Label="Configuration">
    <PlatformToolset>v90</PlatformToolset>
</PropertyGroup>
```

---

[2] Note that targeting v90 does not use VCBuild.

When you build the project now, you can confirm that the v90 toolset is used by looking at the paths of the invoked tools. This information is emitted to the Output window, as the snippet here shows (you need to set the Output window verbosity to *detailed* or *diagnostics*). The snippet shows that the compiler used is from the v90 toolset as the presence of "Microsoft Visual Studio 9.0" in the cl.exe path indicates.

```
C:\Program Files\Microsoft Visual Studio 9.0\VC\bin\CL.exe /c /ZI /nologo /W3 /WX- /Od
/Oy- /D WIN32 /D _DEBUG /D _CONSOLE /D _UNICODE /D UNICODE /Gm /EHsc /RTC1 /MDd /GS /
fp:precise /Zc:wchar_t /Zc:forScope /Yc"StdAfx.h" /Fp"Debug\ConsoleProj.pch" /Fo"Debug\\" /
Fd"Debug\vc110.pdb" /Gd /TP /analyze- /errorReport:prompt stdafx.cpp
```

Since the PlatformToolset property is stored in the project file, building the project from the command line uses the same toolset. If you want to build from the command line using a different toolset than the one specified in the project file, you can always pass in the toolset using /p: PlatformToolset=value as a switch to msbuild.exe (recall that properties passed using the /p switch override the values defined in the project files).

How Does Native Multi-targeting Work?

How does Visual C++ 2010 achieve native multi-targeting? The mechanism is simple and follows directly from the way information about platforms and platform toolsets are stored, as described in the section entitled "Platform and Platform Toolsets," earlier in this chapter. To target a particular toolset, such as v90, Visual C++ needs to use the tools and libraries of that toolset. All this requires is that Visual Studio set the ExecutablePath (PATH), IncludePath (INCLUDE), ReferencePath (LIBPATH), LibraryPath (LIB), SourcePath, ExcludedPath to point to the Visual Studio 2008 installation and Windows software development kit (SDK) installation, respectively. Visual C++ achieves this by defining values of these properties in a property sheet and having multiple property sheets for each of the platform toolsets. These property sheets are stored in the platform toolset directories mentioned in the section entitled "Platforms and Platform Toolsets," earlier in this chapter. When you change the value of the PlatformToolset property, the build system simply picks the property sheets and targets from the appropriate toolset directory. This mechanism allows you to add multi-targeting support for your own toolset. For example, you can create a directory called v80 and author property sheet and targets files for targeting the VS2005 platform. In the section entitled "Adding a New Platform/Platform Toolset," in Chapter 12, we will show how to add support for a new toolset.

Managed Multi-targeting

Note that you need to have Visual Studio 2008 SP1 or later installed to make managed multi-targeting work. For a Visual C++ CLR project, you can know the .NET Framework that it targets by going to the project properties user interface and looking under Common Properties/Framework And References for the Targeted Framework property (see Figure 11-9).

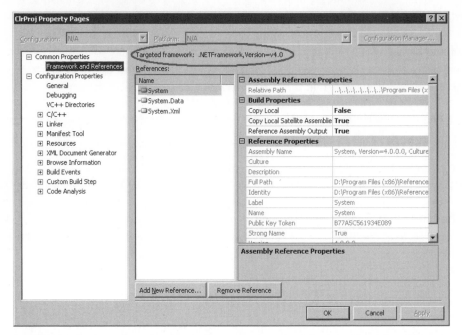

FIGURE 11-9 Property pages showing the Target Framework version for a Visual C++ CLR project

This property was a drop-down list in Visual Studio 2008 that allows you to change the framework version and thus target a different framework directly from the property page. Unfortunately, this is read-only in Visual C++ 2010. However, it is still possible to change the target framework version with a little bit of work.

Open the .vcxproj file for editing in Notepad (or Visual Studio itself) and in the Globals property group, change the value of the TargetFrameworkVersion property to the version that you want. For example, make it *v3.5* if you want to target .NET Framework version 3.5. If this property is not there, simply define one in the Globals property group before setting its value. The following code snippet shows this property set with a value of v3.5.

```
<PropertyGroup Label="Globals">
    <TargetFrameworkVersion>v3.5</TargetFrameworkVersion>
</PropertyGroup>
```

You can confirm that it takes effect by reloading the project and looking at the framework version displayed in the property pages (see Figure 11-9).

Default Visual C++ Tasks and Targets

Visual C++ 2010 ships with a set of tasks and targets that make it possible to build Visual C++ projects created from the IDE. We discuss these topics in the next two sections.

Default Visual C++ Tasks

We will use the term *Default Visual C++ Tasks* to refer to those tasks that are referred to by default by a newly created Visual C++ project. You already know that tasks and targets are the currency for builds in MSBuild. So, when you build a Visual C++ project from the IDE or the command line, you are in effect invoking some targets and tasks. Where are these targets and tasks located, and how are they connected to the Visual C++ projects that you create from the IDE?

We will talk about the targets in the next section, but the tasks referred to by these targets are defined in the following three assemblies (not counting the various incarnations of the last one):

- **Microsoft.Build.Tasks.v4.0.dll**   This is located at $(MSBuildToolsPath), which has a default value of %windir%\Microsoft.NET\Framework\v4.0.30319 and contains generic tasks, such as CopyFile and Exec, that would useful for any language-type project.

- **Microsoft.Build.CPPTasks.Common.dll**   This is located at $(VCTargetsPath) and contains Visual C++–specific tasks whose set of options/switches and behavior is common across the various platforms. Examples include BSCMake and CPPClean.

- **Microsoft.Build.CPPTasks.$(Platform).dll (for example, Microsoft.Build .CPPTasks.Win32.dll)**   This assembly is present in the appropriate platform directory (for example, $(VCTargetsPath)\Platforms\Win32) and contains tasks whose tools/ options or behavior is platform-dependent. For example, Microsoft.Build.CPPTasks. Win32.dll contains CL and Link tasks that call the compiler and linker, respectively, to produce binaries for the Win32 platform. If you are a platform extender, then you may need to provide your own task implementations for these two and other relevant tasks.

Default Visual C++ Targets

We use the term *Default Visual C++ Targets* to refer to those targets that are imported by default into a newly created Visual C++ project. The Default Visual C++ targets are defined in multiple targets files in the $(VCTargetsPath) directory and its subdirectories. All these targets are brought into your project via the following single import in your project file:

```
<Import Project="$(VCTargetsPath)\Microsoft.Cpp.targets" />
```

Let us dig further into the import hierarchy behind this import. Figure 11-10 shows an abbreviated hierarchy showing the most important targets files. What purpose does such a hierarchy have? Why not put all the Targets into one targets file and import it into every project? There are two reasons:

- Visual C++ projects can target different platforms (Win32, x64, and so on) and within them different platform toolsets (v90, v100, and so on). Each platform/platform toolset may require a different set of targets to be invoked. In addition, Visual C++ supports platform extensibility allowing users to add their own platforms. Therefore, it is not only inflexible but also impossible to add all the targets required for all possible platforms in one targets file.

■ By factoring out the targets into logical groupings, we leave the possibility open for extensibility points at each one of these groupings. For example, it is possible to include your custom targets files for only a particular platform toolset or a particular platform. We explain this more next.

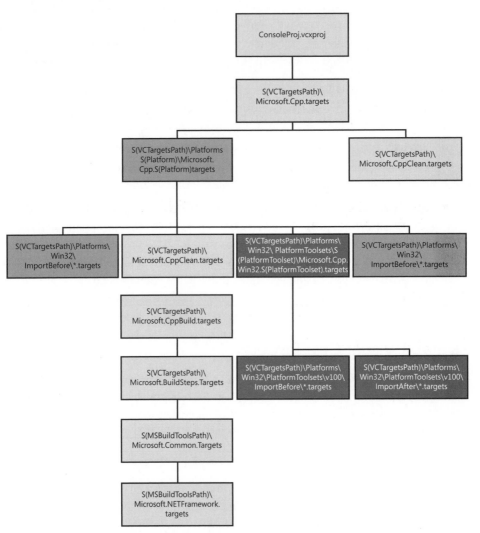

FIGURE 11-10 A simplified ordered hierarchy of the targets file imports that is brought into a Visual C++ project via Microsoft.Cpp.targets

We will explain the targets brought in by each of the targets files listed here. Note that Figure 11-10 shows only the most important targets files in the actual hierarchy. There are other targets files that handle edge cases and/or error scenarios, but these are not shown.

- **$(VCTargetsPath)\Microsoft.Cpp.targets** Connects the Visual C++ target hierarchy to a Visual C++ project. Contentwise, it defines targets that set the Visual C++ Directories and certain user macros as environment variables. Its major import is Microsoft.Cpp.$(Platform).targets, located in the Platforms directory. Finally, this targets file also provides an extensibility point in the form of ForceImportBeforeCppTargets and ForceImportAfterCppTargets (described in the next section).

- **$(VCTargetsPath)\Platforms\$(Platform)\Microsoft.Cpp.$(Platform).targets** The entry point into the world of platform-specific targets. Notice that the location of this property sheet is in a particular platform directory. This file defines targets specific to the particular platform. For example, the Win32 version of this defines targets for compiling and linking for the Win32 platform. It uses the tasks from Microsoft .Build.CppTasks.Win32.dll and Microsoft.Build.CppTasks.Common.dll. It contains two extensibility points in the ImportBefore and ImportAfter directories. See the next section for more details on this. This targets file imports the $(VCTargetsPath)\Platforms\ Win32\PlatformToolsets\$(PlatformToolset)\Microsoft.Cpp.Win32.$(PlatformToolset) .targets file. This is where an individual platform toolset is given the opportunity to define or override any targets specific to that toolset.

- **$(VCTargetsPath)\Platforms\\$(Platform)\ImportBefore*.targets** Represents all targets files in the ImportBefore directory under the platform directory. These targets files are imported at the beginning of the platform targets file (Microsoft .Cpp.$(Platform).targets). This is an extensibility point. See the next section for more details.

- **$(VCTargetsPath)\Microsoft.CppCommon.targets** Defines targets for a number of tools such as Lib, Midl, RC, MT, and so on, whose options/switches and behavior do not vary across platforms. It also contains targets that implement the extensibility points available in earlier (and current) editions of Visual C++, such as PreBuildEvent, PreLinkEvent, PostBuildEvent, and CustomBuildStep.

- **$(VCTargetsPath)\Microsoft.CppBuild.targets:** Is the director of the build, it controls the flow of the build in both execution order and the flow of information between tools. For example, it maps .cpp files to .obj files, and it handles native project-to-project references. It defines targets for selective file build (compiling a single file). It also defines the execution order among the various targets. Finally, this is the file that includes most of the Rule files that results in the pages that you see in the Property Pages user interface. Examples include cl.xml and link.xml.

- **$(VCTargetsPath)\Microsoft.BuildSteps.targets** Defines entry point targets for *Build*, *Rebuild*, and so on. These map to the Build, Rebuild menus in the IDE. This targets file also defines wrapper targets that conceptually divides the build process into multiple passes such as generate source, compile, link, and so on. These targets can be utilized to set up a multiple pass build system when the code base is complicated and the dependencies among projects not easy to determine.

- **$(MSBuildToolsPath)\Microsoft.Common.targets** This file defines the steps in the standard build process for .NET projects. It contains all the steps that are common among the different .NET languages, such as Microsoft Visual Basic and Microsoft Visual C#. It also provides general tools and functionality for managed components. Targets in here may be invoked for C++/CLI projects types.

- **$(MSBuildToolsPath)\Microsoft.NETFramework.targets** This file contains .NET Framework–specific targets. This file encapsulates the multi-targeting and framework-specific build process.

- **$(VCTargetsPath)\Platforms\ \$(Platform)\PlatformToolsets\$(PlatformTools et)\Microsoft.Cpp.\$(Platform).$(PlatformToolset).targets** This is the entry into the world of platform toolset–specific targets. For Win32 platforms and v100 platform toolsets, this file is currently empty except for the imports to the targets files in the ImportBefore and ImportAfter directories. See the next section for more details on the ImportBefore and ImportAfter directories.

- **$(VCTargetsPath)\Platforms\ \$(Platform)\PlatformToolsets\ \$(PlatformToolset)\ImportBefore*.targets** Represents all targets files in the ImportBefore directory under the platform toolset directory. These targets files are imported at the beginning of the platform toolset targets file. This is an extensibility point. See the next subsection for more details.

- **$(VCTargetsPath)\Platforms\Win32\PlatformToolsets\ \$(PlatformToolset)\ ImportAfter*.targets** Represents all targets files in the ImportAfter directory under the platform toolset directory. These targets files are imported at the end of the platform toolset targets file. This is an extensibility point. See the next subsection for more details.

- **$(VCTargetsPath)\Platforms\ \$(Platform)\ImportAfter*.targets** Represents all targets files in the ImportAfter directory under the platform directory. These targets files are imported at the end of the platform targets file. This is an extensibility point. See the next subsection for more details.

- **$(VCTargetsPath)\Microsoft.CppClean.targets** Defines the Clean target for a Visual C++ project.

ImportBefore, ImportAfter, ForceImportBeforeCppTargets, and ForceImportAfterCppTargets

In the previous description of the default Visual C++ targets, we mentioned at various places extensibility points where users can hook in their own targets. We describe these here:

- **ImportBefore and ImportAfter** These are two folders that can be created (if they are not already present) under every individual platform directory, as well as every individual platform toolset directory. For the Win32 platform, the path for the ImportBefore directory would be $(VCTargetsPath)\Platforms\Win32\ImportBefore,

whereas for the v100 toolset under Win32, its path would be $(VCTargetsPath)\
Platforms\Win32\PlatformToolsets\v100\ImportBefore. We will use the platform
scenario for explaining their function; their role for the platform toolset scenario is
similar. Targets files in the ImportBefore directory are imported in the Microsoft
.Cpp.$(Platform).targets file before any other targets files. As you can see in
Figure 11-10, Microsoft.Cpp.$(Platform).targets is the root targets file, and it is
platform-specific. This means that targets defined in ImportBefore directory will
be imported before any other platform-specific targets. You would want to do
something like this if you want to affect the definitions of platform-specific targets
that will be imported down the line. Similarly, targets files in the ImportAfter directory
are imported in Microsoft.Cpp.$(Platform).targets after any other targets files. You
would want to do something like this if you want to override the definitions of
platform-specific targets that were imported earlier. Thus, these two folders provide
the user a place to incorporate his or her targets at deterministic points, for a particular
platform. For example, if the user creates ImportBefore and ImportAfter directories in
the Win32 platform directory ($(VCTargetsPath)\Platforms\Win32), and drops targets
files in these directories, then these will be picked up for every Visual C++ project that
is created after this and that targets the Win32 platform.

- **ForceImportBeforeCppTargets and ForceImportAfterCppTargets**   These two
  extensibility points provide similar hook points as ImportBefore and ImportAfter, but
  at a higher level in the import hierarchy. These two are MSBuild properties, and the
  user can set their values to a semicolon-separated list of valid target names. The target
  names included in ForceImportBeforeCppTargets (ForceImportAfterCppTargets) are
  imported in $(VCTargetsPath)\Microsoft.Cpp.targets before (after) any other targets.
  If you see inside the Microsoft.Cpp.targets file, you will see at the very beginning, the
  following line:

  ```
  <Import Condition=" '$(ForceImportBeforeCppTargets)' != '' and exists('$(ForceImportBe
  foreCppTargets)')" Project="$(ForceImportBeforeCppTargets)"/>
  ```

- As you can see in Figure 11-10, Microsoft.Cpp.targets is the upper-level default targets
  file. Thus, these two properties allow you to include your targets before and after any
  other default Visual C++ targets, respectively.

Default Visual C++ Property Sheets

We use the term *Default Visual C++ property sheets* to refer to those property sheets that
are imported by default in a newly created Visual C++ project. Like the default Visual C++
targets files described in the preceding section, the default Visual C++ property sheets are
organized into logical groupings corresponding to platform, platform toolset, and common
properties. Once again, this factoring is helpful from an organization perspective and also
because it opens up extensibility points. In addition, the default Visual C++ property sheets
are strategically placed to allow proper evaluation among interdependent properties.

The default Visual C++ property sheets are brought into a wizard-generated project via two imports—Microsoft.Cpp.Default.props and Microsoft.Cpp.props. If you look inside a project file, you will notice that these two imports occur almost at the top and are separated by some properties defined in the Configuration PropertyGroup. Here is a snippet from a newly created Visual C++ console project file showing this.

```
. . .

<Import Project="$(VCTargetsPath)\Microsoft.Cpp.Default.props" />

  <PropertyGroup Condition="'$(Configuration)|$(Platform)'=='Debug|Win32'"
                 Label="Configuration">
   <ConfigurationType>Application</ConfigurationType>
   <UseDebugLibraries>true</UseDebugLibraries>
   <CharacterSet>Unicode</CharacterSet>
  </PropertyGroup>

  <!--Configuration properties for Release|Win32 go here-->

  <Import Project="$(VCTargetsPath)\Microsoft.Cpp.props" />
. . .
```

Let us describe each of these three items:

- **Microsoft.Cpp.Default.props**   This property sheet contains the default settings for a Visual C++ project. It contains definitions of all the project settings such as Platform, PlatformToolset, ProjectDir, SolutionDir, OutputPath, TargetName, UseOfATL, and so on. In general, properties in this file are not tool-specific and do not assume anything about the Visual C++ project. This property sheet also imports $(VCTargetsPath)\ Platforms\$(Platform)\Microsoft.Cpp.$(Platform).default.props, which is the entry into the platform-specific property settings.

- **Configuration properties**   This property group hosts configuration-wide properties. These properties control the inclusion of system property sheets in Microsoft. Cpp.props. For example, if we define the property as <CharacterSet>Unicode</ CharacterSet>, then the system property sheet Microsoft.Cpp.unicodesupport.props will be included (as can be seen in the Property Manager). Indeed, in one of the files in the import heirarchy of Microsoft.Cpp.props, we can see the following code:

  ```
  <Import Condition="'$(CharacterSet)' == 'Unicode'" Project="$(VCTargetsPath)\
  microsoft.Cpp.unicodesupport.props"/>
  ```

- **Microsoft.Cpp.props**   This property sheet (directly or via imports) defines the default values for many tool-specific properties. Examples include the compiler's Optimization and WarningLevel properties, the MIDL tool's TypeLibraryName property, and so on. In addition, it imports various system property sheets based on configuration properties defined in the Configuration property group described previously.

The two property sheets bring in a hierarchy of other property sheets, as shown in Figure 11-11. We will now explain the purpose of each one of them (except for

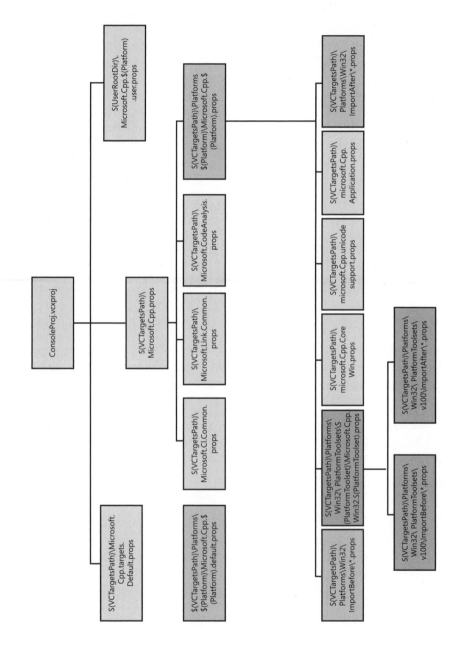

FIGURE 11-11 The Visual C++ property sheet hierarchy for a newly created Visual C++ console project targeting the Win32 platform and using the v100 platform toolset

Microsoft.Cpp.Default.props and Microsoft.Cpp.props, which are described previously). Before that, let us remind you once again of the /preprocess switch discussed in the section entitled "Property Sheets," in Chapter 10, that generates the logical file with all content inline and delineated. The logical file might be useful to see the contributions of all the property sheets in a single file.

- **$(VCTargetsPath)\Platforms\$(Platform)\Microsoft.Cpp.$(Platform).default.props**   Entry into the world of platform-specific default settings. Notice that the location of this property sheet is in a particular platform directory. Like its importing property sheet, the properties whose values are set in this property sheet are non-tool-specific.

- **$(VCTargetsPath)\Microsoft.Cl.Common.props**   Defines default values for compiler switches.

- **$(VCTargetsPath)\Microsoft.Link.Common.props**   Defines default values for linker switches.

- **$(VCTargetsPath)\Microsoft.CodeAnalysis.props**   Includes the property page xml file for code analysis tool. (This is available only in the Premium and Ultimate editions of Visual Studio 2010.)

- **$(VCTargetsPath)\Platforms\$(Platform)\Microsoft.Cpp.$(Platform).props**   This is the exact property sheet where the system property sheets are imported based on the configuration properties. See the previous description of Microsoft.Cpp.props for more information.

- **$(VCTargetsPath)\Platforms\ $(Platform)\ImportBefore*.props**   The extensibility point for the users to include their own platform-specific property sheets. These property sheets are included at the beginning of the importing property sheet. Similar to the ImportBefore folder for default Visual C++ targets (see the section entitled "Default Visual C++ Tasks and Targets," earlier in this chapter).

- **$(VCTargetsPath)\Platforms\ $(Platform)\PlatformToolsets\$(PlatformToolset)\ Microsoft.Cpp.$(Platform).$(PlatformToolset).props**   Provides entry into the world of platform toolset–specific property sheets. The primary purpose is to point the build system to the right toolset directory. The v100 property sheet, for example, sets the EXE, LIB, and WindowsSDK paths to those directories that contain v100 tools.

- **$(VCTargetsPath)\Platforms\ $(Platform)\PlatformToolsets\ $(PlatformToolset)\ ImportBefore*.props**   The extensibility point that allows the user to include the platform toolset–specific property sheets. These property sheets are included at the beginning of the importing property sheet. Similar to the ImportBefore folder for default Visual C++ targets (see the section entitled "Default Visual C++ Tasks and Targets," earlier in this chapter).

- **$(VCTargetsPath)\Platforms\ $(Platform)\PlatformToolsets\ $(PlatformToolset)\ ImportAfter*.props**   The extensibility point that allows the user to include the platform toolset–specific property sheets. These property sheets are included at the end of the importing property sheet. Similar to the ImportAfter folder for default Visual C++ targets (see the section entitled "Default Visual C++ Tasks and Targets," earlier in this chapter).

- **$(VCTargetsPath)\Microsoft.Cpp.CoreWin.props**   Sets core Windows libraries such as kernel32.lib, user32.lib, and so on, as linker additional dependencies.

- **$(VCTargetsPath)\Microsoft.Cpp.unicodesupport.props**   A system property sheet included because of the following property setting in the project file:

  ```
  <CharacterSet>Unicode</CharacterSet>
  ```

- **$(VCTargetsPath)\Microsoft.Cpp.Application.props**   A system property sheet included because of the following property setting in the project file:

  ```
  <ConfigurationType>Application</ConfigurationType>
  ```

- **$(VCTargetsPath)\Platforms\ $(Platform)\ImportAfter*.props**   The extensibility point for users to include their own platform-specific property sheets. These property sheets are included at the end of the importing property sheet. Similar to the ImportAfter folder for default Visual C++ targets (see the section entitled "Default Visual C++ Tasks and Targets," earlier in this chapter).

- **$(UserRootDir)\Microsoft.Cpp.$(Platform).user.props**   This is a user property sheet and is discussed in the section entitled "Visual C++ Directories," in Chapter 10.

Migrating from Visual C++ 2008 and Earlier to Visual C++ 2010

In this section, we describe how you can convert project and solution files in earlier Visual C++ editions to Visual C++ 2010.

IDE Conversion

Visual Studio 2010 comes with a built-in project upgrader—a wizard that springs into action when you try to open a Visual C++ project file created using earlier editions of Visual Studio. The wizard allows you to convert projects in the older .dsp (VC6 project files) and .vcproj (VS2002 – VS2008) formats to .vcxproj format. You can also convert .sln files (solution files in VS2002 – VS2008) and .dsw files (workspace files in VC6) to .sln files in the latest format. The conversion wizard gives you an option to back up your old project files in case you want to go back to your original state for any reason. The mapping between the old and new project files is illustrated in Figure 11-12 and is explained here.

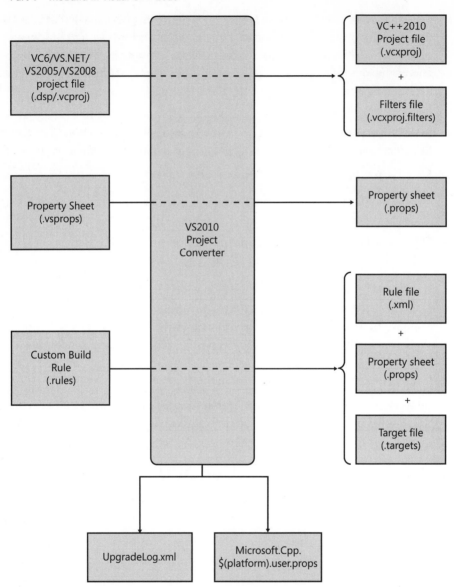

FIGURE 11-12 The Visual C++ 2010 conversion process

■ **Project file (.dsp/.vcproj → .vcxproj + .vcxproj.filters)** The project file in the older formats is converted to a project file that is in the new MSBuild format. This file has the new .vcxproj extension. In addition, another MSBuild file containing the (Solution Explorer) filters information is also created. This has the name *<project name>*.vcxproj .filters and is created in the same directory as the new project file. In Visual C++ 2010, the filters information has been separated into its own file (in the previous format, filters information was included in the project file). This was done to separate the purely user-interface information—the list of filters and their containing files—from other project information. This will ensure that changing the filters in Solution Explorer will not require or result in a build. Note that the filters file must be checked into source control when the project file is. The filters file is not optional. Without the filters file, Solution Explorer will show no filters and simply display all files directly under the project node.

- **Solution file (.dsw/.sln → .sln)**   Although the format for the solution file remains the same—in Visual Studio 2010, it's still not in MSBuild format—some of the content in the previous solution files is moved to the individual project files. When a Visual C++ application from a previous version of Visual Studio is converted to Visual Studio 2010, project dependencies defined at the solution level are converted to project-to-project references. This change ensures that C++ project dependencies are captured in the project file. Here is how a project-to-project reference looks in the .vcxproj project file:

```
<ItemGroup>
    <ProjectReference Include="..\Cpp\Cpp.vcxproj">
      <Project>{c58574bf-9dd8-4cf8-b5b6-6551f2f3eece}</Project>
      <ReferenceOutputAssembly>false</ReferenceOutputAssembly>
    </ProjectReference>
</ItemGroup>
```

There are several advantages of having dependency information in the project file. First, users can build a project without the solution, and the dependent projects will be built automatically. Second, it sets up users for large trees, where they might not use solution files. In addition, many users have several solution files, each with different subsets of the projects. This can save the customers from setting project dependencies for each of the solutions. Another important factor is that build dependencies are more reliable when the dependencies are set through project-to-project references, especially when building with multiple cores.

- **Property sheets (.vsprops → .props)**   Property sheets in the older formats are converted to the MSBuild format. The file extension changes from .vsprops to .props.

- **Build Customizations (.rules → .xml + .props + .targets)**   In older editions, Build Customizations (when they were called Custom Build Rules) were described by a single Extensible Markup Language (XML) file with the .rules extension. As explained in the section entitled "Build Customizations," earlier in this chapter, they are now represented by three files: a Rule file (.xml), a property sheet (.props), and a targets file (.targets). The converter takes the .rules file and generates the three files in the new format.

- **Microsoft.Cpp.$(platform).user.props**   In the section entitled "Visual C++ Directories," in Chapter 10, we explained how the Visual C++ Directories information is now moved to property sheets. During conversion, the converter creates the Microsoft .Cpp.$(platform).user.props for every platform installed on the system. This is created in the %LocalAppData%\Microsoft\MSBuild\v4.0 directory.

- **Upgrade log file**   This is created in the project directory and has the name UpgradeLog.xml. If such a file is already present, then the file is created with the name UpgradeLog2.xml, if two such files exist, the file is given the name UpgradeLog3.xml, and so on. The upgrade log file is an XML file containing status information on the conversion that was just finished. It contains any warning or error messages. The upgrade process will also generate a directory, _UpgradeReport_Files, containing .css files and images used to display the log file in an attractive format in the IDE at the end of the IDE conversion process.

Command-Line Conversion

You can perform project conversion from the command line, too. One reason that you might want to do command-line conversion is if you have a lot of projects to convert, especially if they're not all in the same solution. Two tools are available for you for performing command-line conversion—devenv.exe and vcupgrade.exe. We explain the exact commands to run to perform the conversion described here. You need to run these commands in a Visual Studio 2010 command prompt (and not the regular Windows command prompt), so the path to the tools is already set and available.

Devenv.exe

The devenv.exe file is the executable for the Visual Studio IDE. As was the case with previous editions, you can use this tool to perform a conversion by passing in the /upgrade switch. To upgrade a solution file, type the following:

```
devenv.exe /upgrade YourSolution.sln
```

This will upgrade the solution file along with all the projects in it.

To upgrade a single project file, type the following:

```
devenv.exe /upgrade YourProject.vcproj
```

A few notes about command-line conversion using devenv.exe:

- Unlike IDE conversion, you cannot covert VC6 project (.dsp) and workspace (.dsw) files.
- Since the devenv.exe command is not available for the VC Express SKU edition, this procedure is not applicable for this SKU. Use the IDE to upgrade your old projects.
- Command-line conversion using devenv.exe is preferred to command-line conversion using vcupgrade.exe because of limitations of the latter tool in capturing project dependency information (see the next section for details).

Vcupgrade.exe

The vcupgrade.exe file is a new tool introduced in Visual Studio 2010 and is located in the directory specified by the VS100COMNTOOLS environment variable. It is a tool whose sole purpose is to upgrade VC project files. It performs a role analogous to vcbuild.exe /upgrade in older editions of Visual C++. This, too, is included in the Windows SDK, so users can convert their SDK-based samples even if they do not have Visual Studio installed.

To convert a project file, type the following:

```
vcupgrade.exe YourProject(.dsp/.vcproj)
```

If you wish to convert the same project file again, invoke vcupgrade.exe using the /overwrite switch.

This tool has some limitations, though, as already mentioned. It cannot be used to convert solution files. It can only convert project files, and even here, you want to make sure that a solution referencing this project does not define project dependencies involving this project. As mentioned previously, project dependencies are converted to project-to-project references and converting a single project means that such information cannot be captured. You need to use devenv.exe /upgrade in such cases.

Summary

We started this chapter with the announcement that in Visual Studio 2010, Visual C++ has shifted to using MSBuild as its build system. By moving to MSBuild, Visual C++ has become part of the large migration currently underway by multiple Microsoft and non-Microsoft products to using MSBuild as their build system[3]. Visual C++ customers now not only have an easier way to manage their Visual C++ build setups, but they are also set up to gain from the inevitable improvements to MSBuild going forward.

In this chapter, we described various benefits accrued to Visual C++ by moving to MSBuild. In the next chapter, we delve into advance concepts that mainly deal with extending the Visual C++ build system in various ways.

---

[3] You will be interested to know that MSBuild is used to build the entire Visual Studio product.

Chapter 12
Extending Visual C++ 2010

With the move to MSBuild, all forms of build extensibility offered by MSBuild are now also offered by Visual C++. However, the organization structure of the Visual C++ build system (explained in Chapter 11, "MSBuild in Visual C++, Part 2," in the section entitled "Default Visual C++ Tasks and Targets") also offers alternative extensibility opportunities. This chapter explains the many ways that you can customize and extend the Visual C++ build system.

Build Events, Custom Build Steps, and the Custom Build Tool

Visual C++ 2010, by way of MSBuild, is highly customizable and extensible. However, many times we just need to customize a build in a small way without tapping into the full power of MSBuild extensibility. Build events, custom build steps, and the custom build tool are three ways you can customize your Visual C++ build system in a simple fashion. These three customizations were offered by Visual C++ 2008 as well. In Visual C++ 2010, however, they are powered by MSBuild.

Build Events

Consider a common scenario where we may want to execute a simple operation after the build is done, such as copying the output to a particular directory or registering the output with regsvr32.exe. Build events enable you to specify operations that can be performed at any or all of the following three specific points in the build: before the build starts (the Pre-build Event), before the link process (the Pre-link Event), and after the build finishes (the Post-build Event). Build events are project-level; they execute once per project and not per file. Build events are specified through the property pages.

Figure 12-1 shows the Property Pages user interface with the Post-build Event selected in the left pane. Just above it, you can see Pre-build Event and the Pre-link Event. The user interface allows us to enter a command line that will be executed for any of these events. It also has a Description field that is printed when the command executes. The results of the command line are written to the Output window and the build log files. The description is written to these two places for normal or higher verbosity.

We will illustrate Build Events using the Post-build Event. The other two (Pre-build Event and Pre-link Event) are similar. The command line is a multi-line text field and comes with a multi-line editor. In this editor, you can specify a single command or multiple commands, one per line. You can even call out to external batch files (using the *call* command).

The commands that you enter for the command-line field are emitted to a batch file and executed using cmd.exe. So you can do anything that you can do in a batch file, including using the goto statement. A :VCEnd label is automatically appended to the batch file, which can be used to jump from any point in your command line to the end by using goto VCEnd. A build event can feel free to change the current directory without fear of negatively affecting other parts of the build since the batch file is executed in a subprocess. Figure 12-1 shows that the Post-build Event is set to execute three commands. As we will see later in this chapter, the command line is stored in the project file as item definition metadata. So you can refer to any existing MSBuild properties and metadata. When the command line runs, the Visual C++ environment variables and paths are set. So you can refer to any existing environment variables, too. However, in Visual C++ 2010, to refer to environment variables, you cannot use the % sign because it has special meaning to MSBuild. Instead, use its hexadecimal escape sequence, which is %25. In Figure 12-1, we print the full path of the project using the MSBuild reserved property for the same (MSBuildProjectFullPath). Then we print the computer name using an environment variable. Finally, we execute an external batch file with the name cmds.bat, located in the project directory.

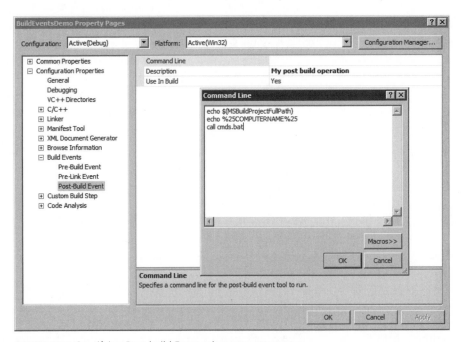

FIGURE 12-1 Specifying Post-build Event using property pages

If you save the project and peek inside the project file, you will see that the information we entered for the Post-build Event is stored as an item definition metadata for the *PostBuildEvent* item definition.

```
<ItemDefinitionGroup Condition="'$(Configuration)|$(Platform)'=='Debug|Win32'">
    ...
    <PostBuildEvent>
      <Message>My post build operation</Message>
      <Command>echo $(MSBuildProjectFullPath)
echo %25COMPUTERNAME%25
call cmds.bat</Command>
    </PostBuildEvent>
</ItemDefinitionGroup>
```

Note that if any of your commands fail, then the build itself fails. Finally, note that the build event operations will not be executed if they are not reached during a build. Therefore, if the build fails, then the Post-build Event will not be executed.

The *PreBuildEvent, PreLinkEvent,* and *PostBuildEvent* targets in the $(VCTargetsPath)\ Microsoft.CppCommon.targets file implement the functionality of these three events. We will copy and paste the definition of the *PostBuildEvent* target to illustrate how this is done.

```
<Target Name="PostBuildEvent" Condition="'$(PostBuildEventUseInBuild)'!='false'">
    <Message Text="Description: %(PostBuildEvent.Message)"
        Condition="'%(PostBuildEvent.Message)' != '' and '%(PostBuildEvent.Command)' != ''"/>
    <Exec Command="%(PostBuildEvent.Command)$(BuildSuffix)"
        Condition="'%(PostBuildEvent.Command)' != ''"/>
</Target>
```

As you can see, the target simply prints the description using the Message task and invokes cmd.exe to execute your commands using the Exec task (the Exec task is implemented to invoke cmd.exe). The value of the BuildSuffix property is *<newline>* :VCEnd. This is the same suffix that was described previously while discussing the command-line format.

Building the project on the author's machine printed the following to the Output window (with verbosity = minimal). Assume that the cmds.bat file contains the single line echo Inside cmds.bat and that MY-PC is the name of the computer on which this is run.

```
C:\InsideMSBuild\Ch12\BuildEventsDemo\BuildEventsDemo.vcxproj

MY-PC

Inside cmds.bat
```

Custom Build Step

Custom Build Step, like build events, allows you to execute arbitrary commands at specific points during the build. Unlike build events, however, you are not limited to a fixed number of points during a build to execute your commands. You have complete freedom to choose when your commands will be executed. Like Build Events, Custom Build Step is a project-level step. Custom Build Step can be specified using property pages, as shown in Figure 12-2.

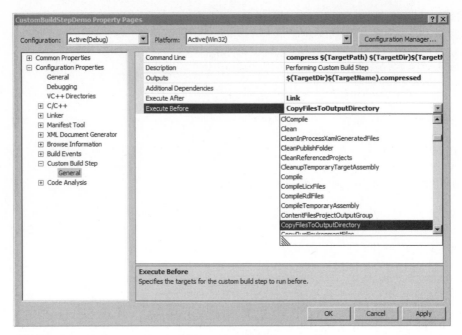

FIGURE 12-2 Specifying Custom Build Step using the property pages

The command-line field has the same qualities as the one for Build Events (described previously). The new fields in here are Execute After, Execute Before, Outputs, and Additional Dependencies.

The Execute After field enables you specify a set of targets, the completion of any one of which will trigger the execution of the Custom Build Step. The Execute Before field enables you to specify that the Custom Build Step should be executed before any of a set of targets is executed. In neither case do the Execute Before or Execute After targets values that you choose cause any of the specified targets to execute. They merely hook the Custom Build Step to build if these other targets happen to execute during the normal course of a build. Note that these two fields do not constitute a strict dependency order, so you don't have to worry about entering incompatible values. The Custom Build Step runs only once during the build, at the first qualifying opportunity—not before *and* after every target you listed.

Each of these two fields can be set to any target or a semicolon-separated list of targets. To help you, each drop-down list includes all the targets in the evaluated project, excluding any that have names starting with an underscore—this tells Visual C++ that they're private implementation details. These two fields directly map to the AfterTargets and BeforeTargets features of MSBuild during run time. See the section entitled "Extending the Build Process," in Chapter 3, "MSBuild Deep Dive, Part 2," for more details on how these work. In fact, if you look at the definition of the CustomBuildStep target in $(VCTargetsPath)\Microsoft.CppCommon.targets (which implements the functionality of Custom Build Step), you will see the mapping between these two concepts. In a moment, we will see that

$(CustomBuildBeforeTargets) and *$(CustomBuildAfterTargets)* are used to represent the
Execute Before and Execute After settings in Figure 12-2.

```
<Target Name="CustomBuildStep"
        Condition="'@(CustomBuildStep)' != '' and '$(SelectedFiles)'==''"
        Inputs="%(CustomBuildStep.Inputs);$(ProjectFileName)"
        Outputs="%(CustomBuildStep.Outputs)"
        DependsOnTargets="ComputeCustomBuildOutput"
        BeforeTargets="$(CustomBuildBeforeTargets)"
        AfterTargets="$(CustomBuildAfterTargets)" >

    <Message Text="Description: %(CustomBuildStep.Message)"
             Condition="%(CustomBuildStep.Message) != ''"/>

    ...

    <Exec Command="%(CustomBuildStep.Command)$(BuildSuffix)" />
</Target>
```

You need to specify the output files generated by the Custom Build Step in the Outputs field.
Without this, the Custom Build Step will not run. The reasoning is explained in detail next.
Similarly, you need to specify files that you want considered as inputs during the up-to-date
check in the Additional Dependencies field.

In Figure 12-2, we entered a simple command line that uses the compress.exe command-line
tool[1] to compress the output executable (we assume that the location of the compress tool
has been added to the PATH environment variable). The compress tool, as we used it, takes
the input file name and the output file name. We entered the same output file name in the
Outputs field. These values are written to the project file as follows. Note that the Execute
After and Execute Before targets are stored as properties, whereas the rest are stored as item
definition metadata. This is because the former values also are used for the Custom Build
Tool (explained in the next section).

```
<ItemDefinitionGroup Condition="'$(Configuration)|$(Platform)'=='Debug|Win32'">
    <CustomBuildStep>
        <Command>compress $(TargetPath) $(TargetDir)$(TargetName).compressed</Command>
        <Outputs>$(TargetDir)$(TargetName).compressed</Outputs>
        <Inputs>$(TargetPath)</Inputs>
    </CustomBuildStep>
 </ItemDefinitionGroup>

...
<PropertyGroup Condition="'$(Configuration)|$(Platform)'=='Debug|Win32'">
    <CustomBuildAfterTargets>Link</CustomBuildAfterTargets>
    <CustomBuildBeforeTargets>CopyFilesToOutputDirectory</CustomBuildBeforeTargets>
</PropertyGroup>
```

---

[1] This tool is freely available from Microsoft as part of the Windows Server 2003 Resource Kit Tools.

The CustomBuildStep target participates in incremental builds. However, it does not use the newer File Tracker mechanism [described in the section entitled "File Tracker–Based Incremental Build," in Chapter 10, "MSBuild in Visual C++ (Part 1)"] for this. It uses an older style that requires us to explicitly specify the inputs and outputs of the target so that MSBuild knows the files it needs to check time stamps for during an incremental build. During an incremental build, if the output file is found to be older than the input file, or if the output file is not found, then the Custom Build Step is run; otherwise, it is not. That is the reason why it is mandatory to specify the Outputs field. If your Custom Build Step doesn't generate any output files but you still want it to execute with every build, make up a fake file name.

Custom Build Tool

A Custom Build Tool allows you to execute a set of commands for a *particular* file during the build. The Custom Build Tool consumes the file and produces one or more output files. Unlike Build Events and Custom Build Step, which are project-level operations, Custom Build Tool is a file-level operation. It runs a maximum of one time for each associated file during a project build. You can also run only the Custom Build Tool for an individual file by right-clicking the file and choosing Compile.

Custom Build Tool should not be confused with Custom Build Rule (which was renamed Build Customization in Visual C++ 2010). Whereas Custom Build Tool acts on a specific file, Build Customizations act on a category of files. Build Customizations are explained in the sections entitled "Creating a Build Customization," later in this chapter, and "Build Customizations," in Chapter 11.

To specify a Custom Build Tool for a particular source file, you need to first set the Item Type property of the source file to Custom Build Tool in the file Property Pages user interface. Clicking Apply makes the Custom Build Tool category appear as in Figure 12-3. This figure shows the property page for a file named File1.xyz that we added to a new Visual C++ console project (although we could have associated any existing file, such as stdafx.cpp, to Custom Build Tool if we wanted). Note that associating a Custom Build Tool for a project changes its MSBuild item type to *CustomBuild* in the project file.

The Custom Build Tool settings page looks very similar to the Custom Build Step settings of Figure 12-2, but that is mostly coincidental. The Command Line field holds the commands to execute. Its format is exactly the same as for the Build Events settings described earlier. For this example, the command is set to simply make a copy of the file on which it acts (specified using the %(*Identity*) metadata). The Description field is used to print a message on the Output window when the Custom Build Tool is executed. The Outputs field indicates the output files produced. Like the Custom Build Step, this field is used to decide whether to execute the Custom Build Tool or not during an incremental build. Without specifying the output, the Custom Build Tool will never run, as explained earlier. The Execute After and Execute Before fields represent the exact same values as the corresponding properties for

Custom Build Step (see Figure 12-2). When they are specified for the Custom Build Step, both the Custom Build Step and the Custom Build Tool execute at the same point, as specified by these two settings. When they are not specified with Custom Build Step, however, these two execute at different points during the build. This behavior is to maintain backward compatibility with older Visual C++ editions.

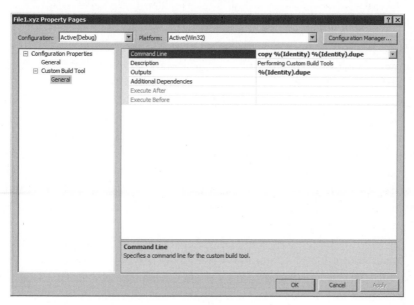

FIGURE 12-3 Custom Build Tool properties for the File1.xyz file

These settings are saved as item metadata for the particular file as shown here. If we had set the Custom Build Tool properties in the *project* Property Pages user interface, then they would have been saved as item definition metadata; and these would apply to every single file whose item type is set to Custom Build Tool.

```xml
<ItemGroup>
    <CustomBuild Include="File1.xyz">
      <Command Condition="'$(Configuration)|$(Platform)'=='Debug|Win32'">copy %(Identity)
%(Identity).dupe</Command>
      <Outputs Condition="'$(Configuration)|$(Platform)'=='Debug|Win32'">%(Identity).dupe</
Outputs>
    </CustomBuild>
</ItemGroup>
```

Building the project prints the following to the Output window (with verbosity = Minimal).

```
1>------ Build started: Project: CustomBuildToolDemo, Configuration: Debug Win32 ------

1>  Performing Custom Build Tools

1>        1 file(s) copied.

. . .
```

Immediately building the same project again will not print this because the Custom Build Tool will not have executed. That is because MSBuild would notice that the output file is not out of date and hence will not execute the Custom Build Tool during this incremental build.

The functionality of Custom Build Tool is implemented by the *CustomBuild* target in the $(VCTargetsPath)\Microsoft.CppCommon.targets file. This target invokes a task by the same name of *CustomBuild*; this task is implemented in the assembly Microsoft.Build.CppTasks. Common.dll.

Finally, we want to discuss briefly the typical usage pattern for the Custom Build Tool. It is used for processing very few files, or even only one specific file. For each of these specific files, we need to manually associate the Custom Build Tool. This means that a Custom Build Tool does not automatically work on a category of files, such as those of a given item type. For example, if you add another file to the project with the same .xyz extension, it will not have its item type defined as CustomBuild in the project file, nor will it have the Custom Build Tool command of the earlier file executed for it. To have the same command executed on this new file, you need to do the same steps as above; that is, changing the item type to Custom Build Tool, setting up the command line, and so on (unless you defined the Custom Build Tool properties at the project level, in which case the latter steps need not be done). If you want to perform custom processing on all items of a specific item type—both existing and future items—use a Build Customization (as described in the section entitled "Creating a Build Customization," later in this chapter). A Build Customization also optionally gives you design-time integration.

Adding a Custom Target to the Build

In this section, we will talk about an extensibility mechanism that directly uses the MSBuild foundation of the Visual C++ build system. The mechanism that we are talking about is to have a custom target execute at an arbitrary point during the build. The Build Events, Custom Build Step, and Custom Build Tool extensibility mechanisms discussed previously are ultimately implemented by targets, but there is a layer of abstraction to make it specific to Visual C++. Further, the command line that can be specified cannot match the power of an MSBuild target that can execute any number of arbitrary tasks.

Suppose that you want to perform some custom processing at a certain point during a build and none of the extensibility mechanisms described previously suffice. Then you can write a custom target that does the desired processing and integrate it into the build. This involves the following steps:

1. Writing a target and the appropriate tasks

2. Specifying the point during a build where you want your target to be executed

3. Including your target in your project(s)

Writing a target and its tasks uses only MSBuild knowledge. See Chapter 4, "Custom Tasks," for information on how to write custom tasks. You can use any of the numerous generic tasks from the MSBuild task library, Visual C++–specific tasks, or even the extensive collection in MSBuild Extension Pack (available online at *http://msbuildextensionpack.codeplex.com*) for this. You can find the Visual C++ tasks in the assemblies mentioned in the section entitled "Default Visual C++ Tasks," in Chapter 11.

You can specify where you want your target to run in numerous ways, including the following:

- You can use the AfterTargets and BeforeTargets features (described in the section entitled "Extending the Build Process," in Chapter 3. This is the most general way of specifying the position in the build. The list of Visual C++ targets that you can use to set these two properties can be obtained from the Execute After and Execute Before drop-down lists of the Custom Build Step property page (see the section entitled "Custom Build Step," earlier in this chapter, for more information).

- You can use Visual C++–specific hooks, such as ForceImportBeforeCppTargets and ForceImportAfterCppTargets, as described in the section entitled "Default Visual C++ Targets," in Chapter 11.

- You can use target injection, as described in the section entitled "Extending the Build Process," in Chapter 3, by putting your target on the list of targets on which a default Visual C++ target depends (the default Visual C++ targets are defined in $(VCTargetsPath)). For example, the *CppClean* target is defined this way in $(VCTargetsPath)\Microsoft.CppClean.targets:

```
<Target Name="CppClean" DependsOnTargets="$(CppCleanDependsOn)">
</Target>
```

MSBuild will execute all of the targets on which a target depends that have not already run before it executes that target itself. Some targets, like CppClean, use a property to capture the list of targets on which they depend. By adding your target to the value list of this property, you can ensure that your target is run before a specific Visual C++ target. You can do this for the CppClean target by defining the following property in your target (named "MyTarget," for instance) or in any of the project files:

```
<PropertyGroup>
    <CppCleanDependsOn>$(CppCleanDependsOn);MyTarget</CppCleanDependsOn>
</PropertyGroup>
```

One other way to get your target to run is to override another one that would otherwise run! For example, you can name your target BeforeClean, AfterCompile, or even CoreCompile itself to override that target (this assumes that your targets file is imported after the default Visual C++ targets files).

How you include your target depends on the scope of its usage.

- If it is meant to be used for only one project, simply import your targets in the project file. A recommended place is the ImportGroup with the label ExtensionTargets. This ImportGroup is located at the bottom of the project file and enables custom targets to override any default targets.

```
<ImportGroup Label="ExtensionTargets">
    <Import Project="MyTarget.targets"/>
</ImportGroup>
```

This is where targets files that are part of Build Customizations are imported (see the section entitled "Build Customizations," in Chapter 11). In fact, since a targets file can be treated as a Build Customization (it is the only mandatory part of a Build Customization), you can simply use the Build Customization user interface to pull in your targets file. As mentioned previously, the user interface places your targets file import at the exact same place.

- If your target is meant to be used for every project targeting a particular platform, then you need to place your targets file in either the ImportBefore or ImportAfter folder of the appropriate platform directory. Your targets file will be automatically imported into projects targeting that platform. For example, to have all projects targeting the Win32 platform to import your target, you can choose to place them in the $(VCTargetsPath)\ Platforms\Win32\ImportAfter folder. See the section entitled "Platforms and Platform Toolsets," in Chapter 11, for more information on these directories.

- If your target is meant to be used for every project targeting a particular platform toolset, you can use the same ImportBefore/ImportAfter mechanism but applied to platform toolsets.

If you plan to deploy your custom targets file with your team, see the section entitled "Deploying Your Extensions," later in this chapter, for details.

Creating a New Property Page

The new data-driven property page architecture has been briefly described in the section entitled "Property Pages," in Chapter 11. The architecture allows you to describe a Rule (a node in the Property Pages user interface under the Configuration Properties node) in a declarative fashion, specifically in the Extensible Application Markup Language (XAML) format. Now, we will describe how to create a property page for your custom tool. This will allow you to provide a design time experience for your tool that is identical to other shipped tools such as the compiler, linker, and so on.

We will take the example of a custom tool that would need both design time and build time integration. This will allow us carry over this example to the section entitled "Creating a Build Customization," later in this chapter. Let us assume that the tool is simple—it converts files in

.docx format (Microsoft Open Office XML Format) to Hypertext Markup Language (HTML). Supposedly, the developers in your team are required to create project documentation such as design documentation, Unified Modeling Language (UML) diagrams, and so on in Microsoft Word files and add it to the project to which the documentation refers to. These Word documents need to be converted to HTML so that they can be hosted on an internal website for easy browsing by other dependent teams. To accomplish this, let us say you already have a command-line tool called Docx2Html.exe that converts .docx files to .html. The tool has options to allow for (1) validating the output in HTML, (2) creating the output file as a single-file web page (.mht) as opposed to an .html page and a folder containing resources such as images, and (3) specifying the output directory where the generated .html file will be placed.

To cleanly integrate this tool into your Visual C++ projects, you would need to do two things:

- Provide a design-time experience akin to the experience for the shipped tools like the compiler and linker. The design-time experience currently includes the Property Pages user interface and the Solution Explorer.

- Build time integration. This means invoking the Docx2Html tool on the docx files during build.

In this section, we will describe how to achieve the design time experience—the first bullet in the previous list. The section entitled "Creating a Build Customization," later in this chapter, will cover the build time integration.

The Property Pages user interface is divided into Rules. Each Rule has categories, and each category has properties. The Rules and the Categories appear in the left pane of the Property Pages user interface, whereas the properties and their values appear in the right pane. To create a Rule node for your custom tool, you simply need to create an XAML file describing these things; for the latest edition of Visual Studio, XAML is just a convenient Extensible Markup Language (XML) format to express information and is not related to Windows Presentation Foundation (WPF) or Silverlight.

For illustration, you can look at the cl.xml Rule file for the compiler tool located on your computer at %ProgramFiles%\MSBuild\Microsoft.Cpp\v4.0\1033 (for non-English-language locales, replace 1033 with the corresponding Locale ID).

If you stripped cl.xml of all data, you will end up with the following skeleton:

```
<?xml version="1.0" encoding="utf-8"?>
<Rule>

  <Rule.DataSource />

  <Rule.Categories>
    <Category />
      . . .
```

```
    </Rule.Categories>

    <BoolProperty />
    <EnumProperty />
    <IntProperty />
    <StringProperty />
    <StringListProperty />
        . . .

</Rule>
```

In other words, a Rule file generally contains a Rule declaration, which in turn includes the declarations for a bunch of categories, a data source, and, most importantly, a collection of properties of various types. The previous snippet shows the five possible types that a property can have.

We will not endeavor to explain every single element type that can occur in a Rule file. You can get that information by going through MSDN documentation for the types defined in the *Microsoft.Build.Framework.XamlTypes* namespace. These types correspond to the deserialization class for the Rule file XAML. More explanation can be found in a blog post by the author entitled "Platform Extensibility - Part 2," on the VS Project Team Blog (*http://blogs .msdn.com/b/vsproject*).

When you include such a file as an item (with item type *PropertyPageSchema*) in your project file, then you will have a node for your Rule in the property pages. Properties set in the Property Pages user interface will be stored in the project file (or any other place, as mentioned in the Rule file). The following Rule file (saved as, say, Docx2Html.xml) makes this happen.

```xml
<?xml version="1.0" encoding="utf-8"?>

<ProjectSchemaDefinitions
   xmlns=http://schemas.microsoft.com/build/2009/properties
   xmlns:x="http://schemas.microsoft.com/winfx/2006/xaml"
   xmlns:sys="clr-namespace:System;assembly=mscorlib">

   <Rule Name="Docx2Html" PageTemplate="tool" DisplayName="Docx2Html" >

     <Rule.DataSource>
         <DataSource Persistence="ProjectFile" ItemType="ProjDoc" />
     </Rule.DataSource>

     <Rule.Categories>
       <Category Name="Conversion" DisplayName="Conversion" />
     </Rule.Categories>

     <StringProperty Name="OutputDirectory" DisplayName="Output Directory"
       Category="Conversion" Subtype="folder"
       Description="Specifies the directory in which to place the output html files" />

     <BoolProperty Name="ValidateHtml" DisplayName="Validate html" Category="Conversion"
       Description="Causes the output html to be validated for standards compliance" />
```

```
<EnumProperty Name="WhichHtmlFileType" DisplayName="Html file type"
  Description="Select the html file type to save in" Category="Conversion" >
  <EnumValue Name="html" DisplayName="Web page (.html)"
    Description="Html page with resources saved in a separate folder" />
  <EnumValue Name="mht" DisplayName="Single file web page (.mht)"
    Description="A single file containing the html code and all resources" />
</EnumProperty>

</Rule>

<ItemType Name="ProjDoc" DisplayName="Project documentation" />
<ContentType Name="ProjDoc" DisplayName="Project documentation" ItemType="ProjDoc" />
<FileExtension Name="*.docx" ContentType="ProjDoc" />

</ProjectSchemaDefinitions>
```

The Rule file, for the most part, is self-explanatory. It defines a Rule with the name Docx2Html with one category named Conversion. This category includes three properties for specifying the output directory, output HTML validation, and output file format. The output directory is a string property of subtype folder; this automatically provides for a file browser to appear as the editor for this property in the Property Pages user interface. The validation property is a Boolean value, whereas the output file format is an enumeration-type property with two possible values. Note that every source file in the project automatically gets associated with a Rule called *General*. This contains two properties—Excluded From Build and Item Type. The former property can be used to exclude a particular document from the conversion process, if needed.

The *DataSource* element for the Rule specifies that the property values set in the property pages must be written to the ProjectFile, which refers to the project file or the property sheet that spawned the property page[2]. Further, the property values must be set for items of type ProjDoc, which is the item type that we gave to the docx files added to our projects (we just made up that name—you could use any syntactically valid MSBuild item name you want).

You can notice a difference between cl.xml and the previous Rule file—we have three additional sibling elements to the Rule element in the latter file, all wrapped up in the *ProjectSchemaDefinitions* root element. These additional ones are the *ContentType*, *ItemType*, and *FileExtension* elements (collectively referred to as the "content type elements"). Notice how these three elements refer to each other. What is their purpose, and why don't we have them in the cl.xml file? These elements identify files ending with .docx files as valid source files to Visual C++ project system. The project file, property sheets, and targets files contain many MSBuild items, yet not all of these items refer to source files. A good example is how we represent project configurations. These are expressed as MSBuild items (of item type ProjectConfiguration; look at the top of a .vcxproj file), yet clearly they don't refer to source

---

[2]   So, if you set the properties in the Property Pages user interface created by right-clicking a property sheet and choosing Properties, then the values will be written to the property sheet. If, instead, the user interface was created from the project node, it would be written to the project file (.vcxproj). Perhaps a better name for this value could have been UnderlyingFile.

files. Unless an item type is explicitly indicated as a source file type, the Visual C++ project system will not display items of that item type in the Solution Explorer. The content type elements in our Rule file indicate exactly that. They also tell that when a .docx file is added to the project, it should be stored as an item of item type ProjDoc. The content type elements for cl.xml are found in the ProjectItemsSchema.xml file in the same directory as cl.xml. This file contains the content type elements, not just for C++ files but also for all the well-known extensions such as .h, .resx, .ico, .html, and so on[3]. You can see the content type names and descriptions displayed in the property pages for an individual file (see the Item Type property in the General category).

To include the Docx2Html.xml Rule file in your project, open the project file in Notepad and add an item of type PropertyPageSchema whose Include path points to the path of the file. Assuming that the Rule file is in the project directory, the inclusion will look like this.

```
<ItemGroup>
    <PropertyPageSchema Include="$(MSBuildProjectDirectory)\Docx2Html.xml" />
</ItemGroup>
```

(See the section entitled "Deploying Your Extensions," later in this chapter, for how to deploy your Rule file for your whole team.)

Now, close and reopen the IDE. If you opened the property pages for the project, you will not see the Docx2Html rule. That is because the project system does not show a Rule when there are no items of the corresponding type. So, add a .docx file to the project. The Solution Explorer should look like Figure 12-4.

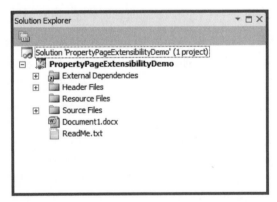

FIGURE 12-4 Adding a .docx file to the project to which we are trying to add the Docx2Html property page

If you opened the project file in Notepad (after first saving the solution), you will note that the document file is added as an item of item type ProjDoc—exactly as we specified in the

---

[3] For design consistency, they should perhaps have been defined in the individual Rule files rather than centralized this way. For example, the content type for C++ files should have been defined in cl.xml.

Docx2Html.xml Rule file. Without the Rule file, it would have been added as an item of item type None—the item type used by the project system for a file type that it does not understand.

Coming back to the main topic, we can now open the Project Properties dialog and see the Docx2Html rule added to the property pages (see Figure 12-5). As expected, the Rule has exactly one category and three properties.

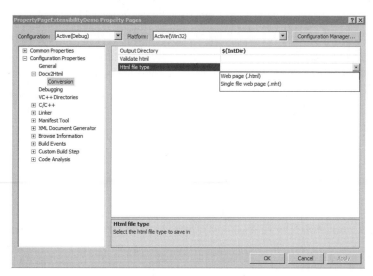

FIGURE 12-5 The Property Pages user interface showing that the Docx2Html Rule has indeed been added

The properties are not set to any value initially. You can specify default values using property sheets. This is explained in the section entitled "Creating a Build Customization," later in this chapter.

When the value of any of these properties is set, the value gets written to the project file. For example, when the Output Directory property is set to *$(IntDir)*, it gets written to the project file as ItemDefinition metadata as shown here[4].

```
<ProjDoc>
    <OutputDirectory>$(IntDir)</OutputDirectory>
</ProjDoc>
```

Troubleshooting

The most common mistake made while developing a new property page is simply inserting XAML syntax errors in the Rule file. Such errors result in failure to load the Rule file, although not the project itself. To debug such failures, you can view the trace messages emitted by

---

[4] If the value were set in the property page obtained from a docx project item, then the value would be written to the project file as an item metadata.

the Visual C++ project system as it loads a project. Viewing the Rule file in an XML editor can reveal basic syntax errors, but errors at a higher abstraction level will need the project system trace messages before they can be debugged. These trace messages mention the exact line number where an error is present. Unfortunately, these messages are not printed to the Output window. We need to use a special tool to view them. We describe how to enable as well as view these messages. It needs to be emphasized that what we describe in this text is a feature of the Visual C++ project system and does not involve MSBuild.

The project system tracing is not switched on by default, so we need to explicitly enable it. After switching it on, we need to use a special tool to view the emitted messages. To enable tracing, add the following xml block to the devenv.exe.config file (found in %ProgramFiles%\ Microsoft Visual Studio 10.0\Common7\IDE) just below the `<configSections />` block (make sure to make a backup of the file first, so you can revert to the previous version in case something goes wrong).

```
<system.diagnostics>
    <switches>
      <add name="CPS" value="4" />
    </switches>
</system.diagnostics>
```

After adding the previous XML block, close and reopen the Visual Studio IDE, but don't load your project yet. Before that you need to install and open the DebugView for Windows tool, which will capture and show you the trace messages emitted by the project system. This tool is available as a free download from *technet.microsoft.com*.

After you open the DebugView tool, load a Visual C++ project that includes your custom property page. A lot of messages will be shown in the DebugView tool window, but you can search for your Rule file name to zero in on any messages specific to that file. For example, missing a closing > tag for an XML node will result in a trace message similar to the following:

```
Failure loading XAML file C:\InsideMSBuild\Ch12\PropertyPageExtensibilityDemo \Docx2Html.
xml': System.Xml.XmlException: ' ' is an unexpected token. The expected token is '>'. Line
15, position 100.
```

To test changes to your Rule file, you need to close and reopen the IDE. The Rule files are loaded only when the solution is opened, and thus reloading the project will not result in your new changes being picked up.

Make sure that the .docx file is added to your project *after* you add the Rule file. Otherwise, the .docx files will not be added with the ProjDoc item type, which means that the project system will not display the Docx2Html Rule in the Property Pages user interface.

Creating a Build Customization

It is possible to add a custom tool to your build process and have it be treated as a first-class citizen by the Visual C++ project system. By "first-class citizen," I mean the project system will treat your custom tool like it would any of the shipped tools like the compiler, linker, and so on. The section entitled "Creating a New Property Page," earlier in this chapter, listed two things that need to be done to achieve such a clean integration. It also described how to achieve the first of those, namely design-time integration. In this section, we will concentrate on the second item, which is to provide build-time integration. Build-time integration that is possible through a Build Customization includes getting invoked during Build/Rebuild/ Clean, incremental build, and selected file build. It however excludes integration with the File Tracker.

The Build Customization architecture was described in the section entitled "Build Customizations," in Chapter 11. To recap, creating a Build Customization involves authoring three files: (1) a Rule file that describes the property page schema for the Rule, as well as acts as a template for a task to be created by the XamlTaskFactory; (2) a property sheet file that contains default values for the properties defined in the Rule file; and (3) a targets file that is at the heart of the Build Customization—it describes the target(s) to be run during the build process. The target almost always refers to the task generated by the XamlTaskFactory. These three files will be presented for the Docx2Html tool introduced in the section entitled "Creating a New Property Page."

Unfortunately, Visual C++ 2010 does not come with an editor that will let you create a Build Customization. You may recall that Visual C++2008 came with one that lets you create a Custom Build Rule. You can however use the editor in Visual C++2008 to create a Custom Build Rule and add it to a dummy Visual C++2008 project, and then use the project upgrader to convert the Custom Build Rule (along with the project) to a Build Customization. With that said, we will proceed to describe the manual creation of these files.

Let's assume that the Docx2Html tool can be run on the command line as follows:

```
Docx2Html.exe [/v] [/m | /h] /outdir:"<output dir>" <list of .docx files to convert>
   Example:   Docx2Html.exe /v /m /outdir:"C:\Foo" Document1.docx Document2.docx
```

where the options mean the following:

- /v: Perform validation on the output HTML

- /m: Output should be in .mht format

- /h: Output should be in .html format

- /outdir: Specified the output directory for the files

Let us start with the targets file, which is the only mandatory file of the three files. The file (Docx2Html.targets) looks like what is listed here. Note that to keep it simple, selected build and chaining (that is, consuming outputs of other tasks) are not presented.

```
<?xml version="1.0" encoding="utf-8"?>
<Project xmlns="http://schemas.microsoft.com/developer/msbuild/2003">

  <ItemGroup>
```

```
      <PropertyPageSchema Include="$(MSBuildThisFileDirectory)$(MSBuildThisFileName).xml" />
    </ItemGroup>

    <UsingTask TaskName="Docx2Html" TaskFactory="XamlTaskFactory"
               AssemblyName="Microsoft.Build.Tasks.v4.0">
      <Task>$(MSBuildThisFileDirectory)$(MSBuildThisFileName).xml</Task>
    </UsingTask>

    <Target Name="Docx2Html" AfterTargets="Build" Condition="'@(ProjDoc)' != ''">
      <Message Importance="High" Text="Converting docx files to html ..." />
      <Docx2Html Condition="'@(ProjDoc)' != '' and '%(ProjDoc.ExcludedFromBuild)' != 'true'"
        CommandLineTemplate="%(ProjDoc.CommandLineTemplate)"
        OutputDirectory="%(ProjDoc.OutputDirectory)"
        ValidateHtml="%(ProjDoc.ValidateHtml)"
        WhichHtmlFileType="%(ProjDoc.WhichHtmlFileType)"
        Inputs="@(ProjDoc)" />
    </Target>

</Project>
```

The targets file includes the Rule file as an item of type PropertyPageSchema. It is a requirement that all three Build Customization files have the same name (ignoring the extension, of course) and be in the same directory. Hence, the path $(MSBuildThisFile Directory)$(MSBuildThisFileName).xml can be used to refer to the Rule file. Recall that MSBuildThisFileDirectory and MSBuildThisFileName are reserved MSBuild properties that refer to the directory and name, respectively, of the file in which they are declared.

Next is the UsingTask statement. Remember that a *<UsingTask>* element defines a task type. You could use this <Docx2Html> task anywhere else in your targets files, with just this one *<UsingTask>* element. This particular statement refers to the XamlTaskFactory and includes the Rule file as a child element. During run time, the net effect of this is that the XamlTaskFactory creates an instance of the Docx2Html task using the Rule file as a template. This saves you from authoring the task (in code) and deploying the task assembly yourself. Most tasks based on tools like Docx2Html simply consist of invoking the tool executable with the appropriate switches and inputs. This simple behavior makes such tasks amenable to being autogenerated, which is exactly what the XamlTaskFactory does. However, we need to write the Rule file in a way that the XamlTaskFactory can consume it. This requires us to add a few more things to the Rule file that we created in the section entitled "Creating a Property Page," earlier in this chapter.

Finally, we have the target that is run during the build to perform the conversion. It consists of a Message task that prints an informational message followed by the Docx2Html task that will be generated by the XamlTaskFactory. Since we refer to the ProjDoc item definition metadata in the task usage, we automatically get batching. So .docx files with different property values will be run through the tool in separate batches.

The Rule file (Docx2Html.xml) is presented here. It is the same as the one in the section entitled "Creating a Property Page" with the following additions:

1. The properties have switches defined for them. These switches correspond to the Docx2Html.exe tool options. This allows the XamlTaskFactory to fashion an appropriate command line for the Docx2Html.exe tool.

2. There is a new category called Command Line, which makes available a command-line page in the Property Pages user interface that displays the command line (minus the inputs) that would be used during the build.

3. We define a new property with the name "CommandLineTemplate." The XamlTaskFactory uses this as a template to create the actual command line and stuff it inside the ITask.Execute() method of the generated Docx2Html task.

4. Then we define a property called Inputs that captures the input files that need to be passed to the tool.

```xml
<?xml version="1.0" encoding="utf-8"?>
<ProjectSchemaDefinitions
xmlns="http://schemas.microsoft.com/build/2009/properties"
xmlns:x="http://schemas.microsoft.com/winfx/2006/xaml"
xmlns:sys="clr-namespace:System;assembly=mscorlib">
<Rule Name="Docx2Html" PageTemplate="tool" DisplayName="Docx2Html" >

    <Rule.DataSource>
        <DataSource Persistence="ProjectFile" ItemType="ProjDoc" />
    </Rule.DataSource>

    <Rule.Categories>
      <Category Name="Conversion" DisplayName="Conversion" />
      <Category Name="Command Line" Subtype="CommandLine" DisplayName="Command Line"/>
    </Rule.Categories>

    <StringProperty Name="OutputDirectory" DisplayName="Output Directory"
      Category="Conversion" Subtype="folder" Switch="/outdir:&quot;[value]&quot;"
      Description="Specifies the directory in which to place the output html files" />

    <BoolProperty Name="ValidateHtml" DisplayName="Validate html"
      Category="Conversion" Switch="/v"
      Description="Causes the output html to be validated for standards compliance" />

    <EnumProperty Name="WhichHtmlFileType" DisplayName="Html file type"
      Description="Select the html file type to save in" Category="Conversion" >
      <EnumValue Name="html" DisplayName="Web page (.html)" Switch="/m"
        Description="Html page with resources saved in a separate folder" />
      <EnumValue Name="mht" DisplayName="Single file web page (.mht)" Switch="/h"
        Description="A single file containing the html code and all resources" />
    </EnumProperty>

    <StringProperty Name="CommandLineTemplate" DisplayName="Command Line"
      Category="Command Line" Visible="False" IncludeInCommandLine="False" />

    <StringListProperty Name="Inputs" Category="Command Line" IsRequired="true">
      <StringListProperty.DataSource>
        <DataSource
          Persistence="ProjectFile"
```

```
                ItemType="ProjDoc"
                SourceType="Item" />
        </StringListProperty.DataSource>
    </StringListProperty>

  </Rule>

  <ItemType Name="ProjDoc" DisplayName="Project documentation" />
  <ContentType Name="ProjDoc" DisplayName="Project documentation" ItemType="ProjDoc" />
  <FileExtension Name="*.docx" ContentType="ProjDoc" />

</ProjectSchemaDefinitions>
```

Figure 12-6 shows the command-line page of the Docx2Html Rule.

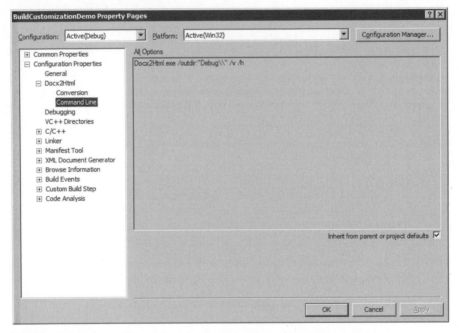

FIGURE 12-6 The Docx2Html Rule showing the command-line page

Finally, we need to define default values for the properties defined in the Rule file. Without this, the user will have to set values for every project and .docx file even if they are the same every time. The default values are defined in the property sheet Docx2Html.props, whose contents are listed here. Notice how we define the CommandLineTemplate property value. The XamlTaskFactory creates the actual command line from this template. Note the reference to the Docx2Html.exe executable, which is based on the assumption that the path to this executable is in the PATH. Otherwise, you need to list the full path. *[AllOptions]* is a placeholder for all the properties defined for the ProjDoc items. Similarly, *[Inputs]* is a placeholder for all the input files, as captured by the Inputs property.

```xml
<?xml version="1.0" encoding="utf-8"?>
<Project xmlns="http://schemas.microsoft.com/developer/msbuild/2003">

  <ImportGroup Label="PropertySheets" />

  <PropertyGroup Label="UserMacros" />

  <PropertyGroup />

  <ItemDefinitionGroup>
    <ProjDoc>
      <WhichHtmlFileType>mht</WhichHtmlFileType>
      <ValidateHtml>true</ValidateHtml>
      <OutputDirectory>$(IntDir)</OutputDirectory>
      <CommandLineTemplate>Docx2Html.exe [AllOptions] [Inputs]</CommandLineTemplate>
    </ProjDoc>
  </ItemDefinitionGroup>
  <ItemGroup />

</Project>
```

Having defined the Docx2Html Build Customization, we need to add it to the project. Simply use the Build Customizations… context menu of the project in the Solution Explorer to get to the user interface that will allow you to do this. Refer to the section entitled "Build Customizations," in Chapter 11, for more information. Once the Build Customization is loaded, you can add files of type .docx. With at least one .docx file in the project, you can see the Docx2Html Rule in the property pages.

To confirm that the Build Customization works, we created a dummy Docx2Html.exe executable. It simply prints "Entered Docx2Html.exe", "Exiting Docx2Html.exe" messages inside its *Main* method. We added the path to this executable to Visual C++ Directories/Executable Directories, and then we rebuilt the project while setting the log file verbosity to diagnostic so we can get as much detail about what happens during the build. The following segment in the log file indicates that the Build Customization indeed took effect (note that we had two .docx files—Document1.docx and Document2.docx—in my project).

```
Target "Docx2Html: (TargetId:109)" in file "C:\InsideMSBuild\Ch12\BuildCustomizationDemo\
Docx2Html\Docx2Html.targets" from project "C:\InsideMSBuild\Ch12\BuildCustomizationDemo\
BuildCustomizationDemo.vcxproj" (target "Rebuild" depends on it):
Task "Message" (TaskId:54)
  Converting docx files to html ... (TaskId:54)
Done executing task "Message". (TaskId:54)
Initializing task factory "XamlTaskFactory" from assembly "Microsoft.Build.Tasks.v4.0".
Using "Docx2Html" task from the task factory "XamlTaskFactory".
Task "Docx2Html" (TaskId:55)
  cmd.exe /C "C:\Users\pavana\AppData\Local\Temp\1559c899bb6b48e286c306e9e020a711.cmd"
(TaskId:55)
  Docx2Html.exe /outdir:"Debug\\" /v /h Document1.docx Document2.docx (TaskId:55)
    (TaskId:55)
  C:\InsideMSBuild\Ch12\BuildCustomizationDemo>Docx2Html.exe /outdir:"Debug\\" /v /h
Document1.docx Document2.docx  (TaskId:55)
  Entered Docx2Html.exe (TaskId:55)
```

```
   Exiting Docx2Html.exe (TaskId:55)
Done executing task "Docx2Html". (TaskId:55)
Done building target "Docx2Html" in project "BuildCustomizationDemo.vcxproj".:
(TargetId:109)
```

To see the effect of batching, change the value of the ValidateHtml property (to use one example) for the Document2.docx file to No, from the default Yes. Building the project indeed shows two invocations of the Docx2Html task, once for each file and with a different command line in each case. This is shown here.

```
Docx2Html.exe /outdir:"Debug\\" /v /h Document1.docx
 . . .
Docx2Html.exe /outdir:"Debug\\" /h Document2.docx
```

Adding a New Platform and Platform Toolset

In this section, we will use the first-class support provided by Visual C++ for adding new platform toolsets and platforms to add a new platform toolset support. We will not discuss adding a new platform in detail because it involves similar concepts. See the section entitled "Platforms and Platform Toolsets," in Chapter 11, for details on how Visual C++ supports multiple platforms and platform toolsets.

As described in the section entitled "Platforms and Platform Toolsets," a Toolset represents a complete set of build tools such as compilers and linkers. Visual C++ comes with default support for v100 and v90 toolsets, representing Visual Studio 2010 and Visual Studio 2008 toolsets, respectively. You can choose between these two toolsets by setting the Platform Toolset property in the Property Pages user interface. In this section, we discuss how to add support for the GCC toolset for the Win32 platform. The GNU Compiler Collection (GCC) is a popular toolset and includes a full set of tools including a compiler, assembler, and linker to build a C++ project. The g++.exe file, which is a part of GCC, provides a front end for these various tools for building C++ source code.

To add support for GCC, we first need to download the tool collection. One option is to download MinGW, which is a port of these tools to Windows. It can be downloaded from *www.mingw.org* (make sure you select the C++ Compiler check box in the MinGW GUI installer). Another option is to download Cygwin, which runs GCC over a Linux emulator. In this section, we use MinGW. We assume that the path to the bin directory of MinGW is added to the PATH environment variable.

As explained in the section entitled "Platforms and Platform Toolsets," Visual C++ considers folders under the PlatformToolsets directory of a platform folder as representing a distinct platform toolset. By default, there are two platform toolset folders under $(VCTargetsPath)\ Platforms\Win32\PlatformToolsets, representing the v90 and v100 toolsets. We add a new folder named gcc to this directory. Recall that this is the same name that will appear in the property pages for the Platform Toolset property drop-down list. In this directory, we need to put a targets file with the name "Microsoft.Cpp.Win32.gcc.targets" and a similarly named property sheet that relates to the GCC platform toolset. However, in the interest of keeping the demonstration simple, we will just have the targets file.

This target has exactly one target that overrides the Build target. This Build target simply invokes g++ to build all the .cpp files into the specified executable. This targets file is sufficient to build a new Visual C++ Win32 console project. It is also possible to selectively override lesser targets, like ClCompile or Link, where the compiler or linker tool is used to perform the compiling or linking action, while leaving the rest of the operations in the overall build to the default tools.

Note that the Build target defined in the toolset directory gets the final say over the similarly named target defined in the platform because it is imported below it. Thus, when a user chooses to build a project in Visual Studio using the gcc toolset for the Win32 platform, the Build target in this targets file gets executed. Figure 12-7 shows the location of the targets file in Windows Explorer.

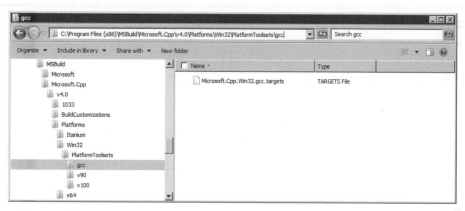

FIGURE 12-7 Location of Microsoft.Cpp.Win32.gcc.targets

The following is the contents of the targets file.

```
<Project ToolsVersion="4.0" xmlns="http://schemas.microsoft.com/developer/msbuild/2003">
  <!-- Override the build target -->
  <Target Name="Build">
    <!-- Create output directory -->
    <MakeDir Directories="$(TargetDir)"/>
    <!--Invoke g++ to build all cpp files. Ask g++ to look into the Windows SDK include
directory.
        Convert semi colon separated ClCompile items into space separated list.
        Add double quotes around all file paths. -->
    <Exec Command="g++ -v @(ClCompile -> '&quot;%(FullPath)&quot;', ' ')
-I &quot;$(ProgramFiles)\Microsoft SDKs\Windows\v7.0A\include&quot; -o
&quot;$(TargetPath)&quot;" />
  </Target>
</Project>
```

The Build target contains two tasks from the MSBuild task library. The first one—the MakeDir task—is used to create the output directory. The second one—the Exec task—invokes the g++ front end. It passes the list of all .cpp files. Because g++ requires items in a space-separated list format, we use an MSBuild item transform (for more information about this, see the section entitled "Item Transformations," in Chapter 2, "MSBuild Deep Dive, Part 1") to convert the default semicolon-separated list to a space-separated list. We also use the " escape sequence to put double quotes around all the file paths. We use the –I switch of g++ to pass in the include directory of Windows SDK because even a simple console project references header files from it. We use the –o switch to specify the output binary name and location. Notice that we simply use the $(TargetPath) path for the output name. Finally, we pass in the –v switch for verbose information from g++. This also gives us a visual indication that g++ has actually run.

To test this, we created a simple Win32 Console project called GccToolsetDemo in the C:\InsideBuild\Cpp directory on our machine. We then changed the Platform Toolset of this project to gcc, as shown in Figure 12-8.

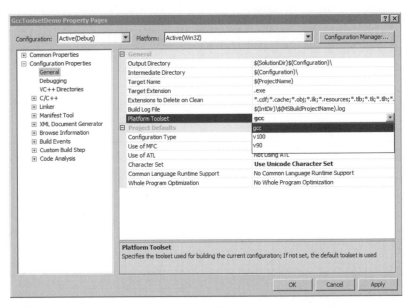

FIGURE 12-8 Choosing the gcc platfrom toolset in the property pages

We build the project by using the Build menu in the IDE. The Output window contains a lot of output from g++, which indicated that g++ was indeed run. More importantly, Visual C++ indicated that the build succeeded[5]. Looking in the output directory also shows the executable as expected, and if we look in the build log file (whose verbosity was set to

---

5 The Error List window will show errors related to Intellisense. You can ignore them, though, because they do not affect the final output generation. It is beyond the scope of this text to discuss how to enable Intellisense.

diagnostic for testing), we reconfirm that our targets file was used. We also see the exact command line that was used to invoke g++.

```
Target "Build: (TargetId:3)" in file "C:\Program Files (x86)\MSBuild\Microsoft.Cpp\v4.0\
Platforms\Win32\PlatformToolsets\gcc\Microsoft.Cpp.Win32.gcc.targets" from project "C:\
InsideMSBuild\Cpp\GccToolsetDemo\GccToolsetDemo\GccToolsetDemo.vcxproj" (entry point):
Using "MakeDir" task from assembly "Microsoft.Build.Tasks.v4.0, Version=4.0.0.0,
Culture=neutral, PublicKeyToken=b03f5f7f11d50a3a".
Task "MakeDir" (TaskId:4)
  Creating directory "C:\InsideMSBuild\Cpp\GccToolsetDemo\Debug\". (TaskId:4)
Done executing task "MakeDir". (TaskId:4)
Using "Exec" task from assembly "Microsoft.Build.Tasks.v4.0, Version=4.0.0.0,
Culture=neutral, PublicKeyToken=b03f5f7f11d50a3a".
Task "Exec" (TaskId:5)
  g++ -v "C:\InsideMSBuild\Cpp\GccToolsetDemo\GccToolsetDemo\GccToolsetDemo.cpp" "C:\
InsideMSBuild\Cpp\GccToolsetDemo\GccToolsetDemo\stdafx.cpp" -I "C:\Program Files (x86)\
Microsoft SDKs\Windows\v7.0A\include" -o "C:\InsideMSBuild\Cpp\GccToolsetDemo\Debug\
GccToolsetDemo.exe" (TaskId:5)
```

As you can see, it is quite easy to integrate a new toolset support into Visual C++. However, to make it bulletproof, many more things need to be done. Although some of them are cleanly supported by Visual C++, the others are not quite at that level yet. We now list what needs to be done to make the previous toolset support production quality:

- Support more GCC switches. In the previous discussion, we used only the –I and –o switches, but there are a lot more switches that can be used to configure GCC. This is similar to cl.exe. In supporting these switches, you have two options: You can repurpose cl.exe switches set by the user through the property pages for g++, and ignore those that do not apply; or you can author a Rule file for GCC, which is explained in the next item.

- You can create Rule files for the tools in GCC (you may want to refer to the section entitled "Creating a New Property Page," earlier in this chapter, for how to author a Rule file) and include it in your target. The Rule file for the compiler can contain exactly those switches that are supported by the GCC compiler tool. Similarly, you can have Rule files for the GCC linker. It would also have been nice if we could remove the existing Rule file for the cl.exe compiler. Unfortunately, this edition of Visual C++ does not provide a way to remove existing Rule files (deleting the cl.xml file will mean that you can set compiler switches for the other toolsets). So you will have to live with property pages for both the CL compiler and GCC compiler, although you can clearly ignore CL properties during run time.

- Provide the Microsoft.Cpp.Win32.gcc.props property sheet in the gcc toolset directory with default values for various GCC switches.

- Add support for Rebuild and Clean targets. Build, Rebuild, and Clean are the trifecta of targets required by any build system.

- Instead of using Exec task to invoke g++, use the XAML task factory along with the corresponding Rule file. Then you can invoke g++ using an elegant syntax: <GCC Sources="..." Include="..." .../>. As well as being prettier, it will be more readable, and it will do some type-checking of its inputs for you.

- Make the task that invokes g++ be File Tracker–enabled. See the section entitled "File Tracker–Based Incremental Build," in Chapter 10, for how this is done. Note that enabling a task to be tracked is relatively difficult to do in this release of Visual C++.

- Provide extension points for your toolset in the form of ImportBefore and ImportAfter. This simply involves adding import statements for all targets files (using the * wildcard) in these folders at the top and bottom of the Microsoft.Cpp.Win32.gcc.targets file.

Deploying Your Extensions

This chapter discussed the various ways that you can extend the Visual C++ build system. However, build systems that are complex enough to need extensions are usually used in a team setting. Suppose that you have a team of 10 developers working on a product, and you want all of them to install and use a certain build extension, such as a new target. How do you deploy it so that all the developers can easily access and use it—automatically if possible? Manually requiring them to install the build extension on their machines is not an elegant or a scalable solution. We will describe an approach to solve this problem.

This approach requires that you check in the whole build system (explained in this section) to your source control system and redirecting all project imports to this folder on the local enlistment. With this kind of setup, sharing extensions becomes easy. Simply check your extension into this build system folder, and it will be picked up when a team member brings in changes from the source control. For example, drop your targets file into the ImportAfter/ImportBefore folders of a checked-in platform folder, and it will automatically be pulled into every team member's projects once the changes are synched. The main steps involved in implementing this approach are listed here. (This is not an exhaustive set of instructions; depending on your build setup, other steps may be required.)

- Checking in the build system: This requires you to check in the folder represented by the property MSBuildExtensionsPath after Visual Studio has been installed. This usually has the value *%ProgramFiles%\MSBuild*. Note that this does not include the common language runtime (CLR) and the framework (which you should not check in).

- Redirection: As you may have noticed, all the default Visual C++ targets are present at the location specified by $(VCTargetsPath) or its subdirectories. The default value for this resolves to %ProgramFiles%\MSBuild\Microsoft.Cpp\v4.0. If you look inside any project file, you will see that the default Visual C++ property sheets and targets files are imported using a path that starts with $(VCTargetsPath). So if we can change the value of this symbol, then redirection is achieved. But, how do we override it?

VCTargetsPath is stored in the registry and is picked up by MSBuild as a toolset property when it starts. Unfortunately, toolset properties can't be overridden using environment variables. So you need to override it as a property in the project file or any of the other imports. There is another way, however. VCTargetsPath is actually defined in the registry as `$(MSBuildExtensionsPath32)\Microsoft.Cpp\v4.0\` and MSBuildExtensionsPath32 *is* overridable by redefining it as an environment variable. Notice that overriding MSBuildExtensionsPath32, unlike with VCTargetsPath, will also cause redirection for C# and VB projects, which may not be unwanted because you may want all project types to build in the checked-in environment. Finally, when you override MSBuildExtensionsPath32, also make sure to override the variants MSBuildExtensionsPath and MSBuildExtensionsPath64 as well.

Part VI
Team Foundation Build

Chapter 13
Team Build Quick Start

MSBuild is a build engine rather than a build automation tool, which is where Team Foundation Build (which we will refer to as *Team Build* for short) comes into the picture. Team Build is a component of Microsoft Visual Studio Application Lifecycle Management. Team Build provides build automation that integrates tightly with the other Visual Studio Application Lifecycle Management components, such as version control, work-item tracking, testing, and reporting.

Why discuss Team Build in a book about MSBuild? Apart from the fact that both are build tools, the good news is that Team Build uses MSBuild to build solutions and projects, so the MSBuild knowledge that you've gained in the previous chapters will be put to good use.

Team Build changed significantly between Visual Studio Team System 2008 and Visual Studio 2010 by moving the build process orchestration from being MSBuild-based to Workflow Foundation–based. This change enables scenarios that were difficult to implement using MSBuild (such as distributing builds across multiple machines), provides a graphical build process designer, and provides a customizable user interface for queuing builds and editing build definitions.

Introduction to Team Build

This section discusses the features and architecture of Team Build to familiarize you with its key components and how they relate to each other. These features and components are covered in more depth in later sections.

Team Build Features

Team Build 2010 has a comprehensive set of features that should meet the needs of almost all build automation requirements, and even if it doesn't, it is highly configurable and extensible.

Some of the key features in Team Build 2010 are as follows:

- Provides a default build process suitable for building most Microsoft .NET Framework applications

- Build process is based on Workflow Foundation and is highly configurable and extensible

- Supports the queuing of builds and multiple build machines

- Supports manual, scheduled, continuous integration, and gated check-in builds

- Private builds (also known as *buddy builds*)

- Retention policies for removing old builds

- Integrates with reporting, testing, version control, and work item–tracking components of Visual Studio Application Lifecycle Management

- Includes an API for automating, extending, and integrating with Team Build

High-Level Architecture

A high-level diagram of Team Build's architecture is shown in Figure 13-1.

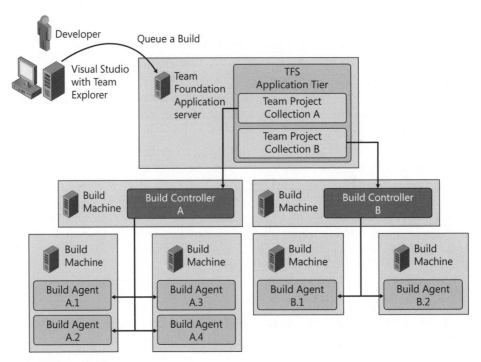

FIGURE 13-1 High-level architecture

The Team Build architecture includes:

- **Team Build client** Visual Studio provides a number of built-in clients for Team Build, including Team Explorer, which is an add-in for Visual Studio; TfsBuild.exe, which is a command-line client for Team Build (and is described in detail in the section entitled "Working with Build Queues and History," later in this chapter); and Team Foundation

Server Web Access, which is a Web interface for Team Build (and other components of the Visual Studio Application Lifecycle Management). Team Build also has an API that can be used to develop your own clients for Team Build, and that will be discussed in Chapter 14, "Team Build Deep Dive."

- **Build controllers**   This Windows Service orchestrates the overall build process and is responsible for initializing the build, reserving build agents, delegating parts of the build process to one or more build agents, and finalizing the build. A Team Project Collection can have one or more build controllers associated with it, but each build controller can be associated with only a single Team Project Collection and a machine can have only a single build controller installed on it.

- **Build agents**   This Windows Service is responsible for executing the bulk of the build process. A build controller can have multiple build agents associated with it, but each build agent can be associated with only a single build controller. Unlike build controllers, a machine can have multiple build agents installed on it. Because builds are CPU- and I/O-intensive, this is generally not recommended, but if you have sufficiently powerful hardware or your build process isn't resource-intensive, you may be able to increase build throughput by running multiple build agents on each physical build machine.

- **Team Project Collection**   Team Project Collections are a new concept in Team Foundation Server 2010, and as you might expect, they are collections of Team Projects. The Team Projects in a Team Project Collection share a database on the database tier and can be backed up, restored, and managed as a single entity. Each Team Project Collection is completely independent, and this is the reason that a build controller can be associated with only a single Team Project Collection.

- **Team Foundation Server application tier**   Any Team Build client that wants to communicate with a build controller does so through the Team Foundation Server's application tier. The application tier is implemented as a number of web services hosted using IIS. Communication from the application tier to build agents is always done via the controller.

- **Team Foundation Server data tier**   The data tier for Team Foundation Server is hosted as a configuration database (TFS_Configuration), a warehouse database (TFS_Warehouse), and a database for each Team Project Collection (for example, TFS_DefaultCollection) in Microsoft SQL Server.

- **Team Project Collection database**   This database stores operational build data such as the list of build controllers and agents, build definitions, build queues, build history, and so on.

- **TFS_Warehouse database**   This database stores historical build data for reporting even after it has been purged from the Team Project Collection database.

- **Cube**   This multidimensional online analytic processing (OLAP) cube is implemented in SQL Server Analysis Services and is populated regularly from the TFS_Warehouse database for high-performance reporting.

- **Drop folder**   When a build completes the build logs, build outputs (if the build is successful or partially successful) and test results are copied to a shared network folder. Public and private builds for the same build definition can be dropped to separate root drop folders.

Preparing for Team Build

In this section, we're going to look at the preparations that you'll need to make to set up the necessary infrastructure before you start automating your build processes using Team Build. Assuming that you've already set up your Team Foundation Server, the first step is to set up at least one build controller and agent to execute your builds. A build controller or build agent is simply a machine that has the Team Build service installed on it and is configured as a build controller, one or more build agents, or both.

Team Build Deployment Topologies

The ability to have multiple build controllers per Team Project Collection and multiple build agents per build controller provides a lot of flexibility, but it also raises questions about when and why you'd want to do this.

Reasons for wanting to have multiple build controllers include:

- **Build agent pooling**   Build controllers are a grouping of build agents so that you can use multiple build controllers to segregate your build agents into pools. You may want to do this to dedicate certain agents for certain types of builds [for example, release builds or continuous integration (CI) builds] or to group build agents by physical location for performance.

- **Using different custom workflow activities or extensions**   Build controllers specify a version control path from where custom workflow activities and extensions are downloaded. Having multiple controllers allows you to have a controller use a different set of custom workflow activities or extensions. For example, you might have a controller dedicated to testing new versions of custom workflow activities or extensions before you roll them out for production builds.

Reasons for wanting to have multiple build agents include:

- **Redundancy**   Having more than one build agent will allow developers to continue to process builds in the event of a build agent failure.

- **Ability to scale out**   Multiple build agents will allow builds to be processed concurrently.

- **Distributed builds**   By customizing the build process template (which is discussed in Chapters 15 and 16), you could enable a single build to be distributed across multiple build agents to reduce build time.

- **Mutually exclusive dependencies**   Different versions of the software that you're building may have dependencies on different versions of third-party software that can't be installed side by side on your build agents. Having multiple build agents enables you to have different versions installed on different build agents. Later in this chapter, we discuss agent tags, which can be used to identify which agents have which dependencies installed.

The other topological consideration is whether you should install build controllers and build agents on the same machine. This is a very valid topology and is especially useful in smaller environments (for example, the build controller has only a single agent) because it requires only one machine. If your build controller is going to manage multiple build agents, then it is recommended to be on its own machine.

What Makes a Good Build Machine?

You should take the following factors into account when selecting and configuring hardware to run Team Build (these factors apply to both build controllers and agents):

- Build machines should be kept as simple as possible. Even minor changes on a build machine can affect the outcome of a build, and if the configuration of a build machine is complex, then it increases the chance of discrepancies if a build agent needs to be rebuilt, when adding additional build machines, or when reproducing an old build.

- Builds usually have to read a large amount of data (the source files) from the Team Foundation Server and write a large amount of data (the build outputs) to the drop folder. Because of this, the build agent should have fast network access to both of these locations. In Chapter 14, we look at how to configure Team Build to use the Team Foundation Proxy to improve performance when the build agent has limited bandwidth to the Team Foundation Server.

- Builds are typically I/O-bound rather than CPU-bound (although there can be exceptions to this), so investing in fast disk and network infrastructure will have a large impact on the performance of your builds.

- Build machines should only be build machines—nothing else. Running other services on the build machine results in Team Build having to compete with them for resources. In particular, avoid disk-intensive services such as the Indexing Service and antivirus software. Many corporate environments require antivirus software; in this case, you should disable scanning for the build agent's working folders to improve performance and reduce the chance that locking issues will cause spurious build failures.

- The build agent needs sufficient disk space to store a copy of the source code and build outputs for each build definition. You should also allow additional disk space for any temporary files produced during the build process.

- The TEMP directory should be located on the same logical drive as the Team Build working directory. The get process is more efficient in this configuration because it can perform move rather than copy operations.

- Team Build 2008 and later have the ability to take advantage of the parallel build functionality introduced in MSBuild 3.5 so multiple processors can improve the performance of your builds.

There might be circumstances where Team Build needs to be installed on developers' workstations. This can be particularly useful when developing, testing, and debugging build customizations or to allow developers to run full end-to-end builds on their local machines.

Installing Team Build on the Team Foundation Server

Although it's technically possible to install a build controller, a build agent, or both on the same machine as the Team Foundation Server, this is not recommended for a number of reasons:

- Compiling software is particularly resource-intensive, and this could be detrimental to the performance of the Team Foundation Server.

- Build scripts and unit tests might be written by people who aren't Team Foundation Server administrators, and having these running on the Team Foundation Server could compromise its security, integrity, and stability.

- Build scripts and the projects being compiled often require third-party software or libraries to be installed on the build agent, and installing these on the Team Foundation Server could also compromise its security, integrity, and stability.

> **Tip** The only time you should consider installing a build controller, a build agent, or both on the same machine as Team Foundation Server is when building a virtual machine for demonstration or testing purposes where it is not practical to have a separate virtual machine acting as the build controller and agent.

Setting Up a Build Controller

The Team Build installation process is quite simple, but it is recommended that you document the process that you use to set up your first build controller and agent so that the process can be repeated if you add additional build controllers or agents to your environment in the future.

Note   When installing any Team Foundation Server component, you should download and refer to the latest version of the Team Foundation Installation Guide for Visual Studio 2010 from *http://go.microsoft.com/fwlink/?LinkId=127730.*

Installing Prerequisites

Before installing a build controller, you will need a domain account for the Team Build service to run if you choose not to use the NT AUTHORITY\NETWORK SERVICE account. This account doesn't need to be, and shouldn't be, that of an administrator on either the build server or the Team Foundation Server, but it does need to be added to the Project Collection Build Service Accounts group of the Team Project Collection for which it will execute builds. See the section entitled "Team Build Security," later in this chapter, for more information about securing Team Build.

Installing a Build Controller

The installation process for build controllers is as follows:

1. Insert the installation media.

2. Run setup.exe from either the TFS-x86 or TFS-x64 directory (for 32-bit or 64-bit machines, respectively).

3. Click Next on the Welcome To The Microsoft Team Foundation Server 2010 Installation Wizard page.

4. Accept the license terms and click Next.

5. Select Team Foundation Build Service on the Select Features To Install page and click Install.

6. Make sure that the Launch Team Foundation Server Configuration Tool check box is selected on the last page of the wizard, and then click Configure.

7. Select the Configure Team Foundation Build Service wizard and click Start Wizard.

8. Click Next on the Welcome To The Build Service Configuration Wizard page.

9. Select the Team Project Collection to which you want to connect the build controller and click Next.

10. On the Build Services page, choose how many build agents that you want to run on the build controller machine (this can be none if it's a dedicated controller machine), choose the Create New Build Controller option, and click Next.

11. On the Settings page, enter the account details for your Team Build service account and click Next.

12. On the Review page, review the settings that you've entered, and then click Next.

13. On the Readiness Checks page, resolve any errors and then click Configure.

14. On the Complete page, click Finish.

Configuring a Build Controller After Installation.

Once a build controller has been installed, you can configure it either from Visual Studio on any computer (as described here) or from the Team Foundation Server Administration Console on the build controller itself.

1. Open Visual Studio 2010.

2. Open Team Explorer.

3. Expand a Team Project.

4. Right-click Builds, and click Manage Build Controllers. This will open the Manage Build Controllers dialog shown in Figure 13-2.

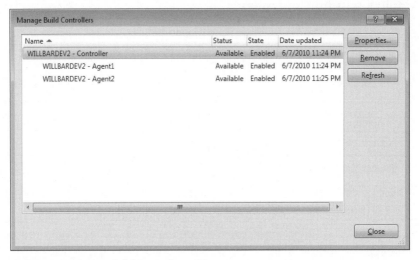

FIGURE 13-2 Manage Build Controllers dialog

5. Select the build controller that you want to configure and click Properties to open the Build Controller Properties dialog shown in Figure 13-3.

The Display Name and Description fields are used to describe the build controller.

The Computer Name field is the host name of the build controller. This will be used by Team Build to communicate with the build controller so the Computer Name should be resolvable from the Team Foundation Server.

The Version Control Path To Custom Assemblies is a server path to a folder containing any custom workflow activities or extensions. The build controller and its agents will download any custom assemblies from the location as required. Creating custom activities is discussed in detail in Chapters 15 and 16.

FIGURE 13-3 Build Controller Properties dialog

Tip To make it easier to test changes to your custom workflow activities and extensions, consider having two separate version control folders for custom workflow activities and extensions (one for production and one for testing), and then set up a dedicated controller for testing that uses the testing version control folder.

Setting Up a Build Agent

The build agent installation process is quite similar to the build controller installation process, but because the majority of the build process is run on the build agent, the prerequisites are more complex.

Installing Prerequisites

Before installing a build agent, the following prerequisites need to be met:

- You will need a domain account for the Team Build service to run if you choose not to use the NT AUTHORITY\NETWORK SERVICE account. This account can, and usually is, the same account used to run the build controller.

- You will need any other software or libraries required by your build process or the software you're building. This would include any utilities or MSBuild tasks called by your build process (such as the MSBuild Extension Pack), as well as any global assembly cache (GAC) references required by the projects you're building (such as the Microsoft Office primary interop assemblies).

- You will need the appropriate version of Visual Studio to use any of the features listed in Table 13-1 as part of your build process.

TABLE 13-1 Team Build Prerequisites

Feature	Required Software
Code Analysis	Visual Studio Premium
Code Coverage	Visual Studio Premium
Coded UI Tests	Visual Studio Premium
Database Projects	Visual Studio Premium
Lab Management	Visual Studio Lab Management
Layer Diagram and Dependency Validation	Visual Studio Ultimate
Load Testing	Visual Studio Ultimate
MSBuild Project Types	.NET Framework SDK
Non-MSBuild Project Types (for example, Deployment Projects)	Any edition of Visual Studio able to build the specific project type
Test Impact Analysis	Visual Studio Premium
Third-Party Build Dependencies	The corresponding third-party software
Third-Party GAC References	The corresponding third-party software
Unit Testing	Visual Studio Professional
Visual C++ Projects	Visual Studio Professional
Web Testing	Visual Studio Ultimate

Installing a Build Agent

The installation process for a build agent is as follows:

1. Insert the installation media.

2. Run setup.exe from either the TFS-x86 or TFS-x64 directory (for 32-bit or 64-bit machines, respectively).

3. Click Next on the Welcome To The Microsoft Team Foundation Server 2010 Installation Wizard page.

4. Accept the license terms and click Next.

5. Select Team Foundation Build Service on the Select Features To Install page and click Install.

6. Make sure that the Launch Team Foundation Server Configuration Tool check box is selected on the last page of the wizard, and then click Configure.

7. Select the Configure Team Foundation Build Service wizard and click Start Wizard.

8. Click Next on the Welcome To The Build Service Configuration Wizard page.

9. Select the Team Project Collection to which you want to connect the build controller and click Next.

10. On the Build Services page, choose how many build agents you want to run on the build agent machine, choose the build controller to which you want to attach them, and click Next.

11. On the Settings page, enter the account details for your Team Build service account and click Next.

12. On the Review page, review the settings that you've entered and then click Next.

13. On the Readiness Checks page, resolve any errors and then click Configure.

14. On the Complete page, click Finish.

Configuring a Build Agent After Installation

A build agent can also be configured either from Visual Studio on any computer (as described here) or from the Team Foundation Server Administration Console on the build agent itself, as follows:

1. Open Visual Studio 2010.

2. Open Team Explorer.

3. Expand a Team Project.

4. Right-click Builds, and then click Manage Build Controllers.

5. Select the build agent that you want to configure and click Properties to open the Build Agent Properties dialog box shown in Figure 13-4.

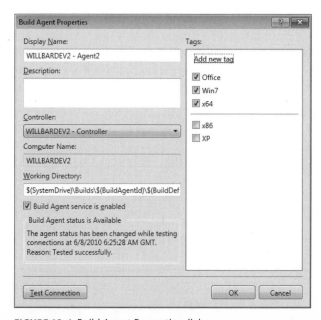

FIGURE 13-4 Build Agent Properties dialog

The Display Name and Description fields are used to describe the build agent.

The Tags allow you to apply arbitrary strings to the agent that can be used to select agents meeting certain criteria. Build definitions can define the tags that they require their agents to have, and then Team Build will automatically select the appropriate agent. Common uses for tags include specifying what operating system and other software the build agent has installed on it, as well as the bit-ness of the build agent. Chapter 14 discusses how you can configure build definitions to require agents with certain tags.

The Controller field allows you to select the build controller that the build agent is associated with.

The Computer Name field is the host name of the build agent. This will be used by Team Build to communicate with the build agent, so the Computer Name should be resolvable from the build controller.

The Working Directory field allows you to specify which directory on the build agent will be used as the working directory during the build. This default working directory is $(SystemDrive)\Builds\$(BuildAgentId)\$(BuildDefinitionPath). For example, if you have a Team Project called Contoso with a build definition called HelloWorldManual running on build agent 12, then the working directory would be C:\Builds\12\Contoso\HelloWorldManual.

You might want to modify the working directory in these scenarios:

- If your build agent has multiple disk partitions, you might want to change the working directory to use one of the additional disk partitions—for example, E:\$(BuildAgentId)\$(BuildDefinitionPath).

- If the source code or build outputs have a particularly deep directory structure or particularly long file names, you may want to use a shorter path—for example, E:\$(BuildAgentId)\$(BuildDefinitionId). This is particularly important when building database projects whose naming conventions result in very long file names.

You should usually include $(BuildAgentId) or $(BuildAgentName) and $(BuildDefinitionPath) or $(BuildDefinitionId) in your working directory so that multiple build agents and definitions can exist side by side in the build agent's working directory. The variables available in the *Working Directory* field are listed in Table 13-2.

TABLE 13-2 Working Directory Variables

Variable Name	Description
BuildAgentId	Contains the integer identifier for the Build Agent in the Team Build database.
BuildAgentName	Contains the Build Agent name.
BuildDefinitionId	Contains the integer identifier for the Build Definition in the Team Build database.

Variable Name	Description
BuildDefinitionPath	Contains the Team Project Name and the Build Definition Name; for example, Contoso\HelloWorldManual.
Environment Variables	Each environment variable on the build agent is available as a property. For example, $(Temp) expands to C:\Documents and Settings\TFSBUILD\Local Settings\Temp\ if the Team Build service account is TFSBUILD.

You can toggle whether or not the build agent is enabled using the Build Agent Service Is Enabled check box. When the agent is disabled, builds can still be queued on it, but they won't be processed until it's enabled.

Clicking Test Connection will verify connectivity from the Team Foundation Server to the build controller and from the build controller to the build agent. If the build controller detects that the build agent is offline, then it will automatically disable the build agent. Team Build will automatically enable the agent when it comes back online, but you can force this to occur earlier by clicking Test Connection.

> **Note** Chapter 14 discusses the advanced configuration options that are available for build controllers and build agents.

Drop Folders

The final piece of infrastructure that needs to be in place before you create a build definition is a drop folder, where the build agent puts the build logs and outputs.

Because a Team Build environment may have multiple build agents, drop folders are typically located on a separate network share that all the build agents use. This means that developers, testers, and other users can access drop folders from a single central location.

The drop folder is typically a share on a file server of some description, but it could just as easily be a Network Attached Storage device or some other shared storage device. There are only a few requirements for the drop folder:

- It must be accessible via a UNC path from all of the build agents.

- The Team Build service account must have Full Control permission to it. This is required for the build agent to be able to drop the build logs and outputs.

- It must have sufficient space available to store the number of builds retained by the retention policies that you define.

Tip There is nothing worse than builds failing simply because there is not enough space available in the drop location, especially because you don't find this out until the very end of the build process. It is recommended that you set up monitoring of the available space in the drop location so that you are alerted if it falls below a threshold.

Creating a Build Definition

Now that the necessary infrastructure is in place, you can create your first build definition. Build definitions define the information required to execute a build, such as what should be built, what triggers a build, and how long these builds should be retained.

To create a new build definition, perform the following steps:

1. Open Visual Studio 2010.

2. Open Team Explorer.

3. Expand a Team Project.

4. Right-click Builds, and click New Build Definition.

5. Enter the desired information on each of the tabs, as described in the remainder of this section.

6. Click Save.

General

The General tab shown in Figure 13-5 allows you to name the build definition and optionally describe it. The description is displayed when a developer queues the build, so this can be useful to communicate additional information about what the build definition is for.

You can also temporarily disable the build definition from here as well, which can be used to prevent developers from queuing builds for obsolete or archived build definitions without having to delete the build definition. If using gated check-ins (as discussed in the section entitled "Gated Check-in," later in this chapter) and if the build definition is disabled, then developers will be able to check in without running a validation build.

Tip Be aware that the build definition name is often used from the command line and as a part of the build agent's working directory path, so you should minimize the length of the name (to avoid exceeding maximum path lengths) and avoid unnecessary special characters, including spaces.

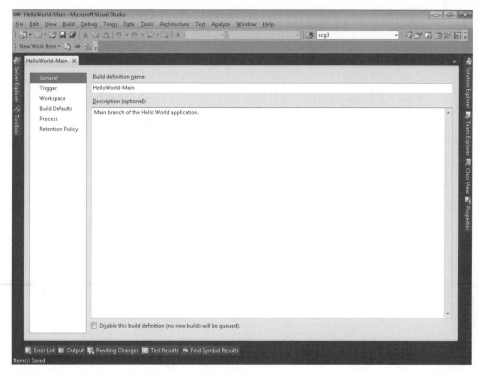

FIGURE 13-5 Build Definition: General

Trigger

Team Build 2005 only provided the ability for builds to be triggered manually, either from within Team Explorer, using the *TfsBuild.exe start* command, from Team Foundation Server Web Access, or using the Team Build API. These methods of starting builds provided build administrators and developers with a large amount of flexibility in how they started builds, but common requirements, such as scheduled builds and continuous integration, required additional programming, scripting, or third-party solutions to implement.

These are now implemented in Team Build 2010 by allowing build administrators to specify what triggers a build in the build definition. The triggers implemented are:

- Manual
- Continuous integration
- Rolling builds
- Gated check-in
- Scheduled

These triggers are configured on the Trigger tab of the Build Definition window, shown in Figure 13-6.

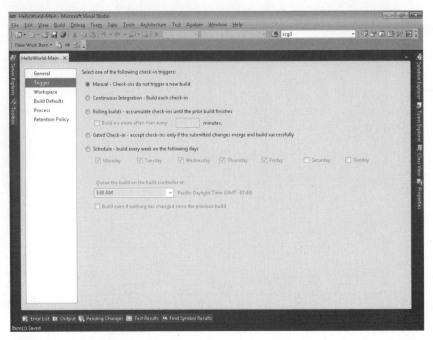

FIGURE 13-6 Build Definition: Trigger

Manual

The simplest (and default) trigger is that builds need to be started manually. This trigger provides exactly the same experience that was available in Team Build 2005, with the exception that in Team Build 2008 and later, builds can be queued rather than failing if a build is already in progress.

Continuous Integration

Continuous integration (CI) is a set of practices from the agile community that provides early warning of bugs and broken code. By building and testing each changeset that has been checked in, any issues can be identified and resolved quickly, minimizing the disruption caused to other developers.

When Team Build 2005 was released, many saw the lack of a CI capability as a huge oversight, especially given its popularity at the time. Microsoft rectified this oversight in Team Build 2008 by adding a CI trigger that removes the need to rely on third-party CI solutions.

The CI trigger causes each check-in to the build definition's workspace to queue a new build, as shown in Figure 13-7.

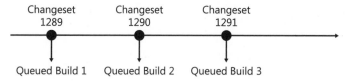

FIGURE 13-7 Changeset to queued build mapping for CI rolling builds

For long-running builds or workspaces that have a large number of check-ins, the CI trigger may result in unacceptably long build queues. The Rolling Builds trigger minimizes this issue by accumulating any check-ins to the build definition's workspace until the currently running build completes; once the build completes, a single build will be queued to build the changesets.

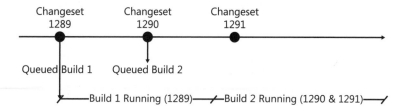

FIGURE 13-8 Changeset to queued build mapping for rolling builds

Even this trigger may result in build queues being dominated by a few build definitions. To add a lag between the builds to allow builds from other build definitions to be executed, you can enable the Build No More Than Every *X* Minutes option of this trigger, shown in Figure 13-9, to ensure that the builds are not executed back to back.

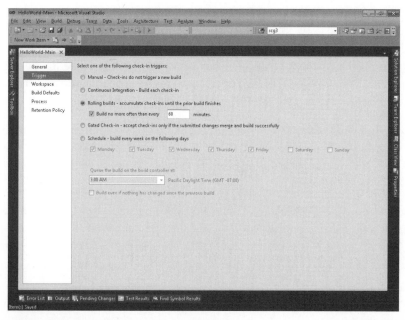

FIGURE 13-9 Build Definition: Trigger (with lag)

Gated Check-in

Team Build 2010 introduces a new trigger called *Gated Check-in*. This trigger behaves similarly to the CI trigger, except that it intercepts the developer's changes before they're checked into version control, builds them, and then, if they build successfully, checks them in on the developer's behalf.

> **Tip** If you think of CI as something that detects bad changes that have made it into version control, then think of Gated Check-in as a mechanism to stop them getting in there in the first place.

Whenever a developer checks changes into a file or folder that is part of the workspace of a build definition that uses the gated check-in trigger, they will be presented with the dialog shown in Figure 13-10.

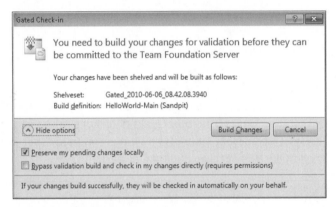

FIGURE 13-10 Gated Check-in dialog

This dialog informs the developer that their changes need to pass a validation build before they're checked in. At this point, the developer's changes have been automatically shelved, and they can choose whether they want to preserve their changes locally or not.

If they've been granted the Override Check-in Validation By Build permission, they also have the option of bypassing the validation build and checking their changes in directly. See the section entitled "Team Build Security," later in this chapter, for more information about this and other Team Build permissions.

Once a gated check-in build completes, the developer will be alerted via the Build Notifications tray to either reconcile their workspace (if the build succeeds) or unshelve their changes (if the build fails). You can also explicitly perform these actions when the build completes by right-clicking the build in the Build Explorer or from the build's Build Details window.

If you did not keep pending changes, then reconciling your workspace is unnecessary, although you should perform a get to bring your workspace up to date. If you did keep your pending changes, then the Reconcile Workspace dialog (shown in Figure 13-11) can be used to undo any redundant pending changes and bring these files up to date with the changeset that was checked in.

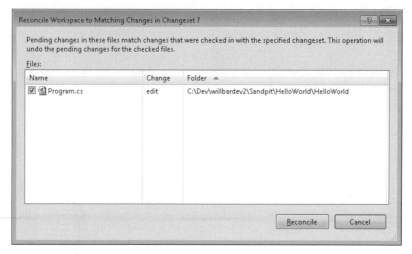

FIGURE 13-11 Reconcile Workspace dialog

Schedule

The Schedule trigger allows builds to be scheduled to run on specific days at a certain time rather than having to use third-party scheduling applications. By default, scheduled builds will be skipped if no changes have been checked in since the previous build. However, this behavior can be overridden by selecting the Build Even If Nothing Has Changed Since The Previous Build check box.

> **Note** One limitation of the scheduling functionality is that you can't schedule a build to be run multiple times a day. If you need this capability, you can either create a new build definition for each time you'd like the build to be run or use a scheduler (such as the built-in Windows Scheduler) to call the TfsBuild.exe command-line client to queue builds.

Workspace

The Workspace tab shown in Figure 13-12 allows you to define which version control folders Team Build will get to execute the build. You can specify multiple folders to get by adding additional working folder mappings with a status of Active, or you can prevent Team Build from getting a folder by changing the status of the mapping from Active to Cloak, as demonstrated in Figure 13-13, which shows that the HelloWorld folder will download but not the HelloWorld/HelloWorld.Tests folder.

Tip If you create a build definition while you have a solution open, then the build definition's workspace mappings will default to the workspace mappings for the workspace containing the solution.

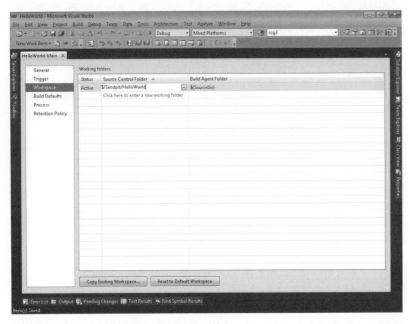

FIGURE 13-12 Build Definition: Workspace tab

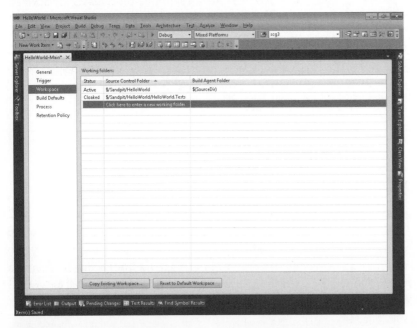

FIGURE 13-13 Build Definition: Workspace tab (multiple working folders)

By default, any other mapping that you add will be mapped to a local folder with the same name as the source control folder. You can override the default by changing the value in the Build Agent Folder column.

If one of the developers already has a workspace that contains the necessary working folder mappings, you can click Copy Existing Workspace to copy the mappings from that workspace into the build definition.

> **Tip** The default working folder mapping on the Workspace tab will download all of the files in the Team Project (or, if you have a solution open when you create the build definition, the workspace containing that solution). If these contain a large number of files and folders that aren't needed by a build definition, you can significantly improve its performance by mapping only the required folders or by cloaking folders that aren't required.

Build Defaults

The Build Defaults tab, shown in Figure 13-14, allows you to specify the default build controller that the build will be queued on and, optionally, where the build outputs will be dropped when the build completes. These are defaults and can be overridden by the developer when they queue the build.

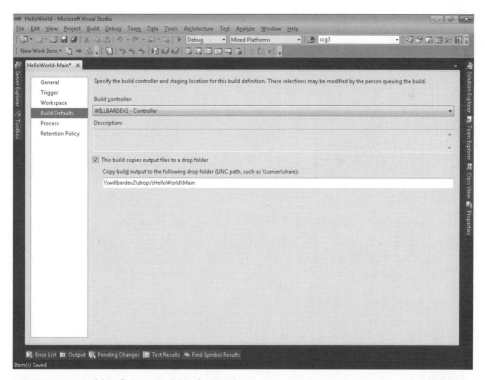

FIGURE 13-14 Build Definition: Build Defaults tab

Process

Build definitions are linked to a Build Process Template that defines the build workflow that will be used. In fact these Build Process Templates are implemented using Workflow Foundation workflows. Chapters 15 and 16 discuss in detail how to customize existing Build Process Templates, as well as how to create your own.

A default Build Process Template will be selected when you create your build definition, but by clicking Show Details, you can select a different Build Process Template, as shown in Figure 13-15.

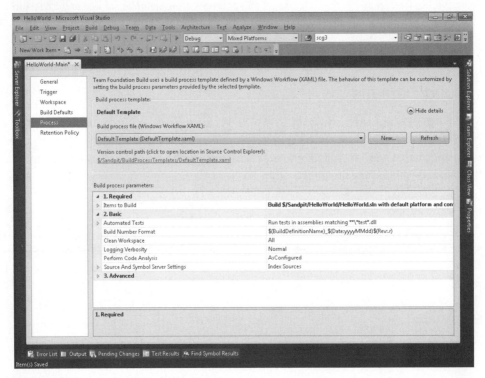

FIGURE 13-15 Build Definition: Process tab

In addition to selecting the Build Process Template, this tab is where you specify the Build Process Parameters. Each Build Process Template defines its own Build Process Parameters, so if you select a different Build Process Template, then you will see different Build Process Parameters selected.

In this section, we'll cover the minimum Build Process Parameters for the Default Template that are needed to get your new build definition working. Chapter 14 will cover all of the Build Process Parameters for the Default Template and the Upgrade Template; and Chapter 16, "Process Template Customization," will cover how to customize Build Process Templates and define your own Build Process Parameters.

The only Build Process Parameter that we need to provide to get our first build definition working is Projects To Build. To provide this parameter, select Items To Build and click the ellipsis to open the Items To Build dialog. Now click Add, browse to the solution or project that you want to build, and then repeat this for each additional solution or project that you want to build. If the solutions or projects have a build order dependency, then you can use the Move Up and Move Down buttons to arrange them in the order they need to be built.

> **Tip** When you create a new build definition, if you have a solution open that's in a version-controlled folder, then the path to that solution will be automatically placed into the Projects To Build build process parameter.

If you don't specify any configurations, then each solution's default configuration will be built, the Configurations tab shown in Figure 13-16 allows you to specify configurations and platforms to be built for the selected solutions. If you specify multiple entries, then the solutions will be built multiple times (once per entry) and the build outputs placed in separate subfolders of the drop folder. In this example, the solution will be built four times, and the build outputs will be placed in the subfolders Release, Debug, Release\x86, and Debug\x86.

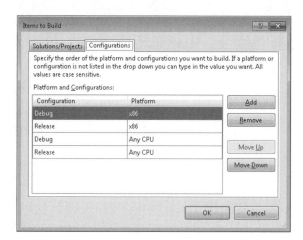

FIGURE 13-16 Configurations tab

> **Tip** If the configuration or platform that you would like to build isn't listed, you can type the name of it into the appropriate combo box.

Retention Policy

In Team Build 2005, build administrators often ran out of disk space in their drop folder. The reason for this is that Team Build 2005 did not provide a solution to automatically remove builds that were no longer required.

Enterprising build administrators worked around this by either scripting the `TfsBuild.exe delete` command or by using third-party solutions (such as the Build Clean-up service, written by Mitch Denny).

Team Build 2008 and later solve this problem by introducing retention policies that allow you to specify which builds should be retained based on criteria in the build definition. The current version of this functionality is limited to retaining builds based on the type of build (Manual And Triggered or Private), the outcome of the build (that is, successful, partially succeeded, stopped, and failed) and the number of builds (for example, retain the last two successful builds). If your requirements are more complex, such as wanting to retain builds based on number of days or on build quality, then you will still need to implement your own solution.

The Retention Policy tab, shown in Figure 13-17, allows you to configure how many builds will be retained for each build outcome.

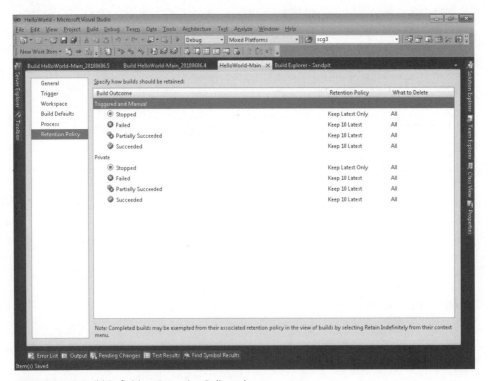

FIGURE 13-17 Build Definition: Retention Policy tab

Tip It's easy to think that you wouldn't want to retain any failed builds, but when builds are removed by the retention policy, everything associated with them, including the build log, is removed. If you don't retain at least one failed build, it might be very difficult to determine the cause of a build failure so that it can be resolved.

When a build is removed by the retention policy, the following items are also removed by default:

- Build details

- Drop folder, including the build logs and binaries

- Test results

- Version control label

- Symbols

> **Note** Although the build details are removed, they are still available for reporting in the TFSWarehouse database and OLAP cube if the warehouse was updated between when the build completed and when it was deleted.

In the What To Delete column, you can override this default for a particular build type and outcome using the Build Delete Options dialog shown in Figure 13-18.

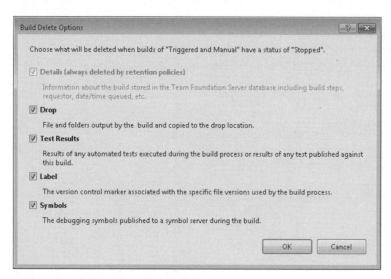

FIGURE 13-18 Build Delete Options dialog

Even if retention policies are enabled for a build definition, individual builds can still be explicitly retained or deleted as discussed in the next section.

Working with Build Queues and History

Congratulations—you've now created your first build definition. Once you have a build definition, you can use Team Build clients such as Visual Studio or the TfsBuild.exe command line to queue builds and work with the build queues and history.

Visual Studio

Developers spend the majority of their time in Visual Studio, so it is logical to be able to work with builds from there. Team Explorer is the entry point to Team Foundation Server functionality within Visual Studio, and Team Build is no exception to this. The Builds node within a Team Project allows build administrators and developers to queue builds and view and manage build queues and individual builds.

Queuing a Build

To queue a build, you right-click the Builds node in Team Explorer and choose Queue New Build to open the Queue Build dialog shown in Figure 13-19. Alternatively, you can right-click a specific build definition and choose Queue New Build, which opens the same dialog but will automatically select that build definition.

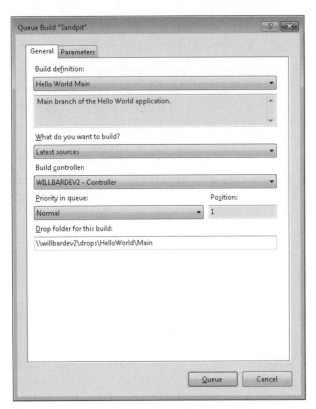

FIGURE 13-19 Queue Build dialog: General tab

The What Do You Want To Build? drop-down list will default to Latest Sources, but developers can change this to Latest Sources With Shelveset to queue a private build against a shelveset containing the changes they'd like to validate. This is discussed in more detail in the section entitled "Queuing a Private Build," later in this chapter.

The Build Controller and Drop Folder For This Build will default to the values selected when you created the new build definition, but developers can override these if desired.

The Position setting indicates where this build will be in the queue if queued on the selected build controller. This is refreshed whenever a different build controller is selected, but there can be a small delay while the position is calculated. You can also change the priority that the build is queued with. As you might expect, the higher the priority, the higher in the queue it will be placed.

On the Parameters tab, shown in Figure 13-20, the developer can override the parameters specified in the build definition for this build process template. Chapter 14 discusses the parameters available for the templates that ship with Team Build, and Chapter 16 discusses how you can define parameters and custom parameter user interfaces for your custom build process templates.

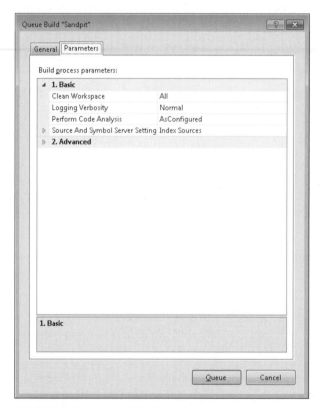

FIGURE 13-20 Queue Build dialog: Parameters tab

If developers always have to override certain parameters, they could create specific build definitions specifying these parameters so they can just queue these build definitions instead.

Clicking Queue will then queue the build on the selected build controller and open the Build Explorer window so you can monitor the progress of your build.

Queuing a Private Build

Private builds (also known as *buddy builds*) allow developers to run a build based on the contents of a shelveset and, optionally, check in the shelveset after a successful build. This can be used to detect compilation errors and test failures before changes are checked in and can affect other developers.

In Team Build 2008, private builds were done by running MSBuild on the TFSBuild.proj in the developer's local workspace. This approach was simple, but it suffered from a number of drawbacks:

- Private builds could be done only from the command prompt.

- The developer's workspace could be out of date, and as such, the build and test results would be inconsistent with the results of building and testing against the latest source code.

- Developers' workstations needed all the prerequisites of the end-to-end build process installed on them.

- Configuration differences between the developer's workstation and the build machines would reduce confidence in the changes actually building successfully when checked in.

- The desktop build process and the end-to-end build process had significant differences that would further reduce confidence in the changes building successfully.

- The build outputs weren't dropped in the same way as the end-to-end build process and couldn't be easily shared with others.

Team Build 2010 takes a different approach and allows developers to shelve their changes and queue an end-to-end build against this shelveset and optionally check the changes in automatically if the build completes successfully.

 Note The only shipping template that supports private builds is the Default Template.

Private builds are queued against a build controller, just like triggered and manual builds are, and as such, they use the same hardware, software, configuration, and build process as a triggered or manual build. This increases a developer's confidence that the changes will build and test successfully when checked in.

In some circumstances, it can be seen as a negative that private builds no longer support building on the developer's workstation, but this can be enabled by installing a Team Build controller and agent and choosing that controller when queuing the build. You should be aware of the drawbacks discussed previously of using a developer's workstation for validating changes before check-in.

To enable a build definition to drop the build outputs for private builds, you must configure a Private Drop Location. If you do not do this, then the build will still validate that the shelveset compiles and passes tests, but the build outputs will not be dropped.

> **Tip** You should drop private builds to a separate location from your triggered and manual builds so they aren't accidentally shipped or used as production builds. Private builds contain changes that aren't checked into version control, are based on non-versioned and auditable shelvesets, and as such, they are not reproducible.

To set the Private Drop Location, edit the build definition, and in the Advanced category of the Process tab, enter a UNC path in the Private Drop Location parameter, as shown in Figure 13-21.

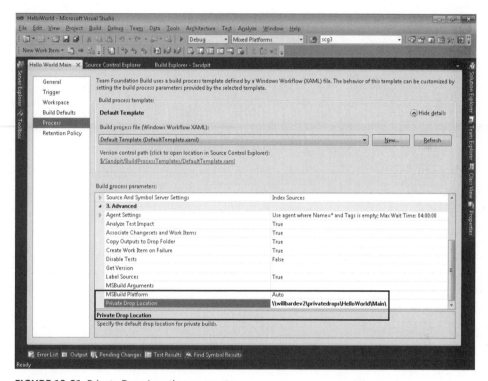

FIGURE 13-21 Private Drop Location parameter

The developer can queue a private build by performing the following steps:

1. Right-click the build definition in Team Explorer and choose Queue New Build.

2. In the What Do You Want To Build? drop-down list, select Latest Sources With Shelveset.

3. Click the ellipsis button and choose the shelveset containing the changes they want to validate. Alternatively, you can create a shelveset based on the pending changes in the workspace by clicking Create.

4. Choose the Check In Changes After Successful Build check box if you want your changes checked into version control if the build completes successfully.

5. Click Queue.

Figure 13-22 shows the Queue Build dialog when queuing a private build of Hello World Main for the shelveset Increase Exclamation.

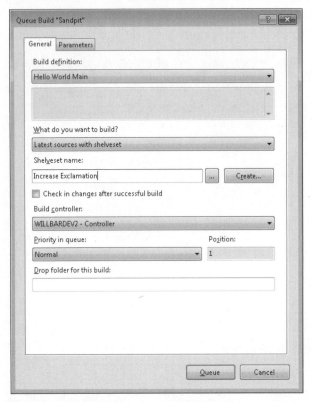

FIGURE 13-22 Queue Private Build dialog

Note In the Team Build 2010 RTM, there is a bug such that the What Do You Want To Build drop-down list sometimes becomes disabled and you won't be able to select Latest Sources With Shelveset. Restarting Visual Studio will usually resolve this.

Private builds need to strike the right balance between speed and completeness to ensure that developers can validate their changes in a reasonable amount of time and still have a high level of confidence that a successful private build will typically mean a successful triggered or manual build.

If private builds take too long or have too much friction, then developers will bypass them and check in without validating their changes (although this can be prevented with the gated check-in trigger discussed in the section entitled "Trigger," earlier in this chapter). For this reason, it can be beneficial to have a dedicated build definition for private builds that is configured to reduce build times (such as doing incremental gets and builds, running a smaller set of tests, and so on). Chapter 14 discusses the different properties that can be set to modify the default build process provided by Team Build.

Build Explorer

The Build Explorer window, shown in Figure 13-23, is the main way to manage build queues and view the build history. The Build Explorer can be opened by right-clicking the Builds node in Team Explorer and choosing View Builds. You can also double-click a build definition, which will open the Build Explorer and automatically filter it to builds of that build definition.

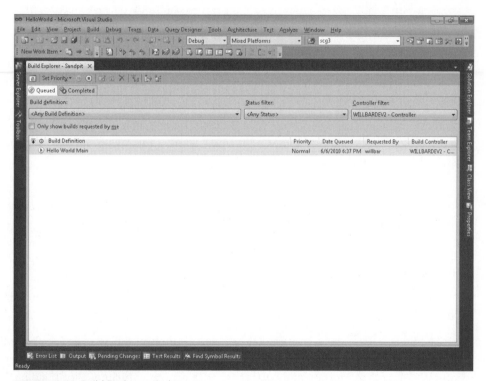

FIGURE 13-23 Build Explorer window

When first opened, the Build Explorer window will show only queued builds, which can be confusing if you expect to see the completed builds as well (as was the case in Team Build 2005). To see completed builds, you need to click the Completed tab at the top of the window.

Note Queued builds will remain on the Queued tab for up to five minutes after they complete.

The Queued build list can be filtered by selecting the filter criteria from the Build Definition, Status Filter, and Controller Filter lists at the top of the window. The Completed build list can be filtered as well, but by Build Definition, Quality, Date, and to builds requested by you.

Cancelling, Stopping, Postponing, and Reprioritizing Builds

If a build is queued but isn't running yet, you can right-click it and choose Cancel to remove it from the queue. Similarly, if a build is currently running, you can stop it by right-clicking the build in the Queued tab of the Build Explorer and choosing Stop.

> **More Info** The actions described in this section are significantly easier to do than they were in Team Build 2005, which required builds to be stopped using the TfsBuild.exe command-line client (which is still possible, as described in the section entitled "Working with Builds from the Command Line," later in this chapter).

Rather than cancelling a queued build, you can postpone it by right-clicking it and choosing Postpone. This places the build on hold, and it won't be built until you right-click the build again and clear the Postpone option.

Builds can be reprioritized to change their position in the queue by right-clicking the build, choosing Set Priority, and then choosing the new priority; the queue will then be refreshed to display the new queue order.

> **Important** The ability to manage the build queue can be restricted via permissions. See the section entitled "Team Build Security," later in this chapter, for details.

Viewing Build Details

Double-clicking a running or completed build in the Build Explorer will open the Build Details window. Note that you can't open the Build Details window for a queued build.

This window has two main views: the Activity Log view, which shows an activity hierarchy for the build; and the Summary view, which summarizes the build results. As shown in Figure 13-24, both views show the build number, latest result, build quality, build history graph, information about how the build was triggered and by whom, how long the build ran, on which controller it ran, and when it completed. You can also change the build quality, open the build's drop folder, toggle retain indefinitely, and delete the build.

 HelloWorld-Main_20100606.5 - Build succeeded - <No Quality Assigned>   ▾

View Summary │ View Log - Open Drop Folder │ Retain Indefinitely │ Delete Build

willbar triggered HelloWorld-Main (Sandpit) for changeset 7
Ran for 13 seconds (WILLBARDEV2 - Controller), completed 53.3 minutes ago

FIGURE 13-24 Build Details header

The build history graph provides an "at a glance" view of the build definition's history. The current build is indicated with a small triangle, the relative height of the bars indicates how long the build ran, and the color indicates the build's outcome (green for successful, orange for partially succeeded, and red for failed). Clicking a bar will take you to the build details for that particular build.

While the build is running, you can only see the Activity Log view (and it will automatically refresh until the build completed) but once the build has completed, you will be shown the Summary view by default. You can toggle between the views using the View Summary and View Log hyperlinks at the top of the window.

The Activity Log view (shown in Figure 13-25) shows a tree of the activities being executed and how long the activity took, which provides an easy way of monitoring the progress of the build and allows you to quickly see what step caused the build to fail.

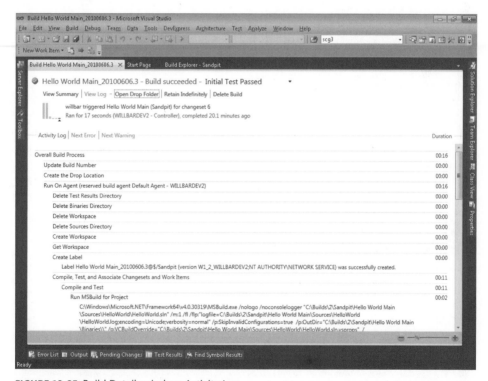

FIGURE 13-25 Build Details window: Activity Log

In Figure 13-26, you can see that the activities preceding compilation succeeded but the compilation itself failed, and you can see exactly what project or configuration caused the build failure. In addition, you can click that project's MSBuild log file to open it.

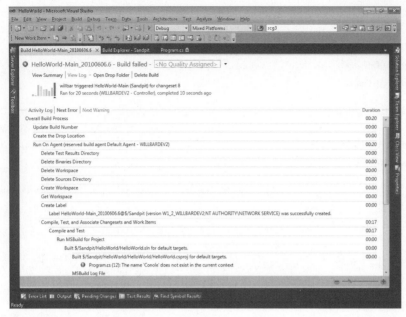

FIGURE 13-26 Build details for a failed build

The Summary view, shown in Figure 13-27, shows the latest activity on the build, a summary of the build results for each configuration and platform (including compilation warnings and errors, test results, and code coverage data), associated changesets and work items, and impacted tests. If the build fails, the Latest Activity section will link to the build failure work item that is created automatically and show its current status, as well as to whom it's assigned.

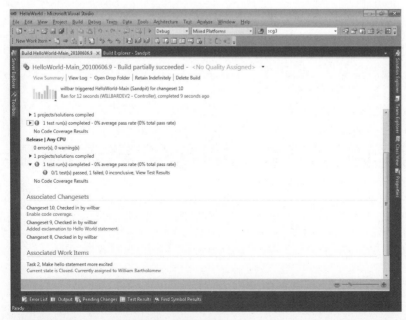

FIGURE 13-27 Build Details window: Summary

The Associated Changesets and Associated Work Items sections list the changesets and work items that are associated with this build, but not earlier builds of the same build definition. This information is extremely useful for providing traceability and in identifying what change caused a build failure or to guide the testing of specific builds. Clicking the changeset number opens the changeset in the standard Changeset dialog, and clicking the work item number opens the work item in the standard Work Item window.

Changing Build Qualities

Once a build has completed, it often goes through a number of other processes before it is released. For example, a build might be installed in a testing environment, pass testing, and then be released.

To provide the ability to track the status of a build, Team Build allows you to flag builds with a build quality. The first step is to define the list of build qualities with which you'd like to be able to flag builds. You can open the Edit Build Qualities dialog, shown in Figure 13-28, by right-clicking the Builds node of Team Explorer and choosing Manage Build Qualities. Figure 13-28 shows the default list of build qualities provided with Team Build, but these can be customized to meet your requirements.

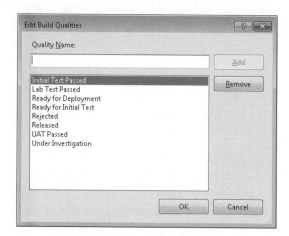

FIGURE 13-28 Edit Build Qualities dialog box

Once the list of build qualities has been defined, you can assign a build quality to a build by opening the build's Build Detail window and changing the drop-down list at the top, as shown in Figure 13-29. You can also change the build quality from the Build Explorer by right-clicking the build and choosing Edit Build Quality. Assigning or changing a build's build quality requires the user to be assigned the Edit Build Quality permission.

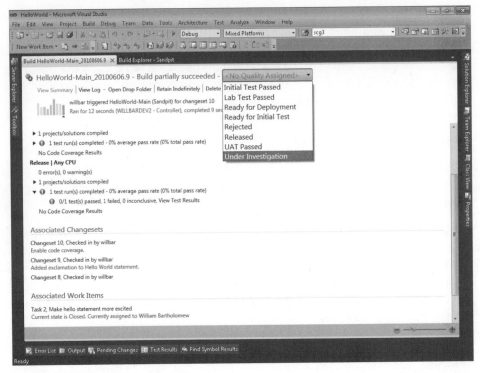

FIGURE 13-29 Changing a build's quality

Retaining Builds

There are situations where you may want to retain builds that otherwise would be removed by the build definition's retention policy, such as builds that you are in the process of testing or that you have released to customers.

You can flag a build to be retained indefinitely by opening the build's Build Details window and clicking Retain Indefinitely at the top. In addition, you can turn this flag on by right-clicking the build in the Completed tab of the Build Explorer window and choosing Retain Indefinitely. If in the future you decide that you no longer want to retain the build, you can repeat this process to turn off the Retain Indefinitely flag.

Deleting Builds

Sometimes you might want to explicitly remove a build even though retention policies haven't been enabled for the build definition or before the retention policy would have removed the build automatically. One reason you might want to do this could be to recover disk space or to remove extraneous builds from the build history.

You can explicitly remove a build by opening the build's Build Details window and clicking Delete Build at the top. You can also delete the build by right-clicking the build on the

Completed tab of the Build Explorer window and choosing Delete. You will be prompted to choose which build artifacts you want to delete, as shown in Figure 13-30.

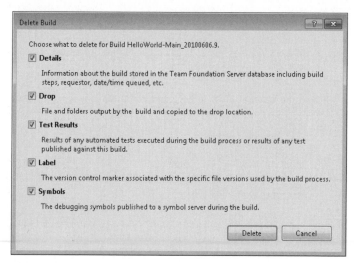

FIGURE 13-30 Delete build options

Working with Builds from the Command Line

Build administrators (and most developers) are command-line fans at heart, and Team Build provides a command-line client for queuing, stopping, and deleting builds. Even if you're not overly fond of using the command line, it also provides a simple way to script Team Build commands as part of a larger process.

The command-line client is called TfsBuild.exe and is installed in the %ProgramFiles%\ Microsoft Visual Studio 10.0\Common7\IDE directory as part of the Team Foundation Client. The easiest way to run it is from the Visual Studio 2010 command prompt, which includes this directory in its default path.

The first parameter to TfsBuild.exe is the command to execute. The available commands are listed in Table 13-3.

TABLE 13-3 TfsBuild.exe Commands

Command	Description
Help	Prints general help for the TfsBuild.exe command-line client as well as command-specific help
Start	Starts a new build either synchronously or asynchronously
Stop	Stops one or more running builds
Delete	Deletes one or more completed builds and their artifacts
Destroy	Destroys (purges) previously deleted builds permanently

To print general help and a list of available commands, run TfsBuild.exe help.

To print help for a specific command, run the following code:

```
TfsBuild.exe help <command>
```

where *<command>* is the command in question (for example, TfsBuild.exe help start).

> **Note** Any arguments containing a space should be enclosed in double-quotation marks.

Queuing a Build

The TfsBuild.exe command line provides two variations of the start command. The first has the following syntax, and its parameters are described in Table 13-4:

```
TfsBuild start /collection:<teamProjectCollectionUrl> /buildDefinition:<definitionSpec>
              [/dropLocation:dl] [/getOption:go] [/priority:p]
              [/customGetVersion:versionSpec] [/requestedFor:userName]
              [/msBuildArguments:args] [/queue] [/shelveset:name [/checkin]] [/silent]
```

TABLE 13-4 TfsBuild.exe Start Parameters

Parameter	Description
/collection:<teamProjectCollection Url>	The full URL of the Team Project Collection (for example, *http://TFSRTM10:8080/tfs/defaultcollection*).
/buildDefinition:<definitionSpec>	The full path of the build definition in the format \<*Team Project*>\<*BuildDefinitionName*> (for example, \Contoso\ HelloWorldManual).
/dropLocation:<dl>	If specified, overrides the drop location in the build definition.
/getOption:<go>	If specified, states what version of the source code Team Build will get. Table 13-5 lists the available *get* options.
/priority:<p>	Set to either *Low*, *BelowNormal*, *Normal*, *AboveNormal*, or *High*. This parameter will default to *Normal* if not provided.
/customGetVersion:<versionSpec>	If /getOption:Custom is specified, this parameter must be supplied and specifies the version of the source code that Team Build should get. The available *versionspec* options are listed in Table 13-6.
/requestedFor:<userName>	By default, the build will be requested for the user that runs the TfsBuild.exe command line, or if you wish, you can pass this parameter to request a build on behalf of another user if you have sufficient permissions.
/msBuildArguments:<args>	Quoted arguments to be passed to MSBuild when executing TFSBuild.proj. For example, to enable optimizations and increase the logging verbosity to diagnostic, you would specify /msBuildArguments:"/p:Optimize=true /v:diag".

Parameter	Description
/queue	By default, the TfsBuild.exe command line will return an error immediately if the build won't be processed immediately by a build controller (that is, if it needs to be queued). If the build is processed immediately by a build controller, TfsBuild.exe won't return until the build has completed. If this parameter is used, TfsBuild.exe will return as soon as the build has been queued on the build controller.
/shelveset:name	Includes a shelveset in the build by unshelving it after the get has completed.
/checkin	Specifies that the shelveset should be checked in if the build completes successfully.
/silent	If specified, suppresses any output from the TfsBuild.exe command line other than the logo information.

TABLE 13-5 Get Options

Option	Description
LatestOnQueue	Builds the latest version of the source code at the time the build is queued.
LatestOnBuild	Builds the latest version of the source code at the time the build starts (this is the default).
Custom	Builds the version specified by the /customGetVersion parameter.

TABLE 13-6 Versionspec Options

Name	Prefix	Example	Description
Date/Time	D	D07/22/2010 or D07/22/2010T18:00	Builds the source code at a specific date and time. Any string that can be parsed into a System.DateTime structure by the .NET Framework is supported.
Changeset Version	C	C1133	Builds the source code at a specific changeset number.
Label	L	Lcheckpoint2label	Builds the source code at the version specified by the label.
Latest Version	T	T	Builds the latest version of the source code.
Workspace Version	W	Wmyworkspace; my-username	Builds the version of the source code currently in the specified workspace.

The second variation of the start command provides the same functionality as the first but mimics the syntax of the start command in Team Build 2005:

```
TfsBuild start <teamProjectCollectionUrl> <teamProject> <definitionName>
            [/dropLocation:dl] [/getOption:go] [/priority:p]
            [/customGetVersion:versionSpec] [/requestedFor:userName]
            [/msBuildArguments:args] [/queue]
            [/shelveset:name [/checkin]] [/silent]
```

Stopping a Build

You can also stop a running build from the TfsBuild.exe command line by using the stop command.

There are three variations of the stop command, and their parameters are described in Table 13-7:

```
TfsBuild stop [/noPrompt] [/silent] /collection:<teamProjectCollectionUrl>
          /buildDefinition:<definitionSpec> <buildNumbers> ...

TfsBuild stop [/noPrompt] [/silent] /collection:<teamProjectCollectionUrl>
          <buildUris> ...

TfsBuild stop [/noPrompt] [/silent] <teamProjectCollectionUrl> <teamProject>
          <buildNumbers> ...
```

TABLE 13-7 TfsBuild.exe Stop Parameters

Parameter	Description
/noPrompt	If specified, suppresses TfsBuild.exe confirming you want to stop the build
/silent	If specified, suppresses any output from the TfsBuild.exe command line other than the logo information
/collection:<teamProjectCollectionUrl>	The full URL of the Team Project Collection (for example, *http://TFSRTM10:8080/tfs/defaultcollection*)
/buildDefinition:<definitionSpec>	The full path of the build definition in the format \<*Team Project*>\<*BuildDefinitionName*> (for example, \Contoso\ HelloWorldManual)
buildNumbers	Space-separated list of build numbers to be stopped
buildUris	Space-separated list of build Uniform Resource Identifiers (URIs) to be stopped

Deleting a Build

You can also delete a build from the TfsBuild.exe command line by using the delete command.

There are five variations of the delete command, and their parameters are described in Table 13-8:

```
TfsBuild delete [/noPrompt] [/silent] [/preview] [deleteOptions:do]
          /collection:<teamProjectCollectionUrl> /buildDefinition:<definitionSpec>
          <buildNumbers> ...

TfsBuild delete [/noPrompt] [/silent] [/preview] [deleteOptions:do]
          /collection:<teamProjectCollectionUrl> <buildUris> ...
```

```
TfsBuild delete [/noPrompt] [/silent] [/preview] [deleteOptions:do]
                <teamProjectCollectionUrl> <teamProject> <buildNumbers> ...

TfsBuild delete [/noPrompt] [/silent] [/preview] [deleteOptions:do]
                /collection:<teamProjectCollectionUrl>
                /buildDefinition:<definitionSpec>
                /dateRange:<fromDate>~<toDate>

TfsBuild delete [/noPrompt] [/silent] [/preview] [deleteOptions:do]
                /collection:<teamProjectCollectionUrl>
                /dateRange:<fromDate>~<toDate> <teamProject>
```

TABLE 13-8 **TfsBuild.exe Delete Parameters**

Parameter	Description
/noPrompt	If specified, suppresses TfsBuild.exe confirming that you want to delete the build.
/silent	If specified, suppresses any output from the TfsBuild.exe command line other than the logo information.
/preview	Outputs a list of the artifacts that would be deleted without actually deleting them.
/collection:<teamProjectCollectionUrl>	The full URL of the Team Foundation Server (for example, *http://TFSRTM10:8080/tfs/defaultcollection*).
/buildDefinition:<definitionSpec>	The full path of the build definition in the format \<*Team Project*>\<*BuildDefinitionName*> (for example, \Contoso\ HelloWorldManual).
/deleteOptions:<do>	If specified, specifies which build artifacts should be deleted. Table 13-9 lists the available delete options. Multiple delete options can be comma-separated (for example, /deleteOptions: Details,DropLocation). The delete command can be run multiple times on the same builds if different delete options are specified.
/dateRange:<fromDate>~<toDate>	The date range of builds that should be deleted. Dates can be specified in any .NET-parsable date format.
buildNumbers	Space-separated list of build numbers to be deleted.
buildUris	Space-separated list of build URIs to be deleted.

TABLE 13-9 **Delete Options**

Option	Description
All	Deletes all the build artifacts listed in this table.
Details	Marks the build as deleted so that it is hidden in the Team Foundation Client. The build will be permanently deleted only if purged.
DropLocation	Deletes the build outputs from the build's drop location.
Label	Deletes the build's version control label.
TestResults	Deletes the build's test results.
Symbols	Deletes the build's symbols from the symbol store.

Team Build Security

Securing Team Build is a critical part of configuring Team Foundation Server and installing new build agents. Even if your Team Foundation Server environment is safely contained within your corporate firewall, this is still important to prevent inadvertent changes to your build agents and the builds that they produce.

Service Accounts

The first consideration when installing Team Build is to decide under what account to run the Team Build service. There are two options:

- **NT AUTHORITY\NETWORK SERVICE**   This built-in Windows account is a limited-privilege account that can access network resources using the computer account's credentials. The account does not have a password and cannot be used to log on to the computer interactively or remotely. For more information about the NETWORK SERVICE account, refer to *http://www.microsoft.com/technet/security/ guidance/serversecurity/serviceaccount/sspgch02.mspx#EBH.*

- **Domain Account**   Team Build can also run as an arbitrary domain account. Using a domain account allows you to log on to the build machine using this account to install or configure applications that use per-user settings (which you can't do with the NETWORK SERVICE account because you can't log on interactively with it). This can also be useful to debug build problems related to permissions on the build machine or other network resources.

To change the service account used by a build agent or build controller, you should use the Team Foundation Server Administration Console rather than the Services MMC snap-in because it will correctly configure the permissions required by Team Build. The steps are as follows:

1. Log on to the build agent or controller for which you want to change the service account.

2. Open the Team Foundation Server Administration Console (shown in Figure 13-31).

3. Click Stop at the top of the console to stop the build service.

4. Click Properties (shown in Figure 13-32).

5. Enter new credentials for the build service.

6. Click Start.

Note   The Team Build service account should not need to be a member of the build machine's Administrators security group. The account should be granted the specific permissions needed by your build processes rather than granting it administrator access to the build machine. This is to minimize the damage of malicious or badly written build scripts.

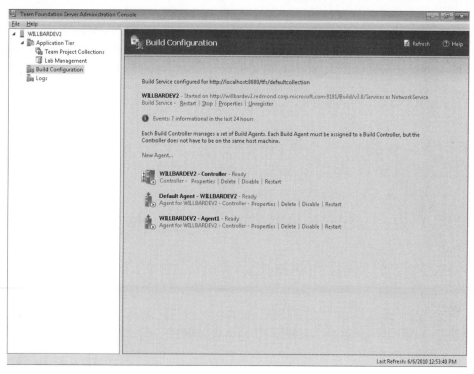

FIGURE 13-31 Team Foundation Server Administration Console

FIGURE 13-32 Configure Team Build service account

The account also needs to be added to the Project Collection Build Service Accounts group for the Team Project Collection for which it will execute builds, as shown in Figure 13-33. This group grants Team Build access to the source, as well as the Team Project Collection permissions required to execute builds. To do this, perform the following steps:

1. Open Visual Studio 2010.

2. Open Team Explorer.

3. Right-click the Team Project Collection.

4. Click Team Project Collection Settings.

5. Click Group Membership.

6. Select the Project Collection Build Service Accounts security group.

7. Click Properties.

8. Click Windows User Or Group.

9. Click Add.

10. Select the domain account that the Team Build service is running as, or the build machine's computer account if it is running as NT AUTHORITY\NETWORK SERVICE.

11. Click OK.

12. Click OK.

13. Click Close.

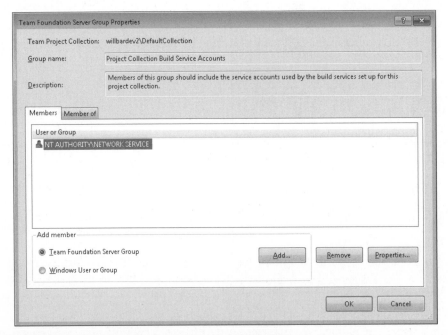

FIGURE 13-33 Build Services Security Group Properties dialog

> **Note** The Team Build service account should not be the Team Foundation Server service account or a member of the Project Collection Administrators, Project Collection Service Accounts, or [Team Project]\Project Administrators security groups. If the Team Build service account is a member of any of these groups, then malicious or badly written build scripts could cause irreparable damage to the Team Foundation Server.

The Team Build service account also requires Full Control file system permission to the drop location.

Permissions

Permissions to both Team Foundation Server or Windows users and groups can be allowed or denied (or left unset). When there is a conflict between allow and deny permissions for a user, deny will take precedence. For more information about how permissions are granted and evaluated in Team Foundation Server, refer to *http://msdn.microsoft.com/en-us/library/ms252587.aspx*.

Team Build provides a number of Team Project Collection–level permissions for controlling access to Team Build functionality. These permissions are detailed in Table 13-10.

TABLE 13-10 Team Project Collection–Level Permissions

Permission	Description	Granted by Default To
Manage Build Resources	Permits the user to manage the build controllers and build agents associated with the Team Project Collection, as well as managing the Use Build Resources and View Build Resources permissions.	Project Collection Administrators; Project Collection Build Administrators; Project Collection Build Service Accounts
Use Build Resources	Permits the user to reserve and allocate build agents. This permission should be granted only to build service accounts.	Project Collection Administrators; Project Collection Build Service Accounts
View Build Resources	Permits the user to see the build controllers and build agents associated with the Team Project Collection.	Project Collection Administrators; Project Collection Build Administrators; Project Collection Build Service Accounts; Project Collection Valid Users

The permissions in Table 13-11 can be managed at either the Team Project level (by right-clicking Builds in Team Explorer and clicking Security) or at the build definition level (by right-clicking the build definition in Team Explorer and clicking Security). Permissions that haven't been overridden at the build definition level will inherit the Team Project level permissions.

Certain Team Build operations (such as creating build definitions and modifying permissions) are limited to users that have the Destroy Builds, Manage Build Queue, and Delete Build Definition permissions.

TABLE 13-11 Team Project– and Build Definition–Level Permissions

Permission	Description	Granted by Default To
Delete Build Definition	Permits the user to delete build definitions.	Project Collection Administrators; [Team Project]\Builders; [Team Project]\Project Administrators
Delete Builds	Permits the user to delete completed builds.	Project Collection Administrators; [Team Project]\Builders; [Team Project]\Project Administrators
Destroy Builds	Permits the user to permanently delete completed builds.	Project Collection Administrators; [Team Project]\Builders; [Team Project]\Project Administrators
Edit Build Definition	Permits the user to create new build definitions (only if applied at the Team Project level) or to edit existing build definitions.	Project Collection Administrators; [Team Project]\Builders; [Team Project]\Project Administrators
Edit Build Quality	Permits the user to set or change the build quality for an individual build.	Project Collection Administrators; Project Collection Build Service Accounts; [Team Project]\Builders; [Team Project]\Contributors; [Team Project]\Project Administrators
Manage Build Qualities	Permits the user to maintain the list of build qualities.	Project Collection Administrators; [Team Project]\Builders; [Team Project]\Project Administrators
Manage Build Queue	Permits the user to cancel, postpone, or change the priority of queued builds. Users without this permission can still cancel their own builds, but they won't be able to postpone or change the priority of any builds, including their own.	Project Collection Administrators; [Team Project]\Builders; [Team Project]\Project Administrators

Permission	Description	Granted by Default To
Override Check-In Validation By Build	Permits the user to bypass gated check-in by checking changes in directly without running a gated check-in build.	Project Collection Administrators; Project Collection Build Service Accounts
Queue Builds	Permits the user to queue a new build.	Project Collection Administrators; Project Collection Build Service Accounts; [Team Project]\Builders; [Team Project]\Contributors; [Team Project]\Project Administrators
Retain Indefinitely	Permits the user to exclude builds from the retention policy.	Project Collection Administrators; [Team Project]\Builders; [Team Project]\Project Administrators
Stop Builds	Permits the user to stop a build that's in progress. Users without this permission can still stop their own builds.	Project Collection Administrators; [Team Project]\Builders; [Team Project]\Project Administrators
Update Build Information	Permits the user to add arbitrary information to the build. This permission should be granted only to build service accounts.	Project Collection Build Service Accounts
View Build Definition	Permits the user to view the details of a build definition.	Project Collection Administrators; Project Collection Build Service Accounts; Project Collection Test Service Accounts; [Team Project]\Builders; [Team Project]\Contributors; [Team Project]\Project Administrators; [Team Project]\Readers
View Builds	Permits the user to view queued and completed builds.	Project Collection Administrators; Project Collection Build Service Accounts; Project Collection Test Service Accounts; [Team Project]\Builders; [Team Project]\Contributors; [Team Project]\Project Administrators; [Team Project]\Readers

The Team Project–level permissions in Table 13-12 are not specific to Team Build but are granted to build service accounts by default.

TABLE 13-12 Other Build-Related Permissions

Permission	Description	Granted By Default To
Create Test Runs	Permits the user to publish test results against any build. Also permits the user to modify test runs or remove test results from any build. Note that this permission can be set only at the Team Project level.	Project Collection Administrators; Project Collection Build Service Accounts; Project Collection Test Service Accounts; [Team Project]\Builders; [Team Project]\Contributors; [Team Project]\Project Administrators
View Project-Level Information	Permits the user to view Team Project–level group membership and permissions.	Project Collection Administrators; Project Collection Build Service Accounts; Project Collection Test Service Accounts; [Team Project]\Builders; [Team Project]\Contributors; [Team Project]\Project Administrators; [Team Project]\Readers;
View Test Runs	Permits the user to view test runs for the Team Project.	Project Collection Administrators; Project Collection Build Service Accounts; Project Collection Test Service Accounts; [Team Project]\Builders; [Team Project]\Contributors; [Team Project]\Project Administrators; [Team Project]\Readers

Chapter 14

Team Build Deep Dive

Team Build ships with a default build process that is suitable for building most applications based on Microsoft .NET Framework 2.0 and later, but to get the most value out of Team Build, you can customize this default process to your needs. You can even build non-.NET-based applications if you like.

Process Templates

Build processes in Team Build 2010 are based on build process templates that are implemented as Workflow Foundation workflows based on Extensible Application Markup Language (XAML). Each build definition is associated with a build process template stored in version control. In Chapters 15 and 16, we'll discuss how to customize existing build process templates, as well as how to create your own from scratch.

Team Build ships with three build process templates:

- **Default Template**   As the name suggests, this is the default build process template and is feature-rich and geared towards building applications based on .NET Framework 2.0 and later. This build process template is discussed in detail in this chapter and is a good basis for creating customized build process templates, as we'll discuss in Chapters 15 and 16.

- **Upgrade Template**   Provides backward compatibility with Team Build 2008 by enabling Team Build 2010 to execute TFSBuild.proj. This template isn't as feature-rich as the Default Template, but it provides an easy transition to Team Build 2010 without having to migrate existing build process customizations from TFSBuild.proj (and MSBuild) to workflow-based build process templates. In Appendix C (available online), "Upgrading from Team Foundation Build 2008," we'll walk through how to configure and use the Upgrade Template.

- **Lab Default Template**   Provides integration between Team Build and Lab Management to allow building an application, deploying it to a test environment, and executing tests in it. Lab Management is a large-enough topic to devote an entire book to it, so we won't be covering it in this one.

These templates will be automatically checked into $/*TeamProject*/BuildProcessTemplates whenever you create a Team Project.

Default Template

The Default Template is the "bread and butter" of Team Build build process templates; it has a large number of features, including build number allocating, cleaning, syncing, building, testing, and indexing source and publishing symbols. This section will explain in depth how these features work, as well as how to tweak them for your needs.

Logging

Team Build logs the execution of each activity to the Build Detail window, as well as logging the output from MSBuild to files so that you can view the progress of a build, examine its results, and diagnose build failures or other issues.

The MSBuild log outputs (with the exception of warnings and errors, which also appear in the Build Details window) will be written to disk and copied to the Logs subdirectory of the drop folder. The section entitled "Copy Files to the Drop Location," later in this chapter, discusses the dropping of logs in more detail.

The logging verbosity can be set using the Logging Verbosity process parameter in the Basic category to one of the values listed in Table 14-1. Viewing and setting process parameters is discussed in the Process subsection of the section entitled "Creating a Build Definition," in Chapter 13, "Team Build Quick Start."

TABLE 14-1 Logging Verbosity Settings

Setting	Logging Effects
Minimal	Workflow will log errors, warnings, and messages with an importance of *High*.
	MSBuild's logging verbosity will be set to *Minimal*.
Normal	Workflow will log errors, warnings, and messages with an importance of *Normal* or *High*.
	Sets MSBuild's logging verbosity to *Normal*.
Detailed	Workflow will log errors, warnings, and messages with an importance of *Low*, *Normal*, or *High*.
	Sets MSBuild's logging verbosity to *Detailed*.
Diagnostic	Workflow will log errors, warnings, and messages with an importance of *Low*, *Normal*, or *High*.
	Workflow will log the inputs to and outputs from each activity. Figure 14-1 shows the Build Detail window when the Logging Verbosity is set to *Diagnostic*.
	Sets MSBuild's logging verbosity to *Diagnostic*.

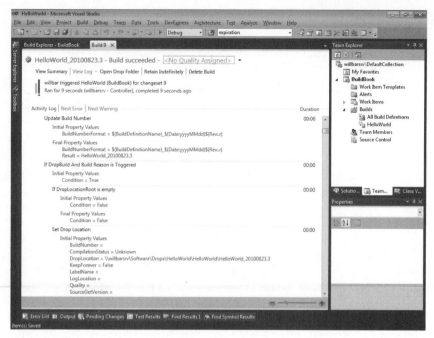

FIGURE 14-1 Build Details window with Diagnostic logging verbosity

Build Number

The Default Template's build numbering scheme is $(BuildDefinitionName)_$(Date:*yyy yMMdd*)$(Rev:.r), where $(Rev:.r) increments starting at 1 and resets whenever the first part of the build number format changes. For example, the first build of the HelloWorld definition on 8/21/2010 will be HelloWorld_20100821.1, the second on that date will be HelloWorld_20100821.2, and the first build on 8/22/2010 will be HelloWorld_20100822.1.

This default build numbering scheme can be customized using the Build Number Format process parameter in the Basic category. The tokens that can be used in the Build Number Format are described in Table 14-2 and any non-tokens will be included in the generated build number as specified.

TABLE 14-2 Build Number Tokens

Token	Description
Environment Variable Name	Any environment variable can be used as a token by surrounding the environment variable name with $(…). For example, $(USERNAME).
$(BuildID)	A unique number allocated to the build by Team Build. This is the number that appears in a build's Uniform Resource Indicator (URI); for example, the *12* in vstfs:///Build/Build/12. The BuildID is unique to the Team Project Collection.
$(BuildDefinitionName)	The name of the build definition (for example, HelloWorld).

Token	Description
$(Date:*format*)	The date that the build was created. The *format* is a standard .NET Framework Date and Time format string. For example, $(Date:*yyyyMMdd*).
$(DayOfMonth)	The day of month that the build was created (for example, 13). This will always be two digits, with a leading zero if necessary.
$(DayOfYear)	The day of the year that the build was created (for example, 233). This will always be three digits, with leading zeros if necessary.
$(Hours)	The hour of day, expressed in 12-hour format, that the build was created (for example, 11). This will always be two digits, with a leading zero if necessary.
$(Minutes)	The minutes part of the time that the build was created (for example, 30). This will always be two digits, with a leading zero if necessary.
$(Month)	The month of year that the build was created (for example, 08). This will always be two digits, with a leading zero if necessary.
$(Rev:*format*)	Returns a unique revision number for the build (based on the rest of the build number format). If used, this token must be at the end of the build number format. The format must begin with a period and be followed with one or more *r*'s indicating how many digits it should be. Leading zeros will be added if necessary. For example, $(Rev:.r) will have one digit, and $(Rev:.rr) will have two digits.
$(Seconds)	The seconds part of the time that the build was created (for example, 30). This will always be two digits, with a leading zero if necessary.
$(TeamProject)	The name of the Team Project containing the Build Definition that the build was created from (for example, MSBuildBook).
$(Year:yy)	The two-digit year that the build was created (for example, 10). This will always be two digits, with a leading zero if necessary.
$(Year:yyyy)	The year that the build was created, expressed in four digits (for example, 2010).

The build number format you use should ensure that each build for a build definition receives a unique build number. Otherwise you'll receive a BuildNumberAlreadyExistsException when the build number is allocated. Build numbers must be 64 characters or less in length, can't end in either a space or a period, and can't contain the characters @":<>\|*?.

Agent Reservation

The majority of the work done by the Default Template is executed on the build agent rather than the controller. By default, the Default Template will select any idle build agent associated with the controller to run the build, but you can change this using the Agent Settings process parameter in the Advanced category.

The first two properties configure the agent reservation timeouts listed in Table 14-3.

TABLE 14-3 Agent Reservation Timeout Properties

Property	Description
Maximum Agent Reservation Wait Time	The maximum amount of time that Team Build can wait for an available build agent to run this build before timing out and failing the build.
Maximum Agent Execution Time	The maximum amount of time that the build process is allowed to execute on the build agent before it is cancelled and the build stopped.

The remaining three properties, which are listed in Table 14-4, configure which agents can be used for the build.

TABLE 14-4 Agent Reservation Properties

Property	Description
Name Filter	Filters build agents by display name (not computer name). This property supports wildcards (* for zero or more characters and ? for one character).
Tags Filter	Filters build agents having the selected tags based on the operator specified in the Tag Comparison Operator.
Tag Comparison Operator	Either *MatchExactly*, to select agents that have the exact tags listed in the Tags Filter and no others, or *MatchAtLeast*, to select agents that have at least the tags listed in the Tags Filter.
	The Tag Comparison Operator is used even if no Tags Filter is specified, so if you leave Tags Filter blank and don't want to exclude agents that have tags, you should change the Tag Comparison Operator from the default of *MatchExactly* to *MatchAtLeast*.

Clean

To provide the ability to do full builds, incremental gets with full builds, and incremental gets with incremental builds, the Default Template provides three levels of cleaning. The type of clean is configured by setting the Clean Workspace process parameter in the Basic category to one of the values in Table 14-5.

TABLE 14-5 Clean Workspace Type Values

Value	What Will Happen	Get Type	Build Type
None	Nothing.	Incremental	Incremental
Outputs	The Clean target will be executed for each project, platform, and configuration. The Binaries directory will be deleted.	Incremental	Full
All (Default)	Binaries and Sources directories will be deleted, as well as the workspace.	Full	Full

Sync

Although they have some similarities, there are significant differences between the sync process for triggered builds and that for private (aka buddy) builds, so we'll discuss them separately. Before performing either sync, the Default Template will undo any pending changes in the workspace that may have been left over from previous builds.

Triggered Builds

The sync process for triggered builds is relatively simple, and the Default Template just performs a get operation on the workspace. The version of this get defaults to the latest changeset at the time of queuing, but this can be overridden by specifying any valid version spec for the Get Version process parameter in the Advanced category. A list of valid version specs is described in Table 13-6 in the previous chapter.

Private (aka Buddy) Builds

Private builds are more complex because they need to merge the contents of a shelveset with the source being synced.

First, the shelveset will be unshelved into the workspace. If the shelveset contains any items outside the build definition's workspace (unmapped items), then the folders containing these items will be temporarily mapped and the unshelve operation repeated.

Next, the get operation will be performed against the workspace. One restriction is that the Get Version process parameter cannot be specified if the Check In Changes After Successful Build check box on the Queue Build dialog is checked when queuing a private build.

Next, any conflicts will attempt to be resolved by performing an auto-merge resolve on the workspace, and if any conflicts remain, the build will fail.

Finally, the resulting pending changes will be reshelved. The shelveset will be created under the build's service account and have a name of _Build_*BuildId,* where *BuildId* is a unique identifier given to the build. This reshelved shelveset can be used to resolve any errors resulting from the auto-merge if the build fails (by unshelving this shelveset, resolving any issues, and resubmitting the shelveset), if the build succeeds, the reshelved shelveset will be automatically deleted.

Label

Version control labels are an integral piece of build reproducibility because they allow you to sync exactly the same sources that the build originally synced. The Default Template will create version control labels for all non-shelveset builds by default, but you can disable it completely by setting the Label Sources process parameter in the Advanced category to False.

The version control label is based on the contents of the workspace and will be linked to the build. This linkage is usually used for determining the version control changes between two builds, as shown in the build summary in Figure 14-2.

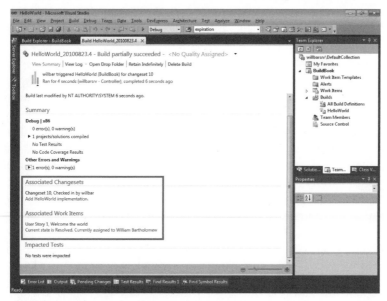

FIGURE 14-2 New Changesets in build summary

The version control label will be named after the build number, will be scoped to the Team Project, and replaces any labels with the same name. Figure 14-3 shows a number of labels created by the Default Template.

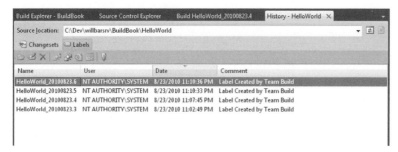

FIGURE 14-3 Labels created by Team Build

Compile and Test

Once the workspace has been prepared, the Default Process Template will begin compiling and testing the sources. It will loop through each platform and configuration specified (in the Items To Build\Configurations To Build process parameter in the Basic category), compile all the projects specified (in the Items To Build\Projects To Build process parameter in the Basic category), and then test them. If Configurations To Build are not specified, then the default platform and configuration (the one selected by default when you open the solution in Microsoft Visual Studio) will be used.

Compile

The major tasks of compilation are left to MSBuild, so this part of the Default Process consists only of looping through each Project To Build, converting the server path to the project to a local path, and executing MSBuild against the project.

Team Build will default to running the x86 version of MSBuild on an x86 operating system and the x64 version on an x64 operating system. You can force Team Build to use the x86 version on an x64 operating system by setting the MSBuild Platform process parameter in the Advanced category to x86. This is often needed when the build process depends on MSBuild tasks that are 32-bit only.

As you've seen in previous chapters, MSBuild itself has a number of arguments, and MSBuild projects can be controlled via properties. Table 14-6 lists the arguments that will be passed by the Default Process.

TABLE 14-6 MSBuild Arguments Passed by the Default Process

MSBuild Argument	Value
/fl	Always passed.
/flp	`"logfile={0};encoding=Unicode;verbosity={1}"`, where {0} is the path to log file and {1} is the value of the Logging Verbosity process parameter discussed in the section entitled "Logging," earlier in this chapter.
/maxcpucount	Always "1".
/noconsolelogger	Always passed.
/nologo	Always passed.
/p:Configuration	Name of the configuration being built.
/p:FxCopDir	Path to the Visual Studio 2005 test tools (particularly FxCop) if they're installed and Perform Code Analysis is not set to Never.
/p:OutDir	The output directory for the platform and configuration being built.
	If only a single platform and configuration is being built, this will be the root of the Binaries subdirectory of the build agent's working directory.
	If the platform is AnyCPU, this will be a subdirectory of the Binaries subdirectory named after the configuration (for example, ...\Debug).
	Otherwise, this will be the subdirectory of the Binaries subdirectory named after the platform and the configuration (for example, ...\x86\Debug).
/p:Platform	Name of the platform being built.

MSBuild Argument	Value
/p:RunCodeAnalysis	This argument is set to *true* if the Perform Code Analysis process parameter in Basic category is Always, *false* if Perform Code Analysis process parameter is Never, and isn't specified if Perform Code Analysis is AsConfigured.
/p:SkipInvalidConfigurations	This argument is always set to *true*.
/p:TeamBuildConstants	This argument is set to *TEAM_BUILD_* if Perform Code Analysis is not Never; and the Visual Studio 2005 test tools (particularly FxCop) are installed on the build server.
/p:VCBuildOverride	The path to the .vsprops file generated by the Default Process.
Additional arguments	The value specified for the MSBuild Arguments process parameter in the Advanced category is passed as is to MSBuild.

Test

Once a platform and configuration has been compiled, it can then be tested using the test specifications in the Automated Tests process parameter in the Basic category. Each test specification can either be a test assembly file specification and an optional test settings file (recommended) or a test metadata (.vsmdi) file and either all of the tests in that file or selected test lists.

Figure 14-4 shows the default test specification, which searches recursively under the Binaries subdirectory (which contains the build outputs) for dynamic link libraries (DLLs) whose name contains the letters *test*.

FIGURE 14-4 Add/Edit Test dialog

For each test specification, you can choose whether a test failure should fail the build, and you can filter the tests to be run using the Criteria/Arguments tab shown in

Figure 14-5. In this example, we're limiting tests to those in the BVT category and (&&) not (!) in the Integration category that have a priority greater than 100. You can also use the *or (|)* operator to include tests from multiple categories, and you can specify arbitrary command-line arguments to be passed to MSTest.

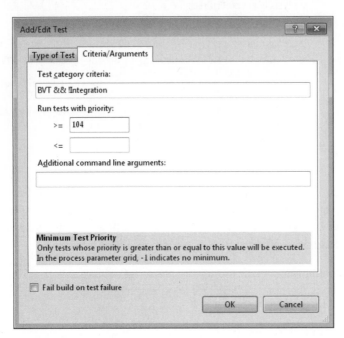

FIGURE 14-5 Criteria/Arguments tab

From time to time, you may want to temporarily disable the running of tests, and, because test specifications can be quite complex, removing and re-adding them would be cumbersome and time-consuming. You can temporarily disable tests by setting the Disable Tests process parameter in the Advanced category to True.

Another new feature in Team Build 2010 is the ability to produce test impact analysis data as part of the build. This information associates code paths with the tests that execute them, and this data can be used to identify subsets of tests that should be run when you're modifying code or are comparing builds. This collection of analysis data can be disabled by setting the Analyze Test Impact process parameter in the Advanced category to *False*.

Source Indexing and Symbol Publishing

Source indexing and symbol publishing are features designed to make it easier to debug your application and to allow you not to ship symbols with your application without hampering your ability to debug it. Source indexing and symbol publishing were commonly requested features in Team Build 2008 (so much so that there was a procedure in the last edition of this book to implement this), but they are now built-in features of Team Build 2010.

Source Indexing

Source indexing is a process where the symbols produced by the compiler (*.PDB) have additional information about the source embedded in them. This information includes the Team Foundation Server URL they came from, the location of the source files in version control, and the particular version of each file.

This information allows Visual Studio to automatically download and show the correct version of each source file while you're debugging. For security reasons [because it allows Visual Studio to connect to whatever Team Foundation Server Uniform Resource Locator (URL) is in the .PDB] you need to enable source server support before debugging. You can do this from Tools\Options\Debugging\General\Enable Source Server Support, as shown in Figure 14-6.

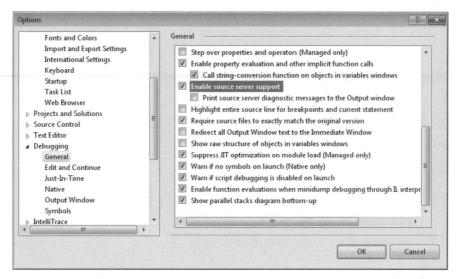

FIGURE 14-6 Enabling source server support

The Default Process enables the indexing of sources by default, but this feature can be disabled by setting the Source And Symbol Server Settings\Index Sources process parameter in the Basic category to *False*.

Symbol Publishing

Symbol stores allow you to store your application's PDBs in a central location so that you can debug instances of your application that didn't ship symbols. Once symbols have been published to the symbol store, you can still debug your application without having to ship the PDBs.

You configure the Default Process to publish symbols by providing the path to the symbol store in the Source And Symbol Server Settings\Path To Publish Symbols process parameter in the Basic category, as shown in Figure 14-7. Initially, this path should be an empty folder on a Universal Naming Convention (UNC) share that is accessible by anyone needing to debug your application.

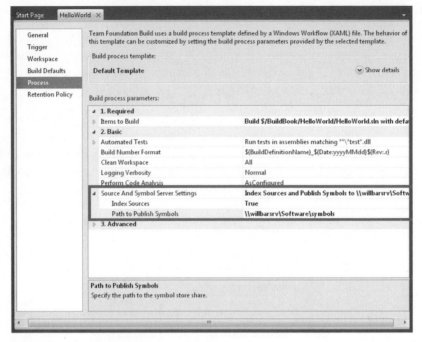

FIGURE 14-7 Enabling publishing of symbols

Because each developer needs to configure the symbol store path in Visual Studio, it's recommended that you have as few symbol stores as possible (ideally just one). To prevent concurrency issues, the Default Process allows only one build to publish symbols to a symbol store at a time, so if you are suffering performance issues for this reason and there is a logical split, you may want to consider multiple symbol stores.

To use the symbol store, the developer needs to add its path to Tools\Options\Debugging\Symbols\Symbol File (.pdb) Locations, as shown in Figure 14-8.

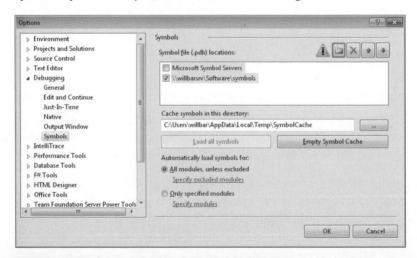

FIGURE 14-8 Configuring Visual Studio symbol file locations

Associate Changesets and Work Items

One important aspect of traceability is being able to trace builds to the changes that were included in it. The Default Process provides this capability by analyzing the changesets between the last good build and the current build and associating them and their work items with the build. The result of this analysis appears in the Build Summary of a completed build, as shown earlier in this chapter in Figure 14-2.

This functionality was also included in Team Build 2008, but due to its performance, it was often disabled. Two things have changed in Team Build 2010 to reduce its performance impact. First, the overall performance of the algorithm was tuned; second, it is performed in parallel with compiling and testing, so the overall build time is not affected.

That being said, the feature can still be disabled by setting the Associate Changesets and Work Items process parameter in the Advanced category to False. This analysis will not occur for private builds regardless of this setting.

Copy Files to the Drop Location

Regardless of the outcome of the build, the Default Process will copy the logs and whatever build outputs are available to the drop location. The root drop location is specified on the Build Defaults tab of the build definition, as shown in Figure 14-9, or you can disable dropping entirely by clearing the This Build Copies Output Files To A Drop Folder check box, but if you do this, you won't even get the log files.

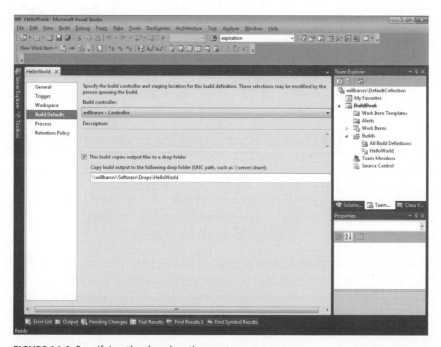

FIGURE 14-9 Specifying the drop location root

The location specified here isn't the final destination of the build outputs. Otherwise, each build would overwrite the previous build. The Default Process will append both the build definition's name and the build's build number to the drop location root to form the drop location; for example, if the drop location root is \\dropserver\drops and you're building the HelloWorld definition, your drop location will be \\dropserver\drops\HelloWorld\ HelloWorld_20100824.1.

To avoid confusion, private builds don't drop to the same drop location root as triggered builds. The private drop location root is specified using the Private Drop Location process parameter in the Advanced category, as shown in Figure 14-10. If this is not specified, private builds will still run, but their outputs won't be dropped and a warning will be logged.

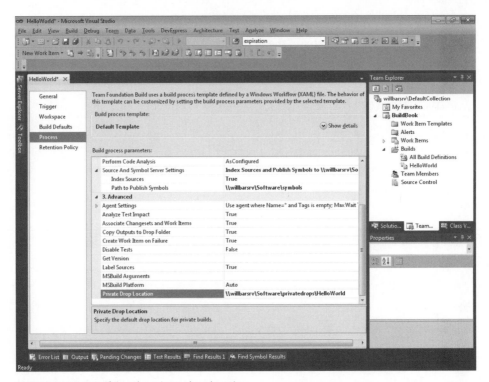

FIGURE 14-10 Specifying the private drop location

The drop location will be created from the controller under the context of the build service account, so this account will require read/write permissions to the drop location root. Refer to Chapter 13 for more information about Team Build security.

The Default Process recursively copies contents of the Binaries directory to the drop location regardless of outcome (even unhandled exceptions), the resulting structure is as described for the /p:OutDir MSBuild argument in the section entitled "Compile," earlier in this chapter. Logs are also dropped in the same structure but under the logs subdirectory of the drop location.

Revert Files and Check in Gated Changes

Whenever a private build completes (whether it's successful or not), any pending changes in the workspace will be undone. If the build (and its tests) are successful and the build is a gated check-in, or the Check In Changes After Successful Build check box on the Queue Build dialog is selected, then the Default Process will check in the shelveset.

The shelveset is checked in server-side (the equivalent of executing `tf checkin /shelveset`), bypassing gated check-in (to avoid the gated check-in trigger) on behalf of the person that queued (or caused to be queued) the build. Finally, it is deleted.

Create Work Items for Build Failure

If compilation fails for a project, then the Default Process will open a Bug work item against the build's requestor with the values in Table 14-7.

TABLE 14-7 Build Failure Work Item Field Values

Work Item Field	Value
Comment	"This work item was created by TFS Build on a build failure."
Priority	"1"
Reason	"Build Failure"
Repro Steps	"Start the build using TFS Build"
Severity	"1 – Critical"
Title	"Build Failure in Build: {0}", where {0} is the build number.

Configuring the Team Build Service

Although most settings are configured at the build definition, service-level settings are configured by running the Team Foundation Server Administration Console on the build server (either the build controller or build agent) itself.

Changing Communications Ports

By default, Team Build listens on port 9191, but this can be changed using the Team Foundation Server Administration Console with the following procedure:

1. Open the Team Foundation Server Administration Console.

2. Click Build Configuration.

3. Stop the build service by clicking Stop.

4. Click Properties to open the Build Service Properties dialog, shown in Figure 14-11.

FIGURE 14-11 Build Service Properties dialog

5. Click Change to open the Build Service Endpoint dialog, shown in Figure 14-12.

FIGURE 14-12 Build Service Endpoint dialog

6. Enter a new port number in the Port Number text box.

7. Click OK.

8. Click Start.

Requiring SSL

Team Build can also require clients to use Secure Sockets Layer (SSL) to encrypt the requests to and responses from the build service's endpoint. This is recommended when the network between the Team Foundation Server application tier and the build agent is untrusted.

The first step is to issue and install an X.509 certificate in the build service account's certificate store. To be used for securing Team Build, the issued certificate must have an intended purpose of client authentication and be issued by a certificate authority trusted by the Team Foundation Server application tier.

Once the certificate has been issued, you need to configure Team Build to use it by doing the following:

1. Open the Team Foundation Server Administration Console.
2. Click Build Configuration.
3. Stop the build service by clicking Stop.
4. Click Properties to open the Build Service Properties dialog.
5. Click Change to open the Build Service Endpoint dialog.
6. Select the HTTPS protocol.
7. Select the SSL certificate to use, as shown in Figure 14-13.

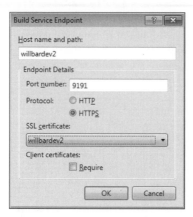

FIGURE 14-13 Build Service Endpoint dialog—selecting the SSL certificate

8. Click OK.
9. Click Start.

From this dialog, you can also require the application tier or build controller to authenticate to the build service endpoint by selecting the Require check box in the Client Certificates group.

Running Interactively

By default, Team Build runs as a service, which is typically desirable because it doesn't require the build agent to be logged in. However, because services can't access the desktop, if your build process runs unit tests that display a user interface, then they will fail.

To work around this, Team Build can be run as an interactive process by doing the following:

1. Open the Team Foundation Server Administration Console.

2. Click Build Configuration.

3. Stop the build service by clicking Stop.

4. Click Properties to open the Build Service Properties dialog.

5. Select Interactive Process, as shown in Figure 14-14.

FIGURE 14-14 Build Service Properties dialog—selecting Interactive Process

6. Enter the account details under which you'll run Team Build.

7. Click Start.

The Team Foundation Server Administration Console will start the interactive process for you automatically. To stop it, you can press Esc. To run the interactive process without opening the Team Foundation Server Administration Console, you can run this command:

```
%ProgramFiles%\Microsoft Team Foundation Server 2010\Tools\TFSBuildServiceHost.exe
```

Running Multiple Build Agents

When you first install Team Build on a build server, you'll be asked how many build agents you want to run on the build server. If you want to run a different number of build agents on the build server at a later stage, you can delete agents or add new agents from the Team Foundation Server Administration Console, as shown in Figure 14-15.

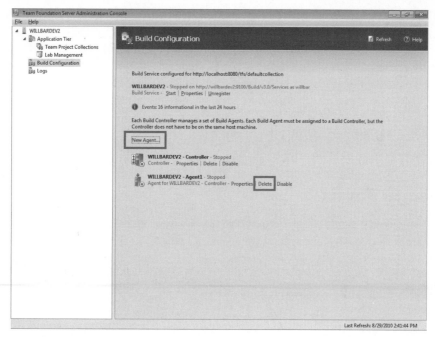

FIGURE 14-15 Adding or deleting build agents

Build Controller Concurrency

Build controllers default to concurrently running as many builds as it has agents; you can configure this in the Build Controller Properties dialog, shown in Figure 14-16.

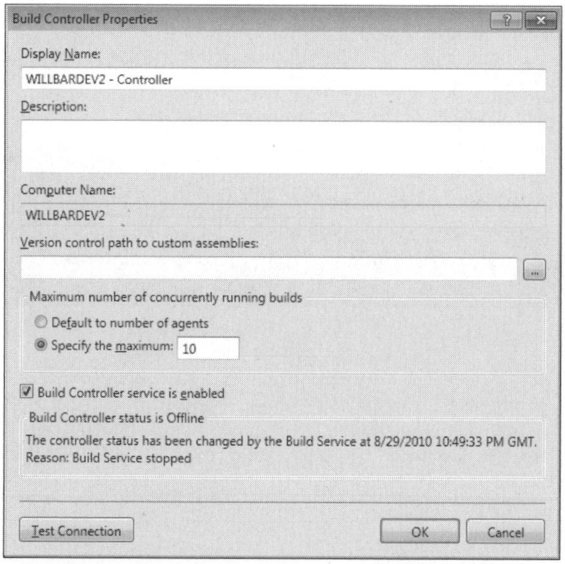

FIGURE 14-16 Build Controller Properties dialog

Team Build API

Team Build provides a rich application programming interface (API) that allows you to query and manage the build server, process templates, build definitions, and individual builds. There are a number of scenarios where the Team Build API is useful:

- Automating administration tasks
- Integrating Team Build into other processes
- Extending the build process

Creating a Project

The first step is to create a project that references the required assemblies. In this example, we'll create a new console application called TeamBuildAPI, as shown in Figure 14-17.

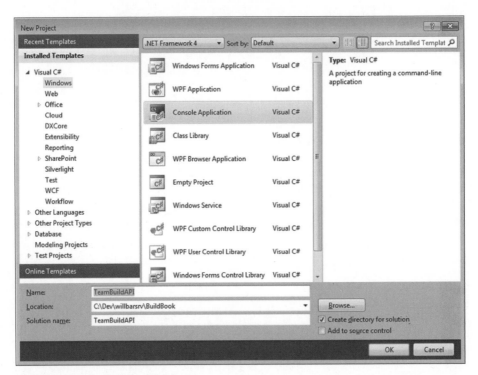

FIGURE 14-17 New Project dialog box

Using the Team Build API requires at least three references:

- **Microsoft.TeamFoundation.Client.dll** Provides the necessary classes to connect to Team Foundation Server

- **Microsoft.TeamFoundation.Common.dll**   Contains common classes such as exception classes

- **Microsoft.TeamFoundation.Build.Client.dll**   Contains the classes and interfaces relating to Team Build

These references can be added from the .NET tab of the Add References dialog, but make sure that you select the 10.0.0.0 assemblies, which are for Team Build 2010.

Connecting to Team Project Collection

Once you've referenced these assemblies, you need to obtain a *TfsTeamProjectCollection* object, which represents a connection to a Team Project Collection. This object provides access to all of the services offered by the Team Project Collection, such as build, version control, and work-item tracking.

The recommended way to create a *TfsTeamProjectCollection* object is to pass the URL or Registered Server Name to the *GetTeamProjectCollection* method of the *TfsTeamProjectCollectionFactory* class.

```
TfsTeamProjectCollection tpc = TfsTeamProjectCollectionFactory
    .GetTeamProjectCollection(new Uri("http://TFSRTM10:8080"));
```

The advantage of using the factory over creating an instance of the *TfsTeamProjectCollection* class directly is that the factory will cache connections based on the URL and will return these cached connections, which can increase the performance of the application.

The API will attempt to authenticate the user automatically using integrated authentication, but if this fails, the API will throw a TeamFoundationServerUnauthorizedException exception. This behavior is inconsistent with Visual Studio, which instead prompts users for their credentials if they can't be authenticated automatically. You can achieve this same behavior by passing an instance of UICredentialsProvider to the *GetTeamProjectCollection* method.

```
TfsTeamProjectCollection tpc = TfsTeamProjectCollectionFactory.GetTeamProjectCollection(
    new Uri("http://TFSRTM10:8080"),
    new UICredentialsProvider()
);
```

When this overload is used, then the API will try to authenticate the user automatically; and if that fails, it will display the credentials prompt shown in Figure 14-18 and then use those credentials to authenticate the user to the Team Foundation Server.

FIGURE 14-18 Credentials prompt

Connecting to Team Build

In Team Foundation Server 2010, the Team Build functionality is exposed via the IBuildServer interface. You can't directly create an instance of IBuildServer (because it is an interface), but the *TfsTeamProjectCollection* class has a *GetService<T>* method that returns a concrete implementation that you can use:

```
IBuildServer buildServer = tpc.GetService<IBuildServer>();
```

Working with Build Service Hosts

The build service host is a feature internal to Team Build that represents a build server running a build controller, one or more build agents, or both.

Querying Build Service Hosts

To list the build service hosts (either controllers or agents) that have been defined for a specific Team Project Collection, you call IBuildServer.QueryBuildServiceHosts, as shown here:

```
IBuildServiceHost[] buildServiceHosts = buildServer.QueryBuildServiceHosts("*");
```

The *QueryBuildServiceHosts* method returns an array of objects that implement the IBuildServiceHost interface shown here:

```
namespace Microsoft.TeamFoundation.Build.Client
{
    public interface IBuildServiceHost
    {
        ReadOnlyCollection<IBuildAgent> Agents { get; }
        Uri BaseUrl { get; set; }
        IBuildServer BuildServer { get; }
        IBuildController Controller { get; }
```

```
        string Name { get; set; }
        bool RequireClientCertificates { get; set; }
        Uri Uri { get; }

        void AddBuildAgent(IBuildAgent agent);
        IBuildAgent CreateBuildAgent(string name, string buildDirectory);
        IBuildAgent CreateBuildAgent(string name, string buildDirectory,
            IBuildController buildController);
        IBuildController CreateBuildController(string name);
        void Delete();
        bool DeleteBuildAgent(IBuildAgent agent);
        void DeleteBuildController();
        IBuildAgent FindBuildAgent(string controller, string name);
        void Save();
        void SetBuildAgentStatus(IBuildAgent agent, AgentStatus status, string message);
        void SetBuildController(IBuildController controller);
        void SetBuildControllerStatus(ControllerStatus status, string message);
    }
}
```

We can determine if a build service host has a build controller by checking if the Controller property is non-null, and you can determine if it has one or more build agents by checking if the Agents property contains any objects.

Working with Build Definitions

Being able to work with build definitions programmatically allows you to update build definitions in bulk, create them automatically, and query them.

Querying Build Definitions

The list of build definitions can be retrieved in a similar manner using the *QueryBuildDefinitions* method of the IBuildServer interface, as shown here:

```
IBuildDefinition[] buildDefinitions = buildServer.QueryBuildDefinitions("Contoso");
```

This method returns an array of objects that implement IBuildDefinition, as shown here:

```
namespace Microsoft.TeamFoundation.Build.Client
{
    public interface IBuildDefinition : IBuildGroupItem
    {
        IBuildController BuildController { get; set; }
        Uri BuildControllerUri { get; }
        IBuildServer BuildServer { get; }
        [Obsolete("This property has been deprecated. Please remove all references.")]
        string ConfigurationFolderPath { get; set; }
        int ContinuousIntegrationQuietPeriod { get; set; }
        ContinuousIntegrationType ContinuousIntegrationType { get; set; }
        [Obsolete("This property has been deprecated. Please remove all references.", true)]
        IBuildAgent DefaultBuildAgent { get; set; }
```

```
        [Obsolete("This property has been deprecated. Please remove all references.", true)]
        Uri DefaultBuildAgentUri { get; }
        string DefaultDropLocation { get; set; }
        string Description { get; set; }
        bool Enabled { get; set; }
        string Id { get; }
        Uri LastBuildUri { get; }
        string LastGoodBuildLabel { get; }
        Uri LastGoodBuildUri { get; }
        IProcessTemplate Process { get; set; }
        string ProcessParameters { get; set; }
        [Obsolete("This property has been deprecated. Please remove all references.", true)]
        Dictionary<BuildStatus, IRetentionPolicy> RetentionPolicies { get; }
        List<IRetentionPolicy> RetentionPolicyList { get; }
        List<ISchedule> Schedules { get; }
        IWorkspaceTemplate Workspace { get; }

        IRetentionPolicy AddRetentionPolicy(BuildReason reason, BuildStatus status,
            int numberToKeep, DeleteOptions deleteOptions);
        ISchedule AddSchedule();
        IBuildRequest CreateBuildRequest();
        IBuildDetail CreateManualBuild(string buildNumber);
        IBuildDetail CreateManualBuild(string buildNumber, string dropLocation);
        IBuildDetail CreateManualBuild(string buildNumber, string dropLocation,
            BuildStatus buildStatus, IBuildController controller, string requestedFor);
        [Obsolete("This method has been deprecated. Please remove all references.", true)]
        IProjectFile CreateProjectFile();
        IBuildDefinitionSpec CreateSpec();
        void Delete();
        IBuildDetail[] QueryBuilds();
        void Save();
    }
}
```

In this example, we use the array of build definitions to change each of their default build controllers to the first build controller.

```
IBuildController defaultBuildController = buildServer.QueryBuildServiceHosts("*")
    .Where(bsh => bsh.Controller != null).Select(bsh => bsh.Controller).First();

foreach (IBuildDefinition buildDefinition in buildDefinitions) {
    buildDefinition.BuildController = defaultBuildController;
    buildDefinition.Save();
}
```

Creating a Build Definition

Build definitions can be created using the *CreateBuildDefinition* method on the IBuildServer interface. This method returns IBuildDefinition, which can be populated with the required values before calling Save to persist the build definition to the TfsBuild database.

This example creates a new build definition, which is configured to build on each check-in, defaults to the first build controller, and retains only two successful builds.

```
IBuildDefinition buildDefinition = buildServer.CreateBuildDefinition("Contoso");
buildDefinition.Name = "HelloWorld";
buildDefinition.ContinuousIntegrationType = ContinuousIntegrationType.Individual;
buildDefinition.BuildController = defaultBuildController;
buildDefinition.DefaultDropLocation = @"\\CONTOSO\Projects\HelloWorld\drops";


IRetentionPolicy retentionPolicy = buildDefinition.RetentionPolicyList.Where(
    rp => rp.BuildReason == BuildReason.Triggered
        || rp.BuildStatus == BuildStatus.Succeeded)
    .First();
retentionPolicy.NumberToKeep = 2;
retentionPolicy.DeleteOptions = DeleteOptions.All;

buildDefinition.Save();
```

Working with Builds

Working with builds programmatically allows you to automate launching builds from other systems, develop a build status dashboard, and develop alerting systems.

Queuing a Build

Queuing builds using the API can be useful for integrating builds into other processes and can give more control than what is available via the command-line interface or Visual Studio.

The most flexible way to queue a build is by creating IBuildRequest by calling the *CreateBuildRequest* method on the IBuildDefinition interface and then passing this to the *QueueBuild* method on the IBuildServer interface.

As you can see here, the IBuildRequest interface allows you to specify all of the options available in the Queue Build dialog in Visual Studio.

```
namespace Microsoft.TeamFoundation.Build.Client
{
    public interface IBuildRequest
    {
        [Obsolete("This property has been deprecated. Please remove all references.
            Use the BuildController property instead.", true)]
        IBuildAgent BuildAgent { get; set; }
        [Obsolete("This property has been deprecated. Please remove all references.
            Use the BuildControllerUri property instead.", true)]
        Uri BuildAgentUri { get; }
        IBuildController BuildController { get; set; }
        Uri BuildControllerUri { get; }
        IBuildDefinition BuildDefinition { get; }
        Uri BuildDefinitionUri { get; }
        IBuildServer BuildServer { get; }
        [Obsolete("This property has been deprecated. Please remove all references. To pass command
            line arguments to MSBuild.exe, set the ProcessParameters property.", true)]
```

```
        string CommandLineArguments { get; set; }
        string CustomGetVersion { get; set; }
        string DropLocation { get; set; }
        string GatedCheckInTicket { get; set; }
        GetOption GetOption { get; set; }
        int MaxQueuePosition { get; set; }
        bool Postponed { get; set; }
        QueuePriority Priority { get; set; }
        string ProcessParameters { get; set; }
        BuildReason Reason { get; set; }
        string RequestedFor { get; set; }
        string ShelvesetName { get; set; }
    }
}
```

In this example, we queue a build for each build definition that has been defined in the Contoso Team Project.

```
foreach (IBuildDefinition buildDefinition in buildServer.QueryBuildDefinitions("Contoso")) {
    IBuildRequest request;
    request = buildDefinition.CreateBuildRequest();

    buildServer.QueueBuild(request);
}
```

Querying Build Queues

Accessing the queued builds is slightly more complicated than querying build agents and build definitions. First, you need to create an *IQueuedBuildsView* object using the *CreateQueuedBuildsView* method on the IBuildServer interface.

```
IQueuedBuildsView queuedBuildsView = buildServer.CreateQueuedBuildsView("Contoso");
```

You then need to define the filters for the view. You can filter based on the build agent, build definition, or build status using the ControllerFilter, DefinitionFilter, and StatusFilter properties, respectively. You can also determine for how long a completed build should remain in the build queue using the CompletedWindow property. We'll include just builds that have a status of Queued.

```
queuedBuildsView.StatusFilter = QueueStatus.Queued;
```

We then define how much information about each build should be returned using the QueryOptions property. This enumeration allows you to specify whether the build agent, build definition, or workspace details should be returned; in addition, you can request multiple objects to be returned by OR-ing the values. We'll return the details about the build definitions and the build controllers.

```
queuedBuildsView.QueryOptions = QueryOptions.Definitions | QueryOptions.Controllers;
```

Finally, we call the *Refresh* method to retrieve the list of queued builds. The Boolean parameter indicates whether recently completed builds should also be returned, in this case because we want only queued builds. The list of queued builds can then be accessed from the QueuedBuilds property, which returns an array of objects implementing the IQueuedBuild interface. Finally, we cancel all of the queued builds returned by the view.

```
queuedBuildsView.Refresh(false);
foreach (IQueuedBuild queuedBuild in queuedBuildsView.QueuedBuilds) {
    queuedBuild.Cancel();
}
```

Querying Build History

Completed builds can be queried using the *QueryBuilds* method on the IBuildServer or IBuildDefinition interface. If you call the *QueryBuilds* method on an object implementing IBuildDefinition, it will return all builds for that build definition, whereas calling it on an object implementing IBuildServer allows you to filter the builds based on different criteria. All of these variants of *QueryBuilds* return an array of objects implementing the IBuildDetail interface, as shown here:

```
namespace Microsoft.TeamFoundation.Build.Client
{
    public interface IBuildDetail
    {
        [Obsolete("This property has been deprecated. Please remove all references.", true)]
        IBuildAgent BuildAgent { get; }
        [Obsolete("This property has been deprecated. Please remove all references.", true)]
        Uri BuildAgentUri { get; }
        IBuildController BuildController { get; }
        Uri BuildControllerUri { get; }
        IBuildDefinition BuildDefinition { get; }
        Uri BuildDefinitionUri { get; }
        bool BuildFinished { get; }
        string BuildNumber { get; set; }
        IBuildServer BuildServer { get; }
        [Obsolete("This property has been deprecated. Please remove all references.", true)]
        string CommandLineArguments { get; }
        BuildPhaseStatus CompilationStatus { get; set; }
        [Obsolete("This property has been deprecated. Please remove all references.", true)]
        string ConfigurationFolderPath { get; }
        [Obsolete("This property has been deprecated. Please remove all references.", true)]
        Uri ConfigurationFolderUri { get; }
        string DropLocation { get; set; }
        string DropLocationRoot { get; }
        DateTime FinishTime { get; }
        IBuildInformation Information { get; }
        bool IsDeleted { get; }
        bool KeepForever { get; set; }
        string LabelName { get; set; }
        string LastChangedBy { get; }
        DateTime LastChangedOn { get; }
```

```
        string LogLocation { get; set; }
        string ProcessParameters { get; }
        string Quality { get; set; }
        BuildReason Reason { get; }
        string RequestedBy { get; }
        string RequestedFor { get; }
        string ShelvesetName { get; }
        string SourceGetVersion { get; set; }
        DateTime StartTime { get; }
        BuildStatus Status { get; set; }
        string TeamProject { get; }
        BuildPhaseStatus TestStatus { get; set; }
        Uri Uri { get; }

        event PollingCompletedEventHandler PollingCompleted;
        event StatusChangedEventHandler StatusChanged;
        event StatusChangedEventHandler StatusChanging;

        void Connect();
        void Connect(int pollingInterval, ISynchronizeInvoke synchronizingObject);
        IBuildDeletionResult Delete();
        IBuildDeletionResult Delete(DeleteOptions options);
        void Disconnect();
        void FinalizeStatus();
        void FinalizeStatus(BuildStatus status);
        void Refresh(string[] informationTypes, QueryOptions queryOptions);
        void RefreshAllDetails();
        void RefreshMinimalDetails();
        void Save();
        void Stop();
        void Wait();
    }
}
```

In this example, we use a build detail specification to filter the list of all builds in the Contoso
Team Project to those finished in the last five days.

```
IBuildDetailSpec spec = buildServer.CreateBuildDetailSpec("Contoso");
spec.MinFinishTime = DateTime.Now.AddDays(-5);
IBuildDetail[] builds = buildServer.QueryBuilds(spec).Builds;

foreach (IBuildDetail build in builds) {
    Console.WriteLine(build.BuildNumber);
}
```

Chapter 15
Workflow Foundation Quick Start

Workflow Foundation (WF), included in Microsoft .NET Framework 4.0, has been completely re-engineered to increase performance and make developers more productive. The changes made were necessary in many respects in order to provide the best experience for developers adopting Workflow Foundation and to enable Workflow Foundation to continue being a strong platform for use in your applications.

This chapter, written by Jason Ward, is about Workflow Foundation and how it is a set of tools for declaring your workflow (also known as *business logic*), activities to define the logic and control flow, and a run time for executing the resulting application definition. Workflow Foundation is about using a higher-level language for writing applications, with the goal of making applications easier to manage while simultaneously increasing productivity and facilitating quicker implementation of changes.

Introduction to Workflow Foundation

This section discusses the types of workflows available and demonstrates a basic "Hello World" workflow.

Types of Workflows

Workflow Foundation provides three types of workflows:

- **Sequential** Executes activities in sequence, one after another. Execution must always move forward.

- **Flowchart** Executes activities one after another, like a Sequence activity, but also allows control to return to an earlier step. This is new in the .NET Framework 4.0 release of Workflow Foundation and more in alignment with how we think, and indeed how real processes actually work.

- **State Machine** Provides a modeling style with which you can model your workflow in an event-driven manner. Each state can have a set of transitions that specify the execution logic between the states.

> **Note** The State Machine workflow type is shipped as an Activity Pack, available at *http://wf.codeplex.com*.

Building a Simple Workflow Application

No introduction is complete without the stereotypical "Hello World" example, and this one is no different! Let's go ahead and build a simple "Hello World" application to walk you through how to get started.

1. Open Microsoft Visual Studio 2010.

2. Click the New Project link.

3. Under Installed Templates, navigate to Microsoft Visual C#, Workflow and select the Workflow Console Application, as shown in Figure 15-1. Enter the name as **HelloWorldExample**, and select a suitable location of your choice.

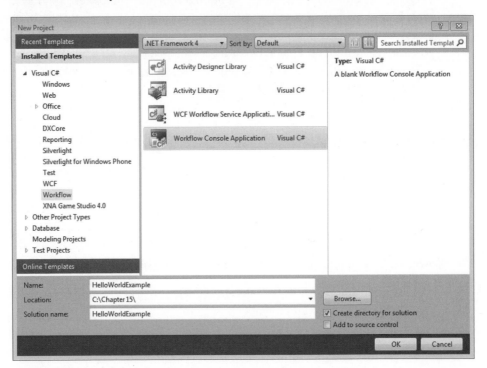

FIGURE 15-1 Creating a new Workflow project

4. Click OK. The project will be created, and you should see an empty Workflow Designer, as shown in Figure 15-2.

5. In the Toolbox, click the Control Flow tab and drag a Sequence activity onto the Workflow Designer.

6. In the Toolbox, click the Primitives tab and drag a WriteLine activity onto the sequence that you created in step 5.

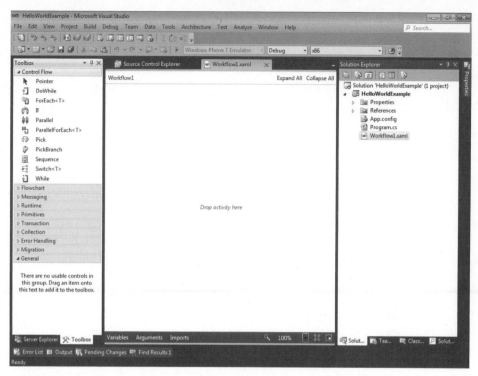

FIGURE 15-2 The Visual Studio IDE showing an empty Workflow Designer window

7. Double-click inside the Text text box and type **"Hello World!"**. The Workflow should now look like Figure 15-3.

FIGURE 15-3 The completed Workflow

8. In Solution Explorer, locate and open the Program.cs file. You should see the following code:

```
using System;
using System.Linq;
using System.Activities;
```

```
            using System.Activities.Statements;

            namespace HelloWorldExample
            {
                class Program
                {
                    static void Main(string[] args)
                    {
                        WorkflowInvoker.Invoke(new Workflow1());

                        Console.WriteLine("Press the ENTER key to exit");
                        Console.ReadLine();
                    }
                }
            }
```

The static *Workflow Invoker* class is used to start the Workflow. The additional two lines shown in bold are not part of the default implementation. I added these lines to prevent the console application from exiting before you see the output. You should also add these two lines to your Program.cs file in the same location.

Running the Application

Press F5 to run the application. You should see the following output:

```
Hello World!
Press the ENTER key to exit
```

Workflow Design

In order to get started designing your Workflows, it's important that you understand some of the basic concepts and functionality available. This includes the built-in activities, as well as passing arguments between activities and how to handle exceptions.

Built-in Activities

Workflow Foundation ships with a number of activities. In the next sections, you'll find a summary of the commonly used activities.

Sequence

A container activity that allows you to categorize activities into logical groups, each of which are executed in sequential order. It's important to point out that all activities must be placed inside a Sequence.

DoWhile

Executes the Body activities while its Condition equals True. The Body will be executed at least once.

ForEach<T>

Contains a list of Values and a Body. At run time, the list is iterated and the Body is executed for each value in the list.

If

Chooses a child activity to be executed based on a Boolean expression value. If the condition equals True, the Then activity is executed. If False, the Else activity is executed.

Parallel

Allows parallel execution of its child activities. It completes when all child activities have completed, or when its CompletionCondition evaluates to True.

ParallelForEach<T>

Enumerates the values of its collection, executing an activity for each element in the collection. Similar to the ForEach activity, although each activity is executed in parallel. Also similar to the Parallel activity, ParallelForEach<T> has a CompletionCondition, which can allow early termination should it evaluate to True. The CompletionCondition is evaluated after each iteration is completed.

Pick

Provides event-based control flow modeling. A Pick activity can contain only PickBranches activities. The Pick activity is similar in concept to the C# switch statement, although unlike the switch statement, which executes a branch based on a value, the Pick activity executes based on how an activity completes.

PickBranch

Represents a branch in a Pick. A PickBranch activity can be added only to a Pick activity.

Switch<T>

The Switch<T> activity is similar in concept to the C# switch statement, although rather than executing a branch based on a value, Switch<T> schedules an activity to be executed based on the result of an expression.

While

Executes the Body activites while its Condition equals True.

Working with Data

Arguments

Data is passed in and out of Workflows using arguments. You can define the arguments for each activity in the Workflow Designer by selecting the activity and clicking the Arguments tab at the bottom of the Workflow Designer to display the Arguments Designer, shown in Figure 15-4.

FIGURE 15-4 The Arguments Designer

To create a new argument, simply click in the Create Argument line and define the following properties for your argument:

- **Name** The name of your argument. This will essentially be the property you will set in your workflow from your host application.

- **Direction** Defines whether this argument is passed into the workflow, passed out of the workflow, or both.

- **Argument Type** The type of object you are using. This can be a simple type, such as String, or a complex type you define, such as a custom *Person* class.

- **Default Value** Allows you to set a value in case the argument isn't passed into the Workflow.

To demonstrate how we can use an argument, let's expand on the simple application we built at the beginning of this chapter to use the FirstName argument shown in Figure 15-4.

1. Double-click inside the Text text box and change the value to **"Hello " & FirstName & "!".** The Workflow should now look like Figure 15-5.

2. In Solution Explorer, locate and open the Program.cs file. Modify your code so it looks like this:

```
using System;
using System.Linq;
using System.Activities;
using System.Activities.Statements;
```

```csharp
using System.Collections.Generic;

namespace HelloWorldExample
{
    class Program
    {
        static void Main(string[] args)
        {
            var inArguments = new Dictionary<string, object>();
            inArguments.Add("FirstName", "Jason");

            Workflow1 workflow = new Workflow1();
            WorkflowInvoker.Invoke(workflow, inArguments);

            Console.WriteLine("Press the ENTER key to exit");
            Console.ReadLine();
        }
    }
}
```

FIGURE 15-5 The updated Workflow showing the use of the FirstName argument

Tip Even though I could have simply set the FirstName property of my workflow object, it is best practice to use a *Dictionary* object because not all types will be exposed with properties.

Running the Application

Press F5 to run the application. You should see the following output:

```
Hello Jason!
Press the ENTER key to exit
```

Variables

Variables are storage locations for data and are declared as part of the workflow definition. A variable definition is made using the Variables Designer, shown in Figure 15-6, to specify the name of the variable, the type of the variable, the scope, and (if you want) the default value. Variables can also have modifiers (available in the Properties window), which allow you to set a variable as Read-Only, for example. The lifetime of a variable is equal to the lifetime of the associated activity that contains the variable declaration.

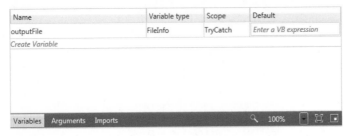

FIGURE 15-6 Declaring a variable in the Variables Designer

Imports

The Imports Designer, a new feature added in WF 4.0, allows you to pick out the namespaces that you want to import, making it easier to resolve types. This saves you from having to fully qualify types when using expressions. An example of importing a namespace using the built-in search functionality is shown in Figure 15-7.

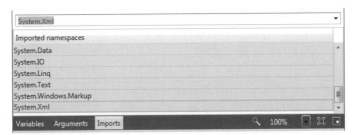

FIGURE 15-7 Importing a new namespace using the Imports Designer

Exception Handling

Like other exception handling that you may be familiar with, workflow exceptions will propogate up the hierarchy until they are caught. If you like, you can choose to rethrow them, which will cause them to continue propogating up the stack until they are caught again.

It's very important to choose where to place exception handling in your application. For example, surrounding your entire workflow in a TryCatch activity might seem like a good idea, but it doesn't allow you to handle exceptions in the proper way and may not provide you with the behavior you expect.

There are two ways of dealing with exceptions in Workflow Foundation. In this section, I will provide a brief overview of each, as well as examples on how to use them.

TryCatch

The TryCatch activity is useful when you want fine control over which activities should react to errors, and indeed *how they should react to errors*. By using the TryCatch activity, you're assuming the activity may run into problems, and you'd like to handle the issue without terminating the workflow. This is very similar to the role of the Try/Catch statement in languages such as C# and VB.NET.

To demonstrate the use of the TryCatch activity, let's modify the application that we've created so far in this chapter.

1. Drag a TryCatch activity from the Toolbox and place it inside the Sequence activity, directly above the WriteLine activity, as shown in Figure 15-8.

FIGURE 15-8 The empty TryCatch activity inside our Workflow

2. Drag a Throw activity from the Toolbox into the Try area of the TryCatch activity.

3. Right-click the Throw activity and choose Properties.

4. Click the ellipses next to the Exception text box to display the Expression Editor, and enter the value, as displayed in Figure 15-9.

5. Click OK.

6. Inside the TryCatch activity, click the Add New Catch line under the Catches category header displayed in bold. This will display a drop-down list, asking which exception type you'd like to catch.

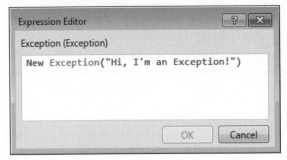

FIGURE 15-9 The Expression Editor for the Throw activity's Exception property

7. Choose System.Exception from the list of options and press Enter.

8. Drag a WriteLine activity into the Exception catch area.

9. Set the Text for the WriteLine activity to match the value shown in Figure 15-10.

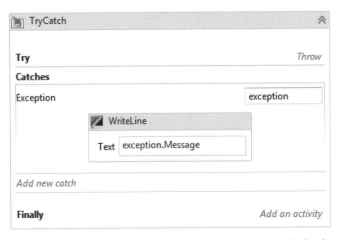

FIGURE 15-10 The value for the WriteLine activity inside our TryCatch activity

10. Press F5 to run the application, and you should see the following output:

```
Hi, I'm an Exception!
Hello Jason!
Press the ENTER key to exit
```

Global Exception Notification

There is often a requirement to be notified of any unhandled exceptions in the workflow. For example, perhaps you want to send an email every time an unhandled exception error occurs in the workflow. You can do this using the OnUnhandledException callback available in the *WorkflowApplication* class. The code here shows an example of how to use the callback in a modified version of the Program.cs file that we have been using in our sample application throughout this chapter.

```
using System;
using System.Linq;
using System.Activities;
using System.Activities.Statements;
using System.Collections.Generic;

namespace HelloWorldExample
{
    class Program
    {
        static void Main(string[] args)
        {
            var inArguments = new Dictionary<string, object>();
            inArguments.Add("FirstName", "Jason");

            Workflow1 workflow = new Workflow1();

            var workflowApp = new WorkflowApplication(workflow, inArguments);

            workflowApp.OnUnhandledException = e =>
                {
                    Console.WriteLine(e.UnhandledException.Message);
                    return UnhandledExceptionAction.Terminate;
                };

            workflowApp.Run();

            Console.WriteLine("Press the ENTER key to exit");
            Console.ReadLine();
        }
    }
}
```

Note Because the workflowApp.Run method executes asynchronously, you may now see the "Press the ENTER key to exit" line before the exception message in the console output.

Custom Activities

As with almost everything in the .NET Framework, you can also extend the provided activities or create the following custom activities to cater to your needs:

- **Composite activities**   A composite activity is essentially the same as a workflow. It allows you to embed other activities inside of it.

- **XAML activities**   These are activities where the logic is encapusulated in the XAML file—hence, the .xaml file extension.

- **Native activities**   Also referred to as code activities, these are activities where the logic is encapusulated in a code file.

Creating a Custom Activity

It's always a best practice to create custom activities in a separate library. Let's go ahead and create a custom WriteLine activity that we can use to replace the default WriteLine activity we've been using in our sample application.

1. In Solution Explorer, right-click the HelloWorldExample solution and select Add\New Project from the context menu.

2. Under Installed Templates, navigate to Visual C#, Workflow and select Activity Library, as shown in Figure 15-11. Enter the name as **HelloWorldExample.CustomActivities** and select a suitable location of your choice.

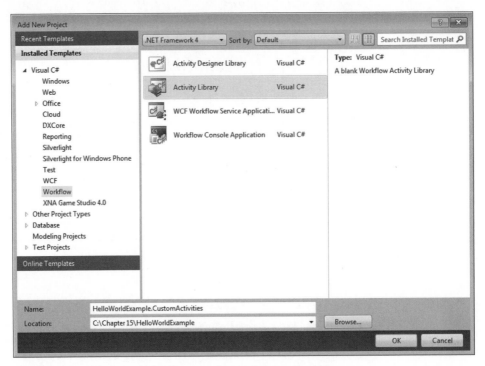

FIGURE 15-11 Adding an Activity Library project to the current solution

3. Click OK. The project will be created, and you should see that the new project has been added to the solution, as shown in Figure 15-12.

4. In Solution Explorer, right-click the Activity1.xaml file and select Delete from the context menu.

5. In Solution Explorer, right-click the HelloWorldExample.CustomActivities project and select Add\New Item . . . from the context menu.

6. Navigate to Workflow in the list of Installed Templates, and then choose Code Activity, as shown in Figure 15-13. Enter the name as **CustomWriteLine.cs.**

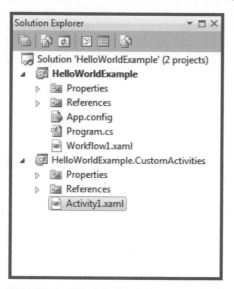

FIGURE 15-12 Solution Explorer showing the newly added project

FIGURE 15-13 Adding the custom code activity to the HelloWorldExample.CustomActivities project

7. Click Add. The file will be created, and the code will show in the editor.

8. Modify the generated code in the CustomWriteLine.cs file so the Execute method looks identical to the following code.

```csharp
protected override void Execute(CodeActivityContext context)
{
    // Obtain the runtime value of the Text input argument
    string text = context.GetValue(this.Text);

    Console.WriteLine("Hello from the Custom WriteLineActivity, {0}!", text);
}
```

Build the solution by pressing Ctrl + Shift + B.

9. Navigate back to the Workflow and delete all activities. Drag a new Sequence activity onto the Workflow Designer.

10. Scroll to the top of the Toolbox and drag the CustomWriteLine activity from the Toolbox onto the Workflow, inside the Sequence activity, as shown in Figure 15-14.

FIGURE 15-14 Adding the CustomWriteLine activity to the Workflow Designer

11. Right-click the CustomWriteLine activity and select Properties. Double-click inside the Text property text box and type FirstName, as shown in Figure 15-15.

FIGURE 15-15 Setting the Text property on the CustomWriteLine activity

12. Press F5 to run the application. You should see the following output in the Console window:

```
Hello from the CustomWriteLine activity, Jason!
Press the ENTER key to exit
```

Note Because the workflowApp.Run method executes asynchronously, you may see the "Press the ENTER key to exit" message in the first line of the console output.

Workflow Extensions

One of the core features of Workflow Foundation is its ability to be hosted in any .NET application domain. Although, since it can operate in different domains, chances are that it's going to need customized execution semantics, which means various aspects of the run-time behaviors need to be externalized from the run time. This is where Workflow Extensions provide a benefit—they enable you, as the developer, to add behavior to the run time with custom code.

The two extensions that the run time is aware of are the tracking and persistence extensions.

Persistence

The persistence extension provides the core functionality for saving workflow state to permanent store (such as a database) and retrieving that state when needed. As part of the standard functionality, the persistence extension supports Microsoft SQL Server, but extensions can be written to support other databases or storage formats.

Persistence is useful for long-running workflows, load balancing, and fault tolerance.

Tracking

Once a workflow is complete, the state of a workflow is often deleted from the data store because it is no longer required. Having information about what a workflow is currently doing can be useful in managing a workflow and gaining insight into a process. This is where tracking comes into play. The ability to track what is happening in your application is, after all, one of the compelling features of Workflow Foundation.

Tracking consists of two primary components—participants and profiles. A *profile* defines the events and data that you want to track. A *participant* is an extension that can be added to the run time, whose job it is to process tracking records as they are emitted. This can be accomplished by deriving from the *TrackingParticipant* base class, which defines a property to provide a tracking profile as well as a *Track* method to handle the tracking.

Putting It All Together—Workflow Foundation Image Resizer Sample Application

This sample project has been designed to utilize some of the concepts you're learned so far in this chapter. This project is fairly extensive, with a large amount of code, so in order to save you some time, you can also download a copy of the completed sample from

Overview

This application, exposed as a console application, allows you to resize, and optionally automatically attempt to correct the orientation, of photographs in a folder that you specify.

Some of the key workflow concepts that will be demonstrated are custom activities, error handling, parallelization, arguments, and variables.

Let's go ahead and get started!

Building the Application

1. Open Visual Studio 2010.

2. Click the New Project link.

3. Under Installed Templates, navigate to Visual C#, Workflow and select the Workflow Console Application, as shown in Figure 15-16. Enter the name as **WFImageResizer** and select a suitable location of your choice.

FIGURE 15-16 Creating a new Workflow project

4. Click OK. The project will be created, and you should see an empty Workflow Designer, as shown in Figure 15-17.

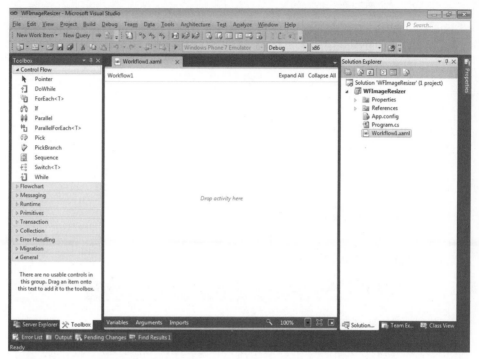

FIGURE 15-17 The Visual Studio IDE showing an empty Workflow Designer window

5. In Solution Explorer, right-click the solution, select Add, and then select New Project.

6. Under Installed Templates, navigate to Visual C#, Workflow and select the Activity Library, as shown in Figure 15-18. Enter the name as **WFImageResizer.Components** and select a suitable location of your choice.

7. Click OK. The project will now be added to the solution.

8. In the WFImageResizer.Components project, locate the Activity1.xaml file. Right-click and select Delete from the context menu. Click OK to confirm the deletion.

9. Right-click the WFImageResizer.Components project and select Add New Item.

10. Under Installed Templates, navigate to Visual C# Items, Workflow and select the Activity item. Enter the name as **ResizeImageActivity.xaml** and then click Add.

11. Right-click the WFImageResizer.Components project and select AddNew Item.

12. Under Installed Templates, navigate to Visual C# Items, Workflow and select the Code Activity item. Enter the name as **ResizeImage.cs** and then click Add.

13. Right-click the WFImageResizer.Components project and select Add New Item.

14. Under Installed Templates, navigate to Visual C# Items, Code and select the Class item. Enter the name as **Options.cs** and click Add.

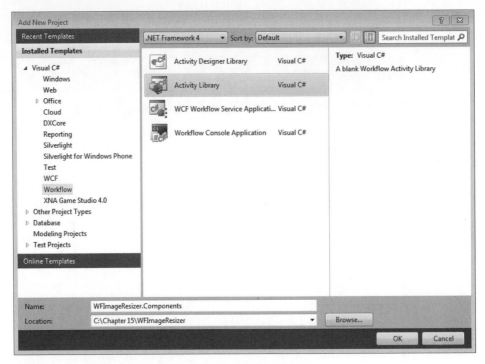

FIGURE 15-18 Adding the Activity Library project to the solution

15. Your solution should now look identical to Figure 15-19.

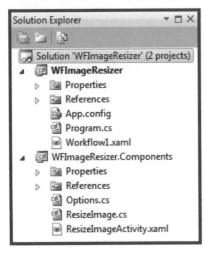

FIGURE 15-19 The solution with all projects and files added

16. Right-click the WFImageResizer.Components project and select Add Reference.

17. Add a reference to the System.Drawing (version 4.0.0.0) assembly.

18. In Solution Explorer, locate and open the Options.cs file. Modify the code to match the following code.

```csharp
using System;
using System.Collections.Generic;
using System.Linq;
using System.Text;
using System.IO;

namespace ImageResizer.Components
{
    public class Options
    {
        private List<FileInfo> files;

        public string SourceDirectory { get; set; }
        public string TargetDirectory { get; set; }
        public bool AutoRotate { get; set; }
        public bool Parallelize { get; set; }
        public int Height { get; set; }
        public int Width { get; set; }

        public List<FileInfo> Files
        {
            get
            {
                if (files == null || files.Count == 0)
                {
                    files = new List<FileInfo>();
                    var imagepaths = Directory.GetFiles(SourceDirectory, "*.jpg");

                    foreach (string path in imagepaths)
                    {
                        FileInfo fileInfo = new FileInfo(path);
                        files.Add(fileInfo);
                    }
                }

                return files;
            }
        }
    }
}
```

19. In Solution Explorer, locate and open the ResizeImage.cs file. Modify the code to match the following code:

```csharp
using System;
using System.Activities;
using System.Drawing.Imaging;
using System.IO;
using System.Linq;
```

```
namespace ImageResizer.Components
{
    public sealed class ResizeImage : AsyncCodeActivity
    {
        public InArgument<FileInfo> InputFile { get; set; }
        public InArgument<Options> Options { get; set; }
        public OutArgument<FileInfo> OutputFile { get; set; }

        protected override IAsyncResult BeginExecute(AsyncCodeActivityContext context,
AsyncCallback callback, object state)
        {
            // Obtain the runtime value of the Text input argument
            FileInfo image = context.GetValue(this.InputFile);
            Options options = context.GetValue(this.Options);

            Func<FileInfo, Options, AsyncCodeActivityContext, FileInfo> resizeDelegate =
new Func<FileInfo, Options, AsyncCodeActivityContext, FileInfo>(ResizeImageFile);
            context.UserState = resizeDelegate;
            IAsyncResult result = resizeDelegate.BeginInvoke(image, options, context,
callback, state);

            return result;
        }

        protected override void EndExecute(AsyncCodeActivityContext context,
IAsyncResult result)
        {
            Func<FileInfo, Options, AsyncCodeActivityContext, FileInfo> resizeDelegate =
context.UserState as Func<FileInfo, Options, AsyncCodeActivityContext, FileInfo>;
            FileInfo resizedFile = resizeDelegate.EndInvoke(result);

            OutputFile.Set(context, resizedFile);
        }

        public FileInfo ResizeImageFile(FileInfo image, Options options,
AsyncCodeActivityContext context)
        {
            // Get the image codec info
            ImageCodecInfo CodecInfo = GetEncoderInfo("image/jpeg");

            //Save the bitmap as a JPEG file with quality level 75.
            System.Drawing.Imaging.Encoder encoder = System.Drawing.Imaging.Encoder
.Quality;
            EncoderParameter encoderParameter = new System.Drawing.Imaging
.EncoderParameter(encoder, 100L);
            EncoderParameters encoderParameters = new EncoderParameters();
            encoderParameters.Param[0] = encoderParameter;

            System.Drawing.Image img = null;
            System.Drawing.Bitmap bitmap = null;
            string savePath = string.Empty;

            try
            {
                img = System.Drawing.Image.FromFile(image.FullName);
```

```
            if (options.AutoRotate == true)
            {
                var pi = img.PropertyItems.FirstOrDefault(p => p.Id == 0x0112);
                if (pi != null)
                {
                    switch (pi.Value[0])
                    {
                        case 6:
                            img.RotateFlip(System.Drawing.RotateFlipType
.Rotate90FlipNone);

                            break;
                        case 8:
                            img.RotateFlip(System.Drawing.RotateFlipType
.Rotate270FlipNone);

                            break;
                        default:
                            break;
                    }
                }
            }

            //set the width and height, using the original values if not specified
            int width = options.Width == 0 ? img.Width : options.Width;
            int height = options.Height == 0 ? img.Height : options.Height;

            if (img.Width < img.Height)
            {
                int tempWidth = width;
                width = height;
                height = tempWidth;
            }

            bitmap = new System.Drawing.Bitmap(img, new System.Drawing.Size(width,
height));

            //make sure the target directory exists. If not, create it!
            if (!Directory.Exists(options.TargetDirectory))
                Directory.CreateDirectory(options.TargetDirectory);

            savePath = Path.Combine(options.TargetDirectory, image.Name);
            bitmap.Save(savePath, CodecInfo, encoderParameters);

            if (!string.IsNullOrWhiteSpace(savePath))
                return new FileInfo(savePath);

            return null;
        }
        catch
        {
            throw new Exception
                (
                    string.Format("Cannot resize '{0} as it is not a valid image
file!", image.Name)
                );
        }
```

```
        finally
        {
            if (bitmap != null)
                bitmap.Dispose();

            if (img != null)
                img.Dispose();
        }
    }

    private static ImageCodecInfo GetEncoderInfo(String mimeType)
    {
        var encoders = ImageCodecInfo.GetImageEncoders();

        var codec = Array.Find<ImageCodecInfo>(
            encoders,
            e => e.MimeType.Equals(mimeType, StringComparison.
CurrentCultureIgnoreCase)
            );

        if (codec != null)
            return codec;

        return null;
    }

  }
}
```

20. Build the solution. This is to verify the changes so far and to add the activity to the Toolbox.

21. In Solution Explorer, locate and open the ResizeImageActivity.xaml file.

22. Open the Arguments Designer and add the following arguments:

TABLE 12-1 The Required Arguments for the ResizeImageActivity Activity

Name	Direction	Argument Type	Default Value
Options	In	ImageResizer.Components.Options	
InputFile	In	System.IO.FileInfo	

 Note When adding these arguments, you will need to select custom Argument Types. This can be accomplished by selecting the Browse For Types … option in the combo box that appears after selecting the Argument Type cell in the Arguments Designer.

23. In the Toolbox, select the Error Handling tab and drag a TryCatch activity onto the Workflow Designer.

24. With the TryCatch activity selected in the Workflow Designer, add the following variable using the Variable Designer.

TABLE 12-2 The Required Variable for the TryCatch Activity

Name	Variable Type	Scope	Default
outputFile	System.IO.FileInfo	TryCatch	

25. In the Toolbox, click the Control Flow tab and drag a Sequence activity onto the Workflow Designer, inside the Try section of the TryCatch activity. Your workflow should now look the same as Figure 15-20.

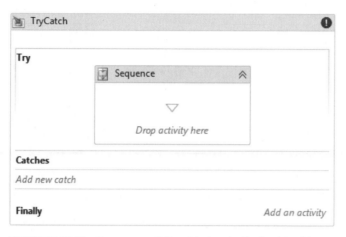

FIGURE 15-20 The Sequence activity added to the TryCatch activity

26. In the Toolbox, click the ImageResizer.Components tab and drag the ResizeImage activity on the Workflow Designer, inside the Sequence activity that you just added.

27. Right-click the ResizeImage activity and choose Properties.

28. Enter the necessary property values for the ResizeImage activity as shown in Figure 15-21.

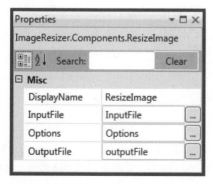

FIGURE 15-21 Setting the required values of the ResizeImage activity

29. In the Toolbox, click the Primitives tab and drag the WriteLine activity on the Workflow Designer, still inside the Sequence activity and just below the ResizeImage activity that you just added.

30. Right-click the WriteLine activity and choose Properties.

31. Click the ellipses next to the Text text box to display the Expression Editor, and enter the value, as displayed in Figure 15-22.

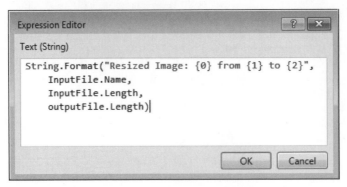

FIGURE 15-22 Setting the value of the WriteLine activity

32. Click OK. This completes the changes in the Try section of the TryCatch activity.

33. Click the Add New Catch link in the Catches section of the TryCatch activity.

34. Choose System.Exception from the drop-down list that appears and press Enter.

35. In the Toolbox, click the Primitives tab and drag the WriteLine activity on the Workflow Designer, inside the Catch block you just created.

36. Double-click the Text area in the WriteLine activity and type **exception.Message** as the value. Your workflow should now look the same as Figure 15-23.

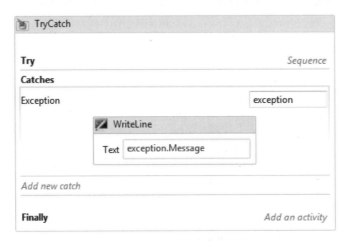

FIGURE 15-23 Completing the Catch block by setting the value of the WriteLine activity

37. Right-click the WFImageResizer project and select Add Reference.

38. Add a reference to the WFImageResizer.Components project.

39. Build the solution.

40. In Solution Explorer, locate and open the Workflow1.xaml file in the WFImageResizer project.

41. Open the Arguments Designer and add the following argument:

TABLE 15-3 **The Required Argument for the Workflow1.xaml File**

Name	Direction	Argument Type	Default Value
Options	In	ImageResizer.Components.Options	

42. In the Toolbox, click the Control Flow tab and drag a Sequence activity onto the Workflow Designer.

43. In the Toolbox, click the Control Flow tab and drag an If activity onto the Workflow Designer, inside the Sequence activity that you just added.

44. In the If Condition, enter `Options.Parallelize = True`.

45. In the Toolbox, click the Control Flow tab and drag a Sequence activity onto the Workflow Designer, inside both the Then and Else statements of the If activity.

46. In the Toolbox, click the Primitives tab and drag the WriteLine activity on the Workflow Designer, inside the sequence you just added for the Then statement.

47. Double-click the Text area in the WriteLine activity and type **"Resizing Images in parallel!"** as the value.

48. In the Toolbox, click the Primitives tab and drag the WriteLine activity on the Workflow Designer, inside the sequence that you just added for the Else statement.

49. Double-click the Text area in the WriteLine activity and type **"Resizing Images sequentially!"** as the value.

50. Your workflow should now look the same as Figure 15-24.

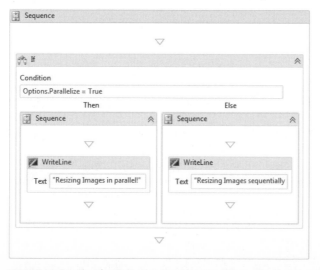

FIGURE 15-24 The If activity showing the Condition as well as the start of each sequence.

51. In the Toolbox, select the Control Flow tab and drag a ParallelForEach<T> activity onto the Workflow Designer, inside the Then statement of the If activity, just below the WriteLine activity.

51. Right-click the ParallelForEach<T> activity and change the TypeArgument property to have a value of *System.IO.FileInfo*.

53. Double-click the first text box in the ParallelForEach<T> activity and enter **file** as the value.

54. Double-click the second text box in the ParallelForEach<T> activity and enter **Options .Files** as the value.

55. In the Toolbox, click the WFImageResizer.Components tab and drag the ResizeImageActivity activity onto the Workflow Designer, inside the Body of the ParallelForEach<T> activity that you just added.

56. Right-click the ResizeImageActivity activity and select Properties.

57. Enter **file** as the value for the InputFile property.

58. Enter **Options** as the value for the Options property.

59. The completed Then sequence should now look identical to Figure 15-25.

FIGURE 15-25 The completed Then sequence in the Then statement of the If activity

60. In the Toolbox, click the Control Flow tab and drag a ForEach<T> activity onto the Workflow Designer, inside the Else statement of the If activity, just below the WriteLine activity.

61. Right-click the ForEach<T> activity and change the TypeArgument property to have a value of *System.IO.FileInfo*.

62. Double-click the first text box in the ForEach<T> activity and enter **file** as the value.

63. Double-click the second text box in the ForEach<T> activity and enter **Options.Files** as the value.

64. In the Toolbox, select the WFImageResizer.Components tab and drag the ResizeImageActivity activity onto the Workflow Designer, inside the Body of the ForEach<T> activity that you just added.

65. Right-click the ResizeImageActivity activity and select Properties.

66. Enter **file** as the value for the InputFile property.

67. Enter **Options** as the value for the Options property.

68. The completed Else sequence should now look identical to Figure 15-26.

FIGURE 15-26 The completed Else sequence in the Else statement of the If activity

69. In Solution Explorer, locate and open the Program.cs file. Modify the code to match the following code.

```
using System;
using System.Activities;
using System.Collections.Generic;
using System.IO;
using ImageResizer.Components;

namespace WFImageResizer
{
    class Program
    {
        private static Options options;
```

```csharp
static void Main(string[] args)
{
    options = new Options();

    if (ParseArgs(args))
    {
        var inArguments = new Dictionary<string, object>();
        inArguments.Add("Options", options);

        Workflow1 workflow = new Workflow1();
        WorkflowInvoker.Invoke(workflow, inArguments);
    }
    Console.WriteLine("Press ENTER to exit");
    Console.ReadLine();
}

private static bool ParseArgs(string[] args)
{
    int intResult;
    bool boolResult;

    foreach (var arg in args)
    {
        string[] argParts = arg.Split('=');
        if (argParts.Length != 2)
            return false;

        switch (argParts[0].ToLower())
        {
            case "/source":
                options.SourceDirectory = argParts[1];
                break;
            case "/target":
                options.TargetDirectory = argParts[1];
                break;
            case "/width":
                if (!int.TryParse(argParts[1], out intResult))
                {
                    Console.WriteLine("Width must be numeric!");
                    return false;
                }
                options.Width = int.Parse(argParts[1]);
                break;
            case "/height":
                if (!int.TryParse(argParts[1], out intResult))
                {
                    Console.WriteLine("Height must be numeric!");
                    return false;
                }
                options.Height = int.Parse(argParts[1]);
                break;
            case "/autorotate":
                if (!bool.TryParse(argParts[1], out boolResult))
                {
                    Console.WriteLine("AutoRotate must be either 'True' or
```

```
'False'!");
                                    return false;
                    }
                    options.AutoRotate = bool.Parse(argParts[1]);
                    break;
                case "/parallelize":
                    if (!bool.TryParse(argParts[1], out boolResult))
                    {
                        Console.WriteLine("Parallelize must be either
'True' or 'False'!");
                        return false;
                    }
                    options.Parallelize = bool.Parse(argParts[1]);
                    break;
            }
        }

        if (string.IsNullOrWhiteSpace(options.SourceDirectory) || string.
IsNullOrWhiteSpace(options.TargetDirectory))
        {
            Console.WriteLine("USAGE: WFImageResizer /Source:DIR /Target:DIR [/
AutoRotate:TRUE|FALSE] [/Width:SIZE] [/Height:SIZE] [/Parallelize:TRUE|FALSE]");
            Console.WriteLine();
            Console.WriteLine("Options:");
            Console.WriteLine();
            Console.WriteLine("/AutoRotate:[TRUE|FALSE]\tAutomatically attempts to
rotate images to the correct orientation.");
            Console.WriteLine("/Width:[SIZE]\t\t\tSets the width (in pixels) of
the target image.");
            Console.WriteLine("/Height:[SIZE]\t\t\tSets the height (in pixels) of
the target image.");
            Console.WriteLine("/Parallelize:[TRUE|FALSE]\tParallelizes the
resizing operation to increase performance.");
            Console.WriteLine();
            return false;
        }

        if (!Directory.Exists(options.SourceDirectory))
        {
            Console.WriteLine("The source Directory '{0}' does not exist!",
options.SourceDirectory);
            return false;
        }

        if (!Directory.Exists(options.SourceDirectory))
        {
            Console.WriteLine("The Target Directory '{0}' does not exist!",
options.TargetDirectory);
            return false;
        }

        return true;
    }
  }
}
```

Running the Application

Press F5 to run the application. You should see the following output:

```
USAGE: WFImageResizer /Source:DIR /Target:DIR [/AutoRotate:TRUE|FALSE]
[/Width:SIZE] [/Height:SIZE] [/Parallelize:TRUE|FALSE]

Options:

/AutoRotate:[TRUE|FALSE]        Automatically attempts to rotate images
to the correct orientation.

/Width:[SIZE]                   Sets the width (in pixels) of the
target image.

/Height:[SIZE]                  Sets the height (in pixels) of the
target image.

/Parallelize:[TRUE|FALSE]       Parallelizes the resizing operation to
increase performance.

Press any key to exit
```

> **Tip** If you have trouble running the application, one important setting to check is the Target Framework setting. To do this, perform the following steps:
>
> 1. In Solution Explorer, right-click the WFImageResizer project and select Properties.
> 2. Click the Application tab.
> 3. Verify that the Target Framework is set to .NET Framework 4.0. Often, this is set to .NET Framework 4 Client Profile, which is insufficient for our requirements.

To run the application manually, simply open a command prompt and navigate to the output folder of the WFImageResizer project and manually run the WFImageResizer.exe executable. This will show the output above if run without any arguments, so you'll need to make sure to pass at least the source and target directories as options.

Debugging the Application

In order to assist with debugging the application, you will need to set some default settings. Without these settings, the application will continue to show the Help screen (showing example usage) and won't progress any further. Luckily, Visual Studio provides a way to pass parameters to the application when debugging by providing an option called Command line arguments.

1. In Solution Explorer, right-click the WFImageResizer project and select Properties.

2. Click the Debug tab.

3. Enter the following text in the Command line arguments text box, making sure to modify the Source and Target directories as applicable for your system:

   ```
   /source=c:\images /target=c:\images\resized /autorotate=true /width=320 /height=240
   ```

> **Note** In the arguments above, I have chosen c:\images as the path for my photos. You should change this to reflect the path of the photos stored on your file system.

4. Press F5 to run the application. You should now see output showing the images being resized.

Summary

The goal of this chapter was to provide you with an introduction to Workflow Foundation and demonstrate how it can be used in conjunction with, or indeed independently of, Team Build. Hopefully, you now have a basic understanding of the technology and the tools required to begin exploring and using the capabilities of Workflow Foundation. Good luck!

Chapter 16
Process Template Customization

This chapter will give you the basics needed to take an existing build process template and customize it or to create a build process template from scratch. This customization process is critical to making the most of Team Build and to automate your end-to-end build process. Example build process templates and additional guidance are available in the ALM Rangers Build Customization Guide which will be available in early 2011 at *http://msdn.microsoft.com/ en-us/vstudio/ee358786.aspx*.

Getting Started

While it is possible to open and edit process template Extensible Application Markup Language (XAML) files directly (often referred to as "naked XAML"), you're limited to using the activities that ship with Team Build and Workflow Foundation. In this section, we'll describe how to set up your development environment to enable a full fidelity experience for creating, testing, debugging, and deploying custom process templates and activities.

Creating a Process Template Library

The first step is to create a Workflow Activity library that will contain our custom process templates. Even if you only ever plan to customize the process templates that ship with Team Build, you should still add them to a Workflow Activity Library so that you can use custom activities.

1. In Microsoft Visual Studio 2010, click File, New Project….
2. Ensure that .NET Framework 4 is selected, as shown in Figure 16-1.
3. Expand your preferred language and click Workflow.
4. Select Activity Library.
5. Enter a Name (for example, Processes), verify the Location, and click OK.

At this point, you should have a solution containing a workflow Activity Library called Processes.

By default, workflow Activity Libraries are created that target the .NET Framework 4 Client Profile. You will need to change that profile to the .NET Framework 4 Full Profile by doing the following:

1. Right-click the Processes project, and click Properties.
2. Click the Application tab.
3. Change the Target Framework from .NET Framework 4 Client Profile, as shown in Figure 16-2, to .NET Framework 4.

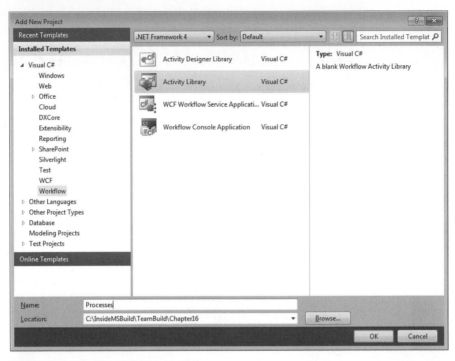

FIGURE 16-1 Selecting .NET Framework 4

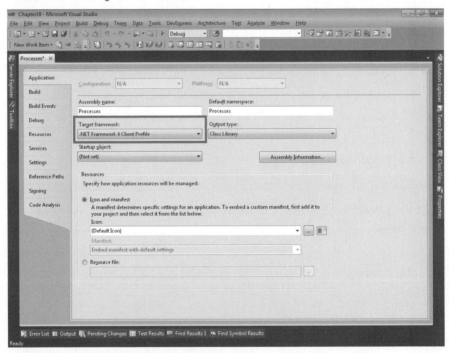

FIGURE 16-2 Changing the Target Framework

4. Click Yes in the Target Framework Change message box that appears.

To build your process template library, you will need to add references to the following assemblies:

- Microsoft.TeamFoundation.Build.Client (%ProgramFiles(x86)%\Microsoft Visual Studio 10.0\Common7\IDE\ReferenceAssemblies\v2.0\Microsoft.TeamFoundation.Build .Client.dll)

- Microsoft.TeamFoundation.Build.Workflow (%ProgramFiles(x86)%\Microsoft Visual Studio 10.0\Common7\IDE\PrivateAssemblies)

- Microsoft.TeamFoundation.TestImpact.BuildIntegration (%ProgramFiles(x86)%\ Microsoft Visual Studio 10.0\Common7\IDE\PrivateAssemblies)

- Microsoft.TeamFoundation.TestImpact.Client (%windir%\assembly\GAC_MSIL\Microsoft .TeamFoundation.TestImpact.Client\10.0.0.0__b03f5f7f11d50a3a\Microsoft .TeamFoundation.TestImpact.Client.dll)

- Microsoft.TeamFoundation.VersionControl.Client (%ProgramFiles(x86)%\Microsoft Visual Studio 10.0\Common7\IDE\ReferenceAssemblies\v2.0\Microsoft .TeamFoundation.VersionControl.Client.dll)

- Microsoft.TeamFoundation.WorkItemTracking.Client (%ProgramFiles(x86)%\Microsoft Visual Studio 10.0\Common7\IDE\ReferenceAssemblies\v2.0\Microsoft .TeamFoundation.WorkItemTracking.Client.dll)

- System.Drawing (%ProgramFiles(x86)%\Reference Assemblies\Microsoft\Framework\ .NETFramework\v4.0\System.Drawing.dll)

- System.Activities.Presentation (%ProgramFiles(x86)%\Reference Assemblies\Microsoft\ Framework\.NETFramework\v4.0\System.Actvities.Presentation.dll)

- PresentationFramework (%ProgramFiles(x86)%\Reference Assemblies\Microsoft\ Framework\.NETFramework\v4.0\PresentationFramework.dll)

- WindowsBase (%ProgramFiles(x86)%\Reference Assemblies\Microsoft\Framework\ .NETFramework\v4.0\WindowsBase.dll)

- Microsoft.TeamFoundation (%ProgramFiles(x86)%\Microsoft Visual Studio 10.0\ Common7\IDE\ReferenceAssemblies\v2.0\Microsoft.TeamFoundation.dll)

- Microsoft.TeamFoundation.VersionControl.Common (%ProgramFiles(x86)%\Microsoft Visual Studio 10.0\Common7\IDE\ReferenceAssemblies\v2.0\Microsoft .TeamFoundation.VersionControl.Common.dll)

Once you add these references, you should check each of their properties to ensure that they're not copied to the project's output directory, by doing the following:

1. In Solution Explorer, expand the Process Template Library, and then References. If you're using Microsoft Visual Basic, you'll need to click the Show All Files button at the top of the Solution Explorer to see the References node.

2. Select the first reference you added and open the Properties window (by pressing F4 or clicking View, Properties Window).

3. Set the Copy Local property to False, if it isn't already, as shown in Figure 16-3.

4. Repeat steps 1–3 for each of the references that you added.

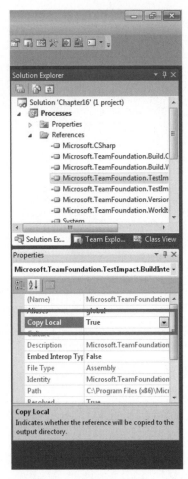

FIGURE 16-3 Setting the Copy Local property

If you want to customize a process template that ships with Team Build, such as DefaultTemplate.xaml, you need to add it to your process template library as follows:

1. Download DefaultTemplate.xaml from the BuildProcessTemplates folder in the root of your Team Project's version control folder.

2. Add it to the project by right-clicking the process template library, clicking Add, Existing Item, browsing to DefaultTemplate.xaml, and clicking Add.

If you want to create a process template from scratch, you need to add an empty Activity to the process template library, as follows:

1. Right-click the process template library and click Add, New Item.
2. Select Workflow, and then select Activity.
3. Enter a Name for the process template, and click Add.

If you open DefaultTemplate.xaml (or any other process template that ships with Team Build), you'll find two new tabs in the Toolbox:

- Team Foundation Build Activities
- Team Foundation LabManagement Activities

However, if you open your new process template, you'll find that these tabs don't exist. The problem is a chicken-and-egg one: These tabs are shown only if the process template contains a Team Foundation Build workflow activity, but you can't add a Team Foundation Build workflow activity unless they're in the Toolbox.

To work around this issue, we need to add any Team Foundation Build workflow activity manually to the process template. We'll use the GetBuildDetail activity because it has no required inputs. We do this as follows:

1. Open the process template in the Workflow Designer.
2. Click Imports at the bottom of the Workflow Designer surface, enter **Microsoft .TeamFoundation.Build.Workflow.Activities,** and press Enter to add the namespace to the list of Imported Namespaces.
3. Save the process template.
4. Click View, Code to open the process template in the XML editor.
5. Within the Activity element, add the XAML:

```
<Sequence>
  <mtbwa:GetBuildDetail />
</Sequence>
```

Now, when you switch back to the Workflow Designer, the Team Foundation Build workflow activities will be shown in the Toolbox and you can drag the activities you need and remove the temporary GetBuildDetail activity from your process template.

If you build the process template library and then open the project's output directory, you'll find (as you'd expect) a compiled binary. However, as we'll discuss later in this chapter when we deploy process templates, it's the naked XAML files themselves that we need to deploy. Although we could manually copy the XAML files from the project directory, it would be ideal if they were automatically copied to the output directory so that when we build our process template library using Team Build, the XAML files are dropped to the drop folder.

At first you might think you can achieve this by setting the Copy To Output Directory property for the XAML file to Copy Always or Copy If Newer. Unfortunately, this works only if we change the Build Action from XamlAppDef to Content, and by doing this, we'll lose compile time validation of our process templates. So we can work around this by creating a Post-Build Event that will copy the process templates to the output directory:

1. Right-click the Process Template Library in the Solution Explorer and click Properties.

2. Click the Build Events tab.

3. In the Post-Build Event Command Line box, add this code:

```
del "$(TargetDir)$(TargetName).*"
copy /Y "$(ProjectDir)\*.xaml" "$(TargetDir)"
```

4. Save and close the project properties.

Because we'll never deploy the compiled assembly for the process template library but still need to produce it to get compile time validation, the first command will delete the compiled assembly so that it doesn't get dropped, cause confusion, or accidentally get deployed. The second command will copy any XAML files in the root of the project to the project's output directory. If you create subdirectories in your process template library, then you will need to replace this with XCopy.

Once this is done, if you compile your process template library and open your output directory, you shouldn't find anything except the XAML files that you added to it.

Creating a Custom Activity Library

Once you've created a Process Template Library, you're in a place where you can create customized process templates using existing workflow activities. If you want to create custom activities, then you'll also need to create a Custom Activity Library.

You might be tempted to just add your custom activities to the Process Template Library, but this won't work. If you add a custom activity to the same project as the process template, the Workflow Designer will add an unqualified reference (that is, one that doesn't specify the assembly name) when you use it (because it is in the same project). However, process templates are deployed as naked XAML files and the custom activities as compiled binaries, so when Team Build tries to resolve the custom activities in the process template, it will be unable to find them because of these unqualified references.

The good news is that because both process template libraries and custom activity libraries are simply workflow activity libraries, you can create custom activity libraries exactly the same way as you created the process template library in the previous procedure:

1. Create a workflow activity library.

2. Switch the project from the Client Profile to the Full Profile.

3. Add references to the required assemblies.

Note You shouldn't add the Post-Build Event that was added to the process template because custom activity libraries are deployed compiled rather than as naked XAML.

Once you've created the custom activity library, you can add a reference to it from the process template library so that you can use your custom activities:

1. Right-click the Process Template Library in Solution Explorer and click Add Reference.

2. Click the Projects tab in the Add Reference dialog.

3. Select your Custom Activity Library and click OK.

You can now use any custom activities that you create in your custom process templates.

Process Parameters

Process parameters provide a way to configure a process template on a per-definition or even per-build basis. This allows you to make process templates somewhat generic so they can be reused across multiple definitions. For example, in the Default Template described in Chapter 14, "Team Build Deep Dive," the projects to be built are specified using a process parameter, allowing this one process template to be used for building different projects.

Process parameters appear in the user interface on the Process tab when editing a build definition, and they appear on the Parameters tab when queuing a build. It is also possible to create custom editors to provide a richer user experience when editing process parameter values; this is discussed in more detail in the section entitled "User Interface," later in this chapter. When authoring a process template, you can choose whether each process parameter will appear when editing a build definition, queuing a build, or both. This is discussed in more detail in the section entitled "Metadata," later in this chapter.

Defining

Process parameters are defined by the In arguments to the process template. To add a new process parameter, do the following:

1. Open the process template in the Workflow Designer.

2. Click the Arguments tab at the bottom of the Designer.

3. Scroll to the bottom of the arguments list and click Create Argument. A new row will be added to the list of arguments.

4. Enter a Name, leave the Direction as its default setting of In, select an Argument Type, and, if you want, provide a Default Value.

> **Note** When specifying defaults for enumerations, you should specify the fully qualified value (namespace, type, and value) rather than the unqualified value (just type and value). For example, specify Microsoft.TeamFoundation.Build.Workflow.BuildVerbosity.Normal instead of BuildVerbosity.Normal.

In Figure 16-4, we've defined a new process parameter called FirstVersion of type String with a default value of "1.0.0.0".

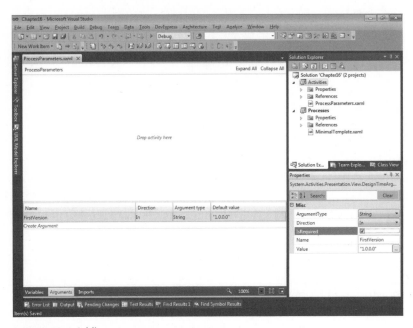

FIGURE 16-4 Adding a process parameter

Once we deploy this customized process template, when we edit the build definition, we'll see our new process parameter as shown in Figure 16-5.

Process parameters aren't restricted to simple types (such as Boolean, string, and integer); they also can be complex types (such as enumerations, arrays, and custom classes) that can be further comprised of simple types and other complex types. Process parameters are stored against the build definition or the build itself by serializing them as XAML, so the only requirement is that your complex type supports this.

Any custom types that you create need to be accessible to Visual Studio and the build controller and build agents, by either registering them in the global assembly cache (GAC) or, preferably, by checking the assembly containing them into version control and configuring the controller with the appropriate version control path. This is discussed in more detail in the section entitled "Deployment," later in this chapter.

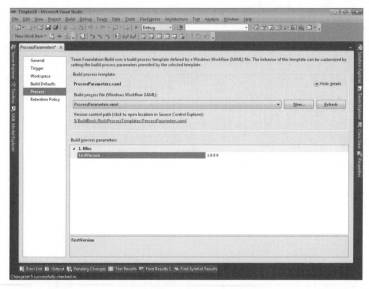

FIGURE 16-5 Process parameter in edit build definition

Metadata

By default, any process parameters you define will be shown in the Misc category, use the argument's name as the process parameter name, have no description, and be shown when both editing a build definition and queuing a build.

Team Build provides a way to attach additional metadata to arguments that allows you to customize the category it's displayed in; the name and description that's displayed; whether the process parameter is available when editing a build definition, queuing a build, or both; whether or not it's required; and the editor to use to edit its value.

The first step is to add an argument called Metadata in which to store the metadata (if you're editing an existing process template, it may already have this argument; if so, skip this procedure).

1. Open the process template in the Workflow Designer.
2. Click the Arguments tab at the bottom of the Designer.
3. Scroll to the bottom of the arguments list and click Create Argument. A new row will be added to the list of arguments.
4. Enter the Name **Metadata**, select the Direction as Property, and browse for the Argument Type Microsoft.TeamFoundation.Build.Workflow. ProcessParameterMetadataCollection.

The argument should look like Figure 16-6 when you're finished.

Once the process template has a Metadata property, you can add, edit, and delete metadata by clicking the ellipsis in the Default Value column, which will produce the Process Parameter Metadata Editor dialog shown in Figure 16-7.

The Parameter Name field is used to link the metadata entry to the argument it relates to and should match the argument's name.

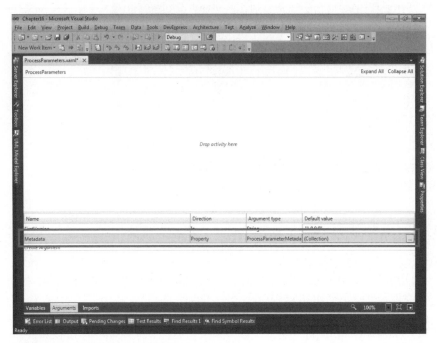

FIGURE 16-6 Metadata argument

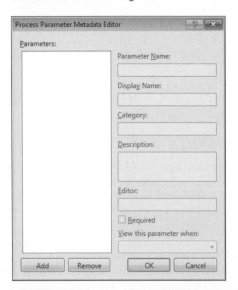

FIGURE 16-7 Process Parameter Metadata Editor

The Display Name field provides a friendly name for the argument to be displayed in the user interface.

The Category field specifies the category that the argument should be grouped under in the user interface. If left blank, the argument will be shown in the Misc category. If you have arguments in a category called Advanced, the category will be collapsed by default, and all other categories will be expanded by default.

Categories are shown in the user interface in alphabetical order by default. You can specify to order category names by prefix with *#ddd,* where *d* is any digit. For example, the category #020Required will display in the user interface as "Required" and positioned before the category #030Optional, which will display as "Optional" even though "Optional" comes before "Required" alphabetically. Categories that don't have a numeric prefix will be listed after those that do. This numeric prefix is independent of the number that is shown before the category name in the user interface, which is based entirely on the order they're displayed.

The Description field provides additional information about the argument, which will be displayed at the bottom of the user interface, as shown in Figure 16-8.

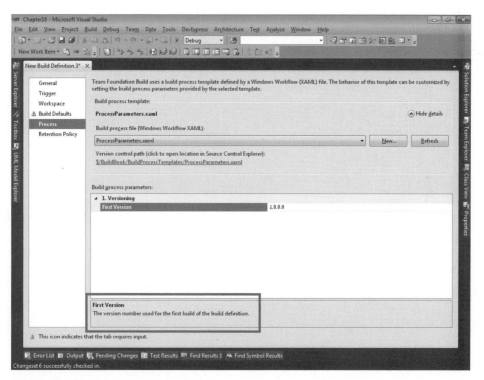

FIGURE 16-8 Process parameter description

The Editor field specifies the editor class that will be used to specify the value for custom types in the user interface. The editor class is specified in the standard .NET *TypeName,*

AssemblyName form, such as *MyEditors.VersionNumberEditor, MyEditors*. Custom editors are discussed in more detail in the section entitled "User Interface," later in this chapter.

The Required field specifies whether the argument is required. If the argument has a default value, then making it required means that the value specified needs to differ from the default value. If a required field isn't provided, the Process tab and the field in question will be marked with a warning icon, as shown in Figure 16-9. If required fields aren't specified, the build definition can still be saved, and you can even queue a build, but the build will fail with an error that the required argument hasn't been provided.

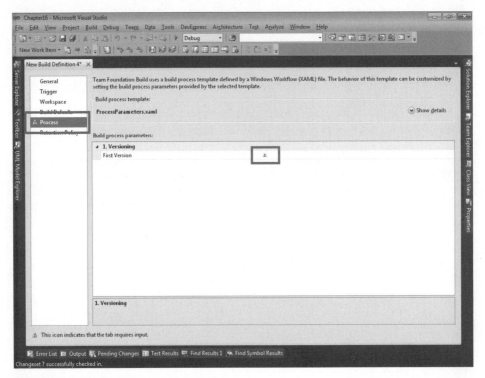

FIGURE 16-9 Required process parameters

The View This Parameter When field specifies when the argument is visible. It can be set to Never, Only When Editing A Definition (which will show on the Process tab of the definition), Only When Queuing A Build (which will show on the Parameters tab of the Queue Build dialog), or Always (which will show on both).

User Interface

Team Build provides default editors for a number of built-in types, including Booleans, strings, integers, enumerations, and arrays of these types. For custom types, you can provide your own editor to display a custom user interface.

The first step is to add the required references to the project containing your editors (which will either be your custom activity library project or a dedicated editors project). These references are:

- System.Design

- System.Drawing

- System.Windows.Forms

Then, create a public class that inherits from System.Drawing.Design.UITypeEditor (in the System.Drawing assembly) and override the *EditValue* and *GetEditStyle* methods. This simple editor opens a dialog to edit a *System.Version* object:

```
using System;
using System.ComponentModel;
using System.Drawing.Design;
using System.Windows.Forms;
using System.Windows.Forms.Design;

public class VersionEditor : UITypeEditor {
    public override object EditValue(ITypeDescriptorContext context,
        IServiceProvider provider,
        object value) {

        var editorService = (IWindowsFormsEditorService)provider.GetService(
            typeof(IWindowsFormsEditorService)
        );

        if (editorService != null) {
            var versionDialog = new VersionDialog(value);
            if (editorService.ShowDialog(versionDialog) == DialogResult.OK) {
                value = versionDialog.Version;
            }
        }

        return value;
    }

    public override UITypeEditorEditStyle GetEditStyle(ITypeDescriptorContext context) {
        return UITypeEditorEditStyle.Modal;
    }
}
```

> **Tip** If your editor needs to access information about the build definition being edited, you can access its associated IBuildDefinition by calling `provider.GetService(typeof(IBuildDefinition))`.

Next, create a Windows Form to edit your custom type (in this case, VersionDialog), whose constructor takes the value to be edited and then returns the edited value via a property (in this case, Version). We won't walk through creating the dialog.

Finally, associate your custom editor with the process parameter using the Editor metadata described in the section entitled "Metadata," earlier in this chapter.

Supported Reasons

The SupportedReasons argument allows you to define what triggers are supported by the process template, and this will be automatically reflected in the user interface by disabling options that aren't available. For example, if your process template doesn't support being queued with a shelveset, you can select all reasons other than ValidateShelveset and CheckinShelveset.

To add the SupportedReasons argument to your process template, do the following:

1. Open the process template in the Workflow Designer.

2. Click the Arguments tab at the bottom of the Designer.

3. Scroll to the bottom of the arguments list and click Create Argument. A new row will be added to the list of arguments.

4. Enter the Name **SupportedReasons**, select the Direction as Property, and browse for the Argument Type Microsoft.TeamFoundation.Build.Client.BuildReason.

The argument should look like Figure 16-10 when you're done.

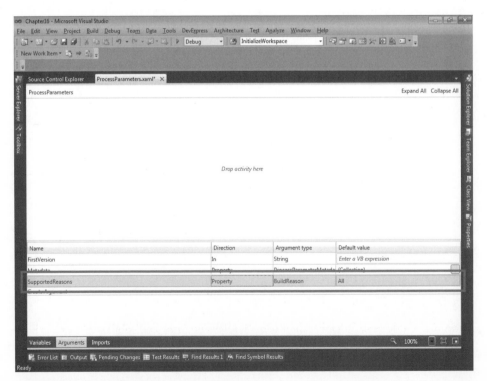

FIGURE 16-10 SupportReasons process parameter

You can now specify the supported reasons by clicking the drop-down list in the Default Value column and selecting the supported reasons.

Backward and Forward Compatibility

There are two behaviors you need to be aware of to maintain backward and forward compatibility of your build definitions with respect to process parameters:

- How default values are handled.
- Compatibility of the serialized XAML.

As mentioned earlier, Team Build serializes the process parameter values specified when editing a build definition and queuing a build as XAML. More precisely, Team Build serializes the delta between the default values and the current values (that is, if a process parameter has the default value, it isn't serialized). This means that if you change the default value in the process template and deploy it, any build definition that is currently using the default value for that process parameter will automatically appear to upgrade to the new default value. (It doesn't actually change, however, because of the way that data is stored.)

Breaking changes to the process parameter's interface (such as changing the parameter's name or type) will cause it to fail to deserialize, and builds using the process template will fail. You can work around this by editing each build definition that uses that process template. When you edit the build definition, any process parameters that can't be deserialized will revert to their default values, and you can simply save the build definition to update the serialized XAML.

> **Note** In rare circumstances, we have seen all of the process parameters revert to default. If this occurs, we recommend that you don't save the build definition, and review the changes you made to your process template.

Team Build Activities

This section describes a subset of the activities shipped by Team Build. These activities are those that are pivotal to creating customized build processes and have nontrivial or nonobvious arguments.

AgentScope

This is one of the most important activities provided by Team Build because it allows the build controller to delegate work to a build agent. This is a composite activity, and any logic that it contains will automatically be executed on the appropriate build agent.

The decision of which build agent to execute on is governed by the ReservationSpec argument. The ReservationSpec argument is of type AgentReservationSpec and allows you to specify agents to consider by name (with wildcards supported) and tags (tag comparison can either be *MatchExact* or *MatchAtLeast,* as discussed in the section entitled "Agent Reservation," in Chapter 14). For example, the following ReservationSpec will find an agent whose name starts with *NEW* and has at least the tag *x86*.

```
New AgentReservationSpec() With {
    .Name = "NEW*",
    .Tags = { "x86" },
    .TagComparison = TagComparison.MatchAtLeast }
```

The AgentScope activity has two arguments for controlling timeouts. The first, MaxWaitTime, defines the maximum amount of time to wait for an agent matching the ReservationSpec to become available before failing. The second, MaxExecutionTime, defines the maximum amount of time that the AgentScope can execute on the agent before failing.

Any workflow arguments and variables that are in scope will automatically be serialized and will be available within AgentScope. This can cause issues if any of the variables that are in scope can't be serialized. You can avoid this by adding the variable's name to the DataToIgnore property of AgentScope or by ensuring that the variable isn't in scope when AgentScope is reached.

CheckInGatedChanges

This activity will check in the shelveset associated with the current build and return the resulting Changeset object in the Result argument. The check-in will be performed only if both the compilation and test phases passed or the IgnoreErrors argument is set to *True*.

ConvertWorkspaceItem/ConvertWorkspaceItems

This activity converts server paths to local paths and vice versa (depending on the Direction argument) using the workspace specified in the Workspace argument.

ExpandEnvironmentVariables

This activity takes a string containing environment variable references (for example, %TEMP%) and returns a string with the environment variable references expanded.

FindMatchingFiles

This activity takes a path containing wildcards (either the standard wildcards * and ? or a recursive wildcard **) and returns the list of files matching that wildcard.

GetBuildAgent

This activity returns the *IBuildAgent* object associated with the current build agent. This activity can be used only within AgentScope.

GetBuildDetail

This activity returns the *IBuildDetail* object associated with the current build.

GetBuildDirectory

This activity returns the path to the working directory for the current build agent. This activity can be used only within an AgentScope.

GetBuildEnvironment

This activity returns a *BuildEnvironment* object that allows you to determine whether you're running on a controller or agent, as well as to determine the path to custom build activities and extensions.

GetTeamProjectCollection

This activity returns a *TfsTeamProjectCollection* object for the Team Project Collection that the build is running against.

InvokeForReason

This composite activity allows you to execute the contained activities only if the build was started for one or more specified reasons. For example, you could execute certain activities only if the build were a scheduled one.

InvokeProcess

This activity is very useful when customizing build processes because it allows you to execute any existing tools on which your build process depends. Most arguments on the activity are self-explanatory, but you'll see that the activity has a different appearance to the other activities and composite activities you've used so far. The InvokeProcess activity has two Drop Activity Here areas, where you can drop an activity (or multiple activities wrapped in a composite activity) that will be executed whenever the process writes a line to standard output or standard error.

In Figure 16-11, we use the InvokeProcess activity with the WriteBuildMessage and WriteBuildError activities to log the outputs from the process as messages (for standard output) or errors (for standard errors).

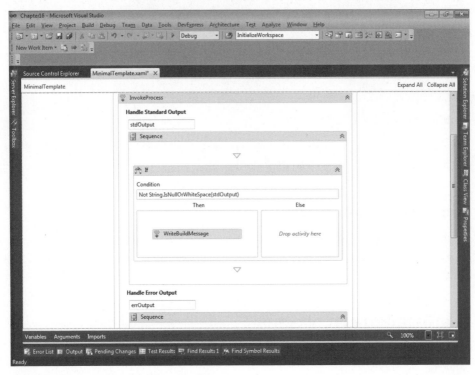

FIGURE 16-11 InvokeProcess output handling

MSBuild

This activity is the core of most build processes because it is used to execute MSBuild. Rather than using the InvokeProcess activity, this activity provides a rich set of arguments for specifying inputs to MSBuild as well as processing its outputs.

SetBuildProperties

This activity provides a convenient way to update commonly set properties on the *IBuildDetail* object. To use this activity, set the appropriate arguments on the activity to the values you want to set and set the PropertiesToSet property to the properties to be updated.

To set properties not supported by SetBuildProperties in a process template or composite activity, you'd have to combine GetBuildDetail (to get the *IBuildDetail* object), Assign (to set the appropriate properties), and InvokeMethod (to call the *Save* method).

SharedResourceScope

This composite activity provides a cross-controller and cross-agent critical section. Team Build guarantees that activities with SharedResourceScope activities with the same ResourceName (which is any arbitrary string) won't execute at the same time and will be processed in a first-in-first-out (FIFO) manner. The SharedResourceScope activity also provides the same timeout arguments (MaxWaitTime and MaxExecutionTime) as the AgentScope activity.

UpdateBuildNumber

This activity provides a convenient way to update the running build's build number. The UpdateBuildNumber activity will create a build number based on the specified build number format that supports the tokens discussed in the section entitled "Build Number," in Chapter 14.

Custom Activities

Although Workflow Foundation and Team Build ship with a large number of activities for everything from creating directories to running code in parallel, a time will come when you need to perform some action that's not available in the shipped activities. Building custom activities allows you to bridge the gap between what the product provides and what you require.

Team Build supports any of the activity base classes supported by Workflow Foundation, including:

- *Activity* (declarative XAML activities)
- CodeActivity
- AsyncCodeActivity
- NativeActivity

Creating custom workflow activities was discussed in Chapter 15, "Workflow Foundation Quick Start," so in this section, we'll just discuss things specific to creating custom activities for Team Build.

BuildActivity Attribute

Team Build–specific custom activities are identified by their being decorated with a *Microsoft .TeamFoundation.Build.Client.BuildActivity* attribute. This attribute also allows you to restrict whether the activity can run on controllers, agents, or both, which can be used to ensure that activities aren't used in inappropriate places (such as using activities that require a workspace on a controller).

Here, we can see the *BuildActivity* attribute being used to identify the ScorchWorkspace activity as one that can be run only within an AgentScope activity:

```
using Microsoft.TeamFoundation.Build.Client;

[BuildActivity(HostEnvironmentOption.Agent)]
public class ScorchWorkspace : CodeActivity {
    ...
}
```

Note Team Build uses the *BuildActivity* attribute to decide which assemblies to load. By default, only assemblies containing at least one type marked with the *BuildActivity* attribute (or the *BuildExtension* attribute) will be loaded. This behavior can be overridden using the CustomActivitiesAndExtensions.xml file, as discussed later in this chapter.

Extensions

Team Build uses workflow extensions to make certain objects always available to custom activities without their having to be passed as arguments throughout the workflow. These extensions are accessible using the *GetExtension* method on the context object passed to the custom activity's *Execute* method.

In this example, we retrieve the IBuildDetail instance associated with the running build from a custom activity:

```
using Microsoft.TeamFoundation.Build.Client;

[BuildActivity(HostEnvironmentOption.Agent)]
public class ScorchWorkspace : CodeActivity {
    protected override void Execute(CodeActivityContext context) {
        var buildDetail = context.GetExtension<IBuildDetail>();
        ...
    }
}
```

Table 16-1 lists some of the types that are accessible as extensions.

TABLE 16-1 Extension Types

Type	Available on Controller?	Available on Agent?
Microsoft.TeamFoundation.Build.Client.IBuildAgent	No	Yes
Microsoft.TeamFoundation.Build.Client.IBuildDetail	Yes	Yes
Microsoft.TeamFoundation.Build.Workflow.BuildEnvironment	Yes	Yes
Microsoft.TeamFoundation.Build.Workflow.Tracking.BuildTrackingParticipant	Yes	Yes
Microsoft.TeamFoundation.Client.TfsTeamProjectCollection	Yes	Yes

You can create your own extensions by creating a class with the *Microsoft.TeamFoundation .Build.Client.BuildExtension* attribute. These extension classes (which are stateful) can then be accessed using *GetExtension* in the same way. For example:

```
using Microsoft.TeamFoundation.Build.Client;

[BuildExtension(HostEnvironmentOption.Agent)]
public class ScorchWorkspaceStatistics {
    public int ExecutionCount { get; set; }
}

[BuildActivity(HostEnvironmentOption.Agent)]
public class ScorchWorkspace : CodeActivity {
    protected override void Execute(CodeActivityContext context) {
        var statistics = context.GetExtension<ScorchWorkspaceStatistics>();
        statistics.ExecutionCount += 1;
        ...
    }
}
```

Logging

Effective investigation of failed builds and debugging of process templates and custom activities depend heavily on the logging performed by Team Build. As with most things, excessive logging is just as dangerous as insufficient logging because it makes it easy to overlook important information.

Logging in Team Build is controlled through a combination of the specified logging verbosity, attached properties on custom activities, and explicit calls to Team Build's logging API (either in code or using the logging activities provided by Team Build).

Logging Verbosity

The verbosity of Team Build's logging is controlled by the Verbosity argument to the process template. If this argument doesn't exist, the logging verbosity value will default to *Normal.* The available verbosity levels are defined by the enumeration Microsoft.TeamFoundation .Build.Workflow.BuildVerbosity and are described in Table 14-1.

To add the Verbosity argument to your process template, do the following:

1. Open the process template in the Workflow Designer.

2. Click the Arguments tab at the bottom of the Designer.

3. Scroll to the bottom of the arguments list and click Create Argument. A new row will be added to the list of arguments.

4. Enter the Name as **Verbosity**, leave the Direction setting as its default of In, and browse for the Argument Type "Microsoft.TeamFoundation.Build.Workflow .BuildVerbosity".

The argument should look like Figure 16-12 when you're done.

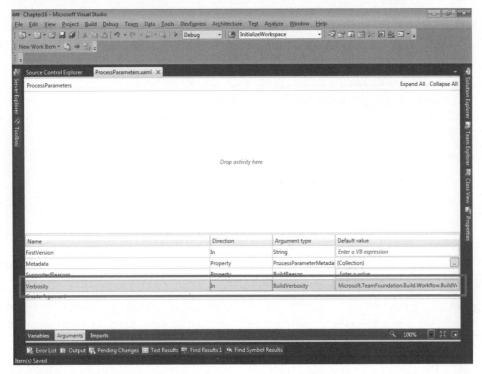

FIGURE 16-12 Verbosity process parameter

Typically, this logging verbosity is honored by activities within AgentScope regardless of how deeply it is nested in the workflow; however, if AgentScope is used inside a composite activity, you will notice that the logging verbosity reverts to Normal rather than the specified logging verbosity. You can avoid this by adding a Verbosity argument to the composite activity and binding the Verbosity argument of the process template to that of the composite activity.

Logging Activities

Team Build ships three activities for logging from within the process template. They can be found in the Team Foundation Build Activities tab in the Toolbox and are as follows:

- WriteBuildMessage
- WriteBuildWarning
- WriteBuildError

All three activities take a Message parameter (of type String) that specifies the message to be added to the log. The WriteBuildMessage activity also takes an Importance parameter (of type Microsoft.TeamFoundation.Build.Workflow.BuildVerbosity) that defines in which verbosity levels the message should appear. Messages from the WriteBuildWarning and WriteBuildError activities are always logged because of their implicit importance. If any errors are logged (either using the WriteBuildError activity or using the Team Build API), the build's outcome will become Partially Succeeded instead of Succeeded.

Because Team Build automatically logs messages for each activity that executes, any messages, warnings, and errors that are logged from within composite or container activities will automatically be nested appropriately, as shown in Figure 16-13.

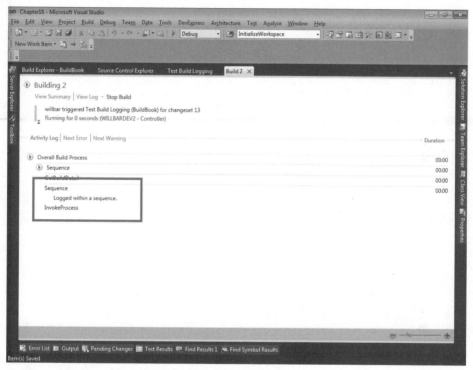

FIGURE 16-13 Nested log messages

Logging Programmatically

Although the logging activities are useful for logging from composite activities, you can't use them to log from custom activities. To log from a custom activity that inherits from CodeActivity or CodeActivity<T>, you can use the extension methods in the *Microsoft .TeamFoundation.Build.Workflow.Activities* namespace. For example:

```
using Microsoft.TeamFoundation.Build.Client;
using Microsoft.TeamFoundation.Build.Workflow.Activities;


[BuildActivity(HostEnvironmentOption.Agent)]
```

```
public class ScorchWorkspace : CodeActivity {
    protected override void Execute(CodeActivityContext context) {
        context.TrackBuildWarning("The ScorchWorkspace activity is obsolete and should no longer be
            used.");
        ...
    }
}
```

Logging from custom activities that don't inherit from CodeActivity can't use the extension methods and need to use the more verbose syntax:

```
using Microsoft.TeamFoundation.Build.Client;
using Microsoft.TeamFoundation.Build.Workflow.Activities;
using Microsoft.TeamFoundation.Build.Workflow.Tracking;

[BuildActivity(HostEnvironmentOption.Agent)]
public class ScorchWorkspace : NativeActivity {
    protected override void Execute(NativeActivityContext context) {
        context.Track(new BuildWarning() { Message = "The ScorchWorkspace activity is obsolete and
            should no longer be used." });
        ...
    }
}
```

Adding Hyperlinks

In addition to just static text, you can add hyperlinks to the build log:

```
using Microsoft.TeamFoundation.Build.Client;

[BuildActivity(HostEnvironmentOption.Agent)]
public class ScorchWorkspace : CodeActivity {
    protected override void Execute(CodeActivityContext context) {
        var buildDetail = context.GetExtension<IBuildDetail>();
        var externalLink = InformationNodeConverters.AddExternalLink(buildDetail.Information,
            "ScorchWorkspace has been obsoleted. Click for more information.",
            new Uri("http://buildweb/help/scorchworkspace.html"));
        externalLink.Save();
    }
}
```

The resulting hyperlink is shown in Figure 16-14.

You can also add the hyperlink under the log message for the particular activity being executed by adding it to the activity's information node rather than the build's information node, as shown here:

```
using Microsoft.TeamFoundation.Build.Client;

[BuildActivity(HostEnvironmentOption.Agent)]
```

```
public class ScorchWorkspace : CodeActivity {
    protected override void Execute(CodeActivityContext context) {
        var buildLoggingExtension = context.GetExtension<IBuildLoggingExtension>();
        var activityTracking = buildLoggingExtension.GetActivityTracking(context);
        activityTracking.Node.Children.AddExternalLink("ScorchWorkspace has been
obsoleted.",
            new Uri("http://buildweb/help/scorchworkspace.html"));
        activityTracking.Save();
    }
}
```

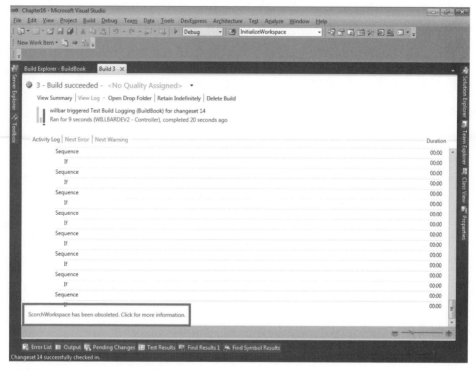

FIGURE 16-14 Hyperlink in build detail

Tracking Attributes

By default, Team Build will log every activity's name to the build log when it executes. Although this makes the build log complete, it does reduce the signal-to-noise ratio and makes important information harder to find. Team Build provides an attached property that we can apply to activities in XAML to choose what logging verbosity they appear at (if they appear at all). The downside is that this attached property can be set only by editing XAML (that is, it can't be set in the Workflow Designer).

The first step (and this is best done in the Designer) is to import the *Microsoft .TeamFoundation.Build.Workflow.Tracking* namespace. To do this, complete the following steps:

1. Open the process template (or composite activity) in the Workflow Designer.

2. Click the Imports tab at the bottom of the Designer.

3. Type **Microsoft.TeamFoundation.Build.Workflow.Tracking** and press Enter.

4. Save the workflow.

To make this same change in XAML (if you prefer), perform the following steps:

1. Open the process template (or composite activity) in the XML editor by right-clicking the file in Solution Explorer and clicking View Code.

2. Add `xmlns:mtbwt="clr-namespace:Microsoft.TeamFoundation.Build.Workflow .Tracking;assembly=Microsoft.TeamFoundation.Build.Workflow"` to the root *Activity* element.

3. Save the workflow.

Once you've imported this namespace (using either technique), you can now set the attached property on any activities called by that workflow (or custom activity), as follows:

1. Open the process template (or composite activity) in the XML editor by right-clicking the file in Solution Explorer and clicking View Code.

2. Locate the call to the activity for which you want to change the logging settings.

3. Add the attribute `mtbwt:BuildTrackingParticipant.Importance="<Importance>"`, where *<Importance>* is None, Low, Normal, or High.

The rules that we typically apply when setting importance are:

- **Assigns**   Set to Low. These activities rarely add value to the build log.

- **Ifs**   Set to Low. These activities usually add confusion in the build log because the log messages for either the Then branch or the Else branch will be nested directly beneath the If's log message with no clear indication which branch executed.

- **Sequences**   Set to None unless the sequence represents a logical grouping for the viewer of the build log.

Before applying these attributes, a build log would look like Figure 16-15.

Afterward, the build log would look like Figure 16-16.

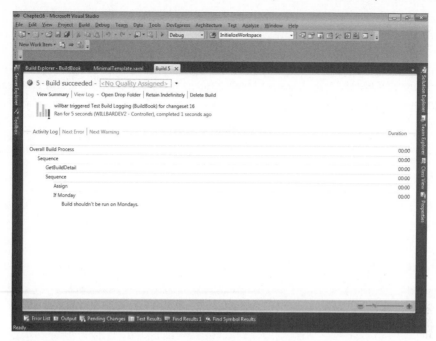

FIGURE 16-15 Build log before tracing participant attached properties are added

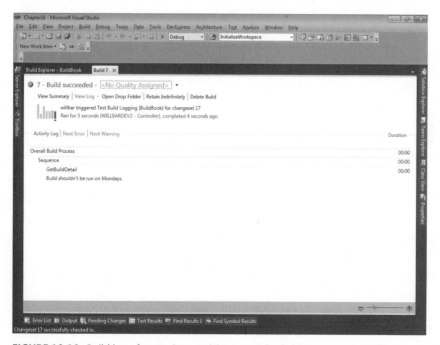

FIGURE 16-16 Build log after tracing participant attached properties are added

Exceptions

If an unhandled exception occurs during the execution of a process template, the exception message will automatically be logged as an error, the workflow terminated, and the build status changed to Failed. If you want to fail the build as part of your workflow, then you can use the Throw activity (which ships as part of Workflow Foundation) on the Error Handling tab of the Toolbox.

Deploying

Once you've created your customized process templates and custom assemblies, you need to deploy them to version control so they can be consumed by Team Build.

Process Templates

Two steps are involved in deploying process templates:

1. Check the process template into version control.

2. Configure Team Build so that it is aware of the process template.

Process templates are typically checked into $/<TeamProject>/BuildProcessTemplates directly. This is not a requirement, however, and you can check in process templates wherever makes most sense in your branching structure. I normally create folders under BuildProcessTemplates for each process template and a folder within that for each environment.

For example:

```
$/BuildBook/
    BuildProcessTemplates/
        MyBuildProcess/
            Development/
                MyBuildProcess.xaml
                ...
            Production/
                MyBuildProcess.xaml
                ...
```

Once the process template has been checked in, you need to tell Team Build about it. To do this, perform the following steps:

1. Create or edit a build definition.

2. Click the Process tab.

3. Click Show Details in the Build Process Template group.

4. Click New.

5. Click Select An Existing XAML File.

6. Click Browse, browse to the process template you checked in, and then click OK. The process template that you selected will appear under Version Control Path, as shown in Figure 16-17.

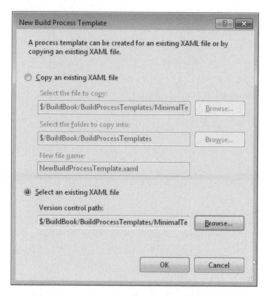

FIGURE 16-17 Selecting an existing process template

7. Click OK.

Custom Assemblies

Custom assemblies also need to be checked into version control, and two steps to having Team Build recognize them:

1. Check the custom assemblies and any dependencies into version control.

2. Configure the build controllers to download the custom assemblies.

A tightly coupled relationship usually exists between process templates and custom assemblies, so we normally deploy them in a subfolder of the process templates. The reason we deploy them in a subfolder is that whenever you check in custom assemblies, the build controllers and agents transition to offline until they're idle and can pick up the new custom assemblies. By having them in a separate folder from the process template, it is possible to deploy process template updates without triggering the build controllers and agents to restart.

For example:

```
$/BuildBook/
    BuildProcessTemplates/
        MyBuildProcess/
            Development/
                MyBuildProcess.xaml
                CustomAssemblies/
                    MyCustomAssembly.dll
                    MyDependency.dll
            Production/
                MyBuildProcess.xaml
                CustomAssemblies/
                    MyCustomAssembly.dll
                    MyNewDependency.dll
```

Once the custom assemblies have been checked in, you need to configure the build controllers to download them. To do this, do the following:

1. Right-click the Builds node in Team Explorer.

2. Click Manage Build Controllers.

3. Select the build controller that you want to configure and click Properties.

4. Click the ellipsis next to Version Control Path To Custom Assemblies, browse to the folder you checked the custom assemblies into, and click OK. The resulting version control path appears in the dialog, as shown in Figure 16-18.

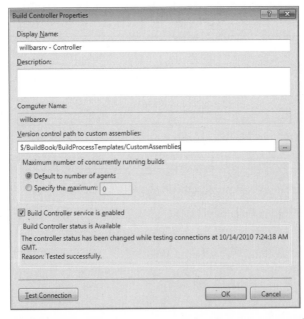

FIGURE 16-18 Setting the version control path to custom assemblies

5. Click OK.

Downloading and Loading Dependent Assemblies

By default, Team Build will download all files in the custom assemblies directory. However, only assemblies containing types marked with either the *BuildActivity* or *BuildExtension* attribute will be loaded into the Team Build process. If your activities depend on assemblies that don't contain any types meeting these criteria, you will run into assembly loading exceptions.

To work around this, you can check a file into the custom assemblies path called CustomActivitiesAndExtensions.xml with the following contents:

```
<?xml version="1.0" encoding="utf-8"?>
<Assemblies>
  <Assembly FileName="MyDependency.dll">
    <Extensions>
      <Extension FullName="MyDependency.CustomException" />
    </Extensions>
  </Assembly>
  <Assembly FileName="MyNewDependency.dll">
    <Extensions>
      <Extension FullName="MyNewDependency.CustomEventArgs" />
    </Extensions>
  </Assembly>
</Assemblies>
```

The class name listed in the *FullName* attribute of the *Extension* element can be any class within the assembly that is public and has a parameterless public constructor. This class will be constructed and loaded into memory, so choose a type whose constructor does as little as possible and has as few dependencies as possible (look for exception classes, data transfer objects, and the like).

This will force the assemblies listed to be downloaded and loaded into the Team Build process so that they're available to your workflow and custom assemblies.

Part VII
Web Development Tool

Chapter 17
Web Deployment Tool, Part 1

Deployment of ASP.NET web applications has historically been very challenging and widely varied across different teams. In fact, if you put 10 different ASP.NET developers in a room and ask them how they deploy their applications today, you may hear a slew of different answers, some of which are outlined in the list that follows.

- Manual FTP transfer
- RoboCopy
- psexec.exe
- MSBuild
- Microsoft System Center
- .msi files that are manually installed

And the list goes on—you probably have a few others as well. Different groups use different tools for several reasons, including the fact that there is no single recommended practice today, and that many tools that exist today don't cover the broad spectrum of scenarios that exist. For instance, web deployments can be categorized into three different high-level scenarios, which include the following:

- Deployment to web servers hosted with third parties
- Deployment to web servers hosted in an organization's network
- Deployment to the local web server on the same machine

Most tools are optimized to perform a deployment to one of the scenarios listed, but not all three. That is where the Web Deployment Tool, also known as *MSDeploy*, comes in. MSDeploy handles deployment for all three scenarios, and in a consistent manner. In this chapter, we will introduce the Web Deployment Tool, show you how it integrates into Microsoft Visual Studio 2010, show its integration into IIS 7 and later, and show how to perform deployments.

 Note Since we are dealing with deploying to the local IIS server in this chapter, you will need administrator rights for many of the examples in this chapter. For example, you will have to open Visual Studio as an administrator as well as opening the command prompt as an administrator.

Web Deployment Tool Overview

The Web Deployment Tool (MSDeploy) is a tool that is provided by Microsoft to assist in the following areas:

- Deployment of web applications and sites

- Migration of web applications and sites

- Synchronization of web applications and sites from one location to another

MSDeploy consists of two major components; the tool itself and the Remote Agent Service. There are a few different ways that you can interact with MSDeploy; one is through the IIS 7 extension and the other is through the msdeploy.exe command-line utility. The Remote Agent Service is a Windows service that you can install on machines that you would like to deploy applications to. We will discuss the Remote Agent Service later in this chapter.

Synchronization is the heart of MSDeploy. With MSDeploy, we can synchronize a "source" with a "destination." The concepts of source and destination are intentionally abstract and extensible. Source and destination targets are accessed via providers. Many different providers are built into MSDeploy, but you can create your own as well. We cover more providers later in this chapter in detail, but to give you an idea now, the providers include web applications, websites, web packages, and folders. You may be wondering what web packages are. Web packages are a new concept introduced with MSDeploy and Visual Studio 2010. We will now move on to discuss web packages in detail.

Working with Web Packages

When you are developing web applications using Visual Studio, there comes a time to deploy that application to different environments. Previous versions of Visual Studio did not have any built-in support for creating a self-contained artifact for the entire web application. Many times, people would take the contents of the website, throw them into a .zip file, and use that file to deploy from one environment to another. We are happy to say that with Visual Studio 2010, there now exists a way to create that much-needed artifact, which is known as a web package or deployment package. A web package is a self-contained .zip file that can be used to set up the application, along with its required files and related resources.

Inside Visual Studio 2010, you can right-click a web application and select Build Deployment Package to create this package. That menu option is shown in Figure 17-1.

If you click the Build Deployment Package option shown in this figure, then you should find a .zip file under the obj*CONFIGURATION*\Package folder, where *CONFIGURATION* is the name of the current configuration that Visual Studio is using. In this case, the configuration was set to Debug, and the name of the project is HelloWorldMvc, so the package is located at obj\Debug\Package\HelloWorldMvc.zip. A web package can include the following:

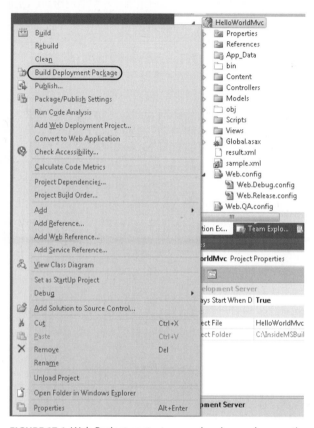

FIGURE 17-1 Web Project context menu showing package option

- Files
- Access control lists (ACLs)
- Certificates
- Registry settings
- Database scripts to be executed
- Parameters (the user will be prompted for values upon sync)
- Assemblies to be installed in the GAC

Now that we have discussed what packages are, and we've even shown how to create a package using all the default options, we will cover the different options when creating packages, and after that, we will show how you can take the created package and directly import it into an IIS 7 web server.

> **Note** There are some limitations to the number of files and the total size of the packages that you should be familiar with. Those include the fact that the maximum file size that can be placed in a package is 2,147,483,647 bytes (*Int.MaxValue*) and the maximum number of files is 65,536. If you need to support more files, then you will have to use archiveDir instead of a package.

Package Creation

In the previous section, we showed how you can create a package using the Build Deployment Package context menu option in Visual Studio. We will now take a look at some of the different ways that you can customize the package that gets created. There are a few options inside Visual Studio that you can use to customize package creation. You can get to these options from the project's Properties page. To get there, you can right-click the project, select Properties, and then click the Package/Publish Web tab. Figure 17-2 shows this tab.

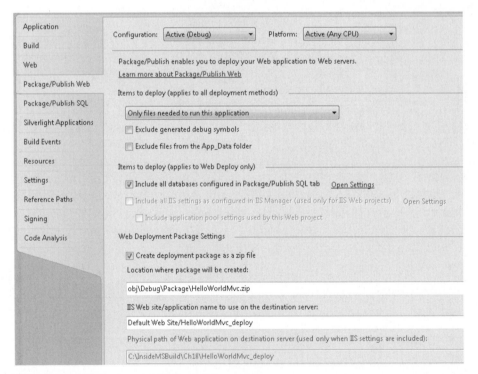

FIGURE 17-2 Web Deployment Package options page

From this tab, we can set a few options, including which files to include in the package, whether a database should be included, where the package should be written to, and a few IIS settings that will be used when the package is imported. We will go over these options here, but you should keep in mind that you can have much more control over the package creation process by editing the project file. We will thoroughly cover this in the next chapter, "Web Deployment Tool, Part 2".

You can specify what file should be included in the package by selecting one of the options in the Items To Deploy drop-down list. These options are covered in Table 17-1.

TABLE 17-1 Items to Deploy Options

Option	Description
Only Files Needed To Run This Application	MSDeploy will attempt to determine all the files that are required by your web application. It will include only those files.
All Files In This Project	Selecting this option will include all the files needed to run the application, plus all the other files that are a part of the project.
All Files In This Project Folder	This will include all the files needed to run the web application, as well as other files located in, or under, the projects directory. Some files are excluded, when it's known that they are not needed. For instance, all files under obj\, as well as any file with an extension including .scc, .vsssc, and vspscc, which are common extensions for files containing version control information.

Underneath the Items To Deploy option, there are two check boxes that you can select:

- Exclude Generated Debug Symbols
- Exclude Files From The App_Data Folder

By default, your debug symbols will be included in the created package. This is true even for builds using Release configuration. It is a good idea to keep your .pdb (program debug database) files in case you need to debug that particular build at some time in the future. Also, you may want to exclude the files from App_Data if your deployed applications will not be using a data source contained in that folder.

When you are creating a package, you can include database deployment with it. In order to do that, you will have to click the Include All Databases Configured In Package/Publish SQL Tab and set the database options on that tab. We will not cover database deployment in this chapter but we do discuss it in the next chapter "Web Deployment Tool, Part 2" in the "Database" section.

Only a couple other options allow you to specify inside Visual Studio. By default, the Create Deployment Package As A Zip File option is selected. When this is selected and the Build Deployment Package operation is executed, then your files are placed into a .zip file package. If this option is cleared, then the package is created to an archive directory. The archive directory contains all the files that the .zip file would.

Earlier, we stated that the package would be located in the obj folder. This is the default, but you can specify another location using the Location Where Package Will Be Created option. Note that if you have specified that the package be created as a .zip file, then you should specify a file name ending in *.zip*. Otherwise, you will receive an error when building the package.

The other three options are IIS settings that can be included in the deployment package. The first is the default value for the website name and application name that should be used. The default value for that will follow this pattern: *Default Web Site/WEB-PROJ-NAME_deploy,* where *WEB-PROJ-NAME* is the name of the web project being packaged. If the package is imported using IIS 7, the user will be given the option to change those values. We will discuss that later in this chapter. If you are developing your web application or website using IIS instead of the ASP.NET Development Server ("Cassini"), then you will be allowed to specify the physical path. Otherwise, you will not be able to do that, and the default path (under inetpub) will be used when the application is imported. In the case of the sample application, IIS was not used, so the option is dimmed. If you have any deployment settings marked as secure, then you can enter the encryption password in the text box shown. You should know that those values are stored in plain text and not safely guarded, so use them with caution. Now that we have discussed how to create packages, we will move on to the topic of how packages can be installed.

Installing Packages

There are primarily two different ways to install packages: using the IIS 7 extension or using msdeploy.exe. We will first go over using IIS to install packages, and then we will show how to install them using msdeploy.exe. Although only IIS 7 and later support MSDeploy packages through its user interface, you can still install MSDeploy packages to IIS 6 using msdeploy.exe.

Installing Packages Using IIS 7

When you install MSDeploy (it is installed automatically with Visual Studio) on a machine that is running IIS 7, it will automatically install the IIS manager user interface (UI) module by default (you can disable this via a custom install). After installing MSDeploy, you should see a new Deploy section (when a website is selected in the Connections pane), as shown in Figure 17-3.

From Figure 17-3, you can see three actions: Install Application From Gallery, Export Application, and Import Application. Install Application From Gallery uses the Web Platform Installer to allow you to easily install some popular web applications. We will not cover the Web Platform Installer in this book, because it is outside the scope of typical web deployments, but you can get more info on it at *http://www.iis.net/webpi*. The action that we will look at now is Import Application, and later in this chapter we'll cover Export Application.

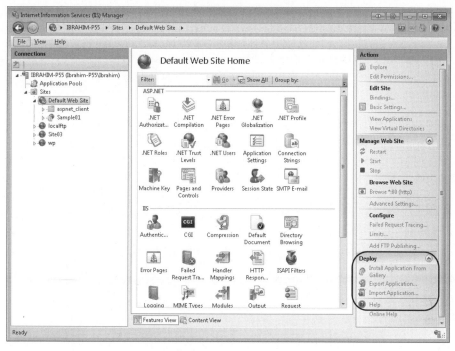

FIGURE 17-3 Deploy actions for a website

When you click the Import Application link, you will see a dialog prompting you to select a package to import. Then select the package that was just created using the HelloWorldMvc project and click Next to get the dialog shown in Figure 17-4.

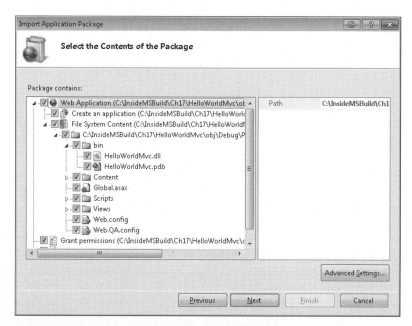

FIGURE 17-4 IIS Manager Import Application Package dialog

This dialog shows the preview of the changes that the package will make to the local IIS server. When the package is being imported, certain operations can be skipped if necessary.

For instance, if you choose not to deploy the HelloWorldMvc.pdb file or if you do not want to include the web.config file, then you can simply clear it. You can also choose to skip other operations.

At this point, you can click Next to continue with the import, or you can choose to tweak the advanced settings through the Advanced Settings dialog. Once you click Next on this page, you will be shown a dialog to input all the values for the parameters that the package contains. In this case, you should see the dialog shown in Figure 17-5.

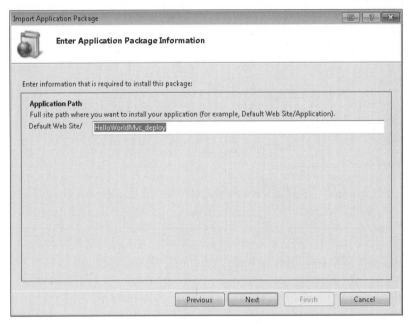

FIGURE 17-5 Input Application Package Information dialog

Since we created the default package from Visual Studio, the only parameter that is defined is the IIS application that will be created. You can customize the package creation process to include other parameters, and when the package is imported, the user will be given a chance to update those values. For instance, you can create a package that will prompt the importer for a connection string that will be placed in the web.config file. We will discuss parameters in more detail in the section entitled "MSDeploy Parameters," later in this chapter.

In the dialog shown in Figure 17-5, when you click Next, the import will start. Following that, you will be shown a report of all the actions that were performed during the import process. Figure 17-6 shows the Details view of those results.

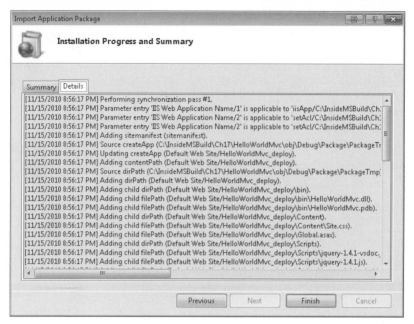

FIGURE 17-6 Details report after a package import

The messages that are shown in Figure 17-6 are the same ones that you would have seen from the console if you had performed the import using msdeploy.exe. We will now move on to show that process.

Installing Packages Using MSDeploy.exe

As stated previously, you can also use the command-line utility, msdeploy.exe, to import packages. This utility is located in the %ProgramFiles(x86)%\IIS\Microsoft Web Deploy folder. It is a good idea to add this value to your PATH environment variable if you regularly use msdeploy.exe. First we will show you the command to perform the same sync as in the previous section, and then we will discuss the different options when invoking the command.

In the previous section we created a new IIS application by importing the package that was created by Visual Studio. We can achieve the same thing using the msdeploy .exe command-line utility. The command to do that is `msdeploy -verb:sync -source:package=HelloWorldMvc.zip -dest:auto`. Don't worry about the syntax now; we will discuss that shorty. The result of executing this command is shown in Figure 17-7.

If you are thinking that those messages look familiar, they are. They are the same messages that you saw in Figure 17-6, when we were importing the package using the IIS Manager user interface. Now that we have deployed this to the local IIS server, let's see what happens if we execute the exact same command again. Take a look at the new results in Figure 17-8.

```
C:\InsideMSBuild\Ch17\HelloWorldMvc\obj\Debug\Package>msdeploy -verb:sync -source:package=HelloWorl
dMvc.zip -dest:auto
Info: Adding sitemanifest (sitemanifest).
Info: Updating createApp (Default Web Site/HelloWorldMvc_deploy).
Info: Adding contentPath (Default Web Site/HelloWorldMvc_deploy).
Info: Adding dirPath (Default Web Site/HelloWorldMvc_deploy).
Info: Adding child dirPath (Default Web Site/HelloWorldMvc_deploy\bin).
Info: Adding child filePath (Default Web Site/HelloWorldMvc_deploy\bin\HelloWorldMvc.dll).
Info: Adding child filePath (Default Web Site/HelloWorldMvc_deploy\bin\HelloWorldMvc.pdb).
Info: Adding child dirPath (Default Web Site/HelloWorldMvc_deploy\Content).
Info: Adding child filePath (Default Web Site/HelloWorldMvc_deploy\Content\Site.css).
Info: Adding child filePath (Default Web Site/HelloWorldMvc_deploy\Global.asax).
Info: Adding child dirPath (Default Web Site/HelloWorldMvc_deploy\Scripts).
Info: Adding child filePath (Default Web Site/HelloWorldMvc_deploy\Scripts\jquery-1.4.1-vsdoc.js).
Info: Adding child filePath (Default Web Site/HelloWorldMvc_deploy\Scripts\jquery-1.4.1.js).
Info: Adding child filePath (Default Web Site/HelloWorldMvc_deploy\Scripts\jquery-1.4.1.min.js).
Info: Adding child filePath (Default Web Site/HelloWorldMvc_deploy\Scripts\jquery.validate-vsdoc.js
).
Info: Adding child filePath (Default Web Site/HelloWorldMvc_deploy\Scripts\jquery.validate.js).
Info: Adding child filePath (Default Web Site/HelloWorldMvc_deploy\Scripts\jquery.validate.min.js).
Info: Adding child filePath (Default Web Site/HelloWorldMvc_deploy\Scripts\MicrosoftAjax.debug.js).
Info: Adding child filePath (Default Web Site/HelloWorldMvc_deploy\Scripts\MicrosoftAjax.js).
Info: Adding child filePath (Default Web Site/HelloWorldMvc_deploy\Scripts\MicrosoftMvcAjax.debug.j
s).
Info: Adding child filePath (Default Web Site/HelloWorldMvc_deploy\Scripts\MicrosoftMvcAjax.js).
Info: Adding child filePath (Default Web Site/HelloWorldMvc_deploy\Scripts\MicrosoftMvcValidation.d
ebug.js).
Info: Adding child filePath (Default Web Site/HelloWorldMvc_deploy\Scripts\MicrosoftMvcValidation.j
s).
Info: Adding child dirPath (Default Web Site/HelloWorldMvc_deploy\Views).
Info: Adding child dirPath (Default Web Site/HelloWorldMvc_deploy\Views\Account).
Info: Adding child filePath (Default Web Site/HelloWorldMvc_deploy\Views\Account\ChangePassword.asp
x).
Info: Adding child filePath (Default Web Site/HelloWorldMvc_deploy\Views\Account\ChangePasswordSucc
ess.aspx).
Info: Adding child filePath (Default Web Site/HelloWorldMvc_deploy\Views\Account\LogOn.aspx).
Info: Adding child filePath (Default Web Site/HelloWorldMvc_deploy\Views\Account\Register.aspx).
Info: Adding child dirPath (Default Web Site/HelloWorldMvc_deploy\Views\Home).
Info: Adding child filePath (Default Web Site/HelloWorldMvc_deploy\Views\Home\About.aspx).
Info: Adding child filePath (Default Web Site/HelloWorldMvc_deploy\Views\Home\Index.aspx).
Info: Adding child dirPath (Default Web Site/HelloWorldMvc_deploy\Views\Shared).
Info: Adding child filePath (Default Web Site/HelloWorldMvc_deploy\Views\Shared\Error.aspx).
Info: Adding child filePath (Default Web Site/HelloWorldMvc_deploy\Views\Shared\LogOnUserControl.as
cx).
Info: Adding child filePath (Default Web Site/HelloWorldMvc_deploy\Views\Shared\Site.Master).
Info: Adding child filePath (Default Web Site/HelloWorldMvc_deploy\Views\Web.config).
Info: Adding child filePath (Default Web Site/HelloWorldMvc_deploy\Web.config).
Info: Adding child filePath (Default Web Site/HelloWorldMvc_deploy\Web.QA.config).
Info: Adding setAcl (Default Web Site/HelloWorldMvc_deploy).
Info: Adding setAcl (Default Web Site/HelloWorldMvc_deploy).
Total changes: 41 (40 added, 0 deleted, 1 updated, 0 parameters changed, 1158641 bytes copied)
```

FIGURE 17-7 Using msdeploy.exe to deploy the HelloWorldMvc project

```
C:\InsideMSBuild\Ch17\HelloWorldMvc\obj\Debug\Package>msdeploy -verb:sync -source:package=HelloWorldMvc.zip -dest:auto
Info: Updating setAcl (Default Web Site/HelloWorldMvc_deploy).
Info: Updating setAcl (Default Web Site/HelloWorldMvc_deploy).
Total changes: 2 (0 added, 0 deleted, 2 updated, 0 parameters changed, 0 bytes copied)
```

FIGURE 17-8 Using msdeploy.exe to update the HelloWorldMvc application

That's kind of interesting; the output is much shorter than it was last time. That's because
MSDeploy will examine the source and destination and push through only the relevant
changes. In this case, we do not see any messages about adding files; we just see the setAcl
command executing, which specifically does not skip by design. In this scenario, the project
doesn't have many files, and the deployment is on the same machine, so it wouldn't have
mattered if a full deployment was executed. But suppose you have a website that has
thousands of files, and you change only a few of them. If you then had to deploy your full
application again, this would be far from ideal. MSDeploy is designed to solve this problem.
Since MSDeploy will send only the changed content in most cases, you will save not only time
but also bandwidth. Now let's take a closer look at the msdeploy.exe options.

msdeploy.exe Usage Options

The msdeploy.exe file, simply referred to as *msdeploy* in command examples, has a very rich
command-line syntax. We will not fully cover it here, but we will go over the most important
options. For full coverage of this subject, you should visit *http://technet.microsoft.com/en-us/*

library/dd569106.aspx. The basic syntax for invoking MSDeploy takes the form `msdeploy` `–verb:`*VerbHere* `–source:`*SourceHere* `–dest:`*DestHere*, where *VerbHere, SourceHere,* and *DestHere* are values that you provide. The –verb option, which is required, allows you to indicate to MSDeploy what action to perform. The six different possible values are outlined in Table 17-2.

TABLE 17-2 MSDeploy Verb Options

Value	Description
dump	Returns the details of the source object
sync	Synchronizes the source object with the destination object
delete	Deletes the destination object
getDependencies	Can be used to get information about any dependencies that the destination object may have
getParameters	Will return all parameters that are defined on the source object
getSystemInfo	Will return system information for the source object

Note A really good way to learn about the msdeploy.exe command-line usage is to invoke the partial or full command in which you are interested and appending the /? switch. For example, if you wanted to learn more about the sync verb, you can invoke the command `msdeploy.exe` `–verb:sync /?`.

The most useful option is the sync verb followed by dump, so let's just focus on those two for now. From Table 17-2, we know that we can use the dump verb to get information about the source object, so let's show an example of that. If you were following along with the examples in this chapter, then you recall from the previous section that we have created a new application, HelloWorldMvc_deploy, in the Default Web Site. In order to get information about that application, you can execute the following command:

```
msdeploy -verb:dump
    -source:appHostConfig="Default Web Site/HelloWorldMvc_deploy"
```

When you do this, you should see a result similar to Figure 17-9.

From the results shown in Figure 17-9, we can see the different files that the application contains, as well as some information about the application itself, such as the path to the application. Now is a good time to call out the –xml option. From the previous command, we saw a raw text representation of an IIS application. If you want to see the XML representation that MSDeploy uses internally, then you can attach the –xml option to the command. So in our case, the new command would be

```
msdeploy -verb:dump
    -source:appHostConfig="Default Web Site/HelloWorldMvc_deploy" -xml
```

```
C:\InsideMSBuild\Ch17\HelloWorldMvc\obj\Debug\Package>msdeploy -verb:dump -source:appHostConfig="De
fault Web Site/HelloWorldMvc_deploy"
MSDeploy.appHostConfig
Default Web Site/HelloWorldMvc_deploy
MSDeploy.appHostConfig/appHostConfig[@path='Default Web Site/HelloWorldMvc_deploy']/application[@pa
th='/HelloWorldMvc_deploy']
MSDeploy.appHostConfig/appHostConfig[@path='Default Web Site/HelloWorldMvc_deploy']/application[@pa
th='/HelloWorldMvc_deploy']/virtualDirectoryDefaults
MSDeploy.appHostConfig/appHostConfig[@path='Default Web Site/HelloWorldMvc_deploy']/application[@pa
th='/HelloWorldMvc_deploy']/virtualDirectory[@path='/']
C:\inetpub\wwwroot\HelloWorldMvc_deploy
C:\inetpub\wwwroot\HelloWorldMvc_deploy\bin
C:\inetpub\wwwroot\HelloWorldMvc_deploy\bin\HelloWorldMvc.dll
C:\inetpub\wwwroot\HelloWorldMvc_deploy\bin\HelloWorldMvc.pdb
C:\inetpub\wwwroot\HelloWorldMvc_deploy\Content
C:\inetpub\wwwroot\HelloWorldMvc_deploy\Content\Site.css
C:\inetpub\wwwroot\HelloWorldMvc_deploy\Global.asax
C:\inetpub\wwwroot\HelloWorldMvc_deploy\Scripts
C:\inetpub\wwwroot\HelloWorldMvc_deploy\Scripts\jquery-1.4.1-vsdoc.js
C:\inetpub\wwwroot\HelloWorldMvc_deploy\Scripts\jquery-1.4.1.js
C:\inetpub\wwwroot\HelloWorldMvc_deploy\Scripts\jquery-1.4.1.min.js
C:\inetpub\wwwroot\HelloWorldMvc_deploy\Scripts\jquery.validate-vsdoc.js
C:\inetpub\wwwroot\HelloWorldMvc_deploy\Scripts\jquery.validate.js
C:\inetpub\wwwroot\HelloWorldMvc_deploy\Scripts\jquery.validate.min.js
C:\inetpub\wwwroot\HelloWorldMvc_deploy\Scripts\MicrosoftAjax.debug.js
C:\inetpub\wwwroot\HelloWorldMvc_deploy\Scripts\MicrosoftAjax.js
C:\inetpub\wwwroot\HelloWorldMvc_deploy\Scripts\MicrosoftMvcAjax.debug.js
C:\inetpub\wwwroot\HelloWorldMvc_deploy\Scripts\MicrosoftMvcAjax.js
C:\inetpub\wwwroot\HelloWorldMvc_deploy\Scripts\MicrosoftMvcValidation.debug.js
C:\inetpub\wwwroot\HelloWorldMvc_deploy\Scripts\MicrosoftMvcValidation.js
C:\inetpub\wwwroot\HelloWorldMvc_deploy\Views
C:\inetpub\wwwroot\HelloWorldMvc_deploy\Views\Account
C:\inetpub\wwwroot\HelloWorldMvc_deploy\Views\Account\ChangePassword.aspx
C:\inetpub\wwwroot\HelloWorldMvc_deploy\Views\Account\ChangePasswordSuccess.aspx
C:\inetpub\wwwroot\HelloWorldMvc_deploy\Views\Account\LogOn.aspx
C:\inetpub\wwwroot\HelloWorldMvc_deploy\Views\Account\Register.aspx
C:\inetpub\wwwroot\HelloWorldMvc_deploy\Views\Home
C:\inetpub\wwwroot\HelloWorldMvc_deploy\Views\Home\About.aspx
C:\inetpub\wwwroot\HelloWorldMvc_deploy\Views\Home\Index.aspx
C:\inetpub\wwwroot\HelloWorldMvc_deploy\Views\Shared
C:\inetpub\wwwroot\HelloWorldMvc_deploy\Views\Shared\Error.aspx
C:\inetpub\wwwroot\HelloWorldMvc_deploy\Views\Shared\LogOnUserControl.ascx
C:\inetpub\wwwroot\HelloWorldMvc_deploy\Views\Shared\Site.Master
C:\inetpub\wwwroot\HelloWorldMvc_deploy\Views\Web.config
C:\inetpub\wwwroot\HelloWorldMvc_deploy\Web.config
C:\inetpub\wwwroot\HelloWorldMvc_deploy\Web.QA.config
```

FIGURE 17-9 MSDeploy dump for Default Web Site/HelloWorldMvc_deploy

When using MSDeploy in many cases, you have to provide XPath values to locate elements. This view can help you construct that XPath. Now that we've discussed the dump verb, let's move on to the more useful sync verb.

> **Note** MSDeploy uses *object* as a generic term to refer to different things, including but not limited to IIS applications, IIS websites, web packages, web archives, folders, and other objects.

The sync verb is the one that you are most likely to use the most. This is the verb that you will use when you want to deploy an application somewhere, but it can be used for other things as well, such as backing up an object. When you perform a sync, you always have to specify a source and a destination. The source and destination have to be compatible, but they don't have to be the same type. For example, you can sync an IIS application to a web package, to a folder, and so on. You might be wondering what it means for two object types to be compatible. It just means that the source and destination providers are designed to interact with each other. So the appHostConfig provider is compatabile with the package provider, and vice versa. Now let's look at some of the providers that are included with MSDeploy.

MSDeploy Providers

We have touched on the concept of providers already in this chapter, but we have not yet discussed them in depth. We now will continue our discussion from the last section and put an emphasis on MSDeploy providers. According to the MSDeploy documentation at *http://technet.microsoft.com/en-us/library/dd569040.aspx,* "Providers process specific source or destination data for Web Deploy." If it sounds like this description is a bit vague, it is—for a reason. A provider is an abstract concept by design. MSDeploy will accept a source and destination represented by a provider and some settings for each. The providers are to figure out the exact actions that are to be performed. This abstraction is one that enables MSDeploy to handle a source and destination object in an independent manner. Many providers are shipped with MSDeploy. The most commonly used providers are listed in Table 17-3; for the full list, you can execute msdeploy.exe /?.

TABLE 17-3 MSDeploy Providers

Provider Name	Description
appHostConfig	A provider used for IIS 7 applications.
archiveDir	Used to create, or synchronize to and from, an archive directory (.zip file).
auto	When this provider is used, the destination uses the same provider as the source.
contentPath	Allows you to use a folder as a source or destination object.
createApp	Used to create an IIS application. *Note: This provider is not intended for direct use; instead, it should be used inside a manifest.*
dbFullSql	This can be used to synchronize either a Microsoft SQL Server database or a script to another SQL Server database or script.
dbMySql	This can be used to synchronize either a MySQL database or script to another MySQL Server database or script.
dirPath	This allows you to perform operations to a directory.
filePath	This provider is used to sync individual files.
gacAssembly	This provider allows you to add a file to the GAC.
iisApp	A provider that can be used for IIS 7 or IIS 6 applications.
manifest	This provider will enable you to call many different providers in sequence by using a manifest XML file.
metaKey	This can be used to perform operations against IIS 6 metabase keys.
package	This can be used to perform operations against a web package (.zip file).
runCommand	This can be used to execute arbitrary commands.
setAcl	This can be used to set permissions on a given folder.

The best way to learn how to use different providers is to demonstrate some of them in action. We've already seen how we can use a package to create an IIS application. Now let's reverse that and see how to back up an IIS application to a package. For example, if we wanted to do this with the HelloWorldMvc_deploy application, the command would be

```
msdeploy -verb:sync -source:appHostConfig="Default Web Site/HelloWorldMvc_
deploy" -dest:package=HelloWorldMvc01.zip.
```

Once you execute this command, you will see that the file HelloWorldMvc01.zip is created in the current working directory. If the package already existed at the destination, then only the changes would be made to the package. You can test this by removing a file from the package and running the command again. Now let's take a look at another commonly used provider, dbFullSql.

> **Note** While you are experimenting with msdeploy.exe, you should know that you can use the –whatif switch to determine what actions would be performed if you executed the command. Using –whatif will not make any changes; it only simulates them.

In many cases, your application relies on a database. With MSDeploy, you can deploy a SQL Server database using the dbFullSql provider. This provider was designed for *first-time publishing*. It is not designed to do incremental publishing, although you can do it if there are no conflicts between the source and destination. Also, you should note that this provider is not capable of creating server-level objects such as logons. On this local machine, the AdventureWorks sample database is installed, which you can download at *http://msftdbprodsamples.codeplex.com/*. In order to sync that database with another one on my machine, the following command can be used:

```
msdeploy -verb:sync
    -source:dbFullSql="Data Source=localhost;
        Integrated Security=SSPI;Initial Catalog=AdventureWorks"
    -dest:dbFullSql=C:\InsideMSBuild\Ch17\advWorksFull.sql.
```

As you can see, the dbFullSql provider is used as the source and is provided the connection string to the AdventureWorks database. For the destination, the full path to where the script should be stored is provided. When scripting to a file, you are required to provide a full path, but you can use an environment variable such as %temp% to help you construct the path. When you perform this operation, this will sync both schema and data by default. So if you open the generated script, you will see operations, such as create table, as well as inserts. You can change that behavior by specifying options to the provider.

Many providers accept options to enable you to customize their behavior. The dbFullSql provider can accept 122 different options. You can see all the options with the `msdeploy -verb:sync -source:dbFullSql /?` command. In order to pass an option to a provider, you just insert a comma followed by the option in the form *<option>=<value>*. For example, if you want to script only the schema of the AdventureWorks database, then you would modify the command to `msdeploy -verb:sync -source:dbFullSql="Data Source=localhost;Integrated Security=SSPI;Initial Catlog=AdventureWorks", includeData=false -dest:dbFullSql=C:\InsideMSBuild\Ch17\advWorksFull -NoData.sql`.

Every provider is free to define what options it can accept, but some common options are outlined in Table 17-4. We will show how to use some of these settings in the subsequent discussion.

TABLE 17-4 Common MSDeploy Provider Options

Option	Description
computerName	The name of the remote server, or URL. If the Remote Agent service is running on a nondefault port, then you should specify the full URL instead of just the name of the computer as you normally would.
userName	The user name that will be used to authenticate to the remote server.
password	The password that will be used to authenticate to the remote server.
includeAcls	This option can be used to determine if ACLs should be included in the sync operation.
tempAgent	If you want to use the temp agent, then you can specify this value to be true.

To demonstrate how to use some of these settings, we have installed the MSDeploy Remote Agent service on a virtual machine with the name WIN-MCX6WTF4J4R. In order to sync the HelloWorldMvc_deploy application from my local IIS server to that machine, we would invoke the command `msdeploy -verb:sync -source:iisApp="Default Web Site/HelloWorldMvc_deploy" -dest:auto,computerName=WIN-MCX6WTF4J4R,username=deploy,password=p@ssw0rd`.

In this command, we are using the iisApp provider to sync the application to the target remote server. As you can see, we are specifying the following options: computerName, username, and password. If the two machines were in the same domain, then the credentials could have been omitted if the user invoking msdeploy.exe had the necessary rights on the target machine. As you can see, we are using the auto provider here so that we do not have to repeat the iisApp provider and settings for the target. Those are implied when using the auto provider. After executing that command you will see the results shown in Figure 17-10.

```
C:\InsideMSBuild\Ch17\HelloWorldMvc\obj\Debug\Package)msdeploy -verb:sync -source:iisApp="Default W
eb Site/HelloWorldMvc_deploy" -dest:auto,computerName=WIN-MCX6WTF4J4R,username=deploy,password=p@ss
w0rd
Info: Updating createApp (Default Web Site/HelloWorldMvc_deploy).
Info: Adding contentPath (Default Web Site/HelloWorldMvc_deploy).
Info: Adding dirPath (Default Web Site/HelloWorldMvc_deploy).
Info: Adding child dirPath (Default Web Site/HelloWorldMvc_deploy\bin).
Info: Adding child dirPath (Default Web Site/HelloWorldMvc_deploy\Content).
Info: Adding child dirPath (Default Web Site/HelloWorldMvc_deploy\Scripts).
Info: Adding child dirPath (Default Web Site/HelloWorldMvc_deploy\Views).
Info: Adding child dirPath (Default Web Site/HelloWorldMvc_deploy\Views\Account).
Info: Adding child dirPath (Default Web Site/HelloWorldMvc_deploy\Views\Home).
Info: Adding child dirPath (Default Web Site/HelloWorldMvc_deploy\Views\Shared).
Info: Adding child filePath (Default Web Site/HelloWorldMvc_deploy\bin\HelloWorldMvc.dll).
Info: Adding child filePath (Default Web Site/HelloWorldMvc_deploy\bin\HelloWorldMvc.pdb).
Info: Adding child filePath (Default Web Site/HelloWorldMvc_deploy\Content\Site.css).
Info: Adding child filePath (Default Web Site/HelloWorldMvc_deploy\Global.asax).
Info: Adding child filePath (Default Web Site/HelloWorldMvc_deploy\Scripts\jquery-1.4.1-vsdoc.js).
Info: Adding child filePath (Default Web Site/HelloWorldMvc_deploy\Scripts\jquery-1.4.1.js).
Info: Adding child filePath (Default Web Site/HelloWorldMvc_deploy\Scripts\jquery-1.4.1.min.js).
Info: Adding child filePath (Default Web Site/HelloWorldMvc_deploy\Scripts\jquery.validate-vsdoc.js
).
Info: Adding child filePath (Default Web Site/HelloWorldMvc_deploy\Scripts\jquery.validate.js).
Info: Adding child filePath (Default Web Site/HelloWorldMvc_deploy\Scripts\jquery.validate.min.js).

Info: Adding child filePath (Default Web Site/HelloWorldMvc_deploy\Scripts\MicrosoftAjax.debug.js).

Info: Adding child filePath (Default Web Site/HelloWorldMvc_deploy\Scripts\MicrosoftAjax.js).
Info: Adding child filePath (Default Web Site/HelloWorldMvc_deploy\Scripts\MicrosoftMvcAjax.debug.j
s).
Info: Adding child filePath (Default Web Site/HelloWorldMvc_deploy\Scripts\MicrosoftMvcAjax.js).
Info: Adding child filePath (Default Web Site/HelloWorldMvc_deploy\Scripts\MicrosoftMvcValidation.d
ebug.js).
Info: Adding child filePath (Default Web Site/HelloWorldMvc_deploy\Scripts\MicrosoftMvcValidation.j
s).
Info: Adding child filePath (Default Web Site/HelloWorldMvc_deploy\Views\Account\ChangePassword.asp
x).
Info: Adding child filePath (Default Web Site/HelloWorldMvc_deploy\Views\Account\ChangePasswordSucc
ess.aspx).
Info: Adding child filePath (Default Web Site/HelloWorldMvc_deploy\Views\Account\LogOn.aspx).
Info: Adding child filePath (Default Web Site/HelloWorldMvc_deploy\Views\Account\Register.aspx).
Info: Adding child filePath (Default Web Site/HelloWorldMvc_deploy\Views\Home\About.aspx).
Info: Adding child filePath (Default Web Site/HelloWorldMvc_deploy\Views\Home\Index.aspx).
Info: Adding child filePath (Default Web Site/HelloWorldMvc_deploy\Views\Shared\Error.aspx).
Info: Adding child filePath (Default Web Site/HelloWorldMvc_deploy\Views\Shared\LogOnUserControl.as
cx).
Info: Adding child filePath (Default Web Site/HelloWorldMvc_deploy\Views\Shared\Site.Master).
Info: Adding child filePath (Default Web Site/HelloWorldMvc_deploy\Views\Web.config).
Info: Adding child filePath (Default Web Site/HelloWorldMvc_deploy\Web.config).
Info: Adding child filePath (Default Web Site/HelloWorldMvc_deploy\Web.QA.config).
Total changes: 38 (37 added, 0 deleted, 1 updated, 0 parameters changed, 1158641 bytes copied)
```

FIGURE 17-10 msdeploy.exe used to sync HelloWorldMvc_deploy to a remote server

From the results in Figure 17-10, we can see that the application was successfully deployed to the WIN-MCX6WTF4J4R machine. Now that we have discussed providers, we will move on to discuss MSDeploy rules.

MSDeploy Rules

Along with providers, MSDeploy includes the concept of rules that govern behavior during syncs. When a sync operation is executed, MSDeploy will check to see whether there is a defined and enabled rule that applies to the current add, update, or delete operation. If there is, then the rule is given a chance to modify the behavior of the action. This will become more concrete as we take a closer look at rules. There are many rules shipped with MSDeploy, and some of them are disabled by default. We will not discuss all of the rules here, but you can get a list of them, along with descriptions, by executing the command msdeploy -enableRule /?. To give you an idea of the types of rules that are available, take a look at a Table 17-5, which lists just a few rules.

TABLE 17-5 **MSDeploy Rules**

Name	Description
DoNotDeleteRule	This is the rule that can be used to block deletions from occurring on the destination. This rule is disabled by default.
EnvironmentVariableNormalize	This rule is responsible for expanding environment variables such as %temp% and %windir%. It is enabled by default.
Parameterization	This rule enables support for parameterization via –declareParam and –setParam. This rule is not intended to be used directly, and it is enabled by default.
SkipNewerFilesRule	This rule can be used to ensure that only out-of-date files are written to the destination. It is disabled by default.
SyncGeneral	This rule facilitates general sync operations. This rule is not intended to be used directly, and it is enabled by default.

In order to enable a rule when you invoke msdeploy.exe, you can use the –enableRule switch, and to disable a rule, use –disableRule. As an example, let's take another look at the HelloWorldMvc_deploy application that we deployed earlier. This time, before we perform a sync, we will copy another file where the application is running with the command copy ExtraFile.txt C:\inetpub\wwwroot\HelloWorldMvc_deploy. The lt rules enabled are shown in Figure 17-11.

```
C:\InsideMSBuild\Ch17>copy ExtraFile.txt C:\inetpub\wwwroot\HelloWorldMvc_deploy
        1 file(s) copied.

C:\InsideMSBuild\Ch17>msdeploy -verb:sync -source:package=HelloWorldMvc\obj\Debug\Package\HelloWorl
dMvc.zip -dest:auto
Info: Deleting filePath (Default Web Site/HelloWorldMvc_deploy\ExtraFile.txt).
Info: Updating setAcl (Default Web Site/HelloWorldMvc_deploy).
Info: Updating setAcl (Default Web Site/HelloWorldMvc_deploy).
Total changes: 3 (0 added, 1 deleted, 2 updated, 0 parameters changed, 0 bytes copied)
```

FIGURE 17-11 Sync showing removal of target object

From Figure 17-11, we can see that the file that we just copied, ExtraFile.txt, was deleted from the destination because it didn't exist in the source package. This is by design. When you tell MSDeploy to perform a sync, it will make sure that the destination object looks just like the source object. In many cases, this can be undesirable. For example, if you have a blog that writes entries as a file on disk, you do not want to destroy all of your entries. In order to perform a sync without destroying those files, we can just enable DoNotDeleteRule. Now, let's do the same copy and sync operation, but this time, we will enable that rule. The result is captured in Figure 17-12.

```
C:\InsideMSBuild\Ch17>copy ExtraFile.txt C:\inetpub\wwwroot\HelloWorldMvc_deploy
        1 file(s) copied.

C:\InsideMSBuild\Ch17>msdeploy -verb:sync -source:package=HelloWorldMvc\obj\Debug\Package\HelloWorl
dMvc.zip -dest:auto -enableRule:DoNotDeleteRule
Info: Updating setAcl (Default Web Site/HelloWorldMvc_deploy).
Info: Updating setAcl (Default Web Site/HelloWorldMvc_deploy).
Total changes: 2 (0 added, 0 deleted, 2 updated, 0 parameters changed, 0 bytes copied)
```

FIGURE 17-12 Sync with DoNotDelete rule enabled

The command for that would be

```
msdeploy -verb:sync
    -source:package=HelloWorldMvc\obj\Debug\Package\HelloWorldMvc.zip
    -dest:auto -enableRule:DoNotDeleteRule
```

From the results shown in Figure 17-12, we can see that no files were deleted, which is exactly what we wanted to accomplish. Now let's briefly discuss the –replace and –skip command-line switches.

When you invoke msdeploy.exe, you can also include –replace and –skip directives. Let's see how they work. From the HelloWorldMvc example, you might have noticed the presence of a Web.QA.config file in the root of the project, along with a Web.config file. Let's say that we wanted to deploy the package and replace Web.config with Web.QA.config. We could achieve that by using the –replace rule. First, we will see the example in action; then, we will dissect the syntax in more detail. The command to perform the sync and replace is here.

```
msdeploy -verb:sync
    -source:package=HelloWorldMvc\obj\Debug\Package\HelloWorldMvc.zip
    -dest:auto
    -replace:objectName=filePath,match=Web.QA.config,replace=Web.config
```

The results of running this code are shown in Figure 17-13.

```
C:\InsideMSBuild\Ch17>msdeploy -verb:sync -source:package=HelloWorldMvc\obj\Debug\Package\HelloWorl
dMvc.zip -dest:auto -replace:objectName=filePath,match=Web.QA.config,replace=Web.config
Info: Deleting filePath (Default Web Site/HelloWorldMvc_deploy\ExtraFile.txt).
Info: Adding child filePath (Default Web Site/HelloWorldMvc_deploy\Web.config).
Info: Deleting filePath (Default Web Site/HelloWorldMvc_deploy\Web.QA.config).
Info: Updating setAcl (Default Web Site/HelloWorldMvc_deploy).
Info: Updating setAcl (Default Web Site/HelloWorldMvc_deploy).
Total changes: 5 (1 added, 2 deleted, 2 updated, 0 parameters changed, 2945 bytes copied)
```

FIGURE 17-13 MSDeploy Replace example

Here, we can see that the application was synced and the Web.config file was updated. If you open that file, you will see that it is the Web.QA.config file. Now let's take a closer look at this command. The new part of this command is `-replace:objectName=filePath,` `match=Web.QA.config,replace=Web.config`. In this syntax, we always use the –replace switch and then pass it some parameters for the replacement. In order to help to create the values for the options, you can use the –xml option against the source to see the XML representation that MSDeploy uses internally. In this example, since our source is the HelloWorldMvc.zip file, we would execute the command `msdeploy -verb:dump` `-source:package=obj\Debug\Package\HelloWorldMvc.zip -xml > result.xml` to place the XML content into result.xml file. Here, we are using the > directive to pipe the result of the command to a file, result.xml. In the next code snippet, you will see a version of that file (which has been abbreviated to save space).

```
<output>
  <sitemanifest>
    <iisApp path="C:\InsideMSBuild\...\PackageTmp">
      <createApp path="C:\InsideMSBuild\...\PackageTmp" isDest="False" ... />
      <contentPath path="C:\InsideMSBuild\...\PackageTmp">
        <dirPath path="C:\InsideMSBuild\...\PackageTmp" ...>
          <dirPath path="bin" ...>
            ...
          </dirPath>
          <dirPath path="Content" ...>
            ...
          </dirPath>
          <filePath path="Global.asax" .../>
          <dirPath path="Scripts" ...>
            ...
          </dirPath>
          <dirPath path="Views" ...>
            <dirPath path="Account" ...>
              ...
            </dirPath>
            <dirPath path="Home" ...>
              ...
            </dirPath>
            <dirPath path="Shared" ...>
              ...
            </dirPath>
            <filePath path="Web.config" ...>
          </dirPath>
          <filePath path="Web.config" ...>
          <filePath path="Web.QA.config" ...>
        </dirPath>
      </contentPath>
    </iisApp>
    <setAcl path="C:\InsideMSBuild\...\PackageTmp"...>
    <setAcl path="C:\InsideMSBuild\...\PackageTmp" ...>
  </sitemanifest>
</output>
```

From this snippet, you can see the presence of the Web.config and Web.QA.config files inside a filePath element. In basic terms, when each element is encountered, an MSDeploy provider is started to process it. For files, this would be the filePath provider. The provider is invoked with all the attribute values to perform its operation. What we need to do is locate the element that we want to replace and use them in the –replace expression, the expression we used again was `-replace:objectName=filePath,match=Web.QA.config,replace=Web.config`.

For objectName, you will specify a regular expression that can be used to identify the element. In this case, it is just filePath. Then the match option is passed to identify the specific filePath entry that we want to replace. Following that, the replacement value is specified. So the name "Web.QA.config" is replaced with "Web.config" during the sync operation. Note when performing a replace like this it is important to follow the naming convention {Filename}.{Identifier}.{Extension} where {Filename} and {Extension} are taken from the file you are replacing and {Identifier} is any string. This is because you must ensure that the operation which writes the original file occurs before the replacement, otherwise the replaced file may be overwritten by the original file.

Now, we will look at another replace example so that we can provide a bit more clarity. From the same package, we just sync the package up to the initial state with the command `msdeploy -verb:sync -source:package=obj\Debug\Package\HelloWorldMvc.zip -dest:auto="Default Web Site/HelloWorldMvc_deploy"` from the C:\InsideMSBuild\ Ch17\HelloWorldMvc directory. For the sake of giving an example, let's say that when we performed the sync, we want the Scripts folder to be renamed ScriptsProd. In order to achieve that, we could use the command shown here.

```
msdeploy -verb:sync
        -source:package=obj\Debug\Package\HelloWorldMvc.zip
        -dest:auto
        -replace:objectName=dirPath,match=Scripts,replace=ScriptsProd
```

This is very similar to the file replacement that we performed last time. After you execute that command, you should see the result shown in Figure 17-14.

In the result shown in Figure 17-14, you can see that all of the files under Scripts were removed and then files added under ScriptsProd. If it were a fresh sync, then the Scripts folder would have never been created. You can include multiple –replace values for a single sync. For example, if you wanted to perform both of the previous replacements, you could use the combined command shown next.

```
msdeploy -verb:sync
    -source:package=obj\Debug\Package\HelloWorldMvc.zip
    -dest:auto
    -replace:objectName=filePath,match=Web.QA.config,replace=Web.config
    -replace:objectName=dirPath,match=Scripts,replace=ScriptsProd
```

```
C:\InsideMSBuild\Ch17\HelloWorldMvc>msdeploy -verb:sync -source:package=obj\Debug\Package\HelloWorl
dMvc.zip -dest:auto -replace:objectName=dirPath,match=Scripts,replace=ScriptsProd
Info: Adding child filePath (Default Web Site/HelloWorldMvc_deploy\abc.config).
Info: Deleting filePath (Default Web Site/HelloWorldMvc_deploy\Scripts\jquery-1.4.1-vsdoc.js).
Info: Deleting filePath (Default Web Site/HelloWorldMvc_deploy\Scripts\jquery-1.4.1.js).
Info: Deleting filePath (Default Web Site/HelloWorldMvc_deploy\Scripts\jquery-1.4.1.min.js).
Info: Deleting filePath (Default Web Site/HelloWorldMvc_deploy\Scripts\jquery.validate-vsdoc.js).
Info: Deleting filePath (Default Web Site/HelloWorldMvc_deploy\Scripts\jquery.validate.js).
Info: Deleting filePath (Default Web Site/HelloWorldMvc_deploy\Scripts\jquery.validate.min.js).
Info: Deleting filePath (Default Web Site/HelloWorldMvc_deploy\Scripts\MicrosoftAjax.debug.js).
Info: Deleting filePath (Default Web Site/HelloWorldMvc_deploy\Scripts\MicrosoftAjax.js).
Info: Deleting filePath (Default Web Site/HelloWorldMvc_deploy\Scripts\MicrosoftMvcAjax.debug.js).
Info: Deleting filePath (Default Web Site/HelloWorldMvc_deploy\Scripts\MicrosoftMvcAjax.js).
Info: Deleting filePath (Default Web Site/HelloWorldMvc_deploy\Scripts\MicrosoftMvcValidation.debug
.js).
Info: Deleting filePath (Default Web Site/HelloWorldMvc_deploy\Scripts\MicrosoftMvcValidation.js).
Info: Deleting dirPath (Default Web Site/HelloWorldMvc_deploy\Scripts).
Info: Adding child dirPath (Default Web Site/HelloWorldMvc_deploy\ScriptsProd).
Info: Adding child filePath (Default Web Site/HelloWorldMvc_deploy\ScriptsProd\jquery-1.4.1-vsdoc.j
s).
Info: Adding child filePath (Default Web Site/HelloWorldMvc_deploy\ScriptsProd\jquery-1.4.1.js).
Info: Adding child filePath (Default Web Site/HelloWorldMvc_deploy\ScriptsProd\jquery-1.4.1.min.js)
.
Info: Adding child filePath (Default Web Site/HelloWorldMvc_deploy\ScriptsProd\jquery.validate-vsdo
c.js).
Info: Adding child filePath (Default Web Site/HelloWorldMvc_deploy\ScriptsProd\jquery.validate.js).
Info: Adding child filePath (Default Web Site/HelloWorldMvc_deploy\ScriptsProd\jquery.validate.min.
js).
Info: Adding child filePath (Default Web Site/HelloWorldMvc_deploy\ScriptsProd\MicrosoftAjax.debug.
js).
Info: Adding child filePath (Default Web Site/HelloWorldMvc_deploy\ScriptsProd\MicrosoftAjax.js).
Info: Adding child filePath (Default Web Site/HelloWorldMvc_deploy\ScriptsProd\MicrosoftMvcAjax.deb
ug.js).
Info: Adding child filePath (Default Web Site/HelloWorldMvc_deploy\ScriptsProd\MicrosoftMvcAjax.js)
.
Info: Adding child filePath (Default Web Site/HelloWorldMvc_deploy\ScriptsProd\MicrosoftMvcValidati
on.debug.js).
Info: Adding child filePath (Default Web Site/HelloWorldMvc_deploy\ScriptsProd\MicrosoftMvcValidati
on.js).
Info: Updating setAcl (Default Web Site/HelloWorldMvc_deploy).
Info: Updating setAcl (Default Web Site/HelloWorldMvc_deploy).
Total changes: 29 (14 added, 13 deleted, 2 updated, 0 parameters changed, 1083297 bytes copied)
```

FIGURE 17-14   MSDeploy replacing a directory name

The –replace directive is able to digest a few other options, but we will not discuss them here. You can see those options by executing the command `msdeploy.exe -replace /?`. Now that we have discussed the replace command, we can now move on to discuss the skip command.

You can use the –skip directive to ensure that the specified operation(s) are not performed on the target object. For example, you could use –skip to keep files or directories from being synced or to keep ACLs from being updated, and any other operation that MSDeploy performs. In our HelloWorldMvc example, there are two config files in the root, Web.config and Web.QA.config, inside the package. In our development environment, when we sync we do not want to drop the Web.QA.config file on the target server. In order to skip the Web.QA.config file, you need to add the following to the sync command `-skip:objectName=filePath,keyAttribute=Web.QA.config`. Here, we have used the –skip switch in a similar fashion as –replace. The only difference here is that for skip, we have used keyAttribute instead of match. Since we are dealing with a filePath element, the key attribute is path, so when we specify keyAttribute. MSDeploy will try and match the value provided for the path value. For other providers, keyAttribute may be different. When you perform a sync and specify an object to be skipped, the object will not be removed if it already exists on the target. This is because the comparison of source and target does not take skip directives into account. To show you the skip, let's first get rid of the HelloWorldMvc_deploy application from the local IIS server with the command `msdeploy -verb:delete -dest:iisApp="Default Web Site/HelloWorldMvc_deploy"`. This will create a clean slate. The full command, including the skip, is shown in the next snippet.

```
msdeploy -verb:sync
    -source:package=obj\Debug\Package\HelloWorldMvc.zip
    -dest:auto
    -skip:objectName=filePath,keyAttribute=Web.QA.config
```

The result of this is shown in Figure 17-15.

```
C:\InsideMSBuild\Ch17\HelloWorldMvc>msdeploy -verb:sync -source:package=obj\Debug\Package\HelloWorl
dMvc.zip -dest:auto -skip:objectName=filePath,keyAttribute=Web.QA.config
Info: Adding sitemanifest (sitemanifest).
Info: Updating createApp (Default Web Site/HelloWorldMvc_deploy).
Info: Adding contentPath (Default Web Site/HelloWorldMvc_deploy).
Info: Adding dirPath (Default Web Site/HelloWorldMvc_deploy).
Info: Adding child dirPath (Default Web Site/HelloWorldMvc_deploy\bin).
Info: Adding child filePath (Default Web Site/HelloWorldMvc_deploy\bin\HelloWorldMvc.dll).
Info: Adding child filePath (Default Web Site/HelloWorldMvc_deploy\bin\HelloWorldMvc.pdb).
Info: Adding child dirPath (Default Web Site/HelloWorldMvc_deploy\Content).
Info: Adding child filePath (Default Web Site/HelloWorldMvc_deploy\Content\Site.css).
Info: Adding child filePath (Default Web Site/HelloWorldMvc_deploy\Global.asax).
Info: Adding child dirPath (Default Web Site/HelloWorldMvc_deploy\Scripts).
Info: Adding child filePath (Default Web Site/HelloWorldMvc_deploy\Scripts\jquery-1.4.1-vsdoc.js).
Info: Adding child filePath (Default Web Site/HelloWorldMvc_deploy\Scripts\jquery-1.4.1.js).
Info: Adding child filePath (Default Web Site/HelloWorldMvc_deploy\Scripts\jquery-1.4.1.min.js).
Info: Adding child filePath (Default Web Site/HelloWorldMvc_deploy\Scripts\jquery.validate-vsdoc.js
).
Info: Adding child filePath (Default Web Site/HelloWorldMvc_deploy\Scripts\jquery.validate.js).
Info: Adding child filePath (Default Web Site/HelloWorldMvc_deploy\Scripts\jquery.validate.min.js).

Info: Adding child filePath (Default Web Site/HelloWorldMvc_deploy\Scripts\MicrosoftAjax.debug.js).

Info: Adding child filePath (Default Web Site/HelloWorldMvc_deploy\Scripts\MicrosoftAjax.js).
Info: Adding child filePath (Default Web Site/HelloWorldMvc_deploy\Scripts\MicrosoftMvcAjax.debug.j
s).
Info: Adding child filePath (Default Web Site/HelloWorldMvc_deploy\Scripts\MicrosoftMvcAjax.js).
Info: Adding child filePath (Default Web Site/HelloWorldMvc_deploy\Scripts\MicrosoftMvcValidation.d
ebug.js).
Info: Adding child filePath (Default Web Site/HelloWorldMvc_deploy\Scripts\MicrosoftMvcValidation.j
s).
Info: Adding child dirPath (Default Web Site/HelloWorldMvc_deploy\Views).
Info: Adding child dirPath (Default Web Site/HelloWorldMvc_deploy\Views\Account).
Info: Adding child filePath (Default Web Site/HelloWorldMvc_deploy\Views\Account\ChangePassword.asp
x).
Info: Adding child filePath (Default Web Site/HelloWorldMvc_deploy\Views\Account\ChangePasswordSucc
ess.aspx).
Info: Adding child filePath (Default Web Site/HelloWorldMvc_deploy\Views\Account\LogOn.aspx).
Info: Adding child filePath (Default Web Site/HelloWorldMvc_deploy\Views\Account\Register.aspx).
Info: Adding child dirPath (Default Web Site/HelloWorldMvc_deploy\Views\Home).
Info: Adding child filePath (Default Web Site/HelloWorldMvc_deploy\Views\Home\About.aspx).
Info: Adding child filePath (Default Web Site/HelloWorldMvc_deploy\Views\Home\Index.aspx).
Info: Adding child dirPath (Default Web Site/HelloWorldMvc_deploy\Views\Shared).
Info: Adding child filePath (Default Web Site/HelloWorldMvc_deploy\Views\Shared\Error.aspx).
Info: Adding child filePath (Default Web Site/HelloWorldMvc_deploy\Views\Shared\LogOnUserControl.as
cx).
Info: Adding child filePath (Default Web Site/HelloWorldMvc_deploy\Views\Shared\Site.Master).
Info: Adding child filePath (Default Web Site/HelloWorldMvc_deploy\Views\Web.config).
Info: Adding child filePath (Default Web Site/HelloWorldMvc_deploy\Web.config).
Info: Adding setAcl (Default Web Site/HelloWorldMvc_deploy).
Info: Adding setAcl (Default Web Site/HelloWorldMvc_deploy).
Total changes: 40 (39 added, 0 deleted, 1 updated, 0 parameters changed, 1155696 bytes copied)
```

FIGURE 17-15 MSDeploy skip example

From these results, you can see that the Web.QA.config file was indeed not synced with the destination, which is exactly what we wanted. In that screen, toward the bottom, you can see that two setAcl actions were executed. If you wanted to skip these actions as well, you could add the switch -skip:objectName=setAcl. To demonstrate this once again, we will delete the IIS application using the command msdeploy -verb:delete -dest:iisApp="Default Web Site/HelloWorldMvc_deploy". Then we will execute the command shown here, which contains both skip operations.

```
msdeploy -verb:sync
    -source:package=obj\Debug\Package\HelloWorldMvc.zip
    -dest:auto
    -skip:objectName=filePath,keyAttribute=Web.QA.config
    -skip:objectName=setAcl
```

The result of executing this command is shown in Figure 17-16.

```
C:\InsideMSBuild\Ch17\HelloWorldMvc>msdeploy -verb:sync -source:package=obj\Debug\Package\HelloWorl
dMvc.zip -dest:auto -skip:objectName=filePath,keyAttribute=Web.QA.config -skip:objectName=setAcl
Info: Updating createApp (Default Web Site/HelloWorldMvc_deploy).
Info: Adding contentPath (Default Web Site/HelloWorldMvc_deploy).
Info: Adding dirPath (Default Web Site/HelloWorldMvc_deploy).
Info: Adding child dirPath (Default Web Site/HelloWorldMvc_deploy\bin).
Info: Adding child filePath (Default Web Site/HelloWorldMvc_deploy\bin\HelloWorldMvc.dll).
Info: Adding child filePath (Default Web Site/HelloWorldMvc_deploy\bin\HelloWorldMvc.pdb).
Info: Adding child dirPath (Default Web Site/HelloWorldMvc_deploy\Content).
Info: Adding child filePath (Default Web Site/HelloWorldMvc_deploy\Content\Site.css).
Info: Adding child filePath (Default Web Site/HelloWorldMvc_deploy\Global.asax).
Info: Adding child dirPath (Default Web Site/HelloWorldMvc_deploy\Scripts).
Info: Adding child filePath (Default Web Site/HelloWorldMvc_deploy\Scripts\jquery-1.4.1-vsdoc.js).
Info: Adding child filePath (Default Web Site/HelloWorldMvc_deploy\Scripts\jquery-1.4.1.js).
Info: Adding child filePath (Default Web Site/HelloWorldMvc_deploy\Scripts\jquery-1.4.1.min.js).
Info: Adding child filePath (Default Web Site/HelloWorldMvc_deploy\Scripts\jquery.validate-vsdoc.js
).
Info: Adding child filePath (Default Web Site/HelloWorldMvc_deploy\Scripts\jquery.validate.js).
Info: Adding child filePath (Default Web Site/HelloWorldMvc_deploy\Scripts\jquery.validate.min.js).

Info: Adding child filePath (Default Web Site/HelloWorldMvc_deploy\Scripts\MicrosoftAjax.debug.js).

Info: Adding child filePath (Default Web Site/HelloWorldMvc_deploy\Scripts\MicrosoftAjax.js).
Info: Adding child filePath (Default Web Site/HelloWorldMvc_deploy\Scripts\MicrosoftMvcAjax.debug.j
s).
Info: Adding child filePath (Default Web Site/HelloWorldMvc_deploy\Scripts\MicrosoftMvcAjax.js).
Info: Adding child filePath (Default Web Site/HelloWorldMvc_deploy\Scripts\MicrosoftMvcValidation.d
ebug.js).
Info: Adding child filePath (Default Web Site/HelloWorldMvc_deploy\Scripts\MicrosoftMvcValidation.j
s).
Info: Adding child dirPath (Default Web Site/HelloWorldMvc_deploy\Views).
Info: Adding child dirPath (Default Web Site/HelloWorldMvc_deploy\Views\Account).
Info: Adding child filePath (Default Web Site/HelloWorldMvc_deploy\Views\Account\ChangePassword.asp
x).
Info: Adding child filePath (Default Web Site/HelloWorldMvc_deploy\Views\Account\ChangePasswordSucc
ess.aspx).
Info: Adding child filePath (Default Web Site/HelloWorldMvc_deploy\Views\Account\LogOn.aspx).
Info: Adding child filePath (Default Web Site/HelloWorldMvc_deploy\Views\Account\Register.aspx).
Info: Adding child dirPath (Default Web Site/HelloWorldMvc_deploy\Views\Home).
Info: Adding child filePath (Default Web Site/HelloWorldMvc_deploy\Views\Home\About.aspx).
Info: Adding child filePath (Default Web Site/HelloWorldMvc_deploy\Views\Home\Index.aspx).
Info: Adding child dirPath (Default Web Site/HelloWorldMvc_deploy\Views\Shared).
Info: Adding child filePath (Default Web Site/HelloWorldMvc_deploy\Views\Shared\Error.aspx).
Info: Adding child filePath (Default Web Site/HelloWorldMvc_deploy\Views\Shared\LogOnUserControl.as
cx).
Info: Adding child filePath (Default Web Site/HelloWorldMvc_deploy\Views\Shared\Site.Master).
Info: Adding child filePath (Default Web Site/HelloWorldMvc_deploy\Views\Web.config).
Info: Adding child filePath (Default Web Site/HelloWorldMvc_deploy\Web.config).
Total changes: 37 (36 added, 0 deleted, 1 updated, 0 parameters changed, 1155696 bytes copied)
```

FIGURE 17-16 MSDeploy skip command

In Figure 17-16, you can see that the Web.QA.config file was skipped, as well as the setAcl actions. As with the replace operation, sync has more options than what has been shown here. To see the full set of options, execute the command `msdeploy.exe -skip /?`. We will now move on to discuss MSDeploy parameters.

MSDeploy Parameters

With MSDeploy, you can parameterize a package or an archive, which is a package that is unzipped. For this discussion, we will only cover packages, but much of the same information applies to archives. When a package is imported via the IIS 7 Import Application interface, as discussed previously in this chapter, the user will be given a chance to specify the value for that parameter. In order to create a package with a parameter, from the command line, you have to use the –declareParam option. When you perform the sync, you use the –setParam switch. We will see how to use both of these in this section. Before we start defining parameters on packages, let's first see how to create a package from an IIS application. You can create a package from the HelloWorldMvc_deploy application with the following command.

```
msdeploy -verb:sync
    -source:iisApp="Default Web Site/HelloWorldMvc_deploy"
    -dest:package=C:\InsideMSBuild\Ch17\HelloFromIIS.zip
```

Once you execute this command, you will see that the HelloFromIIS.zip file will be created. This is the most basic way of creating a package from an IIS application. Now, let's see if we can decorate the created package with some parameters. First, let's go through the process of creating a package with a parameter; and then, using that package to sync, after that, we will take a closer look at the syntax to create and set parameter values.

For this example, we will use the HelloWorldMvc_deploy IIS application. In the Web.config file for that application, two connection strings are defined. The *connectionStrings* element is shown here.

```
<connectionStrings>
  <add name="customersDb"
      connectionString="Data Source=.;Integrated Security=SSPI;Initial Catalog=Customers"/>
  <add name="recordsDb"
      connectionString="Data Source=.;Integrated Security=SSPI;Initial Catalog=Records"/>
</connectionStrings>
```

It would be great if we could create a package and define a parameter to update these connection string values. First, let's start with one connection string; then we will show you how to create a package with multiple parameters. We have already seen the syntax to create the package from the application. Now, take a look at the syntax to create the package with a parameter.

```
msdeploy -verb:sync
  -source:iisApp="Default Web Site/HelloWorldMvc_deploy"
  -dest:package=HelloFromIIS.zip
  -declareParam:
    name=recordsDbConnString,
    kind=XmlFile,
    scope=Web.config,
    match=/configuration/connectionStrings/add[@name='recordsDb']/@connectionString,
    defaultValue="Data Source=default;Integrated Security=SSPI;Initial Catalog=Records"
```

We will go over this syntax in more detail later in this section, but let's go over the basics now. In this statement, you can see that we have added the –declareParam option, along with a few arguments passed to it. The parameter that we are creating here is named recordsDbConnString. We have indicated that the file that it needs to update is an XmlFile and that the file path is Web.config. After that, we have specified the XPath expression to locate the attribute that needs to be updated. Once again, we will go over all of this syntax in more detail soon. After this command executes, the package HelloFromIIS.zip is created. Now, we will remove the HelloWorldMvc_deploy application using the delete command. That command is `msdeploy -verb:delete -dest:iisApp="Default Web Site/HelloWorldMvc_deploy"`. If you imported this package using the IIS Manager's Import Application feature, then the Parameters page would look like Figure 17-17.

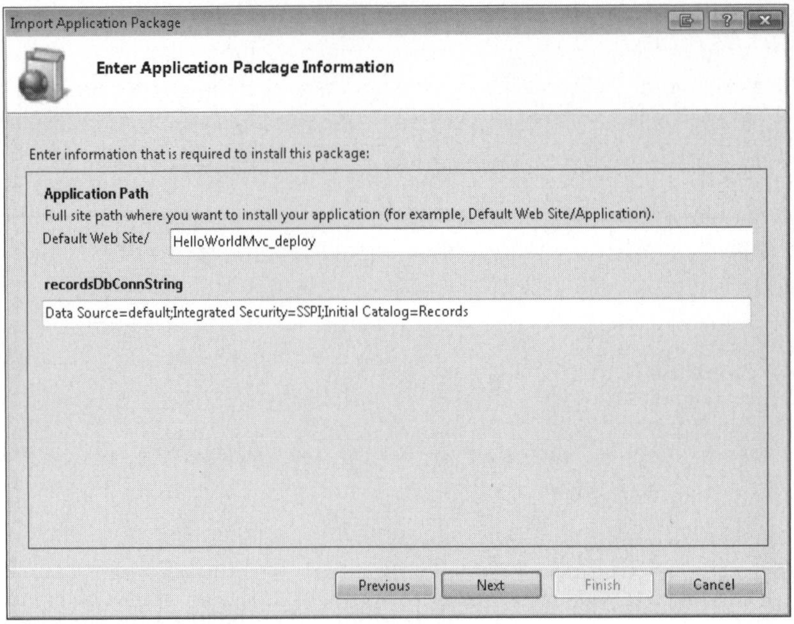

FIGURE 17-17 Import Application Package dialog

In Figure 17-17, you can see that the new parameter is displayed with the default value. For this example, we will cancel the import because we want to specify the value for that parameter on the command line. In order to specify the value for a parameter during a command-line sync, you will use the –setParam option. You will have to pass that option the name and value of the parameter that you want to specify. In this case, the name of the parameter is 'recordsDbConnString' and the value is Data Source=qa01.records .sedotech;Integrated Security=SSPI;Initial Catalog=Records. The full command in this case is shown in the next code snippet.

```
msdeploy -verb:sync
  -source:package=HelloFromIIS.zip
  -dest:auto
  -setParam:
    name=recordsDbConnString,
    value="Data Source=qa01.records.sedotech;Integrated Security=SSPI;Initial
Catalog=Records"
```

From this command, you can see how the –setParam option is used. It is much simpler to specify the value for a parameter than it is to create the parameter. We can use the –setParam option to actually create a new parameter and set its value at the time the sync operation is occurring. This is a really useful feature because many times, it is difficult to know ahead of time what values you want to parameterize. We will cover this technique in this chapter, but for now, let's talk about the –declareParam syntax in more detail.

–declareParam

Earlier in this chapter, we discussed the –declareParam option at a high level. Now we will delve into it a little bit deeper. This option is capable of parameterizing many different things. Because of this, unfortunately, it has a complicated syntax. The full syntax for this option is shown here.

```
-declareParam:name=<ParameterName>
    ,kind=<ParameterKind>
    ,scope=<ParameterScope>
    ,match=<RegularExpression>
    ,defaultValue=<string>
    ,description=<ParameterDescription>
    ,tags=<tag>[,<tag>,...]
```

In the previous example, we have used many of the arguments. But now let's inspect each one individually.

–declareParam kind Argument

This argument defines the behavior that will be executed for the parameter when the sync is performed. This will be defined by where the value exists that you want to parameterize. The values of the –declareParam kind are listed in Table 17-6.

TABLE 17-6 –declareParam Kind Values

Kind Setting	Description
XmlFile	This kind is used when you need to create a parameter that can be used in any XML file. In many cases, you will use this with Web .config, but you can use this against any XML file.
TextFile	This kind is used to specify a replacement in a text file by using a regular expression.
TextFilePosition	This kind is used to specify a replacement in a text file by using the line and column position of the string, along with its length.
ProviderPath	You can use this kind when you want to change the site name during the sync process.
DestinationVirtualDirectory	This kind can be used to change the physical path where the application will be placed on the target machine.
DestinationBinding	You can use this kind to define a different binding on the target object than what is defined in the source.
DeploymentObjectAttribute	You can use this kind to change other attribute values. For example, you can use it to create a parameter for the user name under which the application pool should execute.

–declareParam scope Argument

The general definition of the scope argument, according to the MSDeploy documentation at *http://technet.microsoft.com/en-us/library/dd569084.aspx*, is that it is "a required regular expression which specifies the scope of the parameter kind." The scope argument is tightly coupled to the kind argument, so let's see how this argument behaves for each kind argument, as shown in Table 17-7.

TABLE 17-7 –declareParam Scope Values

Kind Setting	Description
XmlFile	This scope is a regular expression that can be used to identify the path to the XML file on which the replacement will occur.
TextFile	This scope is a regular expression that can be used to identify the path to the text file on which the replacement will occur.
TextFilePosition	This scope is a regular expression that can be used to identify the path to the text file on which the replacement will occur.
ProviderPath	This scope is a regular expression that will be used to identify on which MSDeploy provider the replacement will occur. If you are not using a manifest, then this value will default to the current provider. If you are using a manifest, then this value will be used to determine which provider(s) it affects.
DestinationVirtualDirectory	This scope is a regular expression that will identify which directory, or directories, will be affected by the parameterization.
DestinationBinding	This scope is a regular expression that is used to determine the website that the binding will target. For IIS 7, this would be Default Web Site. For IIS 6, this should be the ID of the site.
DeploymentObjectAttribute	This scope is a regular expression that specifies the absolute path of the affected object.

–declareParam match Argument

The match argument is much the same as the scope argument. Its definition will vary depending on the parameter kind being used. Table 17-8 lists the definition of this argument for each provider.

TABLE 17-8 –declareParam Match Values

Kind Setting	Description
XmlFile	This match is the XPath expression that will be used to identify the attribute which will be updated.
TextFile	This match is a regular expression. It could just be the actual text, which is used to identify what text will be replaced.
TextFilePosition	For this provider, the match expression should be defined using the following syntax: match=`<Line>;<Column>;<CharCount>`. The values *Line*, *Column*, and *CharCount* identify where in the file the replacement should occur. Note that all of these values are based on 1 instead of 0.

Kind Setting	Description
ProviderPath	For this parameter kind, the match argument is used only when a manifest is being synced. In this case, the match argument is used to determine which providers will be affected.
DestinationVirtualDirectory	The match argument is not applicable with this parameter kind.
DestinationBinding	This is a regular expression, which is optional, that is used to determine the binding that will be modified.
DeploymentObjectAttribute	This is a regular expression that identifies which attribute will be updated.

–declareParam defaultValue Argument

The –declareParam defaultValue argument is the value that will be applied for the parameter if no other value is given. If your properties have meaningful defaults then it is a good idea to supply their values here.

–declareParam tags Argument

The –declareParam tags argument is a location where you can place metadata about the parameter that is being declared. For example, if you have a parameter that relates to a database connection, you could indicate this via a DatabaseConnectionString tag, or if you have a parameter that is a user name, then you could indicate this with the a Username tag. You are free to use this as you see fit.

–setParam

Now that we have discussed some of these parameters, let's see how we can put them to use. First, let's create a package from the HelloWorldMvc_deploy site, defining a parameter for the IIS application name and a parameter that will define the physical path where we want the application stored. To do that, we use the simple command shown here.

```
msdeploy -verb:sync
    -source:appHostConfig="Default Web Site/HelloWorldMvc_deploy"
    -dest:package=C:\InsideMSBuild\Ch17\HelloWorld.zip
```

Once you execute this command, the zip file is dropped to C:\InsideMSBuild\Ch17\ HelloWorld.zip. After that, we can delete that site from the IIS server using the command `msdeploy -verb:delete -dest:appHostConfig="Default Web Site/HelloWorldMvc_ deploy"`. Up until this point, we have been discussing the –declareParam switch. Now, let's discuss the –setParam switch. We can use this switch to set the value for any defined parameter, and even to define and set the value for a new parameter during a sync. For example, if you take the package that you just created, there are no defined parameters, but you can use the –setParam switch to change the physical path where the application will be stored. In order to do that, you could execute the command shown here.

```
msdeploy -verb:sync
  -source:package=C:\InsideMSBuild\Ch17\HelloWorld.zip
  -dest:appHostConfig="Default Web Site/HelloWorldMvc_deploy"
  -setParam:kind=DeploymentObjectAttribute,
    scope=virtualDirectory,
    match=virtualDirectory/@physicalPath,
    value="C:\inetpub\wwwroot\Mvc01"
```

When you look at this command, you might be wondering how to construct this yourself. First, the source and dest parts are easy to determine, and we also know that we need to use –setParam to change any values during a sync operation. Now, we need to determine what the parameter kind should be. This is basically a matter of elimination: if there is no specific parameter kind for your situation and you want to change an IIS setting, then you must use the DeploymentObjectAttribute. Following this, we need to figure out what the required values should be for scope and match. In order to determine this, we have to look at the created package to see how MSDeploy represents it. In order to do this, you can use the –verb:dump operation with the –xml option. In this case, you can execute the command.

```
msdeploy -verb:dump
  -source:package=C:\InsideMSBuild\Ch17\HelloWorld.zip -xml
  > C:\InsideMSBuild\Ch17\HelloWorldDump.xml
```

This will write the XML representation of the package to the file C:\InsideMSBuild\Ch17\HelloWorldDump.xml. We have included the file here (but with several substitutions to conserve space), so that you can get a feel for what it looks like.

```
<output>
  <MSDeploy.appHostConfig>
    <appHostConfig path="Default Web Site/HelloWorldMvc_deploy">
      <application path="/HelloWorldMvc_deploy" ...>
        <virtualDirectoryDefaults path="" physicalPath="" userName="" ... />
        <virtualDirectory
          path="/"
          physicalPath="%SystemDrive%\inetpub\wwwroot\HelloWorldMvc_deploy" ...>
          <dirPath path="C:\inetpub\wwwroot\HelloWorldMvc_deploy" ...>
            <dirPath path="bin" securityDescriptor="D:" ...>
              <filePath path="HelloWorldMvc.dll" size="17920" .../>
              <filePath path="HelloWorldMvc.pdb" size="32256" .../>
            </dirPath>
            <dirPath path="Content" securityDescriptor="D:" ...>
              <filePath path="Site.css" size="5379" attributes="Archive" .../>
            </dirPath>
            <filePath path="Global.asax" size="105" attributes="Archive" ... />
            <dirPath path="Scripts" securityDescriptor="D:" ...>
              <filePath path="jquery-1.4.1-vsdoc.js" size="242990"... />
                ...
            </dirPath>
            <dirPath path="Views" ...>
```

```
          <dirPath path="Account" ...>
            <filePath path="ChangePassword.aspx" size="2141" ...>
          </dirPath>
          <dirPath path="Home" securityDescriptor="D:" ...>
            <filePath path="About.aspx" size="390" .../>
            <filePath path="Index.aspx" size="507" .../>
          </dirPath>
          <dirPath path="Shared" securityDescriptor="D:" ...>
            <filePath path="Error.aspx" size="439" attributes="Archive" .../>
            <filePath path="LogOnUserControl.ascx" size="352" .../>
            <filePath path="Site.Master" size="1253" .../>
          </dirPath>
          <filePath path="Web.config" size="1570" .../>
        </dirPath>
        <filePath path="Web.config" size="11932" .../>
        <filePath path="Web.QA.config" size="2945" .../>
      </dirPath>
    </virtualDirectory>
   </application>
  </appHostConfig>
 </MSDeploy.appHostConfig>
</output>
```

In this contents shown here, we have boldfaced the text that represents the attribute that we want to change. In this case, we need to use scope=virtualDirectory to locate the element that we want to update, and then we use the match value to narrow it down to the specific attribute using the XPath expression virtualDirectory/@physicalPath. This is basically the method that you will use to create other parameters. Now that we have discussed parameters a bit, let's move on to the manifest provider.

MSDeploy Manifest Provider

Once you start using MSDeploy, you will notice pretty quickly that it would be really beneficial if you could invoke many providers with the same command—it would be like having a "super" provider that can invoke all other providers. This is pretty much what the manifest provider will do. It allows you to declare, in an XML file, what providers need to be invoked and the values for the options for each provider. This is an advanced concept, and we do not have much space to cover it, but in this section, you should get a good introduction to using manifests. As always, though, the best way to learn something is by doing it. The best way to describe how to use a manifest is to see it in action. Since the package and publish features work only with Web Application Projects (WAPs), we will now see how we can do something similar manually for a website project. To do this, we have created an IIS website project named Website01. You can find the solution file at C:\InsideMSBuild\Ch17\Website01\Website01.sln. You'll need to open Visual Studio in administrator mode because when you open that site, it will create the IIS virtual directory for you. We will use a manifest provider to craft a package that we can use to deploy to another server. Inside the Website01 folder, you will find a file named SourceManifest.xml. The contents of that file are shown on the following page.

```
<sitemanifest>
  <appHostConfig path="Default Web Site/Website01" />
  <dirPath path="C:\InsideMSBuild\Ch17\Website01\"/>
  <setAcl
    path="Default Web Site/Website01\App_Data" setAclAccess="ReadAndExecute,Write,Delete" />
  <setAcl
    path="Default Web Site/Website01\logs" setAclAccess="Write" />
  <runCommand path="echo after finished"/>
</sitemanifest>
```

Let's take this apart a bit before we use it. The first element is the *appHostConfig* element with the path to the virtual directory that IIS is using. This indicates to MSDeploy to take all of the IIS settings from that application. After that, we have a dirPath provider listed with the file path. This indicates to MSDeploy that you want to pull the content from the specified location. The next two providers listed are both setAcl. By using this provider, you can set the access rights that are needed for the application to run. In this case, we are granting read and write (along with execute and delete) access to the App_Data folder, which is the location of my SQL Express database. After that, write access is given to the logs folder. The application will write to a file in this folder. Then, you will see that we use the runCommand provider to send a message to the console. In this case, the action is not useful; but a good way to use this could be to start or stop Windows services or to make a call to an .exe file to initialize your application.

The manifest provider, along with many other providers, does not have to be synced with the same provider. A common scenario when using a manifest provider is to sync it to a package and then use that package to deploy the application to different locations. This is exactly what we are going to do. First, we need to create a package from this manifest; you can do so with the following command.

```
msdeploy -verb:sync
    -source:manifest="C:\InsideMSBuild\Ch17\Website01\SourceManifest.xml"
    -dest:package=C:\InsideMSBuild\Ch17\Website01.zip
```

Once you execute this command, the package is written out to C:\InsideMSBuild\Ch17\Website01.zip. Now, what we need to do is to deploy this to another server. When we do this, we want to set the location where the virtual directory should reside because we do not want the files to be dropped to C:\InsideMSBuild\Ch17\Website01 on my web server. The server that we are deploying to is named WIN-MCX6WTF4J4R, as discussed previously, which has the MSDeploy Remote Agent Service installed and running. The command to deploy this application is shown next.

```
msdeploy -verb:sync
    -source:package=C:\InsideMSBuild\Ch17\Website01.zip
    -dest:auto,computerName=WIN-MCX6WTF4J4R,username=deploy,password=p@ssw0rd
    -setParam:type=DestinationVirtualDirectory,
        scope="Default Website/Website01",
        value="%systemdrive%\inetpub\wwwroot\Website01"
```

In this command, we are using the package as my source and then deploying it to my remote server, which doesn't have the application installed. The results of executing this command are shown in Figure 17-18.

```
C:\InsideMSBuild\Ch17>msdeploy -verb:sync -source:package=C:\InsideMSBuild\Ch17\Website01.zip -dest
:auto,computerName=WIN-MCX6WTF4J4R,username=deploy,password=p@ssw0rd -setParam:type=DestinationVirt
ualDirectory,scope="Default Website/Website01",value="%systemdrive%\inetpub\wwwroot\Website01"
Info: Adding sitemanifest (sitemanifest).
Info: Adding appHostConfig (Default Web Site/Website01).
Info: Updating application (sitemanifest/appHostConfig[@path='Default Web Site/Website01']/applicat
ion[@path='/Website01']).
Info: Adding child virtualDirectory (sitemanifest/appHostConfig[@path='Default Web Site/Website01']
/application[@path='/Website01']/virtualDirectory[@path='/']).
Info: Adding dirPath (C:\InsideMSBuild\Ch17\Website01).
Info: Adding dirPath (C:\InsideMSBuild\Ch17\Website01\).
Info: Adding child dirPath (C:\InsideMSBuild\Ch17\Website01\App_Data).
Info: Adding child dirPath (C:\InsideMSBuild\Ch17\Website01\logs).
Info: Adding child dirPath (C:\InsideMSBuild\Ch17\Website01\Scripts).
Info: Updating setAcl (Default Web Site/Website01\App_Data).
Info: Updating setAcl (Default Web Site/Website01\logs).
Info: Updating runCommand (echo after finished).
Info: The process 'C:\Windows\system32\cmd.exe' (command line '/c "echo after finished"') exited wi
th code '0x0'.
Info: Updating application (sitemanifest/appHostConfig[@path='Default Web Site/Website01']/applicat
ion[@path='/Website01']).
Info: Adding child filePath (C:\InsideMSBuild\Ch17\Website01\App_Data\Database.mdf).
Info: Adding child filePath (C:\InsideMSBuild\Ch17\Website01\App_Data\Database_log.LDF).
Info: Adding child filePath (C:\InsideMSBuild\Ch17\Website01\Default.aspx).
Info: Adding child filePath (C:\InsideMSBuild\Ch17\Website01\Default.aspx.cs).
Info: Adding child filePath (C:\InsideMSBuild\Ch17\Website01\Scripts\jquery-1.4.1-vsdoc.js).
Info: Adding child filePath (C:\InsideMSBuild\Ch17\Website01\Scripts\jquery-1.4.1.js).
Info: Adding child filePath (C:\InsideMSBuild\Ch17\Website01\Scripts\jquery-1.4.1.min.js).
Info: Adding child filePath (C:\InsideMSBuild\Ch17\Website01\SourceManifest.xml).
Info: Adding child filePath (C:\InsideMSBuild\Ch17\Website01\web.config).
Info: Adding child filePath (C:\InsideMSBuild\Ch17\Website01\Website01.sln).
Info: Adding child filePath (C:\InsideMSBuild\Ch17\Website01\Website01.suo).
Info: Updating setAcl (Default Web Site/Website01\App_Data).
Info: Updating setAcl (Default Web Site/Website01\logs).
Info: Updating runCommand (echo after finished).
Info: The process 'C:\Windows\system32\cmd.exe' (command line '/c "echo after finished"') exited wi
th code '0x0'.
Total changes: 27 (19 added, 0 deleted, 8 updated, 0 parameters changed, 2330321 bytes copied)
```

FIGURE 17-18 MSDeploy Publish result

From this result, we can see that the application was successfully deployed to the remote server, as we expected. Also, look at the last few messages in the figure. You can see that the ACLs were set for App_Data folder and the logs folder. After this, you can see that the runCommand executed as we expected.

There is a lot more that you can do with the Manifest provider; this is really just a good starting point. In the next chapter we will move on to discuss how the Web Deployment Tool is integrated into Visual Studio and how you can customize packages that are created.

Chapter 18
Web Deployment Tool, Part 2

In the last chapter, we discussed how the Web Deployment Tool (MSDeploy) can be used from the command line via the msdeploy.exe command. We also touched a bit on the integration that exists inside Microsoft Visual Studio. Along with Visual Studio, there is some integration by way of MSBuild tasks and targets. Together, the entire package is referred to as the *Web Publishing Pipeline* (WPP). In this chapter, we will discuss the WPP in more detail and how you can extend it to suit your needs.

Web Publishing Pipeline Overview

As we just described briefly, the Web Publishing Pipeline (WPP) is the "workflow" that your project undergoes in order to take your project from its source to the destination server. Most of this is captured in MSBuild scripts that get imported into your Web Application Project (WAP) projects. Unfortunately, website projects are left behind in this scenario, but after you understand the WPP, you can reuse many of the tasks and targets for use with website projects. Before we discuss the details behind the WPP, let's discuss a related technology that is used to transform Extensible Markup Language (XML) configuration files.

 Note In many of the examples here, you will have to start Visual Studio, or the command prompt, in administrator mode. In order to do so, you can right-click and select Run As Administrator.

XML Document Transformations

In Visual Studio 2010, when you create a new WAP, there are two files nested under the Web.config by default: Web.Debug.config and Web.Release.config. Take a look at Figure 18-1, which shows them in the Solution Explorer.

The files under the Web.config file are not config files—*they are transform files.* You can use these files to transform your Web.config easily when you publish or package your web. If you crack open the Web.Debug.config file, you should see the following content:

```
<?xml version="1.0"?>
<!-- For more information on using web.config transformation visit
http://go.microsoft.com/fwlink/?LinkId=125889 -->
<configuration xmlns:xdt="http://schemas.microsoft.com/XML-Document-Transform">
```

```
<!--
    In the example below, the "SetAttributes" transform will change the value of
    "connectionString" to use "ReleaseSQLServer" only when the "Match" locator
    finds an atrribute "name" that has a value of "MyDB".

<connectionStrings>
<add name="MyDB"
connectionString="Data Source=ReleaseSQLServer;Initial Catalog=MyReleaseDB;
        Integrated Security=True"
xdt:Transform="SetAttributes" xdt:Locator="Match(name)"/>
</connectionStrings>
    -->
<system.web>
<!--
    In the example below, the "Replace" transform will replace the entire
<customErrors> section of your web.config file.
    Note that because there is only one customErrors section under the
<system.web> node, there is no need to use the "xdt:Locator" attribute.

<customErrorsdefaultRedirect="GenericError.htm"
        mode="RemoteOnly" xdt:Transform="Replace">
<error statusCode="500" redirect="InternalError.htm"/>
</customErrors>
     -->
</system.web>
</configuration>
```

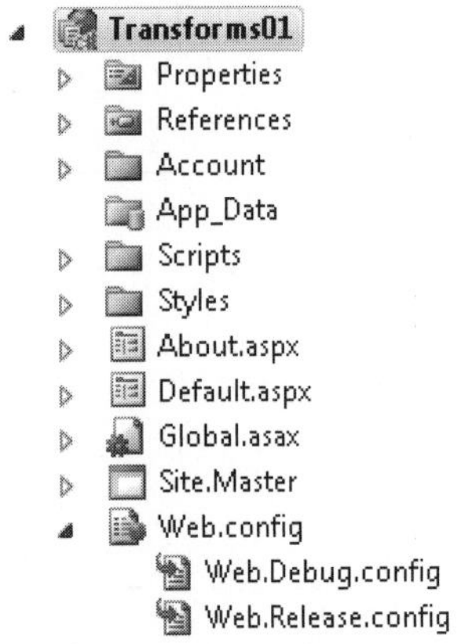

```
▲  📄 Transforms01
  ▷  📄 Properties
  ▷  📄 References
  ▷  📁 Account
      📁 App_Data
  ▷  📁 Scripts
  ▷  📁 Styles
  ▷  📄 About.aspx
  ▷  📄 Default.aspx
  ▷  🔧 Global.asax
  ▷  📄 Site.Master
  ▲  📄 Web.config
        📄 Web.Debug.config
        📄 Web.Release.config
```

FIGURE 18-1 Web.config transform files in the Solution Explorer

The first thing that you should notice is that this looks a lot like a Web.config file. In fact, the only difference is the presence of the xmlns declaration in the root element. The comments in the config file will get you started when you want to create transformations without a reference at hand. Before we get into the details, let's first see all this in action. In the next code snippet, you will find the contents of the Web.config file (with some changes formatting changes to fit the page) from the Transform01 project.

```
<configuration>
<appSettings>
<add key="pageSize" value="2" />
<add key="IncludesConfigPath" value="~/Config/includes.xml.config"/>
<add key="IncludesApplicationName" value="inlinetasks.com"/>
</appSettings>

<connectionStrings>
<add name="recordsDb"
connectionString="Data Source=localhost;Initial Catalog=RecordsDb;
            Integrated Security=True"/>
<add name="accountsDb"
connectionString="Data Source=localhost;Initial Catalog=RecordsDb;
            Integrated Security=True"/>
<add name="partnersDb"
connectionString="Data Source=localhost;Initial Catalog=RecordsDb;
            Integrated Security=True"/>
</connectionStrings>

<system.web>|
<customErrors mode="Off" defaultRedirect="/error.html" />
<compilation debug="true" targetFramework="4.0" />
</system.web>
</configuration>
```

This config file is pretty basic; it just contains a few app settings and connection strings, as well as the compilation element that enables debugging. Let's start by changing the value of one of the app settings, pageSize. Currently, the value is set to a low number, 2, but when we deploy it, we want to increase the value. Let's say that we want to replace the value *2* with *25*. Inside the Web.Debug.config file, I place the following:

```
<?xml version="1.0"?>
<configuration xmlns:xdt="http://schemas.microsoft.com/XML-Document-Transform">

<appSettings>
<add key="pageSize" value="25"
xdt:Transform="Replace" xdt:Locator="Match(key)"/>
</appSettings>

</configuration>
```

To create this, I simply copied the appSettings section, pasted it in the Web.Debug.configfile, and then removed the other elements. After that, I just added the attributes xdt:Transform= "Replace" xdt:Locator="Match(key)". We will discuss the details of all this pretty soon, but first let's see how to use it. When you are using transform files, you need to be aware of the fact that when you are running or debugging your application locally, you will be using the Web.config file itself. A transformation will not occur; they execute only when you publish or package your application. Because of this, you will need to package the application to see the result of the transformation. You can do this by right-clicking the project and selecting Build Deployment Package. After you do this, there will be a PackageTmp folder under the obj\Debug\Package folder. This assumes that you have Debug set as your active configuration. The Web.config transform files are tied to the configuration that you are building. So if you are building Debug configuration, then Web.Debug.config will be used, and the same goes for Release or any other configuration that you define. Inside the PackageTmp folder, the transformed Web.config file can be found. The value for pageSize is set to *25*. I won't show the contents here, but you should take a look for yourself to check them.

Now that you have seen how easy it is to create and transform your Web.config file, let's go over the syntax a bit. The XML Document Transform (XDT) syntax is pretty simple; there are only three attributes and they are described in Table 18-1.

TABLE 18-1 XDT Attributes

Attribute	Description
xdt:Transform	This attribute identifies what type of transformation will be occurring. There are eight possible values available by default: *Replace, Insert, InsertBefore, InsertAfter, Remove, RemoveAll, RemoveAttributes*, and *SetAttributes*. You can create your own transforms so that this value could contain other values.
xdt:Locator	This attribute will be used to help identify the source element that is being transformed. In many cases, you can use the *Match()* function with the name of the unique attribute.
xdt:SupressWarnings	When this attribute is set to *true*, warnings will not be logged.

Even though the syntax is very simple, it is very powerful. Let's take a look at the different transforms that are available by default. They are listed in Table 18-2.

TABLE 18-2 XDT Transforms

Transform Name	Description
Replace	This transform can be used to replace an entire element.
Insert	This transform can be used to insert an element as a sibling to the selected element(s). The new element will be added at the end, if any others exist.
InsertBefore	Similar to the Insert transform, but it will insert the element before the selected element.
InsertAfter	Similar to the Insert transform, but it will insert the element after the selected element.
Remove	Removes all selected elements.
RemoveAll	Removes all elements that match the selection criteria.
RemoveAttributes	Removes the indicated attributes from the selected element.
SetAttributes	Sets the value of one or more attributes on the selected element.

To show you how to use these different transforms, I've created many different transform files in the Transform01 project. By default, how transformations work is that you need to create a transform with the name *Web.{Configuration}.config*, where *{Configuration}* is the value of the configuration that you are currently building. That is why there is Web.Debug .config and Web.Release.config: they correspond to the two default configurations for new projects. Following this pattern, we would have to create many different configurations for this project. In order to avoid that, I am going to show you how to manually perform transformations from any MSBuild script. When you publish your web application or package it, the Web.config file is transformed using the TransformXml task, which is contained in the Microsoft.Web.Publishing.Tasks.dll assembly. We will be using this same task to transform the files ourselves. In the Transforms folder of the Transform01 project, I have created the transform.proj file whose contents are shown in the next snippet:

```
<Project xmlns="http://schemas.microsoft.com/developer/msbuild/2003"
ToolsVersion="4.0"
DefaultTargets="TransformAll">

<UsingTaskTaskName="TransformXml"
      AssemblyFile="$(MSBuildExtensionsPath)\Microsoft\VisualStudio\v10.0\
      Web\Microsoft.Web.Publishing.Tasks.dll"/>

<PropertyGroup>
<DestDirectory>..\obj\TransformedFiles\</DestDirectory>
</PropertyGroup>

<ItemGroup>
<TransformFiles Include="$(FilesToTransform)"/>
</ItemGroup>

<Target Name="TransformAll" DependsOnTargets="ValidateSettings">
<MakeDir Directories="$(DestDirectory)"/>
<TransformXml Source="..\web.config"
Transform="%(TransformFiles.Identity)"
      Destination="@(TransformFiles->'$(DestDirectory)%(Filename).transformed.config')" />
</Target>

<Target Name="ValidateSettings">

<Error Text="FilesToTransform cannot be empty"
          Condition=" '$(FilesToTransform)'=='' "/>
<Error Text="Couldn't find transform file at [%(TransformFiles.Fullpath)]"
          Condition =" !Exists('%(TransformFiles.Fullpath)') "/>
</Target>

</Project>
```

This MSBuild file is pretty simple; in order to use it, you just need to specify the file(s) that will be transformed at the command line in the FilesToTransform property. One example of this is the command `msbuildtransform.proj /t:TransformAll /p:FilesToTransform=trans01.config`. Inside the TransformAll target, you can see that the TransformXml task is being used to transform the Web.config file, and the results are dropped into the \obj\TransformedFiles\ directory. With that out of the way, let's start creating some other transformations.

In order to insert a new element, you can use the Insert transform. This will insert a new element as a sibling of the selected element. It will be appended to any existing elements. For example, take a look at the trans01.config file shown here:

```
<configuration
xmlns:xdt="http://schemas.microsoft.com/XML-Document-Transform">


<appSettings>
<add key="helpUrl" value="http://inlinetasks.com/help"
xdt:Transform="Insert" />
</appSettings>


</configuration>
```

In this transformation, I am adding a new application setting, helpUrl, using the Insert transformation. As we indicated earlier, you do not have to specify where the node will be inserted because it is inferred based on its location in the transform file. Also, you should note that with the Insert transform, you do not have to use xdt:Locator because you are not modifying an existing element. When I run the command `msbuildtransform.proj /t:TransformAll /p:FilesToTransform=trans01.config`, the result will be dropped into the trans01.transformed.config file. The appSettings node of that file is shown here:

```
<appSettings>
<add key="pageSize" value="2" />
<add key="IncludesConfigPath" value="~/Config/includes.xml.config"/>
<add key="IncludesApplicationName" value="inlinetasks.com"/>
<add key="helpUrl" value="http://inlinetasks.com/help"/>
</appSettings>
```

As you can see from the previous snippet, the *helpUrl* value was successfully added to the list of settings in the Web.config file. As we mentioned earlier, and as shown here, the new element is just appended to the end of any preexisting elements. What if you needed to insert an element at a specific location? You can use the *InsertBefore* and *InsertAfter* elements for this.

In order to demonstrate *InsertBefore* and *InsertAfter*, I created trans02.config, which is shown next:

```
<configuration xmlns:xdt="http://schemas.microsoft.com/XML-Document-Transform">
<configSections
xdt:Transform="InsertBefore(/configuration/*[1])">
<section
        name="pageAppearance"
        type="Samples.AspNet.PageAppearanceSection"
allowLocation="true"
allowDefinition="Everywhere"
    />
</configSections>
```

```
<connectionStrings>
<add name="employeeDb"
connectionString="Data Source=prod.sedotech01;
Initial Catalog=EmployeeDb;Integrated Security=True"
     xdt:Transform="InsertAfter(/configuration/connectionStrings/add[2])"/>
</connectionStrings>

</configuration>
```

In this example, two transformations are taking place. First, take a look at the
configSections element. You can see the *InsertBefore* usage here. It takes an argument that
an XPath expression is used to locate the selected element. The new element will be inserted
before that. From the XPath expression shown here, we will be inserting the *configSections*
element before the first element under the configuration element. In effect, this will
make *configSections* the first element in the transformed Web.config file. After that, take
a look at the *employeeDb* connection string element. This element is using the InsertAfter
transformation and it is passing in the XPath expression /configuration/connectionStrings/
add[2]. This will cause the *employeeDb* element to be inserted after the second connection
string. Now let's take a look at the result. The transformed Web.config file is shown here:

```
<configuration>
<configSections>
<section name="pageAppearance"
      type="Samples.AspNet.PageAppearanceSection"
allowLocation="true"allowDefinition="Everywhere"/>
</configSections>
<appSettings>
<add key="pageSize" value="2" />
<add key="IncludesConfigPath" value="~/Config/includes.xml.config"/>
<add key="IncludesApplicationName" value="inlinetasks.com"/>
</appSettings>

<connectionStrings>
<add name="recordsDb"
connectionString="Data Source=localhost;
          Initial Catalog=RecordsDb;Integrated Security=True"/>
<add name="accountsDb"
connectionString="Data Source=localhost;
          Initial Catalog=RecordsDb;Integrated Security=True"/>
<add name="employeeDb" connectionString="Data Source=prod.sedotech01;
          Initial Catalog=EmployeeDb;Integrated Security=True"/>
<add name="partnersDb"
connectionString="Data Source=localhost;Initial Catalog=RecordsDb;Integrated
Security=True"/>
</connectionStrings>

<system.web>
<customErrors mode="Off" defaultRedirect="/error.html"/>
<compilation debug="true" targetFramework="4.0" batch="true" />
</system.web>
</configuration>
```

I've boldfaced the inserted elements in this code. As you can see, they have been inserted in the locations where we expected. Now we will look at the Remove and RemoveAll transformations.

As you might have guessed from their names, the Remove and RemoveAll transformations are used to remove elements from the XML file. When you are using either of these transformations, you can choose to specify a value for xdt:Locator. If you do so, this will be used to narrow down the selected elements. If this locator value is missing, then the selected element will be determined strictly by the element placement in the transform file. Take a look at the trans03.config file shown in the following code:

```
<configuration xmlns:xdt="http://schemas.microsoft.com/XML-Document-Transform">

<appSettings>
<add xdt:Transform="Remove"/>
</appSettings>

<connectionStrings>
<add name="accountsDb"
xdt:Transform="Remove" xdt:Locator="Match(name)"/>
</connectionStrings>

</configuration>
```

In this transform file, the Remove transform is used on the *add* element in appSettings. Since we did not specify a value for xdt:Locator here, this will remove the first *add* element inside appSettings. Even if we had specified other attributes there, like *key="IncludesConfigPath"*, that would be ignored without the *xdt:Locator* attribute. Next, in the connectionStrings section, you will see that I again use the Remove transform, but this time with the locator value asMatch(name). What this will do is remove the first *add* element under connectionStrings that has an attribute name set to *accountsDb*. Take a look at the result shown here:

```
<configuration>
<appSettings>
<add key="IncludesConfigPath" value="~/Config/includes.xml.config"/>
<add key="IncludesApplicationName" value="inlinetasks.com"/>
</appSettings>

<connectionStrings>
<add name="recordsDb"
connectionString="Data Source=localhost;
        Initial Catalog=RecordsDb;Integrated Security=True"/>
<add name="partnersDb"
connectionString="Data Source=localhost;
        Initial Catalog=RecordsDb;Integrated Security=True"/>
</connectionStrings>

<system.web>
<customErrors mode="Off" defaultRedirect="/error.html"/>
```

```
<compilation debug="true" targetFramework="4.0" batch="true" />
</system.web>
</configuration>
```

As you can see the first app settings value, *pageSize,* has been removed. In addition, the connection string pointing to *accountsDb* is removed. The RemoveAll transform works very similarly to the Remove transform. The only difference is that Remove will remove only the first matched element, but RemoveAll will remove all matched elements. Now let's move on to see how we can modify attributes.

Thus far, we have just shown how to add and remove elements. However, if you want to modify attributes, then you can use the SetAttributes and RemoveAttributes transforms to do this. When you use these transforms, you can choose to specify an xdt:*Locator* element to narrow down the element that is being modified. If there is only one such element, then you can leave that out. In the example here, we will omit that attribute. Both of these transforms require that an argument be passed into it, indicating which attributes should be set or removed. If you are modifying a single attribute, then just pass in the name of that attribute. For more than one, then just pass in a comma-separated list. Take a look at the content of the trans04.config file shown here:

```
<configuration xmlns:xdt="http://schemas.microsoft.com/XML-Document-Transform">

<system.web>
<customErrorsxdt:Transform ="RemoveAttributes(defaultRedirect)" />
<customErrors mode="RemoteOnly" redirectMode="ResponseRedirect"
xdt:Transform ="SetAttributes(mode,redirectMode)"/>
<compilation xdt:Transform="RemoveAttributes(debug,batch)" />
</system.web>

</configuration>
```

In this case, I am going to change some of the elements under the *system.web* element. One of the first things that you should notice here is that I have declared two *customErrors* elements here. In a normal Web.config file, this is not allowed; but in a transform, it just means that you are transforming the same element multiple times. Here, you see the original *system .web* element:

```
<system.web>
<customErrors mode="Off" defaultRedirect="/error.html" />
<compilation debug="true" targetFramework="4.0" batch="true" />
</system.web>
```

Now let's discuss what the transformations are doing. The first transformation is removing the *defaultRedirect* attribute from the *customErrors* element. After that, you can see that I am using the SetAttributes transform to update the mode attribute and to insert the *redirectMode* attribute. Following that, I remove the debug and batch attributes from the compilation element. The resulting system.web section is shown on the following page.

```
<system.web>
<customErrors mode="RemoteOnly"
redirectMode="ResponseRedirect"/>
<compilation targetFramework="4.0" />
</system.web>
```

From this result, we can see that the modifications were executed as expected. Web.config transformations are not limited to what you see here. The XDT transforms are built with a plug-in architecture, so you can create your own transformations and apply them. We will not discuss that here, though. Now that we have discussed Web.config transformations, we will continue our discussion of the WPP.

Web Publishing Pipeline Phases

If you take a look at the project file for your WAP, you will see the following import statement towards the bottom:

```
<Import Project="$(MSBuildExtensionsPath32)\Microsoft\VisualStudio\v10.0\
WebApplications\Microsoft.WebApplication.targets" />
```

This will import the Microsoft.WebApplicaiton.targets file into your project; this file will in turn import the Microsoft.Web.Publishing.targets file. Between these two files, the WPP is fully described. There are many targets, properties, items, and tasks that are used to orchestrate the process of taking your source and preparing it for your web servers. In this chapter, we will attempt to demystify that process a bit so that you can fully customize and extend the process. The targets in these files are used to both publish and package your web. As you read this chapter, it may seem as though we are focusing on packaging your application instead of publishing it, but everything that applies for packaging also applies to publishing. The reason that we discuss packaging here is because it is easier to debug locally.

There are three big phases to the WPP: collect, transform, and output. The collect phase is used to determine what files are needed for your web to run. The transform phase is when files are transformed based on the current build configuration. The output phase is when your web is published or packaged to its destination. You can tweak some of the options for the publish and package operation on the Package/Publish Web tab. This tab is shown in Figure 18-2.

Along with this tab, there is the Package/Publish SQL tab. We will discuss how databases are deployed shortly, so we will not cover that tab just yet. On the Package/Publish Web tab, you can tweak a few of the more common properties. For instance, you can specify what items are gathered during the collect phase. The Items To Deploy drop-down list, shown in Figure 18-2, has three possible values: Only Files Needed To Run This Application, All Files In This Project, and All Files In This Project Folder. The default is to simply gather the files needed to run the application. If you are curious how this works, this drop-down list corresponds to three targets files in the same directory as the Microsoft.Web.Publishing

.targets. Depending on the value of the drop-downlist, one of the three files is imported. The names of these files are Microsoft.Web.Publishing.OnlyFilesToRunTheApp.targets, Microsoft.Web.Publishing.AllFilesInTheProject.targets, and Microsoft.Web.Publishing. AllFilesInProjectFolder.targets. Each of these targets extends the PipelineCollectFilesPhase to include the correct set of files. We will cover this more in Chapter 19. The next two check boxes correspond to the following property values: *ExcludeGeneratedDebugSymbol* and *ExcludeApp_Data*.

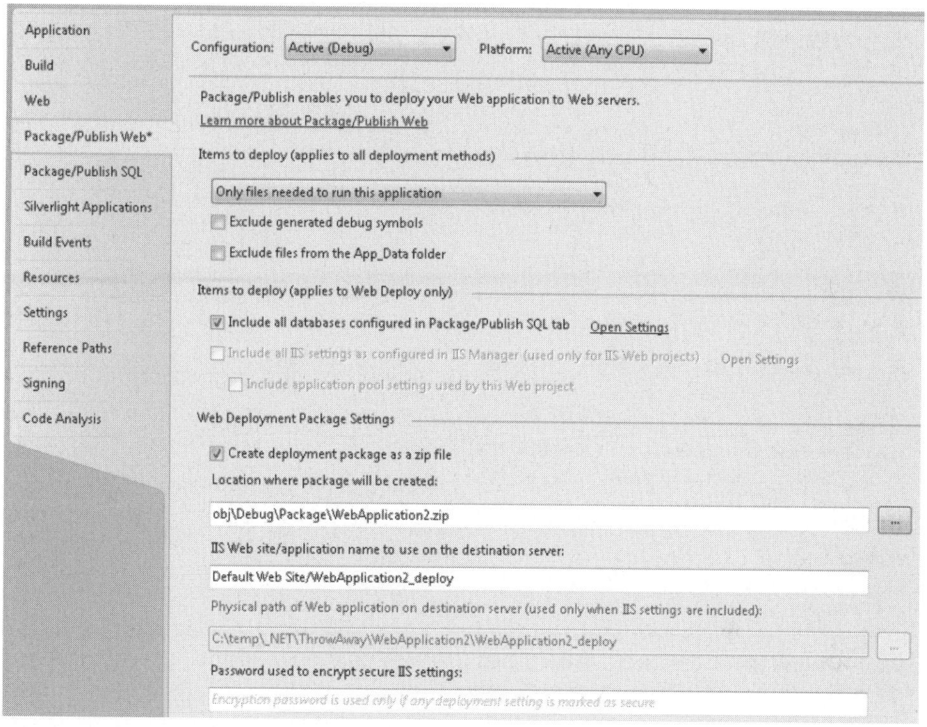

FIGURE 18-2 Package/Publish Web tab settings

Now, let's discuss how you can customize the collect phase. The main target for the collect phase is PipelineCollectFilesPhase. It chains together, via a depends on property, all the other targets that need to be executed, gathering all of the files to be packaged. For example, from the Microsoft.Web.Publishing.OnlyFilesToRunTheApp.targets file, you can see in the following snippet how the collect phase is extended:

```
<PropertyGroup>
<PublishPipelineCollectFilesCore>
    $(PublishPipelineCollectFilesCore);
CollectFilesFromIntermediateAssembly;
CollectFilesFromContent;
CollectFilesFromAddModules;
CollectFilesFrom_SGenDllCreated;
CollectFilesFromIntermediateSatelliteAssembliesWithTargetPath;
```

```
CollectFilesFromReference;
CollectFilesFromAllExtraReferenceFiles;
CollectFilesFrom_SourceItemsToCopyToOutputDirectory;
CollectFilesFromDocFileItem;
CollectFilesFrom_WebApplicationSilverlightXapFiles;
</PublishPipelineCollectFilesCore>
<ExcludeTransformAssistFilesFromPublish
    Condition="'$(ExcludeTransformAssistFilesFromPublish)'==''">True
</ExcludeTransformAssistFilesFromPublish>
</PropertyGroup>
```

By adding more targets to this property, these targets are injected into the file collection phase. Let's take a look at one of these targets to better understand what it is doing:

```
<Target Name="CollectFilesFromContent"
DependsOnTargets="$(CollectFilesFromContentDependsOn)"
        Condition="'@(Content)'!=''">
<!--Get Localized string before display message-->
<GetPublishingLocalizedString
    ID="PublishLocalizedString_GatherSpecificItemsFromProject"
ArgumentCount="1"
    Arguments="Content"
LogType="Message" />
<Message Text="@(Content)" />

<ItemGroup>
<FilesForPackagingFromProject Include="@(Content)"
        Condition="'%(Content.Link)'==''">
<DestinationRelativePath>%(Content.Identity)</DestinationRelativePath>
<FromTarget>CollectFilesFromContent</FromTarget>
<Category>Run</Category>
</FilesForPackagingFromProject>
<FilesForPackagingFromProject Include="@(Content)"
            Condition="'%(Content.Link)'!='' And $(EnableCollectLinkFilesInProject)">
<DestinationRelativePath>%(Content.Link)</DestinationRelativePath>
<FromTarget>CollectFilesFromContent</FromTarget>
<Category>Run</Category>
<Exclude>$(ExcludeLinkFilesInProject)</Exclude>
<ProjectFileType>Link</ProjectFileType>
</FilesForPackagingFromProject>
</ItemGroup>
<CallTarget Targets="$(OnAfterCollectFilesFromContent)" RunEachTargetSeparately="false" />
</Target>
```

From this target, you can see that the Content item is enumerated and added to the FilesForPackagingFromProject item list if one of two conditions are met. From that declaration, we can see that some metadata is also set on the items. This metadata will be used when the package is being constructed. As you are investigating these targets files, you will find that items and their metadata are being used frequently. Now, you might be wondering how we can customize the collection process to include or exclude other files. That's what we're going to discuss next.

Excluding Files

Let's take a look at what it would take to exclude files from the package being created. In order to get a sense of how to properly do this, let's look at how the WPP scripts themselves exclude files. In Figure 18-2, we saw options to exclude the App_Data contents as well as excluding the debug symbols. When you select these, you are setting a couple of properties, which are used to determine if two targets will execute or not. Those targets are ExcludeApp_Data and ExcludeGeneratedDebugSymbol. I have copied those two targets and placed them in the next code fragment, minus some comments to save space here:

```
<Target Name="ExcludeApp_Data"
DependsOnTargets="$(ExcludeApp_DataDependsOn)"
        Condition="$(ExcludeApp_Data)">

<GetPublishingLocalizedString
    ID="PublishLocalizedString_ExcludeAllFilesUnderFolder"
ArgumentCount="1"
    Arguments="App_Data"
LogType="Message" />

<ItemGroup>
<ExcludeFromPackageFolders Include="App_Data">
<FromTarget>ExcludeApp_Data</FromTarget>
</ExcludeFromPackageFolders>
</ItemGroup>
</Target>

<Target Name="ExcludeGeneratedDebugSymbol"
DependsOnTargets="$(ExcludeGeneratedDebugSymbolDependsOn)"
        Condition="$(ExcludeGeneratedDebugSymbol)">

<GetPublishingLocalizedString
    ID="PublishLocalizedString_ExcludeAllDebugSymbols"
LogType="Message" />

<ItemGroup>
<ExcludeFromPackageFiles Include="@(FilesForPackagingFromProject)"
Condition="'%(FilesForPackagingFromProject.Extension)'=='.pdb'">
<FromTarget>ExcludeGeneratedDebugSymbol</FromTarget>
</ExcludeFromPackageFiles>
</ItemGroup>
</Target>
```

From the first target shown, ExcludeApp_Data, we can see that the exclusion is folder-based. In order to get the App_Data contents excluded, the folder is appended to the ExcludeFromPackageFolders item list. Any file underneath any folder contained in that item list will be automatically excluded by the ExcludeFilesFromPackage target. Now looking at the ExcludeGeneratedDebugSymbol target, it employs another item list, ExcludeFromPackageFiles, which lists individual files that will be excluded from the generated package. In the implementation of ExcludeFilesFromPackage, the files contained in any of the folders contained in ExcludeFromPackageFolders are placed in the ExcludeFromPackageFiles item list. Also, you might have noticed that in the declaration of these two targets, each item list contained a bit of metadata, FromTarget. This metadata value is captured to help discover why the item(s) were excluded. You can set this value to anything you want; the default value is *Unknown.*

If you want to extend this process, you have two choices as to where you can put the customizations. You can place them in your project file directly, as you could any other MSBuild customization. With the WPP, however, you are given another option. You can create another MSBuild file named *{ProjectName}*.wpp.targets, where *{ProjectName}* is the name of the project file. For example, I have created a new WAP named ExcludeFiles01. To extend the build process for this file, I just need to create ExcludeFiles01.wpp.targets in the same directory as the project file. You can actually change the name of this file if you want, but we will keep it simple. Take a look at Figure 18-3; the circled items are the ones that I want to exclude from the packages generated for the ExcludeFiles project.

FIGURE 18-3 Items to be excluded from the generated package

In this figure, you can see that I have a folder called Internal, which I want to exclude, and two specific .js files that should be excluded as well. In order to exclude these files, I have placed the following content into the ExcludeFiles01.wpp.targets file:

```
<Project ToolsVersion="4.0"  xmlns="http://schemas.microsoft.com/developer/msbuild/2003">

<ItemGroup>
<ExcludeFromPackageFolders Include="Internal">
<FromTarget>ExcludeFiles01.wpp.targets</FromTarget>
</ExcludeFromPackageFolders>
```

```
<ExcludeFromPackageFiles Include="Scripts\jquery-1.4.1-vsdoc.js;
                                  Scripts\jquery-1.4.1.js">
<FromTarget>ExcludeFiles01.wpp.targets</FromTarget>
</ExcludeFromPackageFiles>
</ItemGroup>

</Project>
```

In this file, you can see that I used ExcludeFromPackageFolders to exclude the contents of the Internal folder. As for the two .js files, they are excluded using the ExcludeFromPackageFiles item list. Also, note that I gave the value of FromTarget as ExcludeFiles01.wpp.targets. You could have given it any value you wanted, or you could have left it off altogether. Now, let's see if the files are successfully excluded. To do this, I am going to build the project from the command line, specifying that target to be Package. The command would be `msbuild ExcludeFiles01.csproj /t:Package`. The end of the log messages is shown in Figure 18-4.

```
Adding child filePath (C:\InsideMSBuild\Ch18\ExcludeFiles01\obj\Debug\Package\PackageTmp\Account
\Register.aspx).
Adding child filePath (C:\InsideMSBuild\Ch18\ExcludeFiles01\obj\Debug\Package\PackageTmp\Account
\Web.config).
Adding child dirPath (C:\InsideMSBuild\Ch18\ExcludeFiles01\obj\Debug\Package\PackageTmp\bin).
Adding child filePath (C:\InsideMSBuild\Ch18\ExcludeFiles01\obj\Debug\Package\PackageTmp\bin\Exc
ludeFiles01.dll).
Adding child filePath (C:\InsideMSBuild\Ch18\ExcludeFiles01\obj\Debug\Package\PackageTmp\bin\Exc
ludeFiles01.pdb).
Adding child filePath (C:\InsideMSBuild\Ch18\ExcludeFiles01\obj\Debug\Package\PackageTmp\Default
.aspx).
Adding child filePath (C:\InsideMSBuild\Ch18\ExcludeFiles01\obj\Debug\Package\PackageTmp\Global.
asax).
Adding child dirPath (C:\InsideMSBuild\Ch18\ExcludeFiles01\obj\Debug\Package\PackageTmp\Scripts)
.
Adding child filePath (C:\InsideMSBuild\Ch18\ExcludeFiles01\obj\Debug\Package\PackageTmp\Scripts
\jquery-1.4.1.min.js).
Adding child filePath (C:\InsideMSBuild\Ch18\ExcludeFiles01\obj\Debug\Package\PackageTmp\Site.Ma
ster).
Adding child dirPath (C:\InsideMSBuild\Ch18\ExcludeFiles01\obj\Debug\Package\PackageTmp\Styles).
Adding child filePath (C:\InsideMSBuild\Ch18\ExcludeFiles01\obj\Debug\Package\PackageTmp\Styles\
Site.css).
Adding child filePath (C:\InsideMSBuild\Ch18\ExcludeFiles01\obj\Debug\Package\PackageTmp\Web.con
fig).
Adding child setAcl (C:\InsideMSBuild\Ch18\ExcludeFiles01\obj\Debug\Package\PackageTmp).
Adding child setAcl (C:\InsideMSBuild\Ch18\ExcludeFiles01\obj\Debug\Package\PackageTmp).
Adding declared parameter 'IIS Web Application Name'.
Adding declared parameter 'ApplicationServices-Web.config Connection String'.
Successfully executed Web deployment task.
Package "ExcludeFiles01.zip" is successfully created as single file at the following location:
file:///C:/InsideMSBuild/Ch18/ExcludeFiles01/obj/Debug/Package
To get the instructions on how to deploy the web package please visit the following link:
http://go.microsoft.com/fwlink/?LinkId=124618
GenerateSampleDeployScript:
Sample script for deploying this package is generated at the following location:
C:\InsideMSBuild\Ch18\ExcludeFiles01\obj\Debug\Package\ExcludeFiles01.deploy.cmd
For this sample script, you can change the deploy parameters by changing the following file:
C:\InsideMSBuild\Ch18\ExcludeFiles01\obj\Debug\Package\ExcludeFiles01.SetParameters.xml
Done Building Project "C:\InsideMSBuild\Ch18\ExcludeFiles01\ExcludeFiles01.csproj" (Package target
(s)).

Build succeeded.
    0 Warning(s)
    0 Error(s)
```

FIGURE 18-4 Package target results

I have included Figure 18-4 to point out a few things. If you take a look at the first line under PackageUsingManifest, it states that the package will be created at the obj\Debug\Package\ ExcludeFiles01.zip location. This is the same value that you saw previously in the Package/ Publish Web tab. When your application is preparing for packaging (or publishing), the files that will be included are placed into the obj*{Configuration}*\Package\PackageTmp, where *{Configuration}* is the current build configuration. In order to verify that the items were successfully excluded from the package, you can check that location.

Previously, when we discussed the FromTarget metadata value, we said that it is used to help debug files that were excluded from the package. You might have been wondering how that happens. A "magic" property, EnablePackageProcessLoggingAndAssert, can be set to *true* to enable this. Once you set this value to *true,* several log files will be written to the obj*{Configuration}*\Package\Log folder. So, in my case, I can convert the previous command to `msbuild ExcludeFiles01.csproj /t:Package /p:EnablePackageProcess LoggingAndAssert=true`. Once I execute this command, one of the many files written out is ExcludeFromPackageFiles.txt. This file enumerates the files that were excluded and why. Take a look at its contents, shown in the following snippet. I modified the format of the file a bit so it would fit the page better.

```
Files:Scripts\jquery-1.4.1-vsdoc.js
FromTarget:ExcludeFiles01.wpp.targets
DestinationRelativePath:

Files:Scripts\jquery-1.4.1.js
FromTarget:ExcludeFiles01.wpp.targets
DestinationRelativePath:

Files:Internal\model01.xml
FromTarget:ExcludeFiles01.wpp.targets
DestinationRelativePath:

Files:Internal\model02.xml
FromTarget:ExcludeFiles01.wpp.targets
DestinationRelativePath:

Files:Internal\model03.xml
FromTarget:ExcludeFiles01.wpp.targets
DestinationRelativePath:

Files:Internal\sub\sub01.xml
FromTarget:ExcludeFiles01.wpp.targets
DestinationRelativePath:

Files:Internal\sub\sub02.xml
FromTarget:ExcludeFiles01.wpp.targets
DestinationRelativePath:
```

From this snippet, you can see that all of the files that we were expecting to be excluded were. Also, you can see in that file how FromTarget might come in handy if you are trying to figure out why a certain file was excluded. Now, let's discuss how to include extra files.

Including Additional Files

Many times you will need to include files that are not a part of the project, but need to be published. I have created a new project in the Ch18 folder namedIncludeFiles01. In addition, to demonstrate including additional files, I have included a bunch of image files in the

C:\InsideMSBuild\Ch18\OtherFiles folder, which is outside the IncludeFiles01 project folder. Following in the spirit of the previous example, in order to determine how to add extra files, let's look at one of the built-in targets, which includes files. To do this, I have included the definition of the CollectFilesFromIntermediateAssembly in this next code block:

```
<Target Name="CollectFilesFromIntermediateAssembly"
        DependsOnTargets="$(CollectFilesFromIntermediateAssemblyDependsOn)"
        Condition="'@(IntermediateAssembly)'!=''">

<GetPublishingLocalizedString
    ID="PublishLocalizedString_GatherSpecificItemsFromProject"
ArgumentCount="1"
    Arguments="IntermediateAssembly"
LogType="Message" />
<Message Text="@(IntermediateAssembly->'
    $(OutDir)%(FileName)%(Extension) to bin\%(FileName)%(Extension)')" />


<ItemGroup>
<FilesForPackagingFromProject
        Include="@(IntermediateAssembly->'$(OutDir)%(FileName)%(Extension)')">
<DestinationRelativePath>bin\%(FileName)%(Extension)</DestinationRelativePath>
<FromTarget>CollectFilesFromIntermediateAssembly</FromTarget>
<Category>Run</Category>
</FilesForPackagingFromProject>
</ItemGroup>
<Message Text="@(IntermediateAssembly->'$(OutDir)%(FileName).pdb to bin\%(FileName).pdb')"
            Condition="$(_DebugSymbolsProduced) AND !$(ExcludeGeneratedDebugSymbol)
            AND Exists(@(IntermediateAssembly->'$(OutDir)%(FileName).pdb')) "/>
<ItemGroup Condition="$(_DebugSymbolsProduced) AND !$(ExcludeGeneratedDebugSymbol)
            AND Exists(@(IntermediateAssembly->'$(OutDir)%(FileName).pdb'))">
<FilesForPackagingFromProject
    Include="@(IntermediateAssembly->'$(OutDir)%(FileName).pdb')"
    Condition="Exists(@(IntermediateAssembly->'$(OutDir)%(FileName).pdb'))">
<DestinationRelativePath>bin\%(FileName).pdb</DestinationRelativePath>
<FromTarget>CollectFilesFromIntermediateAssembly</FromTarget>
<Category>Debug</Category>
</FilesForPackagingFromProject>
</ItemGroup>

<CallTarget Targets="$(OnAfterCollectFilesFromIntermediateAssembly)"
RunEachTargetSeparately="false" />
</Target>
```

In this snippet, I have boldfaced the item declaration that is important. This target uses the FilesForPackagingFromProject task to include additional files. Make note of the DestinationRelativePath metadata. This value defines the relative location in the package where they will be placed. The reason for this is that many times the physical location of a file in a project is not always where you want it to be in your deployed application. What we need to do is to create something similar to include the image files that were previously mentioned. To do this, I have created the file IncludeFiles01.wpp.targets and placed it inside the code on the following page.

```
<Project xmlns="http://schemas.microsoft.com/developer/msbuild/2003"
ToolsVersion="4.0">

<ItemGroup>
<FilesForPackagingFromProject
      Include="..\OtherFiles\**\*">
<DestinationRelativePath>
images\%(RecursiveDir)%(FileName)%(Extension)</DestinationRelativePath>
<FromTarget>IncludeFiles01.wpp.targets</FromTarget>
</FilesForPackagingFromProject>
</ItemGroup>

</Project>
```

In this snippet, I am including files into the FilesForPackagingFromProject item list. I have boldfaced the important parts of this file. You can see that all the files under ..\OtherFiles will be picked up in the item list, and for the destination, they will be placed in the images\ folder. This folder doesn't exist in the source, but it will be created when the project is packaged or published. In order to see this at work, just execute the following command:

```
msbuild IncludeFiles01.csproj /t:Package /p:EnablePackageProcessLoggingAndAssert=true
```

Once you do this, the project will be packaged, and because I set the EnablePackageProcessLoggingAndAssert property to *true,* the log files will be written again. This time, we are not interested in the log files themselves, but rather the files that make up the final package. In order to see this list, you can take a look at the contents of the AfterExcludeFilesFilesList.txt file. I have just a few of the results here so that you can see what the code looks like:

```
From:..\OtherFiles\05.png
DestinationRelativePath:images\05.png
Exclude:False
FromTarget:IncludeFiles01.wpp.targets
Category:Run
ProjectFileType:Default

From:..\OtherFiles\sub01\01.png
DestinationRelativePath:images\sub01\01.png
Exclude:False
FromTarget:IncludeFiles01.wpp.targets
Category:Run
ProjectFileType:Default

From:..\OtherFiles\sub01\02.png
DestinationRelativePath:images\sub01\02.png
Exclude:False
FromTarget:IncludeFiles01.wpp.targets
Category:Run
ProjectFileType:Default
```

From the results shown here, you can see that the files were indeed included in the package, and in the correct location, under images\. In this section, as well as the last one, the approach has been to identify a behavior in the existing WPP and then use that same process to extend the WPP. This is the best way to learn the WPP—look for a similar functionality and then try to customize it to make it work for you. Don't be afraid to dive into those shared targets file—just make sure not to modify any of them. I suggest you copy them to another location and then view the copies. Now that we have covered the collect phase, we can discuss how to extend the transform phase a bit.

Database

Up to this point, we have been discussing how to deploy your web application itself. In many cases, a database is commonly used with web applications. In this section, we will discuss some of the built-in features for deploying your database and with your site itself. In the previous chapter, we showed how you could use the dbFullSql MSDeploy provider to deploy a database to a target server. Visual Studio uses those features for database deployment. Before we dive into the details of database deployment, let's first take a look at the user interface (UI) elements that you can use to tweak this.

In order to show some of the capabilities of database deployment, I have created a sample, Data01, which contains a very basic Microsoft SQL Express database inside the App_Data folder called *RecordsDb*. This database consists of two tables: Person and Account. In the Properties pages for that project, which is a WAP, we can configure database deployment on the Package/Publish SQL tab. This is where we will indicate what database items should be deployed and to what database servers. You can see this tab in Figure 18-5.

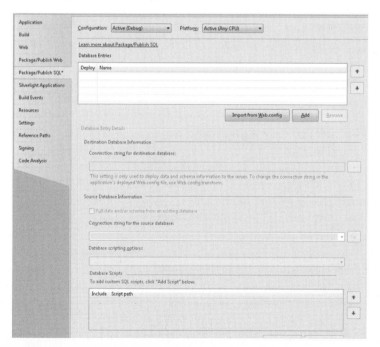

FIGURE 18-5 Package/Publish SQL tab

Note If you intend to deploy databases with your web application, then you need to configure that on the Package/Publish SQL tab. You also need to make sure that the Include All Databases Configured In Package/Publish SQL Tab check box on the Package/Publish Web tab is selected.

Figure 18-5 can be a bit daunting if you are not accustomed to using it. The grid named Database Entries contains a list of database identifiers. I use the term *identifiers* because the values that it contains has no impact on what is deployed or to where—it is just a means of identifying that particular row in the grid. Beneath this grid are some fields that are currently dimmed, which specify the behavior of what to deploy and where to deploy it. An important note here is that the contents beneath the Database Entries grid depend on the selected entry in the grid. This explains why the bottom portion is dimmed: I have not yet defined any database entries. Typically, you are deploying a database with a web application because you are using it, and in most cases, the connection string is located in the Web.config file. Because of this, Visual Studio 2010 has enabled easy importing of database source information from the Web.config file. For example, take a look at the connectionStrings section of the web.config file for the Data01 project:

```
<connectionStrings>
        <add name="RecordsDb"
connectionString="data source=.\SQLEXPRESS;Integrated Security=SSPI;
AttachDBFilename=|DataDirectory|\RecordsDb.mdf;User Instance=true"
providerName="System.Data.SqlClient"/>
</connectionStrings>
```

This Web.confg file contains a single connection string to RecordsDb, which is a SQL Express database as mentioned earlier. You can use the Import From Web.config file to import the databases, which are contained in the Web.config file. When you do this, a new row is added to the Database Entries grid for every connection string, and the connection string to the database is inserted into the Connection String For The Source Database text box. You must enter the value for the destination database in the Connection String For Destination Database text box. In this case, the destination connection string that I provided is "Data Source=Ibrahim-P55;Initial Catalog=RecordsDb;Integrated Security=True". You can see the results in Figure 18-6.

From Figure 18-6, you can see how the source and destination connection strings are captured on the page. The only other important element on this page is the Database Scripting Options drop-down list. This drop-down list has three options, which are used to determine what content will be deployed to the target server. Those options are Schema Only, Schema And Data, and Data Only. These values are self-explanatory, so I won't expand on them. The default value here is Schema Only. If you were interested in executing other SQL scripts on the same destination server, then you could add more scripts using the Add Script button. We will not cover that here.

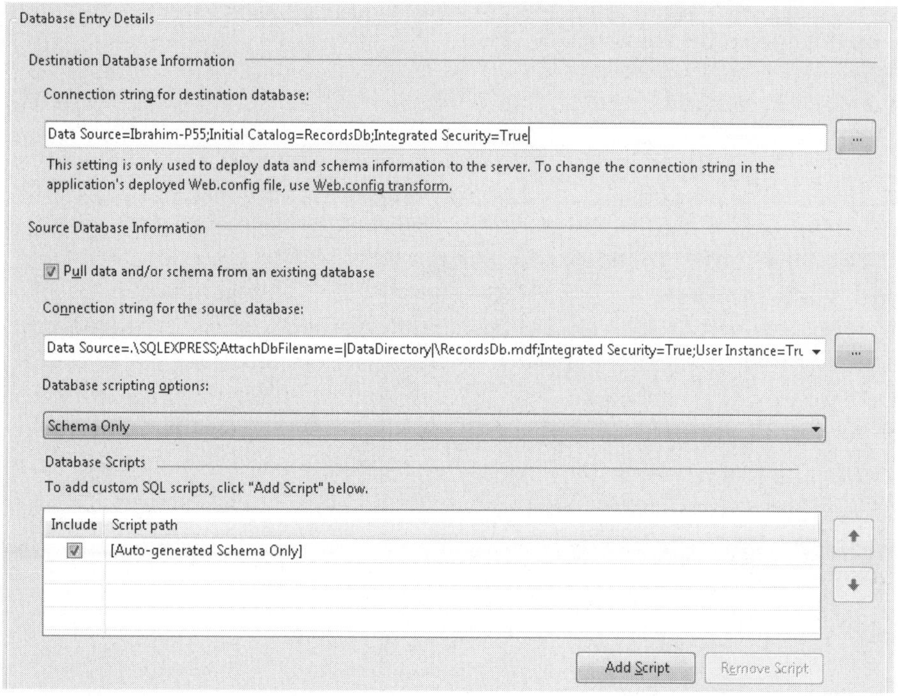

FIGURE 18-6 Database entry details

Now that we have set up our database for deployment, let's perform a publish and see what happens. In my example, I have created an empty database on the Ibrahim-P55 server, which is the value found in the destination database connection string. Now, I will publish this project. To do so, right-click on the Data01 project and then select Publish. This will bring up the Publish Web dialog box, in which I configured the settings to point to my web server. In this case, that is the same as my database server, Ibrahim-P55. You can see the value that I have populated in Figure 18-7.

In Figure 18-7, you can see that I have chosen Web Deploy as my publish method and then specified a few other values here. Database deployment is supported only when you use the Web Deploy publish method. Once I click Publish, I will see several messages in the Output window. I won't include the entire log here, but take a look at the very end of it in the next snippet:

```
Adding child dirPath (Default Web Site/Data01\Styles).
Adding child filePath (Default Web Site/Data01\Styles\Site.css).
Adding child filePath (Default Web Site/Data01\Web.config).
Adding setAcl (Default Web Site/Data01).
Adding setAcl (Default Web Site/Data01).
Adding setAcl (Default Web Site/Data01/App_Data).
Updating dbFullSql (data source=Ibrahim-P55;initial catalog=RecordsDb;integratedsecurity=
True;pooling=False).
Adding child sqlScript (sitemanifest/dbFullSql[@path='data source=Ibrahim-P55;initial
```

```
catalog=RecordsDb;integrated security=True;pooling=False']/sqlScript).
Successfully executed Web deployment task.
Publish is successfully deployed.
Task "MSdeploy" skipped, due to false condition; ($(UseMsdeployExe)) was evaluated as
(False).
Done building target "MSDeployPublish" in project "Data01.csproj".
Done building project "Data01.csproj".
========== Build: 1 succeeded or up-to-date, 0 failed, 0 skipped ==========
```

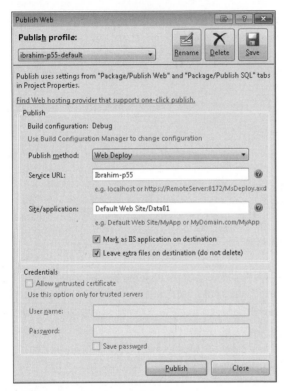

FIGURE 18-7 Publish Web dialog

From the results shown here, I have highlighted the portion that relates to the database deployment. You can see that the database is being deployed, along with the actual files and settings of the web application itself. Now that we have seen this at work, we will talk a little bit about how this is accomplished.

> **Note** You can increase the number of messages written to the Output window by going to Tools/Options/Projects and Solutions/Build and Run, and then specifying a value in the MSBuild Project Build Output Verbosity setting. When you are publishing from Visual Studio, the publish status is being written to the Output window, so it is a good idea to have this value set to Normal or Detailed.

As we saw in the previous chapter, MSDeploy has a dbFullSql provider, which can be used to execute a database script against a given database. Also in the last chapter, we discussed the Manifest provider and how it can be employed to invoke several different providers during the same sync operation. When you publish your application from Visual Studio or from the command line, a manifest is created behind the scenes, and then this is used to deploy your application. If you had a WAP and no database, then by default, the manifest generated would contain an element to create the application and two elements to set up the ACLs for the site. Now that we are deploying a database from the App_Data folder, let's take a look at the generated manifest file. After you perform a publish or create a package, you can take a look at the manifest used at obj*{Configuration}*\\Package*{ProjectName}*.SourceManifest .xml, where *{Configuration}* is the build configuration and *{ProjectName}* is the name of the project. Here is the Data01.SourceManifest.xml file:

```
<sitemanifest>
<IisApp path="C:\InsideMSBuild\Ch18\Data01\obj\Debug\Package\PackageTmp" />
<setAcl path="C:\InsideMSBuild\Ch18\Data01\obj\Debug\Package\PackageTmp"
setAclResourceType="Directory" />
<setAcl path="C:\InsideMSBuild\Ch18\Data01\obj\Debug\Package\PackageTmp"
setAclUser="anonymousAuthenticationUser" setAclResourceType="Directory" />
<setAcl path="C:\InsideMSBuild\Ch18\Data01\obj\Debug\Package\PackageTmp\App_Data"
setAclResourceType="Directory" setAclAccess="Write" />
<dbFullSql path="C:\InsideMSBuild\Ch18\Data01\obj\Debug\AutoScripts\RecordsDb-
Deployment_SchemaOnly.sql" Transacted="True" />
</sitemanifest>
```

From the contents of this file, you can see that the last element uses the dbFullSql provider to execute a script. The script was generated from the source database, which is defined on the Package/Publish SQL tab. It is generated using the dbFullSql provider. For example, to generate a script for the schema of a database to a file, you can use the command `msdeploy -verb:sync -source:dbFullSql="`*{ConnectionString}*`"` `-dest:dbFullSql="`*{FilePath}*`"`, where *{ConnectionString}* is the connection string to the database, including Initial Catalog, and *{FilePath}* is the path to the file where you want to write the script. The following command would script out the schema for the RecordsDb database from the server Ibrahim-P55 and place it into a file at C:\InsideMSBuild\Ch18\recordsDb.sql.

```
msdeploy -verb:sync
-source:dbFullSql="Data Source=Ibrahim-P55;Integrated Security=true;Initial
Catalog=RecordsDb"
-dest:dbFullSql="C:\InsideMSBuild\Ch18\recordsDb.sql".
```

The results of executing this command are shown in Figure 18-8.

From Figure 18-8, we can see that the dbFullSql provider was used to create the recordsDb. sql file. In this case, the command used will only script out the schema of the database with the default settings. The dbFullSql provider has more than 100 different settings, one of which is scriptData. If you want to script the data of your database along with its schema, just set the scriptData setting to *true*. For example, the previous command would change to something like the following:

```
msdeploy -verb:sync
-source:dbFullSql="Data Source=Ibrahim-P55;Integrated Security=true;Initial
Catalog=RecordsDb",scriptData=true

-dest:dbFullSql=C:\InsideMSBuild\Ch18\recordsDb-withData.sql
```

```
C:\InsideMSBuild\Ch18\IncludeFiles01>msdeploy -verb:sync -source:dbFullSql="Data Source=Ibrahim-P55
;Integrated Security=true;Initial Catalog=RecordsDb" -dest:dbFullSql="C:\InsideMSBuild\Ch18\records
Db.sql"
Info: Adding MSDeploy.dbFullSql (MSDeploy.dbFullSql).
Info: Adding dbFullSql (C:\InsideMSBuild\Ch18\recordsDb.sql).
Info: Adding child sqlScript (MSDeploy.dbFullSql/dbFullSql[@path='C:\InsideMSBuild\Ch18\recordsDb.s
ql']/sqlScript).
Total changes: 3 (3 added, 0 deleted, 0 updated, 0 parameters changed, 0 bytes copied)
```

FIGURE 18-8 Using the dbFullSqlprovider to script out a database schema

In this command, I have bolded the setting that was passed in. To pass in more than one setting, just separate the settings with a comma. I won't list all the settings here, but if you are interested in seeing the full list, then execute `msdeploy -verb:sync -source:dbFullSql /?`. You might want to redirect the output to a file by appending `>{Filename}`, where *{Filename}* is the name of the file where the usage information should be placed. This is helpful because the usage information typically will not fit into the console buffer. With that, we will conclude this chapter. In this chapter and the previous one, we have laid the foundation for using MSDeploy to publish your application. In Chapter 19, we will take a look at MSDeploy and show some examples of how you can use it to solve common problems.

Chapter 19

Web Deployment Tool Practical Applications

In Chapter 17, "Web Deployment Tool, Part 1," we introduced msdeploy.exe and how you could use it to deploy your Web (where Web can be either a Web application or website, we will use this throughout this chapter) to a local or remote server. In Chapter 18, "Web Deployment Tool, Part 2," we introduced the Web Publishing Pipeline and discussed how you could create packages which could be used to deploy your Web to IIS servers, either with msdeploy.exe or through the IIS Manager interface. In this chapter, we will take the knowledge that we have learned in those two chapters and apply it to real-life programming. We will show a number of simple applications, such as excluding ACL providers from packages built from Microsoft Visual Studio, as well as a few things that are a bit more complex, such as deploying to multiple environments from Team Build. We will first take a look at how to deploy your application using MSBuild.

Publishing Using MSBuild

In Chapter 17, we saw how to use msdeploy.exe to publish your application from the command line. In Chapter 18, we showed how you could use Visual Studio 2010 to perform the publish for you. From the last chapter, you might have been wondering how you could automate the publish process from the command line using MSBuild. In this example, we will look at exactly that.

In order to start the publish process on your Web Application Project (WAP) using MSBuild, you have to invoke the MSDeployPublish target on the project. This is the target that will perform the deployment for you. There are two ways to invoke this target: by invoking it directly when building the project with the /t switch, or indirectly using the DeployOnBuild and DeployTarget properties. You might be wondering why we are giving you the option of invoking it indirectly. The answer is that if you are building a solution file, you cannot invoke the MSDeployPublish target directly, but you can set properties that get propagated down to each project. This is especially useful for Team Build builds, which many times will be building a solution instead of a lone project file. Because of this, we will cover the indirect method, which will also work for Team Build 2010. Note that neither of these approaches will work with Team Build 2008.

When you are deploying from the command line, you unfortunately do not have the luxury of being able to tap into the values that were entered into the Publish dialog in Visual Studio. Because of this, you will have to pass in some details about the destination for the Web application. Because we are going to be talking about these options here, we have shown the Publish Profile dialog here in Figure 19-1 for your reference.

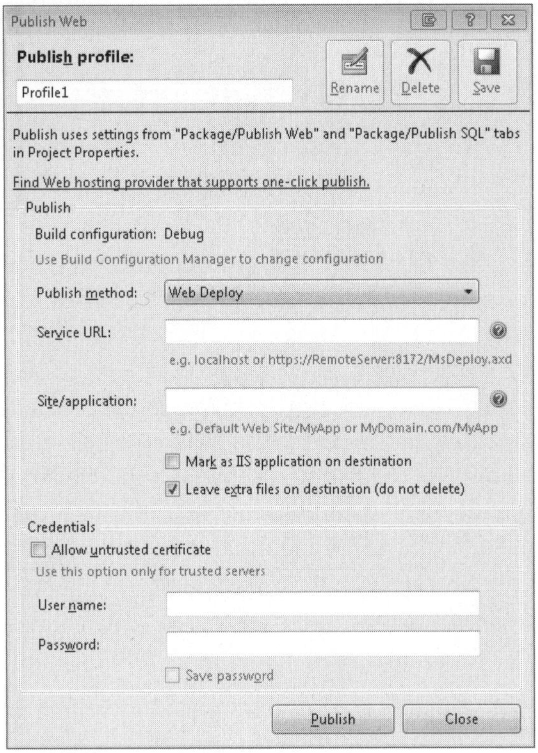

FIGURE 19-1 Publish Profile dialog

From Figure 19-1, we can see that when publishing from Visual Studio using Web Deploy, the inputs that you could specify include the following:

- Service URL
- Site/application
- Mark as IIS application on destination
- Leave extra files on destination
- Allow untrusted certificate
- User name
- Password

For each of these values, there is a corresponding MSBuild property that you can set. In fact, when you are publishing from the command line, there are many useful properties. We have described some of them in Table 19-1. Table 19-1 starts with the properties that correspond with the Publish Profile dialog and then introduces others.

TABLE 19-1 MSBuild Properties or Publish Profile

Property Name	Description
MSDeployServiceUrl	This is the endpoint that will be contacted to perform the publish. This is the same as the Service URL option in the Publish Profile dialog.
DeployIisAppPath	This is the application path for the Web, and it is the same as the Site/Application option.
DeployAsIisApp	This will determine if your content will be marked as an IIS application. This is the same as the Mark As IIS application On Destination option. The default value for this is *true*.
SkipExtraFilesOnServer	This will determine if any files that exist on the server but not in the deploy package should be left on the server or deleted. If *false*, then extra files on the server will be deleted. If *true*, then they will not be deleted. This is the same as the Leave Extra Files On Destination (Do Not Delete) check box.
AllowUntrustedCertificate	If *true*, then untrusted certificates will be allowed for use with deployments; otherwise, they will not be. The default value (empty string) will block untrusted certificates.
UserName	The user name to use in order to contact the Web Deploy remote agent service.
Password	The password to use in order to contact the Web Deploy remote agent service.
DeployOnBuild	If *true*, then the targets declared in the *DeployTarget* property will be executed. The default value is *false*.
DeployTarget	This is the target that will be called when a deployment should occur. The default value for this is *PipelineDeployPhase*. If you want to use MSDeploy for publishing, then you should pass in the value *MSDeployPublish*.
FilesToIncludeForPublish	Determines what files get deployed when a publish occurs. The possible values include *OnlyFilesToRunTheApp, AllFilesInProjectFolder,* and *AllFilesInTheProject*. The default is *OnlyFilesToRunTheApp*. This corresponds to the Items To Deploy drop-down list on the WAP Properties page.
TransformWebConfigEnabled	If *true*, then the Web.config file will be transformed if a transform file exists for that build configuration. The default value is *true*.
IncludeIisSettings	If your WAP is using IIS as the Web server and you set this property to *true*, then MSDeploy can grab the IIS settings and include them for publishing. The default is *false*.

Property Name	Description
IncludeSetAclProviderOnDestination	If this is set to *true,* then ACL information will be included in the publish; otherwise, it will not. The default is *true.*
MarkApp_DataWritableOnDestination	If this is set to *true,* then ASP.NET will be given permission to write to the App_Data folder; otherwise, it will not. The default is *true.*
IncludeAppPool	If this is *true,* then the application pool will be included in the published settings.
PackageEnableLinks	This can be used to enable MSDeploy links. By default, this is an empty string. In order to enable more than one, just pass in a semicolon-separated list. MSDeploy links are not covered in this book.
PackageDisableLinks	This can be used to disable MSDeploy links. By default, the value for this is *AppPoolExtension;ContentExtension; CertificateExtension,* so those three links will be disabled by default. If you have passed in the property `IncludeAppPool=true`, then the value of this will be *"ContentExtension;CertificateExtension".*
ExcludeApp_Data	Set this to *true* to exclude the contents of the App_Data folder from being deployed. The default is *false.*
ExcludeGeneratedDebugSymbol	If you want to exclude debug symbols from being deployed, then set this value to *true.* By default, if debug symbols are produced, then they will be deployed.
ProjectParametersXMLFile	If you want to specify a file other than parameters.xml for parameters, then pass the path and name of the file for this property.
EnablePackageProcessLoggingAndAssert	You can set this property to *true* in order to write out log information to the obj\{Configuration}\Package\ Log\ folder.
PackageTraceLevel	This defines the amount of detail written to the logs.

The list of useful properties in Table 19-1 is not exhaustive. If you need more information, take a look at the Microsoft.Web.Publishing.targets file. It's a good idea to familiarize yourself with that file anyway if you are doing a lot of work deploying WAPs. Now that we've discussed some of these properties, let's move on to the example.

In the samples for this chapter, we have created a new WAP named Deploy01. This is a simple Web application that also contains a SQL Express database inside the App_Data folder. On the Package/Publish SQL properties page, we have given the destination values for the database. With Visual Studio 2010, it is not straightforward to deploy a database using the Web Publishing Pipeline if the destination values are not entered on the Properties page. In order to deploy this application, we are going to use the following code.

```
msbuild Deploy01.csproj
        /p:DeployOnBuild=true;
        DeployTarget=MSDeployPublish;
        MSDeployServiceUrl=WIN-MCX6WTF4J4R;
        DeployIisAppPath="Default Web Site/Data01";
        MSDeployPublishMethod=RemoteAgent;
        Username=deploy;
        password=p@ssw0rd
```

After executing this code, the last part of the console log showing the MSDeploy target
appears as shown in Figure 19-2.

```
MSDeployPublish:
    Start Web Deploy Publish the Application/package to http://WIN-MCX6WTF4J4R/MSDEPLOYAGENTSERVICE
    ...
    Starting Web deployment task from source:manifest(C:\InsideMSBuild\Ch19\Deploy01\obj\Debug\Packa
    ge\Deploy01.SourceManifest.xml) to Destination:auto().
    Adding sitemanifest (sitemanifest).
    Updating createApp (Default Web Site/Data01).
    Updating setAcl (Default Web Site/Data01).
    Updating setAcl (Default Web Site/Data01).
    Updating setAcl (Default Web Site/Data01/App_Data).
    Adding dbFullSql (data source=WIN-MCX6WTF4J4R;initial catalog=RecordsDb;persist security info=Tr
    ue;user id=dbDeploy;pooling=False).
    Adding child filePath (Default Web Site/Data01\About.aspx).
    Adding child filePath (Default Web Site/Data01\Account\ChangePassword.aspx).
    Adding child filePath (Default Web Site/Data01\Account\ChangePasswordSuccess.aspx).
    Adding child filePath (Default Web Site/Data01\Account\Login.aspx).
    Adding child filePath (Default Web Site/Data01\Account\Register.aspx).
    Adding child filePath (Default Web Site/Data01\Account\Web.config).
    Adding child filePath (Default Web Site/Data01\App_Data\Records2.ndf).
    Adding child filePath (Default Web Site/Data01\App_Data\Records2_log.ldf).
    Adding child filePath (Default Web Site/Data01\bin\Deploy01.dll).
    Adding child filePath (Default Web Site/Data01\bin\Deploy01.pdb).
    Adding child filePath (Default Web Site/Data01\Default.aspx).
    Adding child filePath (Default Web Site/Data01\Global.asax).
    Adding child filePath (Default Web Site/Data01\Scripts\jquery-1.4.1-vsdoc.js).
    Adding child filePath (Default Web Site/Data01\Scripts\jquery-1.4.1.js).
    Adding child filePath (Default Web Site/Data01\Scripts\jquery-1.4.1.min.js).
    Adding child filePath (Default Web Site/Data01\Site.Master).
    Adding child filePath (Default Web Site/Data01\Styles\Site.css).
    Adding child filePath (Default Web Site/Data01\Web.config).
    Updating setAcl (Default Web Site/Data01).
    Updating setAcl (Default Web Site/Data01).
    Updating setAcl (Default Web Site/Data01/App_Data).
    Updating dbFullSql (data source=WIN-MCX6WTF4J4R;initial catalog=RecordsDb;persist security info=
    True;user id=dbDeploy;pooling=False).
    Adding child sqlScript (sitemanifest/dbFullSql[@path='data source=WIN-MCX6WTF4J4R;initial catalo
    g=RecordsDb;persist security info=True;user id=dbDeploy;pooling=False']/sqlScript).
    Successfully executed Web deployment task.
    Publish is successfully deployed.
Done Building Project "C:\InsideMSBuild\Ch19\Deploy01\Deploy01.csproj" (default targets).

Build succeeded.
    0 Warning(s)
    0 Error(s)
```

FIGURE 19-2 Publishing Using MSBuild and MSDeploy

In Figure 19-2, we can see that the package was deployed to the target machine. Now
let's explain a few of the properties that are being passed in to the code that we executed.
You need to set DeployOnBuild to *true* so that the deploy will be kicked off after the build
completes. DeployTarget is the name of the target that will execute after the build. This
target will always be MSDeployPublish unless you have your own target that you want to
use. MSDeployPublishMethod is set to RemoteAgent in this case because we want the
MSDeploy Remote Agent Service to perform the deployment. The other options for this
property are *InProc,* which you use only when you want to publish to the same machine
running the build, and *WMSVC,* which you use if you want the Web Management Service to
perform the deployment for you.

One thing that you should take note of is that the SQL deployment will be performed from the target machine. In this case, we started the deployment from my machine, Ibrahim-P55, and the target machine was WIN-MCX6WTF4J4R, which is a virtual machine. So in my case, the SQL script was executed from the WIN-MCX6WTF4J4R machine, and the target SQL database is on the Ibrahim-P55 machine. Since both machines are not on a domain, we had to specify the SQL credentials in the connection string because Windows Authentication would not have worked.

Parameterizing Packages

In Chapter 17, we saw how to use the –declareParam and –setParam switches when using msdeploy.exe to create and set parameters. You might have been wondering if we could parameterize packages created from Web Application Projects. The answer is yes: You can customize the parameters two different ways for packages created from WAPs. You can either create the parameters using MSBuild, or you can create a parameters.xml file, which will be used to create them for you. We will look at the first approach, and then the second.

Using MSBuild to Parameterize the Created Package

When you create a package from Visual Studio, or msbuild.exe, the Web Publishing Pipeline (WPP) is very extensible so you can hook into it to customize the package that is generated. It uses an item list, MsDeployDeclareParameters, to gather the parameters that will be created for the package. When you execute the Package target, it will then call the PackageUsingManifest target to actually create the package. The task that creates the package is shown in the next snippet.

```
<VSMSDeploy Condition="!$(UseMsdeployExe)"
    Source="@(MsDeploySourceProviderSetting)"
    Destination="@(MsDeployDestinationProviderSetting)"
    DeploymentTraceLevel="$(PackageTraceLevel)"
    DisableLink="$(PackageDisableLinks)"
    EnableLink="$(PackageEnableLinks)"
    DeclareParameterItems="@(_Package_MsDeployDeclareParameters)"
    OptimisticParameterDefaultValue="$(EnableOptimisticParameterDefaultValue)"
    ImportDeclareParametersItems="$(_VsPackageParametersFile)"
    ReplaceRuleItems="@(MsDeployReplaceRules)"
    RetryAttempts="$(RetryAttemptsForDeployment)">
  <Output TaskParameter="Result" PropertyName="PackageResult" />
</VSMSDeploy>
```

From this code, we can see that the item list, _Package_MsDeployDeclareParameters, is passed in for the *DeclareParameterItems* value. _Package_MsDeployDeclareParameters is based on the MsDeployDeclareParameters item list. If you need to create your own parameters, you can add extra values to this item list. In order to successfully create the parameters when you add values to that item list, you have to include the correct metadata.

The best way to describe this is to see it in action. In the sample for this chapter, we have included a WAP named Deploy02. The next snippet shows the *appSettings* element from the Web.config file for that WAP.

```
<appSettings>
  <add key="pageSize" value="2"/>
  <add key="IncludesConfigPath" value="~/Config/includes.xml.config"/>
  <add key="IncludesApplicationName" value="inlinetasks.com"/>
</appSettings>
```

Here, what we would like to do is to create a parameter for each of these values. Let's start with the pageSize value. Since we want to parameterize this using MSBuild, we need to extend the build/package process. If you remember from Chapter 18, we can create a .wpp.targets file to do this. In this case, the file would be named Deploy02.wpp.targets. Inside this file we have created a new target named AddCustomParameters. Inside this target, we will append the parameters to the MsDeployDeclareParameters item list. Take a look at the snippet here, which shows this target and what is needed to create the parameter for pageSize.

```
<Target Name="AddCustomParameters" BeforeTargets="Package">
  <ItemGroup>
    <MsDeployDeclareParameters Include="PageSize">
      <Kind>XmlFile</Kind>
      <Scope>Web.config</Scope>
      <Match>/configuration/appSettings/add[@key='pageSize']/@value</Match>
      <Description>desc-here</Description>
      <DefaultValue>25</DefaultValue>
      <Tags>applicationSettings</Tags>
    </MsDeployDeclareParameters>
  </ItemGroup>
</Target>
```

In this target, you can see that we are adding to the MsDeployDeclareParameters item list. Now let's break it down a bit. If you are familiar with the –declareParam switch from Chapter 17, then the metadata names should look familiar. The value for the *Include* attribute will be the name of the parameter being created, which is the value for the name that is passed to –declareParam. Now let's let look at the metadata values. They all match the corresponding names when using the –declareParam switch. Since we've covered –declareParam, it should be pretty straightforward to create new parameters in this method. The following code block shows the target that creates the parameters for all three app settings.

```
<Target Name="AddCustomParameters" BeforeTargets="Package">
  <ItemGroup>
    <MsDeployDeclareParameters Include="PageSize">
      <Kind>XmlFile</Kind>
      <Scope>Web.config</Scope>
      <Match>/configuration/appSettings/add[@key='pageSize']/@value</Match>
      <Description>Enter the value for page size</Description>
      <DefaultValue>25</DefaultValue>
```

```
          <Tags>applicationSettings</Tags>
        </MsDeployDeclareParameters>

        <MsDeployDeclareParameters Include="IncludesConfigPath">
          <Kind>XmlFile</Kind>
          <Scope>Web.config</Scope>
          <Match>/configuration/appSettings/add[@key='IncludesConfigPath']/@value</Match>
          <Description>Enter the value for the pate to the include file</Description>
          <DefaultValue>~/Config/includes.xml.config</DefaultValue>
          <Tags>applicationSettings</Tags>
        </MsDeployDeclareParameters>

        <MsDeployDeclareParameters Include="IncludesApplicationName">
          <Kind>XmlFile</Kind>
          <Scope>Web.config</Scope>
          <Match>/configuration/appSettings/add[@key='IncludesApplicationName']/@value</Match>
          <Description>Enter the value for the includes application name</Description>
          <DefaultValue>inlinetasks.com</DefaultValue>
          <Tags>applicationSettings</Tags>
        </MsDeployDeclareParameters>
      </ItemGroup>
    </Target>
```

When this target is executed, the three values will be added to the item, and then, when the package is created, it will be included in the parameters.xml file. If you open the package at C:\InsideMSBuild\Ch19\Deploy02\obj\Debug\Package\Deploy02.zip, you will find the parameters.xml file. The contents of that file are shown here:

```
<parameters>
  <parameter name="IIS Web Application Name"
             defaultValue="Default Web Site/Deploy02_deploy"
             tags="IisApp">
    <parameterEntry kind="ProviderPath" scope="IisApp"
      match="^C:\\InsideMSBuild\\Ch19\\Deploy02\\obj\\Debug
             \\Package\\PackageTmp$" />
    <parameterEntry kind="ProviderPath" scope="setAcl"
      match="^C:\\InsideMSBuild\\Ch19\\Deploy02\\obj\\Debug
             \\Package\\PackageTmp$" />
  </parameter>
  <parameter name="PageSize"
             description="Enter the value for page size" defaultValue="25"
             tags="applicationSettings">
    <parameterEntry kind="XmlFile" scope="Web.config"
                    match="/configuration/appSettings/add[@key='pageSize']/@value" />
  </parameter>
  <parameter name="IncludesConfigPath"
             description="Enter the value for the pate to the include file"
             defaultValue="~/Config/includes.xml.config" tags="applicationSettings">
    <parameterEntry kind="XmlFile" scope="Web.config"
                    match="/configuration/appSettings/add[@key='IncludesConfigPath']/@value" />
  </parameter>
  <parameter name="IncludesApplicationName"
             description="Enter the value for the includes application name"
             defaultValue="inlinetasks.com" tags="applicationSettings">
```

```
      <parameterEntry kind="XmlFile" scope="Web.config"
                match="/configuration/appSettings/
                       add[@key='IncludesApplicationName']/@value" />
  </parameter>
</parameters>
```

From this file, we can see that our parameters were created as we had expected. You might have noticed a couple of extra parameters for the application name and provider path. Those are included by default in the WPP. Now that your package has been parameterized, you can import the package from the command line and specify the values, or hand off the package to someone else, who can import it using the IIS Manager. The IIS Manager will prompt the user for all parameters defined in the package. If you were to import this package using IIS Manager, the package parameters dialog that you would see is shown in Figure 19-3.

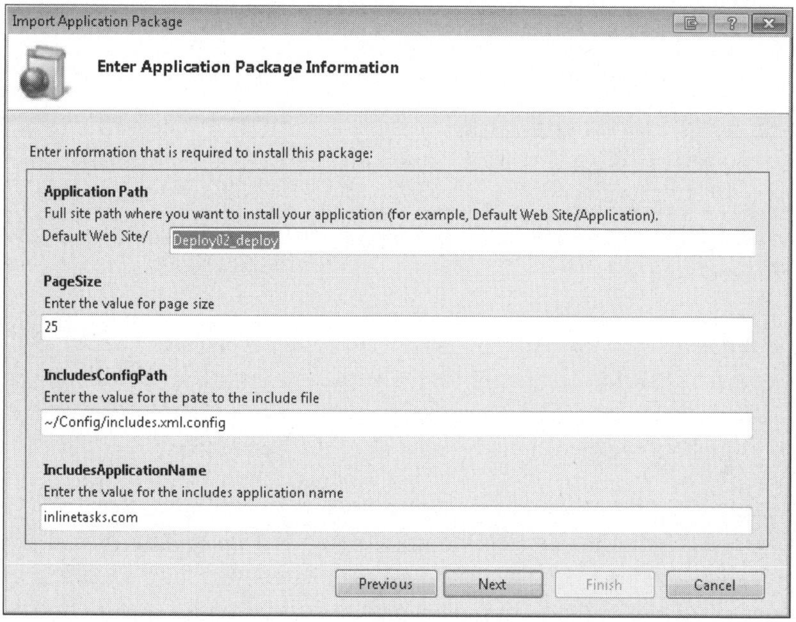

FIGURE 19-3 IIS Manager Import Application Package Parameters dialog

The parameters that were declared are shown in this dialog, including the values for the name, description, and default value for each one. Now that we have seen how to use MSBuild to parameterize the package, let's make it a bit simpler by using a parameters .xml file.

Using Parameters.xml to Parameterize the Create Package

In the previous example, we saw the "rough and dirty" method of customizing the parameters that are included in the generated package. There is a much simpler way to do this, though. Instead of declaring your parameters using MSBuild, you can just hand-craft a parameters.xml file and then drop it into the projects directory. Once you do this, all of the parameters declared in that file will be included in the final parameters.xml file, which ends up in the created package. For this example, we have created another project called Deploy03 and we have included the same appSettings values as the previous example. We added the paramters.xml file with the following contents:

```
<parameters>
  <parameter name="PageSize"
             description="Enter the value for page size" defaultValue="25"
             tags="applicationSettings">
    <parameterEntry kind="XmlFile" scope="Web.config"
                    match="/configuration/appSettings/add[@key='pageSize']/@value" />
  </parameter>
  <parameter name="IncludesConfigPath"
             description="Enter the value for the pate to the include file"
             defaultValue="~/Config/includes.xml.config" tags="applicationSettings">
    <parameterEntry kind="XmlFile" scope="Web.config"
                    match="/configuration/appSettings/add[@key='IncludesConfigPath']/@value" />
  </parameter>
  <parameter name="IncludesApplicationName"
             description="Enter the value for the includes application name"
             defaultValue="inlinetasks.com" tags="applicationSettings">
    <parameterEntry kind="XmlFile" scope="Web.config"
                    match="/configuration/appSettings/add[@key='IncludesApplicationName']/@value" />
  </parameter>
</parameters>
```

This file looks very similar to the parameters.xml file in the package for the Deploy02 project. The only difference is that the parameter for the application name is not found here. You do not have to include that in your parameters.xml—it will be added automatically. From this point, after you create a package, it will contain all of the parameters.

If for some reason you did not want to create parameters from this file, then you could disable this by setting the property ImportParametersFiles to false. Also, if you wanted to change which file is used to create the parameters, just set the value of the ProjectParametersXMLFile property to the full path.

Using –setParamFile

In the previous example, we discussed how you can easily parameterize your packages. We have shown two techniques to set the values of those parameters when the package was imported: through the IIS Manager or by using –setParam. Using –setParam works all right, but after just a couple of parameters, it becomes very unwieldy. Fortunately, there is another way: You can create a file that is used to store the values for these parameters. When you create a package from a WAP in the Package directory, you might have noticed that there is a SetParameters.xml file. That is a file that you can use for this purpose. Let's take Deploy03 as an example. We have copied the package to a new location, C:\InsideMSBuild\Ch19\

Deploy03-Package\Deploy03.zip, and then we have created the file Deploy03
.qa.SetParameters.xml, which would contain the parameter values for the package. When
we created this file, we just copied the Deploy03.SetParameters.xml from the Deploy03
Package directory. The contents of this file are shown next:

```
<parameters>
  <setParameter name="IIS Web Application Name" value="Default Web Site/Deploy03QA" />
  <setParameter name="PageSize" value="125" />
  <setParameter name="IncludesConfigPath" value="~/Config/includes.xml.qa.config" />
  <setParameter name="IncludesApplicationName" value="qa.inlinetasks.com" />
</parameters>
```

In this file, all you need is a *setParameter* element, which gives the name of the parameter
and its value. In this case, we are setting a value for each parameter. You can see from the IIS
Web Application Name parameter that the destination application will be Default Web Site/
Deploy03QA. Now let's see how we can use this file with msdeploy.exe to create or update
the site.

When you are using msdeploy.exe in order to use a file as the source for the parameter
values, you just have to use the –setParamFile switch. In this case, the command we used is
shown in the next snippet:

```
msdeploy -verb:sync
         -source:package=Deploy03.zip
         -dest:auto
         -setParamFile=Deploy03.qa.SetParameters.xml
```

You can see here that the syntax to pass in the file containing the parameter values is very
simple and straightforward. If you execute the command, you should see the result shown in
Figure 19-4.

```
C:\InsideMSBuild\Ch19\Deploy03-Package>msdeploy -verb:sync -source:package=Deploy03.zip -dest:auto
-setParamFile=Deploy03.qa.SetParameters.xml
Info: Adding sitemanifest (sitemanifest).
Info: Updating createApp (Default Web Site/Deploy03QA).
Info: Adding contentPath (Default Web Site/Deploy03QA).
Info: Adding dirPath (Default Web Site/Deploy03QA).
Info: Adding child filePath (Default Web Site/Deploy03QA\About.aspx).
Info: Adding child dirPath (Default Web Site/Deploy03QA\Account).
Info: Adding child filePath (Default Web Site/Deploy03QA\Account\ChangePassword.aspx).
Info: Adding child filePath (Default Web Site/Deploy03QA\Account\ChangePasswordSuccess.aspx).
Info: Adding child filePath (Default Web Site/Deploy03QA\Account\Login.aspx).
Info: Adding child filePath (Default Web Site/Deploy03QA\Account\Register.aspx).
Info: Adding child filePath (Default Web Site/Deploy03QA\Account\Web.config).
Info: Adding child dirPath (Default Web Site/Deploy03QA\bin).
Info: Adding child filePath (Default Web Site/Deploy03QA\bin\Deploy03.dll).
Info: Adding child filePath (Default Web Site/Deploy03QA\bin\Deploy03.pdb).
Info: Adding child filePath (Default Web Site/Deploy03QA\Default.aspx).
Info: Adding child filePath (Default Web Site/Deploy03QA\Global.asax).
Info: Adding child filePath (Default Web Site/Deploy03QA\parameters.xml).
Info: Adding child dirPath (Default Web Site/Deploy03QA\Scripts).
Info: Adding child filePath (Default Web Site/Deploy03QA\Scripts\jquery-1.4.1-vsdoc.js).
Info: Adding child filePath (Default Web Site/Deploy03QA\Scripts\jquery-1.4.1.js).
Info: Adding child filePath (Default Web Site/Deploy03QA\Scripts\jquery-1.4.1.min.js).
Info: Adding child filePath (Default Web Site/Deploy03QA\Site.Master).
Info: Adding child dirPath (Default Web Site/Deploy03QA\Styles).
Info: Adding child filePath (Default Web Site/Deploy03QA\Styles\Site.css).
Info: Adding child filePath (Default Web Site/Deploy03QA\Web.config).
Info: Adding setAcl (Default Web Site/Deploy03QA).
Info: Adding setAcl (Default Web Site/Deploy03QA).
Total changes: 27 (26 added, 0 deleted, 1 updated, 0 parameters changed, 542476 bytes copied)
```

FIGURE 19-4 msdeploy.exe Deploying a site using –setParamFile

From this result, you can see that it was successfully deployed to the site Default Web Site/ Deploy03QA, as described in the Deploy03.qa.SetParameters.xml file.

Using the MSDeploy Temp Agent

All of the examples that we have shown when deploying to a remote machine have been using the MSDeploy Remote Agent Service. If you have anything more than a few servers, then it quickly becomes problematic to install and maintain the service on all the servers to which you need to deploy. Fortunately, there is another option: You can use a temporary agent, or "temp agent." In this case, you will initiate a deployment to a remote machine and a temp agent will be installed on the machine. Once the deployment completes, the temp agent will be removed. If you want to deploy using the temp agent, then you need to initiate the deployment from a user that is an administrator on the target machine. Also, the machine where you are issuing the command must have the Remote Agent Service installed. In my case, we will be deploying to a virtual machine called WIN-MCX6WTF4J4R. Nether the virtual machine nor the machine that we are using, Ibrahim-P55, is joined to a domain, and therefore, we will have to issue a net use command in order to use a remote resource as a remote user. For example, we issued the following command:

```
net use "\\WIN-MCX6WTF4J4R\C$\Windows" /USER:deploy
```

Only after doing this can we use the temp agent against the WIN-MCX6WTF4J4R machine. For this example, we have turned off the Remote Agent Service on that machine. When using the temp agent, you do not have to install MSDeploy on the remote server.

When you are using the temp agent, you can execute the same commands as you could with the Remote Agent Service. For example, in order to get a dump of the application at Default Web Site/Data01, you would use the following command:

```
msdeploy -verb:dump
         -source:iisApp="Default Web Site/Data01",
             computerName=WIN-MCX6WTF4J4R,username=deploy,password=p@ssw0rd,tempAgent=true
```

The only difference between this command and one that uses the Remote Agent Service is the usage of tempAgent=true. In order to show you a bit better what is happening, we executed and added the –verbose option to include more details in the log. The result of executing this command is shown in Figure 19-5.

From the results shown in Figure 19-5, we have highlighted the portions showing that the temp agent is being initialized and shut down. Using the temp agent is a great technique to deploy your applications to remote servers without having to install the Remote Agent Service on every target server.

```
C:\InsideMSBuild\Ch20>msdeploy -verb:dump -source:iisApp="Default Web Site/Data01",computerName=WIN
-MCX6WTF4J4R,username=deploy,password=p@ssw0rd,tempAgent=true -verbose
Verbose: Using ID '1ab22ddd-2017-473e-a5c2-5227545725d7' for connections to the remote server.
Verbose: Creating temporary directory '\\WIN-MCX6WTF4J4R\C$\Windows\TEMP\MSDEPLOY\1ab22ddd-2017-473
e-a5c2-5227545725d7' on remote target.
Verbose: Copying temporary agent file C:\Program Files\IIS\Microsoft Web Deploy\Microsoft.Web.Deleg
ation.dll to \\WIN-MCX6WTF4J4R\C$\Windows\TEMP\MSDEPLOY\1ab22ddd-2017-473e-a5c2-5227545725d7\Micros
oft.Web.Delegation.dll.
Verbose: Copying temporary agent file C:\Program Files\IIS\Microsoft Web Deploy\Microsoft.Web.Deplo
yment.dll to \\WIN-MCX6WTF4J4R\C$\Windows\TEMP\MSDEPLOY\1ab22ddd-2017-473e-a5c2-5227545725d7\Micros
oft.Web.Deployment.dll.
Verbose: Copying temporary agent file C:\Program Files\IIS\Microsoft Web Deploy\MsDepSvc.exe to \\W
IN-MCX6WTF4J4R\C$\Windows\TEMP\MSDEPLOY\1ab22ddd-2017-473e-a5c2-5227545725d7\MsDepSvc.exe.
Verbose: Copying temporary agent file C:\Program Files\IIS\Microsoft Web Deploy\x64\axnative.dll to
\\WIN-MCX6WTF4J4R\C$\Windows\TEMP\MSDEPLOY\1ab22ddd-2017-473e-a5c2-5227545725d7\x64\axnative.dll.
Verbose: Copying temporary agent file C:\Program Files\IIS\Microsoft Web Deploy\x86\axnative.dll to
\\WIN-MCX6WTF4J4R\C$\Windows\TEMP\MSDEPLOY\1ab22ddd-2017-473e-a5c2-5227545725d7\x86\axnative.dll.
Verbose: Copying temporary agent file C:\Program Files\IIS\Microsoft Web Deploy\Extensibility\Custo
mFileProvider.dll to \\WIN-MCX6WTF4J4R\C$\Windows\TEMP\MSDEPLOY\1ab22ddd-2017-473e-a5c2-5227545725d
7\Extensibility\CustomFileProvider.dll.
Verbose: Executing command line 'C:\Windows\TEMP\MSDEPLOY\1ab22ddd-2017-473e-a5c2-5227545725d7\MsDe
pSvc.exe -listenUrl:http://+:80/1ab22ddd-2017-473e-a5c2-5227545725d7/' on remote target.
Verbose: Temporary agent started on remote target. Process ID 3532.
Verbose: Pre-authenticating to remote agent URL 'http://WIN-MCX6WTF4J4R/1ab22ddd-2017-473e-a5c2-522
7545725d7' as 'deploy'.
Verbose: Pre-authenticating to remote agent URL 'http://WIN-MCX6WTF4J4R/1ab22ddd-2017-473e-a5c2-522
7545725d7' as 'deploy'.
MSDeploy.iisApp (name=MSDeploy.iisApp)
Default Web Site/Data01 (name=iisApp) (keyAttribute=Default Web Site/Data01) (linkName=Child1)
Default Web Site/Data01 (name=createApp) (keyAttribute=Default Web Site/Data01) (linkName=createApp
)
Default Web Site/Data01 (name=contentPath) (keyAttribute=Default Web Site/Data01) (linkName=content
Path)
Default Web Site/Data01 (name=dirPath) (keyAttribute=Default Web Site/Data01) (linkName=contentPath
)
Default Web Site/Data01\About.aspx (name=filePath) (keyAttribute=About.aspx)
Default Web Site/Data01\Account (name=dirPath) (keyAttribute=Account)
Default Web Site/Data01\Account\ChangePassword.aspx (name=filePath) (keyAttribute=ChangePassword.as
px)
Default Web Site/Data01\Account\ChangePasswordSuccess.aspx (name=filePath) (keyAttribute=ChangePass
wordSuccess.aspx)
Default Web Site/Data01\Account\Login.aspx (name=filePath) (keyAttribute=Login.aspx)
Default Web Site/Data01\Account\Register.aspx (name=filePath) (keyAttribute=Register.aspx)
Default Web Site/Data01\Account\Web.config (name=filePath) (keyAttribute=Web.config)
Default Web Site/Data01\App_Data (name=dirPath) (keyAttribute=App_Data)
Default Web Site/Data01\App_Data\Records2.mdf (name=filePath) (keyAttribute=Records2.mdf)
Default Web Site/Data01\App_Data\Records2_log.ldf (name=filePath) (keyAttribute=Records2_log.ldf)
Default Web Site/Data01\bin (name=dirPath) (keyAttribute=bin)
Default Web Site/Data01\bin\Deploy01.dll (name=filePath) (keyAttribute=Deploy01.dll)
Default Web Site/Data01\bin\Deploy01.pdb (name=filePath) (keyAttribute=Deploy01.pdb)
Default Web Site/Data01\Default.aspx (name=filePath) (keyAttribute=Default.aspx)
Default Web Site/Data01\Global.asax (name=filePath) (keyAttribute=Global.asax)
Default Web Site/Data01\Scripts (name=dirPath) (keyAttribute=Scripts)
Default Web Site/Data01\Scripts\jquery-1.4.1-vsdoc.js (name=filePath) (keyAttribute=jquery-1.4.1-vs
doc.js)
Default Web Site/Data01\Scripts\jquery-1.4.1.js (name=filePath) (keyAttribute=jquery-1.4.1.js)
Default Web Site/Data01\Scripts\jquery-1.4.1.min.js (name=filePath) (keyAttribute=jquery-1.4.1.min.
js)
Default Web Site/Data01\Site.Master (name=filePath) (keyAttribute=Site.Master)
Default Web Site/Data01\Styles (name=dirPath) (keyAttribute=Styles)
Default Web Site/Data01\Styles\Site.css (name=filePath) (keyAttribute=Site.css)
Default Web Site/Data01\Web.config (name=filePath) (keyAttribute=Web.config)
Verbose: Terminating the temporary agent process (ID 3532) on the remote target.
Verbose: Deleting temporary directory '\\WIN-MCX6WTF4J4R\C$\Windows\TEMP\MSDEPLOY\1ab22ddd-2017-473
e-a5c2-5227545725d7' on remote target.
```

FIGURE 19-5 Result from a dump using a temp agent

Deploying Your Site from Team Build

Building and deploying your site using Team Build is incredibly easy if you've grasped the concepts presented in this chapter as well as the previous two. Deploying from Team Build is about as easy as deploying from msbuild.exe using the techniques described in the first section of this chapter, "Publishing Using MSBuild." In that section, we showed how you can deploy your Web by building the solution file and providing some properties on the command line. We will use this same exact technique in order to deploy from Team Build.

If you want to deploy from Team Build, your best option is first to create the command to deploy using msbuild.exe. We have created a new project, TfsDeploy01, in the samples for this chapter. We want to take the WAP that is contained in that project and deploy that to the WIN-MCX6WTF4J4R machine. In order to do that, we will use the command listed next:

```
msbuild TfsDeploy01.sln
            /p:Configuration=Release;
                DeployOnBuild=true;
                DeployTarget=MSDeployPublish;
                MSDeployServiceUrl=WIN-MCX6WTF4J4R;
                DeployIisAppPath="Default Web Site/TfsDeploy";
                MSDeployPublishMethod=RemoteAgent;
                Username=deploy;
                Password=p@ssw0rd
```

Note If you want to deploy from Team Build, then you must ensure that the build agent machine has the WPP tasks and targets installed.

Now that we've got the command that we need to execute, it is very easy for me to create a new Team Build definition that can deploy this site. When you are creating your new build definition, you would set everything up as you normally would. On the Process tab of the build definition for Items to Build, pick TfsDeploy01.sln. Then you need to pass all the properties to msbuild.exe as arguments. You can do this under the Advanced node in the MSBuild Arguments row. Take a look at Figure 19-6 to see this.

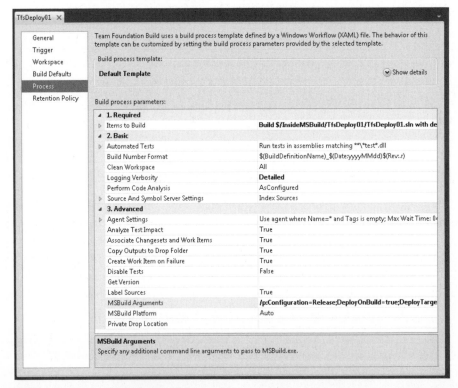

FIGURE 19-6 Team Build definition Process tab

From Figure 19-6, you can see that we have set the Items to Build to TfsDeploy01.sln. The value for MSBuild Arguments is the following:

```
/p:Configuration=Release;
   DeployOnBuild=true;
   DeployTarget=MSDeployPublish;
   MSDeployServiceUrl=WIN-MCX6WTF4J4R;
   DeployIisAppPath="Default Web Site/TfsDeploy";
   MSDeployPublishMethod=RemoteAgent;
   Username=deploy;
   Password=p@ssw0rd
```

The value here is the same set of properties that we used when building the solution. Once we set up this Team Build definition, we can queue a new build that will build the WAP and then deploy it to the target machine, WIN-MCX6WTF4J4R. After the build completes, if you expand the build log, you should see something like what is captured in Figure 19-7.

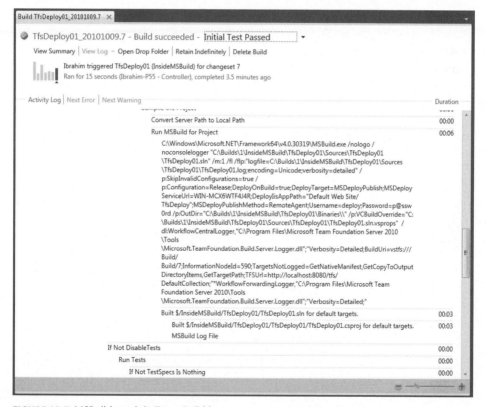

FIGURE 19-7 MSBuild result in Team Build log

In Figure 19-7, you can see the portion of the log that shows MSBuild getting invoked. As you can see, the properties that we specified were passed in. Because we were able to pass in the properties after the build completes, we know that the site will be deployed to the target server—and it was.

Deploying to Multiple Destinations Using Team Build

Now, let's say that you wanted to do something a bit more complicated. Let's say that your QA environment had two Web servers and you wanted to deploy that same package to both environments. Not only that, while doing so, you needed to make small changes to the Web.config file. You can do this pretty easily. First, we'll walk you through doing it on the command line with msbuild.exe, and then I'll show you how that translates to Team Build.

There are many different ways to do this, but here is one approach. For each environment, create a SetParameters.xml file and place it somewhere in source control. Then, you should create a .wpp.targets file. Since you don't want to use this file for each build, you should not name this file to start with the project name. For example, in this case, we named the file qa.wpp.targets. Inside this target is where we will use the MSDeploy task to deploy our application to the different sites. The MSDeploy task contained with the tasks and targets for the WPP. When you perform a deploy, either it or another task, VSMSDeploy, will be used. In this case, you could use either task, but we will use the MSDeploy task because you will see the actual command that is getting executed. The VSMSDeploy task doesn't use msdeploy .exe; it interfaces with MSDeploy via its API.

The MSDeploy task has many different properties that you can pass into it. We have outlined just a few of them in Table 19-2.

TABLE 19-2 MSDeploy Task Properties

Parameter Name	Description
Verb	This is the verb value passed to MSDeploy. A common value here would be *sync*.
Source	An item that is used to populate the values for the –source parameter passed to msdeploy.exe.
Destination	An item that is used to populate the values for the –dest parameter passed to msdeploy.exe.
ImportSetParametersItems	The path to a file that will be passed as the –setParamFile value.
RetryAttempts	The number of times that operation will be retried if the operation is not completed.
AllowUntrusted	If set to *true*, then untrusted certificates will be allowed.
Verbose	You can set this to *true* to enable more verbose output.
WhatIf	If set to *true*, then the –whatif flag will be passed to msdeploy.exe.

Now that we have outlined the MSDeploy task and some of the properties of this task, we will see how it is used shortly. Before we get around to showing how to use the MSDeploy task to perform the deployment, however, it's always best to create the msdeploy.exe command that you need to mimic first. In this case, the command that we need to execute is

```
msdeploy -verb:sync
        -source:package=TfsDeploy01.zip
```

```
    -dest:auto,
        computerName=WIN-MCX6WTF4J4R,
        username=deploy,
        password=p@ssw0rd
    -setParamFile=C:\InsideMSBuild\Ch19\TFS\TfsDeploy01\DeploySettings\
                    TfsDeploy01.QA01.SetParameters.xml
```

The command outlined in the previous block will take the TfsDeploy01.zip package and then deploy it to the WIN-MCX6WTF4J4R machine. In this example, the value for –setParamFile is set to the TfsDeploy01.QA01.SetParameters.xml file. The contents of that file are shown next:

```
<parameters>
  <setParameter name="IIS Web Application Name"
                value="QA01 Web Site/TfsDeploy" />
  <setParameter name="PageSize"
                value="150" />
  <setParameter name="IncludesConfigPath"
                value="~/Config/includes.xml.qa01.config" />
  <setParameter name="IncludesApplicationName"
                value="qa01.inlinetasks.com" />
</parameters>
```

Along with this file, there is another file that contains the settings for the QA02 site. The contents of that file are shown here:

```
<parameters>
  <setParameter name="IIS Web Application Name"
                value="QA02 Web Site/TfsDeploy" />
  <setParameter name="PageSize"
                value="500" />
  <setParameter name="IncludesConfigPath"
                value="~/Config/includes.xml.qa02.config" />
  <setParameter name="IncludesApplicationName"
                value="qa02.inlinetasks.com" />
</parameters>
```

Now we need to create a .wpp.targets file, which can perform the deployment for us. Take a look at the contents of the qa01.wpp.targets file, which is shown in the following snippet:

```
<Project xmlns="http://schemas.microsoft.com/developer/msbuild/2003">

  <Target Name="DeployToQA" DependsOnTargets="Package">
    <Message Text="Deploying to QA01 now"/>
    <!--msdeploy -verb:sync
                 -source:package=TfsDeploy01.zip
                 -dest:auto,
                     computerName=WIN-MCX6WTF4J4R,
                     username=deploy,
                     password=p@ssw0rd
                 -setParamFile=C:\InsideMSBuild\Ch19\TFS\TfsDeploy01\
                  DeploySettings\TfsDeploy01.QA01.SetParameters.xml
    -->
```

```xml
<!--******************************************************
Deploy to QA01
******************************************************-->
<ItemGroup>
  <QAMsDeploySourceProviderSetting Include="package">
    <Path>$(PackageFileName)</Path>
  </QAMsDeploySourceProviderSetting>

  <QAMsDeployDestinationProviderSetting Include="auto">
    <ComputerName>WIN-MCX6WTF4J4R</ComputerName>
    <UserName>$(Username)</UserName>
    <Password>$(Password)</Password>
  </QAMsDeployDestinationProviderSetting>

  <QASetParamFile Include="..\DeploySettings\TfsDeploy01.QA01.SetParameters.xml"/>
</ItemGroup>

<PropertyGroup>
  <_QASetParamFileFullPath>%(QASetParamFile.FullPath)</_QASetParamFileFullPath>
</PropertyGroup>

<MSDeploy
    Verb="sync"
    Source="@(QAMsDeploySourceProviderSetting)"
    ImportSetParametersItems="$(_QASetParamFileFullPath)"
    Destination="@(QAMsDeployDestinationProviderSetting)"/>

<!--******************************************************
Deploy to QA02
******************************************************-->
<Message Text="Deploying to QA01 now"/>
<ItemGroup>
  <QASetParamFile02 Include="..\DeploySettings\TfsDeploy01.QA02.SetParameters.xml"/>
</ItemGroup>

<PropertyGroup>
  <_QASetParamFileFullPath>%(QASetParamFile02.FullPath)</_QASetParamFileFullPath>
</PropertyGroup>

<MSDeploy
    Verb="sync"
    Source="@(QAMsDeploySourceProviderSetting)"
    ImportSetParametersItems="$(_QASetParamFileFullPath)"
    Destination="@(QAMsDeployDestinationProviderSetting)"/>
  </Target>

</Project>
```

In this file, you'll notice that we are using the MSDeploy task without declaring it with a UsingTask. Since we are going to set it up such that this file gets imported by the WPP during the build, we do not need to declare that. The Microsoft.Web.Publishing.targets file takes care of this for us. Now let's try and dissect this file a bit. When we are using the MSDeploy task in this case we are passing four properties to it. We will take a look at each of these.

The first of these parameters is Verb="sync", which identifies the value for the –verb switch. In this case, we are setting it to sync. The next parameter is source="@ (QAMsDeploySourceProviderSetting)", which is used to specify the value for the –source switch. The value for identity will be used to determine the source provider. In this case, the source provider is package. Each metadata value that this item value contains will be added to the source switch as an option. For example, in this case, we have declared a path option. So the resultant –source switch will be –source:package,path=*{PackageFileName}*, where *{PackageFileName}* is the path to the package that is created during the build. The value for the Destination property is similar to the Source property. The include value determines the provider type for the –dest switch, and then each metadata value that it contains will be passed in as an option. The only other property that is passed in is ImportSetParametersItems, and the value of this property is passed as the –setParamFile value. Now let's see this at work.

When we build the project, we will specify that this new target should be our DeployTarget, and we also need to pass in the qa.wpp.targets file as the .wpp.targets file. Normally, when your project is being built, the .wpp.targets file that will be included is *{ProjectName}* .wpp.targets. Since our project name is TfsDeploy01, the qa.wpp.targets file will not be picked up. Let's take a look at the region in the Microsoft.Web.Publishing.targets file that includes this code.

```
<PropertyGroup>
  <WebPublishPipelineCustomizeTargetFile
      Condition="'$(WebPublishPipelineCustomizeTargetFile)'==''">
      $(WebPublishPipelineProjectDirectory)\$(WebPublishPipelineProjectName).wpp.targets
  </WebPublishPipelineCustomizeTargetFile>
</PropertyGroup>

<Import Project="$(WebPublishPipelineCustomizeTargetFile)"
      Condition="Exists($(WebPublishPipelineCustomizeTargetFile))"/>
```

When looking at this snippet, keep in mind that this file is under the %ProgramFiles% directory. We really have two options to change the name of the file that gets imported. We can change the value for the entire property, WebPublishPipelineCustomizeTargetFile, or we can change the value for WebPublishPipelineProjectName. Since we are going to be using Team Build and we know the relative location of the file to the project itself, it is easiest to just replace the value for WebPublishPipelineProjectName. In this case, we simply need to set that property to be qa since the file is in the same directory as the project file itself.

Now that we have explained this file a bit, let's see the command that is used to tie all of this together, shown in the following code block:

```
msbuild TfsDeploy01.csproj
    /t:Build
    /p:DeployOnBuild=true;
        DeployTarget=DeployToQA;
        username=deploy;
        password=p@ssw0rd;
        WebPublishPipelineProjectName=qa
```

From this command, you can see that we set the value for DeployTarget as DeployToQA, which is the target that we were just looking at. Then we set the value for WebPublishPipelineProjectName to be qa, as we had discussed earlier. Once this command is executed, MSDeploy will be invoked to update both sites. The result of the DeployToQA target is captured in Figure 19-8.

```
For this sample script, you can change the deploy parameters by changing the following file:
C:\InsideMSBuild\Ch19\TFS\TfsDeploy01\TfsDeploy01\obj\Debug\Package\qa.SetParameters.xml
DeployToQA:
  Deploying to QA01 now
  Running msdeploy.exe.
  C:\Program Files (x86)\IIS\Microsoft Web Deploy\msdeploy.exe -source:package='obj\Debug\Package\
  qa.zip' -dest:auto,ComputerName='WIN-MCX6WTF4J4R',UserName='deploy',Password='p@ssw0rd' -verb:sy
  nc -setParamFile:"C:\InsideMSBuild\Ch19\TFS\TfsDeploy01\DeploySettings\TfsDeploy01.QA01.SetParam
  eters.xml"
  Info: Updating setAcl (QA01 Web Site/TfsDeploy).
  Info: Updating setAcl (QA01 Web Site/TfsDeploy).
  Info: Updating setAcl (QA01 Web Site/TfsDeploy).
  Info: Updating setAcl (QA01 Web Site/TfsDeploy).
  Total changes: 4 (0 added, 0 deleted, 4 updated, 0 parameters changed, 0 bytes copied)
  Successfully execute msdeploy.exe.
  Publish is successfully deployed.
  Deploying to QA02 now
  Running msdeploy.exe.
  C:\Program Files (x86)\IIS\Microsoft Web Deploy\msdeploy.exe -source:package='obj\Debug\Package\
  qa.zip' -dest:auto,ComputerName='WIN-MCX6WTF4J4R',UserName='deploy',Password='p@ssw0rd' -verb:sy
  nc -setParamFile:"C:\InsideMSBuild\Ch19\TFS\TfsDeploy01\DeploySettings\TfsDeploy01.QA02.SetParam
  eters.xml"
  Info: Updating setAcl (QA02 Web Site/TfsDeploy).
  Info: Updating setAcl (QA02 Web Site/TfsDeploy).
  Info: Updating setAcl (QA02 Web Site/TfsDeploy).
  Info: Updating setAcl (QA02 Web Site/TfsDeploy).
  Total changes: 4 (0 added, 0 deleted, 4 updated, 0 parameters changed, 0 bytes copied)
  Successfully execute msdeploy.exe.
  Publish is successfully deployed.
Done Building Project "C:\InsideMSBuild\Ch19\TFS\TfsDeploy01\TfsDeploy01\TfsDeploy01.csproj" (Buil
d target(s)).

Build succeeded.
    0 Warning(s)
    0 Error(s)
```

FIGURE 19-8 Result of the DeployToQA target

From Figure 19-8, you can see that only a few updates were performed. This is because those sites were essentially up to date to begin with. We did this in order to show you the log of the DeployToQA target. If both sites were not up to date, then the log would have taken up too much space. From this figure, you can clearly see that the package is deployed first to the QA01 website, then after that to the QA02 website. In this example, we are deploying both sites to the same machine; but if you were deploying to multiple machines, then you would just have to tweak the qa.wpp.targets file. Now, let's see how to create a Team Build definition to do the same thing.

Now that we have created an msbuild.exe command to invoke the deploy that we want, creating a Team Build definition for it is essentially trivial. At this point, all we need to do is create a new Team Build definition specifying that we want the TfsBuild01.sln file to build and then pass in the same properties as the MSBuild Arguments value. Take a look at the TfsDeploy02 Team Build definition process tab shown in Figure 19-9.

From this figure, you can see that we passed in the same properties that we discussed previously. From now on, whenever we need to deploy to QA, we can just execute the TfsDeploy02 build.

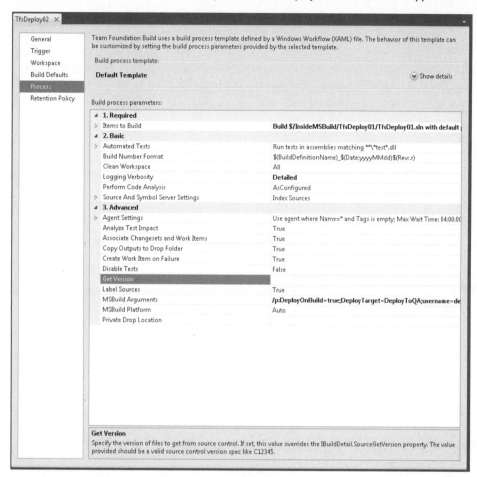

FIGURE 19-9 TfsDeploy02 Team Build definition Process tab

Excluding ACLs from the Package

In all the samples where we deploy a package, you might have noticed that there is always a setAcl action or actions. There may be some cases where you do not want this to occur, though. First, let's create a package and see the setAcl providers in the manifest; then, we will disable and check the manifest again to ensure that we have done the appropriate work. In the samples for this chapter, we have created a new WAP named Deploy04. When we create a deployment package, here is the manifest that is being used:

```
<sitemanifest>
  <IisApp path="C:\InsideMSBuild\Ch19\Deploy04\obj\Debug\Package\PackageTmp"
          managedRuntimeVersion="v4.0" />
  <setAcl path="C:\InsideMSBuild\Ch19\Deploy04\obj\Debug\Package\PackageTmp"
          setAclResourceType="Directory" />
```

```
    <setAcl path="C:\InsideMSBuild\Ch19\Deploy04\obj\Debug\Package\PackageTmp"
           setAclUser="anonymousAuthenticationUser" setAclResourceType="Directory" />
</sitemanifest>
```

In order to disable the setAcl providers in this manifest, you can create a .wpp.targets file. In this case, it would be named Deploy04.wpp.targets file and be in the same directory as the project file. Inside that file, you just need to include the following property declaration:

```
<Project xmlns="http://schemas.microsoft.com/developer/msbuild/2003">

  <PropertyGroup>
    <IncludeSetAclProviderOnDestination>false</IncludeSetAclProviderOnDestination>
  </PropertyGroup>

</Project>
```

After you do this, you can build a new deployment package. The manifest will look like the following:

```
<sitemanifest>
  <IisApp path="C:\InsideMSBuild\Ch19\Deploy04\obj\Debug\Package\PackageTmp"
         managedRuntimeVersion="v4.0" />
</sitemanifest>
```

As you can see, the setAcl providers have been removed as expected. Also, if you didn't want to do this every time, then you could pass in this value on the command line using the /p switch.

Synchronizing an Application to Another Server

Throughout this book, we have discussed MSDeploy only in the context of deployment, but fundamentally it is a synchronization tool. You can use MSDeploy to synchronize a source object to a given destination. For example, if you have an application installed on a given server, you can use MSDeploy to synchronize that site to a different server. For example, we have an application called Deploy03 running on my local machine, Ibrahim-P55, under the Site03 website. If we wanted to sync this site to a site named Backup on the WIN-MCX6WTF4J4R machine, all we have to do is issue the following command:

```
msdeploy -verb:sync
-source:appHostConfig="Site03/Deploy03"
 -dest:appHostConfig="Backup/Deploy03",
                   computerName=WIN-MCX6WTF4J4R,
                   username=deploy,
                   password=p@ssw0rd
```

In this command, the source is the Site03/Deploy03 application and the destination is the Backup/Deploy03 site on my remote server. The result of running this is shown in Figure 19-10.

```
C:\InsideMSBuild\Ch19)msdeploy -verb:sync -source:appHostConfig="Site03/Deploy03" -dest:appHostConf
ig="Backup/Deploy03",computerName=WIN-MCX6WTF4J4R,username=deploy,password=p@ssw0rd
Info: Adding MSDeploy.appHostConfig (MSDeploy.appHostConfig).
Info: Adding appHostConfig (Backup/Deploy03).
Info: Updating application (MSDeploy.appHostConfig/appHostConfig[@path='Backup/Deploy03']/applicati
on[@path='/Deploy03']).
Info: Adding child virtualDirectory (MSDeploy.appHostConfig/appHostConfig[@path='Backup/Deploy03']/
application[@path='/Deploy03']/virtualDirectory[@path='/']).
Info: Updating application (MSDeploy.appHostConfig/appHostConfig[@path='Backup/Deploy03']/applicati
on[@path='/Deploy03']).
Info: Adding child dirPath (C:\inetpub\www3\Deploy03\Account).
Info: Adding child dirPath (C:\inetpub\www3\Deploy03\bin).
Info: Adding child dirPath (C:\inetpub\www3\Deploy03\Scripts).
Info: Adding child dirPath (C:\inetpub\www3\Deploy03\Styles).
Info: Updating application (MSDeploy.appHostConfig/appHostConfig[@path='Backup/Deploy03']/applicati
on[@path='/Deploy03']).
Info: Adding child filePath (C:\inetpub\www3\Deploy03\About.aspx).
Info: Adding child filePath (C:\inetpub\www3\Deploy03\Account\ChangePassword.aspx).
Info: Adding child filePath (C:\inetpub\www3\Deploy03\Account\ChangePasswordSuccess.aspx).
Info: Adding child filePath (C:\inetpub\www3\Deploy03\Account\Login.aspx).
Info: Adding child filePath (C:\inetpub\www3\Deploy03\Account\Register.aspx).
Info: Adding child filePath (C:\inetpub\www3\Deploy03\Account\Web.config).
Info: Adding child filePath (C:\inetpub\www3\Deploy03\bin\Deploy03.dll).
Info: Adding child filePath (C:\inetpub\www3\Deploy03\bin\Deploy03.pdb).
Info: Adding child filePath (C:\inetpub\www3\Deploy03\Default.aspx).
Info: Adding child filePath (C:\inetpub\www3\Deploy03\Global.asax).
Info: Adding child filePath (C:\inetpub\www3\Deploy03\parameters.xml).
Info: Adding child filePath (C:\inetpub\www3\Deploy03\Scripts\jquery-1.4.1-vsdoc.js).
Info: Adding child filePath (C:\inetpub\www3\Deploy03\Scripts\jquery-1.4.1.js).
Info: Adding child filePath (C:\inetpub\www3\Deploy03\Scripts\jquery-1.4.1.min.js).
Info: Adding child filePath (C:\inetpub\www3\Deploy03\Site.Master).
Info: Adding child filePath (C:\inetpub\www3\Deploy03\Styles\Site.css).
Info: Adding child filePath (C:\inetpub\www3\Deploy03\Web.config).
Total changes: 27 (24 added, 0 deleted, 3 updated, 0 parameters changed, 542469 bytes copied)
```

FIGURE 19-10 MSDeploy Synchronizing an Application to a Remote Server

From this result, you can see that the application was synchronized. This included the content as well as the IIS settings. Note that this will synchronize the settings of only this application, not of the entire website.

Index

Symbols and Numbers

About the Author

Sayed Ibrahim Hashimi has a computer engineering degree from the University of Florida. He is currently working at Microsoft as a program manager, creating better web development tools. Previously, he was a Microsoft Visual C# MVP. Along with this book he is also a coauthor of *Deploying .NET Application: Learning MSBuild and Click Once* (Apress, 2006), and has written several publications for magazines such as the *MSDN Magazine*. He has previously worked as a developer and independent consultant for companies ranging from Fortune 500 to startups. He is an expert in the financial, education, and collection industries.

William Bartholomew is a software development engineer at Microsoft Corporation in Redmond, Washington. He is a member of the Developer Division Engineering Systems group, which includes the build lab responsible for building and shipping Microsoft Visual Studio.

Pavan Adharapurapu is a software developer at Microsoft. He was part of the team that was responsible for migrating Microsoft Visual C++ over to MSBuild in Visual Studio 2010. He is currently working in the Cloud Computing space and is part of the Azure AppFabric Services team.

Jason Ward is a development manager at Microsoft. He has more than two decades of experience as a software developer, having worked in Australia and the United Kingdom before moving to Redmond, Washington, where he currently lives with his wife and two daughters.

Best Practices for Software Engineering

**Software Estimation:
Demystifying the Black Art**
Steve McConnell
ISBN 9780735605350

Amazon.com's pick for "Best Computer Book of 2006"!
Generating accurate software estimates is fairly straightforward—once you understand the art of creating them.
Acclaimed author Steve McConnell demystifies the
process—illuminating the practical procedures, formulas,
and heuristics you can apply right away.

**Code Complete,
Second Edition**
Steve McConnell
ISBN 9780735619678

Widely considered one of the best practical guides to
programming—fully updated. Drawing from research,
academia, and everyday commercial practice, McConnell
synthesizes must-know principles and techniques into
clear, pragmatic guidance. Rethink your approach—and
deliver the highest quality code.

Agile Portfolio Management
Jochen Krebs
ISBN 9780735625679

Agile processes foster better collaboration, innovation,
and results. So why limit their use to software projects—
when you can transform your entire business? This book
illuminates the opportunities—and rewards—of applying
agile processes to your overall IT portfolio, with best
practices for optimizing results.

**Simple Architectures for
Complex Enterprises**
Roger Sessions
ISBN 9780735625785

Why do so many IT projects fail? Enterprise consultant
Roger Sessions believes complex problems require
simple solutions. And in this book, he shows how to
make simplicity a core architectural requirement—as
critical as performance, reliability, or security—to achieve
better, more reliable results for your organization.

The Enterprise and Scrum
Ken Schwaber
ISBN 9780735623378

Extend Scrum's benefits—greater agility, higher-quality
products, and lower costs—beyond individual teams to
the entire enterprise. Scrum cofounder Ken Schwaber
describes proven practices for adopting Scrum principles
across your organization, including that all-critical
component—managing change.

ALSO SEE

**Software Requirements,
Second Edition**
Karl E. Wiegers
ISBN 9780735618794

**More About Software
Requirements:
Thorny Issues and
Practical Advice**
Karl E. Wiegers
ISBN 9780735622678

**Software Requirement
Patterns**
Stephen Withall
ISBN 9780735623989

**Agile Project
Management
with Scrum**
Ken Schwaber
ISBN 9780735619937

Solid Code
Donis Marshall, John Bruno
ISBN 9780735625921

microsoft.com/mspress

Collaborative Technologies—
Resources for Developers

**Inside Microsoft®
SharePoint® 2010**

Ted Pattison, Andrew Connell,
and Scot Hillier

ISBN 9780735627468

Get the in-depth architectural insights, task-
oriented guidance, and extensive code samples
you need to build robust, enterprise content-
management solutions.

**Programming for
Unified Communications
with Microsoft Office
Communications
Server 2007 R2**

Rui Maximo, Kurt De Ding,
Vishwa Ranjan, Chris Mayo,
Oscar Newkerk, and the
Microsoft OCS Team

ISBN 9780735626232

Direct from the Microsoft Office Communications
Server product team, get the hands-on guidance
you need to streamline your organization's real-time,
remote communication and collaboration solutions
across the enterprise and across time zones.

**Programming
Microsoft
Dynamics® CRM 4.0**

Jim Steger, Mike Snyder,
Brad Bosak, Corey O'Brien,
and Philip Richardson

ISBN 9780735625945

Apply the design and coding practices that
leading CRM consultants use to customize,
integrate, and extend Microsoft Dynamics
CRM 4.0 for specific business needs.

**Microsoft
.NET and SAP**

Juergen Daiberl,
Steve Fox, Scott Adams,
and Thomas Reimer

ISBN 9780735625686

Develop integrated, .NET-SAP solutions—
and deliver better connectivity, collaboration,
and business intelligence.

For C# Developers

Microsoft® Visual C#® 2010 Step by Step
John Sharp
ISBN 9780735626706

Teach yourself Visual C# 2010—one step at a time. Ideal for developers with fundamental programming skills, this practical tutorial delivers hands-on guidance for creating C# components and Windows–based applications. CD features practice exercises, code samples, and a fully searchable eBook.

Microsoft XNA® Game Studio 3.0: Learn Programming Now!
Rob Miles
ISBN 9780735626584

Now you can create your own games for Xbox 360® and Windows—as you learn the underlying skills and concepts for computer programming. Dive right into your first project, adding new tools and tricks to your arsenal as you go. Master the fundamentals of XNA Game Studio and Visual C#—no experience required!

CLR via C#, Third Edition
Jeffrey Richter
ISBN 9780735627048

Dig deep and master the intricacies of the common language runtime (CLR) and the .NET Framework. Written by programming expert Jeffrey Richter, this guide is ideal for developers building any kind of application—ASP.NET, Windows Forms, Microsoft SQL Server®, Web services, console apps—and features extensive C# code samples.

Windows via C/C++, Fifth Edition
Jeffrey Richter, Christophe Nasarre
ISBN 9780735624245

Get the classic book for programming Windows at the API level in Microsoft Visual C++®—now in its fifth edition and covering Windows Vista®.

Programming Windows® Identity Foundation
Vittorio Bertocci
ISBN 9780735627185

Get practical, hands-on guidance for using WIF to solve authentication, authorization, and customization issues in Web applications and services.

Microsoft® ASP.NET 4 Step by Step
George Shepherd
ISBN 9780735627017

Ideal for developers with fundamental programming skills—but new to ASP.NET—who want hands-on guidance for developing Web applications in the Microsoft Visual Studio® 2010 environment.

microsoft.com/mspress

For Visual Basic Developers

**Microsoft®
Visual Basic® 2010
Step by Step**
Michael Halvorson
ISBN 9780735626690

Teach yourself the essential tools and techniques for Visual Basic 2010—one step at a time. No matter what your skill level, you'll find the practical guidance and examples you need to start building applications for Windows and the Web.

**Microsoft Visual Studio® Tips
251 Ways to Improve Your
Productivity**
Sara Ford
ISBN 9780735626409

This book packs proven tips that any developer, regardless of skill or preferred development language, can use to help shave hours off everyday development activities with Visual Studio.

**Inside the Microsoft Build
Engine: Using MSBuild and
Team Foundation Build,
Second Edition**
Sayed Ibrahim Hashimi,
William Bartholomew
ISBN 9780735645240

Your practical guide to using, customizing, and extending the build engine in Visual Studio 2010.

**Parallel Programming
with Microsoft
Visual Studio 2010**
Donis Marshall
ISBN 9780735640603

The roadmap for developers wanting to maximize their applications for multicore architecture using Visual Studio 2010.

**Programming Windows®
Services with Microsoft
Visual Basic 2008**
Michael Gernaey
ISBN 9780735624337

The essential guide for developing powerful, customized Windows services with Visual Basic 2008. Whether you're looking to perform network monitoring or design a complex enterprise solution, you'll find the expert advice and practical examples to accelerate your productivity.

What do you think of this book?

We want to hear from you!

To participate in a brief online survey, please visit:

microsoft.com/learning/booksurvey

Tell us how well this book meets your needs—what works effectively, and what we can do better. Your feedback will help us continually improve our books and learning resources for you.

Thank you in advance for your input!

Stay in touch!

To subscribe to the *Microsoft Press® Book Connection Newsletter*—for news on upcoming books, events, and special offers—please visit:

microsoft.com/learning/books/newsletter